THE NEW SUPERGARDENER

Alan Titchmarsh

SEVEN
DIALS

**FOR MY MOTHER,
WHO BOUGHT ME MY FIRST PACKET OF SEEDS,
AND MY FATHER,
WHO WAS RELIEVED TO HAND OVER THE SPADE**

This edition first published in the United Kingdom in 1999 by
Ward Lock

This paperback edition first published in 2000 by
Seven Dials, Cassell & Co
Wellington House, 125 Strand
London, WC2R 0BB

First published 1983
Second edition 1988
Third edition 1993
First paperback edition 1994
Second paperback edition, revised, 1997

A CIP catalogue record for this book is available
from the British Library

ISBN 1 84188 046 9

THE NEW
SUPERGARDENER

contents

Introduction 6

PART I
THE BASICS

1 How to start 10
2 Plant propagation 20
3 The toolshed 28

PART II
THE PLANTS

4 Trees 38
5 Shrubs 52
6 Hedges 80
7 Climbers and wall plants 88
8 Roses 100
9 Border plants 112
10 Annuals, biennials and bedding plants 138
11 Garden bulbs 152

PART III
THE FEATURES

12 Rock gardens 166
13 Water gardens 178

14 Wildlife in the garden 188
15 Lawns 192
16 Patio gardening 202

PART IV
THE FOOD CROPS

17 Fruit growing 214
18 Vegetable growing 232

PART V
THE UNDER COVER GARDEN

19 Greenhouse gardening 250
20 House plants 268

PART VI

Pests, diseases and disorders 282

Index 300
Acknowledgements 304

introduction

'THE MAN WHO COULD CALL A spade a spade should be compelled to use one. It is the only thing he is fit for', said Oscar Wilde. So it is that gardeners have acquired a reputation as down-to-earth dullards who possess most of nature's secrets and few social graces. But the days of the crumbling conservatory presided over by a grumbling gardener have long since gone. The mystery of supposed 'green fingers' certainly lingers on, but folk who tackle the land with a handful of common sense as well as a bucketful of manure, will find that this oldest of crafts offers satisfaction and excitement as well as frustration and fury.

Don't believe that all expert gardeners have the patience of Job. Some of them are itching for their seeds to come up and grow into cabbages overnight; others want a mature garden in a matter of weeks. But all of them, if they have a feeling for the soil and for plants, will curb their impatience and learn that there's no rushing nature, though occasionally she'll let you cheat a bit.

I started gardening when I left school – having shown singular lack of success in any subject remotely academic. Off I plodded to the local nursery where I was astounded to find that someone would pay me to grow plants – something that I'd been doing in my spare time for the previous five years. Gardening doesn't grab everybody this way. Lots of folk look upon it as a chore that has to be done on a Sunday after the car has been washed. And it's easy to see why. They find that everything that shouldn't grow fast does – weeds, the hedge and the lawn – and everything that should be bursting into leaf and flower doesn't: the hastily planted tree, the summer bedding and the bulbs.

The secret of success is to adopt the right attitude to your garden. For a start, stop worrying about it, and stop worrying about what the neighbours will say if you don't cut the lawn or the hedge with monotonous regularity. Look upon your garden as a haven where you can escape the high-speed living of today; then the fact that things move slowly within its leafy confines will soon be welcomed as a positive advantage.

Hopefully *New Supergardener* will give you a bit of inspiration as well as practical, down-to-earth advice. Everybody considers that their garden is a problem plot, so there are suggestions of plants that will put up with all sorts of soils and situations. If you've never lifted a spade before, you should still be able to understand what I'm rambling on about. Above all, remember that this is one man's choice of plants and one man's way of growing them, though both plants and techniques have been filched from other gardeners during the couple of decades that count as my apprenticeship in the craft.

I've had to garden, so far, on heavy clay in the north, on dust-like sand, and now on chalk, clay and flints in the south, so I know that time spent tending the earth is not always rewarded with bumper crops and a bounty of blooms. But the failures make the successes that much more enjoyable. If the book makes gardening seem faintly interesting and even encourages you to grow just one plant to perfection, then I'll be well pleased. I hope you will be too.

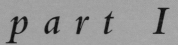

THE BASICS

Here you'll find sound practical advice on the essential elements of successful gardening: planning, techniques, propagation and tools

A secluded haven, with outdoor dining area, has been created in this small urban garden. Plants in containers can be moved around to provide changing seasonal interest.

how to start

Before you buy a plant or a

packet of seeds, there are two

vital preliminary stages in

creating your dream garden:

one is to draw up a plan; the

other is to prepare your soil

T'S A DAUNTING PROSPECT BUT AN IRRESISTIBLE challenge – a weed-infested patch of earth from which must be sculpted a garden. So what should you do first? Most experts are united in their opinions on this: you must draw up a plan.

PLANNING YOUR PATCH

Say the word 'plan' to an architect and he'll immediately take out his pencil and a sheet of graph paper. The pencil will be of use to you; the graph paper is not essential. However, it is a good idea to consult with all members of the family so that you know just what they want of a garden: somewhere to sit, somewhere to play football, somewhere to put a swing or a sandpit, in fact it might seem at times as if there will be no room for plants. But don't make the mistake of thinking that gardens are planned on paper; I reckon the best ones are planned on soil. Get out there with an armful of bamboo canes and a hosepipe and draw patterns and shapes on the earth.

I'm not going to tell you much about the elements of garden design; there are a lot of them and they've been covered in depth in many books on garden planning. What I will say is that your garden should be both practical and pleasing to look at. If you want a formal plot (all circles and squares) then have one, but most folk like an informal scheme that utilizes gentle curves that are easy on the eye, sympathetic to plants, and totally divorced from the symmetry of motorways, traffic roundabouts and office layouts.

With your list of desirable attributes to hand you'll have fun plotting the shape of your potential garden. View it from all angles – both on the ground and from upstairs windows – and use your imagination to tell you that a bamboo cane will, in time, be a tree of sizeable proportions. Avoid fiddly corners on lawns (they'll be difficult to mow) and in beds (they'll be difficult to plant up), but make sure that one or two parts of the garden are invisible as you walk down it – that way you'll be drawn to explore the hidden nooks and crannies.

There are not many rules in gardening, but there are a few that will prevent disasters in garden design:
1 Make sure you know the aspect of your garden – a tall row of conifers planted on the south side will cast heavy shade over most of the plot. Find out where north is and plant with the sun's path in mind.
2 Garden features that need sun (a pond, a vegetable plot or a greenhouse) must be sited in the open.

What do you want from your garden?

Whether you are designing a garden from scratch or intend to make changes to an existing one, think carefully about what you want from your garden and work out how you can successfully achieve this before rushing out to buy new plants or to chop down unwanted shrubs. As well as making a list of desirable features, make sure that you know the aspect of your plot, as this will have a vital bearing on where some of the features can be situated.

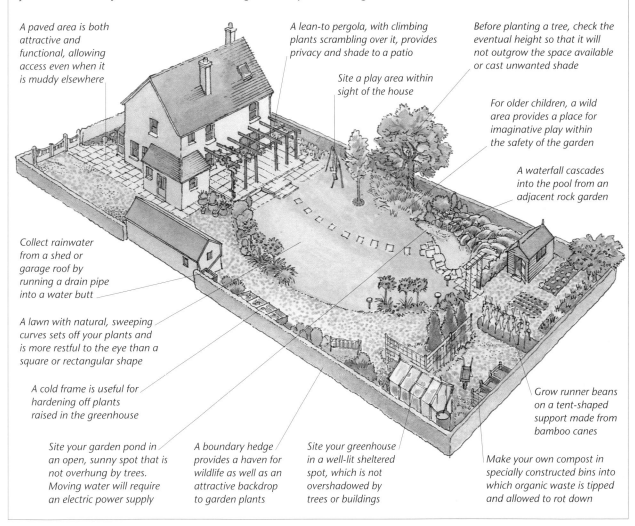

A paved area is both attractive and functional, allowing access even when it is muddy elsewhere

A lean-to pergola, with climbing plants scrambling over it, provides privacy and shade to a patio

Before planting a tree, check the eventual height so that it will not outgrow the space available or cast unwanted shade

Site a play area within sight of the house

For older children, a wild area provides a place for imaginative play within the safety of the garden

A waterfall cascades into the pool from an adjacent rock garden

Collect rainwater from a shed or garage roof by running a drain pipe into a water butt

A lawn with natural, sweeping curves sets off your plants and is more restful to the eye than a square or rectangular shape

A cold frame is useful for hardening off plants raised in the greenhouse

Site your garden pond in an open, sunny spot that is not overhung by trees. Moving water will require an electric power supply

A boundary hedge provides a haven for wildlife as well as an attractive backdrop to garden plants

Site your greenhouse in a well-lit sheltered spot, which is not overshadowed by trees or buildings

Grow runner beans on a tent-shaped support made from bamboo canes

Make your own compost in specially constructed bins into which organic waste is tipped and allowed to rot down

3 Make sure that your soil is well drained and in good shape before you plant anything.

4 Be nosey. Look at gardens in your area and take note of plants that do well and those that don't. Avoid the poor 'doers' and save yourself some money.

5 Use trees and shrubs as the backbone of your planting scheme. Make sure that some of them are evergreens, and try to ensure that there's something to look at all the year round.

6 If you can't afford the time or money to plant all your garden at once (and few of us can), start in one corner and work slowly outwards. If you start near the house, you'll always have something to take your mind off the squalor that lies beyond.

7 Make it simple, sweeping and bold, even if the plot is small. Lots of twiddly bits will drive you nuts.

8 Remember that plant foliage is more important and more enduring than flowers. The predominant foliage colour should be green (too many purples and greys will be overpowering), and each plant should be put next to a neighbour that in some way contrasts with or complements its shape, form or colour. It sounds a bit pretentious but it makes for much more impact than a jumbled scheme of assorted flowers.

Whatever design you settle on, don't make the mistake of thinking that one day your garden will be finished. No garden is a museum (those that are preserved as such invariably go downhill) and constant adjustment of shapes and replanting can be carried out when you tire of your original plantings. Mind you, the trees will appreciate being left alone.

LAND CLEARANCE

I'm afraid there's no magic formula – it's basically hard graft. For a start, all tall weeds, brambles and seedling trees should be hacked down as close to ground level as possible with a sickle, scythe or powered 'strimmer', and the compostable greenstuff stacked on the compost heap. Woody stems can be burned, but dry them off a bit first so that they don't smoke out the neighbours.

I don't much like using weedkillers, but if the plot is vast then you might feel it's essential. They act best in spring and summer on growing weeds. For full details and the right way to use them see p.18.

Whether you kill off the weeds or not, the soil will still have to be turned, and I can't get out of the habit of pulling out thick weed roots, even if they are supposed to be dead, thanks to a herbicide. It's tempting to use a rotavator to turn over the soil. Do so if you're really short of time and energy, but remember that weed roots which are not dead will be chopped up by the blades, and each small piece will make a new plant. Added to this, it is difficult to incorporate organic soil enrichment with a rotavator, and the soil is seldom cultivated as deeply as it is with a spade. Pay your money and take your choice.

When soil has been cleared and dug, keep an eye on it and deal quickly with any weeds that emerge. Better still, mulch it immediately with a 5–8 cm (2–3 in) thick layer of organic matter such as leaf mould, pulverized bark, compost or manure to prevent weed emergence. Neglect it and you'll have to do the whole job again – it's heartbreaking.

Don't overdo the hard work. A little slog every couple of days is better than one back-breaking blitz.

GETTING TO KNOW YOUR SOIL

Soil is pretty boring stuff on the face of it, but it is the staff of life as far as your plants are concerned. Remember: what goes in must come up – you only get out of your soil what you put into it.

The ideal garden soil is something called a medium loam. It exists but I don't know anyone who's got it! It consists of a mixture of sand, clay and rotted organic matter known as 'humus'. It doesn't become too sticky when wet nor too dusty when dry.

SANDY SOILS are 'light' and easy to work but they tend to be lacking in nutrients (which are rapidly washed through) and quick to dry in summer.

CLAY SOILS dry like rock and become squidgy when wet. They are difficult to cultivate whatever the time of year. They are slow to warm up in spring, too.

STONY SOILS may be sandy or they may have a high proportion of clay.

PEATY SOILS are good to work, moisture retentive in summer, but they are inclined to be too acidic for certain plants.

Soil drainage

If soil drainage is poor you'll know about it: pools of water may lie on the surface, or the ground may be like a paddy field in wet weather. Where drainage problems are severe, some kind of piped, underground drainage system will have to be invested in, but such cases are, thank goodness, rare. More often than not, poor drainage is caused either by the fact that the soil is almost pure clay, or because the surface has been compacted by heavy traffic, or because there is a hard and impenetrable layer in the subsoil. The way to deal with these problems is as follows:

1 Clay soil is easy to identify: it is rock-hard when dry and very plastic when wet. Rub it between your finger and thumb and it has a polished sheen. Improve its drainage by working in as much sharp sand, grit and organic matter as you can lay your spade on. All these materials will break up the clay and prevent the individual particles from adhering quite so firmly to one another. Winter digging allows frost to shatter clay but the effect is only temporary.

2 If the surface of the soil refuses to allow water to drain away, fork or dig over the area. If this is not possible – on a lawn for instance – spike the area deeply with a special aerator or a garden fork. Work grit and organic matter into the soil to prevent a recurrence of the problem.

3 If a 'subsoil pan' (a hard, impervious layer below the topsoil) is causing poor drainage, break up the stiff or rocky layer with a pick or a crowbar to allow water through. In large gardens the job might have to be done with a tractor attachment.

IMPROVING YOUR SOIL

Whatever your soil, the chances are that it needs improving. Sandy, stony or clay soil will be much easier to cultivate, and more conducive to plant growth, if some organic nourishment is added, not just at the start of cultivation but regularly over the years. Manure and compost (well-rotted) are best, but leaf mould and composted bark will do wonders too if they can be supplemented with a sprinkling of general fertilizer (they lack the nutrients contained in compost and manure, which will fuel both beneficial soil bacteria and plants). A bucketful to the square metre (square yard) will do for all.

Dig in bulky enrichment like this during autumn and winter. Clay soils can be broken down and 'opened up' if plenty of grit and sharp sand is dug in. This stuff has a longer-lasting effect than organic matter, but will not have the same effect on soil fertility as good old muck – use both if you can.

Stones you will have to live with. Don't try to dig them all out – you'll be at it for ever. Instead, work in plenty of enrichment and let the plants' roots find their way around obstructions.

Sharp sand and grit can be added to peaty soils and liming may also be necessary.

Autumn leaves are a pain, but you can make them work for you too. Avoid the evergreen types, but put all others in black polythene dustbin liners that have been perforated at intervals to allow a little air

Making compost

There's real mystery attached to compost making, which is a shame because it puts a lot of people off. Don't be intimidated. Make yourself a couple of post and wire-netting enclosures 1.2 m (4 ft) square (or buy a proprietary bin if you haven't the space for these) and start from there.

Line the first netting bin with newspaper (to prevent the sides of the heap from drying) and start off your heap. Tip into it anything organic (except waste food such as bread, meat and the like, which can tempt the odd rat or two). Grass clippings, vegetable tops, potato peelings, annual weeds, dead flowers, crushed eggshells, tea leaves and even a few torn up newspapers can be put into the bin, but make sure they are mixed together well. Trample the heap every time you add more. Concentrations of any one substance can slow down rotting. Over every 23 cm (9 in) layer sprinkle a little compost activator or sulphate of ammonia, and keep the top of the heap covered with a bit of carpet or sacking. Pour on a canful or two of water if the surface looks dry. Unfirmed and dry compost heaps don't rot. When the first bin is full, start to fill the second one.

Some compost buffs claim to have their stuff ready to use in a matter of weeks; I'd give it three to six months if I were you. Then it will be fairly brown, fairly crumbly and just the thing for any plant in any soil.

1 Make a post and wire-netting compost bin and fill it with vegetable waste. Mix everything together well and trample the heap every time you add more.

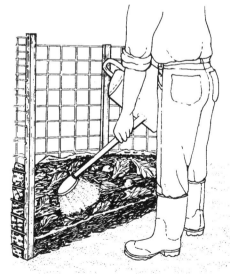

2 Scatter sulphate of ammonia or compost activator over each 23 cm (9 in) layer and water in dry weather. Cover the heap with a piece of old carpet.

circulation. Tread the leaves firm as the bag fills up (to expel air pockets), then seal the top. The leaves should be moist or rotting will not take place, and remember, it's fungi that break down dead leaves rather than bacteria, so the sulphated ammonia won't help much.

Stack the bags in an out-of-the-way corner and crumbly leaf mould, ideal for a mulch, should be yours within about three months. Oak, beech and other small leaves are best; horse chestnut, plane and other toughies can be slower to rot down.

Acid or alkali?

Don't worry about this complicated chemical state of affairs. Certainly it will affect the type of plants you can grow, but there is an easy way to discover the lime content – or pH value – of your soil. There are now plenty of soil-testing kits that allow a small sample of soil to be put in a test tube, treated with a special solution and checked against a colour chart to tell you its pH value. Lots of gardeners get by without ever knowing the pH of their soil, but it's fun to find out and it can save you a lot of frustration.

> *"Choose plants that can cope with your conditions, rather than trying to change the status quo."*

The desirable pH for most plants is a reading of between 6.0 and 6.5 on the pH scale. This is a slightly acid soil. Readings between 4.0 and 6.0 are very acid; and those between 6.5 and 8.0 are very alkaline (and probably very chalky). What does all this mean to you? Well, if your soil is very acid, rhododendrons, heathers and many woodland plants will be blissfully happy; almost all plants will grow well in a soil that is slightly acid. In alkaline soil, real lime haters will not thrive, but many plants will. Choose those that can cope with your conditions, rather than trying to change the status quo. Throughout the book I've indicated which plants are suitable for which conditions.

Making a chalky soil more acidic is not really practical in the long term, but acid ground can be ameliorated by the addition of ground limestone or chalk. Only on the vegetable plot is such adjustment made on a regular basis, when lime is applied in autumn several weeks after manuring (if you do the two jobs at the same time undesirable chemical reactions can take place). Brassicas (members of the cabbage family) in particular are best on a soil that is not too acid, and liming also discourages clubroot, that deadly disease that distorts the roots.

The kit you use to test your soil will indicate how much lime is necessary to bring an acid soil into a more hospitable state. If you can't be bothered with all this palaver, stick your nose over the fence and see what grows well in your neighbour's garden.

Using fertilizers

Cast your eye along the fertilizer shelf in a garden centre or hardware shop and you'll be surprised just how many different concoctions there are. Most of them you can happily do without, but a few of them at your elbow will make sure that you always have a tonic ready for your plants. These are the fertilizers that are most useful:

SULPHATE OF AMMONIA is high in nitrogen, which boosts plant growth. Leafy crops will enjoy a light dusting over the surrounding soil in spring and summer. Apply it very sparingly at the rate of half a clenched handful to the square metre (square yard) and use it only between March and August when plants are actively growing. It's useful to keep bacteria fuelled within the compost heap.

BLOOD, BONE AND FISHMEAL is a general fertilizer that supplies the three most important plant foods – nitrogen for leaf and shoot growth; phosphates for root development, and potassium for flower and fruit production. Use it at the rate of one or two handfuls to the square metre (square yard) during the growing season and one week before sowing or planting. It is an organic fertilizer that encourages bacterial activity within the soil. Inorganic fertilizers supply more concentrated nutrition that the plant can utilize more rapidly, but they make beneficial soil bacteria (which would otherwise break down the stuff) redundant. Use inorganic fertilizers (such as sulphate of ammonia) to give crops a rapid boost, and organic fertilizers to improve fertility.

GROWMORE is an inorganic granular general fertilizer. It is readily available and reasonably priced but I find that blood, bone and fishmeal is more effective and a better tonic for the soil.

BONEMEAL is high in phosphates but, to be fair, most of them are held onto so tightly by the soil that few are made available to the plants. Bonemeal is always recommended as a suitable fertilizer to dust around the hole when you're planting trees and shrubs, but in reality the plants probably see little benefit. Use it if it makes you feel better – I don't bother any more!

ROSE FERTILIZER is just the job for getting plants to flower and fruit well, thanks to its high potash and magnesium content. Use it on well-established plants that are coming into flower or fruit – tomatoes, dahlias and other greedy types. Half a clenched handful to the square metre (square yard) is ample.

TOMATO FERTILIZER in liquid form is high in potash and can be diluted and used on *all* flowers and fruits. It is invaluable and quick-acting.

FOLIAR FEEDS are useful where growing crops need a quick boost. They are diluted in water and sprayed on to the foliage, preferably on a dull day. The leaves rapidly absorb the nutrients that perk up the plant. The effect is not as long-lasting as when fertilizers are applied to the soil.

Many gardeners are mean to their plants. Don't be: they need regular feeding just as we do. Give everything a dusting of general fertilizer every spring, and again in summer if you can.

WHY IS DIGGING NECESSARY?

A lot of folk are appalled at the thought of digging, but tackled a little at a time it's a grand way of getting a bit of exercise. Once you're into the rhythm of the job, you'll really enjoy seeing the fresh soil appearing in your wake. But until you've passed the pain barrier it's a real slog, so take it slowly and dig for just half an hour a day until you're ready for more.

But before you start, consider why digging is necessary. First of all it relieves compaction of the soil, so allowing plant roots to penetrate the soil more easily. It allows in air, which is as vital to plants as water, even around the roots. It improves surface drainage, allows weeds to be removed and organic enrichment such as muck and compost to be worked in. And dug soil looks good too!

There are those who advocate the 'no-dig' technique, in which the ground is never cultivated. Instead a layer of muck or compost is spread over the surface of the soil where it keeps down weeds, keeps in moisture and is incorporated by the worms. This is a fine system to adopt after an initial digging over if you have unlimited supplies of organic matter. Once any border or bed has been planted up it works a treat. On previously uncultivated ground and on the vegetable plot I'm not convinced of its usefulness, except in avoiding work. I'm all for short cuts where possible but, for me, digging is essential.

Mulching and watering

A well-nourished soil that has been mulched is less likely to dry out than poor earth that hasn't, and it will grow better plants. If you can possibly afford to mulch your beds and borders, then do so. The job might cost you a few pounds but it will save you both labour and plants.

When to water is a vexed question, and there are more old wives' tales about this than anything else. Forget them all and remember a few simple rules:

1 Water any newly planted tree, shrub or border plant thoroughly during its first season whenever the soil looks dry on the surface.

2 Water established ornamental plants thoroughly when they show signs of wilting.

3 Don't wait for vegetable or fruit crops to wilt before you water.

4 Don't use a watering can or an open-ended hosepipe to water garden plants. Invest in a sprinkler that can be attached to the end of the hosepipe and leave it running over one patch of earth for at least two hours. That way the plants will be thoroughly soaked. Damping down the soil surface does more harm than good.

Digging techniques

There are two main methods of digging: single digging and double digging. Cynics assume that double digging is so called because it's twice as tiring as single digging. That's absolutely true, but the term was originally used to indicate that in double digging the soil is cultivated to a depth of two 'spits' or spade blades, while in single digging it's worked to a depth of just one spit.

Now there really is no need to double dig ground unless it is packed hard 30 m (12 in) down and hasn't been cultivated for donkey's years. Even then I'd get out of double digging it if I possibly could. Only when trees and shrubs are to be established on really hard soil is double digging worthwhile – unless you aim to be a prize parsnip grower, in which case you can double dig your vegetable plot – but not every year, please!

DOUBLE DIGGING If you're pining for exercise or genuinely feel that you have to double dig, this is how to do it: Start by excavating a trench one spit deep and 60 cm (2 ft) wide at one end of the plot to be dug; barrow the excavated soil to the other end.

Now fork over the base of the trench to the full depth of the tines of the fork – that way the soil is

Digging techniques

DOUBLE DIGGING

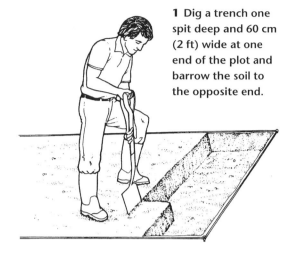

1 Dig a trench one spit deep and 60 cm (2 ft) wide at one end of the plot and barrow the soil to the opposite end.

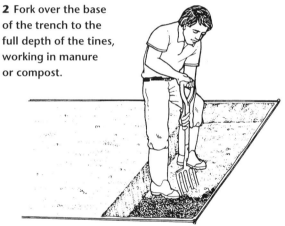

2 Fork over the base of the trench to the full depth of the tines, working in manure or compost.

Fill the last trench in the plot with the soil you removed from the first

3 Dig a second trench behind the first, throwing the soil, inverted, into the first trench. Continue to the end, filling the last trench with soil removed from the first.

SINGLE DIGGING

1 Excavate a trench one spit deep and 45 cm (18 in) wide at one end of the plot to be dug. Barrow the soil to the other end of the plot.

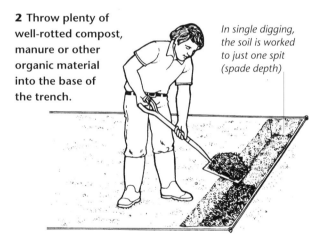

2 Throw plenty of well-rotted compost, manure or other organic material into the base of the trench.

In single digging, the soil is worked to just one spit (spade depth)

To bury short-lived weeds, invert the soil as you throw it forward into the trench in front

3 Dig up the soil immediately behind the trench and throw it forward, inverting it and removing thick-rooted weeds. When the second trench has been created, repeat the operation until the entire plot has been dug.

CHEAT'S DIGGING

1 Start to dig across one end of the strip to be cultivated, lifting up each spadeful of soil, inverting it and throwing it forward a little so that a slight V-shaped trench is created. Remove any thick-rooted weeds.

2 Spread compost or manure along the sloping side of the soil facing you.

Remove any thick-rooted perennial weeds before throwing organic matter over the soil

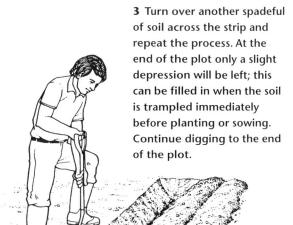

3 Turn over another spadeful of soil across the strip and repeat the process. At the end of the plot only a slight depression will be left; this can be filled in when the soil is trampled immediately before planting or sowing. Continue digging to the end of the plot.

cultivated in two spits. Work in some compost or manure to perk up the earth.

Now dig another trench immediately behind the first, throwing the soil, upside down, into the first trench as you do so. This will bury any short-lived weeds such as groundsel and chickweed, but thick-rooted weeds should be pulled out or they will re-emerge later. Proceed like this until the end of the plot is reached. Then you can use the soil that you removed from the first trench to fill the last.

If the plot is quite wide divide it into two sections, down the centre, and take the first trench out at the end of one half only. Then, instead of barrowing the first soil to the other end of the plot, dump it at the same end of the other half. Now dig down one side and back up the other.

SINGLE DIGGING The difference with single digging is that the soil is dug to the depth of only one spit and the well-rotted manure or compost is scattered over the bottom of the trench rather than being forked into a second spit.

CHEAT'S DIGGING I use this method all the time. It saves the onerous job of barrowing soil around and it allows manure to be spread easily in the upper soil where roots can get at it quickly (see box left).

TRIPLE DIGGING There's another system of digging in which the soil is cultivated to a depth of three spits. I can't believe that anyone would ever want to do it, but for the benefit of masochists it's described in my book *Gardening Techniques* (Mitchell Beazley, 1981).

THE BATTLE AGAINST WEEDS

Although never-ending, weed-control need not be as arduous as many folk assume. The cynic who is convinced that he'll have to spend most of his time in the garden bent double, pulling up nettles and dandelions, probably does just that. The sensible or idle gardener will look for measures that help to prevent the weeds re-emerging once the ground has been cleaned up.

Annual and perennial weeds

When you start to cultivate the soil try to eradicate weeds at the outset. There are two basic kinds: the annuals, which have small root systems but copious amounts of seed; and the perennials, which are often thick-rooted and persistent.

The annuals may not last long as individuals, but the old saying 'One year's seed, seven years' weed' shows that they can be as much of a pain as the longer-lived perennial kinds.

Always try to eradicate annual weeds before they flower. That way they'll have no chance to regenerate. The oldest and most obvious way of weeding is to pull or fork the plants from the soil. It's a practical proposition where ground is being dug or forked over, even though it might be arduous. Where annual weeds are a problem you can use a Dutch hoe. Push it over the soil so that it skims just fractionally below the surface to sever the top half of the plant from the roots. Carried out in dry weather it will leave the weeds to turn crisp on the surface. It's a useful technique on the vegetable plot.

Perennial weeds that are hoed will simply re-emerge from their fat roots, so you'll have to eradicate the underground parts too. If you can't do this by forking or digging you might be tempted to tackle them with a weedkiller.

Using weedkillers

There are three basic types of weedkiller:

CONTACT WEEDKILLERS kill only green parts of the plant that they touch.

TRANSLOCATED OR SYSTEMIC WEEDKILLERS are absorbed by the foliage and transported around inside the plant so that they infect the entire sapstream.

RESIDUAL WEEDKILLERS are watered onto clean soil to prevent weed growth from emerging.

There are also combination weedkillers that can kill off any existing green growth and stop more weeds emerging.

Remember, too, that there are selective and total weedkillers. Those that can be used on lawns are selective in that they kill broad-leaved weeds but not grass. Others are designed to kill couch grass but to leave broad-leaved ornamentals unharmed.

I'm always reluctant to use weedkillers or 'herbicides' among cultivated plants; it's too easy to let the solution stray onto a plant that you want to keep. On paths and drives, though, weedkillers with both a

---

Choosing the correct herbicide

WEED	RECOMMENDED HERBICIDE
● Bindweed (Convolvulus)	Murphy Tumbleweed*
● Bracken	Murphy Tumbleweed (regular cutting back of young growths eventually wipes out plant)
● Bramble	Brushwood Killer or Boots Nettle & Bramble Killer
● Couch grass	Murphy Tumbleweed on uncultivated ground; among plants, wipe leaf blades with Tumbleweed
● Creeping buttercup	Murphy Tumbleweed
● Creeping thistle	Murphy Tumbleweed
● Dock	Murphy Tumbleweed (two applications)
● Ground elder	Murphy Tumbleweed (two applications)
● Japanese knotweed	Murphy Tumbleweed (two applications)
● Marestail (Horsetail)	Murphy Tumbleweed on uncultivated land; Casoron G4 among shrubs and roses
● Mind-your-own-business	Murphy Tumbleweed
● Oxalis	Murphy Tumbleweed
● Pearlwort	Murphy Tumbleweed
● Plantain	Murphy Tumbleweed
● Speedwell	Tar oil winter wash
● Stinging nettle	Murphy Tumbleweed (two applications)

*'Roundup' is the same as 'Tumbleweed'

Troublesome perennial weeds

Perennial weeds are very persistent as their thick roots are difficult to destroy completely by manual methods; you may have to resort to using a systemic weedkiller.

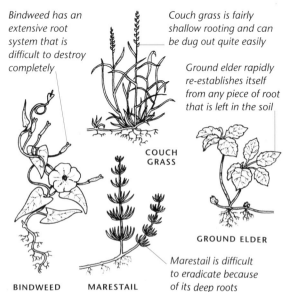

Bindweed has an extensive root system that is difficult to destroy completely

Couch grass is fairly shallow rooting and can be dug out quite easily

Ground elder rapidly re-establishes itself from any piece of root that is left in the soil

COUCH GRASS

GROUND ELDER

Marestail is difficult to eradicate because of its deep roots

BINDWEED   MARESTAIL

contact and a residual action are useful, for they'll kill off any existing growth and prevent its re-emergence for almost 12 months. Choose a herbicide that contains paraquat, diquat and simazine in the form of soluble granules.

Weeding methods for different areas

FLOWER BORDERS Among cultivated plants the best thing to do is to weed the soil properly during preliminary cultivations with the spade or fork and then, immediately after planting (when the soil is moist), lay a 5–8 cm (2–3 in) thick mulch of moist leaf mould, peat, pulverized bark or other organic matter over the surface. Some of these materials may give rise to a few weed seedlings of their own, but such weeds are easy to pull up compared with heavy infestations on bare soil. Top up the mulch when necessary each

A watering can fitted with a dribble bar allows the safe application of herbicides without the danger of spray drifting onto cultivated plants.

spring. A closely planted bed or border will be less likely to support weed growth than one that is sparsely filled. The benefits of ground-cover planting coupled with regular mulching will save you hours of unnecessary hard graft.

FOOD CROPS Among certain fruit and vegetable crops (strawberries, for instance) you can lay a surface mulch of black polythene, pulling the plants through small holes made at the required intervals. This kind of mulch is an effective weed suppressor, but it won't win any prizes in the garden for its good looks.

UNCULTIVATED LAND If you refuse to clean up your land by mechanical means, you can adopt a system that is called, euphemistically, the 'scorched earth policy'. The entire area is treated with a total weedkiller and the application repeated at intervals until nothing else emerges. Then the area is rotavated. Do this, though, and your soil will not be the most hospitable place for plant growth for quite some time.

Specific instructions can be found on the containers of all total weedkillers. There are many to choose from, but avoid sodium chlorate if you can. It stays active in the soil for six months or more; it is highly inflammable; it corrodes metal; and it moves sideways in the soil, often attacking plants that you didn't intend to harm. Others are equally efficient and less lethal.

Where specific weeds are a problem on uncultivated land and you want to use a herbicide to banish them, try to choose the right chemical. The table opposite will give you some idea of the products that are likely to be effective in particular cases.

THE NAMING OF PLANTS

I've no space to go into detail on plant names, but as I've used those terrifying Latin ones throughout I suppose I'd better make my excuses. They're a real mouthful but, unlike common names, they are standard wherever you might be. Even in China or Russia you could ask for *Alcea rosea* and get it; but they'd look puzzled if you asked for a hollyhock. The problem is almost as bad in Britain: common names vary from county to county and some plants have no common name at all, so I've described the plants under their botanical names and given their common names alongside. Both are listed in the index.

plant propagation

Propagating your own plants, whether by seeds (bought or hand-gathered), cuttings or divisions, is surely the most fascinating and rewarding of all gardening activities

MOST OF US ARE COMPELLED TO propagate plants simply to save money, but the compulsion soon becomes an addiction when we find out how easy it is, and how satisfying, to raise a large number of plants with little effort and expense (putting aside the failures, that is). After centuries of gardening there are still a few plants that readily defy attempts at propagation, or which are extremely difficult to multiply in large numbers. This accounts for the relatively high price of certain trees and shrubs. Fortunately, most of the plant kingdom is more obliging and, provided the right conditions are created, most trees, shrubs, flowers and vegetables will increase happily.

There are two basic methods of increase: sexual reproduction (by seeds) and asexual reproduction (by vegetative means such as cuttings and divisions). Seed is a cheap and easy method for many plants, especially vegetables, and is the only way of increasing many annuals (plants that live for just one year before setting seed and dying). Seed-raised plants are almost always vigorous and disease-free.

Vegetative means of propagation must be used where no seed is set, or where such seed will not produce offspring identical to the parent, which is the case with many plant varieties and hybrids. Always take special care to ensure that plants from which cuttings are taken are healthy and disease-free or the problems will be inherited by the offspring.

GROWING FROM SEEDS

Rather like the lady who thought that beans only came out of tins, some folk seem to think that seeds only come out of packets. Don't forget that good seed can often be collected from many plants in the garden. Collected when fully ripe (the pods or capsules usually split at this stage, so you'll have to beat them to it), and stored in a cool, dry place, the seeds will often germinate well the following spring. Keep them in the fridge in an airtight container with a sachet of silica gel to absorb any moisture.

If you're buying seeds always go to a reputable seedsman. There are plenty of them about so it's not difficult. Nowadays all firms are bound by law to test their seeds and guarantee a high viability rate (percentage of germination). If the seeds don't come up when they've been bought from a reputable supplier, the chances are that either you've stored them in too warm a place or you've not given them the conditions they need. Don't rush to blame the seedsman before you check your own treatment.

F1 hybrid seeds are becoming more popular year by year. The first thing you'll notice about them is their price – they cost a bomb! The reason for this is that the seeds have been specially produced by crossing two selected plants known to produce a seed that yields vigorous and uniform offspring with certain desirable qualities – massive flowers or, in the case of a vegetable, whopping roots or leaves.

For the home gardener, F1 hybrid flowers are almost always a good buy. F1 vegetables may not be. They tend to come to maturity with amazing uniformity, providing you with a glut, which might be embarrassing unless you have a freezer!

Don't save seeds from plants that are F1 hybrids – the characteristics they possess will be distributed unevenly in their offspring and you'll have a varied and probably inferior group of plants on your hands.

Pelleted seeds are simply ordinary seeds encased in a coating of clay, sometimes with a fungicide added to aid germination. They make space sowing easy, so cutting out the need for thinning, but they are pricey and, if the soil dries out in the slightest, they may fail to germinate. I never use them, preferring to pay less for a greater number of plain seeds that are not so finicky.

Germination requirements

All seeds need air, moisture and a suitable temperature to trigger off germination. Some also need light (primulas for instance) and should be sown on the compost surface rather than being given the usual burial. Many seeds need exposure to cold before they will germinate (a lot of hardy plants fall into this category), so autumn sowing is practised and the seeds are left in a cold frame during winter.

Some seeds have such tough coats that they have to be chipped a little to allow water to be absorbed; sweet peas are sometimes reluctant to come up unless you 'nick' them, but I've never found them to be difficult provided the compost is kept sufficiently moist.

Berries are usually 'stratified' before being sown. Spread them in alternate layers with sharp sand in a flowerpot during autumn and stand the container outdoors to be frosted all winter. Turn it out into a frame in spring, sift a little compost over the mixture and wait for germination. Some tricky blighters take several years to come up.

'How deep do I sow?' is a regular question. The answer is almost always to one-and-a-half times the diameter of the seed. Dust-fine seeds need no covering at all; large seeds such as beans and nasturtiums can actually be pushed down into the soil with your fingers. Always sow in moist soil but never in cold, soggy earth where the seeds will rot. Seeds sown late in warm soil will always overtake those put in earlier during unfavourable conditions.

Sowing in drills

Most vegetables are sown in straight lines in little V-shaped channels known as drills. The best way to create such drills is to fasten a taut garden line across the soil, resting on the surface, and to draw the soil away from the edge of it with a Dutch or draw hoe. Stand on the line to keep it firm. Sow the seeds thinly in the drill – by thinly I mean at least 0.5 cm (¼ in) apart – and then carefully return the soil to the drill with a rake. Label the row with the name and variety of the crop as well as the date of sowing.

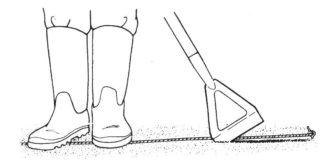

Take out drills for vegetable seeds with a Dutch hoe or a draw hoe. Stand on the garden line to keep it firm while you draw away the soil to create a V-shaped channel.

Sowing broadcast

In the flower border, hardy annual flower seeds can be sown broadcast in irregularly shaped areas known as drifts. Rake the soil so that tiny furrows are left by the rake, and then scatter the seeds over the surface before raking once more in the opposite direction to cover them up.

Don't underestimate the value of thinning out seedlings; do it as soon as possible to give the chosen plants enough light and air to develop.

Sowing under glass

Under any kind of cover, be it greenhouse, frame or windowsill, seeds must be sown in pots of seed compost, not garden soil. However good your soil, it will not be open or well drained enough for plants in pots. Any proprietary seed compost can be used; it should be lightly firmed within the container before sowing so that it rests about 1 cm (½ in) below the rim to allow for a covering of compost and subsequent watering. Make sure the compost is moist before you sow the seeds.

Now read the seed packet. Can you provide the right temperature for germination? The majority of plants you sow under protection will need a temperature of around 18–21°C (65–70°F), though one or two may need a little more heat.

Take the seeds out of the packet and place them in the palm of one hand. Tap the edge of this hand with the other so that the seeds are dislodged a few centimetres (inches) above the compost. They will fall and bounce on the surface, so becoming more evenly distributed. Don't sow too thickly. When you think

you've sown enough seeds, return the rest to the packet and lightly sieve compost over those you have sown. Use a 3 mm (⅛ in) sieve and stop sieving as soon as the seeds disappear from view. Very fine seeds, like *Lobelia*, *Gloxinia*, *Begonia*, *Petunia* and *Calceolaria*, need not be covered at all except with a sheet of paper followed by a sheet of glass, which is a covering recommended for all seeds. The glass helps to keep the compost moist and the paper cuts down the sun's glare, as well as mopping up condensation if it is put over the pots first.

> *"All seeds need air, moisture and a suitable temperature to trigger off germination."*

Label the containers with variety and date and stand them in a warm place – ideally a propagator. These mini-greenhouses can be obtained in all shapes and sizes and at reasonable cost. If you're going in for a bit of propagating, you'll find that the kind that utilizes a plastic seed tray with a transparent dome and a heated base plate will suit you nicely without breaking the bank. Alternatively you can always stick to the airing cupboard if you don't mind compost-covered washing.

Check the pots every day and as soon as the first seedling in each container breaks the surface, remove the pot and stand it in a warm, well-lit place. Should the compost dry out, water it with a watering can fitted with a fine rose.

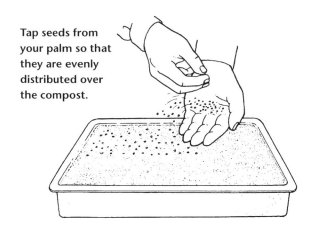

Tap seeds from your palm so that they are evenly distributed over the compost.

Types of propagators

The cheapest propagator consists of a seed tray covered with a transparent dome that is fitted with small vents. An electrically heated panel can be positioned beneath the tray to provide 'bottom heat'. More elaborate structures can be made at home and fitted with thermostatically controlled solid warming cables. A polythene shroud will maintain humidity.

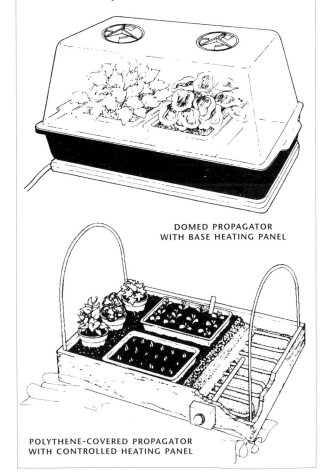

DOMED PROPAGATOR WITH BASE HEATING PANEL

POLYTHENE-COVERED PROPAGATOR WITH CONTROLLED HEATING PANEL

Seeds of hardy plants can be sown in pots of compost, which are then stood outdoors in a garden frame. Spring is the usual time to sow, though many seeds are often best sown as soon as they are ripe – in summer or autumn. A cold winter may be just what they need to spur them into growth.

Pricking out

As soon as the seedlings are large enough to handle, they should be transplanted into seed trays where they will have more room to develop. Lever them from the compost in the pot with a pencil or small dibber, keeping as much compost around their roots as possible. Hold each seedling by one of its seed leaves, not its fragile stem, and lower its roots into a hole made in the compost with the point of the pencil. Firm the compost around the roots so that the seedling stands upright. Space the seedlings about 5 cm (2 in) apart on the square. Water them in when the tray is fully planted up. Grow the seedlings on until they are ready to be hardened off for planting out or potted up into individual containers. Pot plants such as geraniums (*Pelargonium*) can be pricked out straight into 8 cm (3 in) pots to save time.

Prick out seedlings from the compost in which they are growing with a small dibber, holding each one by a seed leaf. Lower it into a pencil-hole made in the new compost and firm it in. Water the seedlings carefully but well.

INCREASING STOCK BY DIVISION

This is one of the easiest means of propagating plants. Simple division, which is best carried out in autumn or spring where hardy border plants are concerned, involves the digging up and prising apart of established clumps. It sounds cruel but it does most plants the

world of good. When you've dug up the clump, chop it into coconut-sized pieces with a spade, discarding the dead central portion (most perennials spread outwards and the old centre gradually dies). Make sure you replant the new plants at the same level as before. Water them well in times of drought. Autumn dividing pays dividends on any well-drained soil for the plants are ready to grow away eagerly come the spring, outstripping spring-divided plants by leaps and bounds. On clay soils, though, they may sit and sulk through the winter.

Irises and other plants that make rhizomes (fat stems at or just below ground level: see p.152) can also be divided. Irises are best split after flowering and fat, healthy rhizomes can be cut into individual portions, each bearing a fan of leaves. Shorten the leaves by half and replant so that the rhizomes sit just beneath the new soil surface.

It is always a good idea to clean up and enrich the soil before replanting your divisions, and it's a good idea to replant in a different spot, too.

Plants that produce suckers (shoots from the roots) can be propagated by severing the new shoot in autumn or spring, with a few roots, and replanting it where it is wanted. Plants grafted onto a different rootstock will, of course, produce suckers inferior to themselves, and these should be removed and discarded.

Tubers (see p.152) can also be divided, provided that each division has a portion of tuber plus a bud.

Any kind of plantlet, be it a strawberry runner or an offset of a *Sempervivum*, makes propagation easy. The youngster can simply be detached and encouraged to make roots of its own in a pot of compost or a bed of soil before being planted out independently. Alternatively it can be encouraged to form roots while still attached to its parent and then removed and transplanted afterwards.

TAKING CUTTINGS

There are three basic types of cutting: stem, leaf and root. All three types are removed from the parent plant and then encouraged to form either roots or shoots, whichever is lacking.

Stem cuttings

Stem cuttings fall into three categories, depending on the time of year at which they are taken and the consequent hardness of the wood.

SOFTWOOD CUTTINGS are taken in spring and early summer and consist of healthy, vigorous shoot tips that are soft and pliable. The finished cutting should be 5–8 cm (2–3 in) long with two or three leaves at the top. The lower leaves should have been removed and the basal cut made just below a leaf joint or node. Insert the cuttings to half their depth in a propagator filled with a half and half peat/sand mix, or around the edge of 10 cm (4 in) pots of the same medium. Bottom heat is helpful in rooting the cuttings quickly. This can be applied via a heated base plate below the propagator or with special soil-warming cables. Some cuttings, such as *Impatiens*, can even be rooted in jars of water stood on a windowsill. Only tricky cuttings need have their bases lightly dipped in hormone rooting powder before insertion in the compost.

Keep the cuttings shaded from brilliant sunshine – but not in the dark – while they root. Humidity is vital in preventing dehydration, hence the desirability of an enclosed propagator or a polythene bag over the pot. Most softwood cuttings root readily in a temperature of around 18°C (65°F). Growth of the shoots is a good indication of rooting and at this stage the plants should be knocked out of their containers and potted up individually. Keep them out of bright sunlight for a few days until their roots are established in the new potting compost.

HALF-RIPE CUTTINGS During July and August the shoots of many plants (especially shrubs) begin to harden. At this stage, but while they are still relatively pliable, they are said to be half-ripe or semi-ripe.

Taking hardwood cuttings

1 Hardwood cuttings of plants such as roses and gooseberries should be taken in autumn. Make them 20 cm (8 in) long and trim them above a bud at the top and below a bud at the base. Insert them to two thirds their depth in narrow trenches into which sand has been trickled.

2 Firm the sand around the stems of the cuttings, then replace the soil around them.

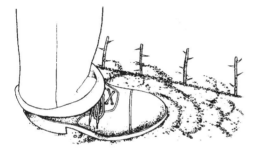

3 Tread the soil firmly back around the cuttings to exclude air pockets, and water them thoroughly.

Types of leaf cuttings

LEAF STALK CUTTINGS

Cut healthy leaves plus stalks from the parent plant. Insert the stalks in a pot filled with peat and sand mixture

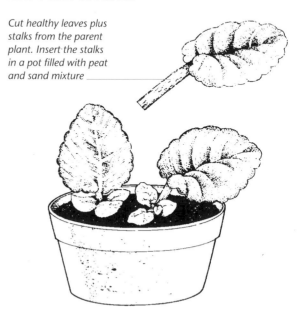

Leaf stalk cuttings of African violets (*Saintpaulia*) can be easily rooted in pots containing a mixture of peat and sand. Keep the cuttings warm while they root.

Cuttings taken at this time should be about 10 cm (4 in) long and prepared and inserted as for softwood cuttings. Half-ripe cuttings of hardy shrubs may also be inserted in a well-drained medium within a cold frame outdoors. Here they can stay until the following spring, when they can be removed and potted up or planted out. Those rooted in a propagator can be potted up and overwintered in a garden frame before being planted out the following year.

Some half-ripe cuttings are found to root better if removed from the parent plant with a heel of older wood. Tear them from the main stem and trim the heel to a length of 1 cm (½ in) before insertion. Many conifers root better with a heel.

HARDWOOD CUTTINGS need no protection at all and they provide an easy means of increasing many deciduous shrubs, including roses. Hardwood cuttings are taken just as the leaves fall in autumn. Young, healthy shoots of pencil thickness should be selected. Trim them above a bud at the top and below a bud at the base so that they are about 20 cm (8 in) long. Roses can be left with two leaves at the top, should these still be present.

Insert the cuttings to two thirds their depth in narrow slit trenches into which a little coarse sand has been trickled. (The vegetable plot may be the most convenient spot for them.) Firm back the earth with your feet. The cuttings should root and grow during the following spring and summer and may be lifted and transplanted the following autumn.

Leaf cuttings

Some plants can be propagated from leaves without any vestige of stem at all. Those of African violets (*Saintpaulia*) and others are removed from the plant, with their leaf stalks intact, and dibbed into sand and peat in a propagator. I've even rooted them in jars of water with the leaf blade supported over the water; the stalk is pushed through a piece of transparent clingfilm fastened over the top of the jar.

Leaves of *Begonia rex* can be cut up into postage-stamp-sized pieces and inserted into the rooting medium like gravestones; provided they are the right way up, they will root and send up youngsters from their bases. The entire leaf of the plant may be laid on the surface of the compost, slit at the main veins and

SLIT LEAF CUTTINGS

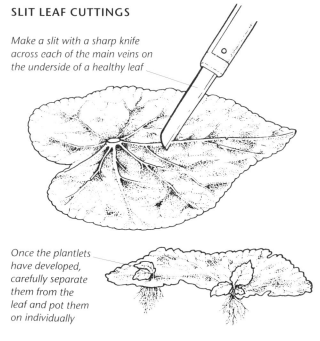

Make a slit with a sharp knife across each of the main veins on the underside of a healthy leaf

Once the plantlets have developed, carefully separate them from the leaf and pot them on individually

A leaf of *Begonia rex*, laid on the surface of moist compost and slit at the main veins, may produce a young plant at each of the slits.

LEAF BUD CUTTINGS

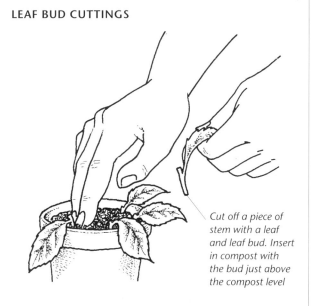

Cut off a piece of stem with a leaf and leaf bud. Insert in compost with the bud just above the compost level

In early summer, leaf bud cuttings from plants with larger leaves, such as *Camellia*, *Ficus* (rubber plant) and *Clematis* can be taken. Once the leaf stem has rooted, a tiny shoot will grow from the base. Leave the original leaf on until it begins to wither.

kept moist. Plantlets will arise at the cuts with any luck.

Leaf bud cuttings include a small portion of stem and a bud. *Camellia*, *Ficus* (rubber plant) and even *Clematis* can be propagated from them. Early summer is generally the best time for this type of propagation.

Root cuttings

These are best taken during the plant's dormant season. Lift the plant to be propagated, wash its roots free of soil and then cut suitable roots (between knitting needle and pencil thickness) into 5 cm (2 in) long sections. To make sure that the roots are the right way up, make a flat cut at the top (the end which was nearer the parent) and a slanting cut at the base. Insert the cuttings in pots of seed compost, planting them vertically with the aid of a dibber. The top of the cutting should be level with the surface of the compost. Scatter a little sharp sand over the surface,

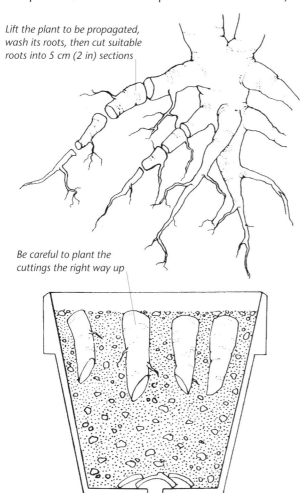

Lift the plant to be propagated, wash its roots, then cut suitable roots into 5 cm (2 in) sections

Be careful to plant the cuttings the right way up

Some plants can be propagated from sections of root that are removed and inserted in pots of compost.

label the pot and stand it in a garden frame or, if the plant is tender, in a propagator. If the compost is moist and the pot is kept lightly shaded, no water should be given until more roots are produced, probably after the shoots appear in early spring.

Not all plants are capable of being propagated by root cuttings; I have indicated in the A–Z sections those that are.

LAYERING

Ordinary stems of garden plants can sometimes be encouraged to form roots if they are bent down and partly buried in the soil. The operation is usually carried out in early spring.

Find a conveniently long and supple stem. Trim off any leaves that occur between 15–38 cm (6–15 in) below the shoot tip so that a healthy cluster is left at the end of the shoot, with a bare length of stem behind. Bend the stem to the soil and make a slight wound in the bark at the point of contact, slitting the stem with a knife to make a tongue. Work peat and sand into the soil immediately below the cut, scoop out a 5–8 cm (2–3 in) hole and lay the cut portion in position. Pin it down with a piece of wire if necessary. Replace the soil and do not let it dry out.

Cut the new plant from its parent in the autumn and leave it for a few weeks before attempting to lift and transplant it. Alternatively wait until spring.

Tip layering can be carried out with plants such as the blackberry. Here the shoot is bent down to the ground and the top 10 cm (4 in) is completely buried. Once a new plant arises it can be transplanted.

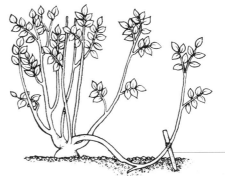

With the stem bent to the soil, make a slight wound in the bark at the point of contact. Peg the stem down

Plants with suitably low-growing stems can often be propagated by layering. Make an incision in the shoot then bend it down and bury it in the soil, holding it firm with a peg. Sever the stem when the new plant is well rooted but leave for a few weeks before transplanting it.

Air layering

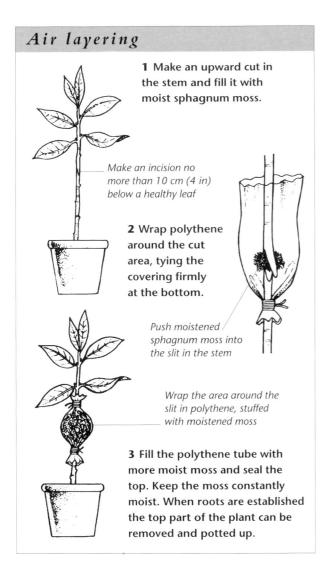

1 Make an upward cut in the stem and fill it with moist sphagnum moss.

Make an incision no more than 10 cm (4 in) below a healthy leaf

2 Wrap polythene around the cut area, tying the covering firmly at the bottom.

Push moistened sphagnum moss into the slit in the stem

Wrap the area around the slit in polythene, stuffed with moistened moss

3 Fill the polythene tube with more moist moss and seal the top. Keep the moss constantly moist. When roots are established the top part of the plant can be removed and potted up.

Many tall house plants and shrubs can be air layered. At a suitable point in the stem – usually about 45 cm (18 in) from the shoot tip and a few centimetres (inches) below a healthy leaf – an upward incision is made, as for ordinary or simple layering. Sphagnum moss (available from florists) is moistened and pushed into the incision then padded around it. Polythene is bandaged around the moss and fastened top and bottom with sticky tape. Keep the moss moist and be patient. Roots are likely to be slow in coming, though the higher the temperature the more quickly they will emerge. In most cases you may have to wait a year before the top half of the plant can be severed from the bottom and potted up on its own. Cherish it for a few months until it becomes established. The bottom part should grow away and become pleasingly bushy.

Plants such as heathers can be propagated by 'dropping'. Dig them up in spring and plant them again more deeply so that only the shoot tips can be seen. In autumn dig up the plants and cut off the shoot tips, which will have formed roots. Replant your new heathers in peat-enriched soil.

BULBS AND CORMS

Most bulbs and corms reproduce themselves naturally, though their rates of multiplication vary. I have no room here to delve deeply into the technicalities of 'scooping' and 'scoring' bulbs, which some aficionados may consider. It's a painfully slow job for use on bulbs that are otherwise hard to propagate in large numbers.

Where most gardeners can cash in is by growing on the smaller bulblets or cormlets produced around the base of larger flowering bulbs. A piece of good soil in full sun should be selected and, at the appropriate planting time, the babies should be set in the soil to twice their depth and allowed to grow on for another year or more until they reach flowering size.

Bulbils – the tiny bulbs produced on the stems of some lilies and one or two other bulbs – can be similarly grown on in pots of sandy compost placed in a garden frame. Remove the bulbils from the plants as soon as they are ripe and press them into the surface of the pot of prepared compost, sifting a little sharp sand over them. Stand them in a garden frame for about a year and then transfer them to their flowering positions in the garden where they may need to grow on for at least another year. It's a job for the patient gardener, but a rewarding one. If your plants don't produce bulbils you may be able to induce them to do so artificially by nipping the flower buds from the stem before they open. Are you prepared to make the sacrifice?

For more detailed information on propagation than I am able to include here, see *The Complete Book of Plant Propagation* by Robert Wright and Alan Titchmarsh (Ward Lock, 1981).

Bulbils that form up the stems of certain lilies can be removed and grown on to flowering-sized bulbs.

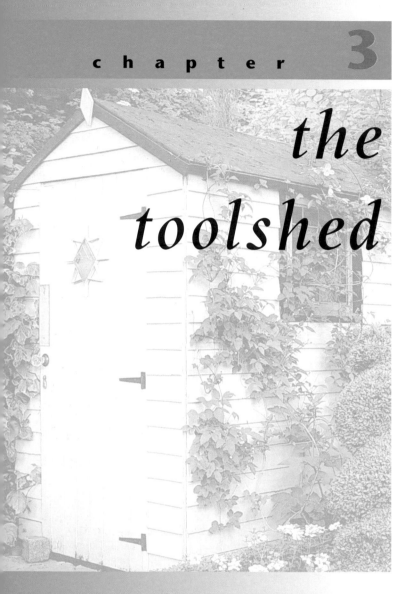

the toolshed

Every job in the garden

is made easier by having

the right tools. If you

choose them carefully

and look after them well,

they will last a lifetime

YOU MIGHT THINK THAT THE BEST PLACE to find a good set of garden tools is the garden centre or the local hardware shop, and sure enough that's where you'll come face to face with a showcase that rivals the Blackpool illuminations for brilliance. But how do you tell which tools are the best buy, and how do you know which are just expensive gimmicks that will end up gathering dust after their first disastrous try-out?

I reckon you'd do far better delaying a visit to the shop and going first to the garage or toolshed of an aged member of the family whose gardening days are numbered. There you might find a set of basic tools that have not only stood the test of time but which have been run in for you. Bright new spades and forks are all very well but they don't half take some breaking in. Until the blades and prongs have been honed to perfection by the soil, they are often difficult and exhausting to work with.

Should your aged relative decide that the tools cannot be parted with, then cast your eye round local auction sales or secondhand shops for spades, forks, rakes and hoes that are well worn. Just make sure that in spite of their age the implements are still strong and that the handles have not cracked or become loose in their sockets. Years of use should have polished the shafts to a silken smoothness, but any splinters can easily be rubbed off with sandpaper. When all attempts at finding secondhand tools fail, then you can visit the local emporium – but beware of being bamboozled into buying something you don't need.

Here's my list of essentials that most gardeners can't do without. Buy them one at a time as you need them.

TOOLS FOR WORKING THE SOIL

Spade

However lazy you are, you'll have to dig sooner or later, even if you're only digging a hole for a tree or shrub. Here the spade is essential but, if your soil is really stony, a fork is much easier to use for general digging over. The spade has the advantage of being able to skim off surface weed growth before digging starts, and you can also use it for mixing composts and for edging the lawn if, like me, you're too mean to buy one of those special half-moon edging tools.

You'll find that there are three sizes of spade: the standard digging spade has a blade measuring 29 x 19 cm (11½ x 7½ in); the medium spade 25 x 16.5 cm (10 x 6½ in); and the border spade

23 x 14 cm (9 x 5½ in). Pick the spade that's most comfortable to use: even if you're in a shop, hold it as if you were about to dig, and go through the motions to see if it's well balanced and feels comfortable. The shaft should be smooth and splinter-free, the socket should be gently cranked to make for better leverage and any rivets should have smooth heads that do not chafe your hands. The handle at the top may be T, D, or YD-shaped. Choose whichever feels the most comfortable, but be warned that the T shape can be more blister-making if you have tender skin. If your soil is very heavy, look for a spade with flattened treads on the upper edges of the blade – they'll be easier on your feet. You'd also be well advised to go for a medium-sized spade on very heavy soil, just to guard against strained muscles.

Most spade shafts are wooden, but some are made from tubular steel or alloy coated with polypropylene. The latter are likely to be more expensive. Nearly all spades and forks now have plastic handles at the top and, in spite of their appearance, they are usually comfortable and long lasting. Which spade you choose will depend on the size of your pocket as well as your physique. The most expensive tools are always made from stainless steel, but they're not essential and can be rather heavy to work with. A good, well-balanced spade, which doesn't feel 'numb' or clumsy, will probably outlast you, so use your common sense when buying and come away with a well-made yet reasonably priced implement.

Powered cultivator

The rotavator is thought of by many gardeners as the only way of cultivating soil. Certainly it's quick and, even though it may pull your arms out of their sockets occasionally, it's easy to use. But it won't rid your ground of weeds and it doesn't work in organic matter very efficiently, so don't think that it replaces the spade completely. Used too regularly at the same depth it will cause a 'pan', or hard, impenetrable layer in the subsoil, so it is best used where its advantages outweigh its disadvantages. Use it for turning over the vegetable plot in winter or for cultivating ground that has been treated with a herbicide to kill off weeds.

It's seldom worth buying a rotavator unless you plan to use it at least once a week – hire it instead and let somebody else worry about the maintenance and storage. If you prepare all the patches of land you want cultivated in advance, you'll be able to romp away with the machine on the day it arrives.

All rotavated land becomes well aerated but rather fluffy so trample it well before you sow or plant to rid it of large air pockets.

Fork

For digging stony or heavy soil, the fork is a better bet than the spade; for pricking over cultivated soil in beds and borders, it is essential. Use it, too, for moving compost and manure and for spiking the surface of the lawn in spring and autumn. When soil has been rough-dug, use the back of the fork rather like a carpet beater to smash up the clods. This action will produce a fine-textured surface, or tilth, without bringing stones to the surface – always a problem if you use a rake for the job.

As to construction, the same general rules apply as for the spade, but two sizes are generally available: the digging fork has a head 30 x 19 cm (12 x 7½ in) and the border fork measures 23 x 14 cm (9 x 5½ in). Both have prongs or tines that are square in cross-section. The potato fork has flattened prongs, supposedly to prevent damage to your spuds when they're being lifted, but I still manage to spear a few of mine whichever fork I use. Again, pick a fork that feels comfortable and not too heavy in your hands.

> *"There's nothing nicer than standing behind a sharp Dutch hoe as it smoothly chops through weeds in the flower border."*

Rake

I reckon that the rake is the most over-used tool in the garden. True enough, it's vital for levelling soil before seed sowing, and it's helpful in clearing up leaves and debris, but it can produce unwanted results if it is used to break down the soil to a fine texture. It brings every available stone to the surface and causes the soil to cake in the first shower of rain. Use the back of the fork for breaking down the soil, and use the rake sparingly in long, sweeping motions to level the surface.

Your average rake has a handle about 1.5 m (5 ft) long and a 30 cm (12 in) wide head, equipped with 5 cm (2 in) teeth. Make sure the handle is smooth and splinter-free if it is wooden, and that the head is securely attached. Rakes with plastic-coated alloy handles are easiest to use, for they are light and less likely to dig up stones. They are also more expensive.

The wire-toothed springbok rake is the best tool for clearing up leaves and lawn mowings and for ripping the thatch, or dead grass, from lawns. It's not too expensive to buy and if you've a lot of grass (or plenty of leaves in autumn) I'd invest in one. Don't fall for the bamboo-toothed kind that will hardly last for a season if you have powerful biceps.

Hoe

You can get by with just one hoe – the Dutch hoe. This is the type that has a long handle and a head shaped like a horseshoe, with a band of metal across the open end. There's nothing nicer than standing behind a sharp Dutch hoe as it smoothly chops through weeds in the flower border or between vegetable rows. Used properly (and kept sharp with a file) it makes light

Tools and equipment for garden care

What you need will depend on the size of your garden and what you plan to do in it. Before buying any tool or piece of equipment hold it and go through the motions of using it, to make sure that it is the right size and weight for you. Often well-honed secondhand tools are the best buy.

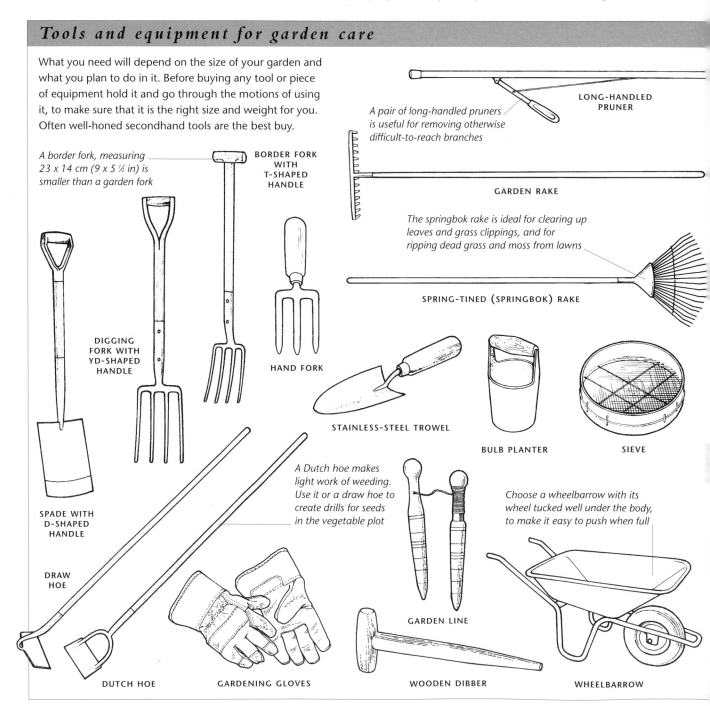

A border fork, measuring 23 x 14 cm (9 x 5 ½ in) is smaller than a garden fork

BORDER FORK WITH T-SHAPED HANDLE

DIGGING FORK WITH YD-SHAPED HANDLE

HAND FORK

SPADE WITH D-SHAPED HANDLE

DRAW HOE

DUTCH HOE

GARDENING GLOVES

A pair of long-handled pruners is useful for removing otherwise difficult-to-reach branches

LONG-HANDLED PRUNER

GARDEN RAKE

The springbok rake is ideal for clearing up leaves and grass clippings, and for ripping dead grass and moss from lawns

SPRING-TINED (SPRINGBOK) RAKE

STAINLESS-STEEL TROWEL

BULB PLANTER

SIEVE

A Dutch hoe makes light work of weeding. Use it or a draw hoe to create drills for seeds in the vegetable plot

Choose a wheelbarrow with its wheel tucked well under the body, to make it easy to push when full

GARDEN LINE

WOODEN DIBBER

WHEELBARROW

work of weed control – the secret is to use it regularly every week or so and to let it skim over the surface of the soil, rather than holding it at an angle so that it digs deeply. That way it's not half as effective at separating the weeds from their roots and they'll probably perk up after the next shower of rain. When you use the Dutch hoe you'll be working backwards so that the soil is left untrampled, but with the draw hoe (a flat-bladed hoe whose blade is at right angles to the shaft) you'll have to walk over the ground you've just scraped over. Both hoes can be used for drawing drills for seeds (those little channels that are taken out against a taut garden line). As with other long-handled tools, a smooth shaft and a secure head are the things to look for, plus a feeling of balance in the implement as a whole. If you're a keen potato and celery grower

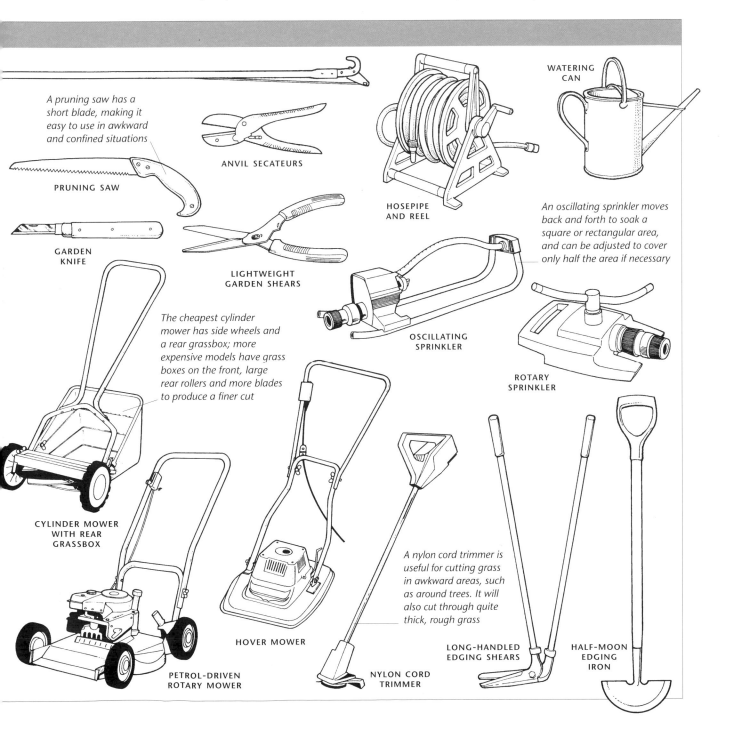

A pruning saw has a short blade, making it easy to use in awkward and confined situations

PRUNING SAW

GARDEN KNIFE

ANVIL SECATEURS

LIGHTWEIGHT GARDEN SHEARS

WATERING CAN

HOSEPIPE AND REEL

An oscillating sprinkler moves back and forth to soak a square or rectangular area, and can be adjusted to cover only half the area if necessary

OSCILLATING SPRINKLER

ROTARY SPRINKLER

The cheapest cylinder mower has side wheels and a rear grassbox; more expensive models have grass boxes on the front, large rear rollers and more blades to produce a finer cut

CYLINDER MOWER WITH REAR GRASSBOX

A nylon cord trimmer is useful for cutting grass in awkward areas, such as around trees. It will also cut through quite thick, rough grass

HOVER MOWER

PETROL-DRIVEN ROTARY MOWER

NYLON CORD TRIMMER

LONG-HANDLED EDGING SHEARS

HALF-MOON EDGING IRON

you'll find the draw hoe useful when it comes to earthing up.

Although it's not strictly a hoe, I'll include the hand cultivator here because it's useful for perking up the soil between all manner of plants. Its head is claw-shaped, usually with three spikes, and it is pulled through the soil with jerky motions to break up the surface crust. Choose a small, lightweight version and you'll find it really comfortable to use.

Trowel

There are some very poor trowels on the market that bend as soon as you show them a tough bit of ground. They'll drive you mad if you have to live with them. Play safe – lash out and buy a stainless-steel trowel; it's the only stainless-steel tool I possess, but I wouldn't be without it. Make sure the handle is smooth and that it fits your hand well and you'll not have to worry a jot about the blade – it will stay clean and sturdy whatever your soil. Short-handled trowels are much easier to use than the long-handled versions, which tend to wobble around. You'll need a trowel for planting everything from bedding plants to young vegetables, and it's a useful weeder in confined spaces.

Rod and line

Not a quick dissertation on fishing, but a note on two pieces of equipment that can be made at home. I do all my planting, both in the flower garden and on the vegetable plot, by eye, but if you don't know what 15 cm (6 in) or 30 cm (12 in) looks like, make yourself a measuring rod from a piece of 5 x 2.5 cm (2 x 1 in) timber marked with shallow saw-cuts at the appropriate distances – a little notch every 15 cm (6 in) and a larger one every 30 cm (12 in).

Two metal spikes (or lengths of broom handle) linked with 10 metres (11 yards) of stout nylon or hemp twine is just what you need to mark the position of drills being drawn on the vegetable plot and for cutting straight edges on the lawn. The line should always be kept as taut as possible when it's being used, and it should rest on the ground to prevent it from moving too much. Keep the line free of knots, which will throw the drill-drawing hoe off course, and wrap it up after use to prevent it from being tangled by children or animals.

Dibber

This is perhaps the most traditional tool in the ancient gardener's armoury, but it's still valuable today. For

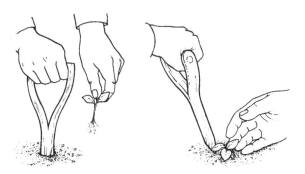

An old spade handle makes a handy dibber. Push it in and wiggle it around to make a hole; lower in the seedling, then use the dibber to firm back the soil.

transplanting or pricking out seedlings into trays, there's no finer dibber than a pencil. For transplanting cabbages and the like on the vegetable plot, an old spade or fork handle is what is needed: if you haven't broken a spade handle in years, go out and buy a new handle to use as a dibber.

With both kinds of dibber, the method of using the tool is the same: wiggle it around in the soil to make a hole; lower the roots into place, and push back the soil with the point of the dibber, firming it as you do so.

TOOLS FOR CUTTING AND PRUNING

Secateurs

A good pair of pruning shears will help you with all cutting operations from flower gathering and deadheading to snipping out dead stems up to finger thickness. Don't try to cut fatter stems than this or you'll strain the secateurs and render them useless. There are several different designs, but the two basic kinds are those with a scissor action and those with what is described as an anvil mechanism. The first type cuts with a slicing motion and the second with a sharp blade that comes down against a flat metal surface. Both are reliable but the anvil type, in particular, must be kept razor-sharp if stems are not to be crushed and disease admitted. I've used a pair of Rolcut anvil secateurs for years and have found them very durable – sharpening is simple with either emery paper or a whetstone. Some secateurs must be returned to the manufacturer for sharpening, and those that look very glossy and chrome-plated are best avoided – they can't keep an edge for half an hour.

By far the best secateurs (if you can afford them) are the type manufactured by Felco; they are superbly made and serviced free for life – not a bad recommendation!

Avoid at all costs those very cheap secateurs that look as if they are made of cast iron. They cut very badly, if at all, and are extremely uncomfortable to hold, trapping your fingers more times than not.

Stems thicker than your finger are best cut with loppers – those long-handled pruners that have tougher blades than secateurs and which can produce more torque. If you have a garden full of shrubs and roses, a pair of loppers is a must.

With all pruning shears remember always to cut back to a point immediately above a bud or a leaf to prevent die-back. Leave a finger of budless stem and it will rot back, probably allowing fungus diseases to enter.

Knife

When I first went to work I was told by the foreman that my pocket should always contain a sharp knife, a piece of string and sixpence. The knife was for taking cuttings, the string to hold my trousers up when all else failed, and the sixpence was for the foreman himself! The knife I always had, but the other two were often missing.

Buy a good knife and it will last for ages; I still use the one I was given on my first day at work, and even then it wasn't new – the propagator decided he'd purloin the one sent for me and I could have his old one. I found I'd got the better of the deal for his old knife was nicely sharpened and well run in. Those sold as budding or grafting knives are good for general purpose work and not too heavy. Do make sure you buy a knife that's specifically made for garden use, but not one of those with a blade you can see your face in – it will be the very devil to keep sharp. A good-tempered steel

A garden shed doesn't have to be an eyesore. This yellow-painted shed has a reclaimed stained glass window, and *Clematis montana* var. *rubens* clambering up the side.

blade is what you should look for in a gardening knife, not a stainless-steel blade that's more at home on the dinner table. Always keep your knife sharp on a whetstone and keep it in your pocket (with or without the string and two-and-a-half new pence).

Shears

A pair of general-purpose garden shears is always handy, whether it's for hedge clipping or for slicing off those tufts of grass that refuse to give in to the lawn mower. Wooden, polypropylene or tubular steel handles can all be comfortable, but check that your wrists are not jarred by the snipping action – rubber

buffers between the blades are a help here. Go for carbon-steel blades and find a pair of shears that has a notch at the base of each blade to allow individual thicker stems to be cut.

In the interests of saving labour, I try to avoid creating bare edges to lawns, but if your garden is full of them, you'll find that edging shears save a lot of time. They have long handles, fitted with blades set at right angles, and they save you bending down to snip off overhanging grass. When you're buying a pair, the same considerations apply as for ordinary shears. When you're using them, try to get into the habit of holding the left hand still and moving just the right hand, which controls the upper blade. That way you'll achieve a more even cut faster and with less exertion – not that this is the most exhausting job in the garden! (See p.82 for how to use electric trimmers.)

Rub the blades of your shears with emery paper after use; this will clear them of dried sap and keep them cutting cleanly.

WATERING EQUIPMENT

Watering cans

After years of using galvanized watering cans, most gardeners have switched to plastic. True enough, the plastic cans cannot be repaired easily, but they are much cheaper and lighter in weight than their metal counterparts and more economical even if thrown away as soon as leaks develop. Long-spouted cans are always easiest to use, and a 10 litre (2 gallon) capacity can is best for general watering, though I'd plump for a 5 litre (1 gallon) can in the greenhouse for its ease of manoeuvrability. The sprinkler heads on the end of the spout are known as roses and brass ones are by far the best.

Use the can for watering anything, and fix the rose to the spout when watering in newly planted seedlings or plants. Use a second can for applying weedkillers, and label it as such. Don't be tempted to use such a can for watering garden plants; herbicide residues hang about in them and can decimate cultivated crops.

Hosepipe

When you tire of using a can it's time you invested in a hosepipe. Only you will know how long a hose you need, but let me persuade you to buy one that's reinforced with nylon thread; it will last far longer than a plain plastic one even though it costs more at the outset. It will also be less likely to kink. Always coil up the hose when you've finished with it and store it out of direct sunlight. If it's left tangled, it will drive you batty every time you come to use it, and where kinks are formed the hose may eventually rupture.

Garden sprinkler

In the interests of spending more time in your deckchair and less time holding on to a hosepipe or watering can, invest in a garden sprinkler, which will do the watering while you stare at it. There are two types – the rotating sprinkler, which soaks a circle of ground, and the oscillating type, which moves back and forth to soak a square or rectangle. As most gardens are square or rectangular, rather than circular, the oscillating sprinkler is more useful (its back and forth motion is also quite soporific if you're trying to doze). Added to this, the oscillating type can usually be adjusted to cover only half the rectangle or square.

Both types of sprinkler apply water more effectively than any hosepipe because they create a fine rain that penetrates the soil very efficiently, getting the moisture to the plant's roots rather than caking the surface of the earth.

Some gardeners are frightened of watering plants in the garden, believing the old wives' tale that if you do the roots come up to the surface. This is rubbish. They will only come to the surface if you constantly keep the surface moist and allow the lower part of the soil to dry out. Give the ground a thorough soak with a sprinkler for two hours when necessary and you'll do the plants nothing but good. Plants hate drought; it stops them from growing, reduces their flowering and fruiting capabilities and may even kill them. So if it hasn't rained for a week or more in summer, and your soil is dry 5 cm (2 in) down when you scoop out a hole with a trowel, turn on the sprinkler. Your plants will show their appreciation while those of your superstitious friends peg out.

On a practical note, remember that you'll need to apply to the water authority for a permit to use a hosepipe, which will cost a few pounds extra on your water rates. You may also require permission to use a sprinkler, so check first to avoid costly embarrassment later.

Hand sprayer

Whether it's for perking up your house plants with a drop of fresh water, or for boosting them with a foliar feed, a small trigger-action hand sprayer is a useful bit of equipment. A 0.5 litre or 1 litre capacity sprayer (roughly 1 or 2 pints) is sufficient for most gardens – and many insecticides are being made to dilute in such small quantities of water nowadays – but a larger pump-up 5 litre (1 gallon) version may be more suited to your needs if you have rolling acres of roses or vegetables. Whichever size you use, wash it out thoroughly after use to rid it of damaging residues. Don't keep made-up spray in the vessel for more than a couple of days – it may go off.

LAWN-CARE TOOLS

Lawn mower

There's still plenty of controversy raging about the different types of mower. Choose one that you find easy to work with and which cuts your grass adequately for your needs. Cylinder mowers give the finest results (the more blades there are in the cylinder the neater the finish) and are essential if you're out to create that bowling green lawn; in this case you can cut as low as 1 cm (½ in) or even 5 mm (¼ in) if you irrigate it regularly and only walk on it occasionally.

Rotary mowers are fine for most hard-wearing lawns, though it's a good idea to find a machine that is fitted with a grassbox. The rotary types won't give you the stripes you get from cylinder mowers, but they can cope with rougher, longer grass. Electric and petrol-driven versions are available.

Hover mowers are useful where the ground undulates too sharply for a wheeled mower and on banks where they can be swung, pendulum fashion, to cut quite long grass.

Electric trimmer

If you've plenty of trees set in grass, a nylon cord trimmer might be useful. This nifty little machine will cut off quite thick and rough grass right against the trunks with its whirling nylon thread.

Care of tools

The longest lasting tools are those that are cared for. Try to get into the habit of scraping off mud and rubbing all metal parts with an oily rag after use. I know it's a real fag but it does make the implements easier to use next time you take them out. The cutting edges of spades and hoes benefit from an occasional honing up with a file so that they cut through soil and weeds quickly, saving your energy.

Store your tools in a dry place, such as a shed or garage, where rust will not be a problem. Good tools are not cheap, but if you take care of them they'll last a lifetime.

Electrical safety outdoors

- Make sure that all electrically powered equipment is fitted with a residual current device (RCD), which cuts off the supply as soon as a fault is detected.
- Avoid trailing leads, which may be severed by moving blades, or tripped over.
- Never use electric tools when it is wet outside.
- Always disconnect the power supply before servicing powered equipment.
- Wear thick rubber-soled footwear when using electric garden tools.

Be guided by information sheets and salesmen when you're buying a mower, but try, whenever possible, to arrange for a demonstration of one or two machines. The mower is the one piece of equipment I would advise you to buy new, and you might as well know what you're in for before you part with your hard-earned cash. Pick one that's comfortable to use, looks sturdily made, and has as wide a cut as possible to lessen the time you need to spend cutting the grass.

When your lawn has had its last mow of the season, clean the mower and rub it down with an oily rag before you store it in a dry shed or garage. Winter is the time to have it repaired – not spring when every gardener is beating on the door of the workshop begging for attention.

WHEELBARROW

Not always essential in a small garden, the wheelbarrow is nevertheless a must where soil, leaves, lawn mowings and rubbish have to be carted any distance. There are all sorts of barrows, made of all sorts of materials, but the vital thing is that it should be easy to push when full. Look for one that has its wheel tucked well under the body so that the weight is carried by the wheel and not by you. Ball-shaped wheels will travel over soft ground more easily than narrower types, but plastic bodies and wheels will not be as durable as those of steel, even though they have the advantage of being lightweight.

Buy a barrow that's large enough for your needs but small enough to go through your gate, and always store it under cover or tipped up so that water does not collect in the body.

part II

THE PLANTS

Plants are what a garden is all about and this section will help you make your selections from the vast range that is available

This herbaceous border with its bold drifts of colour, including the purple spikes of *Nepeta sibirica* 'Souvenir d'André Chaudron', epitomizes the summer garden.

trees

Carefully chosen trees

create a natural framework

in your garden, providing

focal points to draw the eye,

as well as all-year-round

colour, form and fragrance

WHY IS IT THAT MANY FOLK WITH small gardens are terrified of trees? I'll tell you why. It's because they've previously been in gardens where badly chosen trees have dominated the scene: casting shade over most of the plot, moving foundations with their roots, dripping water and leaves everywhere in autumn and threatening to fall onto the house in the first gale of winter. If only the right tree had been planted in the first place the story would be different, and the little job of leaf sweeping in autumn would be a modest price to pay for colour and form during the rest of the year.

So, if you're faced with a treeless plot, let me cajole you into planting a tree that will not foster your neurosis. You own the air space right up to the sky, and there really is no need to worry when the tree rises beyond head height. Provided it's one of the kinds I've recommended in the A–Z section at the end of this chapter, it will not endanger life and limb when planted in the right place.

There's much confusion between trees and shrubs, and some shrubs are often referred to as trees simply because they grow quite tall. But, strictly speaking, a tree is a plant that can reach a height of 5–6 m (15–20 ft) on a single woody stem. If your favourite tree is missing from my selection, take a look at Chapter 5 Shrubs to see if it belongs there instead.

The propagation methods used for increasing trees are exactly the same as for increasing shrubs. Details of the techniques involved are given in Chapter 2 Propagation.

HOW TO USE TREES

In a small garden there's only one way to use a tree, and that is as a single eye-catching specimen around which the rest of the garden revolves. Such a tree takes a lot of choosing: it should be of interest for as much of the year as possible; its shape should be desirable; it should not outgrow its situation; and it should be able to tolerate your garden conditions.

If you can fit in several trees, use them to carry the eye around the garden and to lift your gaze from flatter plantings below, and do try to have at least one tree under which you can sit.

In larger gardens, trees can be used as windbreaks and screens (on smaller plots their place will have to be taken by hedges, shrubs and fences) and as tall backgrounds to plantings of shrubs and border plants.

WHAT TO LOOK FOR IN A TREE

When it comes to choosing a particular tree for a particular spot, there are quite a number of considerations to bear in mind.

FINAL SIZE Uppermost in your mind should be the ultimate height and spread of the tree. Work out how much space you have to spare and select a tree that will fit the bill with a few feet to spare. Do this and you won't have to worry about pruning in the future.

SHAPE AND HABIT Consider the shape and 'habit' of the tree and whether or not it will look right in your chosen spot. Do you want an upright columnar tree, a weeping tree, a round-headed tree, or one with branches that spread horizontally?

SPECIAL FEATURES If you're planting just one tree, tick off its attributes and make sure that it offers as many features as possible. The ideal tree will have attractive foliage, colourful flowers followed by bright fruits, and bark that is good to look at in winter. All right, so your choice may not have all these characteristics but, unless it is exceptional in another area, you should always plump for a tree that offers at least two seasons of interest.

LOCAL CONDITIONS Will the tree be happy in your soil and in the spot you've chosen for it? Check with the nurseryman and cast an eye round local gardens to get some idea of what grows well in your locality. If yours is an area of biting winds, it's no good choosing a tree with tender foliage that will be ripped to shreds in the first strong breeze. If your soil is chalky, don't plant a lime-hater.

BE ADVENTUROUS Even though it's a good idea to be guided by what succeeds in your area, try to plant something a little out of the ordinary: not necessarily a tree that is difficult to grow, but one that doesn't crop

There are many varieties of *Prunus*: **some are chosen for their flowers, some for their foliage and some, like** *P. serrula* **(Tibetan cherry), for their shining coppery bark.**

up on every street corner. If you've room for only one tree, it seems a shame to plant a laburnum or a flowering cherry that can be seen in greater glory in a public park.

CHOOSE A YOUNGSTER When you're choosing your tree at the nursery – and you should always be able to pick the particular plant you want – go for one that has a strong central shoot or 'leader'; this will ensure that the tree will make a shapely specimen when it starts to grow away; and go for a youngster.

Not only are young trees a darned sight cheaper than their older relations, but they always establish themselves far more easily than tall, old ones; they don't need staking and their roots receive little check during transplanting. Sometimes you'll have to settle for an older plant of greater stature. You might think you've got a better deal at the outset, but during its first year the mighty specimen will grow slowly and can often be overtaken by a youngster, which may well develop both a better shape and a better root system.

> *"Try to plant something a little out of the ordinary... one that doesn't crop up on every street corner."*

WHEN TO PLANT

Trees growing in containers can be planted at any time of year provided the soil is in a workable condition. Don't plant them when the ground is so wet that it sticks to your wellies, when it is frosted hard, or when it is dust-dry in the heart of summer. Container-grown trees will be quite happy to wait until soil conditions are right.

Planting bare-root trees
Trees lifted from rows in the nursery are sold as 'bare-root' plants, because precious little soil is left clinging to their roots. The planting season for deciduous bare-root trees (those that lose their leaves in winter) is in the dormant season from November to March.

Planting balled trees
Evergreens are usually sold with their roots and surrounding soil wrapped in a piece of hessian. They are described as being 'balled' and are best planted in April and May when they can grow away actively, rather than in winter when they will sit sulkily in wet soil and a drying wind.

PLANTING METHODS

With the right tree selected for the right spot you can think about planting. But remember the general rules: the site should not be overshadowed; there should be plenty of room for growth; shelter should be provided from strong winds (in the early stages of growth); and the tree should be at least 4.5 m (15 ft) from any building. No tree should be planted on waterlogged soil, though *Salix*, *Metasequoia* and *Alnus* are all tolerant of poor drainage if you're stuck with a bog.

Planting after delivery
You can usually arrange a convenient delivery date with the nurseryman who (if he's worth his salt) will ship the plants to you in good condition. Any bare roots should have been wrapped in damp hessian or straw and polythene, and the branches should be tied together to prevent them from becoming damaged. Remove the ties and any straw from the branches, but leave the wrapping in place around the roots until you are ready to plant, if this can be accomplished within a day or two of their arrival. Stand the trees in an unheated garage or shed.

Delayed planting
If the weather turns nasty and you can't plant for a few days, heel the trees in on a spare patch of ground. All this involves is digging out a hole, freeing the roots of any wrappings and packings and pushing them into the hole. Replace the soil, and the roots will be kept moist until you are ready to plant. Don't position the trees upright; instead lay them on the ground, or at an angle of 45° so that they offer less wind resistance. I've left trees heeled in for far longer than I should (up to four months) and they've come to no harm.

Trees bought from garden centres will usually have to be collected. As most of them will be container-grown, the heeling-in precautions are not necessary.

BEFORE YOU PLANT

Preparing the site
With a bit of luck, any tree is going to be with you for a long time, so it's important to prepare the soil well so that it establishes itself quickly.

Tree planting

1 Excavate a hole that's amply big enough for the roots, knock in the stake and fork well-rotted manure or garden compost into the hole.

2 Trim off any damaged roots then lower the tree into the hole, making sure that there is room for the remaining roots to spread out without restriction.

3 Replace the soil, mixing it with extra compost or manure as you do so. Shake the tree up and down to make sure that soil is distributed around the roots.

4 Replace the rest of the soil and check that the old soil mark on the stem is level with the surface of the soil. Firm the soil into place with your feet.

With both bare-root and container-grown trees, dig a hole one spit (spade blade) deep and 30 cm (12 in) wider all round than the roots or the rootball (the combination of roots and compost within the pot). Fork over the base of the hole and work in a bucketful of well-rotted manure, garden compost, or leaf mould dusted with a general fertilizer such as blood, bone and fishmeal. Mix some of this organic enrichment with the soil removed from the hole to perk that up, too.

I like to bung the roots of all bare-root trees and shrubs in a bucket of water for an hour prior to planting so that they don't have a chance to dry out. Cover the roots with damp sacking when you carry the trees to the planting site.

Stakes for new trees

If the tree needs staking, now is the time to knock the stake into the hole; do it later and the roots will be disturbed. At least 60 cm (2 ft) of stake should be buried below ground level for stability, and the top of the stake should finish below the lowest branch of the tree. Stakes for trees should be about 5 cm (2 in) in diameter but they need not be treated with preservative; if the preservative is fresh it may harm the roots, and after two or three years the tree will be able to support itself anyway. A stake that rots after a year or two is a positive advantage, for it can be removed with little disturbance to the tree.

The current trend is for a short stake, emerging only about 30 cm (12 in) out of the ground. The theory is that this anchors the bare roots or rootball, while allowing the top growth to flex in the wind and so encourage rapid establishment of new roots below. Where children are at large a long stake offers more protection to a newly planted tree.

Trim the roots

With the stake in position and the hole properly prepared, all that remains to be done now is to remove the protective covering from a bare-root tree and examine the roots. With a pair of sharp secateurs, trim off any thick roots that are more than 30 cm (12 in) long, as well as any roots that are torn or damaged. At the same time, snip off any broken or spindly shoots from the branch framework, making all cuts just above a bud. Forget to prune the branches and you may have to find a stepladder once the tree is planted. If there are any leaves or dead flowers present, remove those as well before planting.

PLANTING YOUR TREE

From this point on another pair of hands will be helpful. Stand the tree in the hole and check that when it is planted the old soil mark on the stem will rest just below the new soil level. Add or subtract soil until you are happy with the result. Spread out the roots so that they are not all squashed together.

A container-grown plant should be watered well an hour before planting, and the pot removed carefully at planting time. Any thick roots that are obviously growing inwards can be teased out very gently; if just a fibrous rootball exists, leave it intact. Now replace the soil gradually, adding compost or manure as you do so. Enlist a second pair of hands to hold the tree upright and to jar it up and down occasionally so that the soil particles are shaken down around the roots.

Firm the soil into place with your welly-booted foot – not daintily, but stamping really hard so that no air pockets are left to cause problems of root drying. When planting is completed, leave a slight depression in the soil around the tree trunk so that water can be applied if necessary in dry weather.

Staked and tied for stability, this is the same tree as on p.41, three months later. Make sure the roots never dry out, and slacken the ties as the stem thickens.

Securing the tree

To fasten the tree to the stake, I prefer proprietary tree ties (plastic affairs with buckles) because they can be slackened when necessary; but if funds are short you can use rope cushioned with cloth, or even a pair of old tights. Position one tie about 30 cm (12 in) above ground level and another 2.5 cm (1 in) below the top of the stake. Ideally the stake should be on the windward side of the tree (south-westerlies are the prevailing winds in Britain) but I honestly don't think that the life or death of your tree will depend on this.

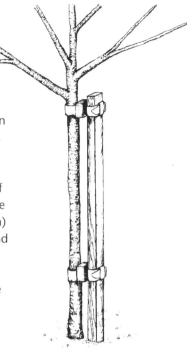

When a long stake is used to protect trees exposed to children and ball games, position one tie just below the top of the stake and the other 30 cm (12 in) above soil level.

Mulching and watering

Immediately after planting, and while the soil is nicely moist, spread an 8 cm (3 in) mulch of garden compost, manure or pulverized bark over the soil around the tree; a 90 cm (3 ft) diameter circle will be sufficient. Trees planted between April and October will almost always need to be watered in before this mulch is laid. Leave a hosepipe running on the soil at the foot of the tree for an hour, or give it at least three 9 litre (2 gallon) cans of water.

Aftercare of newly planted trees

Check the tree ties every month or so to see that they are not constricting the stem. Slacken them if they look too tight.

Do make sure that the tree doesn't run short of water, especially during its first spring and summer. If the roots are allowed to dry out, you stand to lose a lot of money and a whole season's growth.

Trees that are bought as large specimens will often grow very slowly during their first few years. Some gardeners believe that they become 'bark bound' – the bark is so dry and hard that it refuses to allow the trunk to expand and grow. If you think that this is the case after a couple of years, try running a penknife down the length of the trunk so that the bark is split: old hands swear that this gives the tree a chance.

PRUNING

I'm not a great tree pruner: if a tree needs pruning when it's more than a few years old then the chances are that it has been planted in the wrong place. But in its formative years a young tree will need pruning in order to produce that bare stem and a good head of branches.

Early years

In the first two or three years of its life the tree is best left intact: the shoots that arise low down on the stem will encourage it to thicken and support the branches higher up. A tree with such a collection of lower branches is said to be 'feathered'.

If you want a tree that's furnished with leaves to ground level it's still best to remove the lowest branches so that those above can hang down a little. If this is the case the tree will look good and yet still have a strong trunk that may offer winter colour. As soon as your tree is about 2.5–3 m (roughly 8–10 ft) high, make sure that the lower 90 cm (3 ft) of stem is cleared of shoots: cut them off almost flush with the trunk. As the tree grows, trim off more shoots until you have the length of bare stem you require.

In late summer, remove the lower branches of birch trees that need their canopies raised.

Use long-arm pruners to reach shoots that are too high to be removed with secateurs or short-handled loppers.

Trees bought as standards or half-standards should have their trunks trimmed of any emerging shoots. Standard trees are those with about 1.8 m (6 ft) of bare trunk; half-standards have about 1.2 m (4 ft) of trunk.

As with all rules there are exceptions. Trees with an upright columnar habit will never trail their branches to cover the trunk and you may prefer to let them retain all their stems right down to ground level.

Dealing with suckers

Any shoots that arise from below ground level are called suckers, and they should be pulled or cut away from the roots at their point of origin. If you let them remain, or cut them off flush with the soil, they'll develop into a disfiguring thicket. Suckers are an especial problem with some ornamental plums and cherries. Here the upper flowering growth has been grafted onto a rootstock that has no ornamental value whatsoever but which forms a healthy root system governing the vigour of the tree. If you leave suckers to develop on such trees, the upper portion may go into decline.

Pruning ornamental trees

The only regular pruning needed on most ornamental trees will be to remove dead wood. This is easiest to see in summer and can be cut off at that time, as can suckers. The removal of badly placed or dangerous branches may occasionally be necessary and this is done in the dormant season – November to March – when the sap is not rising.

Pleached trees

Pleached trees create a wall or avenue of foliage when the branches, trained to intertwine horizontally, are in leaf. Young trees, with pliable stems, must be used.

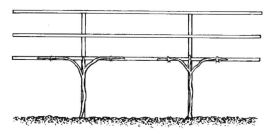

First, erect a framework of uprights and horizontals: the uprights should be about 2.4 m (8 ft) apart. Plant a tree at the base of each upright. Tie in laterals at the height of the first row of horizontal supports and remove any lower side shoots.

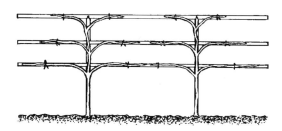

The following year cut back the laterals to encourage new side shoots. Tie in new laterals to the next horizontal support. When the leader reaches the desired height, tie it to the top horizontal support.

Lime trees are one of the traditional choices for pleaching. Hard prune in winter and, in summer, prune long growths back to a well-placed bud.

Tree surgery

This grand-sounding term is usually applied to any kind of tree pruning. On a small scale you can do it yourself, but when large trees are creating a real problem then a reputable firm of tree surgeons should be called in to advise.

Don't agree to let any bunch of cowboys tackle your trees. The sort of 'firm' that knocks on your door asking if you want your trees pruned is not the type to employ. True enough, they may be cheaper than a skilled firm of tree surgeons (who can be found in your Yellow Pages) but they'll leave you heartbroken if you care about trees.

Preventing wound infections

Trees have a natural defence mechanism to prevent wound infection. It is situated at the branch collar (a slight swelling where the branch joins the trunk). The tree will heal itself, without the need for wound paints, if you don't cut into this collar. When you're left with a foot-long stump, make a clean cut at a slight angle away from the trunk. You can find the correct line for the cut by finding the ridge of bark on the trunk, which starts in the crotch where the branch joins the trunk. If you make the cut on the branch at an equal and opposite angle to that made by this ridge, you won't breach the collar that provides the tree's main defence against infection by fungi and other wood-rotting organisms. Undercut the stump first to prevent the bark tearing when the main cut is made.

> *"If a tree needs pruning when it's more than a few years old then it's been planted in the wrong place."*

Removing odd branches

On smaller trees, where just the odd branch needs to be removed, you can tackle it yourself – although a second pair of hands is always helpful, whether it's to hold the ladder steady or to pass the saw. Small branches can be cut off in one go, but anything with a bit of weight to it should be dismantled from the tip inwards. Tie a rope to each section of branch that's being removed before you saw through the stem. Then the wood can be slowly lowered to the ground by your mate on the other end of the rope. That way no damage will be done to the lower branches by falling timber.

If you've a lot of trees you might be tempted by a chain saw, but I always use a bow saw for tree pruning; it is, by far, a much safer option than a chain saw. If you have to remove any branches larger than about 15 cm (6 in) in diameter, call in a professional tree surgeon.

1 Cut off heavy branches in stages. Support the weight of the one to be removed by running a rope from it and over a sturdy, higher branch.

2 Saw through the branch at least 30 cm (12 in) away from its junction with the trunk. That way you'll remove most of the weight before the final cut is made.

3 Undercut the stump flush with the trunk, then cut through from above to meet it. Neaten the surface with a knife and seal it with wound paint.

A-Z

OF

garden trees

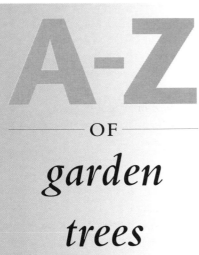

THIS IS A SELECTION OF WHAT I consider to be some of the best garden trees. I've left out the real giants – the oaks, beeches and cedars – and concentrated on those trees that are at home in gardens of modest size. They are not all dwarfs (such trees tend to be lacking in grace) but few of them should present any major problems provided they are planted in the right place.

The height and spread of each tree will depend entirely on the situation in which it is planted; the figures I have given are a rough indication of the ultimate sizes to help you decide if the tree will fit in your garden. Height is the first figure; spread the second.

Acer griseum
Paperbark Maple

6 x 4.5 m (20 x 15 ft)

A maple renowned for its glorious peeling bark of coppery bronze. The three-lobed leaves are orange-tinged on opening, later becoming green, and taking on fiery tints of scarlet in autumn.

Acer japonicum '*Vitifolium*'
Downy Japanese Maple

4.5 x 4.5 m (15 x 15 ft)

This and its more shrub-like relation

A. japonicum 'Aconitifolium' are two of the very best autumn-colouring plants in any garden. The leaves are deep-cut into seven or more lobes and are softly downy. They seem to catch fire in autumn, turning to shades of yellow, pink, orange and bright crimson.

Acer negundo '**Variegatum**'
Box Elder

6 x 4.5 m (20 x 15 ft)

A maple whose foliage is striking in summer rather than autumn. The leaves are pinnate (like those of the rose) and edged with creamy white variegation. The whole effect is delicate and graceful. Occasional all-green shoots will arise and these should be cut out.

There's a form called 'Flamingo' that has pink variegation. It's a real beauty, but bad weather can cause leaf browning. This form is probably best grown as a shrub, and pruned hard each spring.

Acer pseudoplatanus '**Brilliantissimum**'
Sycamore

6 x 4.5 m (20 x 15 ft)

A slow-growing beauty, this is a spectacular form of the sycamore whose leaves are shrimp-pink on opening, gradually turning yellow, then creamy white until they are eventually suffused with green. In spring and early summer it's a sparkling sight. Young specimens may burn a little in brilliant sunlight until their roots are well established.

Alnus glutinosa '**Aurea**'
Golden Alder

4.5 x 3 m (15 x 10 ft)

The yellow-leaved form of the common alder is not as widely planted as it should be. It rarely exceeds 4 m (12 ft) in height, and keeps the yellow colouring of its leaves until late summer in a sunny, sheltered spot.

Arbutus unedo
Strawberry Tree

4.5 x 4.5 m (15 x 15 ft)

This superb evergreen is a slow grower but offers a number of attractive features. The bark is dark brown and peeling; white urn-shaped flowers are carried in clusters in autumn, and these are followed the next autumn by rough-skinned spherical fruits of bright reds, so that flowers and fruits are carried at the same time. The fruits are edible but tart – don't make a pie of them!

Betula ermanii
Erman's Birch

6 x 4.5 m (20 x 15 ft)

Anyone who plants the deformed Young's weeping birch is obviously unaware of the four beautiful species mentioned here. This one makes a broad cone of growth and has bark that is white when young, and pink-flushed as it ages. The young stems are orange-brown.

Betula papyrifera
Paper-bark Birch

10.5 x 4.5 m (35 x 15 ft)

A good 'peeler', this species has white bark marked with orange, pink or dark brown. Pure yellow autumn colour.

Betula pendula '**Laciniata**' (syn. '**Dalecarlica**')
Swedish Birch

10.5 x 4.5 m (35 x 15 ft)

Superb finely cut foliage carried on weeping stems and a good, white bark make this species an excellent choice where a bit of space is available.

Betula utilis var. *jacquemontii*
Kashmir Birch

6 x 4.5 m (20 x 15 ft)

The main branches and trunk are bright white or cream and the saw-edged leaves turn warm yellow before falling in autumn.

Cercis siliquastrum
Judas Tree
4.5 x 4.5 m (15 x 15 ft)

Slow growing and often seen as a shrub rather than a tree, *Cercis* is a fascinating plant. Its leaves are rounded and smooth but, before they emerge, the stems and even the old branches are smothered in rich pink pea flowers during May. These are followed in autumn by flattened pods of crimson-purple. It often grows rather lopsidedly but is still charming. Give it a sunny, sheltered spot and allow it a few years to settle in before expecting flowers – birds can eat the buds, so beware! Reputedly the tree on which Judas hanged himself.

Chamaecyparis lawsoniana
Lawson Cypress
9 x 3 m (30 x 10 ft)

Don't plant the boring ordinary species, but go for one of its varieties such as 'Columnaris', upright and blue-grey; 'Ellwoodii', a rich green; 'Green Pillar', erect green fans of growth; 'Lane' (syn. 'Lanei'), the best yellow form; 'Pembury Blue', rich blue-grey. All these conifers are especially valuable for brightening the winter garden.

Crataegus laevigata 'Paul's Scarlet'
Paul's Scarlet Thorn
4.5 x 2.4 m (15 x 8 ft)

A welcome sight every spring, this hawthorn wreathes its branches in clusters of double pink blossoms. Plant it near shrubs that will please the eye later in the season when it's not much to look at.

Cunninghamia lanceolata
Chinese Fir
9 x 3 m (30 x 10 ft)

This is an unusual conifer that deserves greater popularity. It produces masses of narrow leaves, arranged rather like those of yew, but with an exceptionally shiny texture that is almost metallic. They turn bronzy in autumn and persist to some extent when dead. If you've room to experiment give it a try.

Davidia involucrata
Dove Tree; Pocket Handkerchief Tree
7.5 x 4.5 m (25 x 15 ft)

You'll need patience if you want to grow this tree: it can take 20 years to flower, but what a sight when it does! The shapely head of branches is furnished with bright green lime-shaped leaves and drips with white handkerchief-like bracts that surround the flowers. With luck it will bloom in its tenth year, but be prepared for disappointment. Flowering time is May.

Eucalyptus pauciflora ssp. *niphophila*
Snow Gum
6 x 4.5 m (20 x 15 ft)

This is the species I'd choose, though there are now many on offer. The bark is a marbled python's skin of grey and pale orange, and the leaves are long, grey-green and sickle-shaped. The tree often leans appealingly and, like other eucalypts, it may be damaged in very severe winters, but regeneration from the base of the trunk is common. Growth is rapid with all species, and young specimens should be planted from pots – older ones are difficult to establish. If the snow gum fails with you due to severe winters, try *E. gunnii* which is tougher.

Ginkgo biloba
Maidenhair Tree
7.5 x 3 m (25 x 10 ft) – larger with age

The maidenhair captivates all who set eyes on it. The fan-shaped leaves are rich green, turning to yellow before they fall in autumn, and the tree is of a convenient upright shape. It's the oldest tree in existence, dating back 200 million years.

Trees that thrive on most soil types

All the trees listed will grow on clay or chalky soil. Those marked ✳ are suitable for dry conditions, and those marked ◆ for cold sites.

- *Acer griseum* ◆
- *Acer japonicum* 'Vitifolium'
- *Acer negundo* 'Variegatum' ✳◆
- *Acer pseudoplatanus* 'Brilliantissimum' ✳
- *Alnus glutinosa* 'Aurea' ✳
- *Arbutus unedo* ◆
- *Cercis siliquastrum*
- *Chamaecyparis lawsoniana* varieties ✳◆
- *Crataegus laevigata* 'Paul's Scarlet' ✳◆
- *Cunninghamia lanceolata*
- *Eucalyptus pauciflora* ssp. *niphophila*
- *Ilex* x *altaclerensis* 'Golden King' ✳
- *Laburnum* x *watereri* 'Vossii' ◆
- *Larix decidua* ✳◆
- *Malus floribunda*
- *Malus* 'John Downie'
- *Metasequoia glyptostroboides* ✳
- *Picea breweriana* ◆
- *Picea omorika* ◆
- *Picea pungens* 'Koster' ◆
- *Populus* x *candicans* 'Aurora' ◆
- *Prunus serrula*
- *Prunus serrulata* varieties
- *Prunus* x *subhirtella* 'Autumnalis'
- *Pyrus salicifolia* 'Pendula'
- *Salix* x *sepulcralis* var. chrysocoma ◆
- *Sorbus aucuparia* 'Beissneri' ◆
- *Sorbus* 'Joseph Rock' ✳◆
- *Taxus baccata* 'Fastigiata Aurea' ✳◆
- *Thuja plicata* 'Zebrina' ✳◆

Gleditsia triacanthos 'Sunburst'
Honey Locust

4.5 x 2.4 m (15 x 8 ft)

Pretty as a picture from spring to autumn on account of its finely cut foliage of bright yellow that turns to fizzing lime-green as it ages. Along with *Robinia pseudoacacia* 'Frisia' it is one of the best yellow-leaved trees. Of the two it is the tougher and has smaller leaflets. The leaves turn butter-yellow before they fall in autumn.

Ilex x altaclerensis 'Golden King'
Variegated Holly

4.5 x 2.4 m (15 x 8 ft)

This is, I think, about the best variegated holly: its leaves, though not exceptionally spiny, are margined and splashed with bright butter-yellow. Remember that holly bushes are male or female and only the females carry berries. To add to the confusion 'Golden King' is a female and produces plenty of scarlet fruits in winter. It can be kept much smaller than its ultimate size by Christmas pruning. Other hollies are described in Chapter 5 Shrubs.

Laburnum x watereri 'Vossii'
Voss's Laburnum

4.5 x 3 m (15 x 10 ft)

In early June there is no finer sight than this tree, laden with its pendulous flowers of bright yellow. The green leaves that follow are a bit dull but at least this variety produces few of the poisonous seeds for which laburnums have become feared. Superb when trained over archways and pergolas.

Larix decidua
European Larch

6 x 3 m (20 x 10 ft) and more

Where you've a bit of room to spare, don't forget the larch. It's a pretty conifer that has soft, fresh green needles in spring and summer. In autumn they turn bright yellow before

falling. Neat cones decorate the stems. Larch is a fast grower, but lovely when planted in groups: set the trees 3 m (10 ft) apart and plant them young.

Malus floribunda
Japanese Crab Apple

4.5 x 6 m (15 x 20 ft)

A wide-spreading tree that is magnificent in spring when its white flowers open from rich pink buds. For the rest of the year it's rather dull, so plant it where it can act as a backdrop for other plants when out of flower. In bloom it is absolutely smothered with blossom.

Malus 'John Downie'
Cherry Apple

4.5 x 3 m (15 x 10 ft)

A crab apple with reasonable white flowers and positively superb red and yellow fruits later in the season. They make delicious crab apple jelly if you can bear to rob the tree.

Metasequoia glyptostroboides
Dawn Redwood

9 x 2.4 m (30 x 8 ft) and more

A rotten Latin name for a lovely deciduous conifer. The dawn redwood was thought to be extinct until rediscovered in China in 1941, and now it graces many gardens worldwide. It makes a column of feathery bright green leaves that turn rich coppery shades before falling in autumn. The trunk and stems have russet peeling bark. Few gardens should be without it. Plant young specimens for quick establishment.

Morus nigra
Black Mulberry

3 x 4.5 m (10 x 15 ft) and more with age

The black mulberry makes a rounded, spreading tree with serrated heart-shaped leaves and a gnarled trunk. Red to black fruits are produced on trees over 20 years old and are only fit to eat when really ripe, at which time they fall from the tree. Can be propagated from branches about 1.5 m (5 ft) long, which are relieved of some of their smaller shoots and then pushed into the ground for one third of their length.

Nyssa sylvatica
Tupelo

9 x 3 m (30 x 10 ft) and more with age

For sheltered gardens where there is space to spare, the tupelo is worth planting simply for its autumn colour. The oval leaves are glossy and turn scarlet, orange and crimson in autumn – you'll see no brighter tree at that time.

Ostrya carpinifolia
Hop Hornbeam

4.5 x 3 m (15 x 10 ft)

Here's an oddity. A shapely, upright-growing tree with green hornbeam-like

---

Weeping and spreading trees

TREES WITH A WEEPING HABIT
- *Betula pendula* 'Laciniata'
- *Picea breweriana*
- *Pyrus salicifolia* 'Pendula'
- *Salix* x *sepulcralis* var. *chrysocoma*

TREES WITH A SPREADING HABIT
- *Acer japonicum* 'Vitifolium'
- *Arbutus unedo*
- *Cercis siliquastrum*
- *Eucalyptus pauciflora* ssp. *niphophila*
- *Malus floribunda*
- *Morus nigra*
- *Parrotia persica*
- *Prunus serrulata* varieties
- *Sophora japonica*

Trees with all-year-round interest

- *Acer griseum*
- *Arbutus unedo* ◆
- *Betula ermanii*
- *Betula utilis* var. *jacquemontii*
- *Betula papyrifera*
- *Betula pendula* 'Laciniata'
- *Chamaecyparis lawsoniana* varieties ◆
- *Cunninghamia lanceolata* ◆
- *Eucalyptus pauciflora* ssp. *niphophila* ◆
- *Ilex* x *altaclerensis* 'Golden King' ◆
- *Picea breweriana* ◆

- *Picea omorika* ◆
- *Picea pungens* 'Koster' ◆
- *Prunus serrula* ◆
- *Salix* x *sepulcralis* var. *chrysocoma*
- *Salix babylonica* var. *pekinensis* 'Tortuosa'
- *Sorbus aucuparia* 'Beissneri'
- *Stewartia pseudocamellia*
- *Taxus baccata* 'Fastigiata Aurea' ◆
- *Thuja plicata* 'Zebrina' ◆
- *Trachycarpus fortunei* ◆

◆ Evergreen

leaves among which hang hop-like fruits in summer. Planted behind lower-growing shrubs it makes a fascinating backdrop. Not spectacular but intriguing nevertheless.

Parrotia persica
Persian Ironwood
4.5 x 6 m (15 x 20 ft)

Here's a tree with more than one attribute. For a start the bark is marbled with grey and peels like a plane tree. In winter, tiny red spidery flowers (like those of the witch hazel, *Hamamelis*, to which it is related) bedeck the branches, and the leaves that follow start to turn reddish in summer, colouring brilliant orange, yellow and scarlet by autumn. A good backdrop to shrubs and border plants.

Picea breweriana
Brewer's Weeping Spruce
6 x 2.4 m (20 x 8 ft) and more with age

A beautiful and statuesque conifer for the patient gardener. It makes a conical tree with graceful weeping branches, but it should be planted young and not expected to look at its best until it is almost 20 years old. If you want something to enjoy during your retirement, and you've a bit of space to spare, give it a try.

Picea omorika
Serbian Spruce
9 x 3 m (30 x 10 ft) and more

This is a better choice for the impatient gardener, for it is faster growing than *P. breweriana*. The branches droop but are not as pendulous as those of the previous species. The overall colour is a greyish green and the conical shape makes this one of the most handsome conifers of all.

Picea pungens 'Koster'
Koster's Blue Spruce
6 x 1.8 m (20 x 6 ft)

A conical conifer of blue-grey that will add a lift to green plantings. Excellent with a carpet of heathers surrounding it to make a bright winter garden.

Populus x *candicans* 'Aurora'
Variegated Balm of Gilead Poplar
9 x 2.4 m (30 x 8 ft)

A real stunner where a variegated tree of stature is needed. It is the young foliage that's variegated – splashed with creamy white and tinged with pink. A great sight from a distance or close to. In small gardens it can be pruned hard each winter to encourage the production of plenty of variegated shoots the following spring.

Prunus serrula
Tibetan Cherry
4.5 x 3 m (15 x 10 ft)

Plenty of small white flowers are produced in spring, but the reason why this tree is so popular is that it has shining coppery bark that glows in the sun. Plant it where hands can caress and polish its stems and peel off the older bark. Left untouched the trunk and branches may become dull and moss-covered unless plenty of bright sunshine strikes them.

Prunus serrulata
Sato Cherry; Japanese Cherry
Various sizes

There are dozens of flowering cherries so I've picked just a few of the very best. They are undoubtedly only of value in spring when they bloom, but they flower with such generosity that they cannot be ignored. My selection would be:
'Amanogawa': 4.5 m x 60 cm (15 x 2 ft); upright with pale pink double flowers in April and May.
'Shimidsu': 4.5 x 6 m (15 x 20 ft); spreading, double white flowers in May.
'Shirofugen': 7.5 x 7.5 m (25 x 25 ft); spreading, pale pink to white double flowers in May.
'Taihaku': (Great White Cherry) 6 x 6 m (20 x 20 ft); double white flowers in April, my first choice.
'Ukon': 6 x 9 m (20 x 30 ft); spreading, greenish white double blossoms in April and May.

In most varieties the foliage unfurls with or after the flowers and is tinged bronze. Most develop good autumn colour.

Prunus x *subhirtella* 'Autumnalis'
Winter Cherry
4.5 x 3 m (15 x 20 ft)

A fine back-of-the-border tree where during its dull summer season, it can act as a backdrop. When the summer

border flowers fade, the bare branches of the tree erupt with pink buds that burst into white flowers. There's something to look at from October to April in most years.

Pseudolarix amabilis
Golden Larch

6 x 2.4 m (20 x 8 ft)

This lovely, large-leafed larch should be more widely planted. The deciduous leaves are fresh green in spring and summer, turning bright yellow before they fall in autumn. Give it a sheltered spot in full sun where its change of colour can be admired. Youngsters may be damaged by severe frosts.

Pyrus salicifolia 'Pendula'
Willow-leafed Pear

4.5 x 2.4 m (15 x 8 ft)

A good tree for a restricted space, but of muted rather than spectacular shades. The branches arch downwards and are clothed in narrow leaves of silvery grey, studded with small white flowers in spring. Cheer it up by planting colourful shrubs nearby!

Robinia pseudoacacia 'Frisia'
False Acacia

6 x 3 m (20 x 10 ft)

A favourite of mine, this tree is a stunning spectacle from June to September when its ferny leaves of brilliant acid-yellow stand out against summer skies of blue. Even when the sun is in they will brighten your garden. Compared with *Gleditsia triacanthos* 'Sunburst', this tree is more yellow and, I think, more graceful due to its tissue-thin leaves, which flutter gently in every passing breeze; but it has brittle wood and can suffer in colder countries.

The delicate, ferny leaves of *Robinia pseudoacacia* 'Frisia' remain acid-yellow throughout the summer, providing a brilliant spectacle.

Salix babylonica var. pekinensis 'Tortuosa'
Dragon's Claw Willow
9 x 3 m (30 x 10 ft)

Better where space is restricted, this willow has an upright habit and stems that are twisted like corkscrews, which accounts for the other common name of corkscrew willow. In summer and winter its contorted stems are visible, and the leaves are a fresh green. Raved about by flower arrangers.

Salix x sepulcralis var. chrysocoma
Golden Weeping Willow
9 x 9 m (30 x 30 ft) and more

This is not a tree for small gardens, in spite of the fact that it is often planted there. It is a fast-growing spreader that will rob you of light and shift your foundations if planted too close to your house. Only where there's a vast expanse of lawn, and preferably a lake, or at the very least moist soil, should it be planted. Then it can be allowed to make the magnificent specimen it deserves to be, with its living cascade of yellow stems, thickly decked with narrow green leaves in summer.

Cuttings root so readily that they can even be taken when they are broom-handle-sized and stuck into the ground to grow.

Sophora japonica
Pagoda Tree
6 x 4.4 m (20 x 15 ft)

Rarely planted but often admired, the pagoda tree has pinnate leaves like the rowan, and long clusters of creamy white flowers in late summer when it reaches a reasonable age. It is a tree of grace that relishes a warm, sunny spot.

Sorbus aucuparia 'Beissneri'
Rowan, Mountain Ash
6 x 3 m (20 x 10 ft)

This tree deserves a bright future in gardens for it offers orange-pink bark

---

Trees with attractive flowers or fruit

The following trees have flowers ✳ and/or fruits ◆ of note.

- Arbutus unedo ✳ ◆
- Cercis siliquastrum ✳ ◆
- Crataegus laevigata 'Paul's Scarlet' ✳
- Davidia involucrata ✳
- Ilex x altaclerensis 'Golden King' ◆
- Laburnum x watereri 'Vossii' ✳
- Malus floribunda ✳
- Malus 'John Downie' ✳ ◆
- Morus nigra ◆
- Ostrya carpinifolia ◆
- Parrotia persica ✳
- Prunus serrula ✳
- Prunus serrulata varieties ✳
- Prunus x subhirtella 'Autumnalis' ✳
- Pyrus salicifolia 'Pendula' ✳
- Sophora japonica ✳
- Sorbus 'Joseph Rock' ◆
- Stewartia pseudocamellia ✳

(especially stunning after rain or when a lawn sprinkler has played on it), reddish young stems and bright yellow autumn colour on its ferny foliage. Its habit of growth is attractive too – upright and broadly columnar – and it fits into the smallest gardens. A good choice if there's room for only one tree.

Sorbus 'Joseph Rock'
6 x 3 m (20 x 10 ft)

A stunning rowan of upright habit and with the usual ferny leaves. These take on fiery tints in autumn and are complemented by the generous crop of bright yellow fruits that persist when the leaves are shed. Birds hardly seem to touch them – a great advantage in gardens where fruits are gobbled as fast as they appear.

Stewartia pseudocamellia
4.5 x 2.4 m (15 x 8 ft)

A relative of the camellia, *Stewartia* makes a handsome tree with flaking bark, mottled purplish brown and buff and orange. White, yellow-centred flowers stud the branches in summer, and the leaves (oddly glossy on the undersides and dull above) turn brilliant shades of crimson and yellow in autumn. Plenty of attributes for a modest-sized tree. Sadly it won't put up with chalky soil and it prefers a shady situation to one in full sun.

Taxus baccata
Yew
6 x 6 m (20 x 20 ft)

An oppressive tree to plant where space is limited, the dull green yew is best grown as a backdrop in large shrubberies. But the variety 'Fastigiata Aurea' or 'Fastigiata Aureomarginata' is the yellow-variegated form of the Irish yew, which makes an upright evergreen composed of towering minarets of growth. It cheers up any plot, especially in winter, and grows 3 m x 60 cm (10 x 2 ft).

Thuja plicata 'Zebrina'
Western Red Cedar
9 x 2.4 m (30 x 8 ft) and more

As an alternative to the variegated forms of the Lawson cypress, try this conifer. It makes an upright column of evergreen foliage banded with bright yellow. It is a picture in winter.

Trachycarpus fortunei
Chusan Palm
4.5 x 1.8 m (15 x 6 ft)

If you're feeling frivolous, try planting a palm tree! This one is surprisingly hardy in many parts of the country and makes a thick stem clad in 'coconut matting' and topped with a cluster of fan-shaped fronds. It will be some time before it reaches its maximum height.

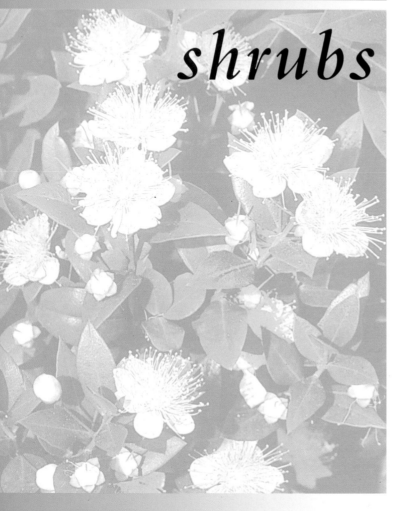

shrubs

Evergreen and deciduous,

flowering and fruiting, with

colourful foliage and

attractive bark and stems,

shrubs lend constant form

and interest to any garden

RIGHTLY DESCRIBED AS THE BACKBONE OF any garden, shrubs are indispensable. You don't have to pack your plot with gigantic bushes: there's a great diversity of shrub material from the positively dwarf to the gargantuan. The secret is to find the right shrub for your particular purpose, and the lists in the A–Z section of this chapter will enable you to do just that.

Shrubs are also good helpmates in keeping down weeds. There's nothing magical in this idea: in the early stages of establishment you'll have to do just as much weeding as in any other part of the garden but, when such shrubs are close-planted, they will eventually form a thicket that beats the weeds, hides the bare soil and saves you work.

HOW TO USE SHRUBS

Providing form

It is most important that you use your shrubs to give form to your garden. Consider the shape and style of any shrub, its ultimate height and its overall effect. Evergreens are valuable because they lend form to the garden all the year round, but plant too many of them and you'll be bored by an unchanging vista. The secret is to mix them up with deciduous kinds that lose their leaves. Do this and you'll retain form without sacrificing the freshness that spring brings to the garden.

Flowers, fruit and foliage

Remember that most flowering shrubs have a brief season of glory – a month is good going when it comes to length of time in bloom. Position these shrubs where they will make a bright pageant in their flowering season, but also where they can act as a plain backdrop to flowers that bloom later. Make them work for a living. A shrub that offers more than one attractive feature is often a better bet than one that puts all its floral eggs in one basket.

A word of warning about coloured foliage: don't overdo it. Green is the colour that should predominate in any garden. Go overboard on the purples and creamy yellows and you'll create a psychedelic nightmare. Choose just a handful of bright-leaved shrubs to show off against the plainer kinds and the effect will be more spectacular.

Contours and focal points

In really small gardens you can avoid trees and select large or medium-sized specimen shrubs to act as your eye-catchers and focal points. I've recommended suitable choices in the A–Z section. Use all your shrubs with their contours in mind: try to create an undulating landscape, positioning the shrubs so that your eye is taken on a gentle tour, not flickering up and down as if you were looking at a castellated battlement. This may sound like pretentious clap-trap, but it makes for a more restful scene if the lines are gradual; then, when you aim to create an eye-catching contrast of form, such as an upright yew among a carpet of lower-growing junipers, you'll achieve the effect you want.

Forgotten art

Topiary, the art of clipping shrubs into fanciful shapes, has rather gone out of fashion today, but it's a useful pursuit if you can't afford to buy statuary for the garden. The secret of making topiary look good is to choose the right plants, and to put them in the right place. You'll have to be patient to succeed but, with plants like box, yew, *Lonicera nitida* and even the humble privet, you can make assorted ornaments that will cheer up odd corners of your garden. Even a simple pyramid of foliage is stunning in a well-chosen spot.

Creating mystery

To give shelter and privacy, shrubs are vital; more than any other plants, they enable you to create a garden that is three-dimensional. Try to turn your patch, however small, into a place that is a little mysterious. There should always be some part that is not quite visible, so that you're tempted to explore its hidden depths. With a bit of imagination you can make hidden crannies on a plot no bigger than 3 m (10 ft) square: I know it's possible, for I've done it!

CHOOSING A HEALTHY SHRUB

Container-grown plants

As well as being able to locate a good nursery, you should also be able to find a good plant once you're there. Container-grown shrubs can be bought and planted at any time of year – they are the stock-in-trade of the garden centre.

Look for a plant that is relatively young and in the peak of health. Don't go for an old and gnarled specimen even though it is larger and therefore more tempting than a youngster. It will probably have a spiralled mass of roots inside the pot and will resent disturbance. Its roots will also be reluctant to leave the safety of the rootball for the soil outside and the plant may sit and sulk rather than grow away.

That's not to say you should buy a plant that's only just been put into its container. No; it should be established and container-grown, but not decrepit.

Choose a shapely, symmetrical plant, furnished with branches down to soil level (unless it is meant to be grown on a bare stem). If it is a columnar grower, it should have a strong central shoot or 'leader'. The compost in the pot should not be dry; neither should there be a gap between compost and pot – a sure sign of previous drying out. Avoid pest- or disease-infected plants and those with brown-edged leaves.

Bare-root plants

Deciduous shrubs are sold for dispatch between November and March, the dormant season, when they can safely be lifted from the nursery rows and transported with little soil around their roots. If the shrub you order is to be delivered 'bare root' in winter, enquire if it is possible to select the plant you want; otherwise you'll have to rely on the reputation of the nurseryman. In general it is possible to transplant quite large bare-root shrubs, provided the nurseryman has occasionally undercut them to encourage the formation of a fairly compact rootball. This involves simply slicing into the soil along the rows of plants to sever any far-roaming roots. The job results in the formation of more fibrous roots – always easier to deal with at planting time than those long roots that are almost as thick as broom handles.

> *"More than any other plants, shrubs will enable you to carve out a garden that is three-dimensional."*

PLANTING SHRUBS

The planting of shrubs is identical to the planting of trees except that staking to prevent wind rock will seldom be necessary (see p.43 for details).

The spacing of shrubs gives rise to much argument. Some folk suggest that they are planted at their final spacing, to allow room for the expected spread; others suggest closer planting and a thinning out of the scheme later on. I'd rather see the plants spaced out to allow for ultimate growth, and the gaps between the shrubs filled with short-term annuals or border plants that can easily be transplanted when the space they occupy is needed.

PRUNING SHRUBS

I think most gardeners hate pruning, probably because they're not quite sure what to do or when to do it. Calm yourself by remembering that the pruning of shrubs is usually necessary for three basic reasons: to remove dead or diseased wood; to keep a plant shapely and within bounds; and to encourage flowering. Some shrubs need hardly any pruning: they don't grow fast, are naturally shapely, seldom suffer from die-back and flower happily without being cut back. Others quickly

become a thicket of flowerless stems where pests and diseases proliferate.

Vital techniques

I've given specific instructions on pruning each shrub in the A–Z, so I won't confuse you by rambling on generally here, except about pruning techniques. Never use anything but a sharp pair of secateurs for pruning, and take a pair of loppers (or long-arm pruners) to any stems thicker than your finger. Make all cuts directly above a leaf or bud: don't leave even a 1 cm (½ in) snag or 'finger' of stem behind – it will only die back and may allow disease to enter. Cuts larger than 2.5 cm (1 in) in diameter can, if you wish, be painted with a proprietary wound sealant to

Transplanting an established shrub

Unless you are exceptionally clear-thinking and full of foresight when it comes to planting, you will occasionally make mistakes. The trouble is that you won't realize it straight away – only after two or three years when the scheme has matured will a plant scream out to be moved. Don't worry; you can still shift it with little danger to its constitution.

THE BEST TIME TO MOVE
Spring and autumn are the best times to transplant, though you can also do the job in winter if you don't mind working in cold weather. Evergreens prefer to be moved in April or May when the sap is starting to rise: it's the deciduous kinds that can tolerate a winter upheaval.

SEVERING THE ROOTS
Start off by taking your spade to the plant and cutting round it about 30–45 cm (12–18 in) away from the stem to sever out-growing roots. If the plant is very large it's a good idea to do this part of the operation some months in advance of the transplanting date. The plant can then recover from the shock while it still has a few roots pushing down underneath the rootball,

Once the rootball has been wrapped in a sheet of sacking or polythene, secure a stout stake to the stem. The shrub can then be lifted easily out of the hole.

and it will form a more fibrous network of roots above these, which can sustain it after transplanting.

WRAPPING THE ROOTBALL
When the sides of the rootball have been cut, push your spade underneath the plant to sever the anchor roots. Now swing the plant carefully to one side and tuck a sheet of sacking or polythene underneath it. Roll up the sheet to just half its size and push the rolled edge underneath the plant; then swing the plant back in the other direction and unroll the sheet so that the plant sits in its centre. Wrap the sheet around the plant as quickly and as tightly as possible, tie it or knot it, then, if it's made of sacking, soak it with a couple of buckets of water.

RE-PLANTING
The plant can stand in a sheltered spot in its wrapping for several weeks if necessary, but for best results it should be planted in its new hole without delay, just as for a balled bare-root plant. Stand it in the prepared hole, unwrap the sacking, swing the plant from side to side so that the wrapping can be removed, and then replace the soil, watering the plant in well if necessary. Anti-desiccant sprays can be used on conifers and evergreens before and after transplanting. These are proprietary solutions that can be sprayed onto foliage to prevent excessive water loss.

Snip out any dead or diseased stems as soon as you notice them, cutting back into healthy wood.

prevent attack by fungus diseases. It's not the end of world if you don't do this because most wounds will heal naturally.

Know your shrub

Whatever else you do, don't tackle all your garden shrubs with the shears as soon as they get out of hand: you'll turn them all into flowerless lollipops of greenery. When you buy a shrub, make sure you know how big it will grow and what pruning it needs, then you can plant with confidence, knowing that you'll get the best out of it without being concerned that it will help to turn your garden into a jungle.

Renovating neglected plants

If you've taken over a garden that's already overgrown with shrubs, renovate them by thinning out the stems. Cut out all old and gnarled branches at ground level, leaving the young ones evenly spaced so that they can breathe and grow. If all the branches are old, cut out two thirds of them and leave the remainder. With any luck (and a bit of feeding) the plants will soon produce healthy young wood at ground level, and then the remainder of the elderly stuff can be cut out. This kind of pruning can be done in summer or autumn and winter. Dead or diseased wood on any shrub, or suckers from rootstocks (see p.104), should be removed the instant they are noticed.

Finally, don't fall into the trap of thinking that because nature doesn't prune her shrubs you needn't. Take a look at a few shrubs in the wild and see how overgrown and full of dead wood they are. They make superb bird nesting sites in a wild part of the garden

but they're not much to look at close to. If you can't bear pruning, there's only one thing to do and that's to select those shrubs that need no cutting back at all.

LOOKING AFTER YOUR SHRUBS

Feeding and mulching

Don't forget that shrubs are just as hungry as other garden plants. Two or three handfuls of blood, bone and fishmeal scattered around each shrub in April will work wonders, especially if it's followed by a mulch of well-rotted garden compost or manure, or pulverized bark. The soil should be moist when you lay the mulch, and the mulch itself should be moist. That way the soil will be protected from excess drying out and weeds will be suppressed. Mulching saves a lot of hard labour.

Providing shelter

In particularly exposed places shrubs can be protected from winter winds by surrounding them with a 'tube' of sacking held in position by four stout canes or stakes, or by cutting the bottom off a plastic sack and slipping this over the canes.

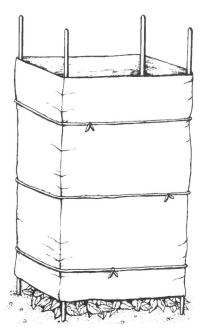

A plastic sack with its bottom slit, held in place by four canes, makes an effective windbreak around a newly planted shrub.

PROPAGATION

It's always great fun to propagate plants. Though not all your cuttings may root, those that do will make all the fuss and bother worth while. All the plants mentioned in the A–Z section can be increased by at least one of these propagation methods: seeds, softwood cuttings, semi-ripe or half-ripe cuttings, leaf bud cuttings, hardwood cuttings, root cuttings, layering and division. Full details of all these methods are given in Chapter 2 Propagation.

A-Z

— OF —

shrubs

I MAKE NO APOLOGIES FOR THE shrub section being so long! The choice is wide and there are so many good garden plants among them that they must be done justice. It's a biased selection; they are all plants that I think deserve a space in your garden but, where the season of interest is limited or the plant has drawbacks, I've said so.

Make sure that any shrub will put up with the soil and situation you have to offer: I've indicated its preferences and its tolerances, and there are lists of plants for particular situations, soils and characteristics throughout this section.

The expected height and spread of each shrub is indicated with the height first and the spread second. Use it as a rough guide to work out whether or not you've room for the plant. Its precise measurements will vary from place to place and from soil to soil.

Abelia x *grandiflora*

90 cm x 1.8 m (3 x 6 ft)

A spreading shrub with small, glossy, oval evergreen leaves and masses of pale pink flowers from summer to autumn. It's the length and timing of the flowering season that makes this a valuable shrub, rather than the spectacle of the individual blooms, which are quite small. Use it near the front of borders or to provide a muted background for more striking plants.
LIKES a warm spot and well-drained soil. May be cut back by frost in hard winters – try it at the foot of a warm wall. Tolerates heavy clay soils and chalk.
PRUNE after flowering, removing older stems that have carried blooms.
PROPAGATE by cuttings of firm shoot tips in summer.

Acer shirasawanum 'Aureum'

Japanese Maple

1.8 x 1.8 m (6 x 6 ft)

A real stunner that is ideal to use as a tree in a tiny garden. The fan-shaped leaves are a glorious acid-yellow when they unfold in spring and they retain much of their brilliance until they fall in autumn.
LIKES a spot sheltered from winds and a soil that never becomes dust-dry. Avoid frost pockets: the new foliage is sensitive. Tolerates clay soil and very occasionally chalky soil; worth a try if you're desperate and can improve the ground with organic matter.
PRUNE at your peril. Remove only dead wood and any inconveniently placed branches in autumn.
PROPAGATE with difficulty. Try layering a low-growing branch in spring; sow seeds outdoors as soon as they are ripe; bud onto seedling stocks in early spring if you are really keen.

Acer palmatum varieties

Japanese Maple

Up to 3 x 4.5 m (10 x 15 ft)

Any gardener with an eye for form admires these supremely elegant plants. There are many varieties, of which these are some of the best:
f. *atropurpureum*, with leaves that are burgundy-purple.
'Dissectum Atropurpureum', the same but very finely cut like lace.
var. *dissectum*, with feathery green leaves.
'Senkaki' has stems of rosy pink and pale green leaves that turn orange-yellow in autumn.
'Osakazuki' is one of the best for autumn tints – the lobed green leaves are burnished rich, warm crimson.

All make shapely bushes or small trees that are ideal where space is restricted. They'll even grow in tubs.
LIKES a sheltered spot where cold winds and early frosts will not damage their leaves. They don't like dry soils. Tolerates clay soil and occasionally chalky soil if the latter is enriched, but they fail in shallow earth over chalk.
PRUNE / PROPAGATE as for *A. shirasawanum* 'Aureum'.

Amelanchier canadensis

Snowy Mespilus

2.4 x 3.6 m (8 x 12 ft)

This is the name under which nurserymen sell their snowy mespilus, but botanists mumble that it's likely to be *A. laevis*. It doesn't matter. Either way you'll obtain a large shrub with oval deciduous leaves that take on dazzling tints of orange, red and yellow before they fall in autumn. Clusters of small white starry flowers are carried in spring so the plant has two seasons of interest, even if it's boring in summer. Position summer bloomers in front of it.
LIKES any open spot in reasonable soil. Tolerates heavy or moist soil, and soils containing chalk.
PRUNE OUT a few old stems each winter.
PROPAGATE by digging up and replanting suckers in autumn.

Aralia elata

Japanese Angelica Tree

3–6 x 3 m (10–20 x 10 ft)

You'll need plenty of space for this whopper, but it has such super architectural form that it's a must where a striking plant is needed. The massive leaves are usually about 90 cm (3 ft) long, but divided into many smaller leaflets. Watch out for the spines! Fluffy flower clusters of creamy green are carried in late summer, and the most striking sight is the variegated form of the plant, *A. elata* 'Aureovariegata', whose leaves are edged with creamy white. Stunning.

LIKES an open spot in any ordinary soil and plenty of room to spread. Tolerates heavy clay soil and chalk.

PRUNE OUT any unwanted stems and any dead wood in spring. Remove unwanted suckers, which these plants can produce rather too freely. Those from the variegated variety will be green-leafed, for it is grafted on to rootstocks of the true species.

PROPAGATE by removing suckers from the true species or, if you've the patience, by grafting shoots of the variegated variety onto rootstocks of the true species in spring.

Arundinaria species
Bamboo

60 cm–3 m x 3 m (2–10 ft x 10 ft)

More folk should grow bamboos. There are midgets for small gardens and others that are so rampant they can only be let loose in relatively wild areas, but all produce a thicket of canes decorated with narrow leaves that may be dazzlingly variegated. These are my own favourites:

A. murieliae (now *Fargesia murieliae*): 3 m (10 ft), yellowish-green canes with arching tips clad in green leaves.
A. nitida (now *Fargesia nitida*): 3 m (10 ft), purplish canes and arching fronds of green leaves.
A. viridistriata (now *Pleioblastus auricomus*): 1 m (3 ft), devastatingly beautiful with short canes and leaves striped with fresh green and butter-yellow. The best for a small garden.

All are fun to grow in tubs and keep their leaves on throughout the year.
LIKES sheltered spots in soil that is unlikely to dry out. Tolerates heavy clay and boggy ground and, surprisingly, relatively dry soil and shady sites under trees. They don't mind chalk and will also put up with coastal exposure, though they certainly grow better without it.
PRUNE OUT a few old and dead canes each spring. Leave in some old wood to support the new and act as a windbreak.

PROPAGATE by lifting and transplanting portions of the clump in spring or autumn.

Aucuba japonica 'Variegata'
Spotted Laurel

2.4 x 2.4 m (8 x 8 ft)

Don't be put off this shrub by the fact that you've seen it, overgrown, in dingy shrubberies. As a single specimen in the right spot it has some sterling attributes: it is clothed with glossy yellow-spotted leaves all year round; it is easy to grow, shapely and produces fat red berries in winter if it's fertilized by a nearby male, which will hopefully be planted in someone else's garden. There are other varieties: some are spotted, some are plain; some are male (producing no berries) and some are female. Plant it where it can be admired from a window in winter.
LIKES good soil and gentle (but not overpowering) shade. Tolerates clay, chalk, heavy shade and coastal exposure.
PRUNE only to remove unwanted branches in spring.
PROPAGATE by cuttings of firm shoot tips in summer.

Azalea See *Rhododendron*

Berberis darwinii
Barberry

1.8 x 1.8 m (6 x 6 ft)

One of the best barberries, good in leaf and flower. The evergreen leaves are dark and glossy, like those of a miniature holly, and the orange flowers, like tiny daffodils in close-up, absolutely smother the stems in spring. Thorny and impenetrable: wear gloves when you prune it! Good for hedges (see p.84).
LIKES an open spot in any reasonable soil. Tolerates clay, chalk, dry soil, cold gardens, some shade and even coastal exposure, though it will burn in really severe salt-laden winds.

PRUNE carefully if you value your arms. Remove a few old stems each winter.
PROPAGATE by cuttings of firm shoot tips in summer.

Berberis x *ottawensis* f. *purpurea*

2.4 x 2.4 m (8 x 8 ft)

Also called *B.* x *ottawensis* 'Superba', this is a nicely vigorous, rather upright shrub whose leaves are a rich maroon-purple. The orange flowers look well against them in early summer, and tiny red berries follow. The leaves are shed in winter. Makes a good hedge. A good contrast to lower growing, grey-leaved plants.
LIKES an open spot in any reasonable soil. Tolerates clay, chalk, dry soil, cold gardens and just a modicum of shade.
PRUNE OUT a few old stems each winter, or cut back really hard at that time each year to encourage the production of new plum-purple shoots from lower down. Very thorny, so beware.
PROPAGATE by cuttings of firm shoot tips in summer.

Berberis x *stenophylla*

2.4 x 3 m (8 x 10 ft)

A spiny, arching thicket-former with tiny evergreen leaves and masses of scented orange-yellow flowers in spring. A really spectacular sight when in flower and one of the densest dog-proof hedges (see p.84).
LIKES most sites and soils.
PRUNE by cutting out overcrowding stems in winter and by digging up unwanted suckers, which it produces generously.
PROPAGATE by replanting the suckers, or by taking shoot tip cuttings in summer.

Berberis thunbergii

30 cm–12 m x 12 m (1–4 ft x 4 ft)

It is the forms of *B. thunbergii* that are valued for their eye-catching foliage. 'Atropurpurea Nana' is purple-leaved and only 30–60 cm (1–2 ft) high; 'Aurea' is also low-growing and has acid-yellow leaves that turn to dazzling green later in the year; 'Rose Glow' is a real curiosity with young leaves splashed and marbled pink on plum-purple. Watch out for a newcomer called 'Bagatelle', which makes domes about 30 cm (12 in) high of dark maroon. All shed their leaves in winter and have unremarkable flowers, but in summer the foliage effect is powerful.

LIKES open but sheltered sites and reasonable soil. Tolerates clay, chalk and a little shade, but is not keen about dry soils in which it will grow rather slowly.

PRUNE only to remove dead or unwanted stems in spring.

PROPAGATE by taking cuttings of firm shoot tips in summer.

Buddleja alternifolia

3 x 3 m (10 x 10 ft) or more

A graceful alternative to *B. davidii*, this species has an arching habit and narrow green leaves that are shed in winter. Lilac-pink flower clusters are carried right along the cascading stems in June, making the bush a real picture. Unlike *B. davidii* this species flowers on older wood, so pruning is rather different. It can be grown as a standard tree if trained to produce one fat stem from which the branches are allowed to cascade.

LIKES full sun and a well-drained soil. Tolerates clay, chalk, dry soil, cold gardens and even a modicum of coastal exposure.

PRUNE OUT the older shoots once the

> *"A large shrub of box is crashingly dull, but smaller bushes kept close-clipped are fun."*

Shrubs for ground cover

The measurement given after each plant is the recommended planting distance when the shrub is used in quantity as ground cover.

VARIETY	DISTANCE APART
● *Cistus*	60 cm (2 ft)
● *Convolvulus*	45 cm (18 in)
● *Cotoneaster dammeri*	45 cm (18 in)
● *Cytisus* (some)	45 cm (18 in)
● *Euonymus fortunei*	45 cm (18 in)
● *Fuchsia*	60 cm (2 ft)
● *Gaultheria* (syn. *Pernettya*)	45 cm (18 in)
● *Genista* (some)	45 cm (18 in)
● Heathers	30 cm (12 in)
● *Hebe*	45 cm (18 in)
● *Hedera*	30 cm (12 in)
● *Hypericum*	45 cm (18 in)
● *Juniperus*	90 cm (3 ft)
● *Lavandula*	45 cm (18 in)
● *Mahonia aquifolium*	60 cm (2 ft)
● *Phlomis*	45 cm (18 in)
● *Potentilla*	60 cm (2 ft)
● *Prunus laurocerasus* 'Otto Luyken'	60 cm (2 ft)
● *Rhododendron* (dependent upon type)	60 cm–1·5 m (2–5 ft)
● *Ruta*	30 cm (12 in)
● *Salix*	60 cm (2 ft)
● *Santolina*	45 cm (18 in)
● *Sarcococca*	45 cm (18 in)
● *Skimmia*	60 cm (2 ft)
● *Symphoricarpos*	60 cm (2 ft)
● *Viburnum tinus*	60 cm (2 ft)
● *Vinca*	45 cm (18 in)

flowers have faded. The stems produced through the rest of the summer will carry next year's crop of flowers.

PROPAGATE by taking cuttings of shoot tips in summer, or by rooting hardwood cuttings outdoors in autumn.

Buddleja davidii

Butterfly Bush

3 x 3 m (10 x 10 ft)

Vigorous, eye-catching and easy to grow, the butterfly bush earns its name by acting as a hostelry to all manner of butterflies when its flower spikes open in July and August. The deciduous leaves are dark green on the upper surface and greyish below, and there are many varieties with flower spikes of pink, white, crimson, purple and violet. There are also two varieties with variegated leaves. Plant any of them at the back of a border or in gaps between paving stones on a patio to bring butterflies close to you in summer. Every garden should have one.

LIKES full sun and a well-drained soil. Tolerates clay, chalk, dry soil, boggy soil, cold gardens and some coastal sites.

PRUNE hard back each winter, reducing

the sideshoots (and even the main stems) to mere stumps. That way you'll maintain a vigorous and flower-laden bush.

PROPAGATE by taking cuttings of flowerless shoot tips in summer and by rooting hardwood cuttings outdoors in autumn.

Buxus sempervirens

Box

Up to 3 x 3 m (10 x 10 ft) and more

A large shrub of box is crashingly dull, but smaller bushes kept close-clipped are fun, as are dwarf hedges around a kitchen garden (see p.84).

B. sempervirens 'Suffruticosa' is the miniature that will grow to just 30–45 cm (12–18 in) tall and it can be clipped into tiny domes or cones in formal gardens, as well as being used as an edger. Try also the variegated varieties whose leaves are edged with creamy white.

LIKES an open or shady spot in reasonably moisture-retentive soil. Tolerates clay, chalk, dry soil and shade.

PRUNE by clipping back in May. Excellent for topiary if you are a fan of vegetative peacocks and chessmen. Never cut back into very old wood.

PROPAGATE by rooting cuttings of shoot tips in summer, or by dividing the dwarf kind in spring.

Calluna See Heathers

Camellia x williamsii

2.4 x 2.4 m (8 x 8 ft)

I reckon that this is the best of the camellias – evergreen spring-flowering shrubs with blooms as big as roses – for it sheds its flowers when they fade, rather than letting them turn brown on the plant as is the case with *C. japonica* (see p.92). The best variety is 'Donation', a double-flowered confection of pink.

LIKES a peaty, moisture-retentive, lime-free soil and a spot in dappled shade.

Avoid frost pockets or the blooms will be damaged as they unfurl. Tolerates bright sun provided that the soil does not become dust-dry. Will tolerates occasional dryness at the expense of making growth.

PRUNE only when absolutely essential, removing old or badly placed stems in spring.

PROPAGATE by inserting cuttings of firm young shoots in summer, or by layering suitably low-slung branches. Leaf-bud cuttings can also be taken.

Caryopteris x clandonensis

Blue Spiraea

90 cm x 1.5 m (3 x 5 ft)

Any shrub of modest size that extends the season of interest in a garden must be worth planting. So it is with the blue spiraea. The deciduous leaves are grey and roughly toothed, and from their axils spring fluffy clusters of blue flowers in late summer and early autumn. Butterflies love it. Superb with other grey-foliage plants and at the front of beds and borders.

LIKES full sun and a well-drained soil. Tolerates dry soil, chalky soil and coastal exposure.

PRUNE BACK all the shoots quite hard each spring to encourage the production of healthy young growth.

PROPAGATE by taking cuttings of shoot tips in summer.

Ceanothus See p.92

Chaenomeles See p.93

Chamaecyparis species

Cypress

Various sizes

There are dozens of different species and varieties of cypress with varying habits, from the squat to the columnar, and varying colours, from golden yellow to blue-grey. I've room to mention just a few favourites, but there are others

recommended in Chapter 4 Trees too:
C. lawsoniana 'Minima Aurea' makes a yellow-tinged pyramid 60 cm (2 ft) high.
C. lawsoniana 'Gimbornii' is a 60 cm (2 ft) high dome of grey-green.
C. pisifera 'Boulevard' grows into a 1.2 m (4 ft) high cone of steel-grey.
C. pisifera 'Filifera Aurea', for all its long name, is a squat spreader with leaves like strands of gold.

They'll all provide you with year-round enjoyment.

LIKES an open site in a well-drained soil enriched with peat. Tolerates clay soils, chalky soils, dry soils and cold gardens.

PRUNE only to cut out damaged or dead branches. 'Boulevard' can be lightly clipped in spring to encourage new growth and prevent browning.

PROPAGATE by taking heel cuttings in summer.

Choisya ternata

Mexican Orange Blossom

1.5 x 2.4 m (5 x 8 ft)

If you want a shrub that really pays ground rent, this is a good one to choose. The fingered evergreen leaves are glossy and aromatic when crushed, and the flowers are certainly a lot like orange blossom. They are white, deliciously scented and carried in large clusters, first in late spring and then again late in summer. It's a shapely plant that is easy to grow in most situations. The variety 'Sundance' has young leaves that are acid-yellow; 'Aztec Pearl' has finely cut leaves and pink-tinged white flowers.

LIKES a sunny and sheltered spot in well-drained soil. Tolerates clay, chalk, shade and a certain amount of coastal exposure.

PRUNE OUT only dead or damaged branches in spring, along with any straggly shoots that make the bush unshapely. One or two old stems can be removed in spring to rejuvenate ageing bushes.

PROPAGATE by taking cuttings of shoot tips in summer.

Cistus species and varieties
Sun Rose
Various sizes

These lovely sun-worshipping shrubs produce some of the best flowers of early summer: large round blooms seemingly made of crumpled tissue paper and centred with a boss of yellow stamens. Each flower is short-lived, but so many are carried that the bush performs well for several weeks. Often the rough, evergreen foliage is rather tacky to the touch. My favourite three are:

C. x purpureus: 90 cm x 1.5 m (3 x 5 ft), rich pink, each petal blotched at the base with maroon.

C. 'Silver Pink': 60 cm x 1.2 m (2 x 4 ft), soft pink.

C. x cyprius: to 1.8 x 2.4 m (6 x 8 ft), white flowers blotched at the base of each petal with maroon.

LIKES full sun and shelter. Tolerates dry soils, chalky soils and coastal exposure.

PRUNE OUT frost-damaged growth in spring.

Propagate by taking shoot tip cuttings in summer.

Convolvulus cneorum
60 cm x 1.2 m (2 x 4 ft)

Deservedly high-ranking among silver-leaved shrubs, this plant has none of the characteristics of its pernicious relative, the bindweed. It makes a sprawling bush with silver-haired spatula-shaped leaves, and the shoots are tipped with white, pink-backed trumpet flowers in summer. A gleaming 'evergrey' treasure.

LIKES a warm, sunny, sheltered spot (preferably at the base of a south- or west-facing wall) and well-drained soil. Tolerates dry or chalky soil.

PRUNE OUT only stems damaged during winter. It is likely to be severely damaged, or even killed outright, by severe winters.

PROPAGATE by layering suitable stems in summer, or by rooting cuttings of firm shoot tips in summer.

Cornus alba
Dogwood
90 cm–1.8 m x 1.8 m (3–6 x 6 ft)

Easily kept low, this shrub is available in three different varieties:

'Elegantissima' has cream-variegated leaves.

'Spaethii' has leaves freely splashed with butter-yellow.

'Sibirica' has bright red stems to cheer you throughout the winter months when the leaves have fallen.

LIKES an open site and any ordinary soil. Tolerates boggy soil, clay, dry soil and chalky soil as well as cold and exposed situations. It also puts up with some shade, though the stems colour up best in full sun.

PRUNE by cutting back all stems really hard in early spring. This keeps the shrub low and produces plenty of new growth for foliage and stem colour. Cut back to ground level if you like. Propagate by layering suitable stems (earth up around them to induce root formation); by taking cuttings of firm shoot tips in summer; or by inserting hardwood cuttings outdoors in autumn.

Cornus kousa
3 x 2.4 m (10 x 8 ft)

A real spectacle in June when the horizontal branches are decorated with flowers, each one surrounded by four white, pointed bracts. They nestle like doves among the green leaves. Superb autumn colour provides another good reason for growing the plant. The variety *chinensis* is rather larger altogether and supposedly freer flowering. I'd have either.

LIKES a deep, lime-free soil and a situation in dappled shade. Tolerates quite heavy shade but hates shallow chalky soils.

PRUNE OUT only dead stems as soon as they are seen.

PROPAGATE by taking cuttings of firm shoot tips in summer, or by seeds sown in pots in a frame in spring.

Corylus avellana 'Contorta'
Corkscrew Hazel
3 x 3 m (10 x 10 ft)

The best time to look at this weird and wonderful shrub is in late winter and early spring when the bare corkscrew branches are dripping with sulphur-yellow catkins. Its other common name of Harry Lauder's walking stick says it all. In summer, when the leaves appear, you'd rather forget about the plant: they are puckered and turned under at the edges as if being attacked by a hidden pest. Plant the shrub where summer flowers will mask its embarrassment at that time of year, but make sure you get a good view in winter.

LIKES an open spot in well-drained soil. Tolerates clay, dry or chalky soils, and even those that are really damp. It also puts up with shade.

PRUNE only to remove overcrowding or dead stems in winter. Propagate by hardwood cuttings in autumn.

Corylus maxima 'Purpurea'
Purple-leafed Filbert
3 x 3 m (10 x 10 ft)

It doesn't do to plant too many purple-leaved shrubs in the garden as the effect becomes rather oppressive, but this shrub must be one of the best. It sends up vigorous stems that are clothed in summer with coarse, bold leaves of deep plum-purple. Probably the largest-leaved purple foliage plant you'll find.

LIKES a spot in the open or dappled shade in ordinary soil. Tolerates clay, chalk, dry soils, cold gardens and quite heavy shade.

PRUNE to remove a few older stems each winter to reduce the density of the thicket.

PROPAGATE by layering or by removing and transplanting rooted suckers.

Sun-loving *Cistus* produces a plentiful supply of papery, pink, white or red flowers. This is *C.* 'Silver Pink'.

Cotinus coggygria
Smoke Tree

1.8 x 2.4 m (6 x 8 ft)

This shrub was designed by a sensitive architect: the rather thin leaves are almost perfectly round, and the buff flowers are a cloud of fluff when they open in midsummer. By autumn they've turned smoke-grey. The bush is shapely, too, and wider than it is tall. Two superb purple-leaved varieties are available: 'Notcutt's Variety' and 'Royal Purple'. Both look terrific when planted near coppery roses such as 'Buff Beauty'. The true variety offers vivid autumn tints, the purple-leaved kinds not as bright, but they certainly make up for it in summer.
LIKES well-drained soil and an open spot. Tolerates clay soil, chalky soil and cold gardens.
PRUNE only to remove one or two old stems and dead wood in late winter.
PROPAGATE by cuttings of firm shoot tips in summer.

Cotoneaster species and varieties
Various sizes

This varied group offers something for almost every situation. Briefly the ones that you'll find most useful are:
C. dammeri: an evergreen ground-hugger with white flowers followed by scarlet berries.
C. conspicuus 'Decorus': 1.8 x 1.8 m (6 x 6 ft), with arching stems clad in evergreen leaves and studded with bird-proof berries in autumn.
C. frigidus 'Cornubia': 3 x 3 m (10 x 10 ft), which is semi-evergreen and laden with hefty clusters of red berries on its cascading stems – not so bird-proof.
C. horizontalis is another good ground coverer, but it is dealt with in Chapter 7 Climbers and Wall Plants. All of the cotoneasters are among the best berry bearers in any garden.
LIKES well-drained soil and positions in the open. Tolerates any soil and any situation.
PRUNE only to remove unwanted or overcrowded growths in spring.

PROPAGATE by rooting cuttings of firm shoot tips in summer.

Cytisus species and varieties
Broom

Various sizes

They don't look much in winter, but the brooms are a treat in spring and early summer when their wiry stems, upright or cascading, are plastered with bright pea flowers. There are many hybrids with flowers of crimson, orange, yellow and creamy white, some of them showing two distinct shades in the same bloom. I'd go for:
C. x beanii: 30 x 90 cm (1 x 3 ft), bright yellow and cascading.
C. x kewensis: 30 cm x 1.2 m (1–4 ft), creamy yellow flowers and rather more upright.

For brighter flowers I'd choose taller hybrids like 'Windlesham Ruby': 1.5 x 1.5 m (5 x 5 ft), bronze-red. Few of them will disappoint you, but in general all are short-lived. Renew them every five to ten years depending on their health.
LIKES a sunny spot in lime-free soil. Tolerates clay soil, dry soil, and some chalky soils, though not those that are really shallow and poor. Also puts up with coastal exposure.
PRUNE OUT most of the flowered shoots when the blooms have faded. Failure to do this will produce an overcrowded bush with plenty of dead wood and little vigour. Try to avoid cutting back into really old wood.
PROPAGATE by taking heel cuttings in late summer.

Daphne species and varieties
30–90 x 30–90 cm (1–3 x 1–3 ft)

Valuable little shrubs that flower in winter and spring with blooms that are deliciously scented. The mezereon, *D. mezereum*, 90 cm x 1.2 m (3 x 4 ft), with its pink or white flower cockades on bare stems in winter, is undoubtedly the most popular species, but there are others offering a greater season of

interest. Try *D. odora* 'Aureomarginata': 1.2 x 1.5 m (4 x 5 ft), with its evergreen leaves margined with cream and its clusters of pale pink perfumed blossoms in spring.
D. x burkwoodii: 90 cm x 1.2 m (3 x 4 ft), is good too: a semi-evergreen, it carries pale pink flowers in May and June, extending your daphne season. No perfumed plot would be complete without them.
LIKES to be planted when young in well-drained organically enriched soil that never dries out completely. Enjoy good light. Tolerates chalky soil, in the case of *D. mezereum* – the others don't like it much.
PRUNE OUT only dead shoots, nothing else.
PROPAGATE by taking cuttings of firm shoot tips in summer.

Deutzia x magnifica
1.8 x 1.8 m (6 x 6 ft)

If you're planting a June border, don't forget the deutzias. This one, like most, grows upright before arching its stems to show off the double rosettes of white flowers against the green summer foliage. The flowering season is brief but glorious and you'd be well advised to use the shrub where it can act as a green backdrop for brighter blooms in late summer. There are other species and varieties of similar build with flowers of pink or white.
LIKES a sunny spot in any well-drained soil. Tolerates clay, dry or chalky soil and cold, exposed gardens.
PRUNE OUT some of the older shoots completely every year as soon as the flowers fade.
PROPAGATE by taking cuttings of firm shoot tips in summer or by rooting hardwood cuttings in autumn.

Elaeagnus pungens 'Maculata'
Oleaster

2.4 x 3 m (8 x 10 ft)

Show-stopping in winter when the sun catches its leaves, this is a variegated

Shrubs for planting as single features

Where there is no room for a small tree, these shrubs can be relied on to act as focal points.

- *Acer japonicum* 'Aureum'
- *Acer palmatum* varieties
- *Aralia*
- *Buddleja alternifolia*
- *Camellia*
- *Chamaecyparis*
- *Cornus kousa*
- *Cotinus coggygria* varieties
- *Cotoneaster conspicuus* 'Decorus'
- *Elaeagnus pungens* 'Maculata'
- *Embothrium*
- *Eucryphia*
- *Fatsia*
- *Genista aetnensis*
- *Hamamelis*
- *Hibiscus*
- *Ilex*
- *Juniperus*
- *Laurus*
- *Lavatera*
- *Leycesteria*
- *Magnolia*
- *Mahonia* x *media* 'Charity'
- *Paeonia*
- *Pieris*
- *Pittosporum*
- *Prunus triloba*
- *Rhododendron*
- *Rhus*
- *Sambucus*
- *Syringa*
- *Tamarix*
- *Viburnum* (some)
- *Yucca*

evergreen that should be on the top of your list. Each oval leaf is margined with dark green and centred with a splash of bright yellow. Handsome all the year round, this shrub really comes into its own in the dreary months. A must for any 'winter garden'. The variety *E.* x *ebbingei* 'Gilt Edge' has yellow rims to its green leaves.

LIKES any good soil and an open position sheltered from biting winds. Tolerates clay, chalk, dry soil, cold gardens and coastal exposure.

PRUNE OUT any shoots that revert to plain green, and remove or shorten unwanted stems in spring.

PROPAGATE by taking cuttings of firm young shoots in late summer and early autumn.

Embothrium coccineum
Chilean Fire Bush
6 x 3 m (20 x 10 ft)

A gambler's treasure. A stunning tree-like shrub with semi-evergreen leaves and, in early summer, masses of fiery orange-red flowers that are long and thin and held in dense clusters along the stems. The *Lanceolatum* Group is also good, but 'Norquinco' is breathtaking and can be seen thriving at Harlow Car Gardens in Yorkshire.

LIKES best a spot in woodland where organic, lime-free soil and dappled shade are found. Tolerates moist ground and cold gardens as long as some shelter can be provided from damaging winds.

PRUNE OUT only dead wood in winter.

PROPAGATE by sowing seeds in a propagator in spring; cuttings of firm shoot tips (or root cuttings) can be taken in summer.

Erica See Heathers

Escallonia 'Donard Star'
1.8 x 1.8 m (6 x 6 ft)

I choose this variety as being representative of a group of plants that should be valued by more gardeners. They are of pleasing habit, bushy and upright or rather arching; most are clothed all the year round in shiny evergreen leaves, and all are generously decorated from summer to autumn with small but profuse flowers of white, pink or deep rose. The cultivar 'Donard Star' has deep pink blooms.

LIKES any reasonably well-drained soil and a position in full sun. Tolerates clay, chalky soil, dry soil and coastal exposure.

PRUNE OUT completely large portions of flowered growth once the blooms have faded. Sideshoots can also be shortened after flowering. After severe winters, badly damaged growth can be cut out in spring when new shoots can be seen growing away.

PROPAGATE by taking cuttings of firm young shoots in summer.

Eucryphia x *nymansensis* 'Nymansay'
6 x 3 m (20 x 10 ft)

This has to be one of my 'Desert Island Shrubs'. The upright branches on this tall bush or tree are clothed all the year round in dark evergreen leaves. In late summer, a feast of white flowers erupts all over them, each pristine blossom being centred with a tuft of fluffy stamens. The timing is as welcome as the spectacle itself – a sort of farewell to summer. Just the plant for the back of a wide border.

There's a handsome eucryphia planted outside the back door of Beatrix Potter's old home, Hill Top Farm at Sawrey in the Lake District, proving that some species (such as *E. glutinosa*) are tougher than many folk would have you believe.

LIKES a moist, preferably lime-free soil that is never likely to dry out. Dappled shade is enjoyed too, but not heavy murk. Tolerates chalky soil better than most eucryphias, and fairly cold gardens provided that shelter can be given from biting winds.

PRUNE not at all, except to remove dead or damaged stems.

PROPAGATE by layering suitable stems, or by taking cuttings of firm shoot tips in early autumn.

Euonymus europaeus
Spindle Tree

3 x 3 m (10 x 10 ft)

Doubly valuable in autumn, our native spindle tree colours its foliage well with tints of orange and crimson, and carries bunches of four-lobed fruits that are rich crimson-pink, splitting to reveal orange seeds. 'Red Cascade' is a particularly good form.

LIKES any reasonable soil and a spot in full sun. Tolerates clay, dry soil, chalky soil and cold gardens. Will put up with shade but you won't get such good autumn colour.

PRUNE only to remove old and overcrowding stems and dead wood.

PROPAGATE by hardwood cuttings or layering.

> *"Most folk think of Fatsia japonica as a house plant, but it's as tough as old boots in the garden."*

Euonymus fortunei 'Emerald 'n' Gold'

30 x 90 cm (1–3 ft)

A bright little carpeter with evergreen leaves that are blotched with butter-yellow and green. They take on pink tinges during cold winter weather, and the shrub will even scale walls if planted against them. There are other varieties of different habits and variegations, such as the green and white 'Emerald Gaiety'.

LIKES ordinary soil and an open site. Tolerates most soils and situations.

PRUNE not at all, except to restrict its spread.

PROPAGATE by cuttings of shoot tips in autumn or by layering.

Fatsia japonica
False Castor Oil Palm

1.8 x 1.8 m (6 x 6 ft)

Most folk think of this as a house plant, but it's as tough as old boots in the garden. True, it might be killed back to the stump by really severe winter weather once every five years, but it always seems to sprout again in spring, and in most years it will remain evergreen, those big, glossy, hand-shaped leaves forming a handsome mound of greenery. Starry white flowerheads are often carried in autumn. A plant has grown happily in my parents' garden in the Yorkshire Dales for over 30 years, and it's also an excellent choice for town gardens.

LIKES good, moisture-retentive soil and full sun. Tolerates gentle shade, cold gardens, clay or chalky soil and coastal exposure.

PRUNE it not at all.

PROPAGATE from shoot tip cuttings taken in summer, or by root cuttings.

Forsythia x intermedia 'Lynwood'
Golden Bells

2.4 x 2.4 m (8 x 8 ft)

All right, so it might be in everybody's garden, but that's only because nothing else can touch it when it comes to brilliant spring colour! This, I think, is the best forsythia to grow as a shrub (see also Chapter 7 Climbers and Wall Plants). It makes an upright bush whose bare khaki stems cannot be seen in spring for the profusion of stemless yellow flowers. The large green leaves emerge to hide the fading blooms and provide pleasant verdure for the rest of the year when other plants are doing their stuff. Site it where you can admire it from a window on dull winter days.

LIKES good, well-drained soil and a sunny spot. Tolerates clay and chalk and cold, exposed gardens, but don't plant it in shade or it won't flower at all well.

PRUNE it immediately after flowering, taking out completely those stems that have carried flowers. The shoots that

form during the summer will carry next year's blooms.

PROPAGATE by layering, by hardwood cuttings in autumn and by shoot tip cuttings in summer.

Fuchsia magellanica varieties

1.8 x 1.8 m (6 x 6 ft)

The hardy fuchsias are a delight in summer and on into autumn, when their ballerina flowers drip from the arching, blushing branches. The blooms of this species have a petticoat of purple held below carmine sepals – a vibrant combination of colour to be found in few plants. The foliage of *F. magellanica* 'Versicolor' is a confection of green, pink and cream; 'Variegata' is similar but without the pink. There are numerous hybrid hardy fuchsias (not to be confused with the more tender greenhouse kinds) but among the very best are 'Mrs Popple' – again with the carmine and purple combination and terribly generous with her flowers; and 'Mrs W. P. Wood', whose little blooms of blush-pink dangle like icicles from shapely bushes. In some years, or in cold gardens, the plants might be killed to ground level by winter frosts; but in milder areas they'll lose their leaves in winter and very little else.

LIKES sunny spots in good, well-drained soil. Tolerates clay, chalk and coastal exposure.

PRUNE BACK to ground level in February in cold gardens or severe winters. Where the stems survive the winter, remove a few of the older ones in February and shorten all sideshoots to three buds. Earthing up with organic matter in autumn gives welcome frost protection to the roots and crown.

PROPAGATE from shoot tip cuttings in summer.

Gaultheria (syn. Pernettya) mucronata
Prickly Heath

60 cm x 1.2 m (2 x 4 ft)

Knee-high thickets of tiny, pointed

evergreen leaves don't sound very interesting, but smother them in purple, pink, red or white berries in autumn and you'll have a sight worth seeing. To get plenty of fruits you'll need several plants to ensure adequate pollination: some have predominantly male flowers, others female. There are named varieties offering berries of certain colours. Good under trees.

LIKES peaty, lime-free soil and a spot in dappled shade. Don't let the earth dry out in summer. Tolerates clay and moist soils and cold, exposed gardens in light or heavy shade.

PRUNE hardly at all. It's sufficient to cut out unwanted stems at ground level in spring.

PROPAGATE by division in spring or by shoot tip cuttings in summer.

Shrubs with evergreen leaves

- *Abelia*
- *Arundinaria*
- *Aucuba*
- *Berberis darwinii*
- *Berberis* x *stenophylla*
- *Buxus*
- *Camellia*
- *Chamaecyparis*
- *Choisya*
- *Cistus*
- *Convolvulus*
- *Cotoneaster* (some)
- *Daphne* (some)
- *Elaeagnus*
- *Escallonia*
- *Eucryphia*
- *Euonymus fortunei*
- *Fatsia*
- Heathers
- *Hebe*
- *Hedera*
- *Hypericum*
- *Ilex*
- *Juniperus*
- *Laurus*
- *Lavandula*
- *Mahonia*
- *Myrtus*
- *Olearia*
- *Osmanthus*
- *Pernettya* (syn. *Gaultheria*)
- *Phlomis*
- *Photinia*
- *Pieris*
- *Pittosporum*
- *Prunus laurocerasus* 'Otto Luyken'
- *Rhododendron*
- *Rosmarinus*
- *Ruta*
- *Santolina*
- *Sarcococca*
- *Skimmia*
- *Viburnum tinus*
- *Vinca*
- *Yucca*

Genista species
Broom
Various sizes

There are four genistas I think you ought to know about, and each one is different. The giant of the race is *G. aetnensis*, the Mount Etna broom, which virtually makes a tree up to 4.5 x 3 m (15 x 10 ft) with wispy, semi-weeping stems, studded in summer with yellow pea flowers. Plant near a patio where it will cast the gentlest shade.

G. lydia: 45 x 90 cm (18 in x 3 ft), is a cascading charmer for a bank or rock garden where its wiry stems drip with bright yellow blooms in spring.

G. hispanica: 30 x 90 cm (1 x 3 ft), is the spitting image of a miniature gorse, which is why it's

The marble-sized berries of *Gaultheria mucronata* (prickly heath) appear first in autumn, and last until the end of winter.

called the Spanish gorse. Its barbarous stems are interlaced with yellow pea flowers in late spring. And finally *G. sagittalis*, 15 cm x 1.2 m (6 in x 4 ft), a carpeting curiosity with flattened, winged stems and the usual yellow flowers in early summer. Scrambling across rocks or paving, it's a real eye-catcher.

LIKES sun and well-drained soil. Tolerates clay, dry soil and some chalky soils, though not the poorest and shallowest. Happy in coastal exposure.

PRUNE OUT most of the flowering shoots when the blooms have faded. Avoid cutting back into old wood.

G. aetnensis can be trained to grow upwards in its youth, and as it matures no pruning, other than the removal of dead wood, is necessary.

PROPAGATE by sowing seeds in gentle heat in spring or by rooting heel cuttings in late summer.

Hamamelis mollis
Witch Hazel
3 x 4.5 m (10 x 15 ft)

A delight to the senses when the shuttlecock of bare branches is colonized by fragrant yellow spider flowers in winter. In the true species the blooms are bright yellow, radiating from a central bronze-red core, while in the variety x *intermedia* 'Pallida' they are a soft sulphur-yellow, making them even more remarkable against a leaden sky. Some varieties, like 'Ruby Glow', have red flowers – a pleasant variation, but not so noticeable in dreary weather. The large, hazel-like leaves unfurl in spring and take on rich autumn tints before they fall.

LIKES good soil that's lime-free and not

prone to drought. Tolerates clay soil and cold gardens.

PRUNE only to remove dead wood.

PROPAGATE by layering suitable stems in spring or summer.

Heathers
Heath, Heather and Ling
15–45 cm x 90 cm (6–18 in x 3 ft)

I've cheated on the naming and grouped *Erica* (heath), *Calluna* (heather) and *Daboecia* (St Dabeoc's heath) together to make life easier. They can be had in flower in most months of the year, many of them have brilliant foliage that takes on vibrant tints of yellow, orange and mahogany red in winter, and all are superb ground coverers. Some species of *Erica* even tolerate chalky soil, the other two will not. I'll draw your attention to two really tall heaths that should be more widely planted: *E. lusitanica*, 3 x 3 m (10 x 10 ft), with wispy green leaves and tiers of tiny white flowers; and *E. arborea*, the tree heath, which is similar but even larger. Both bloom in spring and both need a warm, sheltered spot. They are particularly happy in warm coastal districts.

LIKES acid, peaty soil that never dries out and an open site. Tolerates chalky soil (if you choose varieties of *E. carnea*, *E.* x *darleyensis*, *E. erigena* and *E. terminalis*), clay soil and dry soil. The dwarf species are happy in cold gardens.

PRUNE after flowering, lightly clipping over the foliate with shears.

PROPAGATE by taking short stem cuttings in summer or by removing rooted layers.

Hebe species and varieties
Shrubby Veronica
30 cm–1.5 m x 2.4 m (1–5 x 8 ft)

Rather tender shrubs with opposite and decussate (criss-cross) leaves and bottle-brush sprays of flowers in summer or autumn. They are evergreen, and some species and varieties have coloured foliage – purplish on the undersides or glaucous grey all over. I'll recommend but three, for I've space for no more: *H. pinguifolia* 'Pagei', 30 x 60 cm (1–2 ft), makes hummocks of short grey leaves studded with white flowers in summer; *H.* 'Autumn Glory', 60 cm x 1.2 m (2 x 4 ft), is a valuable late summer and autumn bloomer with purple spikes and glossy green leaves; and *H.* 'Great Orme', 75 cm x 1.2 m (2½ x 4 ft), although not as hardy as some, has slender spikes of such a lovely shade of pink that it's worth the risk.

The so-called 'whipcord' hebes are worth a try. Their leaves are strands of bronze- or golden-green growth, almost like a conifer, and they are hardier than the larger-leaved species. The most popular whipcord is *H. cupressoides*.

LIKES warm, sheltered spots in well-drained soil. Tolerates dry soil, chalky soil and sometimes heavy clay too. They don't mind coastal exposure.

PRUNE OUT frost-damaged stems in spring when new shoots can be seen breaking from lower down. Cut back aged specimens into old wood in spring or summer; they will soon sprout up again. Remove one or two old stems each May and shorten the other growths by half. If you're lazy simply clip over the bushes lightly with shears in spring. Very dwarf species need not be pruned annually.

PROPAGATE by taking cuttings of shoot tips in summer.

Hedera varieties
Ivy
15 cm–15 m x 1.5 m (6 in–5 ft x 6 ft) or more

Although ivy is primarily thought of as a climber, it is invaluable as a weed-suppressing carpeter, particularly in shade and under trees. The varieties of *H. helix* are tremendously varied in appearance, having lobed evergreen leaves that may be dull and dark or shiny and vibrantly coloured in shades of cream, white, yellow and green. The best climbers are mentioned in Chapter 7 Climbers and wall plants, but here I would draw your attention to *H. helix* 'Arborescens', an adult form of the common ivy, with unlobed leaves and woody stems making a bush 1.4 x 3 m (5 x 10 ft). It is the form of ivy that often appears atop trees and walls when the younger stems have done the climbing. *H. hibernica* is unsurpassable as ground cover under trees, making a thick carpet of glossy green, that is impenetrable to weeds. This, too, has an adult form that is taller and more shrubby. *H. helix* 'Erecta', 45 x 90 cm (18 in x 3 ft), makes a neat, upright bush with leaves piled on top of each other in jumbled tiers. It makes a fine

Hydrangeas are deservedly popular for their mass of either mop-head or lace-cap flowerheads. Both types are available in white, pink, red and blue.

feature at the front of a border.

LIKES most sites and soils – variegated varieties prefer good light to shade.

PRUNE most kinds by clipping over with shears in May. The arborescent (shrubby) kinds need no pruning.

PROPAGATE by taking cuttings of shoot tips in summer: adventitious roots may already be present. Layers can be lifted and transplanted in spring.

Helianthemum See p.176

Hibiscus syriacus
2.4 x 1.8 m (8 x 6 ft)

No plant will tax your patience more than a hardy hibiscus. Just when you're about to give it up for dead in June, its grey stems will burst into life with fresh green shoots. The mallow flowers will appear among the green leaves in late summer and autumn before the foliage falls and this lazy plant goes to sleep again. All varieties make upright bushes; 'Woodbridge' has rich rose-pink blooms, 'Hamabo' is white, and 'Blue Bird' a wishy-washy lavender; all are blotched with crimson at the base of the petals. At least the plants do make quite an effort when they're in bloom!

LIKES a warm, sunny, sheltered spot in rich, well-drained soil. Best in the south of England. Tolerates clay, dry or chalky soils and warm coastal gardens.

PRUNE only to remove dead or damaged shoots in summer.

PROPAGATE by taking shoot tip cuttings in summer or autumn and rooting them in a propagator. Sometimes they take an age to root. Suitable stems can be layered.

Hoheria See p.96

Hydrangea macrophylla varieties
1.5 x 3 m (5 x 10 ft)

There are two kinds of common hydrangea, the fat, mop-headed or 'Hortensia' varieties with their cob-loaf-like flowers of white, pink or blue, and the lace-caps with their flattened heads of tiny flowers surrounded by sterile florets with larger petals. The colour range is the same. All are deciduous and bloom in late summer and early autumn. Your local nurseryman will have his own favourite varieties. Enjoyed near front doors, especially in the southern counties, but excellent too in wide borders where they look good with ornamental grasses and other foliage plants.

LIKES sunny spots, sheltered from strong winds, and a rich soil that is unlikely to dry out. Tolerates clay and chalk and very moist soils. Happy by the coast. Blue varieties colour best in acid soils: they usually turn pink in chalky soil. Water them with proprietary hydrangea colorant to help restore their cerulean qualities, or settle for a rosy glow.

PRUNE OUT weak and very old shoots completely in spring before growth starts. At the same time cut off the faded flowerheads above the topmost pair of fat buds. Single fat buds at the stem tips should not be removed for they are certain to flower.

PROPAGATE by taking cuttings of firm shoot tips in summer.

Hydrangea paniculata

1.5 x 1.8 m (5 x 6 ft)

Here the white or pink-tinged flowers are more pyramidal in outline than those of the previous species, though they are carried at the same time, in late summer and autumn. The variety 'Grandiflora' has the largest blooms and is rightly in demand. Plant it where you can get a good look at it during the flowering season.

LIKES sunny spots and a good soil that's not likely to suffer from drought. Tolerates cold gardens more than the previous species. Also happy in clay and chalk.

PRUNE the shoots really hard back to within 2.5 cm (1 in) of the main stem or ground level in late winter; this

species flowers on shoots made during the current season, and if not pruned it gets taller and out of hand.

PROPAGATE by taking cuttings of firm shoot tips in summer.

Hypericum species and varieties
St John's Wort

30 cm–1.5 m x 1.8 m (1–5 ft x 6 ft) or more

Sneers abound when hypericum is mentioned in high horticultural circles, but this is a deserving race of plants whose only failing is a desire to please (and an occasional attack of rust disease). *H. calycinum*, 30 cm x several metres (1 ft x several yards), is the rose of Sharon, a rampant spreader that is a boon to the gardener who wants a bright weed smotherer in dry soil under trees. It's semi-evergreen and carries plenty of yellow, shaving-brush-centred flowers in summer and autumn. *H.* 'Hidcote' is one of the best taller varieties at 50 cm x 1.8 m (5 x 6 ft). The yellow flowers are similar to the rose of Sharon but not so well endowed with bristles.

LIKES reasonably good soil and good light. Tolerates shade, clay, chalk and dry soils and coastal exposure.

PRUNE *H. calycinum* by clipping it back to within about 5 cm (a couple of inches) of ground level in spring, just before growth begins. At the same time, cut out completely any old and weak stems to be found on *H.* 'Hidcote'.

PROPAGATE by lifting and transplanting rooted portions of the plants in autumn or spring. Cuttings may be taken from the shoot tips of *H.* 'Hidcote' in summer.

Ilex aquifolium
Holly

6 x 3 m (20 x 10 ft) at least

As well as making excellent trees and hedges, hollies are very useful evergreen border plants, providing a background of glossy green or green and yellow. Male and female flowers are carried on

separate plants and only the females will carry berries, provided there is a male in the vicinity to pollinate their flowers.

Varieties of *I. x altaclerensis* are as good as those of the common holly, though their leaves are usually larger and less spiny. There are dozens of different variegations described in detail in nurserymen's catalogues: check the sex as well as the colouring.

LIKES good, well-drained soil not prone to drought. Tolerates almost any soil and situation in sun or shade.

PRUNE only to remove Christmas holly, or clip after fruiting to produce a formal shape. Regular pruning is unnecessary.

PROPAGATE by rooting shoot tip cuttings in a propagator in summer/ autumn.

Jasminum See p.96

Juniperus species and varieties
Juniper, Savin

Various sizes

Fuzzy-foliaged conifers of upright or spreading habit, the junipers can be used either as elegant and deep ground cover or as columnar eye-catchers in flat border plantings. Forms of *J. horizontalis* and *J. sabina* (Savin) are among the best spreaders, sending out rocket-like growths over or above the ground. They grow to between 30 cm and 1.5 m (1 and 5 ft) high and to between 1.2 and 3 m (4 and 10 ft) across. *J. communis* provides plenty of upright forms, the favourite being the tiny *J. communis* 'Compressa', a bollard just 45 cm (18 in) high and 15 cm (6 in) across. The spreading forms are superb at covering manhole covers, even if they do make inspection a prickly job!

LIKES soil enriched with peat. Tolerates any soil and situation except severe drought.

PRUNE only to remove dead wood.

PROPAGATE by heel cuttings of young shoot tips in summer.

Kerria japonica 'Pleniflora'
Jew's Mallow
1.8 x 1.8 m (6 x 6 ft)

Nobody would recommend *Kerria* as a specimen front-of-the-border plant – its season is so short – but it is good at the back! Its wiry green canes are bare of leaves in winter and dotted with 3 cm (1 in) wide double chrysanthemum flowers of bright yellow in spring before the foliage unfurls. Soon it becomes an arching shuttlecock of green, but hardly a year goes by without its flowers drawing comments from gardeners unfamiliar with the spectacle. There is a single-flowered variety but it's not as good as the double.

LIKES good soil and a sunny spot. Tolerates clay and chalky soil, some shade and cold, exposed gardens.

PRUNE OUT plenty of older stems completely as soon as the flowers fade.

PROPAGATE by division or layering. Cuttings of firm shoot tips can be rooted in a propagator in summer.

Laurus nobilis
Sweet Bay, Victor's Laurel
Up to 15 x 4.5 m (50 x 15 ft)

Plant your own sweet bay and never buy another packet of bay leaves! Choose a young plant as older ones are prohibitively expensive. It's an evergreen, with leathery oval leaves that are aromatic and fruity flavoured when used in cooking. It can be left to grow unchecked, or clipped quite formally into a pyramid or lollipop – whatever takes your fancy. Only after many years and no clipping or pruning will it reach the given height.

LIKES a warm, sheltered spot and a good soil that's not likely to dry out in summer. Drought or biting winds will burn the foliage. Tolerates sun or light shade, clay or chalky soil and coastal exposure.

PRUNE in spring or summer when necessary.

PROPAGATE by taking cuttings of shoot tips in summer.

Lavandula species and varieties
Lavender
60 cm x 12 m (2 x 4 ft)

Brushing past a bank of lavender on a warm summer's day is a treat to the senses. Nothing else has that sweet and fruity aroma.

Whichever variety you choose the plant will have downy grey foliage (though one or two are nearer grey-green) and spikes of purple-blue flowers on slender stems in summer. There are pink- and white-flowered forms, but both are remarkable for their insipidity. I'd go for 'Hidcote' as first choice – not 'Hidcote Giant', which has longer flower stems that fall over – and then, perhaps, Miss Jekyll's 'Munstead'.

The foliage is just as fragrant as the flowers, and the plants make unsurpassable edging to beds, borders and paths.

LIKES reasonably well-drained soil that is not heavily acid, and a spot in full sun. Tolerates dry soil and chalky soil.

PRUNE by clipping over the plants once the flowers have faded.

PROPAGATE by taking cuttings of shoot tips in summer.

Lavatera 'Rosea'
Tree Mallow
2.4 x 2.4 m (8 x 8 ft)

A smashing shrub for a warm garden, I've never known any plant to be more generous with its flowers. They deck the downy grey stems from July to November – large pink mallow blooms that look a treat with the lobed, grey-green leaves. The shrub grows vigorously in any season, so give it plenty of space to spread its branches. Lovely against a south-facing wall of mellow brick.

LIKES a warm, sheltered spot in full sun and a poor, well-drained soil. Tolerates dry or chalky soil and coastal exposure.

PRUNE hard back each spring, to ground level or to shoots breaking from mature stems.

PROPAGATE from shoot tip cuttings rooted in a propagator in late summer. Plant a young specimen and be prepared to replace it after a few years:

Shrubs for autumn and winter interest

These shrubs provide autumn and winter interest, having colourful berries, attractive bark or stems, or vibrant autumn foliage.

COLOURFUL BERRIES
- *Aucuba*
- *Berberis*
- *Cotoneaster*
- *Euonymus europaeus*
- *Gaultheria* (syn. *Pernettya*)
- *Ilex*
- *Leycesteria*
- *Mahonia aquifolium*
- *Sambucus*
- *Skimmia*
- *Symphoricarpos*

ATTRACTIVE BARK OR STEMS
- *Acer palmatum* 'Sango-kaku' (syn. 'Senkaki')
- *Cornus alba* varieties
- *Corylus avellana* 'Contorta'
- *Deutzia*
- *Kerria*
- *Leycesteria*
- *Pittosporum*
- *Salix*

AUTUMN FOLIAGE COLOUR
- *Acer palmatum* 'Sango-kaku' (syn. 'Senkaki')
- *Amelanchier*
- *Berberis*
- *Cornus kousa*
- *Cotinus*
- *Euonymus*
- *Hamamelis*
- **Heathers**
- *Mahonia*
- *Ruta*
- *Viburnum*

it may flower itself to death or, in the very cold parts of the country, be killed by severe winters.

Leycesteria formosa
Himalayan Honeysuckle
2. x 2.4 m (8 x 8 ft)

Here's a good plant for the impatient gardener. Each spring it sends up a number of bright green bamboo stems that arch at the tips. In July, August and September white flowers drip from the leaf-laden stems in long tassels, but you can hardly see them for the deep maroon bracts that overlap them. Black berries follow. Good for adding beefiness to a border.

LIKES a rich soil in sun. Tolerates chalky soil, clay soil, shade and coastal exposure.

PRUNE everything to ground level in spring, in which case you'll have to make sure the plant is mulched annually with manure at the same time, or prune out older, flowered stems in spring, leaving just the healthy young ones.

PROPAGATE by dividing clumps in spring and by digging up and transplanting self-sown seedlings, of which there will be plenty.

Lippia See p.97

Lonicera See p.97

Magnolia species and varieties
2.4–6 m x 2.4–6 m (8–20 ft x 8–20 ft)

'Ooh' and 'aah' shrubs. There are two species of magnolia that are regularly planted; of these the commoner and, I think, the more beautiful, is *M.* x *soulangeana*. It makes a wide-spreading bush with upturned branches. Examine a plant in winter and you'll see silky hairy buds just waiting to do their stuff in spring. Come April and May, with any luck, they'll erupt into white eggs and then

burst into the typical waxy magnolia flowers. As they fade, the large green leaves will emerge to hide them. There are pure white varieties such as 'Alba Superba', but my heart belongs to 'Rustica Rubra' with its basal flushing of rosy purple.

The other magnolia of renown is *M. stellata*, smaller at 2.4–3 m (8–10 ft) round, and bedecked with starry white flowers earlier in spring. The trouble is that it is frequently burned by frost. *M.* x *loebneri* 'Merrill' is slightly later in bloom and also tolerates my chalky soil. All magnolias need plenty of room to spread.

LIKES a sunny, sheltered spot in a good soil that's not chalky. Tolerates a little shade, clay or moist soil and chalky soil provided the topsoil is deep and suitably enriched.

PRUNE only to remove dead wood.

PROPAGATE by layering in spring.

Mahonia species and varieties
90 cm–2.4 m x 1.8 m (3–8 ft x 6 ft)

Architectural evergreen shrubs that add shape and form to the garden, as well as colour and perfume from their flowers. *M. japonica* is my first choice. Its large leaves composed of holly-like leaflets are held out at right angles to the stem, the top of which is decorated with long yellow flower tassels in winter. It is superbly scented. The most popular mahonia with landscape architects is *M.* x *media* 'Charity' – similar to *M. japonica* but rather more angular and a little taller at around 2.4 m (8 ft). For the improvement in architectural standing you'll have to sacrifice the scent. Everyman's mahonia is *M. aquifolium*, the Oregon grape – so called because of the black spherical fruits that follow the bunches of yellow spring flowers. It makes a 90 cm (3 ft) high thicket of growth on the poorest soil, and its leaves are burnished maroon in winter. Use the first two as specimen plants, especially in town gardens, and the last as deep ground cover.

LIKES any well-drained soil and a spot in dappled shade. Tolerate clay and chalky soil and heavy shade.

PRUNE only to remove dead wood or unwanted stems in winter or spring.

PROPAGATE carefully: these shrubs have spiny leaves. Take shoot tip cuttings in summer, or layer suitable stems in spring. *M. aquifolium* can sometimes be divided in spring.

Myrtus communis
Myrtle
2.4 x 2.4 m (8 x 8 ft)

The sweetly scented myrtle is an old English garden plant that seems to have been unjustly neglected of late. The leaves are dark, glossy, evergreen and quite narrow but thickly carried on the stems of a dense bush. The flowers are white with a tuft of stamens in the centre: there is no daintier sight in the garden than a myrtle bush in flower. Plant one at the end of a border to act as a fragrant full stop.

LIKES a warm and sheltered spot in well-drained soil (it's not a shrub for a cold, exposed garden). Tolerates dry soil, chalky soil and coastal exposure in the warmer counties.

PRUNE only lightly in spring to shorten unwanted stems.

PROPAGATE by taking shoot tip cuttings in summer.

Olearia species
Daisy Bush
1.2–3 m x 1.8–3 m (10 x 6–10 ft)

Underrated shrubs with evergreen leaves and white daisy flowers. Great for adding form to a garden. The commonest is *O.* x *haastii* with oval dark green leaves that are grey and downy beneath. Billowing heads of white daisies smother the plant in summer. It is the hardiest and the easiest of the bunch and grows to about 1.5 m (5 ft) high and 2.4 m (8 ft) wide. *O.* x *macrodonta* is the biggest of my chosen three at up to 4.5 m (15 ft) high and across. Here the

green leaves, downy beneath, are holly-shaped so that even when the summer flower display is over the bush is good to look at. *O.* x *scilloniensis* is 1.8 m x 1.8 m (6 x 6 ft), oval-leaved and a superb sight in flower with its long clusters of daisies. It is the tenderest of the three, but perhaps the most spectacular in bloom.

LIKES warm, sheltered spots in sun and a well-drained soil. Tolerates coastal exposure, clay, dry or chalky soils.

PRUNE OUT unwanted shoots in spring; the bushes will usually produce shoots from quite old wood, but try to avoid leaving a cluster of stumps – thin the stems rather than chopping them all back. Leave unpruned if you like, but after a few years you might possess an overgrown bush.

PROPAGATE by taking shoot tip cuttings in summer.

The sweetly smelling, dainty white flowers of *Myrtus communis* are set off to perfection by the glossy dark evergreen leaves.

Osmanthus delavayi

1.8 x 2.4 m (6 x 8 ft) or taller

Three paces after you've passed this shrub in spring you'll catch the most delectable scent – it travels at least that

the common tamarisk, *T. gallica* (see
Chapter 6 Hedges), but perhaps a
better choice for gardens is
T. ramosissima (sometimes called
T. pentandra), which is a little brighter
and a fraction more shapely. It flowers
at the same time as the common
tamarisk and both are deciduous.
LIKES sun and well-drained soil.
Tolerates clay, dry and chalky soil, cold
gardens and coastal exposure.
PRUNE shoots hard back in spring.
Failure to do this may result in a
straggly bush.

PROPAGATE by hardwood cuttings in
autumn.

Viburnum species and varieties
Various sizes

Here's a real jewel box of plants: some
are deciduous and some are evergreen;
some have superb autumn colour;
some produce fat flowerheads and
others brilliant fruits. Here is the pick of
the crop:
V. farreri (or *V. fragrans*) 2.4 x 2.4 m
(8 x 8 ft) is a deciduous species whose

Both *Vinca major* and the smaller
V. minor make excellent ground
cover plants that thrive in sun or
shade and in most kinds of soil.
This is *V. minor* 'Azurea Flore Pleno'.

bare, upright stems erupt with little
pinkish white flower clusters in winter.
Catch its fragrance in a burst of watery
sunshine and it will keep you going
until spring. The leaves open after the
flowers – bronze at first, changing to
dull green.
V. x bodnantense, in its forms 'Dawn',

pink, and 'Deben', pink in bud, white in flower, beats *V. farreri* by opening a month earlier, in October. It's a rather stiffer, more upright plant and its flowers are not quite as resistant to frost as those of *V. farreri*. *V. carlesii*, 1.5 x 1.5 m (5 x 5 ft), follows in spring, producing large, flat-topped clusters of gloriously fragrant pink and white flowers over the coarse green leaves. These will sometimes take on rich tints in autumn. 'Aurora' is its best variety – a real stunner.

V. plicatum in its forms 'Mariesii' or 'Lanarth' is a heck of a mouthful to quote to your nurseryman, but it will bring you a handsome, horizontally branched plant, naked in winter but furnished with deeply veined leaves in summer. Flat-headed flower clusters like those of a cream lace-cap hydrangea are arranged in rows along the shelf-like stems in late spring. A real treat that eventually makes a shrub 2.4 x 3.6 m (8 x 12 ft).

V. opulus 'Sterile' is the snowball tree – so called because of its spherical heads of ivory-white flowers that are carried on the stems in early summer. It is deciduous, a splendid sight in flower, and a host to blackfly, so give it an occasional spray.

V. tinus is that dingy-foliaged evergreen, but looks quite a treat in its pink-budded form 'Eve Price'. It grows about 1.2 x 1.8 in (4 x 6 ft) or more and blooms in winter and spring, so it's well worth bunging in a border even though its foliage is black as night.

LIKES sun or dappled shade and a soil that is well drained yet never likely to dry out in summer. Tolerates clay, chalk (provided it is not shallow and dry), moist soil (*V. tinus* doesn't mind dry soil), cold gardens and shady spots.

PRUNE OUT a few old stems in later winter and remove dead wood as soon as it is seen. *V. tinus* withstands hard pruning or clipping in summer.

PROPAGATE by layering, or by shoot tip cuttings taken in summer.

Vinca species and varieties
Periwinkle
15 cm x 1.8 m (6 in x 6 ft)

The greater periwinkle (*V. major*) and the lesser periwinkle (*V. minor*) are cheap and cheerful ground coverers that will seldom give you much trouble. They send their long, trailing shoots out over the soil to help smother weeds (eventually) and they brighten early summer with round, five-petalled flowers of blue, white or mauve. The difference in them lies in the size of their leaves. The best periwinkle of all is *V. major* 'Variegata', a vigorous beast with superb evergreen leaves that are fresh green splashed with creamy yellow. It makes a thick rug of growth.

LIKES ordinary soil in sun or shade. Tolerates chalk, clay, dry soil, cold gardens and heavy shade.

PRUNE only to prevent unwanted spread.

PROPAGATE by lifting and transplanting rooted portions – the plant's stems root as they creep.

Weigela
Bush Honeysuckle, Diervilla
1.8 x 1.8 m (6 x 6 ft)

It's impossible for me to think about *Weigela* without thinking about *Philadelphus*: they are both the first spectacular shrubs of late spring and early summer. *Philadelphus* definitely has the edge when it comes to spectacle and perfume, but a well-grown, arching *Weigela* is a welcome addition to any garden during its brief season of bloom. The bare winter stems erupt with leaves in spring, and then in June the bell-shaped flowers of white, pink or crimson appear in close array. Varieties such as 'Bristol Ruby', deep pink, and 'Candida', white, are popular, but don't neglect the two varieties of *W. florida* that will cheer you up for the rest of the summer with their leaves of plum-purple, in the case of 'Foliis Purpureis', and creamy-edged 'Variegata'. Both harmonize delightfully with the pink flowers.

LIKES ordinary well-drained soil and a place in the sun. Tolerates clay or chalky soils, a modicum of shade and even coastal or inland exposure.

PRUNE after flowering, removing older, flowered stems.

PROPAGATE by hardwood cuttings in autumn or by firm shoot tip cuttings in summer.

Yucca filamentosa
Adam's Needle
90 x 90 cm (3 x 3 ft)

Stately plants with upright rosettes of spiky leaves; a must if you're creating a tropical effect. They grow slowly and will eventually produce flower spikes from the top of the rosettes – one spike on each plant. The blooms are beautiful, creamy white and carried thickly up the 15 m (5 ft) stalk in summer. Lovely in pots and tubs on patios, provided you don't walk into them! Be patient; your plant won't flower until it's a few years old.

LIKES ordinary well-drained soil and sun. Tolerates dry and chalky soil and coastal exposure. These blighters are tougher than you'd think.

PRUNE only to remove faded flower spikes.

PROPAGATE by root cuttings or division; pot up or transplant suckers.

chapter 6

hedges

Whether marking boundaries,

providing privacy and shelter,

or dividing up different areas,

hedges are a living feature

of the garden and a haven

for myriad forms of wildlife

IN THE QUEST FOR PRIVACY (AND PERHAPS TO keep the dog in too) you may be tempted to plant a hedge – but before you do, make sure that you know exactly what you're letting yourself in for. The effect will be pleasing so long as you choose the right plant, but there are snags.

WHY PLANT A HEDGE?

The downside of hedges

On a very small plot a tall hedge can cut out light, so avoid planting a vigorous grower if your garden is very narrow. A deciduous hedge (one that loses its leaves in autumn) will let in just a bit more light in winter to brighten shady sites. The roots of any hedge will rob nutrients from adjacent flower borders; privet is a real brute in this respect and in my last garden I made vertical slits with a spade in the soil alongside the hedge and inserted old roofing slates to keep back the roots. In these circumstances, additional feeding of the border plants helps them to win the battle.

The most labour-intensive job of all is clipping: most hedges need at least two cuts a year and one or two, such as privet, will sometimes need three if you're a real stickler for neatness – I'm not!

The benefits

But in spite of all that, hedges are still planted and are still appreciated. You can soon tire of looking at a close-boarded fence, and so many of them pop up on housing estates nowadays that the whole place takes on the appearance of a cattle market packed with pens. Fencing is pricey too.

A hedge will cut down wind, screen you from eyesores and the eyes of your neighbours, cut down noise and act as a lush green backdrop to other garden plants. It's also a haven for many forms of wildlife, from stick insects and moths to birds and mammals. With country hedgerows disappearing at the rate of hundreds of miles a year, planting a hedge will help to conserve a vanishing habitat. Wood-boring beetles are the only form of wildlife supported by a fence.

Don't think of a hedge as always being formally clipped. Some shrubs planted as hedges will grow best if lightly trimmed to shape rather than clipped flat, and many of them offer bright flowers and cheerful berries in addition to the usual leaves. One of these hedges is a far better bet in a small garden than the ubiquitous privet – the magpie of the plant world. The lists in the A–Z section offer suggestions for hedges that are colourful in leaf, flower and fruit. If your hedge has to act as a barrier to livestock (domestic or farm) go for a thorny one that will make a dense thicket. Recommendations are given for those too.

PLANTING YOUR HEDGE

Just like trees, hedges are usually in one place for a very long time. They say you can calculate the age of a hedge in the countryside by counting the number of different species of tree or shrub that are present: each one counts as a hundred years, so if you see a hedge with five different shrubs in it then it's 500 years old. A well-prepared planting site right at the start will give the hedge that kick in the pants it needs to establish itself with a view to outlasting you.

When to plant
Time of planting is as for trees and shrubs: November to March for bare-root plants; September or April/May for bare-root or balled evergreens; and any time of year for container-grown plants (provided the soil is not dust-dry, frozen or muddy). Just as with shrubs and trees, the roots of hedging plants should never be allowed to dry out. Heel them in (see p.40, Delayed planting) if they arrive before you are ready to plant.

Preparing the ground
One of the quickest and most successful ways to plant a hedge is to prepare a strip of ground along the line the hedge is to take. With bamboo canes and string, mark out a 60 cm (2 ft) wide strip of the required length. Dig it, working in two handfuls of bonemeal to each running 30 cm (1 yd), and any organic matter you can lay your spade on. There's great satisfaction to be obtained from digging such a long, narrow strip because you can motor on at a rate of knots. When the strip is dug you can let it settle for a few days. Alternatively you can dig a trench along the line and return the soil at planting time, but don't let too much time elapse or the trench will become a muddy ditch.

Choosing hedge plants
Having decided on the type of hedge you want you'll have to locate the plants, and here one thing is vital – they should be young. Don't waste your money on tall plants just because they'll look good immediately after planting. Smaller plants will settle in much more quickly and even overtake taller ones after only a year

or two. What's more they'll make a thick barrier right down to ground level, and that's the most important requirement of any hedge. They'll be cheaper too. So settle for plants about 30 cm (12 in) high, and buy enough to plant at the distance recommended in the A–Z entries. Most hedges are created by planting a single row of plants, but if you want to make an exceptionally dense thicket, plant two staggered rows 38 cm (15 in) apart.

Which plants?
Privet should be one of your last choices; look for something a little different that's going to offer you more than a green fence. Steer clear, too, of Leyland cypress (x *Cupressocyparis leylandii*) unless you've bags of room to spare. Where there's room for it to grow, it looks a treat, but in tiny gardens it soon outstays its welcome and fills the plot with gloom.

How to plant
Rig up a garden line along the strip to be planted and take out a hole for every plant (unless you're using the trench method). Trim broken roots from bare-root plants and spread out the remainder in the hole (see p.82). Return the soil, firming it into place with your feet, so that the old soil mark on the stem of the plant is just below the new soil level. Water container-grown plants an hour before planting. At planting time, remove the container and tease out any in-growing roots. Don't disturb the rest of the rootball. Plant so that the top of the rootball is just below the surface of the soil. Don't stint on the firming – really put the boot in. If you leave the soil light and fluffy, the roots might dry out, or on heavy soils the trench will act like a sump for the surrounding drainage water, drowning the roots.

> *"Wood-boring beetles are the only form of wildlife supported by a fence."*

Watering and mulching
Water the plants in if the soil is at all dry, and in spring spread a 5 cm (2 in) mulch of leaf mould, pulverized bark, well-rotted compost or manure over the soil – if you have any to spare. If not, keep a close watch on the soil and turn on a sprinkler to soak the earth

Hedge planting

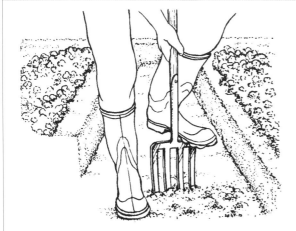

1 Dig a 60 cm (2 ft) wide trench along the line to be occupied by the hedge and fork some compost or manure into the base.

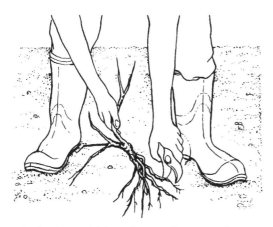

2 Trim back any thick or damaged roots on bare-root plants and keep them in a bucket of water until you're ready to plant.

3 Stand each plant where it is to be planted and feed back the soil, firming it with your foot. The old soil mark on the stem should match the new soil level.

whenever it starts to look dry. Drought will put paid to all your good work.

Autumn-planted hedges will need to be re-firmed into contact with the soil after frosts have lifted them – failure to boot them back in may result in death due to the roots drying out.

CARING FOR YOUR HEDGE

Immediate pruning

Immediately after planting, most hedging shrubs should be pruned to produce really dense growth at ground level. Forget to do this and you'll have a gappy hedge later on. Really vigorous growers such as privet, hawthorn, blackthorn, snowberry, tamarisk and *Lonicera nitida* should be cut back to within 15 cm (6 in) of ground level. Hornbeam, beech, hazel and flowering currant should have all their shoots cut back by one third of their length. Yew, laurel, holly, gorse, osmanthus, laurustinus and all conifers should have their sideshoots shortened a little, but their leading or topmost shoots should be left intact.

All other plants are best relieved just of long and straggling shoots, which should be cut back to a bud or leaf near the base of the offending stem.

Subsequent clipping

Subsequent clippings may have to be carried out twice a year: May and August are the best times. The traditional pruning tool for hedges is a pair of garden shears, which will make a neat job on most shrubs. If you can't rely on your eye when clipping, stretch a taut length of twine between two stakes to mark the cutting line (see opposite). Aim to create a hedge that is a little narrower in cross-section at the top than it is at the bottom. That way it will cast less shade and will be less likely to suffer snow damage. Don't be

Using electric trimmers

Electric trimmers really do make life easier by clipping at a fast rate, but take care: one false move and you'll have made a hole in your hedge! Wear the trimmer cable over your shoulder to keep it out of the way of the blade – or, better still, invest in one of the special harnesses that can be worn to hold the cable out of the way.

Both shears and trimmers should be oiled after use and rubbed down with emery paper to free them of dried sap, which glues the blades together.

If you don't trust your eye when it comes to clipping the top of a hedge, fasten a taut line between two canes to mark the cutting line and clip to this.

frightened of clipping hard in the early years: it will encourage the hedge to thicken up. The top surface of the hedge should also be trimmed back a little each time, even though it has not yet reached the required height. If you don't do this, the hedge will be even more likely to suffer from snow damage, its stems giving way under the lightest powdering.

Clipping informal hedges

Shears or electric trimmers are essential for clipping formal hedges with straight outlines, but informal hedges such as tamarisk, fuchsia, olearia, escallonia, cotoneaster and large-leaved plants such as laurel and aucuba are best pruned with secateurs, unwanted stems being snipped out above a bud or leaf. Where such hedges are very long then shears or trimmers can be used, but some sacrificing of form will have to be accepted.

Clipping flowering and fruiting hedges

Flowering hedges are always best pruned immediately after their blooms have faded; unwanted wood can be removed and the plants will still have time to produce stems that will carry next year's flowers. Berry-bearing hedges should be clipped after the fruits have fallen.

Using hedge-growth retardants

If you really hate hedge clipping then try one of the new hedge-growth retardants. These come in liquid form and are diluted in water and sprayed on to the hedge a few weeks after the spring clipping. No

further pruning is then needed until the same time the following year. There are restrictions on the types of hedge that can be treated with these chemicals, so check the information on the label before you buy. It is also difficult to use them effectively where the hedge abuts a flower border; only on paths and drives or lawn perimeters will they be really useful.

Disposing of clippings

Hedge clippings are difficult to dispose of. They won't really compost because they're too woody, and they produce foul smoke if burned. There are two ways of getting round this: either ferry them to the local tip in your car (or have a gentle word with your dustman to see if he's amenable to shifting bagfuls of clippings), or dry them out in a corner of the garden and then burn them. If the material is crisp and dry, it burns without too much smoke and will not make you unpopular with your neighbours.

When clearing up the clippings, take the opportunity to tidy up the hedge bottom: pull out any weeds that grow there and any waste paper that has lodged among the branches.

RENOVATING AN OLD HEDGE

If you take on a battered old hedge that's riddled with holes you'll want to know what to do with it. Some hedges, such as laurel, privet and yew, will regenerate (produce new shoots) when cut back really hard into old wood. Others, such as box and most conifers, won't. Once the inner parts of conifer branches have gone crisp and brown there's little you can do to perk them up. It's far easier, provided you're not averse to hard labour, to dig out the plants and replant with something else after enriching the soil.

PROPAGATING HEDGES

All hedges can be propagated exactly like other shrubs (see Chapter 2 Propagation), but there's a trick of growing privet, in particular, which any miser should know of. Get hold of some clippings from the hedge – shoots that are firm and woody and about 30–45 cm (1½ ft) long are ideal – and strip off the lower leaves. Push the shoots into the soil for one third of their length along the line the hedge is to take. Stick one shoot in every 15 cm (6 in). Unless you're really out of luck, or you let the soil dry out, you'll soon have a privet hedge where once you pushed in your prunings.

A-Z
OF
hedge
plants

Aucuba japonica
Spotted Laurel

Planting distance 60 cm (2 ft)

5 years to reach 1.5 m (5 ft)

Evergreen. Shiny green leaves sometimes spotted yellow. Victorian effect.

PRUNE in August with shears/trimmers and secateurs. Suitable for formal clipping or informal pruning.

Berberis darwinii
Barberry

Planting distance 45 cm (18 in)

6 years to reach 1.5 m (5 ft)

Evergreen. Dark green thicket plastered with orange flowers in April/May.

PRUNE in May, after flowering, with shears/trimmers. Suitable for formal clipping or informal pruning.

Berberis x *stenophylla*
Barberry

Planting distance 45 cm (18 in)

5 years to reach 1.5 m (5 ft)

Evergreen. Another spiny thicket-former; quite dog-proof. Masses of scented orange-yellow flowers in April/May.

PRUNE in May, after flowering, with shears/trimmers. Suitable for formal clipping or informal pruning.

Buxus sempervirens
Box

Planting distance 30 cm (12 in)

8 years to reach 1.5 m (5 ft)

Evergreen. Dense barrier of round, dark green leaves. Good variegated variety.

PRUNE in May and August with shears/trimmers. Suitable for formal clipping.

Buxus sempervirens 'Suffruticosa'
Dwarf Box

Planting distance 23 cm (9 in)

Grows to 30cm (12 in) maximum

Evergreen. Neat miniature for edging formal beds. Superb around kitchen garden.

PRUNE in May and August with shears/trimmers. Suitable for formal clipping.

Carpinus betulus
Hornbeam

Planting distance 30 cm (12 in)

6 years to reach 1.5 m (5 ft)

A pleasant alternative to beech. Good, plain green leaves.

PRUNE in August with shears/trimmers. Suitable for formal clipping.

Chamaecyparis lawsoniana
varieties
Lawson Cypress

Planting distance 60 cm (2 ft)

5 years to reach 1.5 m (5 ft)

Evergreen. Varieties like 'Green Hedger' are particularly good. Good yellow forms.

PRUNE in August with shears/trimmers. Suitable for formal clipping.

Corylus maxima 'Purpurea'
Purple-leafed Hazel

Planting distance 60 cm (2 ft)

4 years to reach 1.5 m (5 ft)

Bold leaves of dark plum-purple. Don't overdo it.

PRUNE in August with shears/trimmers and secateurs. Suitable for formal clipping and informal pruning.

Cotoneaster simonsii

Planting distance 45 cm (18 in)

5 years to reach 1.5 m (5 ft)

Evergreen. Boring green leaves but super white flowers and orange berries.

PRUNE after fruiting with shears/trimmers and secateurs. Suitable for formal clipping and informal pruning.

Crataegus monogyna
Hawthorn, Quick

Planting distance 30 cm (12 in)

7 years to reach 1.5 m (5 ft)

Thick and dog-proof. Flowering and fruiting restricted by pruning.

PRUNE in May and August with shears/trimmers. Suitable for formal clipping.

x *Cupressocyparis leylandii*
Leyland Cypress

Planting distance 75 cm (2½ ft)

3 years to reach 1.5 m (5 ft)

Evergreen. Don't use this unless you've room to spare. Quick and dense.

PRUNE in August with shears/trimmers. Suitable for formal clipping.

Escallonia rubra var. *macrantha*

Planting distance 45 cm (18 in)

4 years to reach 1.5 m (5 ft)

Evergreen. A marvellous hedge with shiny leaves and pink flowers in summer.

Thorny hedges

The following plants are all suitable for forming a dense thicket to act as a barrier to pets and livestock.

- *Berberis darwinii*
- *Berberis* x *stenophylla*
- *Crataegus monogyna*
- *Ilex aquifolium* varieties
- *Pyracantha rogersiana*
- *Rosa eglanteria*
- *Rosa rugosa*
- *Ulex europaeus*

PRUNE after flowering with shears/trimmers and secateurs. Suitable for formal clipping and informal pruning.

Euonymus japonicus

Planting distance 45 cm (18 in)

6 years to reach 1.5 m (5 ft)

Evergreen. Shiny green leaves, splashed with yellow in variety 'Aureopictus'. **PRUNE** in August with shears/trimmers. Suitable for formal clipping.

Fagus sylvatica

Beech

Planting distance 30 cm (12 in)

5 years to reach 1.5 m (5 ft)

Common but lovely. Bright green leaves in spring; russet in autumn. **PRUNE** in August with shears/trimmers. Suitable for formal clipping.

Forsythia x intermedia 'Spectabilis'

Golden Bells

Planting distance 45 cm (18 in)

4 years to reach 1.5 m (5 ft)

A bit overdone but unsurpassed for spring brightness of yellow blooms. **PRUNE** in May, after flowering, with shears/trimmers and secateurs. Suitable for formal clipping and informal pruning.

Fuchsia magellanica

Planting distance 30 cm (12 in)

5 years to reach 1.5 m (5 ft)

Graceful and colourful with cerise and purple flowers in summer. **PRUNE** in May with secateurs. Suitable for informal pruning.

Ilex aquifolium varieties

Holly

Planting distance 45 cm (18 in)

8 years to reach 1.5 m (5 ft)

Evergreen. Avoid the dark green types, which can be oppressive, and go for a variegated green and yellow variety.

Hedges that will grow anywhere

The following hedge plants do well on chalky or clay soils, on cold and windy sites, and on dry soil. Those marked ◆ also grow well by the seaside.

- *Berberis darwinii*
- *Berberis* x *stenophylla*
- *Corylus maxima* 'Purpurea'
- *Cotoneaster simonsii* ◆
- *Crataegus monogyna* ◆
- x *Cupressocyparis leylandii* ◆
- *Euonymus japonicus* ◆
- *Ilex aquifolium* varieties ◆
- *Lonicera nitida* ◆
- *Potentilla fruticosa* ◆
- *Prunus* x *cistena*
- *Prunus laurocerasus*
- *Pyracantha rogersiana* ◆
- *Tamarix gallica* ◆
- *Taxus baccata*
- *Thuja plicata* varieties
- *Ulex europaeus* ◆
- *Viburnum tinus* ◆

PRUNE after fruiting with shears/trimmers and secateurs. Suitable for formal clipping.

Lavandula varieties

Lavender

Planting distance 30 cm (12 in)

Grows to 60 cm (2 ft) maximum

Evergreen. Superbly aromatic dwarf hedge for paths and borders, with spikes of purple-blue flowers in summer. 'Hidcote' is best. **PRUNE** in August, after flowering, with secateurs. Suitable for informal pruning.

Ligustrum ovalifolium

Privet

Planting distance 30 cm (12 in)

4 years to reach 1.5 m (5 ft)

Evergreen. Overplanted and greedy. Plant the golden form if you have to. **PRUNE** in May and August with shears/trimmers. Suitable for formal clipping.

Lonicera nitida

Planting distance 30 cm (12 in)

5 years to reach 1.5 m (5 ft)

Evergreen. A bit dull but reliable. Tiny, glossy, oval leaves. **PRUNE** in May and August with shears/trimmers. Suitable for formal clipping.

Metasequoia glyptostroboides

Dawn Redwood

Planting distance 60 cm (2 ft)

5 years to reach 1.5 m (5 ft)

Unusual. Feathery foliage of fresh green. Super autumn colour. **PRUNE** in August with shears/trimmers. Suitable for formal clipping.

Olearia x haastii

New Zealand Daisy Bush

Planting distance 30 cm (12 in)

7 years to reach 1.5 m (5 ft)

Evergreen. Leaves dark green above, grey beneath. White daisy flowers. **PRUNE** after flowering with secateurs. Suitable for informal pruning.

Pittosporum tenuifolium

Planting distance 45 cm (18 in)

5 years to reach 1.5 m (5 ft)

Evergreen. Shiny, wavy-edged leaves. **PRUNE** in May with secateurs. Suitable for informal pruning.

Potentilla fruticosa

Planting distance 45 cm (18 in)

Grows to 90 cm (3 ft) maximum

Evergreen. A tumbling charmer with yellow, orange, white or red summer flowers. **PRUNE** in May with secateurs. Suitable for informal pruning.

Prunus x *cistena*
Purple-leaf Sand Cherry

Planting distance 30 cm (12 in)

5 years to reach 1.5 m (5 ft)

Purple leaves and white spring flowers. Best kept to around 90 cm (3 ft). **PRUNE** after flowering with secateurs. Suitable for informal pruning.

Prunus laurocerasus
Cherry Laurel

Planting distance 60 cm (2 ft)

3 years to reach 1.5 m (5 ft)

Evergreen. Victorian favourite. Shiny and green and good in the right place. **PRUNE** in August with shears/trimmers and secateurs. Suitable for formal clipping and informal pruning.

Pyracantha rogersiana
Firethorn

Planting distance 45 cm (18 in)

4 years to reach 1.5 m (5 ft)

Evergreen. Dark leaves; thorny stems; cream flowers in summer, orange berries in winter. **PRUNE** after fruiting with secateurs. Suitable for informal pruning.

Rhododendron ponticum
Common Rhododendron

Planting distance 60 cm (2 ft)

5 years to reach 1.5 m (5 ft)

Evergreen. Dingy of leaf but bright of flower in spring. Good in shade. **PRUNE** after flowering with shears/trimmers and secateurs. Suitable for formal clipping and informal pruning.

Rosa eglanteria
Sweet Briar

Planting distance 45 cm (18 in)

3 years to reach 1.5 m (5 ft)

Deliciously aromatic leaves and pink flowers followed by hips. **PRUNE** after fruiting with secateurs. Suitable for informal pruning.

Hedge plants with good flowers and fruits

The following plants all have either flowers ✳ or fruit ◆ of note.

- *Aucuba japonica* ◆
- *Berberis darwinii* ✳
- *Berberis* x *stenophylla* ✳
- *Cotoneaster simonsii* ✳ ◆
- *Crataegus monogyna* ✳ ◆
- *Escallonia rubra* var. *macrantha* ✳
- *Forsythia* x *intermedia* 'Spectabilis'✳
- *Fuchsia magellanica* ✳
- *Ilex aquifolium* ◆
- *Lavandula* varieties ✳
- *Olearia* x *haastii* ✳
- *Potentilla fruticosa* ✳
- *Prunus* x *cistena* ✳
- *Prunus laurocerasus* ✳ ◆
- *Pyracantha rogersiana* ✳ ◆
- *Rhododendron ponticum* ✳
- *Rosa eglanteria* ✳ ◆
- *Rosa rugosa* ✳ ◆
- *Rosmarinus officinalis* ✳
- *Tamarix gallica* ✳
- *Ulex europaeus* ✳
- *Viburnum* ✳

Rosa rugosa
Ramanas Rose

Planting distance 45 cm (18 in)

5 years to reach 1.5 m (5 ft)

Fresh green leaves, mauve flowers, bright hips. Thorny as hell. **PRUNE** after fruiting with secateurs. Suitable for informal pruning.

Rosmarinus officinalis
Rosemary

Planting distance 45 cm (18 in)

Grows to 1·2 m (4 ft) max.

Evergreen. Aromatic leaves; blue flowers in spring. **PRUNE** in May with secateurs. Suitable for informal pruning.

Tamarix gallica
Common Tamarisk

Planting distance 30 cm (12 in)

4 years to reach 1.5 m (5 ft)

Wispy leaved and beautiful. Fluffy pink flowers in summer. Try it. **PRUNE** in May with secateurs. Suitable for informal pruning.

Taxus baccata
Yew

Planting distance 60 cm (2 ft)

8 years to reach 1.5 m (5 ft)

Evergreen. Green or gold variegated.

PRUNE in August with shears/trimmers. Suitable for formal clipping.

Thuja plicata varieties
Western Red Cedar

Planting distance 60 cm (2 ft)

5 years to reach 1.5 m (5 ft)

Evergreen. Aromatic feathery foliage, shinier than Lawson cypress. **PRUNE** in August with shears/trimmers. Suitable for formal clipping.

Ulex europaeus
Gorse

Planting distance 45 cm (18 in)

6 years to reach 1.5 m (5 ft)

Evergreen. Bright yellow flowers smother thorny stems in spring. **PRUNE** in May after flowering with secateurs. Suitable for informal pruning.

Viburnum tinus
Laurustinus

Planting distance 45 cm (18 in)

5 years to reach 1.5 m (5 ft)

Evergreen. Boring leaves brightened with white flowers in winter to spring. **PRUNE** in May. Suitable for formal clipping and informal pruning.

For an aromatic evergreen hedge, try *Rosmarinus officinalis*; dwarf *Buxus sempervirens* is ideal for edging beds.

climbers and wall plants

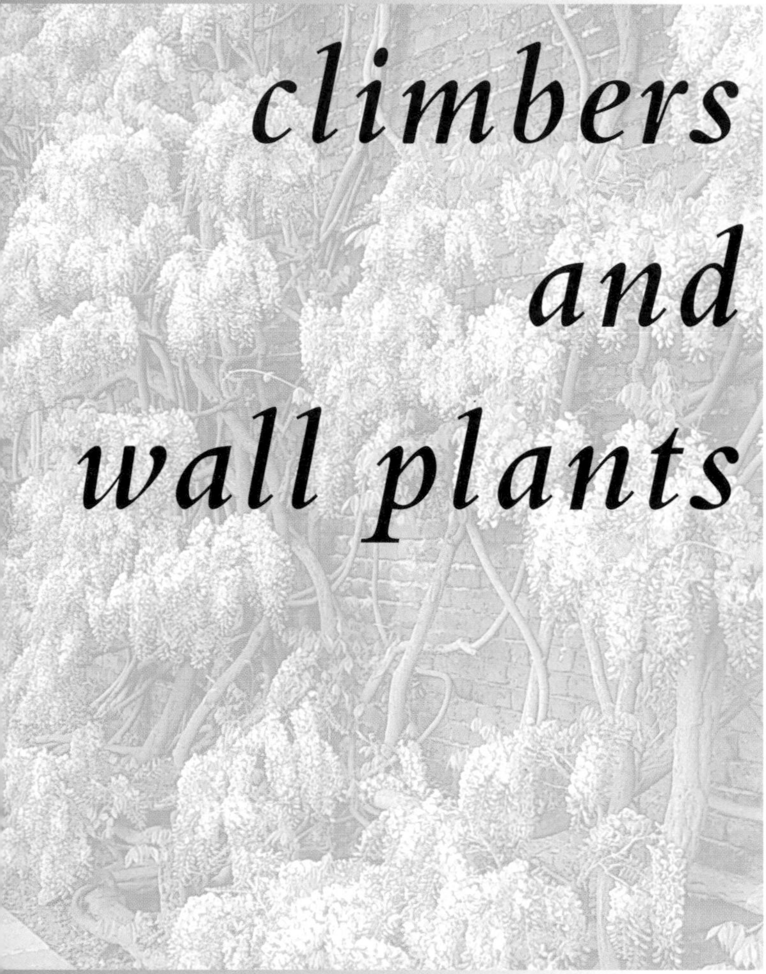

The clinging and twining

habit of climbers, in their rich

variety of colour and foliage,

gives them an enviable ability

to transform charmless

features into things of beauty

HOUSES WITHOUT CLIMBERS ALWAYS LOOK naked to me. I think too many home owners worry about the effect of roots on their foundations and of tendrils on their mortar, but, so long as the right plants are chosen and they are trained properly, the only worry will be an extra spider or two in your bedroom.

SITING CLIMBERS AND WALL PLANTS

Climbing habits

Take into account the habit of any climber or wall plant before deciding where you will grow it. Some of the plants recommended here are twiners, some have sticky pads or aerial roots that need a flat surface to hold on to; others simply scramble and ramble over a support system, and some won't climb at all: they just enjoy the sheltered atmosphere a wall provides.

Against a wall

Trees and some vigorous shrubs can certainly move foundations, but all the plants I've recommended here can safely be planted right up to your walls. Only on badly mortared walls and on pebbledash will clinging climbers ever do any damage. If your house is pebbledashed, rig up a support system that will take the weight of the plant so that the rendering does not peel off in one large sheet.

Mind you, don't think that walls and fences are the only place for climbing plants. They can also be used to cover screens that hide the compost heap, to smother an unsightly garden shed, and to scramble through old and decrepit fruit trees that you can't bring yourself to chop down.

The right plant for the right wall

WALLS FACING NORTH OR EAST	
● Camellia	● Parthenocissus
● Chaenomeles	● Polygonum
● Clematis	(syn. Fallopia)
● Cotoneaster	● Pyracantha
● Garrya	● Tropaeolum
● Hedera	
● Humulus	**WALLS FACING**
● Hydrangea	**SOUTH OR WEST**
● Jasminum	● Abutilon
● Lathyrus	● Actinidia
● Lonicera (some)	● Camellia
	● Carpenteria
	● Ceanothus

There is no better climber than clematis for smothering a wall or arch with flowers. Varieties include this award-winning *Clematis montana* 'Elizabeth'.

- Chaenomeles
- Clematis
- Cotoneaster
- Cytisus
- Eccremocarpus
- Fremontodendron
- Garrya
- Hedera
- Hoheria
- Humulus
- Hydrangea
- Jasminum
- Lathyrus
- Lippia (syn. *Aloysia*)
- Lonicera
- Magnolia
- Parthenocissus
- Passiflora
- Phygelius
- Polygonum (syn. *Fallopia*)
- Pyracantha
- Ribes
- Solanum
- Vitis
- Wisteria

Over arches, pergolas, arbours and tripods

Arches and pergolas (a series of linked arches) are still found in many gardens, but it's time the arbour made a comeback. At one time, this shady retreat was to be found in every garden – an intimate corner where lovers billed and cooed beneath an open-roofed structure over which scrambled a profusion of carefree and colourful climbers.

If you've a sun-dappled corner of the garden that needs brightening up, try making a three-sided enclosure of white-painted trellis fastened to stout posts. Several rails across the top will make a 'roof' over which fragrant honeysuckle, colourful clematis or mysterious wisteria can cascade in summer. Smaller gardens can sport climbers on rustic pole tripods among border plants, or in pots and tubs, which can be equipped with stout cane tripods of their own, or placed against walls fitted with horizontal wires or trellis.

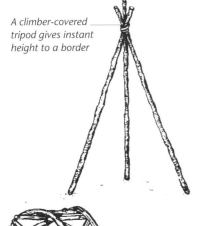

A climber-covered tripod gives instant height to a border

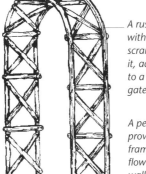

A rustic arch, with climbers scrambling over it, adds charm to a simple gateway

A pergola provides the framework for a flower-covered walkway

Growing plants through shrubs and trees

Remember that many flimsy climbers like clematis can simply be grown alongside other garden shrubs and allowed to scramble through them. It's not a system for tidy-minded gardeners, but it's one for greedy types who can prolong the season of interest of a shrub when its own blooms have faded.

Before you chop down a gnarled and dilapidated tree, consider training a rampant climber through it to brighten its boring boughs. The following plants will happily scramble up through trees and shrubs:

- *Clematis*
- *Eccremocarpus*
- *Humulus*
- *Lathyrus*
- *Parthenocissus*
- *Passiflora*
- *Polygonum* (syn. *Fallopia*)
- *Solanum*
- *Tropaeolum*
- *Vitis*
- *Wisteria*

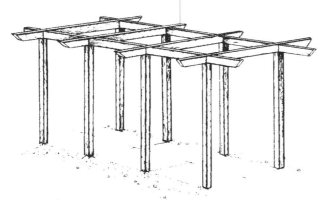

Shown here are three different types of support for climbing plants: tripod, arch, and pergola, each of which will make an attractive feature in your garden.

SITE AND SOIL REQUIREMENTS

There are climbers for walls of all aspects, sunny and shady; each entry in the A–Z section includes advice on this and other cultivation details, while charts throughout the chapter give recommendations for specific situations. What all the plants have in common is a desire for good growing conditions when they are first planted. Your kindness to them in their youth will nearly always be repaid by good growth later in life.

Improve the soil

The soil against a house wall is almost always bone-dry because it's in what is known as a rain shadow area. Dig it well before you plant, and enrich it with plenty of leaf mould, pulverized bark or, better still, well-rotted manure or garden compost. A dusting of blood, bone and fishmeal will also give encouragement to the roots.

Growing climbers in tubs

If climbers are to be grown in tubs, give them a good compost, such as John Innes No. 3 potting compost, over a drainage layer of pebbles. Make sure there are plenty of holes in the base of the tub to allow drainage, and make the container as large as possible if you want the plant to be in residence for some time. It's a good idea to remove 8 cm (3 in) of the old compost each spring and replace it with fresh.

PLANTING CLIMBERS

You can plant pot-grown climbers at any time of year, but they'll grow away best if introduced to their new site in spring when the soil is still a little moist. Bare-root climbers can be planted in autumn but, if the plant is the slightest bit tender, wait until spring.

Set the plants about 30 cm (12 in) away from the tree, shrub, wall, trellis or arch that is to act as the support system. That way the roots have a little more room to explore. Plant when the soil is moist, and water in the plant if necessary. Lay a 5 cm (2 in) thick mulch of organic matter immediately planting is completed to keep in moisture and keep down weeds.

PLANT CARE

Providing support

On walls and fences self-clinging climbers, such as ivy, will need no help at all, though you can paint the surface with manure-water if they refuse to cling at first. Other plants will need to be provided with either horizontal wires held at 30 cm (12 in) intervals, or with trellis. I prefer the wire system: it's cheaper and longer-lasting than trellis. Drill and plug the wall, then insert galvanized vine eyes that will support horizontal strands of plastic-covered wire. If your house wall is painted and will have to be re-painted in future, trellis supports will be better. Fasten the trellis to a batten frame, which can be hinged against the wall at the base and held with butterfly catches at the top. When painting is necessary, the entire framework can be carefully swung away from the wall: most climbers are more flexible than you might think.

Training and pruning climbers

All plants will need to be trained against the support system and their stems spaced out and tied in. I find that wire twist-ties (similar to the kind sold for sealing freezer bags) are the most convenient to use. Pinch out the shoot tips of young plants to encourage a branching habit and good wall coverage.

Detailed instructions on pruning are given in the A–Z section, but remember to use a sharp pair of secateurs or loppers and to cut back, without fail, to a healthy bud or to just above a leaf.

Watering and feeding

Don't, whatever you do, let the soil around the plant dry out during its first year of establishment. Soak it with a hosepipe when necessary and keep the mulch in place. Apply a fresh mulch each spring.

A good feed of a general fertilizer each April will work wonders: use tomato fertilizer to coax any flowering climber to bloom more freely (it contains lots of potash, which is necessary for flower and fruit formation).

Wall support systems

SUPPORTING PLANTS WITH WIRES

Stout horizontal wires fastened to the surface of a wall by metal vine eyes make a cheap, sturdy and unobtrusive support system for climbing plants.

SUPPORTING PLANTS WITH TRELLIS

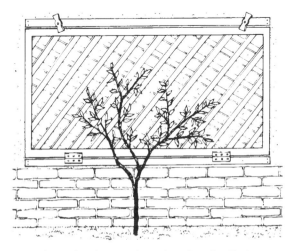

On surfaces that have to be painted, train climbers against a trellis that is hinged to a batten on the wall. The trellis and plant can be swung away as necessary.

A-Z
OF
climbers and wall plants

HERE YOU'LL FIND SOME REAL beauties, valued in leaf, fruit and flower. Don't stick solely to the common stuff: experiment a little with something unusual. All these plants will give value for money, but I've done my best to point out the drawbacks where they exist.

Abutilon vitifolium
3–9 m (10–30 ft)

A little tender it might be, but this abutilon is a treasure worth risking. The leaves are maple-shaped and covered in soft down, and the mallow flowers are a delicate shade of lilac, darker in the variety 'Veronica Tennant', white in var. *album*. All three bloom in early summer and lose their leaves in winter.
ASPECT south or west.
LIKES sun and shelter and a rich, well-drained but not dry soil. Tolerates clay, dry and chalky soils and coastal exposure. Sometimes short-lived.
PRUNE OUT dead stems in spring and remove faded flowerheads.
PROPAGATE by sowing seeds in heat during January, or by rooting cuttings of stem tips in a propagator in summer.

Actinidia kolomikta
1.8–2.4 m (8 ft) and occasionally up to 6 m (20 ft)

This climber needs patience. In the right spot, and when it's settled in, it will turn the tips of its green, heart-shaped leaves bright pink and white. Quite a spectacle. The flowers are insignificant and the leaves deciduous.
ASPECT south or west.
LIKES a sheltered, sunny spot and well-drained soil. Tolerates clay and dry soils, and enriched chalky soils.
PRUNE OUT unwanted growth in summer. Shorten sideshoots to two or three buds in winter and remove a few older stems, replacing them with young ones, which should be tied in.
PROPAGATE in summer by rooting shoot tip cuttings in a propagator or by layering suitable shoots.

Camellia japonica varieties
3 m (10 ft)

I've talked about *C.* x *williamsii*, which I think is a better plant for general garden cultivation, on p.59, but the varieties of *C. japonica* are worth growing on sunny walls, though not those that face east (the early morning sun might damage frosted buds). Their glossy evergreen leaves set off the waxy double or single flowers of red, white, pink or magenta that appear in spring. Ask your nurseryman to suggest suitable varieties from his stock.
ASPECT north, south or west.
LIKES well-drained, lime-free soil enriched with peat and leaf mould. Apply diluted iron sequestrene in spring if the leaves are a bit yellow. Tolerates clay soil and sheltered coastal gardens.

PRUNE OUT only unwanted or badly placed shoots in spring and shorten spindly shoots of older plants by half.
PROPAGATE by taking leaf bud or shoot tip cuttings in summer and rooting them in a propagator.

Carpenteria californica
Californian Mock Orange
1.8–2.4 m (6–8 ft)

Not a climber, but a tender shrub deserving a sheltered spot. The leaves are oval and evergreen and the large, papery white, fragrant flowers are centred with a boss of yellow stamens.
ASPECT south or west.
LIKES light, well-drained soil, shelter and full sun. Tolerates dry or chalky soil and sheltered coastal gardens.
PRUNE OUT one or two older branches and any dead shoots in spring.
PROPAGATE by shoot tip cuttings rooted in a propagator in summer. Sow seeds under glass in spring.

Ceanothus
Californian Lilac
2.4–3 m (8–10 ft)

The upright habit of the ceanothuses makes them a good choice for walls. *C.* 'Delight' is a spring flowerer, and *C.* 'Autumnal Blue' adds colour to the latter part of the year. Both have rough, tiny evergreen leaves and soft blue powderpuff flowers.
ASPECT south or west.

Plants for any situation

The following plants will do well in clay, chalky, or dry soils. Those marked ◆ will also thrive in coastal gardens.

- *Abutilon* ◆
- *Actinidia*
- *Chaenomeles*
- *Cotoneaster* ◆
- *Cytisus* ◆
- *Garrya* ◆
- *Hedera* ◆
- *Humulus*
- *Hydrangea* ◆
- *Jasminum* ◆
- *Lonicera*
- *Magnolia*
- *Parthenocissus*
- *Polygonum* (syn. *Fallopia*) ◆
- *Pyracantha* ◆

LIKES sunny, sheltered spots and a well-drained soil. Tolerates dry or chalky soil and sheltered coastal gardens.
PRUNE the flowering shoots back by half their length when the blooms have faded. Cut out dead stems in spring.
PROPAGATE by rooting shoot tip cuttings in a propagator in summer.

Camellia japonica **will do well on a sunny wall, protected from frost and cold winds. Varieties available include this lovely pink** *C. japonica* **'Tricolor'.**

Chaenomeles
Japonica, Japanese Quince, Cydonia
1.2–3 m (4–10 ft)

Indispensable spring flowers. Varieties of both *C. speciosa* (the earliest to flower, often starting in winter), and *C.* x *superba* are showy. All are deciduous and have apple-blossom-shaped flowers of red, white or pink. Among the best varieties of *C. speciosa* are: 'Brilliant' (scarlet); 'Moerloosii' (pink and white); and 'Nivalis' (white).

C. x *superba* is especially good, and popular, in its variety 'Knap Hill Scarlet'. Most produce aromatic fruits that make sumptuous jelly.
ASPECT north, south, east or west.
LIKES a sunny site if possible, and well-drained soil. Tolerates dry, clay or chalky soil.
PRUNE by shortening sideshoots back to two or three buds after flowering.
PROPAGATE by layering in spring or by rooting firm shoot tips in a propagator in summer.

Clematis
Virgin's Bower
3 m (10 ft) plus

No garden should be without its complement of clematis, scrambling up walls, through trees and shrubs and over arches and pergolas. There are dozens of different varieties, most of them deciduous, which produce their wide-faced single or double flowers at various times during spring and summer. Here's my pick of the large-flowered hybrids:

'Barbara Dibley': magenta; May, June and September.

'Barbara Jackman': lavender, striped magenta; May, June and September.

'Comtesse de Bouchaud': rose-pink; June to August.

'Elsa Späth': lavender-blue; May, June and September.

'Ernest Markham': magenta; June to September.

'Etoile Rose': deep pink, quartered bells with paler edges; June to September.

'Hagley Hybrid': shell-pink; June to September.

'Jackmanii Superba': violet-purple; July to September.

'Lasurstern': lavender-blue with wavy edges; May, June and September.

'Marie Boisselot': pale pink to white; May to October.

'Nelly Moser': pale pink-striped magenta; May, June, August and September.

'Vyvyan Pennell': bluish mauve; double in May and June, single in September.

For covering buildings, *C. montana* is a rampant white-flowered species, most frequently planted in its pink form var. *rubens*. Both are gloriously scented.

C. tangutica offers the best value of any clematis. It produces masses of bright yellow lantern flowers in summer and these are followed by fluffy spherical seedheads that persist through the winter. Grow it through a shrub or over a shed.

C. macropetala produces nodding double blooms of lavender-blue and white in May and June. It looks delightful in tubs and large pots.

ASPECT north, south, east or west.

LIKES their roots in cool, moist soil. Place flagstones or gravel over the soil surrounding them. Most prefer their heads in the sun. Tolerate clay or chalky soil, and sheltered coastal gardens.

PLANT where the soil around the roots will be shaded but the stems will be in full sun, and provide adequate support for the stems. Give all varieties time to settle in before expecting masses of flower. Three years may have to elapse before they really feel at home.

PRUNE clematis according to which group it is in. (See the chart above for all the varieties mentioned here).

PROPAGATE in summer by layering firm stems, or by rooting internodal cuttings in a propagator.

DISEASES Clematis wilt may result in rapid collapse of the entire plant. Cut out any affected stems and spray the plant with a copper fungicide. The plant should soon re-grow, even if it has to be cut back to ground level.

Cotoneaster horizontalis
Fishbone Cotoneaster
1.8–2.4 m (6–8 ft)

Planted against a wall, this cotoneaster sidles up against it to quite a height, spreading out its fans of symmetrical branches. It decorates them with tiny green leaves in summer and red berries in autumn and winter.

ASPECT north, south, east or west.

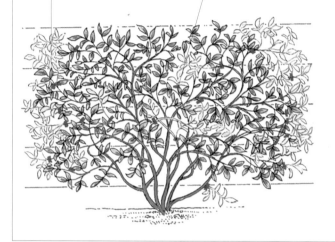

Pruning clematis

GROUP 1
Prune only when they are becoming overgrown. Remove shoots that have carried flowers and any dead growth, as soon as the blooms fade.
- *C. montana*
- *C. macropetala*

To restrict the size or reduce overcrowding, thin out flower-bearing stems after flowering

Remove any dead or damaged stems, cutting back to a healthy pair of buds

LIKES ordinary well-drained soil. Tolerates dry, chalky or clay soil and coastal exposure.

PRUNE OUT only unwanted or overcrowding stems in spring.

PROPAGATE by sowing seeds or by rooting cuttings of firm shoot tips in a propagator in summer.

Cytisus battandieri
Moroccan Broom
3–3.6 m (10–12 ft)

Take a sniff at the bright yellow cockade-like blooms of this open-growing broom and you'll detect the aroma of freshly cut pineapple. Early summer is the time of flowering, and the blooms are carried at the tips of stems that are clad in silky-haired deciduous leaves. Bees love it.

ASPECT south or west.

LIKES full sun and a sheltered spot in well-drained soil. Tolerates dry, clay or

GROUP 2

Remove dead or damaged stems in March and cut back all the rest to a pair of strong buds.

- 'Barbara Dibley'
- 'Barbara Jackman'
- 'Elsa Späth'
- 'Lasurstern'
- 'Marie Boisselot'
- 'Nelly Moser'

Remove any dead or weak stems and cut back healthy stems to a pair of strong buds

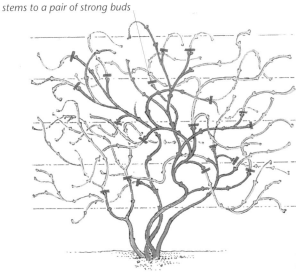

GROUP 3

Cut all stems back to a healthy pair of buds 1 m (3 ft) above ground level in March. Remove completely any damaged stems.

- 'Comtesse de Bouchaud'
- 'Ernest Markham'
- 'Etoile Rose'
- 'Hagley Hybrid'
- 'Jackmanii Superba'
- *C. tangutica*

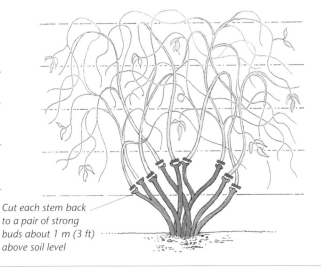

Cut each stem back to a pair of strong buds about 1 m (3 ft) above soil level

chalky soil and sheltered coastal gardens.

PRUNE OUT one or two of the oldest stems each winter, and any that grow straight out from the wall. Never cut into the old wood.

PROPAGATE by sowing seeds in spring, or by rooting firm shoot tip cuttings in a propagator.

Eccremocarpus scaber

Chilean Glory

Flower 3 m (10 ft)

Easy to grow and especially lovely when rambling through other shrubs. The green foliage is ferny and the tubular flowers are burning orange, decorating the plant from summer to autumn.

ASPECT south or west.

LIKES sun and shelter and light, well-drained soil. Tolerates dry or chalky soil; coastal exposure.

PRUNE OUT dead wood in spring. The

plant will be killed back to soil level in severe winters.

PROPAGATE from seeds sown in heat during spring.

Fremontodendron californicum

Fremontia

3 m (10 ft)

A tender evergreen for gambling gardeners. The lobed leaves are a dreary dull green but the starry yellow flowers that appear in summer will make up for the foliar deficiency. Very classy.

ASPECT south or west.

LIKES full sun and shelter and a well-drained soil. Tolerates dry or chalky soil and sheltered coastal gardens.

PRUNE only to remove badly placed or dead branches in spring.

PROPAGATE by seeds sown in heat in spring, or by cuttings of firm shoot tips rooted in a propagator in summer.

Garrya elliptica

Silk Tassel Bush

3.6 m (12 ft)

Funereal in leaf but fabulous in flower, the silk tassel bush produces living icicles of bloom in January and February. The grey-green catkins can be 15 cm (6 in) or more long and show up well against the deep evergreen foliage. A superb plant to floodlight.

ASPECT north, south, east or west.

LIKES a sheltered spot in a well-drained soil. Tolerates dry, clay or chalky soil and coastal exposure. It may suffer in severe winters.

PRUNE OUT dead or out-growing, unwanted branches in spring. Otherwise pruning is not essential.

PROPAGATE by layering low-hanging stems in autumn and by taking cuttings of firm shoot tips in summer any time of year.

Hedera

Ivy

6 m (20 ft) plus

Valuable evergreens with leaves that may be finely cut, crimped or splashed with cream and yellow. They cling by means of tenacious aerial roots: avoid planting them against pebbledash, which they may pull off. All lend colour and form to the garden, especially in winter. (See Chapter 5 Shrubs for other varieties and for use as ground cover.)

The small-leaved ivies are varieties of *H. helix*; among the best for walls are:
'Buttercup': young leaves bright yellow.
'Chicago': green leaves burnished purple.
'Glacier': green leaves edged with white.
'Oro di Bogliasco' (syn. 'Goldheart'): dark green leaves with a yellow centre.
'Parsley Crested': green leaves with wavy edges.
'Sagittifolia': dark green fingered leaves.

Of the larger leafed ivies, the pick of the bunch is the lengthily named *H. colchica* 'Dentata Variegata': its foliage is attractively splashed and marbled with bright creamy yellow.

ASPECT north, south, east or west.

LIKES almost any soil and situation.

PRUNE mature plants by clipping them back with a pair of shears in spring every other year.

PROPAGATE by rooting shoot tip cuttings in a propagator or outdoors in summer. Low-hanging shoots can be layered at any time of year.

Hoheria lyallii

3 m (10 ft) plus

Not half as widely grown as it should be, this shrub is a little tender and benefits from being sheltered by a wall. The deciduous, oval green leaves make a fine backdrop for the thick array of scented white flowers in summer. Try it in the open in sheltered gardens.

ASPECT south or west.

LIKES sun and a well-drained soil. Tolerates dry or chalky soil and coastal gardens.

PRUNE OUT dead wood and one or two older stems each spring.

PROPAGATE by sowing seeds in gentle heat in spring, by layering in summer, or by rooting cuttings of firm shoot tips in a propagator in summer.

Humulus lupulus 'Aureus'

Golden-leafed Hop

4.5 m (15 ft)

This deciduous twiner is stunning in spring and summer when its acid-yellow vine-shaped leaves decorate the questing stems. Good for brightening up dingy corners, and superb with green-flowered euphorbias.

ASPECT south, east or west.

LIKES rich, well-drained soil and sun. Tolerates clay, dry or chalky soil.

PRUNE AWAY all dead growth in spring: it usually dies back to ground level in winter.

PROPAGATE by division or seed in spring.

Hydrangea petiolaris

Climbing Hydrangea

Up to 15 m (50 ft)

If you like the bushy hydrangeas, then you must have a go with the climbing type. The leaves are similar but the stems are rather more tortuous and equipped with aerial roots that enable them to cling to walls. Large white flowerheads open in June.

ASPECT north, south, east or west.

LIKES rich and well-drained soil. Tolerates well-enriched dry, chalky or clay soils, and coastal exposure.

PRUNE OUT only unwanted or dead stems in spring.

PROPAGATE by taking cuttings of firm shoot tips and rooting them in a propagator in summer.

Jasminum nudiflorum

Winter Jasmine

3.6 m (12 ft)

You'll see it squirting through fences in cottage gardens all over the country, and billowing from walls, where it makes a thick mattress of stems. The bright yellow blossoms are especially welcome, for they push out well in advance of the leaves any time from November to March.

ASPECT north, south, east or west.

LIKES almost any soil and situation.

PRUNE OUT flowered shoots immediately after blooming; that way you'll prevent the build-up of that thick mattress of flowerless wood.

PROPAGATE by layering or by rooting hardwood cuttings in the open ground in autumn.

Lathyrus latifolius

Everlasting Pea

2.4 m (8 ft)

Here's something that makes a change from the annual sweet pea: it's a perennial version that will last for years. The foliage is typically pea-like, and the winged flowers are pink or white. Sadly it lacks the powerful fragrance of its annual relations.

ASPECT south, west or east.

LIKES rich, well-drained soil and sun. Tolerates clay or chalky soil.

PRUNE to ground level each autumn.

PROPAGATE by division or seeds in spring.

Climbers of special note

These climbers have either scented flowers or particular winter interest in the form of flowers and berries.

SCENTED FLOWERS
- *Carpenteria*
- *Clematis* (some)
- *Cytisus*
- *Hoheria*
- *Lonicera*
- *Magnolia*
- *Wisteria*

WINTER INTEREST
- *Chaenomeles*
- *Cotoneaster*
- *Garrya*
- *Hedera*
- *Jasminum*
- *Pyracantha*

Lippia citriodora
(syn. Aloysia triphylla)
Lemon Verbena, Aloysia

1.2 m (4 ft)

Never much to look at, this is a shrub valued for its strong citrus scent: crush the leaves and you'll get the full impact. It doesn't climb but certainly appreciates the shelter a wall can give. The leaves are deciduous (and useful for making pot pourri) and the pale lilac flower spikes are pleasing, though hardly spectacular, in summer.

ASPECT south or west.

LIKES sun and shelter and a light, well-drained soil. Tolerates dry or chalky soil and coastal situations.

PRUNE BACK dead stems to suitable buds in spring. Hard winters will kill the bush to ground level but it usually sprouts from below the surface. A winter mulch of dry bracken or straw will help to preserve it.

PROPAGATE by rooting cuttings of firm shoot tips in a propagator in summer.

Lonicera
Honeysuckle, Woodbine

6–9 m (20–30 ft)

The common honeysuckle (and there is none better) is *L. periclymenum*, sold in two varieties: Early Dutch ('Belgica') and Late Dutch ('Serotina'). The first carries its pale yellow, pink-flushed flowers in May, June, and again in September, and the second blooms continuously from July to September. Both are deciduous. If you want an evergreen, try *L. sempervirens* with orange and yellow trumpet flowers. Sadly it lacks the fragrance of its leaf-losing relations. *L. japonica* 'Aureoreticulata' is a good honeysuckle for foliage: its semi-evergreen leaves are oval, fresh green and netted with yellow veins. All these honeysuckles will scramble and twine over anything put in their way.

ASPECT *L. periclymenum* likes a south- or west-facing position; the other two will tolerate any aspect.

LIKES rich, well-drained soil and shelter. Tolerate enriched clay, dry or chalky soil.

PRUNE OUT older, flowered growths of *L. periclymenum* and *L. sempervirens* immediately after flowering. Clip back *L. japonica* 'Aureoreticulata' each spring.

PROPAGATE by layering or by taking cuttings of firm shoot tips and rooting them in a propagator in summer.

Magnolia grandiflora
Bull Bay, Laurel Magnolia

12 m (40 ft)

Now here's a stately wall plant. The leaves, as the second common name suggests, are evergreen and rather like those of laurel except that they often have the additional attraction of russeting on the undersides. You'll have to wait a good many years for the waxy cup-shaped flowers of creamy white to appear, but the plant is still good to look at even when out of flower. The variety 'Exmouth' will bloom earlier in its life than the true species and flowers during summer and autumn. The blooms are scented (if any are within sniffing distance). For large walls only.

ASPECT south or west.

LIKES rich, well-drained soil and a sheltered spot. Tolerates enriched clay, dry or chalky soils.

PRUNE OUT only dead or badly placed branches in spring, otherwise leave it alone.

PROPAGATE by spring layering.

Parthenocissus
Virginia Creeper, Boston Ivy

12 m (40 ft) plus

The true Virginia creeper is *P. quinquefolia* with much divided green leaves that turn brilliant crimson before falling in autumn. *P. tricuspidata*, Boston ivy, is

> ## Plants with evergreen leaves
>
> - Camellia
> - Carpenteria
> - Ceanothus
> - Fremontodendron
> - Garrya
> - Hedera
> - Lonicera (some)
> - Magnolia
> - Passiflora
> - Pyracantha

perhaps the better plant for most walls for it clings more efficiently, needing no support at all. The true Virginia creeper needs a few horizontal wires to give its scrambling stems a bit of a hand. Boston ivy has another advantage too: its maple-shaped leaves are glossy and even better equipped to show off their fiery autumn tints. Keep both plants away from pebbledash.

ASPECT north, south, east or west.

LIKES well-drained soil and a bit of sun for the best autumn colour. Tolerates clay, dry or chalky soil.

PRUNE in winter, clipping back any stems that are growing away from the wall and shortening any that are venturing where they are not wanted.

PROPAGATE by layering in summer or by rooting cuttings of firm shoot tips in a propagator in summer.

Passiflora caerulea
Passion Flower

6 m (20 ft) plus

In spite of its exotic appearance, the passion flower does well in many sheltered British gardens. It is a rampant climber, equipped with tendrils to speed it on its way. The hand-shaped leaves are evergreen and the white, blue-centred flowers are produced in summer, followed by orange, egg-shaped fruits if the weather is kind. They are edible but pippy.

The 'passion' referred to is Christ's passion, not some aphrodisiac property of the fruit. The five petals and five sepals represent the Apostles (minus Judas and either Doubting Thomas or Peter), the blue frill of filaments represents the crown of thorns, the five anthers the wounds, three stigmas the nails, the hand-shaped leaves are the hands of His persecutors and the tendrils the whip with which He was scourged.

ASPECT south or west.

LIKES sun, shelter and a well-drained soil. Tolerates dry or chalky soil and sheltered coastal gardens.

PRUNE in spring cutting back any long, trailing growths to within 10 cm (4 in) of the main stems.

PROPAGATE by cuttings of shoot tips, which can be rooted in a propagator in summer.

Phygelius capensis
Cape Figwort
_1.2–1.8 m (4–6 ft)_

A pretty-flowered shrub that enjoys the protection of a warm and sunny wall. The leaves are unremarkable, but the flowers that appear in branched heads at the stem tips during summer are a jolly sight, little tubular red jobs like tiny trumpets. Tied in, the stems will grow to around 1.8 m (6 ft). Severe winters will kill them back to soil level.

ASPECT south or west.

LIKES sun, shelter and well-drained soil. Tolerates dry or chalky soil and coastal exposure.

PRUNE BACK to ground level or to breaking buds each spring.

PROPAGATE by removing suckers in spring, by sowing seeds in warmth in spring, or by rooting shoot tip cuttings in a propagator in summer.

Polygonum baldschuanicum
(now Fallopia baldschuanica)
Russian Vine, Mile-a-minute
6 m (20 ft) plus

The fastest climber of all, but one I could only recommend to the desperate gardener. It produces a rampant thicket of twining stems and a fluffy mass of creamy white flowers in summer and autumn. The arrowhead-shaped leaves are deciduous, leaving you to look at a mattress of brown stems in winter. But if you want a rapid grower, you can give it a go: it puts on a good 4.5 m (15 ft) each year; for a couple of months in summer it does look quite charming.

ASPECT north, south, east or west.

LIKES almost any site and soil.

PRUNE by clipping back any unwanted stems in early spring.

PROPAGATE by rooting hardwood cuttings outdoors in autumn, or by rooting cuttings of firm shoot tips in a propagator in summer.

Pyracantha
Firethorn
_4.5 m (15 ft)_

Here's a plant that gives good value for money. The dark leaves are evergreen; creamy white flowers are produced in summer and are followed in autumn and winter by a heavy crop of berries: red in _P. atalantioides_, orange in _P. coccinea_ 'Lalandei', and yellow in _P. rogersiana_ f. 'Flava'. The birds love the berries, but then if you enjoy their company what does it matter? Yellow berries are the last to be taken.

ASPECT north, south, east or west.

LIKES ordinary well-drained soil. Tolerate dry, clay or chalky soil and coastal exposure.

PRUNE OUT only those stems that outgrow their allotted space. Prune after flowering but watch those thorns.

PROPAGATE by rooting cuttings of firm shoot tips in a propagator in summer.

Ribes speciosum
Fuchsia-flowered Gooseberry
_2.4 m (8 ft)_

Tiny red tubular flowers, each with a central tuft of stamens, decorate the gooseberry-like stems of this wall shrub in spring, making it look as if it were hung with rosy icicles. The green lobed leaves fall in winter, but the spring show makes cultivation well worth while.

ASPECT south or west.

LIKES sun and shelter and well-drained soil. Tolerates dry or chalky soil.

PRUNE OUT any dead stems and one or two older stems each winter. Shorten to two or three buds any shoots that grow out from the wall in summer.

PROPAGATE by hardwood cuttings in autumn or by inserting cuttings of firm shoot tips in a propagator in summer.

Solanum crispum
Chilean Potato Tree
_7–8 m (25 ft)_

A pretty scrambler with purple and yellow tomato flowers any time between June and September. It looks delightful when allowed to wander through _Abutilon vitifolium_. The best variety is 'Glasnevin': hardier and even longer flowering than the true species. The foliage is deciduous and certainly nothing to write home about, but that doesn't matter if the plant is trained through another.

ASPECT south or west.

LIKES sun, shelter and a light, well-drained soil. Tolerates dry or chalky soil and sheltered coastal gardens.

PRUNE in spring, shortening all sideshoots to three or four buds. Cut out dead or unwanted stems at the same time. Such precise pruning is not necessary where the plant is grown through a shrub or tree.

PROPAGATE by rooting cuttings of firm shoot tips in a propagator in summer.

Tropaeolum speciosum
Scotch Flame Flower
3 m (10 ft) plus

At Hidcote Manor in Gloucestershire, England, and Powys Castle in Wales you'll find dreary yew hedges brought alive by this nasturtium relative that loves to scramble through them. The fresh green hand-shaped leaves are almost as attractive as the tubular scarlet flowers; both are at their best in summer and autumn. The plant dies down completely in winter.

ASPECT north walls and the shady side of shrubs.

LIKES the cooler northern counties and a moist soil enriched with leaf mould and peat. Tolerates coastal gardens.
PRUNE by cutting away all dead growth in winter.
PROPAGATE by division or sow seeds in a frame in spring.

Vitis
Vine
6 m (20 ft) plus

If you want a grape you can eat, on a plant that's ornamental, go for *V.* 'Brandt'. The leaves burnish well in autumn, and the black grapes are delicious at the end of a good summer. For bold foliage colour you'll not do better than the gross *V. coignetiae*, which has massive vine leaves coated in a light down. They turn vivid shades of orange and crimson before they fall to the ground in autumn.
ASPECT south or west.
LIKES sun and a rich soil. Tolerate enriched clay or chalky soil.
PRUNE by shortening the sideshoots to 8 cm (3 in) in winter. Can be left unpruned if growing rampantly over arbours and through trees.
PROPAGATE by layering in spring or autumn or by rooting cuttings of firm shoot tips in a propagator in summer.

Wisteria sinensis
Chinese Wisteria
15 m (50 ft)

This plant brings back fond memories for me; it enveloped our first house, dangling its scented lilac-purple flower trails outside our windows so that the air was permanently scented during the month of May.

The deciduous leaves are pinnate (like those of an ash tree) and make a handsome fresh green covering for a house wall in summer even when there are no flowers are showing. There's a second, lighter flush of bloom later in the summer.

Give it a go over tall tree stumps, arches and pergolas and be patient – it may take a few years to settle in. Correct pruning (and an occasional feed of tomato fertilizer, which has a high potash content) can force young plants to flower more easily.

If your plant still refuses to bloom after about five years, replace it with a wisteria that's been grafted from a free-flowering parent. Some forms are just shy of flowering and a real waste of time. Good ones are stupendous.
ASPECT south or west.
LIKES sun, shelter and a well-drained

The fragrant lilac-purple flowers of *Wisteria sinensis* are a glorious sight in May and June, cascading over walls, pergolas and arches.

soil. Tolerates dry and chalky soil.
PRUNE first in July, shortening all unwanted shoots to about 15 cm (6 in). Prune again in January, shortening all sideshoots to four buds.
PROPAGATE by layering in spring or summer. Cuttings of firm shoot tips can be rooted in a propagator in summer.

chapter 8

roses

Available in a vast number

of varieties, roses offer

breathtaking colour and

scent, glorious flowers, fruit

and foliage, and types to

suit every soil and situation

A FRIEND OF MINE SWEARS THAT ROSES grow in spite of their owners – perhaps that's why most gardeners hold roses dear to their hearts – but they also have romantic connections, delectable scents, glorious colours and one hundred and one uses.

Before you can even begin to choose a rose for your garden you really ought to know the different types that are available. Rose classification is a thorny problem: there are many different groups of plants and a new classification system has just been adopted. But for me and the average gardener, life has to be a little simpler, so here's my offering, which I hope is reasonably clear and enables you to come away from the nursery or garden centre with the right plant.

DIFFERENT ROSE TYPES

Hybrid tea roses

The buffs now call these 'large-flowered roses'. The blooms are fat and fully double and are usually carried in small numbers at the tip of each stem. They will bloom from early summer until the frosts, and sometimes beyond, and the flowers tend to come in flushes. This is the type to grow for winning prizes.

Large-flowered or hybrid tea roses are full centered and carried in small numbers on each stem.

Floribunda roses

Now correctly known as 'cluster-flowered roses', these are the bushes with much-branched flower clusters at the stem tips and usually rather smaller blooms. But don't make the mistake of thinking that all floribundas are single: some of them have decidedly double flowers. The difference is in the size and quantity of flowers. They flower almost continuously through the summer but are usually slightly less vigorous than the hybrid teas. They are easily the best choice for bedding.

Cluster-flowered or floribunda roses carry more blooms than hybrids.

Standard roses

These are simply hybrid tea or floribunda roses (and very occasionally shrub roses) grown on a single, tall stem. They are used as specimen roses to add height to low plantings and should be supported by 2.5 x 2.5 cm (1 x 1 in) stakes that finish just below the head of branches. To my eye, standards look too artificial, but they do make rose-sniffing an easier pastime for elderly gardeners who have trouble bending down!

Miniature or 'patio' roses

Don't think that these are house plants. They might come in pots, but they will turn into spindly, fly-ridden thickets if you grow them indoors for any length of time. Planted out at the edges of beds and borders, on patios, and in tubs and windowboxes, they will perform well, making wiry little shrubs that are peppered with flowers right through the summer. They usually grow between 15 and 45 cm (6 and 18 in) high. The secret of growing miniatures well in containers is to keep the compost gently moist at all times and to give the plants plenty of light.

Climbing roses

These are roses with long and questing stems that can be trained around arches, over pergolas and up walls. There are several different groups of climbing roses, the most useful of these being the 'repeat-flowering climbers' that bloom right through the summer – unlike most rambler roses and many other climbers.

The so-called 'climbing sports' were all derived from hybrid tea or floribunda roses which, for some reason best known to themselves, suddenly sent up a climbing shoot from an otherwise stocky bush. Eagle-eyed gardeners over the years have spotted these shoots and propagated from them, and we now have plenty of climbing sports, all of which can be easily spotted because they are simply referred to as 'Climbing Ena Harkness' or 'Climbing Iceberg'. Sadly, climbing sports do not flower as freely as the bushes

Everyone's idea of the perfect country cottage, with roses cascading round the door.

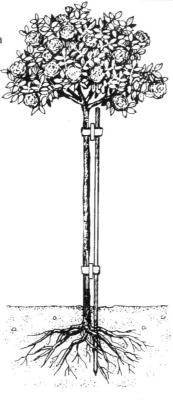

Standard roses need to be supported; use two ties to hold stem to stake.

from which they were propagated. They usually have just one large flush of flowers in early summer.

I'll talk about pruning later, but the important thing about the climbing sports is that they should not be pruned too hard, otherwise they might lose their climbing tendency. Climbers in general have stiffer stems than ramblers.

Rambling roses

Like the climbers, these are useful when they can be planted against tall supports, but preferably not against walls where the lack of air circulation can encourage mildew. They are especially good when planted at the base of old fruit trees and allowed to scramble through the branches above, giving them what appears to be a new lease of life. The stems of ramblers are sometimes more supple than those of climbers but, as explained above, the flush of flowers is usually confined to a grand burst in early summer, and the blooms are usually relatively small.

Shrub roses

Here are to be found roses old and roses new, roses of history, and wild species. The term 'shrub roses' is a sensible one, for these plants should be grown as

shrubs and not as rose bushes. They vary enormously in shape and size and have minimal pruning requirements. Many of them have disease-resistant foliage, attractive fruits or 'hips', flowers that are fully double, or moon-faced and single, and the deepest, most complex scents imaginable. Modern roses have not lost the scent for which nostalgic gardeners yearn. Many of them are as highly fragrant as a cheap tin of talcum powder; what they lack is the thick, sweet aroma that only the old roses seem to possess.

The disadvantages of shrub roses are two-fold: many of them have just one flush of bloom, in early summer; and many are large and look out of place in small gardens. But there are plenty of exceptions: there are repeat-flowering, and continuous-flowering shrub roses, and some that grow no more than 1 m (3 ft) high and as much across. You may have guessed from my enthusiasm that I rather like these roses.

SOIL AND CONDITIONS

Sun or shade

There are a few roses that can tolerate shade but, in general, they like an open, sunny spot that's sheltered from wind at a distance. You'll often be told to avoid planting roses in frost pockets, but something has to be grown there and, quite honestly, roses are more reliable in such situations than most plants.

Improving soil

The other common myth is that roses need heavy soil to do really well. In reality they'll thrive on any soil if you perk it up a bit before planting. You can double dig the site if you really feel better for such exercise, but single digging is all that's necessary on most reasonable soils. Good drainage is essential, as it is for most plants, and work in as much organic matter as you can spare – compost, manure, or even crumbly leaf mould, plus a little fertilizer. The plants will be there for a heck of a long time so you might as well make them feel at home right away. I've seen 30-year-old roses blooming as happily as youngsters in a good soil that has been well prepared and looked after.

Avoid, if you can, planting new roses on ground that was previously occupied by old roses. The soil might be rather tired and in need of a change of crop.

If there's an ideal pH for roses (see p.14) then it's in the region of 6.0 to 6.5, where most plants are happy. They'll still grow, though, on chalky earth, but plenty of organic matter will be appreciated.

Ideal for the larger garden, scrambling shrub roses provide summer blossoms and autumn fruits.

Where to use roses

I've covered some of the many uses of roses in the foregoing explanation of the groups but, just to make sure that you know where they can be used, here are some specific suggestions:

- **In windowboxes and tubs**: miniatures.
- **As hedges**: shrub roses, especially the rugosas and hybrid musks and some gallicas such as *Rosa gallica* 'Versicolor'. (I apologize for the inclusion of more complicated names, but the shrub roses are a mixed and motley band.)
- **Through trees**: climbers and ramblers.
- **Up walls, screens, arches and pergolas**: climbers and ramblers.
- **In beds**: hybrid teas and especially floribundas. Always most effective when planted in large numbers of a single variety.
- **In borders**: hybrid teas, floribundas and shrub roses used as shrubs.
- **As ground cover**: low-growing and miniature varieties. They are compact and spreading in habit, and sometimes root where they touch the ground. The best bloom throughout summer into autumn. Look for the County Series, such as 'Avon' (pearl white), 'Kent' (white) or 'Hampshire' (scarlet).

BUYING ROSES

CONTAINER-GROWN ROSES You can buy and plant container-grown roses at any time of year, and the great advantage is that in summer you can see the bush in flower and check it for scent.

BARE-ROOT ROSES are planted in the dormant season, from November to March. Specialist rose growers despatch most of their plants in this state, and they are undoubtedly the best source of supply if you want unusual varieties and first-class bushes.

PRE-PACKED ROSES Sold in supermarkets and chain stores, pre-packed roses are not usually available in very wide variety, and they are seldom top quality bushes, but I've had some splendid plants that started life in this way. When it comes to price, the pre-packed roses are cheapest, followed by the bare-root plants. Container-grown roses are slightly more expensive: you'll have to pay for the privilege of planting at any time of year.

If you can see what you're buying, go for a shapely bush with at least three stems. If you can't you'll have to rely on the reputation of the grower. If you buy pre-packed roses, make sure they are fresh in and not starting to sprout in the bag.

HOW TO PLANT

The planting technique is exactly the same as that adopted for trees and shrubs (see p.40). Climbers and ramblers that are to be planted against walls, pillars or old trees should be given the same kind of support system and treatment as any other climber (see p.91). Plant hybrid tea and floribunda roses 60 cm (2 ft) apart when they are massed together in beds. Allow shrub roses sufficient room for their indicated spread.

ROSE PRUNING

The pruning of roses need not be the confusing job that it's made out to be. Approach your bush with the courage of your convictions, a sharp pair of secateurs and a clear idea of what you're setting out to achieve. The cardinal rule with all rose pruning is that cuts must be made cleanly and just above a bud; torn cuts will allow in disease, and long snags will simply die back. The different kinds of roses are pruned as follows:

HYBRID TEAS Immediately after planting bare-root hybrid tea roses, shorten all stems to 8–10 cm (3–4 in). It seems cruel, but it will force them into

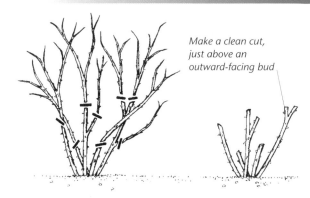

Make a clean cut, just above an outward-facing bud

To prune a rose bush, cut out any dead, diseased, or weak stems, then any that cross the centre. Reduce the open framework that remains to knee height or just below.

producing a healthy framework of new stems. Make clean cuts just above an outward-facing bud.

Container-grown roses planted during spring and summer are treated as mature plants by their first winter: prune between January and March as follows: first remove all dead wood, then any weak, diseased or crossing stems. Leave a cup-shaped framework of well-spaced branches. Cut all these stems back to just below knee height, above an outward-facing bud.

Remove one or two old branches from ageing plants every year so that a relatively young framework is built up. If you can't find an outward-facing bud don't worry; find one that points anywhere other than right into the centre of the bush.

FLORIBUNDAS Prune at the same time as hybrid tea roses, but not quite

> *"Approach your bush with the courage of your convictions, a sharp pair of secateurs and a clear idea of what you're setting out to achieve."*

so low. Prune newly planted bare-root bushes back to 15 cm (6 in) and established bushes to just above knee height. Otherwise the technique is exactly the same.

STANDARD ROSES Depending on whether the variety is a hybrid tea or a floribunda, prune the head of branches exactly as for bush roses (taking a guess at what is knee height).

MINIATURES AND GROUND COVER roses need little or no pruning other than the removal of dead or weak stems and shortening of overlong stems in March.

SHRUB ROSES It is possible to make a real mess of shrub roses by pruning them, so I leave them entirely alone, apart from trimming away dead shoot tips in spring. Occasionally, old stems can be cut out completely, and it's a good idea to remember that total removal of a branch is always likely to produce a more shapely plant than if a branch is cut back by half or a third of its length. There are occasional exceptions to this rule, but not many. *Rosa gallica* 'Versicolor', for instance, can be grown as a small hedge and trimmed back by one third in spring to keep it neat. On most other varieties you must be much more circumspect.

CLIMBING ROSES There are several distinct groups of climbers and they all need slightly different pruning if you want to be really precise. However, it is possible to prune them all in the same way and get away with it, provided you're not too heavy handed. Simply cut off any dead shoot tips in March, and cut back to about 10 cm (4 in) any sideshoots that have previously carried flowers. One or two very ancient stems can be removed each year, but only when they are exhausted and flowering poorly. If in doubt, don't cut it out!

RAMBLING ROSES Most ramblers are pruned right after flowering, when a few very old and gnarled stems are cut out completely at ground level and new ones trained in to replace them. If few new ones have appeared, simply cut back lateral shoots that have flowered to within 10 cm (4 in) of the main stem. Hefty ramblers such as 'Kiftsgate' need not be pruned as drastically (in fact you'll have a job to get at them if they're running through a tree); just trim out visible dead wood.

CARING FOR YOUR ROSES

Watering
Roses are deep rooted and, once established, are capable of resisting mild spells of drought more than most shrubs. During the first spring and summer after planting, however, soak the earth around them whenever it shows signs of drying out. Turn on a sprinkler if you can; otherwise, give each plant at least 10 litres (2 gallons) of water. In succeeding years the plants will only need soaking when drought threatens. It does pay off and can prevent the flowering season coming to an abrupt end.

Feeding
Like all plants that are generous with their blooms, roses like you to be generous with the fertilizer. Give

them a good helping of general fertilizer such as blood, bone and fishmeal in April, scattering it onto the soil at the rate of two handfuls around each bush. In June a specially prepared rose fertilizer based on the Tonks formula will help to give them a boost. One handful to each bush will be sufficient. The general fertilizer supplies all the major nutrients, but the Tonks contains extra magnesium and potash, which keeps the bushes healthy and free-flowering. Hoe both fertilizers into the top few inches of soil.

Mulching
Just as with other shrubs, a mulch laid around your roses will retain moisture, keep down weeds and generally boost plant health. Pulverised bark or garden compost can be used, but well-rotted manure is certainly most enjoyed.

Deadheading
Unless the flowerheads eventually produce decorative hips, snip them off to save the plant's energy and to keep up appearances. Cutting the blooms of hybrid teas actually encourages them to form a second flush of flowers. If you don't cut the blooms for indoor decoration, a bit of light summer pruning won't go amiss – shorten the stems a little when the first flowers have faded.

Sucker removal
Most roses are budded by the nurseryman on to a rootstock or briar because they can be grown to a

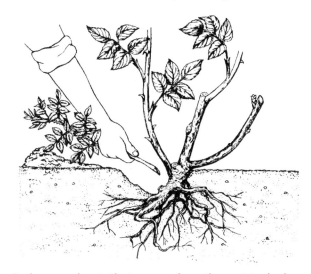

Suckers are shoots that emerge from the rootstock of the rose. Remove them as soon as you see them by tearing them from their point of origin.

saleable size more quickly in this way. Any shoots that emerge from the rootstock will be different in character and appearance from those that arise from the stems above ground. They can usually be differentiated from legitimate shoots by their paler colouring, lack of bronzing and, sometimes, by the presence of more leaflets (though this does not always hold good). Remove suckers as soon as they are seen or they will swamp the bush. Scrape away the soil at the base of the plants until the junction of sucker and rootstock can be seen. Tear away the sucker so that no part of it is left behind (see opposite).

Renovating old roses
Old bushes that have been allowed to grow unchecked can get into a sorry state. Ancient hybrid teas and floribundas can be renovated, if you fancy a challenge, simply by cutting out a portion of old and gnarled wood each year until sufficient new stems have been produced to take over completely. Shorten them gradually each year until they can be pruned to around the regulation knee height. You'll have to be quite patient but the results should be worthwhile.

Weed control
Mulching is the best answer and hoeing the second best but, if you hoe, be careful not to damage the stems or suckers might arise. If you're really idle you can resort to a rose-bed weedkiller that can be watered on to freshly cleaned soil, with the object of keeping it weed-free for an entire season. The trouble is that regular application of the stuff can result in sour soil and damage to the rose stems at ground level. It also stops you growing anything underneath your roses – plants that would, themselves, help to suppress weeds.

Underplanting
I don't much enjoy looking at bare soil, especially when it can be used to grow more plants. Some rose experts seem to like their rose beds bare of anything except roses, but there's no reason why other low-growing plants should not make a pleasant carpet below them. You can choose all manner of things, but

Rose-care calendar	
■ **March**	Complete pruning of established roses.
■ **April**	Apply general fertilizer; start spraying.
■ **May**	Look out for suckers and remove immediately.
■ **June**	Apply Tonks formula rose fertilizer to give roses a boost.
■ **July**	Deadhead hybrid tea and floribunda roses.
■ **August**	Apply general fertilizer.
■ **September**	Deadhead as necessary; tie in new shoots on climbers; watch out for diseases.
■ **October**	Take cuttings of species roses, ramblers, some floribundas and old roses.
■ **November**	Plant new roses as soon as they arrive.
■ **December**	Complete planting new roses during mild weather.

the following are especially good either as edgers or as carpeters: ajuga, alchemilla, arabis, aubrieta, dianthus, geranium, heuchera, lamium, lavender (edging), nepeta, primula (auriculas and polyanthus), pulmonaria, stachys, viola, spring-flowering bulbs.

PESTS AND DISEASES

Roses have their own peculiar band of pests and diseases and some of these occur with such regularity each season that routine spraying is worthwhile. I'm thinking of mildew, blackspot and greenfly (aphids).

Other problems that may strike are rust, leaf-rolling sawfly, leaf-cutter bee, pincushion gall, capsid bug, caterpillars, froghopper (cuckoo spit), and die-back. All are covered in Part VI Pests, Diseases and Disorders.

Routine spraying with one product that controls the big three – mildew, blackspot and aphids – is now possible. Start in April, as growth commences, and repeat at the recommended intervals. Watch for early infestations of aphids which, if left untreated, will cause horrible distortions of leaves and flowers.

PROPAGATION

Although the nurseryman propagates his roses by budding, it is much easier for the home gardener to increase his stock by taking hardwood cuttings in September or October. The plants may take a little while to come into flower (some of my shrub roses have taken five years) but there is no problem with suckers, and the technique is cheap and easy. All you need is patience. It is also easy to propagate climbers and ramblers by layering. Full details of propagation techniques are given in Chapter 2 Propagation.

A-Z

OF

roses

OUT OF THE THOUSANDS OF roses available, these are the ones I'd take with me to a desert island. Other gardeners will have different favourites, but in my roses I look for vigour and shapeliness of the bush, good flower colour for as long a season as possible, and a sigh-provoking scent. Wherever possible, look for roses with leathery, disease-resisting foliage. Now and again some of these attributes may have to be sacrificed if a plant is stunning in other ways. I make no apologies for the fact that the shrub rose list is longer than the others – I love them best.

Roses that are particularly suitable for use as hedging or for planting in shady conditions, and those that are renowned for their fragrance are highlighted in separate listings.

SHRUB ROSES

'Alchymist'

Height 3 m (10 ft)   Spread 2.5 m (8 ft)

Repeat flowering, warm orangey yellow flowers with confused double centre; rich green foliage; very fragrant and excellent disease resistance.

'Ballerina'

Height 1.25 m (4 ft) Spread 1.25 m (4 ft)

Repeat flowering, masses of small, single pink flowers with a white eye; glossy green foliage; slight fragrance and moderate disease resistance.

'Blanche Double de Coubert'

Height 2 m (6 ft)   Spread 1.5 m (5 ft)

Repeat flowering, pure white, semi-double flowers; rich green foliage; very fragrant and excellent disease resistance.

'Buff Beauty'

Height 2 m (6 ft)   Spread 2 m (6 ft)

Repeat flowering, buff-orange, semi-double flowers; purplish green foliage; pleasant fragrance and moderate disease resistance.

'Canary Bird'

Height 2 m (6 ft)   Spread 2 m (6 ft)

Late spring flowering, small, single, bright yellow flowers; light green, ferny foliage; slight fragrance and excellent disease resistance.

'Cardinal de Richelieu'

Height 1.25 m (4 ft) Spread 1 m (3 ft)

Early summer flowering, mauve-purple, fading to dusky purple, double flowers; dull green foliage; very fragrant and moderate disease resistance.

'Chapeau de Napoléon' (syn. *R.* x *centifolia* 'Cristata')

Height 1.5 m (5 ft)   Spread 1.25 m (4 ft)

Midsummer flowering, rich rose-pink double flowers; mid-green foliage; pleasant fragrance and moderate disease resistance.

'Complicata'

Height 2.5 m (8 ft)   Spread 2.5 m (8 ft)

Early to midsummer flowering, rich rose-pink single flowers with a white eye; mid-green foliage; slight fragrance and excellent disease resistance.

'Cornelia'

Height 1.5 m (5 ft)   Spread 2 m (6 ft)

Repeat flowering, apricot-pink, fully double flowers; deep bronze-green foliage; very fragrant and excellent disease resistance.

'Fantin-Latour'

Height 2 m (6 ft)   Spread 1.5 m (5 ft)

Early summer flowering, pale pink, flattened double flowers; dull green foliage; pleasant fragrance and moderate disease resistance.

'Fru Dagmar Hastrup'

Height 1.25 m (4 ft) Spread 1.5 m (5 ft)

Repeat flowering, pale pink single flowers; large red hips; rough bright green foliage; pleasant fragrance and excellent disease resistance. Suitable for ground cover.

'Frühlingsgold'

Height 2.5 m (8 ft) Spread 2 m (6 ft)

Early summer flowering, bright primrose-yellow semi-double flowers; light green foliage; pleasant fragrance and excellent disease resistance.

'Frühlingsmorgen'

Height 2 m (6 ft)   Spread 1.5 m (5 ft)

Early and late summer flowering, rich pink single flowers with primrose-yellow eye; dull green foliage; pleasant fragrance and excellent disease resistance.

'Golden Chersonese'

Height 2 m (6 ft)   Spread 1.5 m (5 ft)

Late spring flowering, bright yellow single flowers; mid-green ferny foliage; pleasant fragrance and excellent disease resistance.

'Königin von Dänemark'

Height 1.5 m (5 ft) Spread 1.25 m (4 ft)

Early summer flowering, pale pink, double, quartered blooms; pale green foliage; very fragrant and excellent disease resistance.

Shrub roses to use as hedging

SHRUB ROSE VARIETY	DISTANCE APART TO PLANT
• 'Ballerina'	60 cm (2 ft)
• 'Blanche Double de Coubert'	60 cm (2 ft)
• 'Buff Beauty'	1 m (3 ft)
• 'Canary Bird'	1 m (3 ft)
• 'Complicata'	1 m (3 ft)
• 'Cornelia'	1 m (3 ft)
• 'Fantin-Latour'	1.25 m (4 ft)
• 'Fru Dagmar Hastrup'	1 m (3 ft)
• 'Frühlingsgold'	1 m (3 ft)
• 'Frülingsmorgen'	1 m (3 ft)
• 'Königin von Dänemark'	60 cm (2 ft)
• 'Lady Penzance'	1 m (3 ft)
• 'Maiden's Blush'	1 m (3 ft)
• 'Marguerite Hilling'	1 m (3 ft)
• 'Nevada'	1 m (3 ft)
• 'Pink Grootendorst'	60 cm (2 ft)
• 'Reine des Violettes'	1 m (3 ft)
• Rosa gallica 'Versicolor' (R. mundi)	60 cm (2 ft)
• Rosa rubrifolia (R. glauca)	1 m (3 ft)
• 'Roseraie de l'Haÿ'	1 m (3 ft)
• 'Scabrosa'	1 m (3 ft)

'Lady Penzance'

Height 2 m (6 ft)   Spread 2 m (6 ft)

Early summer flowering, bright rose-pink, single flowers with tuft of yellow stamens; good hips; the foliage emits an apple-like scent after rain; very fragrant and excellent disease resistance.

'Maiden's Blush'

Height 1.5 m (5 ft) Spread 1.5 m (5 ft)

Early summer flowering, blush-pink, double, quartered blooms; grey-green foliage; very fragrant and excellent disease resistance.

'Marguerite Hilling'

Height 2.25 m (7 ft) Spread 2.25 m (7 ft)

Early and late summer flowering, warm pink overlaid with a deeper shade of pink, semi-double flowers; mid-green foliage; slight fragrance and excellent disease resistance.

'Max Graf'

Height 60 cm (2 ft) Spread 2 m (6 ft)

Midsummer flowering, rich pink, single flowers with tuft of yellow stamens; mid-green foliage; pleasant fragrance and excellent disease resistance. Suitable for ground cover: the prostrate stems spread over the soil surface, rooting as they go.

'Madame Hardy'

Height 1.5 m (5 ft) Spread 1.5 m (5 ft)

Midsummer flowering, pure white, double flowers with green button-eye centre; mid-green foliage; very fragrant and excellent disease resistance.

'Madame Pierre Oger'

Height 1.25 m (4 ft) Spread 1.25 m (4 ft)

Repeat flowering, shell-pink, double and cup-shaped flowers; pale green foliage; pleasant fragrance and slight disease resistance.

'Nevada'

Height 2.25 m (7 ft) Spread 2.25 m (7 ft)

Early and late summer flowering, creamy white, semi-double flowers; mid-green foliage; slight fragrance and moderate disease resistance.

'Pink Grootendorst'

Height 1.25 m (4 ft) Spread 1 m (3 ft)

Repeat flowering, rich pink, small double and frilly flowers in clusters; rough, rich green foliage; no fragrance but excellent disease resistance.

'Reine des Violettes'

Height 2 m (6 ft)   Spread 2 m (6 ft)

Repeat flowering, violet-purple, double, quartered, button-eyed flowers; grey-green foliage; very fragrant and excellent disease resistance.

Rosa gallica 'Versicolor' (R. mundi)

Height 1.25 m (4 ft) Spread 1.25 m (4 ft)

Midsummer flowering, cerise-pink, striped white, semi-double flowers ; light green foliage; no fragrance and only slight disease resistance.

Rosa moyesii 'Geranium'

Height 2.5 m (8 ft) Spread 2.5 m (8 ft)

Early summer flowering, bright red, single flowers; scarlet, flask-shaped hips; mid-green foliage; no fragrance but excellent disease resistance.

Rosa rubrifolia (R. glauca)

Height 2.25 m (7 ft) Spread 2.25 m (7 ft)

Midsummer flowering, rich pink, small, single flowers with white eye and yellow anthers; blue-grey, purple-tinged foliage; excellent disease resistance.

'Roseraie de l'Haÿ'

Height 2 m (6 ft)   Spread 1.5 m (5 ft)

Repeat flowering, rich magenta, fully

double flowers; rough, rich green foliage; pleasant fragrance and excellent disease resistance.

'Scabrosa'

Height 1.25 m (4 ft)   Spread 1.25 m (4 ft)

Repeat flowering, mauve-pink, single flowers with yellow stamens; good hips; rough, rich green foliage; pleasant fragrance and excellent disease resistance.

'Stanwell Perpetual'

Height 1.5 m (5 ft)   Spread 1.5 m (5 ft)

Repeat flowering, blush-pink double flowers; grey-green foliage; pleasant fragrance and excellent disease resistance.

HYBRID TEAS

Alec's Red

Height 1 m (3 ft)

Deep, rich red flowers; glossy green foliage. Very fragrant and excellent disease resistance.

'Ena Harkness'

Height 75 cm (2½ ft)

Dark, velvety crimson flowers with sadly weak necks; mid-green foliage. Pleasant fragrance and moderate disease resistance.

Fragrant Cloud

Height 1 m (3 ft)

Geranium-red is the best description of these flowers; deep glossy green foliage. Very fragrant and moderate disease resistance.

'Grandpa Dickson'

Height 1 m (3 ft)

Light yellow, massively full flowers; deep glossy green foliage. Slight fragrance but excellent disease resistance.

Shrub roses suitable for shade

All of the following shrub roses are suitable for growing in shade. Those marked with the symbol ◆ are also useful as ground cover.

- 'Blanche Double de Coubert'
- 'Canary Bird'
- 'Complicata'
- 'Fru Dagmar Hastrup' ◆
- 'Frülingsgold'
- 'Frülingsmorgen'
- 'Lady Penzance'
- 'Maiden's Blush'
- 'Max Graf' ◆
- 'Pink Grootendorst'
- 'Reine des Violettes'
- 'Rosa rubrifolia (R. glauca)'
- 'Roseraie de l'Haÿ'
- 'Stanwell Perpetual'

Just Joey

Height 75 cm (2½ ft)

Coppery orange, medium-sized, veined red flowers; deep green foliage. Slight fragrance but excellent disease resistance.

Mischief

Height 1 m (3 ft)

Warm salmon-pink flowers; mid-green foliage. Slight fragrance and moderate disease resistance.

Pascali

Height 1 m (3 ft)

The best white hybrid tea; glossy green foliage. Slight fragrance and moderate disease resistance.

Peace

Height 1.5 m (5 ft)

Huge pale yellow blooms edged with pink; deep glossy green foliage. Slight fragrance; excellent disease resistance.

Piccadilly

Height 75 cm (2½ ft)

Blooms carmine red above, yellow beneath; glossy purplish green foliage. Slight fragrance but excellent disease resistance.

'Precious Platinum'

Height 1 m (3 ft)

Brilliant, rich red flowers; glossy green foliage. Slight fragrance but excellent disease resistance.

Roses for fragrance

All of the following roses are strongly fragrant. Those marked with the symbol ◆ also have excellent disease-resistance.

SHRUB ROSES
- 'Alchymist' ◆
- 'Blanche Double de Coubert' ◆
- 'Cardinal de Richelieu'
- 'Cornelia' ◆
- 'Königin von Dänemark' ◆
- 'Lady Penzance' ◆
- 'Maiden's Blush' ◆
- 'Madame Hardy' ◆
- 'Reine des Violettes' ◆

HYBRID TEAS
- Alec's Red ◆
- Fragrant Cloud
- 'Wendy Cussons' ◆
- Whisky Mac

FLORIBUNDAS
- Margaret Merril ◆

CLIMBERS
- Compassion ◆
- 'Climbing Crimson Glory'
- 'Gloire de Dijon'
- 'Madame Grégoire Staechelin' ◆
- 'Zéphirine Drouhin'

RAMBLERS
- 'Albertine'

Rose Gaujard

Height 1 m (3 ft)

Flowers rich pink above, white beneath; deep glossy green foliage. Slight fragrance but excellent disease resistance.

Silver Jubilee

Height 75 cm (4 ft)

Flowers in a mixture of pinks; glossy green foliage. Slight fragrance and excellent disease resistance.

'Wendy Cussons'

Height 1 m (3 ft)

Very vibrant, rich cerise-pink flowers; deep glossy green foliage. Very fragrant and excellent disease resistance.

Whisky Mac

Height 75 cm (2½ ft)

Rich, coppery orange flowers; purplish green, glossy foliage. Very fragrant and moderate disease resistance.

FLORIBUNDAS

Allgold

Height 60 cm (2 ft)

Bright yellow, double flowers; glossy green foliage. Slight fragrance and excellent disease resistance.

City of Belfast

Height 60 cm (2 ft)

Bright scarlet, double flowers; glossy green foliage. Slight fragrance and excellent disease resistance.

Evelyn Fison

Height 75 cm (2½ ft)

Bright scarlet, medium-sized double flowers; deep glossy green foliage. Slight fragrance and moderate disease resistance.

Eye Paint

Height 1.25 m (4 ft)

Masses of small red, single flowers with white eyes; glossy green foliage. No fragrance but moderate disease resistance.

Iceberg

Height 1.25 cm (4 ft)

Plenty of pure white, double flowers; glossy green foliage. No fragrance but moderate disease resistance.

Lilli Marlene

Height 75 cm (2½ ft)

Deep red, double flowers with attractive petal formation; glossy purplish green foliage. Slight fragrance and moderate disease resistance.

Margaret Merril

Height 1 m (3 ft)

White, double flowers with a touch of blush; deep glossy green foliage. Very fragrant and excellent disease resistance.

'Pink Parfait'

Height 1 m (3 ft)

Double flowers in a rich pink mixture; glossy green foliage. No fragrance but excellent disease resistance.

Queen Elizabeth

Height 2 m (6 ft)

Light pink, fully double flowers; deep glossy green foliage; good hedger. Slight fragrance but excellent disease resistance.

'Southampton'

Height 1 m (3 ft)

Large, coppery orange, double flowers; deep glossy green foliage. Slight fragrance but excellent disease resistance.

Sue Lawley

Height 75 cm (2½ ft)

Semi-double, rich pink flowers edged with white; yellow stamens and a white eye; deep glossy green foliage. Slight fragrance but excellent disease resistance.

Trumpeter

Height 60 cm (2 ft)

Vibrant scarlet, double flowers; deep glossy green foliage. No fragrance but excellent disease resistance.

Yesterday

Height 1 m (3 ft)

Rich lilac-pink and white, semi-double flowers; glossy green foliage. Pleasant fragrance and excellent disease resistance.

MINIATURES

Angela Rippon

Height 30 cm (12 in)

Salmon pink, double flowers; rich green foliage. Slight fragrance and excellent disease resistance.

'Baby Faurax'

Height 30 cm (12 in)

Purplish pink, semi-double flowers; glossy green foliage. Pleasant fragrance and excellent disease resistance.

Darling Flame

Height 30 cm (12 in)

Vivid orange and yellow, double flowers; glossy green foliage. Slight fragrance; excellent disease resistance.

'Josephine Wheatcroft'

Height 38 cm (15 in)

Mid-yellow, double flowers; glossy green foliage. No fragrance but excellent disease resistance.

Magic Carrousel

Height 38 cm (15 in)

White, double flowers, deeply flushed pink at the edges; glossy green foliage. Slight fragrance but excellent disease resistance.

'New Penny'

Height 23 cm (9 in)

Rich pink, double, rosette flowers; glossy green foliage. No fragrance but excellent disease resistance.

Snow Carpet

Height 15 cm (6 in)

White, semi-double blooms; deep glossy green foliage; a spreader that makes good ground cover. Slight fragrance but excellent disease resistance.

CLIMBERS

'Aloha'

Height 2.5 m (8 ft)

Repeat flowering, rich rose-pink, double flowers. Slight fragrance but excellent disease resistance.

Bantry Bay

Height 2.5 m (8 ft)

Repeat flowering, soft pink, semi-double flowers. Slight fragrance but excellent disease resistance.

'Climbing Crimson Glory'

Height 3 m (10 ft)

Repeat flowering, deep red, double flowers. Very fragrant with slight disease resistance.

'Climbing Iceberg'

Height 3 m (10 ft)

Repeat flowering, pure white, double flowers. No fragrance but moderate disease resistance.

Compassion

Height 2.5 m (8 ft)

Repeat flowering, pink-flushed apricot flowers. Very fragrant with excellent disease resistance.

Danse du Feu

Height 2.5 m (8 ft)

Repeat flowering, fiery scarlet, double flowers. No fragrance but excellent disease resistance.

'Gloire de Dijon'

Height 4 m (12 ft)

Repeat flowering, large, buff to pale orange, old-fashioned, button-eyed, double blooms. Very fragrant with moderate disease resistance.

Golden Showers

Height 2.5 m (8 ft)

Repeat flowering, bright yellow, double flowers; prolonged flowering season from June until the first frosts. Slight fragrance but excellent disease resistance.

Handel

Height 3 m (10 ft)

Repeat flowering, white, double flowers, boldly edged with deep pink. Slight fragrance but excellent disease resistance.

'Mermaid'

Height 9 m (30) ft)

Repeat flowering, yellow, single flowers with amber stamens. Slight fragrance but excellent disease resistance.

'Madame Grégoire Staechelin'

Height 5 m (15 ft)

Early summer flowering, rich pink, double flowers with wavy-edged petals. Very fragrant with excellent disease resistance.

'Pink Perpetué'

Height 2.5 m (8 ft)

Repeat flowering, rose-pink, double flowers. Slight fragrance and moderate disease resistance.

'Schoolgirl'

Height 3 m (10 ft)

Repeat flowering, apricot, double flowers. Pleasant fragrance and excellent disease resistance.

'Zéphirine Drouhin'

Height 3 m (10 ft)

Repeat flowering, cerise-pink, semi-

double flowers; thornless. Very fragrant with moderate disease resistance.

RAMBLERS

'Albéric Barbier'

Height 5 m (15 ft)

Midsummer flowering, creamy yellow, double flowers with confused centres. The foliage is dark and glossy. Pleasant fragrance and excellent disease resistance.

'Albertine'

Height 5 m (15 ft)

Early summer flowering, pale pink,

double flowers, tinged with salmon. Dark green foliage, reddish when young. Very fragrant with moderate disease resistance.

'Félicité Perpétue'

Height 6 m (20 ft)

Midsummer flowering, creamy white, globular, double flowers. Slight fragrance but excellent disease resistance.

A profusion of pink roses provides a fragrant background to the mounds of magenta *Geranium* (cranesbill) and the pale-green foliage of *Alchemilla* in this exuberant summer border.

'Kiftsgate'

Height 9 m (30 ft)

Midsummer flowering, masses of small, creamy white, single flowers; good through trees or as ground cover. Slight fragrance but excellent disease resistance.

'New Dawn'

Height 4 m (12 ft)

Repeat flowering, pale, blush-pink, double flowers. Pleasant fragrance and excellent disease resistance.

GROUND COVER

Blenheim

Height 1 m (3 ft)

Repeat flowering, palest blush, double flowers. Pleasant fragrance and excellent disease resistance.

Kent

Height 50 cm (20 in)

Repeat flowering, creamy white, double flowers. Slight fragrance but excellent disease resistance.

Pink Bells

Height 75 cm (30 in)

Midsummer flowering, clear pink, fully double, somewhat bell-shaped flowers. Slight fragrance but excellent disease resistance.

Red Meidiland

Height 75 cm (30 in)

Repeat flowering, with deep red, white-eyed, single flowers. Slight fragrance but excellent disease resistance.

Suma

Height 60 cm (24 in)

Repeat flowering, deep pink, fully double flowers. Slight fragrance but excellent disease resistance.

border plants

Whether planted in an

island bed, a mixed border, or

in a formal herbaceous border,

hardy perennials delight us

by springing to life each year

after their dormant period

SHRUBS MIGHT BE THE BACKBONE OF THE garden, but border plants certainly help to flesh out the skeleton. Those that are covered in this chapter are the plants that the gardener calls hardy perennials.

WHAT ARE HARDY PERENNIALS?

'Hardy' means that the plants can stay outdoors all year round, usually putting up with the worst that the British weather can offer; 'perennial' means that they will last indefinitely. True enough there are a few perennials that are short-lived, lasting maybe two or three years, but most of them will outlive you if you treat them well.

Hardy herbaceous perennials form the bulk of the A–Z section, and these are the tough, long-lived plants that die down to soil level each autumn, keeping alive through the winter by means of roots and resting buds at soil level. They may not have the year-round appeal of shrubs, but this gives them a different advantage: they provide seasonal change in the garden so that it's fresh whatever the time of year.

USING BORDER PLANTS

Flower beds and borders
The obvious place for your border plants is in a flower bed or border. The traditional herbaceous border has bitten the dust in all but the most stately of gardens, and it's been replaced by the mixed border, where shrubs, bulbs, bedding and border plants keep each other company in a longer lasting display; the old herbaceous border started its season of glory in late May or June and was spent by September.

There's an awful lot of fuss made about island beds nowadays. These are simply flower beds of regular or informal shape, around which you can walk. Planted up wisely, they show off border plants to perfection. The trouble is that there's seldom room for island beds in very small gardens, unless you want to turn your plot into something resembling a traffic roundabout.

Where space is short, sweeping borders made as wide as possible are the best bet. You'll get plenty of plants into them and they'll be easy to work.

Planning ahead
Think carefully before you plant. Consider all the known characteristics of the plant and compare them with the characteristics of its neighbours. Bear in mind

its season of flowering, its ultimate height and spread and its foliage form, as well as flower colour.

It's a good idea to plant shrubs first and to fill in among them with border plants. The latter are easy to dig up and move when the space they occupy is needed by some expanding shrub. Not only will they tolerate disturbance, but they'll thrive on it. The tattiest border plants are those that are left alone, apart from agapanthus, peonies and one or two others that like to stay in one place for years.

Plan your border for a long display of colour, or for a burst of glory during one particular season. That revered gardener of the Victorian and Edwardian era, Gertrude Jekyll, had borders for every month of the year. Most small gardens would have a job to fit in all twelve, but it's no bad idea to set aside a patch outside a window that can act as a winter border; or another corner that billows with flowers in June.

If you can't or won't do this, make sure that as one plant fades from its season of glory, there is another one nearby to take over and delight the eye. Remember that vivid colour isn't everything: a bright, bold bloomer set in front of some handsome or muted foliage shows up far better than half-a-dozen assorted flowers vying for attention.

Using height in the border

A traditional border relies on a carefully graded series of heights, moving from the shortest at the front to the tallest at the back. As many of the plants used are herbaceous, the full effect will not be seen until early or mid- summer.

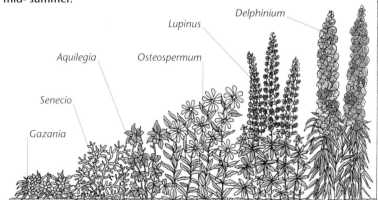

In this island bed, low-growing perennials are blended together with the occasional taller perennial or grass for impact.

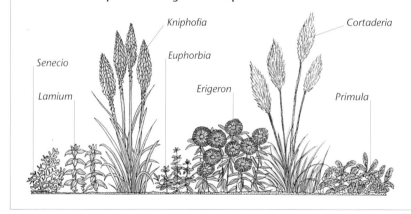

Single-colour themes

The popularity of Sissinghurst Castle in Kent, and its 'white garden' in particular, has encouraged more gardeners to plant borders with a single-colour theme. Yellow, red, blue, grey or white schemes are great fun to create, but do make sure that other parts of the garden act as an antidote to these monochrome amusements, or they'll bore the pants off you.

Ground-cover planting

Some border plants are stately enough to lend themselves to being planted as individual specimens;

others spread into a dense rug or canopy that will smother the weeds and ground once they are well established. Such ground-cover planting is useful, but it needs efficient maintenance in the early stages. For a start, the ground must be dug free of perennial weeds before planting. Watering will have to be attended to, and emerging weeds must be removed by hand or hoe until the plants are large enough to do the smothering. Remember, too, that herbaceous ground-cover plants will disappear in winter.

Gravel beds

Gravel and cobble beds are great fun, very labour saving and will show off foliage plants to great effect. All you need to do is cultivate the ground, plant your chosen specimens or arrangements, pat the soil level with the back of a fork, then lay 5 cm (2 in) of washed pea shingle or a layer of large pebbles or cobbles on top; this will keep down weeds and will always look smart. When you want to change or add to the planting, scrape away the gravel or lift off the cobbles, do your planting and then replace the stony mulch.

CHOOSING THE RIGHT SPOT

You probably won't have much choice when it comes to selecting a site for your bed or border. It is always recommended that hardy perennials are given a spot in full sun and a well-drained soil but, as the lists in the A–Z section show, there are plants for shade as well as sun, and some for heavy clay or chalk.

If you can't pick the ideal site, at least pick the plants that are ideal for your particular situation. Versatile as they are, few plants will thrive in really heavy shade cast by trees whose roots riddle the ground, or in very windy places. Only a handful will enjoy growing in really boggy soil. Do your best to improve the earth, whatever its composition.

PREPARING THE GROUND

Making the best of your soil

Just because a plant is said to tolerate dry soil, it doesn't mean that if, on one baking hot summer day, you dig a hole in the dust and plant it, it will survive. Every plant needs a chance to establish itself before it can settle down and cope with inhospitable conditions.

Soil improvers

Whether you garden on clay, chalk, sand or dust, cultivate the soil well, and work in as much well-rotted garden compost, manure, spent hops, mushroom compost, pulverized bark or leaf mould as you can afford: a bucketful to each square metre (yard) of ground will do nicely. The last two contain few nutrients, so a dusting of general fertilizer can be scattered over them before they are dug in.

When to dig

Digging or forking is essential: it will enable you to remove thick-rooted weeds as well as letting in air and incorporating the organic enrichment. Living soil full of muck, bacteria and worms produces better plants than sterile, tired earth. Soil can be dug at any time of year, but heavy clay will be easier to work in late summer or early autumn when it's gently moist rather

than sodden or baked hard. Leave it through the winter and the frost will have broken it down into a crumbly soil by spring. Sandy soil can be dug in spring: it needs no frost to shatter it and it will only be compacted by winter rains and snow if dug earlier.

The no-dig technique

You might have heard of the 'no-dig' technique: it sounds appealing. If you decide to make a border without digging or forking the soil you'll first have to kill off the weeds with one or two applications of a total weedkiller such as Tumbleweed (glyphosate). Then an 8 cm (3 in) thick mulch of organic matter will have to be laid on the soil and the border plants planted through this into pockets of enriched earth below. It involves a lot of organic matter and I feel rather sorry for any plant that has to push its roots down into poor, compacted earth before it can think of enjoying life. It's digging for me.

PLANNING BEDS AND BORDERS

I've never been one for planning gardens on bits of graph paper, but I suppose it does help to sketch out some idea of the scheme when you're planting up a bed or border; then you can juggle the plants around in the cosy comfort of your fireside until you have the effect you want.

Planting in drifts

I've already mentioned the things you should bear in mind when deciding what plant goes where – height, spread, colour, shape, season of flowering – but remember, too, that the most impact is created by large patches of one particular plant. To this end, stately herbaceous borders possess drifts of three, five, or seven plants (odd numbers always seem to be the order of the day) of one particular species. In tiny gardens, or where the collecting bug has bitten, single

This luxuriant herbaceous border illustrates the effectiveness of planting in bold drifts of colours. In traditional style, the border graduates from smaller plants at the front to the tallest at the back.

plants can be used, but the effect will be more like a patchwork quilt. In cottage gardens there's nothing wrong with that.

If you really can't be bothered to plan the scheme you can go to the garden centre and buy what's pretty. Bring the plants home and juggle with them on the soil around your existing border plants; but you'll still have to consider their height, spread and flowering season if you want good results.

Creating pleasing shapes

A final word on planning: consider carefully the shape of the bed or border. It should be as large as your plot will allow, and arranged so that its shape can be appreciated. Curves should be gradual, to make them easy on the eye and on the mower. Lay a hosepipe on the ground to mark out the shape (run hot water through it first if it's a cold day). Take out a strip of turf or a little V-shaped drill to mark the line, then start digging. In general, tall plants should be set at the back of the border, or the centre of a bed, and shorter ones at the front, but bring a few of the giants forward a little to vary the contours and to create hidden pockets. Even a border should hold a few surprises.

Where to buy the plants?

The garden centre might offer plants in flower, but seldom will it give you the choice that a specialist nursery offers. The larger, specialist firms do a healthy mail order trade, and can be relied on to supply good, healthy plants. They will even replace plants that appear to be dead or damaged on arrival if they are informed immediately. Plan your border and buy the bulk of your plants from a specialist – the garden centre can be used for in-fillers. If you don't like that idea, then go along to the garden centre for a look round before planning your border to include only the stock they offer.

> *"Bring a few of the giants forward a little to vary the contours and to create hidden pockets. Even a border should hold a few surprises."*

PLANTING BORDER PLANTS

Container-grown plants

Almost all border plants sold in garden centres will be container grown; this means that they have been growing for some time in the pot in which they are sold. The advantage with this system is that the plants can be planted in your garden at any time of year provided the soil is not frozen, muddy or bone-dry.

Lifted plants

Plants bought from a specialist nursery by mail order, and plants obtained from friends, are usually lifted from the ground in October or November. If your soil is well drained or on the light side, this is by far the best planting season, for the plants will have time to sink their roots into the soil and become well established before growing away vigorously next spring. If your soil is heavy, avoid autumn planting. It's better to wait and get the plants in during spring when drainage is improving, rather than have them sit in a cold quagmire through their first winter.

How to plant

The planting method for both lifted and container-grown plants is the same. Scatter a handful of blood, bone and fishmeal over each square metre (yard) of soil and hoe it in. Make sure the plant's root system, or the compost in the container, is moist, and dig a hole with a trowel that will take all the roots, allowing an 8 cm (3 in) gap all round. Remove the pot if the plant is container grown and sit the rootball in the hole. Any large and obviously ingrowing roots can be gently teased out, but the rest should be left undisturbed. Spread out all the roots of plants that have been lifted from open ground. Replace and firm back the soil with your feet so that the old soil mark on the stem or crown of the plant is level with the new surface.

Water the plant in thoroughly if necessary, and don't let the soil around it dry out during the first spring and summer. Plant at a spacing that will allow the plant to grow to its full spread before meeting its neighbour, or plant a little closer and thin out later if you want to achieve the full effect more quickly; it will cost you money, though.

LOOKING AFTER YOUR PLANTS

Watering and feeding

Don't neglect your plants once you've bunged them in. Remove any weeds that might compete and water thoroughly with a lawn sprinkler in dry weather (unless the plants are tall or leafy and will be weighed down by water droplets: in this case support a hosepipe, fitted with a sprinkler head, on the handle of a garden fork and let it play on the surrounding soil).

A sprinkling of blood, bone and fishmeal can be scattered on the soil around the plants in April and again in June if you're feeling generous and can get in to do the job. Hoe it into the surface.

Deadheading

Removing faded flowerheads from border plants can be a bore, but it will often encourage a second flush of bloom later in the season – it saves the plants the job

Supporting tall plants

Tall plants such as delphiniums will need individual cane supports for their stems: push a bamboo in by each spike as soon as it is 90 cm (3 ft) tall and gently tie the stem to it as it extends. Bushier plants can be held up either by proprietary wire plant supports such as Link stakes, or by pushing among them twiggy branches pruned from trees and shrubs in winter.

There's an excellent method of supporting border plants to be seen at Crathes Castle in Scotland; stout 2.5 cm (1 in) square dahlia stakes run around the border and black nylon netting with a 10 cm (4 in) wide mesh is stretched between the posts right across the border at a height of about 45 cm (18 in). When the foliage grows through the netting the strands disappear but the plants are well supported. Whatever kind of staking you use, make sure it's in position before the plants need it. You'll never get them to stand up properly once they've fainted. I've indicated in the A–Z section which plants need to be supported and which can stand on their own feet.

Knock in tall bamboo canes by individual delphinium spikes while they are quite small.

As the flower spike extends, tie it gently to the cane

A nifty support system used at Crathes Castle in Scotland. Wooden stakes support wide-mesh black nylon netting through which the plants grow.

of producing unwanted seeds. If the seedheads are needed for decoration or propagation, leave them be.

The benefits of mulching

If you can afford the time and money needed, then do lay a mulch of compost or pulverized bark over the soil in March each year, or even every other year if funds are short. It really does keep the soil in good condition (as well as suppressing weeds and holding in moisture) and the plants will enjoy the benefits it provides, especially on sandy soils. After four years of trying to cope with a dry sandy soil, I resorted to spring mulching with pulverized bark while the soil was moist. The plants grew that summer as they had never grown before.

Renovating old plants

Apart from those plants that are indicated as being best left undisturbed, all border plants can be kept in good condition by regular division of the clumps. With age, the central portion usually dies out, and every three or four years such clumps should be lifted and divided

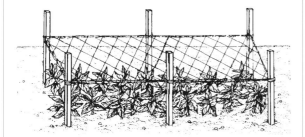

Dig up old clumps of border plants. Chop them into smaller lumps with a spade; discard the dead central portion and replant the youngsters.

into pieces as big as your fist before being replanted in freshly enriched soil. The dead central portions of each clump should be thrown away. Overgrown borders that are inherited when you move house can be completely renovated in this way in autumn or spring.

Winter care

In winter, when the top growth of herbaceous perennials dies down, go over the border and chop off the stems at ground level. Leave 5 cm (2 in) high stumps and you'll stab your fingers when you come to do the job next year. One or two tender plants can be left with a little stem or foliage in place to give them a bit of frost protection, but most need no such coddling. When the stems have been chopped off, a light forking over will tidy the soil for winter.

A-Z
OF
border plants

ERE I'VE INCLUDED NOT ONLY the floriferous border plants, but also a few ferns, bamboos and grasses, which provide a welcome change or a backdrop for the more blatant bloomers. I've indicated how each plant can be increased: methods are given in the order of popularity with which they are used on each plant (see Chapter 2 Propagation for details). I have also indicated which plants need staking for support. Measurements indicate ultimate height and spread.

Acanthus
Bear's Breech

1.5 m x 90 cm (5 x 3 ft)

A. mollis has bold, arching, glossy green leaves that are deeply lobed. Those of *A. spinosus* are more finely cut. Prickly flower spikes of white and rosy purple appear in late summer.
LIKES ordinary, well-drained soil and full sun. Tolerates gentle shade; dry, chalky and clay soils.
PROPAGATE by division, root cuttings, seed.

Achillea
Yarrow

60 cm–1.5 m x 45 cm (2–5 ft x 18 in)

Statuesque plants with flat heads of yellow flowers carried on feathery-leaved stems in summer. A. filipendula 'Gold Plate' is rich yellow: 1.5 m (5 ft) tall; 'Moonshine' is sulphur-yellow: 60 cm (2 ft) tall, and 'Coronation Gold' is mid-yellow: 90 cm (3 ft) tall. The last two have greyish leaves. *A. ptarmica* 'The Pearl' has tiny double white rosette flowers on 60 cm (2 ft) stems.
LIKES well-drained soil and full sun. Tolerates dry, chalky and clay soils; coastal gardens.
STAKING required.
PROPAGATE by division.

Aconitum
Monkshood, Wolfsbane

1.2–2.1 m x 60 cm (7 x 2 ft)

Towering plants with spires of hooded flowers – blue, pink, yellow or white in late summer. A. napellus is the common blue monkshood. The entire plant is very poisonous, as are all aconitums: avoid it where children are at large.
LIKES moisture-retentive soil and full sun. Tolerates chalk, clay and shady spots.
PROPAGATE by division, seed.

Agapanthus
Blue African Lily

60 x 60 cm (2 x 2 ft)

The 'Headbourne hybrids' are among the best and hardiest, producing rounded white or blue heads of 'lily' flowers on stiff stalks amid glossy strap-shaped leaves in midsummer.
LIKES well-drained soil and a sunny, sheltered spot. Tolerates dry or chalky soil; coastal exposure.
PROPAGATE by division, seed.

Ajuga
Bugle

15 x 90 cm (6 in x 3 ft)

Colourful carpeters making dense ground cover. Blue flower spires are carried in spring over leaves that may be deep purple, in the variety 'Purpurea'; cerise, cream and pale green, 'Burgundy Glow'; cream and green, 'Variegata'; or purple with orange marbling, 'Multicolor'.
LIKES moisture-retentive soil and gentle shade. Tolerates clay, chalk, heavy shade, sun (but not dry soil).
PROPAGATE by division.

Alcea
Hollyhock

2.4 m x 90 cm plus (8 x 3 ft)

Tall spires of red, pink, yellow or white mallow flowers open in summer over clumps of lobed leaves. A. rosea has single and double varieties. Best renewed from seed every couple of years to keep rust disease at bay (those orange spots underneath the leaves).
LIKES a sunny spot in well-drained soil. Tolerates clay soil.
STAKING required.
PROPAGATE by seed, divsion.

Alchemilla
Lady's Mantle

45 x 60 cm (18 in x 2 ft)

Scalloped green leaves covered in silky hairs hold water droplets like mercury. Fluffy lime-green flowerheads appear in summer. A. mollis is the commonest species and the loveliest. It seeds itself freely unless faded flowerheads are snipped off.
LIKES gentle shade and a moisture-retentive soil. Tolerates sun, dry soil, chalk and clay.
PROPAGATE by division, seed.

Alstroemeria
Peruvian Lily

60 cm–1.2 m x 45 cm (2–4 ft x 18 in)

Spectacular lily flowers are carried in large clusters atop narrow-leafed stems. The blooms are orange, marked with brown lines in A. aurea, or salmon

Lavender-coloured *Agapanthus*, orange-red *Alstroemeria* and deep pink *Phlox* provide the colour in this leafy border in Butterstream, Eire.

and pink in the beefier, more expensive, *A. ligtu* hybrids, which are trickier to grow. Plant them young and don't disturb. They flower in summer.
LIKES a warm and sunny spot in well-drained soil. Tolerates a fraction of shade; dry or chalky soil; coastal exposure.
STAKING required.
PROPAGATE by division, seed.

Anaphalis
Pearly Everlasting
30 x 45 cm (12 x 18 in)

Neat stems clad in long, grey-haired leaves are topped with clusters of white, bead-like everlasting flowers in summer. The best species is *A. triplinervis*. Essential in any white garden or grey-foliage scheme.
LIKES full sun and a soil not likely to dry out. Tolerates clay and chalky soils; gentle shade.
PROPAGATE by division.

Anchusa
90 x 60 cm (3 x 2 ft)

True gentian-blue flowers are carried over hairy leaves in early summer. *A. azurea* (syn. *A. italica*) offers excellent value in the varieties 'Loddon Royalist' and 'Little John' – the latter grows to just 45 cm (18 in).
LIKES well-drained soil and full sun. Tolerates clay and chalky soil.
STAKING required.
PROPAGATE by division, root cuttings.

Anemone
Windflower
1.5 m x 90 cm (5 x 3 ft)

It is the varieties of *A. x hybrida* that are most valued in borders for their late summer and early autumn display of wide-faced flowers on tall branching stalks. 'Honorine Jobert' is white, and 'Queen Charlotte' (syn. 'Königin Charlotte') is pink. There are others. All have a central crown of gold stamens and are good value when most plants are past it.

LIKES a well-drained but moisture-retentive soil in full sun. Tolerates clay and chalky soil; some shade and coastal exposure.
PROPAGATE by division, root cuttings.

Aquilegia
Columbine
75 x 45 cm (2½ ft x 18 in)

Bright border plants for early summer when their branched heads of bonnet-shaped flowers open above finely cut grey-green leaves. The blooms may be white, blue, pink, yellow and red. There are many hybrids. Most last only a few years but set plenty of seed and can be divided.
LIKES ordinary well-drained soil in a sunny spot. Tolerates clay and chalky soils and gentle shade.
PROPAGATE by seed, division.

Artemisia
Lad's Love
60 x 90 cm (2 x 3 ft)

The true lad's love, southernwood, or old man, is *A. abrotanum*. It makes a fruity-aromatic, feathery thicket of grey-green leaves. There are many other species, of which one of the best is *A. absinthium* 'Lambrook Silver' with exceptionally finely cut silver foliage. Grow any you can lay your trowel on. All are valued for their foliage.
LIKES warm and sunny spots in well-drained soil. Tolerates dry and chalky soil; coastal exposure.
PROPAGATE by stem cuttings, division.

Arum
Cuckoo Pint; Lords and Ladies
30 x 30 cm (12 x 12 in)

Our native cuckoo pint, *A. maculatum*, pops up all over my chalky garden, but *A. italicum* 'Marmoratum' is a better choice for most plots. The arrowhead leaves are veined with cream and, as in the native species, fat clubs of orange berries follow the spring arum flowers in late summer and autumn.

LIKES a shady spot in moisture-retentive soil. Tolerates chalk, clay and full sun (but not drought).
PROPAGATE by division.

Aruncus
Goat's Beard
2.1 x 1.2 m (7 x 4 ft)

Like a massive astilbe, *A. dioicus* (syn. *A. sylvestris*) has ferny dark green leaves, over which tower feathery plumes of creamy white flowers in summer. Give it room to show off.
LIKES dappled shade and a moisture-retentive soil. Tolerates sun, quite heavy shade; clay soil.
PROPAGATE by division, seed.

Asplenium
Hart's Tongue Fern
30 x 45 cm (12 x 18 in)

The crested forms of *A. scolopendrium* with their wavy-edged strops of lime-green leaves are grand front-of-the-border foliage plants. Protect them from spring frosts, which may burn the newly emerging leaves. Chop off old leaves in March.
LIKES moisture-retentive soil. Tolerates sun or shade; clay, chalk and some dry soils.
PROPAGATE by division.

Aster
Michaelmas Daisy
30 cm–1.5 m x 60 cm (1–5 x 2 ft)

Unsurpassable for late summer and autumn colour, most of the asters are super garden plants. The neat *A. amellus* is the shortest at 30 cm (12 in), and has varieties with purple, crimson, pink, violet and white flowers, as have most of the other species. There are dozens of different michaelmas daisies in assorted shades and sizes, but *A. x frikartii* 'Mönch' is an aster to cherish. It has lavender-blue flowers from summer to autumn and lasts longer than any other aster I know.
LIKES full sun and good soil. Tolerates

clay and chalky soils.
STAKING required.
PROPAGATE by division every 3 years.

Astilbe
Spiraea
60 cm–1.2 m x 60–90 cm (2–4 x 2–3 ft)

All the varieties of *A. x arendsii* have ferny leaves and feathery plumes of white, pink, mauve or crimson flowers in summer. Most grow to between 60 cm and 1.2 m high, but 'Sprite' is a charming pink-flowered variety at just 23 cm (9 in). All are good streamside plants. The young foliage is often bronzed.
LIKES moisture-retentive soil and sun. Tolerates shade; some chalky soils and clay soil.
PROPAGATE by division.

Astrantia
Hattie's Pincushion, Masterwort
60 x 60 cm (2 x 2 ft)

Sterling plants making domes of fingered leaves from which spurt stems of starry flowers from early to mid-summer. *A. major* is the best white; *A. major rubra* has rich crimson flowers, and 'Sunningdale Variegated' has leaves that are splashed cream early in the season. *A. maxima* has pink flowers but a weaker constitution.
LIKES moisture-retentive soil in sun or light shade. Tolerates quite heavy shade; chalky, clay and some dry soils (where plenty of organic matter has been worked in).
PROPAGATE by division, seed.

Ballota
60 x 60 cm (2 x 2 ft)

A straggly but endearing shrublet, *B. pseudodictamnus* has rounded leaves about 2.5 cm (1 in) across. Both they and the stems are thickly covered in white wool. The tiny mauve flowers are carried in compact clusters below the leaves but are hardly visible.
LIKES sun and a well-drained soil. Tolerates dry or chalky soil.
PROPAGATE by root cuttings.

Bergenia
Elephant's Ears, Megasea
30 x 60 cm (12 in x 2 ft)

Glossy leaves like table-tennis bats – and in some species just as big – and pink flower clusters on fat stalks in spring make this a cherished ground-cover plant. The most popular species is *B. cordifolia*, and its variety 'Purpurea' is one of the best bergenias for autumn colour, turning reddish purple. Evergreen.
LIKES sun and well-drained soil. A superb path-edger. Tolerates shade; clay, chalky or dry soil; coastal exposure.
PROPAGATE by division.

Blechnum
15 x 90 cm plus (6 in x 3 ft)

The tiny evergreen fern, *B. penna-marina*, is neat and jolly ground cover at the front of a shady border where its upright fronds make a thick, dark rug.
LIKES gentle shade and a peaty, leafy, acid soil. Tolerates full sun if kept moist at the roots.
PROPAGATE by division.

Brunnera
45 x 60 cm (18 in x 2 ft)

A forget-me-not-flowered woodlander with heart-shaped green leaves. *B. macrophylla* blooms in spring and is available in three variegated varieties; 'Dawson's White', roughly bordered with creamy white; 'Hadspen Cream', with deeper cream variegation; 'Langtrees' whose margins are spotted with silvery grey blobs. The last two are the best.
LIKES a shady spot in organic, moisture-retentive soil. Tolerates dry soils (in the case of the true species and the variety 'Langtrees').
PROPAGATE by division, seed.

Calamintha
Calamint
30 x 30 cm (12 x 12 in)

Underrated edgers with aromatic leaves and small, hooded flowers carried in summer and autumn. *C. nepeta* has pale blue flowers; *C. grandiflora* has pink flowers. Good ground coverers.
LIKES sunny spots in well-drained soil. Tolerates dry or chalky soil and shade.
PROPAGATE by division, seed.

Campanula
Bellflower
Various sizes

I'd grow any campanula that came my way, but space allows me to mention just three that I think are the best. *C. persicifolia*, 90 x 30 cm (3 ft x 12 in),

Border plants suitable for all soils

The following plants will do well in clay, chalky and dry soil. Those marked ◆ will also tolerate coastal exposure.

- Acanthus
- Achillea ◆
- Alchemilla
- Asplenium
- Astrantia
- Bergenia ◆
- Centaurea ◆
- Crocosmia ◆
- Curtonus
- Digitalis
- Dryopteris
- Echinops ◆
- Erigeron ◆
- Eryngium ◆
- Galega
- Geranium ◆
- Iris ◆
- Kniphofia ◆
- Lamium
- Lychnis ◆
- Paeonia
- Phlox
- Physalis
- Sedum ◆
- Solidago
- Verbascum
- Veronica

I've discovered in both my gardens. From evergreen clumps it produces tall stalks of pale blue or white bells. *C. latiloba* 'Alba' is a queen among campanulas for shade, producing deep-toothed white bells up its 1.2 m (4 ft) stems in clumps 60 cm (2 ft) wide. *C. glomerata*, 45 x 60 cm (18 in x 2 ft), has densely packed heads of violet-blue, upturned bells. All these species bloom in early to mid-summer. **LIKES** sun and any well-drained but moisture-retentive soil. Tolerates dry soils (*C. persicifolia*), chalky soils (all), and shade (*C. latifolia*).
STAKING required.
PROPAGATE by division, seed.

Carex
Sedge
30 x 30 cm (12 x 12 in)

Fountains of bright yellow leaves spurt up from the soil where *C. morrowii* 'Variegata' is planted. It's an ever-yellow plant to cheer you the year round.
LIKES moist soil and full sun. Tolerates clay, chalky soil (provided it's not dry) and a little shade.
PROPAGATE by division.

Catananche
Cupid's Dart
60 x 45 cm (2 ft x 18 in)

Pale blue dandelion flowers on wiry stems are produced by *C. caerulea* in summer from a clump of narrow leaves. Plant it between beefier foliage plants. It can be short-lived.
LIKES sun and a well-drained soil. Tolerates dry or chalky soil; coastal exposure.
STAKING required.
PROPAGATE by seed, root cuttings.

Centaurea
Cornflower, Knapweed
45–90 cm x 90 cm (18 in–3 ft x 3 ft)

Most gardens boast the spring- and summer-flowering *C. montana* with its spiky blue cornflowers and narrow grey-green leaves. More should give a home to the impressive *C. macrocephala*, 90 x 90 cm (3 x 3 ft), which has large leaves and hefty thistle heads of yellow. They dry well.
LIKES sun and well-drained soil. Tolerates dry, chalky or clay soil; coastal exposure.
STAKING required.
PROPAGATE by division, seed.

Centranthus
Valerian
90 x 60 cm (3 x 2 ft)

The red valerian, *C. ruber*, is a summer beauty beloved of butterflies and gardeners. It makes an upright plant with deep pink flowerheads and there is also a white variety. Both will grow well in crevices in paving and walling.
LIKES sun and a well-drained soil. Tolerates dry or chalky soils and coastal exposure.
PROPAGATE by stem cuttings, seed.

Ceratostigma
Hardy Plumbago
90 x 90 cm (3 x 3 ft)

A rounded bush clad in coarse leaves and topped with bright blue flowers in late summer and autumn. *C. willmottianum* is not totally hardy and may be killed to ground level in winter.
LIKES warm, sunny spots in well-drained soil. Tolerates chalky soil.
PROPAGATE by stem cuttings, seed.

Chrysanthemum
Shasta Daisy
90 x 90 cm (3 x 3 ft)

The white, thick-centred shasta daisy is *C. maximum* (now *Leuchanthemum* x *superbum*), also known by the name of one of its varieties 'Esther Read'. One of the best white flowers of summer and a vigorous clump former.
LIKES full sun and a well-drained soil. Tolerates clay or chalky soil and coastal exposure.
STAKING required.
PROPAGATE by division.

Cimicifuga
Bugbane
1.5 m x 90 cm (5 x 3 ft)

Tricky plants with ferny foliage and arching sprays of white flowers in late summer and early autumn. *C. racemosa* flowers earliest of all.
LIKES shade and a rich, moist soil. Tolerates organically enriched chalk and clay soils.
PROPAGATE by division, seed.

Convallaria
Lily-of-the-valley
23 x 90 cm plus (9 in x 3 ft)

A spreader with upright, pointed, oval leaves and arching flower stalks that carry tiny white bells in spring. Headily scented. *C. majalis* is the true species, and it has several varieties including the pink-flowered var. *rosea* and the larger-flowered 'Fortin's Giant'. All spread greedily.
LIKES dappled shade and well-drained soil. Tolerates full sun or heavy shade; dry or chalky soil.
PROPAGATE by division.

Coreopsis
Tickseed
60 x 60 cm (2 x 2 ft)

The finely cut bright green foliage of *C. verticillata* sits like tangled wire netting below the orange-yellow daisy flowers that open from midsummer to early autumn. It's a showy but graceful plant for the front of a border.
LIKES full sun and well-drained soil. Tolerates clay or chalky soil.
PROPAGATE by division.

Cortaderia
Pampas Grass
2.4 x 2.4 m (8 x 8 ft)

Varieties of *C. selloana* are the most popular, producing plumes of creamy white flowers in early autumn once the plant is a few years old and well suited. Chop off dead foliage in spring.

LIKES a sunny spot in light, well-drained soil. Tolerates some clay or chalky soils.
PROPAGATE by division.

Corydalis
Fumitory
23 x 45 cm (9 x 18 in)

The finely cut green leaves of *C. lutea* make a fine foil for the spires of yellow flowers that bloom from spring to autumn. Good between paving stones.
LIKES dappled shade and well-drained soil. Tolerates full sun; dry soil and chalk.
PROPAGATE by seed.

Crambe
1.8 x 1.2 m (6 x 4 ft)

The massive *C. cordifolia* produces hefty dark green leaves over which splay the billowing flower stems in early summer. The blooms are tiny and white, combining to form a dense cloud. For big borders only.
LIKES a sunny patch of well-drained soil. Tolerates chalky and dry soils; coastal exposure (though strong winds may buckle its stems).
PROPAGATE by division, root cuttings.

Crocosmia
Montbretia
60 cm–1.2 m x 60 cm (2–4 ft x 2 ft)

A popular late summer flower with grassy green leaves carried in dense, upright tufts. The blooms are held on arching stems and may be orange, as in the common *C. x crocosmiiflora*, or brilliant scarlet as in the superb 'Lucifer'. This showy hybrid starts to flower in June and carries on until late summer. It is almost 60 cm (2 ft) taller than the previous species at around 1.2 m (4 ft) and is a hybrid between *C. aurea* and *C. pottsii*.
LIKES sun and a well-drained soil. Tolerates dappled shade; dry, chalky and clay soils; coastal exposure.
PROPAGATE by division.

Crocosmia paniculata
Aunt Eliza
1.2 m x 30 cm (4 x 12 in)

Rather like a giant Montbretia this plant used to be called *Antholyza paniculata*, which explains its common name. Botanists now call it *Crocosmia paniculata*. The orange-red blooms appear in late summer. The leaves are broader and taller than those of *Crocosmia* with marked pleating.
LIKES sun and a well-drained soil. Tolerates dappled shade; dry, chalky and clay soils.
PROPAGATE by division.

Cynara
Cardoon
1.8 m x 90 cm (6 x 3 ft)

Stunning, arching leaves of grey are

Towering spikes of pale mauve and purple *Delphinium* and magenta *Althaea* (hollyhock) are punctuated with the pastel pink of *Aquilegia*.

boldly cut, making *C. cardunculus* an exceptionally attractive foliage plant. Artichoke flowerheads appear on tall stems in summer. Cheap to grow from seed.
LIKES sun and well-drained soil in a sheltered spot. Tolerates dry or chalky soil.
PROPAGATE by seed, division, root cuttings.

Delphinium
Larkspur
1.8 m x 90 cm (6 x 3 ft)

The hybrids of *D. elatum* have become firm towering features in many gardens and always seem to be bracketed with lupins. The flower spikes rise from clumps of serrated leaves in summer, and have dozens of blooms ranging in colour from rich blue through paler shades to pinks, mauves and primrose-yellow as well as white. The red delphinium, no doubt, will be with us shortly.

LIKES sun and a rich, well-drained soil. Tolerates chalky and clay soils.
STAKING required.
PROPAGATE by division, seed.

Dianthus
Carnation, Pink
15–30 x 30–60 cm (6–12 in x 1–2 ft)

There are many named varieties of pink and border carnations and all make superb edgers for beds, borders and paths. Their spiky foliage is usually neat and grey, they bloom freely in summer, and they possess the most exquisite scents. Varieties are available with crimson, pink, mauve, pale yellow and white flowers, single or double. Some are bicoloured.

LIKES sun and well-drained chalky soil. Tolerates other well-drained soils if lime is added; coastal exposure.
PROPAGATE by stem cuttings, seed.

Dicentra
Bleeding Heart, Lady in the Bath
45 x 60 cm (18 in x 2 ft)

The true bleeding heart is *D. spectabilis*, which has finely cut green leaves and arching stems of pink and white locket flowers in late spring. *D. formosa* is a smaller version with leaves like carrot foliage and more slender flowers. Among the best hybrids are 'Stuart Boothman', with filigree grey leaves and pink flowers in spring and summer, and 'Langtrees', grey leaved with white flowers tinged pink. 'Bacchanal' has dusky crimson flowers. The smaller versions grow to around 23 x 45 cm (9 x 18 in).

LIKES gentle shade and moisture-retentive soil. Tolerates sun and chalky

soil (provided the roots do not dry out) and clay.
PROPAGATE by division in autumn or spring; be careful not to break the brittle roots.

Dictamnus
Dittany
75 x 60 cm (2½ x 2 ft)

Both *D. albus* (syn. *D. fraxinella albus*), with white flowers, and its variety *purpureus,* with rich pink flowers, are superb border plants. The leaves are fingered and the flowers rather starry in appearance. They open in early summer and later form seed pods which give off a volatile oil. Hold a lighted match underneath them and you'll hopefully see a minute explosion! The plant is citrus scented.
LIKES full sun and a well-drained soil. Tolerates dry and chalky soils.
PROPAGATE by division, root cuttings, seed.

Dierama
Fairy Wand Flower, Angel's Fishing Rod
1.2 m x 90 cm (4 x 3 ft)

From a clump of grassy evergreen leaves the flower stems erupt in summer, carrying rich pink bell flowers on arching fusewire-thin stalks. Very graceful and always a conversation piece. The smaller *D. dracomontanum*, 30 x 30 cm (12 x 12 in), is similar but even more graceful and a good front-of-the-border plant. Plant in spring.
LIKES full sun and a well-drained but moisture-retentive soil. Tolerates dry soil and chalk; coastal exposure. Be patient – it may die down after planting but will re-emerge.
PROPAGATE by division, seed.

Digitalis
Foxglove
60 x 30 cm (2 ft x 12 in)

A pale yellow foxglove of modest height, *D. grandiflora* is a reliable

perennial where most other foxgloves are biennial (p.150). The flower spikes shoot from downy, evergreen leaf rosettes in summer.
LIKES organically enriched soil in dappled shade. Tolerates sun, quite heavy shade; dry, chalky or clay soil.
PROPAGATE by seed, division.

Doronicum
Leopard's Bane
45 x 45 cm (18 x 18 in)

These bright yellow spring daisies are always welcome heralds of a new season and the variety 'Miss Mason' is one of the best. Doubles like 'Spring Beauty' ('Frühlingspracht') are dazzling but look too much like a summer pot marigold at this time of year. The rounded leaves are a good, fresh green.
LIKES sun and well-drained soil. Tolerates gentle shade; clay and chalky soil.
PROPAGATE by division.

Dryopteris
Male Fern
90 x 90 cm (3 x 3 ft)

The arching green fronds of *D. filix-mas* add an ethereal look to any border. Plant this fern where you can enjoy its form and where the mid-green of its fronds can set off other plants.
LIKES shade and well-drained soil. Tolerates sun; dry, clay and chalky soils.
PROPAGATE by division.

Echinacea
Purple Coneflower
1.2 m x 60 cm (4 x 2 ft)

Rich pink daisies are not plentiful in the garden but *E. purpurea* makes up for the deficiency by producing a good show over its green foliage in summer. 'Robert Bloom' is an exceptionally good variety of a dusky rose colour; it is long-flowering too.
LIKES sun and a rich, well-drained soil. Tolerates chalk and well-worked clay.
STAKING required.
PROPAGATE by division, root cuttings.

Echinops
Globe Thistle
1.2 m x 60 cm (4 x 2 ft)

A real whopper of a border plant with finely cut dark green leaves (grey underneath) and spherical flowerheads of steely blue in late summer. *E. ritro* is the most popular species, but *E.* 'Taplow Blue' is taking over from it and is even more vigorous at around 1.5 or 2 m (5 or 6 ft).
LIKES full sun and a good, well-drained soil. Tolerates dry, chalk and clay soils; coastal exposure.
STAKING required.
PROPAGATE by dividing clumps in autumn or spring, or by root cuttings.

Growing to a height of 1.2 m (4 ft), *Echinops ritro* is a stunning plant for the back of the border, with its large, purplish blue, spherical flowerheads from July to September.

Epilobium
Rose Bay Willowherb
1.2 m x 30 cm (4 ft x 12 in)

When the Emperor of Japan came to Kew Gardens in 1971 he was offered any plant he wanted – and took away a packet of rose bay willowherb seeds. You might not want to plant this invasive, if beautiful, weed, but its white variety *E. angustifolium* var. *album* is a green-and-white-flowered treasure that is not so rampant. It flowers in late summer. Super in white borders.
LIKES well-drained soil and sun or dappled shade. Tolerates clay and chalky soils.
PROPAGATE by division, seed.

Epimedium
Bishop's Hat, Barrenwort
30 x 30 cm (12 x 12 in)

Whichever species you choose you'll inherit a fine ground-cover plant with mitre-shaped leaves that are often burnished with crimson when they unfurl in spring. The tiny, short-lived flowers may be red, yellow or white and they open in spring. The stems and stalks are stiff and wiry, an altogether admirable race of plants valued for foliage contrasts.
LIKES some shade and a moisture-retentive soil. Tolerates sun provided it isn't dry at the roots; chalk and clay. Slow in dry soils.
PROPAGATE by division.

Eremurus
Foxtail Lily
1.5–2.4 m x 60 cm (8 x 2 ft)

You'll find no showier border plants than the hybrids of eremurus that are now freely available. In early summer they send up rocket-like stems, packed for most of their length with starry flowers of white, pink, yellow or orange. The strappy leaves die down in summer so the plants should be clearly marked. Mulch in winter.
LIKES sun and well-drained soil; a

sheltered spot. Tolerates nothing but excellent drainage; chalky soil.
PROPAGATE by division, seed.

Erigeron
Fleabane
45–60 x 60 cm (18 in x 2 ft)

Pretty daisies with petals of pink, mauve, violet or white, surrounding a central disc of yellow. They flower for a good two months in early to mid-summer. Take your pick from the varieties listed in nurserymen's catalogues.
LIKES sun and well-drained soil. Tolerates clay, dry or chalky soil and coastal exposure.
PROPAGATE by division.

Eryngium
Sea Holly
60 cm–1.2 m x 30–60 cm (2–4 x 1–2 ft)

No garden should be without sea hollies. From rosettes or clumps of leaves the branched stems erupt in summer carrying aloft spiky steel-blue flowers – a central knob of tiny florets is surrounded by a ruff of spiny bracts. The flowers are many and miniature on species such as *E. planum*, or large and spectacular in the fuzzy-collared *E. alpinum* or the more open-bloomed *E. x oliverianum*. Sneak the plants between other border inhabitants who will hold them up. They look silly staked. The plant known as Miss Willmott's Ghost is *E. giganteum*, a glorious silver-leaved sea holly of modest size 45 x 30 cm (18 x 12 in) but it is biennial. Grow it in spite of this minor drawback.
LIKES well-drained soil and full sun. Tolerates dry or chalky soil and coastal exposure. Some can put up with clay.
PROPAGATE by division, seed.

Euphorbia
Spurge
Various sizes

Classy plants with leaves arranged in spirals up the fleshy stems. The tallest

and most stately is *E. characias*, 1.5 m x 90 cm (5 x 3 ft), most popular in its subspecies *wulfenii*. The flowerheads are the yellowish green so common in euphorbias. None is more luminous than those of *E. polychroma* (syn. *E. epithymoides*) 45 x 45 cm (18 x 18 in), which makes a neat, rounded dome of acidic yellow heads. *E. amygdaloides* var. *robbiae* 60 x 60 cm (2 x 2 ft) makes a dense, evergreen, weed-suppressing blanket of attractive growth. All these flower in spring and look terrific planted in front of the golden-leafed hop or near yellow-leafed shrubs. The stunning *E. griffithii* 'Fireglow' blooms in early summer, plastering its stems with rounded heads of brick-red blooms.
LIKES sun and a good, well-drained soil. Tolerates shade; dry or chalky soil; coastal exposure.
PROPAGATE by division, seed.

Festuca
Fescue Grass
23 x 30 cm (9 x 12 in)

Big, blue-grey shaving brushes sprouting from the ground; that's the best description I can offer of *F. glauca*, the blue fescue. It's a neat foliage plant to squeeze into any bed or border and looks good among cobbles or gravel. It is evergreen but can be chopped to ground level in spring when tatty; it will soon sprout again.
LIKES sun and well-drained soil. Tolerates dry or chalky soil; coastal exposure.
PROPAGATE by division.

Gaillardia
Blanket Flower
75 x 45 cm (2½ ft x 18 in)

Bright-petalled double daisies of red, orange or yellow that are at their best in summer. There are many varieties, but 'Mandarin' is one of the best; orange-red petals radiate from a central boss of mahogany-brown.
LIKES light, well-drained soil and sun.

Tolerates dry or chalky soil. Propagate by division, root cuttings.
PROPAGATE staking.

Galega
Goat's Rue
1.2 m x 90 cm (4 x 3 ft)

Goat's rue should be much more popular. It makes a thicket of vetch-like stems and leaves, decorated in summer with clusters of white, pink, lilac or pale blue pea flowers. *G. officinalis* is the species from which the varieties are derived.
LIKES sun and well-drained soil. Tolerates chalk, dry and clay and soils.
STAKING required.
PROPAGATE by division.

Gentiana
Gentian
60 x 60 cm (2 x 2 ft)

The willow gentian, *G. asclepiadea* looks a treat in late summer and early autumn when its arching stems produce pairs of blue trumpet flowers among the topmost leaves. The leaves are willow-shaped, which accounts for the common name. One of late summer's most cheering sights.
LIKES rich, leafy soil and gentle shade. Tolerates sun (but not drought); chalky soil.
PROPAGATE by seed.

Geranium
Cranesbill
Various sizes

Vital plants in my garden where they make billowing flower-spotted ground cover from spring to autumn. Grow any of them – they're all worth a try. Among the best are:
G. macrorrhizum: 30 x 60 cm (12 in x 2 ft), aromatic, pink or white.
'Claridge Druce': 45 x 90 cm (18 in x 3 ft), pink.
G. phaeum: 60 x 30 cm (2 x 12 in), the mourning widow, dusky purple.
G. pratense 'Plenum Violaceum': 60 x 60 cm (2 x 2 ft), double blooms of violet and mauve.
G. psilostemon (syn. *G. armenum*): up to 1.8 x 1.8 m (6 x 6 ft) usually less, magenta centred with deep purple.
LIKES sun and well-drained soil. Tolerates shade; dry, chalky or clay soil; coastal exposure.
STAKING required by *G. psilostemon*.
PROPAGATE by division.

Geum
Avens
30–60 x 45 cm (12 in–2 ft x 18 in)

Most hybrid geums have double flowers of red, yellow, orange or pink, held like rosettes at the tips of sturdy stems. 'Mrs J. Bradshaw' is a good, solid red, and 'Lady Stratheden' a double yellow. *G. rivale* 'Leonard's Variety' is altogether more classy with its orange-pink bells that nod on 30 cm (12 in) stems. All bloom from early to midsummer.
LIKES full sun and good, well-drained soil. Tolerates gentle shade; chalky or clay soil.
PROPAGATE by division.

Glyceria
60 cm x 1.5 m (2 x 5 ft)

A clump of upright grassy leaves with blades that are boldly striped in white and green makes *G. maxima* var. *variegata* (syn. *G. aquatica variegata*) a must. It's a stunner and grows itself in any reasonable spot. Give it room – it's invasive.
LIKES moisture-retentive soil and sun. Tolerates gentle shade; chalky or clay soil. Slow in dry soil.
PROPAGATE by division.

Gunnera
Prickly Rhubarb
2.4 x 2.4 m (8 x 8 ft)

For massive gardens only. *G. manicata* makes gargantuan parasols of leaves, dull green above, lighter green below, with prickly stalks. Best by a lake if you happen to have one. Mulch with bracken in winter to protect the tender crowns.
LIKES rich, leafy, moisture-retentive soil; sun. Tolerates gentle shade.
PROPAGATE by division.

Gypsophila
Baby's Breath
Various sizes

Billowing clouds of tiny blooms float over this plant in summer. *G. paniculata*, 1.2 x 1.2 m (4 x 4 ft), is white and single; 'Bristol Fairy', 90 x 90 cm (3 x 3 ft), is a double white; and 'Rosy Veil' a double pink. Can be short-lived.
LIKES a warm, sunny spot in well-drained, chalky soil. Tolerates other well-drained soils; coastal exposure.
PROPAGATE by seed, grafting (varieties).

Helenium
Sneezeweed
60–90 x 60 cm (2–3 x 2 ft)

Summer and autumn daisies of yellow, orange and mahogany–red. There are many varieties, all of which have a prominent central boss of yellow or brown. 'Butterpat', yellow; 'Wyndley', orange-brown; and 'Moerheim Beauty', mahogany, are particularly good.
LIKES good, well-drained soil and sun. Tolerates clay or chalky soil.
STAKING required.
PROPAGATE by division.

Helleborus
Christmas Rose, Hellebore
30–60 x 30 cm (12 in–2 ft x 12 in)

By flowering in winter and spring this group of plants really earns its keep. *H. niger*, the Christmas rose, usually carries its waxy white saucers in January or February (unless cloche covered). *H. orientalis* is the undoubted aristrocrat with its many-flowered 30 cm (12 in) stalks, of creamy white, purple or purple-spotted blooms that precede the leaves. *H. corsicus* is

evergreen with spiny-edged fingered leaves, and in its second year each stem is topped with a cluster of pale green flowers. Most hellebores require a little patience until they settle in.
LIKES gentle shade and well-drained but moisture-retentive soil. Tolerates sun; chalky or well-cultivated clay soils.
PROPAGATE by seed, division.

Hemerocallis
Day Lily
60–90 x 60 cm (2–3 x 2 ft)

Grassy, fresh green leaves make a perfect background to the branched heads of lily flowers carried over them in summer. There are dozens of varieties with short-lived (but regularly produced) blooms of yellow, orange, white, pink or mahogany-red. A good contrast for broader-leaved plants.
LIKES sun and well-drained but moisture-retentive soil. Tolerates gentle shade; chalky or clay soils.
PROPAGATE by division.

Heuchera
Coral Bells, Alum Root
30–60 x 45 cm (12 in–2 ft x 18 in)

Valued as pretty ground cover, the heucheras produce a thick pile of flowering-currant-shaped leaves over which are carried upright stems decorated with little bells of pink or red. The named varieties have now upstaged the true species. They bloom in early summer and some have leaves marbled bronze. 'Pewter Moon' is especially good in leaf.
LIKES rich, well-drained but moisture-retentive soil. Tolerates sun or shade; chalky or clay soils; coastal exposure.
PROPAGATE by division.

Hosta
Plantain Lily, Funkia
30–60 x 60 cm (12 in–2 ft x 2 ft)

Bold foliage plants of great merit. The leaves are always juicy and squeaky,

and tall stems of bell-shaped lily flowers tower over them in summer. The blooms are usually white or pale lilac in colour, but it is the leaves that are the main attraction. They die down in autumn but emerge afresh each spring. *H. sieboldiana* var. *elegans* has whopping blue-grey leaves that are rounded and ribbed; *H. fortunei* var. *albopicta* is striped and blotched with butter-yellow on green in spring, fading to green later; *H. crispula* has narrower leaves, twisted at the edges and margined. with creamy white. Of the many good newcomers 'Frances Williams' is strikingly bold. It has the size and colour of *H. sieboldiana* var. *elegans* but with a pale yellow margin.
LIKES gentle shade and a rich, moisture-retentive soil. Tolerates sun (but not dryness); chalky or well-worked clay soil.
PROPAGATE by division, seed.

Incarvillea
45 x 30 cm (18 x 12 in)

The rich pink trumpets of *I. delavayi* blow a colourful fanfare from the tops of sturdy stalks in early summer. The much-divided leaves are deep bronzy green. Spectacular in sheltered gardens.
LIKES sun and a well-drained soil. Tolerates dry or chalky soil.
PROPAGATE by division, seed.

Iris
Flag
Various sizes

Sword-like or grassy leaves and bright, often bearded flowers combine to make the irises indispensable garden plants. The German bearded irises, which are available in a tremendous variety of colours, make that brilliant June display of bloom, but their glaucous leaves are still useful later in the season for foliage contrasts. Prolong the iris season by growing *I. unguicularis* (syn. *I. stylosa*) in really dry soil at the foot of a sunny wall. Its grassy leaves remain all the year round, but from November to February it can produce pale violet-blue flowers to brighten your winter. Starve it and don't disturb it. *I. pallida* in either its white-variegated or yellow-variegated leafed forms is a superb foliage plant, and *I. foetidissima* is the species that has those fat seed pods that burst to reveal orange seeds in autumn.
LIKES well-drained soil, especially if it's chalky; full sun. Tolerates gentle shade (in the case of *I. pallida* and *I. foetidissima*); dry or clay soils; coastal exposure.
PROPAGATE by division, seed.

Specimen plants

These are plants that strike me as having such good form and appearance that they are worth planting as eye-catchers in a bed or border, or as single specimens on patios or in gravel and cobble beds. Not all of them are huge; some are small and capable of being fitted into the tiniest back yard.

- **Acanthus**
- **Aruncus**
- **Carex**
- **Cortaderia**
- **Cynara**
- **Dierama**
- **Dryopteris**
- **Euphorbia**
- **Festuca**
- **Glyceria**
- **Gunnera**
- **Hemerocallis**
- **Hosta**
- **Iris**
- **Kniphofia**
- **Macleaya**
- **Matteuccia**
- **Phormium**
- **Polygonatum**
- **Polygonum** (syn. **Persicaria**)
- **Rheum**
- **Rodgersia**
- **Sedum**
- **Smilacina**
- **Stipa**

Kirengeshoma

90 x 60 cm (3 x 2 ft)

Not half as widely grown as it should be. Rich green, paired leaves show off a treat the upside-down shuttlecock flowers of pale yellow that dangle from branched, purple-flushed stems in late summer and early autumn. *K. palmata* is its full name.

LIKES a rich, moisture-retentive and lime-free soil in dappled shade. Keep it sheltered from strong winds. Tolerates full sun if it's not dry at the roots.

PROPAGATE by division, seed.

Kniphofia
Red Hot Poker

Various sizes

Striking plants with sceptre-like flower stems that appear from early summer to autumn depending on the species or variety. The leaves are grassy and make a massive clump. Most varieties have red and yellow flowers, but there are now some with pale yellow or green flowers, and a good race of miniatures that can be easily fitted into the small garden. *K. uvaria*, 1.5 m x 90 cm (5 x 3 ft), is the common autumn-flowering poker, but try 'Little Maid', 60 x 30 cm (2 ft x 12 in), with its pale yellow flowers; 'Green Jade', 1.2 m x 60 cm (4 x 2 ft), with cool green blooms, and 'Strawberries and Cream', 45 x 30 cm (18 x 12 in), pale yellow and rich pink, all raised by that observant lady Beth Chatto.

LIKES full sun and well-drained soil. Tolerates dry, chalky or well-worked clay soil; coastal exposure.

PROPAGATE by division.

Lamium
Deadnettle

30 cm x 1.2 m (12 in x 4 ft)

As a ground-cover plant at the front of a border *L. maculatum* has little competition. Choose a variety such as 'Chequers' with white-striped leaves and rich mauve hooded spring flowers, or

'Beacon Silver' whose leaves are almost entirely silver-green. *L. galeobdolon* (syn. *Galeobdolon luteum, Lamiastrum galeobdolon*) is a firework plant – light the blue touch-paper and stand back. In its variety 'Florentinum' it has trailing stems clad in green, grey-spotted leaves, with yellow flowers in early summer. Once established it is unstoppable and thrives where little else will grow. All are evergreen.

LIKES any well-drained soil and sun. Tolerates heavy shade; dry, chalky or clay soil.

PROPAGATE by division, stem cuttings.

Lathyrus

45 x 45 cm (18 x 18 in)

This is a neglected plant that should soon make a comeback. Over a mound of finely cut leaves it produces plenty of pinkish purple pea flowers in spring. *L. vernus* has several varieties, among which is 'Spring Delight' with paler pink flowers. Give it a try.

LIKES sun and well-drained soil. Tolerates dry or chalky soil; coastal exposure.

PROPAGATE by division.

Liatris
Kansas Gayfeather

60 x 30 cm (2 ft x 12 in)

It is *L. spicata* that appears in most catalogues and in most gardens. It has shiny, narrow leaves that make a bold tuft of growth, and in summer it sends up pokers of fluffy pink flowers. Butterflies love them. 'Kobold' is a good purplish pink variety, and 'Alba' is white.

LIKES sunny spots in well-drained soil. Tolerates dry or chalky soil.

PROPAGATE by division.

Linaria
Toad Flax

90 x 30 cm (3 ft x 12 in)

The spires of *L. purpurea* pop up all over my garden and will do so for ever:

the plant seeds itself freely. The stiff stems sport spirals of narrow grey leaves and are topped with spikes of tiny purple snapdragon flowers – pink in the variety 'Canon Went', which seems just as prolific and come true from seed. Good in paving stone crevices and walls and flowering freely from early to late summer.

LIKES sun and well-drained soil. Tolerates dry and chalky soil; coastal exposure.

PROPAGATE by seed, division.

Linum
Flax

45 x 45 cm (18 x 18 in)

If you want a good sky-blue flower, look no further than *L. narbonense*. Its bell-shaped blooms decorate the wiry stems for several weeks in summer. It can be rather short-lived.

LIKES sun and a well-drained soil in a sheltered spot. Tolerates dry and chalky soils.

PROPAGATE by seed, stem cuttings.

Liriope

30 x 30 cm (12 x 12 in)

I'm never quite sure whether I like the appearance of *L. muscari*, but it's so useful that it's worth a mention. It makes a clump of darkest green, grassy leaves that arches into a small fountain, and in autumn stiff stalks appear carrying pale purple blobs of flowers. It's useful because it can put up with dense, dry shade under trees.

LIKES sun or shade and good, well-drained soil. Tolerates well-worked clay or chalky soil.

PROPAGATE by division.

Lobelia
Cardinal Flower

90 x 30 cm (3 ft x 12 in)

As distinct from the bedding lobelia, *L. cardinalis* produces tall stems thickly set with scarlet flowers in summer. *L. fulgens* is similar but redder in leaf.

LIKES sun and rich soil that is unlikely to dry out. Tolerates dappled shade and well-worked, enriched, chalky soil.
STAKING required.
PROPAGATE by division, seed.

Lupinus
Lupin
1.2–1.8 m x 60 cm (4–6 x 2 ft)

George Russell, an assiduous Yorkshireman, raised many different varieties of tall-spired lupin with towers of close-packed pea flowers in shades of blue, pink, red, yellow, mauve, purple and white. They were all grown on allotments and he wouldn't take a penny for them from any nurserymen; instead he distributed them free of charge. We still have many of his excellent varieties, at their best in June. The blooms look well over the fingered green leaves that hold water drops in their centre like globules of mercury.
LIKES good, well-drained soil and full sun. Tolerates well-worked clay soils and, reluctantly, organically enriched

Lupins, delphiniums, irises and pyrethrums epitomize the luxuriance of high summer.

chalky soils. On shallow chalk they sulk.
PROPAGATE by stem cuttings, seed, division.

Lychnis
Maltese Cross
90 x 30 cm (3 ft x 12 in)

There are two species of lychnis that have particularly striking flowers in summer. *L. coronaria* makes upright branching stems covered all over with white down; the leaves are felted too. Atop the stems are magenta flowers in early summer. *L. chalcedonica* has plain green leaves and stems topped with clusters of zingy scarlet flowers – there is no truer red in the garden. Place them carefully to avoid clashes.
LIKES sun and a well-drained soil. Tolerates dry, chalky or clay soils and coastal exposure, though they appreciate shelter from strong winds.
STAKING required.
PROPAGATE by division, seed.

Lysimachia
Loosestrife, Creeping Jenny
Various sizes

The yellow loosestrife, *L. punctata*, makes a clump 60 x 60 cm (2 x 2 ft) and sends up stems of starry yellow flowers in summer. Creeping Jenny (*L. nummularia*) is a sprawling plant with tiny rounded leaves the size of a new penny. Little yellow cup-shaped flowers appear in the leaf axils in early summer. The variety 'Aurea' has leaves of an eye-catching acid-yellow. All are rampant.
LIKES moisture-retentive soil in dappled shade. Tolerates chalk and clay; sun but not drought.
STAKING required by *L. punctata*.
PROPAGATE by division.

Macleaya
Plume Poppy
2.4 m x 90 cm (8 x 3 ft)

The dusky green, lobed leaves of *M. microcarpa* (syn. *Bocconia cordata*) are grey beneath and flash brightly when

disturbed by wind. The plumes of orange-pink flowers appear in summer and are most attractive in the variety 'Kelway's Coral Plume'. A hefty plant that needs room to spread itself. It suckers freely.
LIKES well-drained soil in a sunny, sheltered spot. Tolerates dry or chalky soil.
STAKING required.
PROPAGATE by division, root cuttings.

Malva
Mallow
1.2 x 1.5 m (4 x 5 ft)

The easiest mallow to get hold of is *M. alcea* var. *fastigiata*, which produces upright stems decorated with round, pink flowers in summer. *M.* 'Primley Blue' deserves to be better known, for it makes a spreading, vigorous plant that never ceases to carry myriads of soft blue flowers from early summer to autumn. Give it room to spread. Rust disease can sometimes attack and it can be short-lived.
LIKES sun and well-drained soil. Tolerates chalk and well-worked clay.
PROPAGATE by stem cuttings.

Matteuccia
Ostrich Plume Fern
60 x 60 cm (2 x 2 ft)

Shuttlecocks of bright green fronds unfurl in spring, making *M. struthiopteris* (syn. *Struthiopteris germanica*) one of the most striking ferns, if one of the most unpronounceable. Superb in small colonies.
LIKES dappled shade and leafy, moisture-retentive soil. Tolerates well-enriched chalk or clay; sun and heavy shade.
PROPAGATE by division.

Meconopsis
Himalayan Blue Poppy, Welsh Poppy
Various sizes

The Welsh poppy, *M. cambrica*, 30 x

30 cm (12 x 12 in), is the easiest to please, seeding itself around so freely that it amounts to a weed in my garden. But its bright yellow poppy flowers are a treat in late spring.

The coveted blue poppy, *M. betonicifolia* (syn. *M. baileyi*), 1.2 m x 30 cm (4 ft x 12 in), is showstopper, producing branched heads of almost luminous blue flowers in early summer. But beware: there are wishy-washy varieties, and the plant's performance varies from garden to garden, as does its length of life.

LIKES dappled shade and a rich, lime-free soil. Best in the cooler northern counties. Tolerates full sun if happy at the roots.

PROPAGATE by division, seed.

Milium
Bowles' Golden Grass
60 x 60 cm (2 x 2 ft)

A superb yellow-foliage plant, *M. effusum* 'Aureum' was spotted by that Enfield plantsman E.A. Bowles, which accounts for its common name. It makes dainty, arching clumps of acid-yellow leaves, which produce airy flower stems in summer. It seeds about freely.

LIKES gentle shade and a well-drained soil. Tolerates dry or chalky soil and full sun.

PROPAGATE by division, seed.

Mimulus
Monkey Flower
30–90 x 60 cm (12 in–3 ft x 2 ft)

There are lots of different monkey flowers with fleshy green leaves and trumpet flowers of red, yellow or orange, often contrastingly spotted. They bloom in summer and especially enjoy being planted by ponds and streams.

LIKES sun and moisture-retentive soil. Tolerates dappled shade, chalk and clay; coastal exposure.

STAKING required by taller varieties.

PROPAGATE by stem cuttings, division, seed.

Monarda
Bee Balm, Bergamot, Oswego Tea
60 x 60 cm (2 x 2 ft)

Crush the leaves of monarda and you'll smell Earl Grey tea! The aromatic foliage is just one of the attractions; the main benefit is the summer display of hooded flowers carried in tiers around the stems. 'Cambridge Scarlet' is the best variety with rosy crimson flowers; 'Croftway Pink' is a good paler pink, and 'Prairie Night' (syn. 'Prärienacht') a violet-purple.

LIKES sun and well-drained but moisture-retentive soil. Tolerates chalky or clay soils.

PROPAGATE by division.

Morina
90 x 30 cm (3 ft x 12 in)

The leaves of *M. longifolia* are just like those of a glossy thistle – don't uproot the plant by mistake when it's young. Later the leaves are longer and more handsome: then you'll have no difficulty in distinguishing them. The flower spikes of hooded white blooms appear above the leaf rosettes in summer. They turn to deep rose-pink as they age. A plant deserving greater popularity, and one of my all-time favourites.

LIKES sun and well-drained soil in a sheltered spot. Tolerates chalk and well-worked clay soil; coastal exposure.

PROPAGATE by division, seed.

Nepeta
Catmint
45 x 60 cm (18 in x 2 ft)

Our cat loves this plant so much that she chews it off at ground level every time it tries to emerge. *N. x faassenii* is the one you want. Its aromatic leaves are dusky grey and it has long stems of lavender-blue flowers in summer. 'Six Hills Giant' is the most robust variety.

LIKES sun and well-drained soil. Tolerates dry or chalky soil.

PROPAGATE by division, stem cuttings.

Oenothera
Evening Primrose
23–45 x 60 cm (9–18 in x 2 ft)

The bright yellow cup-shaped flowers of *O. macrocarpa* are held on 23 cm (9 in) stems right through summer, making this grand for the front of a border and a long-lasting display. Taller varieties like 'Fireworks' (*O. fruticosa* 'Fyrverkeri') 45 x 45 cm (18 x 18 in), with masses of yellow flowers and orange buds are even more showy.

LIKES full sun and well-drained soil. Tolerates dry and chalky soils; coastal exposure.

PROPAGATE by division, seed.

Paeonia
Peony
60–90 x 90 cm (2–3 x 3 ft)

Fleeting but fabulous, the spring-flowering Chinese peonies make a stunning show before any summer flowers have time to compete. There are dozens of varieties with double or single blooms of white, pink, crimson and magenta, and single kinds with crested centres. Pick where you like from nurserymen's pictures. Try *P. mlokosewitschii* (you'll have to point at the name if you can't say it). It makes a glorious show of golden goblets centred with yellow stamens and a red 'eye' in May.

LIKES full sun and a rich, well-drained soil, especially if it's chalky. Tolerates dry or clay soils, provided the latter is well worked. Plant peonies and leave them: they don't like disturbance.

PROPAGATE by division.

Papaver
Poppy
90 x 90 cm (3 x 3 ft)

The varieties of *P. orientale*, the oriental poppy, are flowers of June. It's a relatively brief display but one that can truthfully be described as dazzling. The massive bowl-shaped blooms of orange, salmon, pink, scarlet or white are

centred with a crown of black stamens and may be contrastingly blotched or picotee edged. Others have frilly-edged petals. 'Marcus Perry' is a good orange; 'Mrs Perry' a warm salmon-pink; and 'Picotée' is white-edged with orange; 'Black and White' is just as its name.
LIKES sun and well-drained soil, especially if it's chalky. Tolerates dry soil.
STAKING required.
PROPAGATE by division, root cuttings.

Penstemon

60 x 45 cm (2 ft x 18 in)

Many penstemons are rather tender, but there are now a good few hybrids that can be gambled with as hardy plants in the milder counties. All carry their foxglove-like flowers on elegant spikes and bloom generously from mid- to late summer. 'Garnet' ('Andenken an Friedrich Hahn') is rosy red; 'Sour Grapes' is lilac-purple; and 'Firebird' ('Schoenholzeri') is scarlet. There are other varieties with pink and salmon flowers.
LIKES a warm, sunny, sheltered spot in well-drained soil. Tolerates dry or chalky soil and warm coastal gardens.
PROPAGATE by stem cuttings.

Persicaria (syn. Polygonum)
Knotweed

Various sizes

Make a point of exploring this tribe: it offers such a varied and valuable collection of plants. *P. bistorta* 'Superba', 75 x 90 cm (2½–3 ft), is a spring beauty with green, dock-like leaves over which tower pink pokers. It continues to throw up a few blooms right through summer. *P. campanulata*, 90 x 90 cm (3 x 3 ft), is a more frothy treasure with dusky green leaves and branched flowerheads of miniature blush-pink bells from summer to autumn. *P. milettii*, 45 x 60 cm (18 in x 2 ft), is the brightest persicaria I know, with deep rose-red flower spikes carried over lush green leaves in summer. And finally a giant – *Fallopia japonica* 'Spectabilis' (was

P. cuspidatum 'Spectabile'), 1.8 x 2.4 m (6 x 8 ft) and more. Don't let this blighter loose unless you have plenty of room to spare. Where it can be entertained it will certainly entertain you in summer with its vigorous hollow stems that arch at the tips to show off the leaves. These are variegated green and creamy yellow with a tinge of pink, like some revolting foreign cheese. I can never make up my mind whether the plant is lurid or spectacular, but it always attracts gasps from onlookers.
LIKES sun and good, moisture-retentive soil. Tolerates dappled shade and clay or chalky soils; sheltered coastal gardens.
STAKING required by some.
PROPAGATE by division.

Phlox

1.2 m x 60 cm (4 x 2 ft)

Essential ingredients of a summer border, the varieties of *P. paniculata* are lovely plants with fat, rounded heads of flower, each bloom often being marked with a darker central eye. They'll flower from mid- to late summer, in shades of pink, crimson, lavender-blue, mauve, violet-purple and white. Take your pick from the glowing descriptions in nurserymen's catalogues. If your plants develop puckered, twisted leaves and swollen stems they've fallen prey to eelworm. Dig them up, take root cuttings (all else will be affected), and replant in uninfected ground.
LIKES sun and well-drained soil. Tolerates dry, chalky or clay soil but only if all three are enriched with organic matter and well worked.
STAKING required.
PROPAGATE by root cuttings, division.

Phormium
New Zealand Flax

60–90 x 60–90 cm (2–3 x 2–3 ft)

Certainly among the most spectacular foliage plants in the border, the phormiums send up great sword-leafed fountains of tough foliage that may be

rich bronze or striped with green, cream, orange and red. There's a new vogue for these plants, which are hardy (if they are forms of *P. cookianum*) or on the borderline of hardiness (in the case of *P. tenax* varieties). There are now plenty of named varieties of varying heights. Use them for evergreen foliage contrasts.
LIKES sun and a warm, sheltered spot in well-drained soil. Tolerates well-worked clay or chalky soil; coastal exposure in the milder counties. *P. tenax* varieties are only reliably hardy in southern counties.
PROPAGATE by division.

Physalis
Chinese Lantern Flower

60 x 60 cm (2 x 2 ft)

No flower arranger will want to be without this plant in the garden. In autumn the stems of *P. alkekengi* var. *franchetii* are hung with Chinese paper lanterns of bright orange. They keep their colour when dried. An easy-to-grow treasure.
LIKES sun and a well-drained soil. Tolerates dappled shade; dry, chalky or clay soil.
STAKING required.
PROPAGATE by division.

Physostegia
Obedient Plant

75 x 60 cm (2½ x 2 ft)

Here's a curiosity; the obedient plant produces densely packed flower spikes in late summer, and each of the tiny tubular blooms can be nudged on its stalk to any position you want – hence the common name. *P. virginiana* has two good varieties: 'Vivid', which is rich mauve-pink, compact at around 45 x 45 cm (18 x 18 in) and particularly late, flowering in early autumn; and 'Summer Snow', a white form.
LIKES sun and a good, well-drained soil that's not likely to dry out. Tolerates clay and chalky soils; coastal gardens.
PROPAGATE by division.

Platycodon
Balloon Flower
30–45 cm x 45 cm (12–18 in x 18 in)

The inflated buds of platycodon are pushed up over the greyish leaves where they open out into beautiful campanula flowers in mid- to late summer. *P. grandiflorus* has several varieties, of which var. *mariesii* is a good sky-blue, and 'Snowflake' a dainty white. Good front-of-the-border plants which are fun to 'pop'.

LIKES sun and a rich, well-drained but not dry soil. Tolerates clay and chalky soils.

PROPAGATE by division, seed, stem cuttings.

Polemonium
Jacob's Ladder
60–75 cm x 75 cm (2–2½ ft x 2 ft)

Attractive flowering and foliage plants with pinnate leaves carried thickly on upright stems that are topped with lavender-blue flower clusters in early summer. *P. caeruleum* is the commonest species; its white form is lovely. 'Pink Beauty' is mauve-pink. Can be short-lived if neglected.

LIKES sun and a rich, moisture-retentive soil. Tolerates shade; chalky and clay soil.

STAKING required.

PROPAGATE by division (regularly).

Polygonatum
Solomon's Seal
60 x 60–90 cm (2 x 2–3 ft)

I'm lucky enough to have this plant growing wild in my garden and it looks a treat in late spring when its arching stems drip with tiny ivory bells. The bold leaves sprout from the stems like wings. A fine foliage plant for use with other bold beauties like hostas and sword-leafed irises. The British native is *P. multiflorum. P.* x *hybridum* is beefier.

LIKES shade and a leafy, moisture-retentive soil. Tolerates chalk and well-worked, enriched clay.

PROPAGATE by division.

Potentilla
Cinquefoil
45 x 60 cm (18 in x 2 ft)

There are lots of hybrid herbaceous potentillas that can be used to bring brightness to beds and borders in summer. They offer double or single flowers in shades of red, yellow, orange and salmon carried on floppy stems over fingered, downy leaves. 'William Rollison' is a favourite double red, and 'Yellow Queen' a double yellow. The doubles last longer than the singles.

LIKES sun and a well-drained soil. Tolerates dry or chalky soil and coastal exposure.

STAKING required.

PROPAGATE by division.

Primula
Polyanthus
Various sizes

The polyanthus is the pride of spring in most folk's gardens, making neat mounds of primrose leaves that are iced with red, orange, yellow, blue or white flowers over many spring weeks. The plants grow to maybe 23 x 30 cm (9 x 12 in) but repay annual division after flowering. Try also the choice 'Garryarde' varieties of primrose with their dusky pastel flowers and bronze-burnished leaves. The candelabra primulas come in all sorts of colours, carrying their blooms in tiers up stems that may be anything from 30–90 cm (12 in–3 ft) tall. *P. japonica, P. pulverulenta, P. chungensis* and *P. bulleyana* are good examples, and *P. sikkimensis* has nodding clusters of sulphur-yellow bells. The others may be yellow, red, pink, orange, crimson, magenta or white. At Harlow Car Gardens near Harrogate they look better than anywhere else. Late spring and early summer is their season of glory.

LIKES sun or dappled shade and a leafy, peaty, moisture-retentive soil. Tolerates clay soil and chalky soil

(though the candelabra types prefer acid ground and sometimes fail on chalk).

PROPAGATE by seed, division.

Pulmonaria
Lungwort, Soldiers and Sailors
30 x 90 cm (12 in x 3 ft)

The lungwort is one of the earliest and most reliable flowers of spring. Its nodding clusters of pink and blue flowers unfurl in March and look a treat with hellebores. As they fade the bold, oval leaves, splashed with silver-grey, push up to take their place. *P. saccharata* is the type best in leaf, but for flowers (without the foliage spotting) try *P. rubra*, which has glorious, large, rich pink blooms especially early in the season. 'Munstead Blue' is a lungwort with especially good blue flowers.

LIKES gentle shade and a moisture-retentive soil. Tolerates clay and chalky soils; full sun but not drought.

PROPAGATE by division.

> *"No garden should be without sea hollies... the branched stems erupt in summer, carrying aloft spiky steel-blue flowers."*

Rheum
Rhubarb
2.4 x 1.5 m (8 x 5 ft)

The bold maroon leaves of *R. palmatum* 'Atrosanguineum' (syn. 'Atropurpureum') take some spectators aback in spring when they unfurl from huge scarlet buds of rather rude appearance. But soon the deeply cut rhubarb leaves assume stately proportions, eventually being accompanied by a towering rose-red flower spike in summer. By then the upper surfaces of the leaves are dull green, but the ruddiness remains beneath.

LIKES dappled shade and a rich, moisture-retentive soil that's not likely to dry out. Tolerates full sun (but not drought), clay and chalky soil.
PROPAGATE by division.

Rodgersia
Rodger's Bronze Leaf
90 x 90 cm (3 x 3 ft)

Imagine some bronze horse-chestnut leaves stuck on 60 cm (2 ft) stalks and pushed into the soil and you have some idea what rodgersia looks like, except that it is rather more graceful than my crude description implies. *R. pinnata* 'Superba' is perhaps the best form, and it carries frothy plumes of pink flowers over its leaves in summer.
LIKES dappled shade and a rich, moisture-retentive soil. Tolerates well-worked and enriched clay or chalky soils; full sun but not dry soil.
PROPAGATE by division.

Rudbeckia
Coneflower, Black-eyed Susan
75 x 60 cm (2½ x 2 ft)

More bright summer daisies with vivid yellow flowers centred with a prominent brown boss. 'Goldsturm' is the most popular variety and blooms from mid- to late summer. 'Goldquelle' starts and finishes rather later.
LIKES sun and a well-drained soil. Tolerates clay or chalky soils.
STAKING Requires staking.
PROPAGATE by division.

Salvia
Sage
Various sizes

The ornamental sages are a varied bunch, among the best of which are *S. nemorosa* 'Lubecca', 60 x 60 cm (2 x 2 ft), with slender spikes of violet-blue in summer; and a lovely

grey-foliaged plant, *S. argentea*, which produces a rosette of large, rumpled leaves covered in silky white wool. When the flower spike appears the leaves become a greyish green, so try to chop off the stalk as soon as you see it emerging. Older leaves can be cut off too. Best treated as a biennial on heavy soils; longer-lived on lighter earth.
LIKES full sun and a well-drained soil. Tolerates dry and chalky soils; coastal exposure.
STAKING required by all taller varieties.
PROPAGATE by seed, division.

Saponaria
Soapwort, Bouncing Bet
75 cm x 1.2 m (2½ x 4 ft)

Buy a plant by the name of *S. officinalis* 'Rosea Plena' and you'll own a glorious late-summer bloomer that produces masses of double pale pink campion flowers over a thicket of mid-green leaves. It starts in midsummer and doesn't finish until autumn. A treat with blue-grey foliage like that of *Hosta sieboldiana*. Not suitable for tidy gardeners.
LIKES sun and well-drained soil. Tolerates dappled shade; chalk and clay soils.
STAKING Requires staking.
PROPAGATE by division.

Scabiosa
Scabious
60 x 60 cm (2 x 2 ft)

Pale blue scabious always brings back memories of my grandfather, who grew the plant as a cut flower on his allotment. 'Clive Greaves' is the best variety of *S. caucasica*, and it produces masses of sky-blue-petalled flowers with their complicated white and lilac-

pink centres in summer. The green leaves stay low and are finely cut. Lovely among silver-foliaged plants.
LIKES sun and well-drained, especially chalky, soil. Tolerates well-worked clay; coastal exposure.
STAKING required.
PROPAGATE by division.

Late summer colours glow in this border in Waterperry Gardens, Oxfordshire: *Sedum* **'Autumn Joy',** **golden** *Rudbeckia* **and purple and mauve** *Aster.*

Sedum

Ice Plant, Stonecrop

30 x 45 cm (12 x 18 in)

Grow a patch of *S. spectabile* at the foot of a buddleja and you'll have a combination of plants that butterflies find irresistible. The grey-green succulent leaves start to push up in spring, making the plant a fine foliage subject. In late summer and autumn the flat flowerheads of dusky pink open to attract your eyes and the insects (though butterflies are said to be less fond of the variety 'Autumn Joy' than they are of the true species). From the human point of view 'Brilliant' is another good form with flowers of a warmer and rather deeper shade of pink.

LIKES full sun and a well-drained soil. Tolerates dry or chalky soils and well-worked clay; coastal exposure.

PROPAGATE by division, stem cuttings.

Sidalcea

90 x 90 cm (3 x 3 ft)

Like elegant miniature hollyhocks the sidalceas are bright clump formers for summer borders. They produce towering stems of mallow flowers at their best in the glorious pink of 'Rose Queen' or the rather shorter 'Loveliness'. There is also a smaller flowered white species, *S. candida*. The rich pinks are derived from *S. malviflora*.

LIKES full sun and a well-drained but moisture-retentive soil (they resent dryness at the roots). Tolerates chalk and well-worked clay.

STAKING required by taller varieties.

PROPAGATE by division.

Smilacina

False Spikenard

90 x 60 cm (3 x 2 ft)

Take the stems and leaves of Solomon's seal and the creamy white flower plumes of an astilbe; fasten the two together and you've got smilacina. It's a superbly attractive plant at its best in spring. The scent is deliciously overpowering.

LIKES shade and leafy, well-drained lime-free soil. Tolerates well-worked clay.

PROPAGATE by division.

Solidago

Golden Rod

60 cm–1.8 m x 60 cm–1.8 m (2–6 x 2–6 ft)

Railway embankments countrywide are decorated with the sceptre-like stems of golden rod in late summer and autumn, so happy is it to colonize any

Plants for ground cover

The measurement given after each plant is the recommended planting distance when large numbers are used for ground cover. All the plants listed, apart from Kniphofia and Nepeta, will grow in shade: entries in the A–Z section give more a precise indication of the type of shade the plants can tolerate.

VARIETY	PLANTING DISTANCE	VARIETY	PLANTING DISTANCE
● Acanthus	90 cm (3 ft)	● Geranium	45 cm (18 in)
● Ajuga	23 cm (9 in)	● Glyceria	60 cm (2 ft)
● Alchemilla	30 cm (12 in)	● Hemerocallis	60 cm (2 ft)
● Aruncus	60 cm (2 ft)	● Heuchera	30 cm (12 in)
● Astilbe	45 cm (18 in)	● Hosta	60 cm (2 ft)
● Astrantia	45 cm (18 in)	● Kniphofia (some)	60 cm (2 ft)
● Bergenia	45 cm (18 in)	● Lamium	45 cm (18 in)
● Blechnum	30 cm (12 in)	● Liriope	30 cm (12 in)
● Brunnera	30 cm (12 in)	● Lysimachia	30 cm (12 in)
● Calamintha	30 cm (12 in)	● Nepeta	60 cm (2 ft)
● Convallaria	23 cm (9 in)	● Persicaria (syn. *Polygonum*)	60 cm (2 ft)
● Corydalis	23 cm (9 in)	● Primula	23 cm (9 in)
● Crocosmia	30 cm (12 in)	● Pulmonaria	45 cm (18 in)
● Curtonus	45 cm (18 in)	● Saponaria	30 cm (12 in)
● Doronicum	45 cm (18 in)	● Stachys	30 cm (12 in)
● Epimedium	30 cm (12 in)	● Tradescantia	45 cm (18 in)
● Euphorbia	60 cm (2 ft)	● Viola	23 cm (9 in)

ground. Don't let the tall and dead-bottomed stems of sooty yellow flowers put you off growing the better varieties, which are brighter and less rampant. 'Goldenmosa' has an elegance and bright colouring that few others can rival. At 75 x 60 cm (2½ x 2 ft) it fits into any garden.
LIKES sun and well-drained soil. Tolerates dry, chalky and clay soil.
PROPAGATE by division.

Stachys
Betony, Lamb's Ears
45 x 60 cm (18 in x 2 ft)

There are two good species here: S. macrantha 'Superba' has toothed green leaves and dense heads of mauve-purple hooded flowers in summer. It makes deep ground cover and is smart without being prissy.

My second choice is S. byzantina (syn. S. lanata, S. olympica) the white and woolly lamb's ears, tongues or lugs (depending on your part of the

country). It makes a rag-rug of leaves over which tower spikes of tiny mauve flowers, interspersed with leafy bracts. Beth Chatto offers a variety known as 'Cotton Boll', whose flower cluster are orbs of white velvet dotted up the stem. These summer blooms are a treat and sadly lacking in the dreary 'Silver Carpet', often recommended as ground cover. It gets mildew and dies out in places and so needs frequent lifting and dividing.
LIKES full sun and a well-drained soil. Tolerates partial shade (S. macrantha only), dry and chalky soils; coastal exposure.
PROPAGATE by division.

Stipa
Feather Grass
1.8 x 1.2 m (6 x 4 ft)

A massive, elegant, oat-like grass with arching tufts of narrow green leaves over which hover the bronze flowerheads in summer. S. gigantea is a

bold, yet graceful grass that glints in the sun. The heads turn strawy as they age. Don't be without it if you can spare the space it requires.
LIKES full sun and a well-drained soil. Tolerates dry and chalky soil.
PROPAGATE by division.

Thalictrum
Meadow Rue
90 cm–1.5 m x 60 cm (3–5 x 2 ft)

Feathery mounds of columbine foliage, finely cut and grey-green, are topped in summer with airy sprays of fluffy flowers. The blooms are lilac-pink in T. delavayi (syn. T. dipterocarpum) and even more fluffy in 'Hewitt's Double'. Pays ground rent amply on account of both foliage and flowers.
LIKES sun and well-drained but moisture-retentive soil. Tolerates dappled shade; well-worked clay and chalky soils.
STAKING required.
PROPAGATE by division, seed.

Tradescantia
Spiderwort, Flower of a Day
60 x 60 cm (2 x 2 ft)

The varieties of *T. virginiana* (now more correctly known as *T. andersonia* group) are lush border plants with succulent stems and long, fresh-green leaves. In summer and on into autumn the stems are topped with three-petalled flowers of purplish blue – at least that's the colour of the type most frequently seen in gardens. Go to a nurseryman and you can choose from 'Osprey', white; 'Purewell Giant', magenta; and 'J. C. Weguelin', pale blue; as well as that good dark blue 'Isis'.
LIKES sun and well-drained soil. Tolerates dappled shade; well-worked clay and enriched chalky soils (they fail on poor, shallow chalk); coastal exposure.
STAKING required.
PROPAGATE by division.

Trollius
Globe Flower
60–90 x 60 cm (2–3 x 2 ft)

That bright yellow spherical flower of spring, *T. europaeus,* is a good streamside plant where its flowers are shown off well against a mound of rich green buttercup leaves, but the king of the race is *T. chinensis*, a bright orange spring and summer bloomer with flowers that are composed of an outer cup and an inner tuft of spiky petals. There is no brighter orange in the garden.
LIKES sun and moisture-retentive soil. Tolerates dappled shade; well-worked clay and chalky soil but never drought.
PROPAGATE by division.

Tropaeolum
Scotch Flame Flower
Climbing/trailing

Over the gloomy countenance of evergreen hedges the Scotch flame flower, *T. speciosum*, will blaze a trail of bright red tubular flowers in summer and autumn, accompanied by its neat, fingered leaves of fresh green. Once suited it will scramble to 3 m (10 ft) or more. *T. polyphyllum* is a different kettle of fish. It spreads its stems sideways over the soil for 90 cm (3 ft) or more. They are thickly plastered with blue-grey leaves and, in early summer, with pale orange blooms – a brave combination of colours.
LIKES *T. speciosum* likes the cool, damp northern counties better than those in the south, but it will often romp away if planted on the north side of hedges or trees. Plant the tubers on their sides 10 cm (4 in) deep and mark them well. It likes a peaty, moisture-retentive soil. *T. polyphyllum* likes deep, well-drained soil and a sunny spot. Plant its tubers 30 cm (12 in) deep. Both plants die down after flowering.
PROPAGATE by division.

Verbascum
Mullein
45 cm–1.8 m x 30–90 cm

Many mulleins are biennial and die after flowering, but a few will stay with you for years. Two in particular: 'Golden Bush', 60 x 60 cm (2 x 2 ft), with spires of yellow flowers in summer, and *V. chaixii*, 90 x 60 cm (3 x 2 ft), whose yellow blooms are spotted in the centre with purple, are good garden plants. Varieties like 'Gainsborough' are not reliably perennial but can be increased by root cuttings annually.
LIKES sunny spots in well-drained soil. Tolerates dry and chalky soil and well-worked clay.
PROPAGATE by seed, division, root cuttings.

Veronica
Various sizes

If you're seeking upright spires of blue summer flowers, you can safely plump for veronicas. *V. spicata*, 60 x 60 cm (2 x 2 ft), offers them, and provides additional shades in its varieties 'Barcarolle', rose pink, and 'Red Fox', deep rose. 'Icicle' will give you white spikes.
LIKES sun and a well-drained soil. Tolerates dry, clay or chalky soils; coastal exposure.
STAKING required by taller varieties.
PROPAGATE by division.

Viola
Violet, Pansy
30 x 90 cm (12 in x 3 ft)

Charming plants, violas can grow in the tiniest, dimmest corner. I'll pick just two. *V. cornuta*, the horned violet, makes sprawling clumps of green leaves alive with pale lavender or white flowers in summer. Clip over the plants in late July and they'll bloom again in autumn. *V. labradorica* 'Purpurea' (now *V. riviniana* Purpurea Group), much neater at around 10 cm (4 in), makes carpets of maroon leaves, studded with lavender-purple flowers in spring.
LIKES dappled shade and a well-drained but moisture-retentive soil. Tolerates heavy shade or sun; chalky or well-worked clay soil.
PROPAGATE by division, seed, stem cuttings.

Zantedeschia
Arum Lily
90 x 60 cm (3 x 2 ft)

Bold, lustrous, juicy green arrowheads of leaves and white vase-shaped flowers centred with a yellow club-like spadix are the hallmarks of *Z. aethiopica*. It will bloom annually in summer in sheltered gardens. Its variety 'Crowborough' is apparently more tolerant of dry soils. Both need the winter protection of dry straw or bracken until well established.
LIKES sun or gentle shade and a moisture-retentive, preferably boggy soil. Tolerates ordinary well-drained soil but not drought; coastal exposure.
PROPAGATE by division, root cuttings, seed.

annuals, biennials and bedding plants

Annuals and biennials are the

cheerful summer visitors,

bringing a splendid variety

of colour, form and texture

to borders, windowboxes,

hanging baskets and tubs

AKE SOME BLUE LOBELIA AND SOME white alyssum and plant them alternately along the edge of a flowerbed. Plant behind them a dense array of orange French marigolds, and behind these a forest of scarlet salvias, perhaps with a fuchsia or white-leaved *Senecio cineraria* to act as a dot plant. And there you have it: the typical bedding out scheme. Nothing in the garden will be brighter – and nothing will be less inspiring!

PLANNING COLOUR SCHEMES

Persuading gardeners to be adventurous with their bedding out might have been the eighth labour of Hercules, so difficult is it to accomplish. Now I'm not sneering at lobelia, alyssum, French marigolds and salvias (even though I have to try really hard to like the last two), I'm sneering at the way they are used. People who'd never dream of painting a room of their house in contrasting shades of red, orange, blue and white, will do it to a border in their garden. But it's much more fun to think of a different colour scheme for your bedding every year and to avoid planting in serried ranks as though your bedders were advancing troops clad in their ceremonial colours. Plan each bed or border with a particular colour theme: it will have tremendous impact. If you insist on a rainbow border, then plan one on paper so that the colours are displayed gradually as you round a corner or progress along the bed; that way the spectacle can be fun, rather than a reason for taking out the Polaroid.

The beauty of bedders

But before all dedicated bedders flip over a few pages, I'll cool down and sing the praises of a grand bunch of plants. Annuals, biennials and bedding plants are invaluable in any garden for their cheapness, cheerfulness and speedy growth. They are nearly all raised from seeds, which will fill you with a deep sense of achievement; they are valuable gap-fillers, especially in new gardens when the more permanent shrubby occupants have not yet filled their allotted space; and they offer a surprising variety of form, texture and colour. Almost all of them adore full sun and a well-drained soil; those that are shade-tolerant are indicated in the A–Z section.

Consider flower and foliage contrasts when planting annuals; here sweet pea is set off to perfection by the golden foliage of *Gleditsia triacanthos* 'Sunburst'.

WHAT ARE BEDDING PLANTS?

The names given to the different groups of bedding plants (a term that embraces any temporary garden occupant) can be confusing, but basically this is what they mean:

HARDY ANNUALS For a start, annuals are those plants that complete their life cycle – from seed to flowering and setting new seed – within the space of a year. If you want a quick mnemonic, think of *Beano* and *Dandy* annuals: both last for just a year.

Hardy annuals are the bold little blighters that can be sown outdoors in April to bloom *in situ* later on in the summer. Some of them are even so tough that they can be sown outdoors in September to struggle through the winter and flower quite early the following summer. Doesn't this make them biennials? No: they are still flowering within 12 months of being sown.

HALF-HARDY ANNUALS are more lily-livered. They need to be sown in pots in a greenhouse or porch or on a windowsill where they can be coaxed into action with a little warmth. As soon as they emerge they need pricking out (that strange phrase that brings a smirk to the novice's cheeks) into seed trays, and growing on, before being hardened off (that is, gradually accustomed to outdoor temperatures). These are the plants that are bought by the boxful from garden centres and greengrocers all over the country in early summer. Only when all danger of frost is past can they be planted out.

TENDER ANNUALS fall into much the same category, though often these are grown in a greenhouse for all their brief lives. If you simply cannot provide these plants with the protection they need to germinate, don't worry. Some of them can be sown outdoors in late

May as for hardy annuals. They'll flower later, but are nonetheless welcome for that.

BIENNIALS Gardeners are not known for their perversity, but it's a fact that most of the plants they grow as biennials are truly perennials. Take the wallflower for instance: it will make a small shrub if grown on for several years, but it won't be as plastered with flowers as it was in its youth. True biennials complete their life cycle within the space of two years. They are sown during one year and grown on to flower and set seed the next. Here we are not talking so much about calendar years as about 12-month periods. Most biennials are sown in May to bloom the following May and June before they seed themselves and die off, probably during the summer. The whole episode probably takes about 14 months, but this varies from plant to plant.

> *"Plan each bed or border with a particular colour theme: it will have tremendous impact."*

OTHER BEDDING PLANTS Gardeners love exceptions, and there is a host of superb bedding plants that are really tender perennials: pelargoniums (geraniums), greenhouse fuchsias and the like. These must be overwintered in a greenhouse or on a windowsill where the frost can't get at them. Most can be propagated from cuttings each spring or autumn, so youngsters can be used each year, instead of the ancient gnarled parents who have just about exhausted themselves during a summer of over-generous blooming.

RAISING THE PLANTS

The techniques for raising the plants from seed vary slightly according to the plants' hardiness and length of life. The following are the methods generally used for each group:

Hardy annuals

These plants are sown in prepared patches of soil in beds and borders, usually among the permanent inhabitants, but there's nothing to stop you from having a bed devoted entirely to them. Fork over the earth in March and scatter over it a dusting of blood, bone and fishmeal at the rate of about a handful to the square metre (square yard). Don't add too much manure or compost: it turns the plants into Billy Bunters – fat and full of leaf, but short on flowers.

PREPARING THE SOIL April (and on through May for later summer flowers) is a good time to sow, for by then the soil has usually warmed up a little but is still moist. Rake over the surface of the soil to break it down a little (don't over-rake or the surface will cake in the first shower of rain) and mark out the shape or drift that is to be occupied by each plant. Use the rake handle or a trail of sand to show each drift shape.

PLANNING YOUR BORDER You can plan your border or bed in advance on a sheet of paper if you like, or rely on inspiration when you're out in the garden. Either way, try to place most of the taller plants at the back of the bed and the smaller ones at the front, but vary this arrangement occasionally and bring tall plants forward. They will create bays in the bed and make for a few surprises: the smaller plants crouching behind them will be revealed as you stroll along.

SOWING THE SEED With the soil prepared and the drifts marked out you are ready to sow. First, draw the rake across each drift to leave tiny furrows. Scatter the seeds over the surface and lightly rake in the opposite direction to cover them. That's all they need, apart from labelling. Failures usually occur either as a result of the seeds being buried too deeply, or because they've been allowed to dry out during germination. Keep a watering can or lawn sprinkler handy and really soak the soil before it has a chance to dry out. There's also a slight chance that cats might patronize the area when performing their vital functions. Twiggy pea sticks laid on the ground will discourage them. (Remove them after germination.)

THINNING OUT When the seedlings emerge they'll need thinning out to give the survivors room to grow. Thin them twice: once to a spacing of 5 cm (2 in), and finally, when they are touching again, to the recommended spacing. Instead of pulling up the unwanted seedlings, pinch them off at soil level. This prevents the roots of the remaining plants from being disturbed. Alternatively dig them up with a trowel and they'll often transplant quite well to fill other gaps.

PROVIDING SUPPORT Most annuals can support themselves. Some can't. Push twiggy pea sticks among the feeble kinds when they are 15 cm (6 in) high; they'll soon grow to mask the supports.

Half-hardy annuals

Half-hardy annuals are sown in pots, usually during March, in a greenhouse or on a windowsill. Scatter the

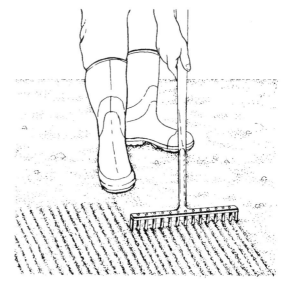

Sowing hardy annuals

Hardy annuals can be sown directly in the garden. Rake over the surface of the soil to break it down, then lightly rake again to create tiny furrows.

Annuals that need supporting, such as chrysanthemums, sunflowers, poppies, and sweet peas, can be held up unobtrusively if a few twiggy branches are pushed into the soil around them when they are about 15 cm (6 in) high. Don't overdo it!

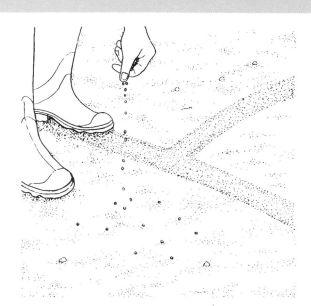

Mark out with trails of sand, or with the rake handle, the areas – or drifts – to be occupied by each plant. Scatter the seeds thinly and evenly over the surface of the soil.

Lightly rake in the opposite direction to cover the seeds; label each drift. Make sure that the soil is kept moist during germination. Plastic netting will deter birds.

seeds thinly on the surface of moist seed compost that has been firmed down to 1 cm (½ in) below the pot rim. Dust-fine seeds such as begonias and lobelia need no further covering, but most seeds can be lightly covered with sieved seed compost. Place a label in the pot, cover with a sheet of glass or polythene, then place a piece of newspaper over it. Stand the pots where they can be kept at a temperature of around 18–21°C (64–70°F). Check them every day and remove glass and paper as soon as the first seedling breaks the surface. Water by immersing the pot to half its depth in a bowl of water whenever the surface of the compost is just beginning to look dry.

PRICKING OUT Transfer the seedlings to trays of potting compost with a pencil, carefully lifting them individually and making a hole into which the roots can be lowered. Firm the compost around each seedling and then water them in.

HARDENING OFF Grow the seedlings on in gentle heat and good light until early May, when they can be gradually accustomed to the temperatures outdoors: stand them out during the day and bring them under cover at night. By late May (or early June in the cooler north) they can stand outdoors at all times, for by then all danger of frost should be past and they can be planted out.

PLANTING Plant them with a trowel (after giving them a really good soak in their trays) at the distances recommended in the chart. Water them in with a lawn sprinkler left running for a good two hours, and soak them again at any time when the earth around them starts to look dry. Forget to water and you'll have wasted your time – they'll turn crisp and die.

Biennials

Biennials are usually sown on the vegetable plot where they can be trickled thinly into drills and transplanted to a wider spacing of 15–23 cm (6–9 in) when they are large enough to lift with a trowel. Sow during May and June, and the first transplanting can be carried out in July – still in rows on the vegetable plot. In September the plants can be dug up and planted at their final spacing in beds and borders. Most biennials are grown for spring bedding schemes but there are exceptions and these are indicated in the A–Z section.

Tender perennials

Tender perennials are usually planted out in late May or early June along with the half-hardy annuals, and lifted and brought under cover during September before the frosts strike. Their cultivation is covered in Chapter 19 Greenhouse Gardening.

A-Z

OF

annuals, biennials and bedding plants

I N THIS A–Z SECTION, THE PLANTS are arranged alphabetically in their respective groups, according to whether they are hardy annuals, half-hardy annuals or biennials.

HARDY ANNUALS

Hardy annuals are grown in profusion all over the country, but what they're called varies from one place to another – common names are anything but common!

To make it easier to find these plants, I've listed them under the names most commonly used in seed catalogues – so it's a weird mixture of botanical and common names.

I have included here some charming flowers that are facing extinction. They are still to be had for a few pence but, if gardeners don't do something about it soon, a host of beautiful hardy

annuals will disappear from the seed catalogues, leaving us with more and more petunias and French marigolds. Try to grow a few of these before the seedsmen scrap them because of lack of demand. (See the list on p.146 for those most in need of your patronage.)

Acroclinium

Rhodanthe chlorocephala ssp. *rosea*

Height 45 cm (18 in)

Final spacing 23 cm (9 in)

Dainty pink and white 'everlasting' flowers.

sow in spring.

staking required.

Adonis aestivalis

Pheasant's Eye

Height 45 cm (18 in)

Final spacing 23 cm (9 in)

Feathery leaves; scarlet, black-eyed flowers.

sow in spring/autumn.

Agrostemma 'Milas'

Corn Cockle

Height 90 cm (3 ft)

Final spacing 23 cm (9 in)

Lovely pink blooms pencilled with darker streaks.

sow in spring/autumn.

staking required.

Alyssum

Sweet Alyssum

Height 10 cm (4 in)

Final spacing 15 cm (6 in)

Pink, white or violet scented flowers in dense bunches.

sow in spring/autumn.

Anchusa capensis 'Blue Angel'

Height 23 cm (9 in)

Final spacing 30 cm (12 in)

Spreading domes of blue forget-me-not flowers.

sow in spring.

Argemone

Prickly Poppy

Height 60 cm (2 ft)

Final spacing 30 cm (12 in)

Prickly, thistle-like foliage and yellow flowers.

sow in spring.

Asperula azurea setosa

Annual Woodruff

Height 30 cm (12 in)

Final spacing 23 cm (9 in)

Pale blue, tubular flowers carried in rounded heads. Tolerates some shade.

sow in spring.

Atriplex hortensis var. *rubra*

Orach

Height 1.2 m (4 ft)

Final spacing 45 cm (18 in)

Dock-like flowerheads and leaves of deep maroon.

sow in spring.

Cabbage, Ornamental

Height 30 cm (12 in)

Final spacing 45 cm (18 in)

Cabbages with cream, white or pink hearts. Stunning!

sow in spring.

Calendula

Pot Marigold

Height 30 cm (12 in) plus

Final spacing 23 cm (9 in)

Cream, yellow or orange daisies; double or single. Thrives in poor soil in sun or partial shade.

sow in spring/autumn.

Canary Creeper

Tropaeolum peregrinum

Climber

Fingered green leaves and frilly yellow flowers.

sow in spring.

staking required.

Candytuft

Iberis

Height 30 cm (12 in)

Final spacing 10 cm (4 in)

Lance-shaped leaves, and clusters of rounded flowers in white, pink, lilac or carmine.

SOW in spring/autumn.

Chrysanthemum carinatum

Height 60 cm (2 ft)

Final spacing 30 cm (12 in)

Single daisies banded in orange, yellow, red and white.

SOW in spring/autumn.

STAKING required.

Clarkia elegans (C. unguiculata)

Height 60 cm (2 ft)

Final spacing 23 cm (9 in)

Double varieties are best. Rosettes of pink, mauve or crimson blooms.

SOW in spring/autumn.

STAKING required.

Convolvulus 'Blue Flash'

Height 15 cm (6 in)

Final spacing 15 cm (6 in)

Blue trumpets centred with yellow and white.

SOW in spring.

Coreopsis

Height 30 cm (12 in) plus

Final spacing 23 cm (9 in)

Single yellow flowers with red centres. Very bright.

SOW in spring/autumn.

Cornflower

Centaurea cyanus

Height 90 cm (3 ft)

Final spacing 23 cm (9 in)

Sprays of blue, white or pink fluffy flowerheads.

SOW in spring/autumn.

STAKING required.

Crepis rubra

Hawksbeard

Height 45 cm (18 in)

Final spacing 15 cm (6 in)

Endearingly dainty pink 'dandelion' flowers.

SOW in spring/autumn.

STAKING Requires staking.

Dimorphotheca

Star of the Veldt

Height 23 cm (9 in)

Final spacing 15 cm (6 in)

Delightful white, yellow or orange daisies.

SOW in spring.

Dracocephalum moldavica

Dragon's Head

Height 60 cm (2 ft)

Final spacing 15 cm (6 in)

Spires of hooded lavender-blue flowers. Aromatic.

SOW in spring.

STAKING required.

Echium

Viper's Bugloss

Height 30 cm (12 in)

Final spacing 23 cm (9 in)

Violet-blue cup-shaped flowers among fluffy buds.

SOW in spring/autumn.

Emilia

Tassel Flower, Cacalia

Height 45 cm (18 in)

Final spacing 15 cm (6 in)

Fluffy 'composite' flowerheads of burning orange.

SOW in spring.

Eschscholzia

Californian Poppy

Height 30 cm (12 in)

Final spacing 15 cm (6 in)

Lacy foliage and poppy flowers of red, pink, yellow, orange or white.

SOW in spring/autumn.

Gilia 'Summer Song'

Height 30 cm (12 in)

Final spacing 15 cm (6 in)

Masses of lilac-blue and white five-petalled flowers.

SOW in spring/autumn.

Godetia

(Dwarf varieties *Clarkia*)

Height 30 cm (12 in)

Final spacing 15 cm (6 in)

Wide-faced blooms in shades of pink, red and white.

SOW in spring/autumn.

Gypsophila elegans

Height 45 cm (18 in)

Final spacing 15 cm (6 in)

Sprays of tiny white or pink flowers.

SOW in spring/autumn.

STAKING required.

Ionopsidium

Violet Cress

Height 8 cm (3 in)

A carpeter with plenty of pale lilac flowers. Enjoys a little shade.

SOW in spring/autumn.

Kochia

Burning Bush, Bassia

Height 60 cm (2 ft)

Final spacing 45 cm (18 in)

Columns of green turning red in autumn.

SOW in spring.

Larkspur

Annual Delphinium

Height 90 cm (3 ft)

Final spacing 23 cm (9 in)

Feathery leaves and spires of blue, pink, violet or white.

SOW in spring/autumn.

STAKING required.

Lavatera
Mallow

Height 60 cm (2 ft)

Final spacing 30 cm (12 in)

Huge trumpet-shaped flowers of pink ('Silver Cup') or white ('Mont Blanc') on a bushy plant. Thrives in sun or light shade.
SOW in spring.
STAKING required.

Layia elegans
Tidy Tips

Height 30 cm (12 in)

Final spacing 15 cm (6 in)

Yellow daisies whose petals are tipped with white.
SOW in spring.

Legousia speculum-veneris
Venus Looking Glass

Height 30 cm (12 in)

Final spacing 10 cm (4 in)

Violet-blue flowers with white eyes.
SOW in spring/autumn.

Leptosiphon
Stardust

Height 10 cm (4 in)

Final spacing 5 cm (2 in)

Small flowers of orange, red, cream or yellow over needle-like leaves.
SOW in spring.

Limnanthes
Poached Egg Flower

Height 23 cm (9 in)

Final spacing 10 cm (4 in)

Feathery green leaves and two-toned white and yellow blooms (hence the common name). The flowers are highly attractive to bees.
SOW in spring/autumn.

Linaria 'Fairy Bouquet'
Toadflax

Height 23 cm (9 in)

Final spacing 10 cm (4 in)

Tiny snapdragon flowers in a bright range of colours.
SOW in spring/autumn.

Linum grandiflorum 'Rubrum'
Scarlet Flax

Height 30 cm (12 in)

Final spacing 10 cm (4 in)

Single wide-faced flowers of bright red.
SOW in spring.

Lonas inodora

Height 30 cm (12 in)

Final spacing 15 cm (6 in)

Clusters of bright yellow powder-puff flowers.
SOW in spring.

Love-lies-bleeding
Amaranthus caudatos

Height 90 cm (3 ft)

Final spacing 60 cm (2 ft)

Oval green leaves and drooping velvet tassels of crimson or green.
SOW in spring.

With its delicate foliage and white-edged yellow flowers, *Limnanthes douglasii* is a delightful edging plant.

Malope

Height 75 cm (2½ ft)

Final spacing 23 cm (9 in)

Single mallow flowers of pink, white or crimson.

sow in spring.

Matthiola longipetula
(syn. ***bicornis***)

Night-scented Stock

Height 23 cm (9 in)

Dingy lilac, strongly perfumed at night.

sow in spring, mixed with Virginian stocks.

Mentzelia

Height 45 cm (18 in)

Final spacing 23 cm (9 in)

Deeply cut leaves and a profusion of scented, pointed-petalled yellow

The glowing colours and parasol-shaped leaves of *Tropaeolum majus* (nasturtium) edge this border, with spikes of purple *Nepeta* behind.

flowers with feathery stamens.

sow in spring.

Mignonette

Reseda odorata

Height 30 cm (12 in)

Final spacing 10 cm (4 in)

Fluffy rusty-orange flowers; strongly perfumed.

sow in spring.

Moluccella

Bells of Ireland

Height 90 cm (3 ft)

Final spacing 23 cm (9 in)

Spires of white flowers that fall to reveal large, green, cockle-shaped calyces borne on graceful stems.

sow in spring.

Nasturtium

Tropaeolum majus

Height 30 cm (12 in)

Final spacing 30 cm (12 in)

Parasol-shaped leaves and red, orange

or yellow flowers that will grow in poor but free-draining soil.

sow in spring.

Nemophila

Baby Blue Eyes

Height 15 cm (6 in)

Final spacing 8 cm (3 in)

Carpeter with sky-blue flowers centred with white.

sow in spring/autumn.

Nicandra

Shoo-fly Plant

Height 75 cm (2½ ft)

Final spacing 30 cm (12 in)

Pale lavender and white flowers; inflated seed cases.

sow in spring.

Nigella

Love-in-a-mist

Height 45 cm (18 in)

Final spacing 15 cm (6 in)

Feathery foliage and blue, white or

pink flowers. The dried seedheads are popular with flower arrangers.
SOW in spring/autumn.

Perilla

Height 60 cm (2 ft)

Final spacing 30 cm (12 in)

Deeply cut purple foliage – like a dark coleus.
SOW in spring.

Phacelia campanularia

Height 23 cm (9 in)

Final spacing 8 cm (3 in)

Pure gentian blue bells with bright yellow stamens – indispensable.
SOW in spring/autumn.

Poppy 'Pink Chiffon'

Height 75 cm (2½ ft)

Final spacing 23 cm (9 in)

Double pink, peony-like blooms.
SOW in spring/autumn.
STAKING required.

Poppy, Shirley

Height 60 cm (2 ft)

Final spacing 15 cm (6 in)

Lovely poppies of pink, yellow, orange and red.
SOW in spring/autumn.
STAKING required.

Rhodanthe

Helipterum manglesii

Height 30 cm (12 in)

Final spacing 15 cm (6 in)

Dainty pink 'everlasting' daisies.
SOW in spring.

Rudbeckia

Coneflower

Height 60 cm (2 ft)

Final spacing 15 cm (6 in)

Orange ('Marmalade') or mahogany ('Rustic Dwarf') daisies.
SOW in spring.

Use them or lose them

Here is a selection of beautiful hardy annuals that desperately need your patronage: do try to grow some of them before the seedsmen decide to remove them from their catalogues because of lack of demand.

- *Adonis aestivalis*
- *Agrostemma 'Milas'*
- *Argemone*
- *Asperula azurea setosa*
- *Bartonia*
- *Campanula speculum 'Violetta'*
- *Crepis rubra*
- *Dracocephalum moldavica*
- *Echium*
- *Emilia*
- *Gilia 'Summer Song'*
- *Ionopsidium*
- *Layia elegans*
- *Leptosiphon*
- *Limnanthes*
- *Linaria 'Fairy Bouquet'*
- *Linum grandiflorum 'Rubrum'*
- *Lonas inodora*
- *Malope*
- *Mignonette*
- *Nemophila*
- *Nicandra*
- *Phacelia campanularia*
- *Saponaria vaccaria*
- *Viscaria 'Blue Angel'*

Salvia viridis

Clary

Height 45 cm (18 in)

Final spacing 15 cm (6 in)

Tall spires of pink, white or blue bracts.
SOW in spring/autumn.

Saponaria vaccaria

Height 60 cm (2 ft)

Final spacing 15 cm (6 in)

Plenty of dainty pink flowers.
SOW in spring/autumn.
STAKING required.

Sunflower

Helianthus

Height 3 m (10 ft) plus

Final spacing 60 cm (2 ft)

Massive yellow or orange daisies atop gigantic stalks.
SOW in spring.
STAKING Requires staking.

Sweet Pea

Lathyrus odoratus

Height 1.8 m (6 ft) plus

Final spacing 30 cm (12 in)

Fragrant pea flowers in assorted colours.
SOW in spring/autumn.
STAKING Requires staking.

Sweet Pea, Jet Set Group

Height 90 cm (3 ft)

Final spacing 15 cm (6 in)

Easy to support with twiggy branches.
SOW in spring/autumn.
STAKING required.

Sweet Sultan

Centaurea moschata, Amberboa moschata

Height 45 cm (18 in)

Final spacing 23 cm (9 in)

Starry 'cornflower' blooms of purple, yellow, pink and white.
SOW in spring.

Viscaria 'Blue Angel'

Height 30 cm (12 in)

Final spacing 10 cm (4 in)

Five-petalled lavender-blue flowers. Thrives in sun or partial shade.
SOW in spring.

Xeranthemum

Height 60 cm (2 ft)

Final spacing 15 cm (6 in)

'Everlasting' daisy flowers of pink, yellow and white.
SOW in spring.
STAKING required.

HALF-HARDY ANNUALS

These slightly tender plants are available in greater variety than you'd think. Steer yourself away from the commoner types to those that are less frequently planted. Generally speaking, those varieties described as F1 hybrids are more expensive than all others, but they usually offer superb value for money, producing high quality and uniform plants. I have indicated which plants can be sown outdoors and, again, I have listed the plants under the names that are usually used in seedsmen's catalogues.

Ageratum
Floss Flower

Height 15–23 cm (6–9 in)

Spacing 15 cm (6 in)

Hairy green leaves topped with fluffy lavender-blue or white pom-poms.

Amaranthus 'Illumination'

Height 75 cm (2½ ft)

Spacing 45 cm (18 in)

Brilliant leaves marked red, bronze, yellow and green.

Anagallis 'Coerulea'

Height 15 cm (6 in)

Spacing 15 cm (6 in)

True blue, large pimpernel flowers over green domes of foliage.

SOWING Can be sown outdoors.

Antirrhinum
Snapdragon

Height 15–90 cm (6 in–3 ft)

Spacing 23 cm (9 in)

Lipped, tubular flowers of every hue except blue or green.

Arctotis
African Daisy

Height 45 cm (18 in)

Spacing 23 cm (9 in)

Vibrant daisies of red, orange, yellow, pink or white.

Half-hardies to sow outdoors

- *Anagallis* 'Coerulea'
- *Aster*
- *Brachyscome*
- *Cleome spinosa*
- *Gourd*
- *Helichrysum*
- *Mesembryanthemum*
- *Mimulus*
- *Nolana* 'Lavender Gown'
- *Phlox drummondii*
- *Portulaca*
- *Statice*
- *Stocks, Ten-week*

Aster

Height 30–45 cm (18 in)

Spacing 23 cm (9 in)

Double or single daisies in a wide range of colours.

SOWING Can be sown outdoors.

Begonia semperflorens

Height 15 cm (6 in)

Spacing 15 cm (6 in)

Shiny leaves of green or brown; red, pink or white flowers.

The fluffy pink blooms of *Ageratum houstonianum* 'Bavaria' flower freely throughout the summer.

Brachyscome
Swan River Daisy

Height 15 cm (6 in)

Spacing 10 cm (4 in)

Finely cut leaves and blue or white daisy flowers.
SOWING Can be sown outdoors.

Calandrinia umbellata
Rock Purslane

Height 15 cm (6 in)

Spacing 15 cm (6 in)

Neat tufts of foliage topped with crimson-magenta flowers.

Calceolaria 'Sunshine'

Height 23 cm (9 in)

Spacing 23 cm (9 in)

Bright yellow pouch-like flowers over green leaves.

Carnation 'Chabaud Mixed'

Height 45 cm (18 in)

Spacing 15 cm (6 in)

'Annual' carnations of mixed colours.

Carnation 'Dwarf Mixed'

Height 30 cm (12 in)

Spacing 23 cm (9 in)

F1 hybrid mixture; pricey but very showy.

Centaurea gymnocarpa

Height 45 cm (18 in)

Spacing 30 cm (12 in)

Finely cut grey leaves; an exceptional foliage plant.

The single, dahlia-like flowers of *Cosmos* seem to float above the delicate ferny foliage.

Cleome spinosa
Spider Flower

Height 75 cm (2½ ft)

Spacing 30 cm (12 in)

Spidery flowers of pink or white.
SOWING Can be sown outdoors.

Cosmos
Cosmea

Height 60–90 cm (2–3 ft)

Spacing 23 cm (9 in)

Single 'dahlia' flowers of red, yellow, orange, pink or white.

Dahlia

Height 30 cm–1.2 m (12 in–4 ft)

Spacing 30 cm (12 in)

Fleshy leaves and double or single mixed flowers.

Dahlia 'Redskin'

Height 45 cm (18 in)

Spacing 30 cm (12 in)

Mixed flowers over deep bronze-purple leaves.

Delphinium 'Blue Butterfly'

Height 45 cm (18 in)

Spacing 30 cm (12 in)

Tall spires of rich blue flowers.

Dianthus heddewigii
Pink

Height 15–30 cm (6–12 in)

Spacing 15 cm (6 in)

Brilliant annual pinks of red, pink, white and bi-coloured flowers; there are some superb F1 hybrids; try 'Queen's Court'.

Gaillardia
Blanket Flower

Height 30–60 cm (12 in–2 ft)

Spacing 23 cm (9 in)

Double or single daisies of orange, red and yellow.

Gazania

Height 30 cm (12 in)

Spacing 15 cm (6 in)

Single starry daisies often bi-coloured in red, orange and yellow. Likes a sunny location.

Gourd

Climber

Spacing 30 cm (12 in)

Cucumber-like vine with decorative fruits of orange, yellow and green.
SOWING Can be sown outdoors.

Helichrysum

Strawflower

Height 45 cm (18 in)

Spacing 15 cm (6 in)

'Everlasting' flowers of orange, yellow, red and white.
SOWING Can be sown outdoors.

Heliotrope

Heliotropium, **Cherry Pie**

Height 45 cm (18 in)

Spacing 30 cm (12 in)

Lilac-purple scented flower clusters.

Impatiens

Busy Lizzie

Height 23 cm (9 in)

Spacing 23 cm (9 in)

Fleshy leaves and stems; red, white, orange or magenta flowers.

Ipomoea

Morning Glory

Climber

Spacing 30 cm (12 in)

Trumpets of sky-blue or carmine.

Lobelia

Height 10 cm (4 in)

Spacing 10 cm (4 in)

Lipped flowers of blue, white or carmine over fresh green leaves.

Marigold, African

Height 45–60 cm (18 in–2 ft)

Spacing 30 cm (12 in)

Double flowers of orange or yellow.

Marigold, Afro-French

Height 45 cm (18 in)

Spacing 23 cm (9 in)

Very floriferous. 'Nell Gwynn' is one of the best.

Marigold, French

Height 10–30 cm (4–12 in)

Spacing 15–23 cm (6–9 in)

Neat aromatic plants with smaller double blooms of orange and yellow.

Matricaria 'Golden Ball'

Feverfew, *Tanacetum*

Height 30 cm (12 in)

Spacing 30 cm (12 in)

Rounded plants covered in yellow 'button' flowers

Mesembryanthemum

Livingstone Daisy

Height 8 cm (3 in)

Spacing 15 cm (6 in)

Trailer with orange, cerise, pink or yellow daisy flowers.
SOWING Can be sown outdoors.

Mimulus

Monkey Flower

Height 30 cm (12 in)

Spacing 15 cm (6 in)

Red, orange or yellow trumpets, often spotted. Tolerates a little shade.
SOWING Can be sown outdoors.

Mirabilis

Four o'clock Plant

Height 45 cm (18 in)

Spacing 30 cm (12 in)

Red, yellow or white trumpets open in late afternoon.

Nemesia

Height 23 cm (9 in)

Spacing 23 cm (9 in)

Large-lipped flowers of red, yellow, orange or white.

Nicotiana

Tobacco Plant

Height 30–75 cm (12 in–2½ ft)

Spacing 23 cm (9 in)

Fragrant starry flowers of red, yellow, green or white.

Nolana 'Lavender Gown'

Height 15 cm (6 in)

Spacing 15 cm (6 in)

Mounds of lavender-blue flowers centred with white and yellow.
SOWING Can be sown outdoors.

Penstemon

Height 60 cm (2 ft)

Spacing 23 cm (9 in)

Spires of colourful foxglove flowers.

Petunia

Height 23 cm (9 in)

Spacing 23 cm (9 in)

Huge trumpets, some fully double, in assorted colours; some are striped.

Phlox drummondii

Height 15–30 cm (6–12 in)

Spacing 15 cm (6 in)

Dense heads of 'primula' flowers in assorted colours.
SOWING Can be sown outdoors.

Portulaca

Purslane

Height 15 cm (6 in)

Spacing 15 cm (6 in)

Succulent leaves and double or single 'poppy' flowers in mixed colours. Good for a dry, sunny bank.
SOWING Can be sown outdoors.

Pyrethrum 'Golden Moss'

Height 10 cm (4 in)
Spacing 15 cm (6 in)

Fluffy acid-yellow leaves; yellow and white daisies.

Pyrethrum 'Silver Lace'

Height 15 cm (6 in)
Spacing 15 cm (6 in)

Finely cut grey filigree foliage.

Ricinus
Castor Oil Palm

Height 90 cm (3 ft)
Spacing 90 cm (3 ft)

Large hand-shaped leaves of dark green or bronze.

Salpiglossis
Painted Tongue

Height 60 cm (2 ft)
Spacing 23 cm (9 in)

Trumpets of mixed colours, contrastingly veined; stunning.

Salvia 'Blaze of Fire'

Height 30 cm (12 in)
Spacing 30 cm (12 in)

Green leaves and scarlet flower spikes. Only scarlet varieties are any good, though pink and purple are available.

Sanvitalia procumbens

Height 15 cm (6 in)
Spacing 23 cm (9 in)

Black-eyed, starry yellow daisies on compact plants.

Scabious
Pincushion Flower

Height 60 cm (2 ft)
Spacing 23 cm (9 in)

Dainty double flowers of pink, crimson, white or lavender. Thrives best in full sun.
SOWING Can be sown outdoors.

Senecio cineraria
Dusty Miller

Height 30 cm (12 in)
Spacing 30 cm (12 in)

Not as finely cut as the above, but more densely felted.

Statice
Sea Lavender

Height 45 cm (18 in)
Spacing 23 cm (9 in)

Branched sprays of pink, blue, white or yellow 'everlasting' flowers.

Stocks, Ten-week

Height 30 cm (12 in)
Spacing 23 cm (9 in)

Columns of fragrant magenta, purple, yellow, pink or white flowers.
SOWING Can be sown outdoors.

Tagetes
African Marigold, French Marigold

Height 23 cm (9 in)
Spacing 23 cm (9 in)

Rounded, aromatic domes studded with single orange or yellow flowers.

Tithonia

Height 1.2 m (4 ft)
Spacing 45 cm (18 in)

Single bright orange 'dahlia' flowers on tall stems.

Ursinia

Height 30 cm (12 in)
Spacing 23 cm (9 in)

Dazzling daisies of orange, yellow or red.

Verbena
Vervain

Height 23 cm (9 in)
Spacing 23 cm (9 in)

Clustered flowerheads of red, violet, pink or white.

Zinnia

Height 30–60 cm (12 in–2 ft)
Spacing 23 cm (9 in)

Double round-petalled flowers in mixed colours – even green!

BIENNIALS

Do remember that all these plants are sown one year to grow the next. Most plants grown as biennials are truly perennials and I have indicated in the entries where this is the case: if you like you can leave these to grow on for another year or so.

Bellis perennis
Double Daisy

Height 15 cm (6 in)
Final spacing 15 cm (6 in)

Neat double daisies with white, pink or crimson pom-poms. True perennial.
SOW in June.

Campanula medium
Canterbury Bell

Height 75 cm (2½ ft)
Final spacing 23 cm (9 in)

Thick spires of pink, white or lavender bellflowers.
SOW in June.

Digitalis
Foxglove

Height 90 cm–1.5 m (3–5 ft)
Final spacing 30 cm (12 in)

Tall spires of pink, mauve, yellow or white bells. Some species are perennial, others true biennials.
SOW in May.

Dipsacus fullonum
Fuller's Teasel

Height 2.4 m (8 ft)
Final spacing 60 cm (2 ft)

Towering flowerheads with spiny blooms that dry well.
SOW in May.

Honesty

Lunaria

Height 60 cm (2 ft)

Final spacing 23 cm (9 in)

Mauve flowers followed by translucent 'pennies' that dry well. A variegated variety that comes true from seed. **sow** in June.

Myosotis

Forget-me-not

Height 30 cm (12 in)

Final spacing 15 cm (6 in)

Sprays of pale blue, pink or white flowers. **sow** in June.

Pansy

Viola

Height 15–23 cm (6–9 in)

Final spacing 15 cm (6 in)

Wide-faced blooms in assorted colours. Especially good in the 'Universal' strains, which will flower in winter as well as in spring and summer. Tolerates some shade. True perennial. **sow** in June.

Papaver nudicaule

Iceland Poppy

Height 75 cm (2½ ft)

Final spacing 23 cm (9 in)

Single, papery blooms of pink, orange, yellow and white. True perennial. **sow** in May.

Penstemon

Height 30–60 cm (12 in–2 ft)

Final spacing 23 cm (9 in)

Spires of foxglove flowers in mixed colours. True perennial. **sow** in May.

Stock, Brompton

Height 45 cm (18 in)

Final spacing 23 cm (9 in)

Columns of mauve, pink, magenta,

violet or white flowers. True perennial. **sow** in June.

Sweet William

Dianthus barbatus

Height 45 cm (18 in)

Final spacing 23 cm (9 in)

Clustered heads of crimson, pink or white flowers, often bi-coloured. Make sure you find a sweetly scented mixture. True perennial. **sow** in June.

Verbascum

Mullein

Height 1.2–1.8 m (4–6 ft)

Final spacing 60 cm (2 ft)

Tall spires of yellow, orange or white flowers; downy leaves. Some species are perennial, others true biennials. **sow** in May.

White *Antirrhimum* and *Digitalis* (foxglove), yellow *Achillea*, and creamy white Siberian wallflower blend together in this gravel garden.

Wallflower

Cheiranthus cheiri, Erysimum cheiri

Height 30–45 cm (12–18 in)

Final spacing 30 cm (12 in)

Gloriously scented blooms of red, yellow, pink, orange and mauve. Massed single colours give the best effect. True perennial. **sow** in May.

Wallflower, Siberian

Cheiranthus allionii, Erysimum × allionii

Height 30 cm (12 in)

Final spacing 30 cm (12 in)

Orange-yellow flowers. True perennial. **sow** in June.

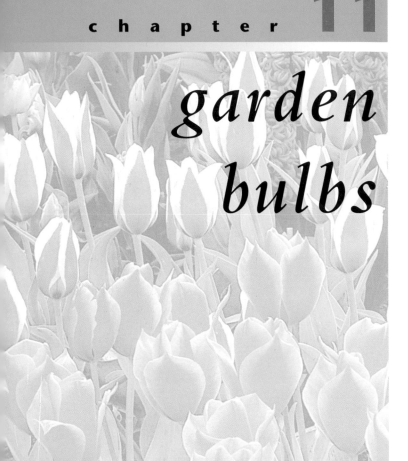

garden bulbs

Unmatched for their ability

to provide colour throughout

the year – not just in spring –

bulbs are also obliging enough

to reproduce themselves

with very little help from us

EVERY BULB IS A DO-IT-YOURSELF KIT. PACKED inside it are roots, shoots, leaves and flowers – all you have to do is add water and stand well back... well, almost.

First of all let's clear up the confusion that exists between bulbs, corms, tubers and rhizomes. I've included plants that arise from all four of these 'storage organs', so it's only fair to tell you how they differ. Basically they are all designed for food storage: like a camel's hump, they keep the plant alive during its dormant season, while it's resting and not growing. **BULBS** (e.g. daffodil) are really condensed shoots or buds. They have a flat bottom called the base-plate, which is really the stem. The fat scales that arise from this are modified leaves and, with any luck, they shield a central flower bud. The roots emerge from the base-plate as soon as moisture is placed within their reach. **CORMS** (e.g. crocus) are modified stems. Roots appear from the base, and buds and shoots from the tip. **TUBERS** may be swollen stems, as in the case of the potato, or swollen roots, as in the case of the dahlia. The potato shows it's a stem because buds appear all over it; they only appear at the top of a dahlia tuber. **RHIZOMES** (e.g. large-flowered border iris) are underground stems that usually grow horizontally, just below the surface of the soil.

So now that you know the technical differences between bulbs, corms, tubers and rhizomes, you can settle down to fitting all of them into your garden. And remember, bulbs are not simply plants that flower in spring; plan your selection carefully and they'll give you blooms in spring, summer, autumn and winter.

CHOOSING GARDEN BULBS

Most folk buy their bulbs from chain stores. There's nothing wrong with this provided the bulbs are fresh in and have not had a chance to dehydrate. However, you'll have a much wider choice of varieties if you order from a specialist catalogue. If you're buying bulbs over the counter, check that they are firm and of a good size. Very tiny or dehydrated bulbs may not flower during their first year, and may even die. One or two types of bulb, such as snowdrops, snowflakes and cyclamen, are best bought 'in the green' – as growing plants. They resent even slight desiccation and will receive less of a check if they are planted when in leaf. Sadly they are usually more pricey when sold like this, and it may be worth risking the loss of a few dry bulbs if the prices are markedly cheaper.

Types of bulbous plants

BULB

A bulb is a condensed shoot. The flattened base-plate is the stem; the scales are leaves and the flower nestles in the centre. Roots emerge from the base-plate.

CORM

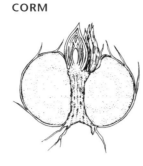

A corm is really a condensed stem. This crocus shows that the flesh is solid – a bud sits on top of the 'stem' and roots emerge below it.

TUBER

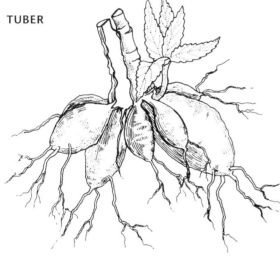

Dahlia tubers are root tubers: shoots arise only at the top, so it's vital that a bud or shoot is attached to any parts of the tuber removed for propagation.

RHIZOME

A rhizome is a flattened stem that grows on or just below the surface of the soil, such as this flag iris.

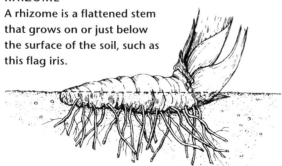

WHERE TO PLANT BULBS

The most obvious place to plant bulbs is in the flower border among herbaceous plants and shrubs. This is undoubtedly the best home for them in small gardens, because bulbs that can remain in the garden undisturbed must always be allowed to make plenty of foliage for at least six weeks after the flowers have faded. They nearly always looks untidy, but this is masked to some extent by the growth of border plants and shrubs. If you chop the foliage off instantly after flowering, you're stopping the plants from building up their food reserves. Tie the leaves in pigtails with elastic bands and you're still impeding feeding, for they need light in order to manufacture food. No: take a firm hold on your tidy-mindedness and let the bulbs go mad for six weeks, then, in most cases, you can chop off the leaves and neaten your border. Mind you, it's a good idea to mark the site they occupy to prevent accidents with a hoe or fork.

Most bulbs are happy left in the soil, in which case they are said to be 'naturalized'; those that are not, and which need to be dried off and ripened, can be dug up as soon as the flowers fade and brought into a dry shed or garage. As soon as their foliage dies off, they can be cleaned up and stored in a cool, dry, dark, frostproof place until planting time the following year. I've indicated which bulbs need this treatment under the individual entries in the A–Z section, so you need worry no more about it here.

Naturalizing bulbs in grass

Naturalizing bulbs in grass (planting them in haphazard formations and letting them grow on undisturbed) is an attractive proposition, but one I would not recommend in small gardens. After they've flowered the grass around them, along with their foliage, must remain uncut for six weeks, and the untidiness and restriction of movement on the lawn may be something you cannot cope with. Where you have space to let a little of your lawn run riot for a few weeks in spring, nothing looks nicer and more promising of a flower-filled summer to come.

Growing bulbs in beds and borders

Spring-flowering bulbs planted in beds with other temporary occupants, such as wallflowers, forget-me-nots, dwarf double daisies and polyanthuses, are always lifted after flowering so that the bed can be made ready for its summer occupants. I always find this a rather tiresome exercise and would rather fit these bulbs into pockets in a mixed border where they can be quickly replaced after flowering without having to clear the entire bed.

Container-grown bulbs

Pot-grown bulbs should be every gardener's joy; they can be fitted into the smallest garden or even onto a windowsill. The time at which the bulbs are potted up will depend on their time of flowering, but don't be conned into thinking that all pot-grown bulbs must be planted in bulb fibre. They'll usually do far better in John Innes No. 1 potting compost, preferably – but not essentially – with a little sharp sand added.

Bulb fibre (a mixture of peat, charcoal and crushed oyster shell) was originally developed for use in containers with no drainage holes, such as the bowls in which most folk plant hyacinths. The charcoal and oyster shell kept the mixture 'sweet' in the face of bad drainage. Today most bulb fibres are nothing more than peat plus a few nutrients; they do nothing to ameliorate the conditions prevalent in a holeless bowl and seem to have become simply a moneymaking proposition for enterprising compost merchants. Spurn them in favour of John Innes, which will feed your bulbs and keep them in good condition, allowing them to be planted out in the garden after blooming to give pleasure in future years.

PLANTING IN CONTAINERS

When you plant large bulbs in containers, leave their 'noses' just showing through the surface of the compost. Smaller bulbs and corms, such as crocuses, can be planted just below the surface. There's a neat trick you can try with daffodils and narcissi (daffodil, by the way, is simply the common name for any narcissus with a large trumpet). Spread 5 cm (2 in) of compost in the bottom of the pot, cram in a layer of bulbs, add a little compost and then cram in a second layer before topping up with compost, leaving the noses of the top layer showing. You'll get twice as many flowers from your pot than if you use a single layer of bulbs.

Choosing bulbs for your garden

Different bulbs are suited to different situations, though the majority of them will grow well in any ordinary well-drained soil. Almost all bulbs will rot in soggy earth, so it's always worth improving matters with grit, sharp sand and organic enrichment such as leaf mould or peat; too much manure can cause leafy growth at the expense of flowers.

TO NATURALIZE IN GRASS
- *Crocus*
- *Fritillaria meleagris*
- *Galanthus*
- *Narcissus*
- *Scilla*

FOR ROCK GARDENS
- *Allium* (dwarf spp.)
- *Anemone*
- *Crocus*
- *Cyclamen*
- *Eranthis*
- *Erythronium*
- *Galanthus*
- *Iris* (dwarf spp.)
- *Leucojum autumnale*
- *Muscari*
- *Narcissus* (dwarf spp.)
- *Tulipa* (dwarf spp.)

FOR BEDDING SCHEMES
- *Crocus*
- *Dahlia*
- *Gladiolus*
- *Hyacinthus*
- *Muscari*
- *Narcissus*
- *Tulipa*

FOR GENTLE SHADE
- *Allium moly*
- *Anemone blanda*
- *Anemone nemorosa*
- *Colchicum*
- *Cyclamen*
- *Eranthis*
- *Erythronium*
- *Fritillaria meleagris*
- *Leucojum*
- *Scilla*

To get as many daffodils as possible from one pot, plant a double layer of bulbs, positioning the upper layer so that the shoots below can squeeze past those above. A few crocks placed in the bottom of the container will improve drainage.

Bulbs for containers

- *Anemone* (some)
- *Chionodoxa*
- *Crocus*
- *Galtonia*
- *Hyacinthus*
- *Iris* (dwarf spp.)
- *Lilium*
- *Muscari*
- *Narcissus*
- *Nerine*
- *Ornithogalum*
- *Tulipa*

In general, pots with drainage holes are always more satisfactory than bowls without them, unless you take exceptional care not to overwater.

Temperature and light

All bulbs appreciate eight weeks of cool temperatures and darkness after potting. You can stand them outdoors and cover them with peat and ashes if you like (it's what the old gardeners used to recommend), but it's far easier to keep them in a cellar or coal shed, or to stand them outdoors and cover them with black polythene. Whatever you do, don't put them in the airing cupboard: your washing will get dirty and your bulbs won't enjoy the heat. They need cool conditions for the first two months so that they can establish their root system; only then can they take more heat, and this should be applied very gradually; bring them first into a cool room (if you're flowering them indoors) and then into a warmer one if you must. Most will bloom better and last longer in well-lit but cool rooms.

Bulbs grown in tubs, pots and windowboxes outdoors need none of this coddling; simply treat the bulbs as though they were being planted in the ground, but use John Innes No. 2 potting compost plus a little sharp river sand for extra drainage.

HOW TO PLANT BULBS OUTDOORS

All outdoor bulbs are best planted with a trowel. As a general rule they should be covered with soil to twice their depth. That is, if a bulb measures 5 cm (2 in) from tip to toe it should be planted in a hole 15 cm (6 in) deep.

Bulb-planting tools that take out a core of soil are useful for planting large numbers of bulbs in grass, but they are hell to use effectively on stony soil. If you do use one, take out all your holes first, push your bulbs in and then replace the divots.

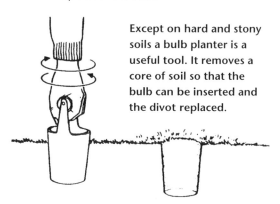

Except on hard and stony soils a bulb planter is a useful tool. It removes a core of soil so that the bulb can be inserted and the divot replaced.

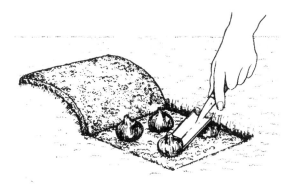

Save time when planting bulbs in grass by lifting a flap of turf. With a trowel, plant the bulbs in the soil below, then replace the turf and firm it into place.

I find it easier when naturalizing bulbs in grass to lift up a flap of turf, plant the bulbs underneath with a trowel, then replace the flap and firm it into place.

Never plant bulbs too shallowly. It's one of the greatest causes of failure. Shallow-planted bulbs will often refuse to flower well because they are short of water and nutrients. Seldom can a bulb be planted too deeply – unless you're daft enough to plant a tiny snowdrop 30 cm (12 in) under.

If you're planting bulbs among spring bedding plants, put the plants in first and the bulbs in afterwards – that way they won't be disturbed by the trowel.

IMPROVE FLOWERING BY FEEDING

People are as rotten to their bulbs as they are to their lawns: they often forget completely about feeding. You'll have better flowers each year if you treat your bulbs to a square meal of general fertilizer as the flowers fade. A light dusting of blood, bone and fishmeal will do them nicely. Lack of food will often cause 'blindness' (failure to flower), especially in bulbs that grow among grass, which robs them of food anyway; but dry springs can also be responsible for the failure of flower formation. If you can water your spring-flowering bulbs well during a parched April and May you might notice a difference the following year.

PROPAGATION OF BULBS

Almost all bulbs are obliging enough to reproduce themselves without any help from us, but I have included a few tips on encouraging them to increase in Chapter 2 Propagation.

A-Z
OF
garden bulbs

THIS SECTION INCLUDES THE bulbs, corms, tubers and rhizomes that are grown in the garden or in containers outdoors – although some of them are brought indoors during their flowering season.

Some bulbous plants are so commonly grown as border plants that I have sneaked them into that chapter: if the plant you seek is not here, check to see if it is included in Chapter 9 Border Plants.

Where a specific planting depth is given for a bulb, it refers to the depth of the hole that should be taken out, not to the depth from the tip of the bulb to the surface.

Allium
Ornamental Onion

Most of these don't smell too strongly of onions unless they're bruised, so don't be put off. They are a tremendously varied and valuable bunch of plants, which can be relied on to bring colour to the garden from spring to autumn. They vary in stature from the very small to around head height, and many have attractive seedheads. I can mention just a few – the ones I'd grow in preference to all others. Some species (none of those mentioned here) can become annoying weeds.

The huge mauve-pink flowerheads of *Allium cristophii* tower above the foxglove-like spires of *Penstemon glaber* and the woolly grey leaves of *Stachys byzantina* in this border.

A. bulgaricum (syn. *A. siculum dioscoridis*, now called *Nectaroscordum*): 1–1.25 m (3–4 ft); towering heads of drooping creamy flowers striped with green and tinted purple; superb seedheads like Bavarian castles; summer flowering; likes sun and well-drained soil.
A. cristophii (syn. *A. albopilosum*): 45 cm (18 in); football-sized flowerheads composed of glistening, mauve-pink metallic stars; dries strawy brown; summer flowering; loves sun.
A. giganteum, 2 m (6 ft): lilac-purple ball-shaped flowerheads on top of its tall stems in early summer; likes sun or very gentle shade.
A. karataviense: 20 cm (8 in); remarkable as its spherical flowerheads of dirty pink nestle between a pair of very broad grey-green leaves in late spring or early summer; likes sun and good drainage.
A. moly: 30 cm (12 in); clusters of starry yellow flowers; early summer flowering; naturalizes well in sun or light shade.
A. oreophilum (syn. *A. ostrowskianum*): 15 cm (6 in); cheap and easy to find; rosy pink flower clusters in early to mid-summer; prefers well-drained soil and sun.
PLANT in autumn or as soon as bulbs become available; cover all bulbs to twice their depth. Rich soil preferred.
SUITABLE for naturalizing, rock gardens (dwarf species), shade (as indicated); most adore sun.
PROPAGATE by division of bulbs in summer.

Amaryllis belladonna
Belladonna Lily

This is the only true amaryllis and one to treasure. It produces green, strap-shaped leaves and, once it is happy, a flowerhead carrying several large, pink,

white-flushed flowers shaped like gigantic stars. It grows to about 60 cm (2 ft) high and flowers in autumn. There are darker-flowered forms and a good white. Only in a sun-baked border will it thrive and become reliably perennial. In colder counties it may be killed in severe winters and it will not tolerate poorly drained soil. Leave clumps undisturbed for many

years for best results. Good against south- and west-facing walls. Feed with blood, bone and fishmeal in late summer and cover with dry straw or bracken in winter.

PLANT in summer 15 cm (6 in) deep and 30 cm (12 in) apart. The leaves die down altogether in summer.

PROPAGATE by division of established clumps in summer.

Anemone
Windflower

Little charmers of small stature but considerable impact. The Mothering Sunday bunches of anemones are generally the De Caen Group (single) and St Brigid Group (double) varieties of *A. coronaria* with flowers of red, pink, white, mauve and lavender-blue. They grow to around 30 cm (12 in) high and will bloom in spring (if planted in October), summer (if planted in April), or late summer and autumn (if planted in June). Give them a well-drained soil that has been laced with a little garden compost.

A. blanda, 10 cm (4 in), is my own favourite. It has starry wood-anemone flowers of white, pink, blue or, in the variety 'Radar', rich magenta. This last-named is iniquitously expensive; the others are very cheap. All flower in early spring and will multiply into large colonies if left alone in any decent soil; they can even be planted in grass.

A. nemorosa, 10 cm (4 in), is our native wood anemone with finely cut leaves and white flowers flushed mauve on the outside. It has a double form and a glorious lavender-blue variety called 'Robinsoniana'; both flower in spring and enjoy a peaty, leafy soil.

PLANT both these species in autumn, 8 cm (3 in) deep.

SUITABLE for naturalizing in sun or gentle shade, or for growing in pots, but keep them cool. Good in rock gardens and under shrubs and trees, but avoid really dry soils.

PROPAGATE by division of the tubers after flowering.

Camassia
Quamash

Variable but always beautiful bulbs with starry flowers in tapering spires. *C. cusickii,* 75 cm (2½ ft) high, is usually pale blue, and *C. quamash* (syn. *C. esculenta*), 45 cm (18 in) high, is usually darker blue, but both vary considerably in colour depending on

source of supply. Both flower in summer and both deserve to be more popular.

PLANT in autumn, 15 cm (6 in) deep and as much apart.

SUITABLE for naturalizing in beds and borders where they can be left undisturbed. They enjoy full sun and a moisture-retentive soil with a bit of body. They resent drought.

PROPAGATE by sowing seeds outdoors in spring (they take three or four years to come to flowering size), or by division in autumn, though increase is slow.

Chionodoxa forbesii
Glory of the Snow

Grows without any fuss at all. It makes 15 cm (6 in) high arching stems of starry blue and white flowers in spring, and produces tufts of glossy green leaves.

PLANT in autumn, 8 cm (3 in) deep.

SUITABLE for naturalizing in beds and borders, for rock gardens and for planting in pots, tubs and window boxes. They enjoy sun or gentle shade and any reasonable soil.

PROPAGATE by division after flowering.

Colchicum
Meadow Saffron, Naked Ladies, Autumn Crocus

It's a shame about the third inaccurate common name. If ever you want to know whether or not you've got a colchicum or a true autumn-flowering crocus, count the stamens: crocuses have three (and a shorter name); colchicums have six (and a longer name). Some species flower in spring, but the most popular are the autumn bloomers such as *C. autumnale,* 15 cm (6 in), with its dainty crocus-shaped flowers of lilac-pink. *C. speciosum,* 23 cm (9 in), is better still and a good deal beefier – absolutely breathtaking in flower. It has various varieties with lighter and darker blooms, and one glorious double called 'Waterlily', which is a warm pink. Some species, such as *C. aggripinum*, have blooms that carry a chequered pattern (the experts refer to them as 'tessellated'), and the species that flower in winter and spring, including a rare yellow one, should be fitted in where there is room. Remember that all have vast leaves like huge leeks that push up after the flowers. If the foliage can be masked by shrubs and border plants, so much the better.

PLANT in late summer 15 cm (6 in) deep and as much apart; plant spring-flowering kinds in autumn.

SUITABLE for naturalizing in beds and borders, under trees and among shrubs. They enjoy a rich, leafy soil, preferably organically mulched, which is not likely to become baked in summer. Bulbs of *C. autumnale* can be stood, quite dry, on a windowsill in late summer where they will flower with no attention whatsoever. Plant them out afterwards.

PROPAGATE by seeds sown outdoors in summer (allow three to four years for flowering) or by division in summer. Most folk simply buy in more bulbs.

Crocus

I hardly know where to begin with the crocuses, they are such a delightfully varied bunch. I've never been a fan of the fat Dutch hybrids, but I rave over the smaller varieties of such species as *C. chrysanthus*, 5–8 cm (2–3 in), that flower in spring. Try the warm yellow 'E. A. Bowles' and 'Ladykiller' with white petals flushed purple on the undersides. *C. ancyrensis*, 8 cm (3 in), is a good orange-yellow that can be in flower in winter in pots or outdoors, and by far the best naturalizer is *C. tommasinianus*, 8 cm (3 in), whose amethyst-purple buds spear the soil in late winter before opening in the sunshine like floral stars. There are several species that flower in autumn – some in September and some in October and November – and it's time more folk knew about them:

C. speciosus, 10 cm (4 in), pale mauve; *C. zonatus*, 10 cm (4 in), pale lilac; *C. niveus*, 10 cm (4 in), white with red stigmas; *C. nudiflorus*, 15 cm (6 in), deep violet-purple, are all worth planting outdoors or in pots.

PLANT or pot up in late summer (for autumn-flowering kinds); in autumn (for spring-flowering kinds). Plant 5 cm (2 in) deep and 8 cm (3 in) apart.

SUITABLE for naturalizing in grass or beds and borders, even under trees and shrubs. Good in the rock garden and in containers. If you plan to bring the containers indoors when the crocuses are in flower, try to keep them cool. In the garden leave the bulbs undisturbed to multiply on their own. All will tolerate any ordinary, well-drained soil.

PROPAGATE by seed if you've the patience: it will be two or three years before the progeny flower. Most gardeners buy in new bulbs and leave their existing ones to increase naturally by both division and seed.

Cyclamen
Sowbread

It's not the large, pot-grown cyclamen so popular at Christmas that can be grown outdoors, but the smaller hardy species such as *C. hederifolium* (syn. *C. neapolitanum*). It grows just 8 cm (3 in) or so high, produces its pretty reflexed-petalled flowers of warm pink from summer to autumn, and then a show of marbled heart-shaped leaves.

PLANT the tubers while they are growing, for preference, or take a gamble and hope that dry ones (which you can buy from department stores and garden centres) will succeed. Plant the tubers so that they rest fractionally below the surface of the soil.

SUITABLE for dappled shade under trees and shrubs, and shady pockets on the rock garden. They like a peaty, leafy soil that doesn't dry out.

PROPAGATE by sowing fresh seeds in pots of compost placed in a garden frame.

Dahlia

The dahlia is a tuber that can grow happily outdoors in summer, but which needs frost protection in winter. There are hundreds of different varieties with flowers in 'pompon', 'cactus' and 'decorative' shapes, in shades of red, orange, yellow, mauve, purple and white. The stems and foliage are juicy and succulent and the plants may grow anything from 45 cm to 1.5 m (18 in to 5 ft) tall.

PLANT dormant tubers 15 cm (6 in) deep in late April or early May; young plants in late May or early June. Stake the plants as they grow. Feed fortnightly in summer and control earwigs (p.294), which will nibble both flowers and leaves.

SUITABLE for beds and borders in full sun. The soil should be rich: work in plenty of compost or manure and a dusting of blood, bone and fishmeal before planting. Water well in dry spells. When the stems are blackened by autumn frosts, lift the plants, cut off the top growth and store the tubers in an airy, cool but frostproof place in trays of dry peat. If you're idle you can risk leaving them in the ground outdoors, in which case mulch the soil above them with a thick layer of compost, manure, straw or bracken. Prepare for total losses in severe winters.

PROPAGATE by taking cuttings from tubers boxed up in compost, watered and kept warm in a greenhouse during early spring. Alternatively, divide these tubers into sections (each with a shoot) as soon as they start to sprout. Grow on a little in heat and plant out when danger of frost is past.

Eranthis hyemalis
Winter Aconite

These pretty yellow buttercup flowers, each with a green ruff, are welcome heralds of spring, flowering in February just 8 cm (3 in) above the cold, damp soil.

Eranthis hyemalis (winter aconite) creates a mass of gold only 10 cm (4 in) from the ground.

PLANT growing plants if you can find them; if you can't, plant dry tubers in autumn and be prepared to wait a few years for the plants to settle in and flower well. Plant 8 cm (3 in) deep and 10 cm (4 in) apart.

SUITABLE for naturalizing in rock gardens or in beds and borders under trees and shrubs in sun or dappled shade. Really dry soils will not be appreciated.

PROPAGATE by division of tubers after flowering.

Erythronium
Dog's Tooth Violet, Trout Lily

Grey-green, liver-spotted leaves and pink or white pagoda-shaped flowers make *E. dens-canis* a popular plant. It grows just 15 cm (6 in) high, but there are taller species such as *E. tuolumnense* at 25 cm (10 in), which has glossy green leaves and yellow flowers. All bloom in spring, and all are well worth growing.

PLANT growing plants in spring or, if this is not possible, dormant, but not

totally desiccated, corms in late summer. Plant 8 cm (3 in) deep and 10 cm (4 in) apart.

SUITABLE for dappled shade under trees and shrubs in a peaty, leafy soil that is never likely to dry out. Happy in shady pockets on the rock garden. A light mulch of leaf mould or pulverized bark will be appreciated after flowering. Once established the corms resent disturbance.

PROPAGATE by division after flowering.

Fritillaria
Crown Imperial, Snakeshead Fritillary

The stately *F. imperialis*, with its 1 m (3 ft) stem, pendant orange or yellow bells and topknot of leafy green bracts, is a startling feature in the May garden and is criticized only for its foxy odour. The daintier *F. meleagris*, 23 cm (9 in), is altogether more coy, with nodding chequered bells of dusky plum-purple, pink or creamy white. Its leaves are narrow and grassy, unlike those of the crown imperial, which radiate in whorls from the thick stem.

PLANT bulbs of *F. imperialis* 15 cm (6 in) deep on their sides; those of *F. meleagris* the right way up, 10 cm (4 in) deep and as much apart. Plant both in autumn.

SUITABLE for rich but well-drained soil in full sun for *F. imperialis*; moisture-retentive soil in dappled shade for *F. meleagris*. Both are best left undisturbed after planting; the snakeshead fritillary can even be naturalized in grass.

PROPAGATE by seeds sown in a garden frame as soon as ripe. A job for the patient gardener – others will buy in fresh bulbs.

Galanthus
Snowdrop

The common snowdrop is *G. nivalis*, usually at its best during February, when its green and white ballerina flowers dangle from 15 cm (6 in)

stems. There are dozens of other species and varieties with quaint markings and broader leaves; some of them possess delightful scents, and some flower earlier, even in autumn if you choose the right species. Many are expensive to buy, but the double form of the common snowdrop is cheap and produces masses of tulle-petticoated flowers at the same time as the true species.

PLANT growing plants 'in the green' immediately after flowering if you can. Dry bulbs can be planted in autumn but may not establish so quickly. Plant the bulbs 8 cm (3 in) deep and 5 cm (2 in) apart.

SUITABLE for naturalizing in beds and borders under trees and shrubs and in grass. Happy in full sun or dappled shade. Good in rock gardens.

PROPAGATE by dividing mature clumps after flowering.

Galtonia candicans
Spire Lily

Stately spires of creamy-white bells 1 m (3 ft) tall are the trademark of galtonia. The blooms are deliciously fragrant and open in July or August.

PLANT in spring 15 cm (6 in) deep and as much apart.

SUITABLE for well-nourished and well-drained soil in beds and borders among summer-flowering perennials and shrubs. Full sun is essential. Galtonia can also be grown in pots for room decoration. Plant one bulb, with its nose just showing, in a pot of compost in autumn. Keep it cool and dark for eight weeks and then gradually introduce to light and warmer temperatures. It will flower in spring.

PROPAGATE by the removal of offsets in autumn.

Gladiolus
Sword Lily

Sword-leafed plants with tapering spikes of wide-faced flowers in shades of red, yellow, orange, pink, mauve and white, as well as a rather lurid green. There are many different forms with strangely shaped flowers such as the 'butterfly' types. They grow to 30 cm–1.5 m (12 in–5 ft) high and flower in summer. Most are not winter hardy and have to be lifted, dried and stored before severe frosts have a chance to kill them, but *G. communis* ssp. *byzantinus*, 60 cm (2 ft), is a magenta-flowered species that can survive outdoors all the year round. It's daintier and flowers earlier, in June.

PLANT *G. communis* ssp. *byzantinus* in autumn 8 cm (3 in) deep and 15 cm (6 in) apart. Plant the hybrid types at intervals between March and May for a succession of flowers. Set the corms 10 cm (4 in) deep and 23 cm (9 in) apart. The hybrids will need staking as soon as the flower spikes appear. Feed fortnightly in summer.

SUITABLE for rich and well-drained soil in full sun. Water well in dry spells. Six weeks after flowering lift the hybrid varieties, cut off the foliage 2.5 cm (1 in) above the corm, remove the old corm, which will be a shrivelled button below the new one, and store the new corms in seeds trays kept in a cool, dry, frostproof place during winter.

PROPAGATE by planting 'cormels' (tiny corms that form around the main one) and allow them to grow on to flowering size. Plant them in spring.

Hyacinthus
Hyacinth

Unsurpassed for fragrance, the hyacinth is part of the Christmas tradition in many homes. The dense spikes of bloom may be rich rose-red, pink, blue, salmon, pale yellow or white. 'L'Innocence' (white), 'Jan Bos' (rich pink), 'Ostara' (blue), and 'City of Haarlem' (pale yellow), are probably the most popular varieties. All bloom in winter (in pots) or in spring (outdoors) and are around 25 cm (10 in) high.

PLANT prepared bulbs in pots or bowls of compost in late August and

September for Christmas flowers. Plant one variety to each container to make sure that all the bulbs flower simultaneously: mix your colours, and blooming may be staggered and less effective. Keep the pots of bulbs cool and dark for eight weeks, bringing them indoors when the flower spikes can be seen nestling among the leaves. Ordinary bulbs can be planted in bowls at the same time but they will not flower quite so quickly.

Plant outdoors during September and October, setting the bulbs 10 cm (4 in) deep and 15 cm (6 in) apart. The bulbs are so expensive nowadays that few folk can afford to grow them outdoors except in tubs and windowboxes.

SUITABLE for beds and borders, pots, tubs, bowls and windowboxes. Plant pot-grown bulbs in the garden when the flowers fade. If the soil is well nourished and in full sun they should bloom again in succeeding years, but plant them a good 10 cm (4 in) deep.

PROPAGATE by scooping and scoring if you're really mean (see Chapter 2 Propagation). Otherwise save up and buy in more bulbs.

Iris

In January, February and March, when most gardeners' hopes are at a low ebb, the varieties of *I. reticulata* burst into flower. Their blooms may be blue or violet in various intensities, and are almost always attractively etched with yellow and white. They're just 15 cm (6 in) tall, but if you can get your nose down to them you'll detect a sweet scent in the winter sun. *I. histrioides* 'Major' is another must. It's slightly shorter but rather larger flowered and

Dwarf bulbs such as *Iris reticulata* and *Scilla sibirica* take up little space but add much-needed colour to the winter border.

coloured blue and white. The foliage follows the flowers and, in all the varieties, is grassy and not too untidy. The Dutch, Spanish and English irises are all much taller at around 45 cm (18 in) and bloom in late spring or early to mid-summer. They are valuable and easy plants that are neglected by too many gardeners.

Plant the Dutch types to bloom in May, the Spanish to bloom in June, and the English to bloom in June and July, offering flowers of blue, violet, yellow and white.

PLANT in autumn 8 cm (3 in) deep. Space the dwarf types 8 cm (3 in) apart and the taller varieties 15 cm (6 in) apart.

SUITABLE for beds and borders in full sun (taller varieties); rock gardens in full sun (dwarf varieties). All appreciate a gritty, well-drained soil. The tall varieties can be lifted and divided every three years in autumn, the others left undisturbed. The dwarfs can also be grown in pots for winter colour indoors. Keep them cool at all times. **PROPAGATE** by division of established clumps in autumn.

Leucojum
Snowflake

There are three snowflakes grown with frequency by discerning plantsmen: the summer snowflake, *L. aestivum*, 45 cm (18 in), white, green-tipped bells in late spring and early summer; the spring snowflake, *L. vernum*, 30 cm (12 in), similar flowers in early spring; and the autumn snowflake, *L. autumnale*, 15 cm (6 in), a dainty miniature with reed-like leaves and papery white or pale pink bells in autumn.

PLANT the spring- and summer-flowering species in early autumn, the autumn-flowering species in late summer. Alternatively, plant 'in the green' after flowering, as for snowdrops. Plant 10 cm (4 in) deep and as much apart. Both *L. aestivum* and *L. vernum* appreciate a leafy, moisture-retentive soil, while *L. autumnale* likes something grittier and well drained. All are happy in full sun or dappled shade.

SUITABLE for beds and borders and, in the case of *L. autumnale*, rock gardens. The bulbs may not flower in their first year.

PROPAGATE by lifting and dividing mature clumps after flowering.

Lilium
Lily

How can I even begin to tell you about lilies in such a small space? I can't, but I can perhaps persuade you to try them in beds and borders among your herbaceous plants and shrubs, and in pots on a patio or doorstep. They possess starry, bell-shaped, trumpet or turk's cap flowers in a wide colour range, and some fragrances that surpass anything that comes out of a bottle. If you've never grown lilies before, start off with *L. regale*, 1.25 m

(4 ft), which has white and pale yellow trumpets flushed with purple on the outside; and *L.* 'Enchantment', 60 cm (2 ft), whose vibrant orange blooms are dotted with brown. Don't be put off by the daunting mystery that surrounds the lily: some are notoriously difficult, it's true, but others are easy if you meet their simple requirements.

PLANT these two species in October or in spring, as soon as the bulbs become available. Plant them 15 cm (6 in) deep and 20 cm (8 in) apart. They need a well-drained soil that is not prone to drought in summer. Winter sogginess will encourage rotting. Alternatively, pot up the bulbs in autumn in gritty compost – one bulb to a 13 cm (5 in) pot or three to a 20 cm (8 in) pot. Cover the bulbs with 8 cm (3 in) compost. Keep cool and dark until growth begins, then gradually introduce to light and warmth. Water carefully at all times: little will be needed until the plants are growing well. Outdoors and in pots the plants may need staking. Plant out the bulbs in the garden after flowering.

SUITABLE for beds and borders in well-drained soil and full sun or dappled shade. Many can be grown in pots. If you plan to specialize in lilies, lay your hands on a book that offers comprehensive advice. Some lilies hate chalk; others don't much care for acid ground, some are 'stem rooting' and need to be planted quite deeply; others, like the madonna lily, need shallow planting in late summer. See how confusing it gets? No wonder some gardeners are frightened of lilies!

PROPAGATE by seed or by the removal and growing on of bulb scales or bulbils – those little bulbs that appear in the leaf axils of some species. (See Chapter 2 Propagation for details.)

Muscari
Grape Hyacinth

Easy spring-flowering bulbs with spires of blue or white flowers held on stout stalks 15 cm (6 in) long. The

commonest species is *M. armeniacum*. **PLANT** in autumn 8 cm (3 in) deep and 8 cm (3 in) apart.

SUITABLE for beds and borders, tubs, windowboxes and pots. Ordinary soil and full sun are appreciated. There is no need to disturb the bulbs once they are planted, but should they become all leaf and no flower in succeeding years, dig them up in June and discard all but the largest bulbs, which can be replanted in freshly fertilized soil.

PROPAGATE by division after flowering.

Narcissus
Daffodil

'King Alfreds' pop up in gardens countrywide, but there are hundreds, and maybe even thousands more varieties that are equally valuable to stately gardeners and windowbox owners alike. Catalogues offer a vast choice of form and colour: large- and small-cupped varieties, doubles and singles, and even blooms that are pale green or salmon-pink. I'll leave you to pick your favourites from the glossy pages, but will sneak in a recommendation for the useful dwarf varieties such as *N. asturiensis*, *N. bulbocodium* and *N. cyclamineus* and some of their hybrids such as 'Little Witch', 23 cm (9 in) (yellow), and 'Tête-à-Tête', 15 cm (6 in) (yellow), which are marvellous for rock gardens, pots and windowboxes. All bloom during spring. Cottage gardeners should not be without 'Van Sion', the double yellow daffodil; and orchard owners can carpet the ground around their trees with the headily fragrant 'Old Pheasant's Eye', which has white petals and a tiny red and yellow centre. Both are just over 30 cm (12 in) tall.

PLANT in September and October, 10 cm (4 in) deep in beds and borders; 15 cm (6 in) deep if naturalizing the bulbs in grass. The miniature varieties should be planted 8 cm (3 in) deep. All varieties can be planted 8 cm (3 in) apart. Plant in groups, not lines. Alternatively plant the bulbs in pots

(see p. 154 for details) in autumn for winter flowering indoors. The varieties 'Soleil d'Or' and 'Paper White' are often potted for Christmas flowering. **SUITABLE** for beds, borders, rough grass, rock gardens (dwarf varieties), pots, tubs and windowboxes. Pot-grown plants can be planted out in the garden after flowering. All appreciate full sun and a well-drained soil. Feeding with a balanced general fertilizer, such as blood, bone and fishmeal, after flowering will encourage regular blooming. Dry springs may account for 'blindness' (lack of flowers) the following year.
PROPAGATE by division after flowering.

Nerine bowdenii
Diamond Lily

Find this September-flowering bulb a sheltered patch of well-drained soil in full sun and it will demand little attention. It will gradually make a congested clump of bulbs from which will spring branched heads of rich pink, wavy-petalled flowers at the end of summer, followed by a small forest of glossy green strap-shaped leaves. The flower stems are about 45 cm (18 in) high, and the leaves persist through winter, dying down in early summer.
PLANT in late summer, positioning the bulbs just below ground level.
SUITABLE for light, well-drained, even dry soils in full sun. A spot at the foot of a south-facing wall is ideal and the plants will usually come through the

"In January, February and March, when gardeners' hopes are at a low ebb, the varieties of Iris reticulata burst into flower."

winter unscathed, though they may suffer in the north and in sticky earth. They can also be grown in pots of gritty compost and protected from winter cold and wet in a frame. Withhold water in summer when the leaves die down. Repot in late summer when the bulbs become overcrowded. Those growing in the garden seem to flower best when jammed close together. Protect them from slugs and snails.
PROPAGATE by division of clumps in late summer.

Ornithogalum umbellatum
Star of Bethlehem

A neat and cheerful little plant with branched heads of white, starry flowers that are green on the undersides. They open on top of 23 cm (9 in) stalks in April and May and make a pretty edging to a bed or border. They open late morning and close again in the afternoon, but they're nice when they're out!
PLANT in autumn, 8 cm (3 in) deep and as much apart.
SUITABLE for ordinary soil in sunny beds, borders or containers.
PROPAGATE by dividing clumps after flowering.

Schizostylis coccinea
Kaffir Lily

Rich pink, starry flowers emerge at the top of slender stems in autumn to make the kaffir lily a valuable border flower. There are several named varieties such as 'Viscountess Byng' and 'Mrs Hegarty' that are paler than the true species. All are around 45 cm (18 in) tall and have grassy leaves.
PLANT in spring, 8 cm (3 in) deep and as much apart.
SUITABLE for warm and sunny borders at the foot of south- and west-facing walls. In cold districts protect with straw or bracken in winter.
PROPAGATE by division of mature clumps in spring.

Scilla
Squill

The two squills most commonly planted are *S. siberica*, 10 cm (4 in), and *S. bifolia*, 15 cm (6 in), both of which have rich blue, bell-like flowers in spring. The native British bluebell is strictly *Endymion nonscriptus* or, if you want to be slap-bang up-to-date, *Hyacinthoides non-scripta*, but it used to be a scilla and for convenience I'm including it here along with its heftier relation the Spanish bluebell *H. hispanica*. Both have variants with white and pink flowers, but the Spanish bluebell is the more imposing plant at around 30 cm (12 in) high with broader bells.
PLANT all the bulbs in autumn to twice their depth.
SUITABLE for bed and border edgings in the case of the two true scillas, or for naturalizing in grass and woodland, in the case of the two bluebells. None of them needs to be disturbed once planted.
PROPAGATE by division after flowering.

Sternbergia
Lily of the Field, Winter Daffodil

Just like a vivid yellow crocus to look at, *S. lutea*, 10 cm (4 in), blooms in autumn and then sends up a neat fountain of lustrous green 'daffodil' leaves. Sometimes it is reluctant to flower but if planted deep enough and allowed a year or two to settle in it should oblige.
PLANT in late summer, 15 cm (6 in) deep and 10 cm (4 in) apart.
SUITABLE for sunny spots in well-drained soil, preferably at the foot of a warm wall where they will receive a welcome baking in summer.
PROPAGATE by division in late summer.

Tulipa
Tulip

As popular and as varied a race as *Narcissus*, with almost as many variations. The hybrids are classified in different groups that vary in stature and time of flowering; it's possible to have tulips in bloom from late winter to late spring. Pick the hybrid types for bedding schemes – the Darwin hybrids have long stems and will bloom at the same time as wallflowers – and the smaller species for rock gardens. Colourful catalogues will give you more detailed information on varieties than I can hope to here, but let me urge you to have a bash with the miniatures like *T. clusiana*, 23 cm (9 in), white, flushed red outside, late April; *T.* var. *chrysantha*, 15 cm (6 in), red and yellow, mid-April, and *T. tarda*, 10 cm (4 in), yellow and white, April. The varieties of *T. kaufmanniana* and *T. greigii* are stocky, large flowered and have leaves attractively streaked with maroon. At 23 cm (9 in) high they are the best types for container planting. There are many others that will delight you year in, year out.

PLANT in October or November – no earlier, and the deeper the better. Plant the miniatures 15 cm (6 in) deep, and the larger hybrids 23 cm (9 in) deep if you want to avoid lifting them every year. I've known them undisturbed at this depth for 30 years, flowering annually. Plant in pots at the same time, just covering the noses of the bulbs. Keep cool and dark for eight weeks, then bring into the light. Avoid a dramatic rise in temperatures.

SUITABLE for bedding, naturalizing in beds and borders, where their foliage will not give offence, tubs, pots and windowboxes. Dwarf species look good in the rock garden. If tulips are used in a spring bedding scheme that has to be shifted to make way for summer flowers, lift the bulbs, leaving their top growth intact, and lay them in a trench on the vegetable plot, replacing some soil over the bulbs. When growth dies down, lift and strip the bulbs of their foliage before storing them in a cool, dry place. Discard the small bulbs and retain only the larger, flowering-sized bulbs for planting next

Massed tulips and hyacinths provide a gloriously colourful and fragrant spring display in beds, borders, and containers, welcoming us back to the garden after the dark winter months.

year. Dry out pot-grown bulbs after flowering and treat as for lifted bulbs.

PROPAGATE tulips by dividing bulb clusters in summer and growing on the small bulbs.

part III

THE FEATURES

The features that we incorporate into our gardens are as vivid an expression of personality as the plants that surround them

This enchanting stretch of water winds its way through the dense planting around its edges, givng it a wholly natural charm that is attractive to both humans and wildlife.

rock gardens

An open, sunny site and good

drainage are the essential

elements for creating a rock

garden to show off and

grow a delightful collection

of alpines and rock plants

EVERY GARDENER HAS HIS FAVOURITE PLANTS: alpines and rock plants happen to be mine – even though they are regularly rivalled by roses, shrubs, house plants, border plants ....

If I do nothing else in this chapter I'd like to encourage you to grow alpines anywhere but on rock-studded mounds that look like large graves. Alpines mostly come from mountainous areas so it may seem natural to create mini-Alps in the garden, but this is really not necessary. They are shown off and grow happily in rock beds (raised or flat), sinks and troughs as well as in properly constructed 'rock outcrops' that fit most naturally into banks or undulating ground.

WHERE TO SITE YOUR ROCK GARDEN

Whatever feature you decide on, the site should be open and sunny. There are one or two alpines that like a shady spot, but the vast majority need all the light they can get. Avoid a site that is overhung by trees or the plants will be dripped on all the year round and smothered with leaves in autumn.

Some shelter from strong winds is desirable and the patch of ground should not be in a frost pocket (a hollow that collects cold air). Most alpines flower in spring and will be damaged if frosted at that time.

As well as hating bad drainage, the plants dislike winter wet. Most of them are protected in the wild by a thick, dry blanket of snow. In Britain they are more likely to be battered by distinctly soggy rain or sleet. Many alpines will reluctantly tolerate our winters; those that will not can be protected with panes of glass supported on wire legs, with cloches, or by being grown in a garden frame or – great luxury – in an alpine house. Hairy-leaved plants in particular suffer from excessive damp in cold weather.

PREPARING THE SOIL

Alpines like that seemingly impossible combination, rapid drainage in winter and adequate moisture retention in summer. You can usually achieve this happy state if you perk up your existing soil. Light earth will need the addition of coarse peat (alpines don't go a bundle on lashings of manure – well, actually they do, but you'll get more foliage than flowers), and heavier soils can take both peat and sharp grit to improve their drainage. A dusting of bonemeal before planting will set your alpines on the road to establishment.

The amount of lime your soil contains (its acidity or alkalinity) will affect the plants you can grow. Most rock plants will be happy in slightly acid earth, but there are dozens (with the exception of some gentians, dwarf rhododendrons and others) that can be grown on chalk. Garden with your soil rather than against it and plant things that will be happy in your conditions.

Really go to town when you prepare the soil. Dig or fork it over, working in the appropriate enrichment and pulling out any weeds. Make sure that you eliminate every last bit or the blighters will be with you for ever once the rock garden is established. Let the soil settle for a while after cultivation; that way you can be sure it is firm and free of air pockets when construction of the rock garden begins. You'll also be able to spot any more weeds that emerge.

Spring and autumn are the customary times to plant, though alpines from pots can be established quite happily in summer provided enough attention is paid to watering. It follows that construction of a rock garden can be carried out at almost any time of the year except the middle of winter, when the soil will cling so fiercely to your spade and wellies as to make cultivation impossible.

WHICH ROCK?

You don't actually need any rock to grow rock plants; it's the state of the soil that matters most. But alpines do look good when displayed against a background of rock or when allowed to tumble over a boulder. This sets the gardener off on the road that leads to the rock-dotted mound. Steady now!

Decide which kind of rock would best fit into your garden. The answer is usually local stone, which will also be cheaper. The two kinds of stone most frequently offered are limestone and sandstone.

WESTMORLAND LIMESTONE is that beautifully water-worn runnelled and layered stone that, to many, typifies a traditional rock garden. Avoid buying new supplies that are destroying rare limestone pavements. Purchase only secondhand stone from old rock gardens.

SANDSTONE hails from all sorts of regions and is a bland, mid-brown stone that looks good in most situations.

GRANITE is sometimes available but is rather difficult to work with and not so easy to blend into the garden.

TUFA is formed from calcium carbonate deposits and is a soft, creamy white rock that rapidly becomes coated with mosses. Use single lumps of it as features (chip out holes and plant them with cushion-forming alpines) rather than incorporating it into a rock garden. It's a bit too pricey for that anyway.

All rock costs money so, if you can't afford it, settle for just one or two pieces set into a flat bed to remind you of the nature of the plants. Once they've been planted up, most rock gardens are covered with a 2.5 cm (1 in) layer of gravel, stone chippings or even pea shingle. This prevents the plants from being splashed by mud, it keeps their 'collars' dry, keeps down weeds, keeps in moisture and generally shows plants off to perfection.

This rock bank was constructed ten years ago. (See the photographs on p.169 of how it looked then and one year later.) It is now totally covered with plants and ready for renovation.

CREATING AN ALPINE GARDEN

Rocky outcrops

If you want to build a traditional rock garden, the best place to do it is on a slight slope. Failing this you'll have to create a mound but, if this is the case, for goodness sake make it sizeable and make the slope gradual. Try to construct an outcrop of rock that looks almost as if it is naturally occurring, pushing up through the soil in your garden.

Look at rocks in the wild and notice how their strata (layers) all run in the same direction. Arrange your rocks similarly so the layers run almost horizontally and the rocks tilt back slightly. Put large rocks in place first – 100 kg (2 cwt) is about the largest anyone can shift on their own – and position smaller ones around them. Leave pockets of firm soil for the plants both above and below the rocks. When rock was plentiful, gardeners used to bury two thirds of it in the soil. There's no need to be so extravagant nowadays; just make sure that the rocks sit firm, and really ram the soil around them with your boot and an old spade handle. Jump from rock to rock and you should not detect any wobble.

> *"You don't need rock to grow rock plants, but alpines do look good against a rocky background or when allowed to tumble over a boulder."*

Trample the soil to firm it when the job is finished so that no root-drying air pockets are left.

Rock beds

In most gardens, rock beds are easier to fit in than rocky outcrops. They're cheaper too. If your soil is sandy, the bed can be made flat on the ground. On heavier soils, it's a good idea to raise the bed up with two or three courses of brick or broken flagstone. There's no need to mortar this low wall; simply stack the bricks in a staggered fashion and make sure that they slope inwards slightly for stability. Dry-mortar the bricks with soil if you want to plant a few alpines in the crevices as you go.

Enrich the soil with peat and/or grit and add extra soil to bring the level up to within 2.5 cm (1 in) of the rim of a raised bed. One or two pieces of stone can be set in the surface of the bed to set the scene, but they are by no means essential. If your bed is too wide to lean across, lay some stepping stones for easy access.

Raised beds can also be built on patios but they will need to be about four bricks high and equipped with a drainage layer of rubble in the base before the soil is tipped in.

Scree beds

Plants that insist on really sharp drainage are those that grow in almost pure rock chippings at the foot of mountain slopes. In the garden they can be catered for in a rock bed that has been filled with a special sharp-draining mixture of 10 parts stone chippings, 1 part soil, 1 part peat or leaf mould (sifted), and 1 part sharp sand. They are really plants for the connoisseur and need a raised rather than a flat bed, which may act as a sump for all rainwater in the vicinity. Mind you, it's amazing how many rock plants will thrive in a bed containing a scree mixture provided they are not allowed to dry out in summer; there are heavy showers even on alpine screes.

Plants for scree beds

- Androsace
- Erigeron
- Erodium
- Hypericum
- Leontopodium
- Nierembergia
- Origanum
- Papaver
- Sedum
- Sempervivum
- Silene
- Verbascum

Dry walls

Where walls have to be constructed in the garden to retain banks or divide off areas, consider making them 'dry' and packing either the cavity or the rear of the wall with soil as building progresses. Pack the joints, too, and, as building progresses, you'll be able to insert sempervivums (house leeks), encrusted saxifrages and other alpines that are happy in vertical crevices. The key to success with dry stone walls is watering, for the plants may bake before their roots become established if you forget to turn on the hosepipe occasionally.

Peat beds

Peat beds are definitely for the connoisseur. They are made to accommodate a choice group of plants that relishes moist, acid soil and usually a modicum of

Creating a rock bank

1 Create a natural-looking outcrop with local rocks on slightly sloping ground. Ram the soil firmly around the rocks to make sure that there are no air pockets.

2 Water a container-grown alpine before planting. Knock it from its pot and plant without disturbing the rootball. Water it in and topdress with gravel.

3 This shows the rock bank immediately after it had been planted. The gravel topdressing helps to suppress weeds, retain moisture, and keep the plants mud-free.

4 After one year the scheme is well established, but there is room for a few more plants. Scrape away the gravel, plant the newcomer and push the gravel back.

shade. Site your peat bed against a north-facing wall and use coir-based compost if you would rather spare the peat bogs. On chalky soil you might as well forget the whole thing, for the plants insist on acidity and need a bed that has been so enriched that it contains as much peat as soil. The edges of the bed are usually raised up with peat blocks, but to conserve peat you can use logs.

The ground must be weed-free from the outset and never allowed to dry out. Peat garden plants are mainly natives of woodland, so provide them with the shade and moisture they enjoy. The peat blocks, and the peat enrichment, must be moist from the very beginning. Soak them both in a tank or tin bath of water before constructing the bed.

Apply a dusting of blood, bone and fishmeal over the entire area, then a 5 cm (2 in) mulch of pure peat before planting. Stepping stones can be laid over wide beds (it's not a good idea to flatten the springy mixture with your size ten wellies), and a close watch must be kept at all times to prevent the medium from drying out. An additional top-dressing of peat should be applied each spring, and any weeds removed as soon as they are seen.

SINK GARDENS

Should you have the good fortune to come across an old porcelain sink, don't kick it out of the way or smash it up for use as hardcore; instead, turn it into a sink garden. No, not a shining white one – a stone one.

First clean it and remove the plug. Coat the outside with a bonding agent (an adhesive that's available from any hardware shop); while this is tacky, pat on a moistened mixture of 2 parts coir, 1 part sand and 1 part cement. A 1 cm (½ in) thick layer all over the outside and 8 cm (3 in) over the lip inside is what's needed to transform the sink into a 'stone' one. The mixture is euphemistically called 'hypertufa'

Coat an old glazed white sink with an artificial stone mixture and plant it with a selection of slow-growing alpines. The dwarf conifer and rock add height and interest.

Plants for sink gardens

- Androsace
- Armeria
- Dianthus
- Erinus
- Gentiana
- Juniperus communis 'Compressa'
- Leontopodium
- Lewisia
- Oxalis
- Saxifraga
- Sempervivum
- Thymus
- Verbascum

(trust the alpine buffs to give it a fancy handle), and when it hardens it's as tough as cement itself.

Stand the sink in its final position before you coat it – afterwards it will be a weighty load. It will be best stood on bricks to keep it clear of the soil, so preventing frosting and faulty drainage. Alpines in sinks need sun just as much as those in the rock garden – although you could aim to grow one sinkful of shade-lovers (see the list on p.173).

Leave the sink to dry and harden for about two weeks, then place a layer of rubble in the base and fill with compost: John Innes No. 2 potting compost plus half its bulk of sharp sand is a good mixture. Plant your alpines – with a piece of rock and a dwarf conifer to add a bit of height and interest – and then water them in. About 20 plants will fit into the average sink if you sensibly choose those that are dwarf and slow growing. Add a 1–2.5 cm (1–2 in) layer of stone chippings to the surface and the job is finished.

Keep a close eye on the sink during summer and soak it whenever the compost shows signs of drying out. Severe frosts may lift off parts of the 'stone' coating after a time but these can easily be patched. Replace any plants that succumb during the winter, rather than removing all the plants and starting again. Only when the sink has become really overgrown and unsightly need it be renovated and totally re-landscaped but, as a general rule, age brings even greater beauty.

PLANTING AND CARING FOR ALPINES

Planting

Now that alpines are sold almost entirely in pots, they can be planted with safety at any time between early spring and autumn. Water the plant well an hour or so before planting, tap it out of its pot and plant it without disturbing the rootball. Replace the soil and firm it down, spread the gravel mulch around the plant, then water it in. Do not plant too deeply.

Planting alpines in sinks

1 Turn an old sink into an alpine garden. Stand the sink on bricks to keep it clear of the soil. Spread a layer of drainage material over the base of the sink.

2 Fill the sink to just below the rim with a mixture of John Innes No. 2 potting compost and sharp grit to improve drainage. Firm down the compost.

3 Arrange your plants over the surface of the compost so that they are roughly 15 cm (6 in) apart.

4 Remove each plant from its pot, scoop out a hole in the compost and lower it in. Firm down the compost.

5 When planting is completed, spread a 1 cm (½ in) layer of grit over the surface of the compost.

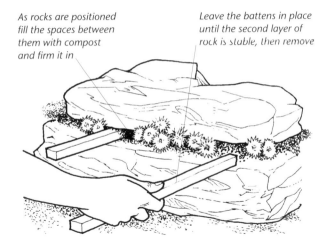

As rocks are positioned fill the spaces between them with compost and firm it in

Leave the battens in place until the second layer of rock is stable, then remove

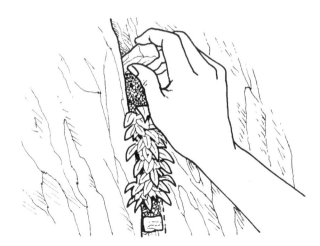

As you construct your rock garden, plant alpines and rock plants between layers of rock, firming a little compost around their roots. Place wooden battens between the plants to protect them while you put the second rock in position. Firm it into place then remove the battens.

Water thoroughly at the first sniff of drought. The plants are capable of coping with prolonged dry spells when they are established, but during their first year they will suffer greatly from drought.

Rock plants for gentle shade

All the rock plants in the A–Z section enjoy an open, sunny spot in well-drained soil, but the following will tolerate gentle shade:

- Ajuga
- Anemone
- Blechnum
- Epimedium
- Lewisia
- Pratia
- Saxifraga
- Trillium

Pruning

As a general rule, all faded flowerheads of alpines can be snipped off. Exceptions occur when you consider the seedheads to be decorative or when you want to collect seed for propagation. Spring is the best time for pruning dwarf shrubs and woody alpines, for then you can cut back to a bud that can be seen to be growing. Dead leaves and rotting tissue can be removed at any time of year, as soon as they are seen.

In this well-established rock garden in Dorset, the basic structure is almost hidden by the mounds of low-growing perennials, shrubs and conifers. The gravel layer between plants helps to retain moisture and keep down weeds.

To plant alpines and rock plants in vertical crevices in a rock garden, place a small stone at the base of the crevice. Position the plant on a layer of compost, cover the roots with more compost, and put a small stone on top of the compost to keep the plant in place.

Labelling

If you can't remember what your plants are, label them – but don't stud your rock garden with those white plastic markers that will make it look like a miniature graveyard. I find that those rigid plastic labels, written on in black indelible ink, can be pushed into the soil by the plant so that only the top 1 cm (½ in) is visible. This prevents the birds from pulling them out and lets you locate them when you need to, without their being blatantly obvious.

Plant care

Rock gardens seldom need wholesale renovation; it is usually sufficient to replace worn-out plants either with new ones or with their own divisions. Spring is the best time for this.

Weeds should be pulled up as soon as they are seen. Annuals will come out of the gravel layer with ease; any perennial weeds can be spot-treated with a touchweeder containing a suitable herbicide, such as glyphosate.

Feed your rock plants once a year in spring. Scatter a light dusting of blood, bone and fishmeal over the surface of the gravel and let the rain wash it in.

PROPAGATION

Like border plants, alpines can be propagated by seed, cuttings or division. Details of these methods can be found in Chapter 2 Propagation.

A-Z
OF
rock
plants

THIS IS A BRIEF ALPHABET OF alpines, including only those plants that are easy to grow in a variety of situations. I have slipped in a couple of tricky customers just to tax you a little, but in the main you'll find them a bright and undemanding bunch.

Some of the plants that grow in rock gardens will also grow happily in beds and borders and may have been included in Chapter 5 Shrubs and Chapter 9 Border Plants. I've indicated where this is the case.

Dwarf bulbs make a significant contribution to winter and spring colour on the rocks, and you'll find a list on p.154 (Chapter 11 Garden Bulbs), which shows some species that look good with alpines. Remember, though, that all bulbs must be allowed to produce leaves after they have flowered, and these may be a bit of a nuisance if they swamp smaller plants.

Acaena
New Zealand Burr
Carpeting

Ferny-leaved plants with burr-like flowers in summer. *A. microphylla* is the tiniest and has bronze-green leaves; *A.* 'Blue Haze' has blue-grey leaves and pink-flushed stems. Both spread freely.
PROPAGATE by division.

Aethionema
Stone Cress
15 x 60 cm (6 in x 2 ft)

A. 'Warley Rose' seems to be everybody's favourite variety. It makes a spreading shrublet and is smothered in pink flowers from late spring to early summer.
PROPAGATE by cuttings.

Ajuga See p.118

Alyssum
Gold Dust, Madwort
30 x 60 cm (12 in x 2 ft)

Alyssum is popular and deservedly so. *A. saxatile* makes mounds of grey-green spatula-shaped leaves, which are decorated with bright yellow flower clusters in spring. Brilliant with purple aubrieta, even if it isn't exactly subtle!
PROPAGATE by cuttings.

Androsace
Rock Jasmine
8 x 30 cm (3 x 12 in)

There are some lovely (and tricky) androsaces, but *A. sempervivoides* is not too difficult. It forms clumps of neat green rosettes over which rich pink flowers appear clustered on stalks in spring. The easiest of the cushion types is *A. cylindrica*, whose domes are smothered in white flowers in May.
PROPAGATE by cuttings and seed.

Anemone See p.157

Arabis
Rock Cress
15 x 60 cm (6 in x 2 ft)

A favourite along with aubrieta and alyssum, this cascading plant tumbles happily down banks to show off masses of blue, pink or white flowers. There is also a variegated variety.
PROPAGATE by cuttings.

Armeria
Thrift, Sea Pink
8 x 23 cm (3 x 9 in)

Neat domes of needle-like leaves are topped in spring with drumstick tufts of rich pink, crimson or white flowers. *A. maritima* 'Düsseldorfer Stoltz' is the best red I've seen.
PROPAGATE by cuttings.

Aubrieta
Purple Rock Cress
10 x 60 cm (4 in x 2 ft)

Another cascader, *A. deltoidea* has a host of varieties with flowers of purple, mauve, lavender, crimson, pink and white, all set off well when they open against the grey-green leaves in spring.
PROPAGATE by cuttings.

Blechnum See p.121

Campanula
Bellflower
Various sizes

There are dozens of dwarf campanulas suitable for the rock garden. Some are upright, others sprawling. Avoid those that are very invasive. Bells of blue or white are produced from spring to autumn if you choose well.
PROPAGATE by cuttings and division.

Cerastium
Snow in Summer
15 cm x 1.25 m (6 in x 4 ft)

Don't let this glorious, grey-leaved, white-flowered trailer loose anywhere near delicate plants – it will smother them. Find a sunny bank where it can romp and delight you in spring.
PROPAGATE by cuttings.

Chamaecyparis See p.59

Cytisus See p.62

Corydalis See p.123

Cyclamen See p.158

Dianthus

Pink

5–15 cm x 60 cm (2–6 in x 2 ft)

The daintiest and most desirable rock pink is *D. alpinus,* which makes a flat cushion topped with 5 cm (2 in) high wide-faced flowers of pale to deep pink. The hybrids of *D. deltoides* are taller at around 15 cm (6 in) but smaller flowered and perhaps best admired for their glowing colours at a distance. **PROPAGATE** by cuttings and division.

Diascia

23 cm x 1 m (9 in x 3 ft)

As yet not widely grown, but it certainly should be. *D.* x 'Ruby Field' produces masses of spurred salmon-pink flowers in dainty spires over low mats of foliage nearly all summer. **PROPAGATE** by cuttings and division.

Dicentra See p.124

Dryas

Mountain Avens

8 cm x 1 m (3 in x 3 ft)

Dark green, glossy, oak-shaped leaves make a dense carpet that is spattered with nodding white wood anemone flowers in early summer. There are two species commonly grown: *D. octopetala* and *D.* x. *suendermannii.* **PROPAGATE** by division.

Epimedium See p.126

Erigeron

Fleabane

23 x 30 cm (9 x 12 in)

Here's a bright alpine daisy with flowers

of white or pink. *E. mucronatus* is an easy plant to grow and blooms sporadically from late spring to autumn. Don't let it loose near dainty alpines or it will swamp them. **PROPAGATE** by division.

Erinus

10 x 15 cm (4 x 6 in)

A neat clump former with tiny saw-edged leaves and pretty pink flowers carried in clusters atop short stalks in late spring. *E. alpinus* is the true species but there is also a white variety. **PROPAGATE** by division.

Erodium

Heron's Bill

10 x 30 cm (4 x 12 in)

There are lots of erodiums valuable in the rock garden but *E. chamaedryoides* (syn. *E. reichardii*) is the most popular. White, pink-veined flowers are carried over low domes of leaves from early to late summer. **PROPAGATE** by cuttings and division.

Euphorbia

Spurge

15 x 60 cm (6 in x 2 ft)

The trailing *E. myrsinites* is a good plant to establish above a boulder or some steps where it can cast its grey-leaved stems downwards. Yellow-green flowers

open at the stem tips in late spring. **PROPAGATE** by cuttings and division.

Festuca See p.126

Genista See p.64

Gentiana

Gentian

15 x 30 cm (6 x 12 in)

The measurements I've given are for *G. septemfida,* a summer-flowering, blue-trumpeted gentian that is easy to grow on any soil. Species from Asia generally hate lime; the European ones don't seem to mind it. Start with *G. septemfida* and progress to others. **PROPAGATE** by division and seed.

Geranium

Cranesbill

8 x 60 cm (3 x 12 in)

You should grow as many geraniums as you can on your rock garden – they flower for such a long time. *G. sanguineum* 'Lancastriense' (now ssp. *striatum*) is one of the best: a sprawling mat with large, white, saucer-shaped flowers veined in pink. **PROPAGATE** by division.

Heathers See p.65

Dwarf conifers for rock gardens

Dwarf conifers offer year-round interest and add height and form to otherwise flat rock beds. When you buy such conifers, make sure that they are dwarf or very slow growing, or they'll quickly turn your rock garden into an arboretum.

- *Abies balsamea* f. *hudsania*
- *Chamaecyparis lawsoniana* 'Gimbornii'
- *Chamaecyparis lawsoniana* 'Minima Aurea'
- *Chamaecyparis obtusa* 'Nana'
- *Chamaecyparis pisifera* 'Nana'
- *Cryptomeria japonica* 'Vilmoriniana'
- *Juniperus communis* 'Compressa'
- *Juniperus horizontalis* 'Glauca'
- *Picea abies* 'Gregoryana'
- *Picea glauca* 'Albertiana Conica'
- *Picea mariana* 'Nana'
- *Pinus mugo* 'Gnom'
- *Thuja plicata* 'Rogersii'

Helianthemum
Rock Rose
23 cm x l m (9 in x 3 ft)

Sun-loving summer bloomers making twiggy rugs of evergreen or evergrey leaves. The flowers may be yellow, orange, red, pink or white. 'Henfield Brilliant' is a striking mahogany-orange. The doubles hold on to their flowers longer than the singles.
PROPAGATE by cuttings and seed.

Juniperus See p.68

Hypericum
St John's Wort
23 x 60 cm (9 in x 2 ft)

The dainty *H. polyphyllum* is a treasure that makes low domes of greyish leaves that are plastered in bright yellow, shaving-brush-centred flowers during early to mid-summer. 'Sulphureum' is a paler yellow.
PROPAGATE by cuttings, division and seed.

Iberis
Perennial Candytuft
23 cm x 1 m (9 in x 3 ft)

Dark, evergreen leaves act as an effective backdrop to the dense heads of white flowers that *I. sempervirens* produces in spring. Needs room to spread.
PROPAGATE by cuttings and division.

Leontopodium
Edelweiss
15 x 23 cm (6 x 9 in)

From tufts of greyish leaves the starry, white-felted flowers of *L. alpinum* rise up in early summer. Soggy soil kills it.
PROPAGATE by division.

Lewisia
15 x 15 cm (6 x 6 in)

Some lewisias are the devil to grow.

L. cotyledon hybrids are among the easiest. They make succulent rosettes from which rise branched flowerheads carrying salmon, pink or white flowers in summer. Lime-free soil is preferred, and walls and crevices are enjoyed.
PROPAGATE by division.

Lithodora
Gromwell
8 x 60 cm (3 in x 2 ft)

A lime-hating trailer with narrow, hairy leaves and starry true-blue flowers in summer. It's the nearest blue to a gentian outside that family. *L. diffusa* 'Grace Ward' has replaced the old favourite 'Heavenly Blue', which is now rather lacking in vigour.
PROPAGATE by cuttings.

Nierembergia
Cup Flower
5 x 30 cm (2 x 12 in)

A low-growing plant with a little carpet of dark green leaves through which appear large, white, cup-shaped flowers in early to mid-summer. *N. repens* (syn. *N. rivularis*) is the species offered.
PROPAGATE by division.

Origanum
Dittany
30 x 30 cm (12 x 12 in)

Its time of flowering alone makes *O. laevigatum* worth growing – it carries tiny crimson-purple tubular flowers on branching stems in late summer and autumn. From a distance you'll see a purple haze mingled with grey-green leaves.
PROPAGATE by cuttings and division.

Othonna
30 x 30 cm (12 x 12 in)

O. cheirifolia has fans of grey, paddle-shaped leaves and yellow daisies, carried in late spring.
PROPAGATE by cuttings.

Oxalis
Wood Sorrel
5 x 23 cm (2 x 9 in)

Neatly pleated grey leaves rise from the tuberous root and are spiced with five-petalled, pale pink, darker-veined flowers in late spring and early summer. *O. adenophylla* is the species I describe; *O. enneaphylla* is more of a spreader: the variety 'Rosea' is also popular.
PROPAGATE by division.

Papaver
Alpine Poppy
15 x 15 cm (6 x 6 in)

Short-lived but self-seeding, *P. alpinum* has finely cut leaves and plenty of pink, white, orange or yellow poppy flowers from early summer onwards.
PROPAGATE by seed.

Persicaria
Knotweed
8–15 cm x 1 m (3–6 in x 3 ft)

There are two splendid plants for the rock garden: *P. affinis*, which has pink 23 cm (9 in) high pokers in summer and autumn, and *P. vacciniifolia*, which is shorter with little pink mousetail flowers that persist right into the colder weather. Both are best when allowed to tumble over rocks.
PROPAGATE by division, or plant non-flowering cuttings in autumn.

Phlox
8 x 45 cm (3 x 18 in)

Thick mats of needle-like leaves and masses of bright, stemless flowers have made the varieties of *P. subulata* justifiably popular. They are easy to grow, too, and have blooms of violet, lavender, crimson, pink, lilac and white. 'Chattahoochee', lavender-blue with a crimson eye, and 'Daniel's Cushion', large pink flowers, are two of the best modern hybrids.
PROPAGATE by cuttings and division.

Pratia

2.5 x 45 cm (1 x 18 in)

Not showy, but nevertheless valuable, *P. angulata* 'Treadwellii' makes a rug of green leaves decorated with tiny white flowers in summer, followed by crimson-purple berries.
PROPAGATE by division.

Primula See p.133

Pulsatilla

Pasque Flower

23 x 30 cm (9 x 12 in)

Early spring favourite with upturned bellflowers of purple, blue, crimson or white, centred with a boss of yellow stamens and swathed in silky hairs. *P. vulgaris* is the most commonly grown species. Loves chalk.
PROPAGATE by root cuttings and seed.

Salix See p.75

Saponaria

Soapwort

15 x 45 cm (6 x 18 in)

The old favourite *S. ocymoides* is a bright plant to put where it can tumble down a bank or boulder. It smothers itself in summer with plenty of pink flowers and as a result it can be rather short-lived.
PROPAGATE by seed.

Saxifraga

Saxifrage, Rockfoil

Various sizes

You could plant up a rock garden with saxifrages and nothing else and still enjoy it for most of the year. The plants are divided into groups. Among the easiest (and the brightest) are the mossy saxifrages, with yellow, red, pink or white flowers carried in spring on 10 cm (4 in) stalks over cushions of bright green leaves; the encrusted saxifrages love crevices and have tough leaves decorated with lime deposits; the kabschias make hard domes of leaves and usually produce short-stemmed flowers very early in spring. They like gentle shade. Try any you can lay your hands on; they offer excellent value.
PROPAGATE by division.

Sedum

Stonecrop

Various sizes

As varied as the saxifrages and even easier to grow, sedums have succulent leaves and bright starry flowers. *S.* var. *kamtschaticum* 'Variegatum', 10 x 45 cm (4 x 18 in), is especially cheering with green and cream leaves and orange summer flowers.
PROPAGATE by cuttings.

Sempervivum

Houseleek

5 x 30 cm (2 x 12 in)

These rosette-forming succulents are quite hardy. They are available in assorted leaf colours, from green through to deep crimson, and have starry flowers of pink, crimson, yellow or white in summer. *S. arachnoideum* is the cobweb houseleek and is covered in silvery silky hairs.
PROPAGATE by division.

Silene

Catchfly

15 x 45 cm (6 x 18 in)

The one catchfly that is easy and obliging on the rock garden is *S. schafta*, which produces plenty of pinkish purple campion flowers in summer.
PROPAGATE by cuttings, division, seed.

Sisyrinchium

23 x 30 cm (9 x 12 in)

Among tufts of small, iris-like leaves, the yellow starry flowers of *S. brachypus* will appear from summer right through to autumn.
PROPAGATE by division and seed.

Thymus

Thyme

Carpeting

Dense little rugs of aromatic foliage studded with pinkish lilac flowers in summer. There are colour variations in both flower and leaf, some plants having variegated or golden foliage. Likes well-drained soil and full sun.
PROPAGATE by cuttings and seed.

Trillium

Wood Lily

23–30 x 30 cm (9–12 x 12 in)

Choice woodlanders for shady, leafy pockets in the rock garden or for a peat bed. *T. grandiflorum* is the favourite species; its three broad leaves at the tip of a strong stalk set off to perfection the large white, three-petalled flowers, which are surrounded by three small green sepals.
PROPAGATE by division.

Verbascum

Mullein

15 x 30 cm (6 x 12 in)

The neat *V.* 'Letitia' makes a mound of grey-felted leaves, topped with spires of yellow flowers from early to late summer. Protect from winter wet.
PROPAGATE by root cuttings.

Viola See p.137

Zauschneria

Californian Fuchsia

30 x 60 cm (12 in x 2 ft)

Tricky in the colder north but usually reliably perennial in the south, *Z. californica* makes a wiry shrublet with narrow greyish leaves and tubular flowers of burning scarlet. *Z.* ssp. *garrettii* 'Glasnevin' is a fraction taller and a better bet than the true species in colder areas. Both bloom from late summer into autumn.
PROPAGATE by cuttings, division, seed.

water gardens

Water adds a whole new dimension to the garden, creating a tranquil spot to relax, enticing wildlife, and providing the environment for a host of different plants

PICTURE, IF YOU CAN, A STILL SUMMER'S day by a limpid pool. Sword-leafed irises and frothy lady's mantle decorate its edges, and a water lily flaunts its shiny pads and starry flowers in the warm light. Bright goldfish dart among the shadowy water while, above the surface, dragonflies and demoiselles buzz from plant to plant, courting in the sunshine. The plate-glass surface is broken only by occasional ripples as a frog plops out of sight, or while the pond skaters dance like dervishes with a gift for walking on water. Now I know that gardening writers are incurable optimists, but this really can be the scene if you play your cards right.

Even in the tiniest garden a sheet of water will provide spicy variety. You'll be able to grow a wider range of plants, both in the water and at its edges, and whether you like it or not you'll find that you've created a miniature nature reserve. You'll always have frogs, the occasional toad and newt, and an abundance of water-loving insects. If you don't like creepy crawlies a pond is not for you. But before you try to expel the toad population, just think of all the slugs they'll eat.

If tiny tots are at large, then you'd better wait a few years before building the pond. Even a few inches of water is potentially dangerous. But there's nothing to stop you from laying a pool liner, filling it with about 15 cm (6 in) of soil, planting bog plants and then laying pebbles over the earth to produce a dry river-bed effect. A hosepipe can be played into the liner occasionally to keep the soil moist. When the children are older it's a simple job to turn the river bed into a fully fledged pool – remove the bog plants, top up with water and treat the area as you would any other new water garden. But I'm racing ahead. If you want to build a simple pool that won't turn into a gigantic bowl of green pea soup, here's what to do.

PLANNING YOUR WATER GARDEN

Choosing the right spot

Just as there's an ideal spot for every other garden feature, so there is for a pool. It should be open and sunny, not overhung by trees, but sheltered at a distance from biting winds. Under trees the water will become a mass of soggy leaf mould in autumn and your fish and aquatic plants will suffer.

If you insist on having a pool under a tree you'll have to be prepared for the task of stretching plastic netting over it every autumn before leaves start to fall, and you'll also have to put up with spindly plants that don't grow or flower as well as those in the sun. Your pool won't be so much limpid as stagnant.

What shape?

Formal pools are for formal gardens. In informal gardens (and most plots fall into that category) irregular shapes are better. I don't mean fiddly: make your pool as sweepingly curved as you can; don't go in for narrow necks and wiggly serpentine shapes.

Fit your pool into the general scheme of the garden so that its outline complements other beds and borders. Make it as large as possible; the bigger the stretch of water, the more impact it will have and the easier it will be to keep in good condition – clear and not green.

How deep?

Make your pool more than 60 cm (2 ft) deep and its bottom will become a stagnant mire of lifeless mud. Make it shallower than 30 cm (12 in) and it will heat up like a pan of water on a summer's day, encouraging those algae that turn the water green. 45 cm (18 in) is the happy medium.

Choosing a lining material

Ancient ponds were made of puddled clay but the art of constructing them went out with button boots. Concrete came next, but the work involved in making a concrete pool is amazingly arduous and life is hell when a concrete pool starts to leak. Fibreglass or rigid plastic liners may look handy little jobs when you see them stacked in the garden centre, but they are iniquitously expensive and almost always useless in the garden. Most are too small, their shapes are weird and, when filled with plant life and fish, the water nearly always turns green.

By far the best bet are the flexible liners made of butyl – a sort of luxury rubber. Thick PVC liners are the next choice (provided they're not a nasty shade of turquoise) and finally, the cheapest liner, polythene. Polythene is also the shortest lived, but where funds are lean it's worth using, for it will almost always last for three years before it needs to be replaced. The other two liners will last for donkeys' years, and repair kits are available should they be encouraged to spring a leak by the clumsy placement of a garden fork.

For goodness sake calculate carefully the size of liner you'll need. Its length will be equal to the length of the pool, plus twice the depth, plus 60 cm (2 ft) to allow it to be tucked under whatever edging material you decide on. The width will be equal to the width of the pool, plus twice the depth, plus 60 cm (2 ft). There's nothing worse than digging out a pool and putting the liner in place only to find that it's too small. The feeling compares with buying a fitted carpet that doesn't.

The handsome, bold foliage of these water plants, in all their contrasting shapes and shades of green, is reflected in the pool, creating an alluring depth and beauty to this tranquil garden feature.

Constructing a pool with a liner

1 Having decided on the shape of your pool, mark out the perimeter with pegs. Level the tops of the pegs so that they correspond with the required final level. The water should come exactly to the top of the liner.

2 Excavate the pool, making it at least 1 m (3 ft) deep at the lowest point and sloping up gradually on one side. Leave shelves about 23 cm (9 in) deep all round to take pots of marginal plants.

3 To prevent the liner being pierced once it is in place, cover the hole with a layer of fibreglass insulating material, trimming it level with the top of the hole. If you prefer, use strong polythene or a layer of sand.

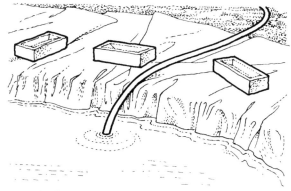

4 Lay the liner in the hole, checking that the material is evenly distributed and smoothing out wrinkles. Weight the edges with bricks. Slowly fill the pool with water, pulling and tugging at the liner to eliminate creasing.

5 When the pool is full to the brim, check that the water and pool edging are level all round. When you are satisfied, trim off the excess liner material, leaving about 15 cm (6 in) all round.

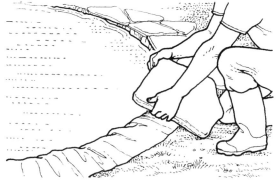

6 Edge the pool by laying flagstones around it, tucking the liner under them. Alternatively, use bricks, laying them so that they overlap the pool. Use fine sand or soil to bed the stones level, but don't cement them in.

CONSTRUCTING THE POOL

Preparing the hole

Once you've marked out the shape of your pool, either with a trail of sand or a curved hosepipe, you'll have to start excavating. April and May are the best months for pondmaking, so start digging in March to allow for unexpected interruptions.

The more help you can get at this stage the better. You'll be surprised how many barrowloads of soil come out of a relatively small hole, leaving you with the problem of deciding what to do with the stuff. The usual solution is to build a rock garden mound at the side of the pool. Avoid it. It will always be patently obvious that the mound is a spoil heap, however hard you try to disguise it with well-placed pieces of rock.

Use the stuff to build a raised bed in another part of the garden or to make a terrace near the house, or by a distant patio. It's the top 23–30 cm (9–12 in) of soil that's valuable as far as plants are concerned. Inhospitable subsoil can be used for raising up hard areas of paving and the like or, as a last resort, it can be dumped in a hired skip and carted away.

The sides of the pool should slope gently at an angle of about 45°. Cut a step into the side if you like, just about halfway up. This will provide you with a shelf on which pots and baskets of marginal aquatic plants (those that like the shallows) can be stood.

It's tempting, at this stage, to get the liner in and fill it with water, but it might be a costly operation should any pieces of sharp stone or glass be protruding. First pat the exposed surfaces of the pool with a spade to knock any protuberances back into the soil, then line the pool with a layer of fibreglass matting; or, if you prefer, spread a 2.5 cm (1 in) layer of sand over the whole area, including a 30 cm (12 in) overlap at the pool edges. With this buffering layer in place the liner can be laid.

Fitting a liner

Unpack the liner carefully and check it for holes; they have been known to exist even before the liner is laid. Stretch it over the hole (you'll need more than one pair of hands) and gently hold the edges down with smooth stones or bricks. Check that the material is evenly distributed so that when the water is in the hole the liner will overlap an equal amount all round.

Now the pool can be filled. Lay a hosepipe on the liner and turn on the tap. This is the exciting bit – as the water flows in you'll see your pool slowly taking shape. Gradually the weight of the water will push the liner flat against the soil, but you'll have to gently pull and tuck in any overlaps to avoid a mass of creases, which are potential leak areas. Turn off the hose when the pool is full to the brim. At this stage you'll be able to see the final level of the water and the level of your pool edging.

I usually incorporate a boggy area into a pool by excavating just 30 cm (12 in) of topsoil at one end, running the liner over it and up to the surface level (see p.182). The soil is then replaced before the pool is filled. Here all sorts of bog plants will be happy and they don't mind the fact that there's no drainage. Some gardeners insist on perforating the liner when it runs under a boggy area but I don't think that this is necessary. What's more, it means that you're for ever topping up the water level in the pool, and topping up encourages green scum.

Edging the pool

The most popular way of edging a pool is to lay flagstones (crazy or sane) around it, tucking the liner under them. I know it's hackneyed but it is the most reliable method. Mind you, bricks will do just as good a job. Lay them (or the flagstones) so that they overlap the edge of the pool by 5 cm (2 in). There's nothing worse than having to look at a strip of pool liner around what should be a clean-edged stretch of water. Lay your edging very carefully, using the surface of the water as a straight-edge and making sure that the liner slopes upwards from the water just a fraction to prevent any leakage. Fine soil or sand can be used to bed your stones or bricks level, but don't consider cementing them into place or repairs and adjustments may become difficult. Take your time over the edging and be meticulous – it will make or mar your pool.

Now comes the difficult bit. You've got to stand back and do nothing for about ten days. This will allow the water to settle down and disperse some of its undesirable chemical contents. After ten days you can introduce plants.

> *"Sword-leafed irises and frothy lady's mantle decorate its edges, and a water lily flaunts its shiny pads and starry flowers in the warm light."*

PLANTS FOR A WATER GARDEN

There are five basic kinds of plant that can be used in or around garden pools:

SUBMERGED AQUATICS spend most of their time below the surface of the water and many of them are vital oxygenating plants, keeping fish happy and preventing the water from becoming stagnant. Some of them produce flowering shoots above the surface, which makes them doubly valuable. No pool can become balanced and clear without oxygenators, so make sure that you have at least two bunches of these plants for every square metre (square yard) of the pool's surface area. You can always thin the plants out when they become overcrowded and give them away to pool owners anxious to clear their water.

FIXED-FLOATING AQUATICS are anchored to the base of the pool (or to a basket of compost within the pool), but their leaves and flowers float on the surface. Water lilies come into this category.

FREE-FLOATING AQUATICS bob about merrily on the surface. Duckweed (*Lemna* spp.) is a classic example, but fairy floating moss (*Azolla*) is a more desirable plant for it is less likely to swamp the pool. In fact, it's best to avoid duckweed like the plague. It will soon plaster your pool from end to end, totally masking its reflective properties, so that it looks like a sunken lawn. Woe betide the unobservant visitor who treads on it.

MARGINAL AQUATICS like to grow in shallow water and are most at home on the shelf especially built for them, just 23 cm (9 in) or so below the surface.

BOG PLANTS are happy in soil that stays constantly moist. It doesn't need to be really muddy but most of the plants are quite tolerant of extreme conditions.

Planting aquatics

Free floaters require no planting at all – just release them on the surface of the water. Bog plants can be planted with a trowel, like any garden plant, but take care not to perforate the liner. Submerged aquatics can be tied to pebbles with bits of fishing line and dropped to the bottom of the pool where they will soon take root in the sediment.

Marginal and fixed-floating aquatics, like water lilies, are best planted in the special plastic baskets that are made for the job. Line the basket with a bit of old sacking to prevent the compost from seeping out, and plant the lily or other aquatic plant in ordinary garden soil. This is the only occasion on which you'll hear me recommending garden soil for container-grown plants. Normally they are far better with a special potting compost, but in this case the chemical content of the compost would only help to foul the water.

Remove any tatty leaves or very long roots from the plants, then set them in the basket of soil so that their crown (junction of roots and shoots) is level with the

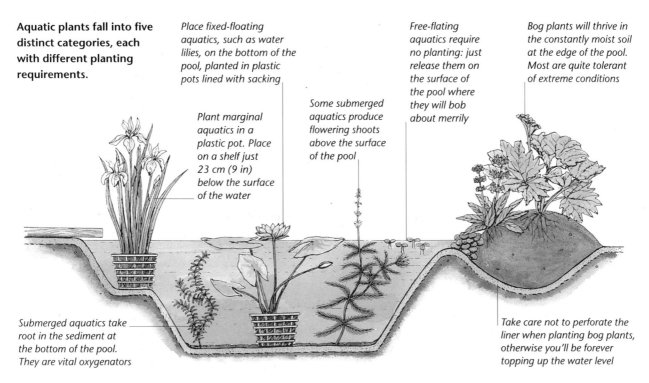

Aquatic plants fall into five distinct categories, each with different planting requirements.

Place fixed-floating aquatics, such as water lilies, on the bottom of the pool, planted in plastic pots lined with sacking

Plant marginal aquatics in a plastic pot. Place on a shelf just 23 cm (9 in) below the surface of the water

Some submerged aquatics produce flowering shoots above the surface of the pool

Free-flating aquatics require no planting: just release them on the surface of the pool where they will bob about merrily

Bog plants will thrive in the constantly moist soil at the edge of the pool. Most are quite tolerant of extreme conditions

Submerged aquatics take root in the sediment at the bottom of the pool. They are vital oxygenators

Take care not to perforate the liner when planting bog plants, otherwise you'll be forever topping up the water level

surface. Firm the earth around their roots and cover its surface with gravel to prevent fish disturbing the soil and muddying the water when the plant is in place.

When the basket is planted up, perfectionists will submerge it in a tank of water so that all air can be driven out (a process that can muddy the water). Only then will they transfer the basket to the pool, standing it on bricks at first so that it rests just 15 cm (6 in) below the surface. Marginal aquatics can go straight on to their shelves, but water lilies will appreciate this gentle introduction to the water. After a couple of weeks the bricks can be removed and the basket allowed to rest on the bottom of the pool.

Never be tempted to plant aquatics in mounds of soil at the bottom of the pool. Fish will forever create havoc down there, turning the water into grey soup as they ferret around for food. All planting up is best carried out in spring, during April and May.

FISH AND OTHER WILDLIFE

No pool should be without its quota of wildlife. You'll probably attract frogs and toads whether you want them or not; newts are not so easy to entice and you may not see them very frequently even if you take the trouble to introduce them.

Iridescent dragonflies and demoiselles, or damsel flies, will doubtless come uninvited, but they are a treat to watch as they perform aerobatics over the water in summer. Other insects will abound, especially pond skaters on the surface and water boatmen beneath. Don't worry about introducing water snails: they're not essential and if you end up with the wrong ones they'll spend all their time eating your water lily leaves instead of clearing up the sediment, for which they are renowned. I've never noticed that they make any difference at all to the state of the water.

Goldfish are a must. Most experienced pond makers recommend golden orfe as being the finest fish for a garden pond. I agree that they look good in shoals, but they're not as bright as your common- or garden-pool goldfish, which move around more slowly, giving you time to admire their vivid coats. I'd settle for a mixture of the two, avoiding those expensive and revolting Koi carp, which look like a fish-breeder's nightmare. Don't overstock your pool: allow at least 30 sq cm (1 sq ft) of surface area to each fish. Introduce your fish gently about two months after planting up the pond and establishing the oxygenators.

Always buy your fish from a reputable supplier, and

Planting water lilies

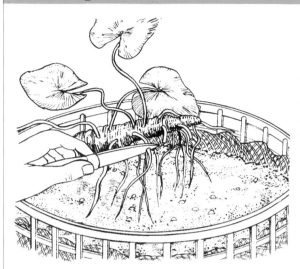

1 Before planting water lilies, cut off any tatty leaves and very long roots. Plant in ordinary garden soil, in plastic baskets lined with a piece of sacking to prevent the soil from seeping out into the water.

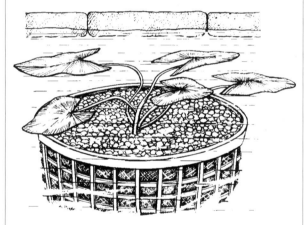

2 Cover the soil with gravel to prevent disturbance once it is submerged. Rest the basket on bricks in the pool for two weeks before lowering to the bottom.

avoid any fish that are listless or showing signs of white fungal growth. Suspend the container in which they are supplied over the edge of the pool for a few hours so that the water temperatures can equalize. Then the fish can be allowed to swim gently out of the bag or bowl into the pool.

There's much argument about feeding fish. I've kept them going for years by dropping pelleted food into the pond once a week from April to September. Allow one pellet per fish. Drop too much food into the water and it will only cause the pool to become cloudy. Between October and March the fish will find all they need among the plants and sediment – they won't need any supplements to their diet.

Diseased or damaged fish are best removed and knocked on the head. Don't be shocked at this callousness. There are all manner of cures given for diseases, most of which involve immersing the fish in a bowl of water containing some thoroughly unpleasant solution. The fish will be miserable and is quite likely to infect the other members of the pool when he's reintroduced. I stand by my seemingly cruel solution. You'll also have to harden your heart if your fish are speared and stolen by herons. This stately grey bird cleared my pond of all but two fish a couple of years ago. All the fish had names and were won at assorted fairgrounds with well-aimed ping-pong balls (so much for reputable suppliers). It was a heavy blow! Only plastic netting stretched over the pool will keep the big birds at bay, but who wants to look at a vista of plastic netting every day?

MAINTAINING YOUR WATER GARDEN

Green water
This is your biggest pool problem, but if you make your stretch of water large enough and deep enough it will only be a temporary nuisance. All pools turn green shortly after they are made but, if plenty of oxygenating plants are present, the water will eventually clear, though it may briefly turn pea-green each spring.

Don't be tempted to drain the pool and start again – the greening will only start again too. Leave the pool alone and only top it up with a hosepipe when the water level starts to get low. Excessive topping-up will exacerbate the problem.

Green blanket weed is easy to fish out with a wire-toothed lawn rake, but take care neither to disturb the sediment at the bottom of the pool nor to puncture the liner. Construct your pool properly, ensuring that the elements are balanced, and be patient: that way you're less likely to encounter long-term problems.

Renovation and cleaning
Just like other garden plants, aquatics and bog plants will need an annual clean-up in autumn and winter. Remove all faded leaves and chop back the stalks of deciduous kinds to within a few centimetres (inches) of soil level. Pull faded leaves from water lilies and remove any rotting vegetation from the water.

If your garden is a moving scene of fallen leaves in autumn it is definitely worthwhile covering the pool with plastic netting to catch the foliage before it falls in. Rotting leaves will cloud the water and poison the fish.

Don't clean the bottom of the pond every year; save the job up and do it when it is really necessary – say once every three years. Empty the pool and divide the plants at the same time, re-basketing those that need it. Before emptying the pool you'll have to catch and safely house your fish.

Create a water garden and it will instantly become a magnet to visitors: for humans it is a haven of tranquillity; for wildlife it forms a miniature nature reserve.

Creating a moving water feature

For a moving water feature you must provide a series of smaller pools at different heights above the main pool. Set a submersible pump on blocks at the bottom of the pool and run a hose from the pump to the header pool. Bury the hose in a trench to one side of the pool.

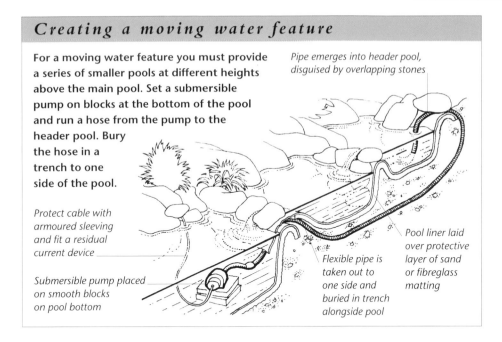

Pipe emerges into header pool, disguised by overlapping stones

Protect cable with armoured sleeving and fit a residual current device

Submersible pump placed on smooth blocks on pool bottom

Flexible pipe is taken out to one side and buried in trench alongside pool

Pool liner laid over protective layer of sand or fibreglass matting

In winter keep a patch of ice melted so that the fish can breathe. Don't clout it with a hammer – the sound waves will stun the fish – but pour a kettle of boiling water on the surface to make a hole. Extract a little water if you can, to leave a greater surface area from which the fish can extract oxygen.

OTHER WATER FEATURES

Moving water

Although fountains, cascades and waterfalls seldom look attractive on a small scale – and plants rarely enjoy growing in moving water – I have to admit that there is nothing more musical than the sound of moving water. The urge to add this feature to a water garden has been aided by the array of inexpensive equipment that is now available – submersible pumps for the circulation of water, preformed cascades and the like. For safety's sake, however, I would urge you to employ an electrician to install a pump or any other electrically powered feature in the garden. Pool lights, for example, bring the water alive at night and are especially worth installing adjacent to a patio or picture window to illuminate the plants, water and fish. Make sure the correct lights are chosen for the job: again rely on your tame electrician.

Tub pools

Finally, for the gardener with no garden, there's the tub pool. Half an oak beer cask, soundly coopered and painted inside with waterproofing bitumen, can be filled with water and used as a home for a pygmy water lily and three goldfish. If you can't lay your hands on a tub, find an old porcelain sink, treat it as described on p.170, put the plug in and fill it with water. The plants and fish will do just as well as in a tub. The fish will need warmer quarters in winter (a friend's pond will do nicely) but in spring and summer the pool will bring life and interest to the tiniest patio.

Pond-care calendar

■ *April/May*	Check that electrics are in good order. Remove, clean and store pool heater. Reconnect pump. Lift and divide overcrowded aquatics. Feed in May with special fertilizer, directly into baskets.
■ *June/July/August*	Top up water level as necessary. Remove weed from surface. Remove faded flowerheads.
■ *September/October*	Clean up pond before winter. Cut down foliage and flower stems as they fade. Remove debris and made sure leaves are kept out. Remove tender aquatics to overwinter in buckets of water in cool, frost-free place. Remove, clean and store pump and replace pool heater in pond.

If space is short create a tub pool from a half barrel. Well coopered and painted inside with bitumen, it will hold a pygmy water lily and a couple of fish.

A-Z

OF

water plants

THE FOLLOWING LISTS INCLUDE some of the most cheering water plants; all are easy to grow in the right situation. They're a self-sufficient little bunch who give of their best in spring and summer.

SUBMERGED AQUATICS

Elodea canadensis
Canadian Pondweed

This, or its larger relative *E. crispa* (syn. *Lagarosiphon major*), is the curly-leaved water plants that one was always given a sprig of with a petshop goldfish. Vital oxygenators.

Hottonia palustris
Water Violet

Feathery underwater leaves and spikes of starry flowers above water in spring.

Myriophyllum spp.
Water Milfoil

Superbly dainty feathery leaves. Spikes of insignificant flowers in summer.

Potamogeton crispus
Curled Pondweed

Narrow, wavy leaves. Insignificant flowers in summer.

Ranunculus aquatilis
Water Crowfoot

Feathery leaves below water; buttercup leaves and white flowers above in late spring.

Utricularia vulgaris
Bladderwort

A neat little insectivorous plant that catches its prey in minute bladders held among the feathery underwater leaves. Yellow snapdragon flowers appear above water in summer.

FIXED-FLOATING AQUATICS

Aponogeton distachyos
Water Hawthorn

Oval leaves sit on the water and are decorated with scented clusters of white, black-anther-dotted flowers in summer.

Nuphar lutea
Brandy Bottle; Yellow Water Lily

Water-lily-like leaves and cup-shaped yellow flowers on stalks that hold them above the water in summer.

Nymphaea species and varieties
Water Lily

The queen of the pool with those rounded, shiny pads of leaves and starry flowers of white, yellow, pink, crimson or violet-blue. I offer a selection for ponds of different sizes. All bloom for most of the summer:
'Caroliniana': pale pink; small pools and tubs.
'Escarboucle': rich rosy crimson; large pools.
'Froebelii': rosy red; small pools.
'Gladstoneana': white; large pools.
'Gonnère': white; large pools.
'James Brydon': rich rosy red; large or small pools.
'Marliacea Chromatella': pale yellow; large pools.
'Mrs Richmond' (*N. fabiola*): deep pink; large pools.
Odorata var. *minor*: tiny white flowers and leaves; small pools.
'Odorata Sulphurea': pale yellow; small pools.
'Pygmaea Alba': minute white flowers and leaves; the best choice for tubs and sinks.
'Rose Arey': rose pink; small pools.

MARGINAL AQUATICS

Acorus calamus
Sweet Flag
75 cm (2½ ft)

Sword-shaped leaves that are sweetly scented when crushed. The variety 'Variegatus' is cream-striped and more compact.

Butomus umbellatus
Flowering Rush
90 cm (3 ft)

Grassy green leaves and umbels of lovely pink flowers in summer.

Calla palustris
Bog Arum
23 cm (9 in)

Glossy, green, heart-shaped leaves and miniature arum lily flowers of clear white in summer.

Caltha palustris
Kingcup; Marsh Marigold
30 cm (12 in)

Heart-shaped green leaves and bright yellow buttercup flowers in spring. The double-flowering variety 'Flore Pleno' is best.

Glyceria maxima var. *variegata*
Reed Meadow Grass
60 cm (2 ft)

A stunning variegated grass with leaves striped green and creamy white. Vigorous.

Houttuynia cordata 'Flore Pleno'

45 cm (18 in)

Pointed, heart-shaped leaves make a dense clump that sports white, pyramidal flowers in summer. Very handsome.

Iris laevigata

Smooth Iris

75 cm (2½ ft)

Sword-shaped leaves and exceptionally handsome wide-petalled flowers of purple, blue, pink or white in early summer.

Iris pseudacorus

Yellow Flag

90 cm (3 ft)

Grey-green leaves and bright yellow iris flowers in early summer.

Juncus effusus 'Spiralis'

Corkscrew rush

45 cm (18 in)

A reed with leaves spiralled just like corkscrews – a conversation piece if nothing else.

Mentha aquatica

Water Mint

45 cm (18 in)

Green leaves and the usual lilac summer flowers of mint. Equally as aromatic as garden mint and just as useful.

Menyanthes trifoliata

Bog Bean

30 cm (12 in)

Three-lobed leaves and white early summer flowers with fringed edges.

Myosotis scorpioides

Water Forget-me-not

23 cm (9 in)

Clouds of pale blue flowers in late spring and early summer.

Orontium aquaticum

Golden Club

30 cm (12 in)

Golden-yellow flower spikes rise up from oval green leaves in early summer.

Pontederia cordata

Pickerel Weed

45 cm (18 in)

Arrow-shaped, glossy green leaves and spires of pale blue flowers in summer.

Sagittaria sagittifolia 'Flore Pleno'

Arrowhead

45 cm (18 in)

The double white flowers are carried up tall stems.

Scirpus (syn. *Schoenoplectus*) *tabernaemontani* 'Zebrinus'

Zebra Rush

90 cm (3 ft)

Porcupine quills of green banded with creamy yellow. Very handsome.

FREE-FLOATING AQUATICS

Azolla caroliniana

Fairy Floating Moss

A pale green, lacy-leaved floater that becomes pinky red with the onset of cold weather.

Hydrocharis morsus-ranae

Frogbit

Miniature water-lily leaves and three-petalled white flowers in summer. Sinks to the bottom in winter.

Stratiotes aloides

Water Soldier

Rosettes of green leaves float half in, half out of the water. White, three-petalled flowers open in summer.

Bog plants

The following plants are described in detail in Chapter 9 Border Plants. They will all do well in a patch of moist soil on the pond bank.

- *Aconitum*
- *Ajuga*
- *Alchemilla*
- *Aruncus*
- *Astilbe*
- *Dicentra*
- *Gunnera* (massive bogs only!)
- *Hemerocallis*
- *Hosta*
- *Iris* (some)
- *Lobelia*
- *Lysimachia*
- *Mimulus*
- *Monarda*
- *Rheum*
- *Rodgersia*
- *Trollius*
- *Zantedeschia*

A pale blue bridge crosses a shallow pool in our garden. Variegated iris and knotweed decorate its banks.

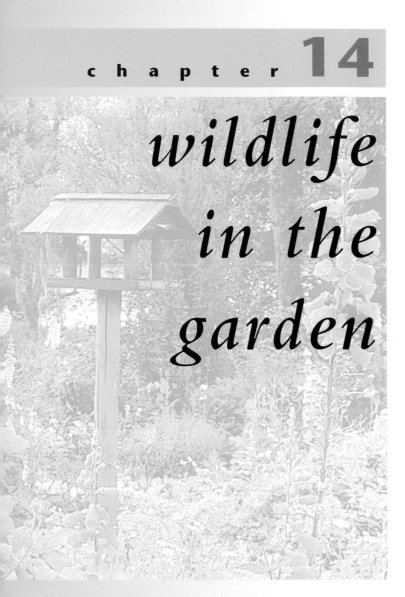

wildlife in the garden

A garden is brought to life

by the wildlife it attracts: by

providing the right conditions,

and by not being too

tidy-minded, you can encourage

a host of creatures to visit

A GARDEN WITHOUT ANIMALS AND BIRDS, butterflies and bees is as dead as a doornail and as dull as ditchwater. Ever since I was a lad I've been just as interested in the wildlife to be found in a garden as in the plants. Serried ranks of lobelia and alyssum, salvias and French marigolds hold no joy for me, but a bank of billowing summer flowers that's perhaps a bit too overgrown for the neat-and-tidy-minded gardener offers great excitement when it's alive with butterflies and abuzz with bees.

I don't carry my love of nature to extremes though: snails and slugs have to be ruthlessly expelled from the rock garden and the vegetable plot – the places where they seem to do most damage – and I can't stand greenfly on roses. So how is a gardener to live with these conflicting ideas? It's not as difficult as it sounds.

The first rule is one that all lazy gardeners will enjoy putting into practice: don't be too tidy. That's not an excuse for letting all parts of the plot lie fallow for the rest of your life; it's simply a matter of selecting certain areas of the garden that can be left relatively undisturbed and where the right weeds can be encouraged to grow. There's planning to be done, even in a wilderness.

ATTRACTING BUTTERFLIES AND MOTHS

Butterflies

Most of us admire butterflies, and a few of us like moths as well. Both can be encouraged to make themselves at home in the garden if the right food plants are present. There are two distinct kinds of food plant: those that nourish the larvae or caterpillars, and those from which the adults drink nectar. You'll need patches of both so that you have vital egg-laying sites for the propagation of the species, and insect pubs where the adults can drink their fill from spring to autumn.

In a large garden, it's easy to let a sunny and sheltered corner run wild with nettles, thistles, grasses and other food-supplying weeds for egg laying; in a small garden it's more difficult to squeeze them in, but a patch of nettles alone (always in a sunny spot) will bring you a surprisingly rich harvest.

If you enjoy watching adult butterflies feeding by day, you'll be pleased to hear that there are plenty of ornamental garden plants whose nectar they love. Your entire plot does not have to be converted to (or allowed to remain) a flowerless jungle.

Plants with purple or yellow flowers are apparently the favourites, but in my own garden the following are the ones that have been as well patronized as any real-ale pub by the butterfly population. Single flowers are always better than doubles for they have large nectaries: ageratum, alyssum, aubrieta, buddleja, caryopteris, echinops, eryngium, grostemma, hebe, honesty, lavatera, lavender, liatris, Michaelmas daisy, nicotiana, petunia (single), phuopsis, sedum, centranthus, nepeta, phlox, scabious, thyme.

Moths

The moths have an equally varied diet from privet to various weeds, cabbages and lettuces. Most of them are nocturnal but they are often disturbed during the day if you brush past their resting sites among plants. In our garden we are plagued with large yellow underwings, but the occasional maiden's blush, magpie moth and hawk moth come to light too.

Finally, remember that a little shelter in the garden, in the form of a thick coat of ivy on a garage or outbuilding, or a thicket of brambles in a corner, will allow hibernating butterflies and moths to shelter through the winter and carry on their good work the following season.

BEE-ATTRACTING PLANTS

If you wave your arms around and do an impersonation of a windmill every time a bee comes near you, the last thing you'll want to do is attract them to your garden. But if you like all forms of wildlife, then the following plants will persuade the bees that your garden really is the place to visit: borage, buddleja, echinops, erica, eryngium, fuchsia, godetia, lavatera, lavender, lime trees, lupins, monarda, nasturtium, nepeta, nigella, phacelia, scabious.

BIRD FEEDING AND NESTING

Faded seedheads on all manner of plants, from thistles to sunflowers and Michaelmas daisies, will keep seed-eating birds such as goldfinches busy for hours, and berrying shrubs, like berberis, pyracantha and symphoricarpos, will feed other species in winter. That's the time at which you should be making a special effort to supplement the diet of all wild birds. Outside my study and our sitting-room windows, wire-netting bird feeders, filled with bits of fat and peanuts, hang from November to March. After years of squirrels destroying flimsy models, I now have sturdy, squirrel-proof ones. The feeder is filled every morning and by evening it's almost empty, proving that the birds have a powerful hunger. The bird bath (kept thawed in winter) is patronized too and, for those species that have no head for heights (though they seem happy enough when flying), mixed wild bird food is scattered on the lawn. The centre of the lawn is the place for bird food: scatter it near beds and borders and cats will stealthily sneak through the undergrowth to wreak havoc.

We never bother with coconuts as they seem to dry up before the birds can really get stuck in. Pieces of bacon rind are ignored too; it's the softer fat or suet that goes down best. Coal tits, blue tits, great tits, nuthatches and greenfinches are regularly in evidence, and a great spotted woodpecker sometimes turns up too. So far, after 11 years of living here, 47 species of bird have appeared at one time or another.

Stop feeding the birds as soon as spring arrives; if their young are fed a diet of peanuts they'll suffer. By egg-hatching time you should be encouraging the adults to help you out with pest-control in the garden; there will be plenty of caterpillars and grubs to devour.

Some birds are irritating pests at certain times of year. Sparrows and bullfinches will strip fruit trees of

> *"Butterflies can be encouraged to make themselves at home in the garden if the right food plants are present."*

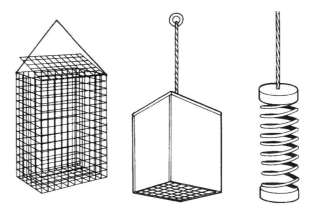

There are various types of bird feeder on the market. Fill them with winter snacks of suet, fat and peanuts to attract tits, nuthatches, and greenfinches to your garden.

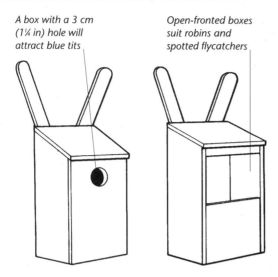

A box with a 3 cm (1¼ in) hole will attract blue tits

Open-fronted boxes suit robins and spotted flycatchers

Choose a nestbox suited to the birds you want to attract, and hang it out of the way of predatory cats.

their buds, often as soon as the leaves fall in autumn. Netting is really the only successful long-term deterrent. Blackbirds will adore your raspberries, but mostly the depredations can be lived with, and both you and the birds will have a substantial diet.

It's always fun to put up nestboxes, but do the job properly. Tits need a box with a hole just 3 cm (1¼ in) in diameter; make it any larger and sparrows will take over. Robins and spotted flycatchers need open-fronted boxes, and there are all manner of different permutations that can be made at home or bought from special firms. Well made from tough plywood, they are highly successful in persuading birds to nest.

The secret is to find the right place for the box. I'm no expert here, but have put all my boxes at a height of around 2 m (7 ft) – out of the way of our marauding cat. I've yet to try them in woodland, but they've lured blue tits with ease on walls facing east and south. Put your boxes up in autumn. That gives the birds a chance to do plenty of prospecting right through the winter. Sometimes they'll roost in the boxes rather than nesting in them; other years they'll ignore them completely. As well as being skilful in placing your boxes, you'll also have to rely on luck.

Don't forget that birds like the cover and nesting sites provided by shrubs, hedges and brambles. Provide these hiding places and you're bound to get more birds.

ENCOURAGING OTHER WILDLIFE

I've no room to launch into a comprehensive natural history of the back garden, but I will remind you of the joys to be had from hedgehogs, who slurp saucers of milk more quickly and noisily than a cat, and the mixed feelings you'll have about foxes, rabbits and deer.

There's nothing as romantic as the sight of a few

Create a water garden and it will become an instant magnet to all manner of wildlife, such as frogs, newts, dragonflies, and pond skaters.

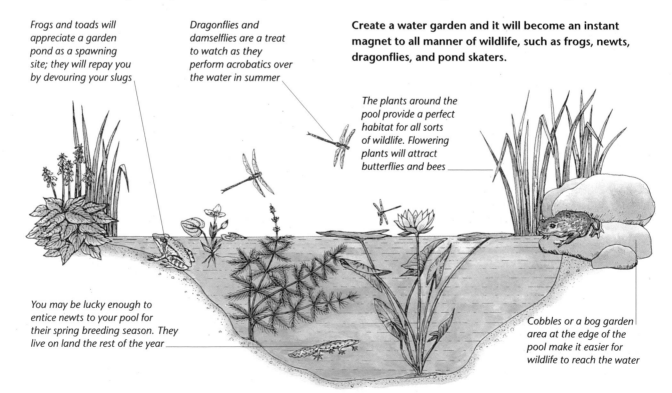

Frogs and toads will appreciate a garden pond as a spawning site; they will repay you by devouring your slugs

Dragonflies and damselflies are a treat to watch as they perform acrobatics over the water in summer

The plants around the pool provide a perfect habitat for all sorts of wildlife. Flowering plants will attract butterflies and bees

You may be lucky enough to entice newts to your pool for their spring breeding season. They live on land the rest of the year

Cobbles or a bog garden area at the edge of the pool make it easier for wildlife to reach the water

deer at the top of our garden in summer or winter, but I go up the hill with a sinking feeling whenever they've been, wondering what they've eaten this time. Once they've ring-barked a pine tree or another favourite it's curtains (for the tree, not the deer). Plastic rabbit guards are a bit of a help, but not much.

A garden pool is less of a worry and more of a magnet for all sorts of creatures from frogs and toads (valuable slug eaters) to dragonflies and damsel flies. You might be lucky enough to have newts, and you'll certainly have pond skaters whose acrobatics defy the laws of gravity. With frog-spawning sites disappearing every year, the back-garden pond is playing a vital role in their continued wellbeing. (See Chapter 13 Water Gardening for further details.)

WILD FLOWER GARDENING

Finally, don't forget the wild flowers. Only where there's space to spare for such luxuries will you want to make a patch of natural 'wild garden' or grassland where the rarer wild flowers can feel safe. But such a patch dovetails into other forms of wildlife encouragement because butterflies, moths, bees and other insects will relish the opportunity to feed in these mini-reserves. To keep the patch as grassland you'll still have to mow, but only three times a year: in early to mid-July, late August and finally in October.

There's just one problem with this type of gardening, and that's the use, or non-use, of chemicals. It's a thorny old problem and I don't want to preach about the wonders of organic gardening, but if you're out to create a reserve that will replace the natural habitats decimated by modern farming methods and pesticides, you'll have to take

A wildflower garden provides a delightful way of encouraging the conservation of native species and attracting wildlife.

extra care. If your plants need feeding, try to use organic fertilizers such as blood, bone and fishmeal, which encourage bacterial activity. Inorganic fertilizers like sulphate of ammonia and superphosphate supply nutrients in a readily accepted form as far as plants are concerned, but they give the bacteria – vital to soil wellbeing – nothing to break down. Avoid using herbicides altogether, except on paths and drives, and learn to live with a weedy lawn. I have! When really severe outbreaks of pests appear, most gardeners feel that they have to take action with a chemical. If this is necessary, do the job in the evening when there are few butterflies and bees around. Choose a still, windless day and a chemical that is known to be fairly specific. There is one chemical at least that will kill aphids (greenfly and blackfly) while leaving beneficial insects such as bees, ladybirds and lacewings unharmed. Any chemical that has these advantages is to be preferred to a lethal insecticidal potion that kills everything and anything, or to a supposedly harmless concoction made from rhubarb leaves, which is equally toxic to other forms of insect life. The choice is yours.

lawns

Restful on the eye, the perfect foil for surrounding plants, and a place for the whole family to play or relax – it is hardly surprising that lawns feature in most gardens

EVERY GARDEN HAS A LAWN – OR SOMETHING that passes for one. It's quite true that in tiny gardens the lawn brings with it a host of problems, but whatever the arguments against it, it has one unassailable advantage: it's cheap. It's all very well for the landscape architect to persuade you that what you really need is York stone paving, granite setts or brick paviors, but if you have to take on a second mortgage to cover the cost it's probably not worthwhile.

Mind you, he has a point about grass being a bad choice in confined spaces. It will be difficult to mow; the clippings might be difficult to dispose of; the grass is not an all-weather surface, so you'll have to steer round it when it's muddy; and you'll likely as not have problems with wear and tear, moss and fungus diseases (but then so will any lawn owner).

Grown well, all the usual compliments levelled at a lawn apply: it sets off the rest of the garden; it shows off the plants a treat; when new-mown, it makes the rest of the garden look tidy even if it isn't. And you can't play croquet on York stone paving.

THE NEW LAWN

If you're faced with the task of making a new lawn, get ready for a bit of hard graft. Whether you sow seed or lay turves the preparation of the ground is exactly the same. It should be cleared of debris, builder's rubble, long grass, all weeds and any piles of subsoil (if it's a new site), then forked or dug over. That's several weeks' work in just one sentence.

It does pay to take a bit of trouble at this stage. If you can dig out completely any tree stumps, for instance, you'll be saved the job of filling in the hole that appears years later when the stump rots. It's at this stage that fungi keep coming up on the lawn too.

A generous helping of moist peat dug into the soil during preliminary cultivations will give the grass some welcome organic matter into which it can sink its shallow roots and obtain a little resistance to drought.

Try to make the site as level as you can. Keen types will hammer pegs into the ground to the required level, and check them against one another with a straightedge and spirit level. To be honest, most gardeners needn't go to this length, but it's a good idea to rake the surface as level as possible, tramp it down with your feet and rake again, crouching down and running your eye over the ground to spot any bumps and hollows that can be flattened or filled in.

Preparing for a new lawn

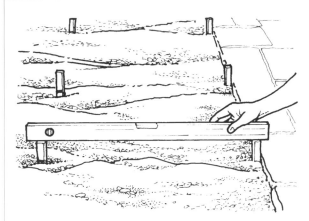

1 Before sowing grass seed or laying turf, it is essential that the site is cleared of debris and weeds, forked over and enriched with organic matter. Then get the site as level as possible, using a spirit level and straightedge set between pegs marked at the required level.

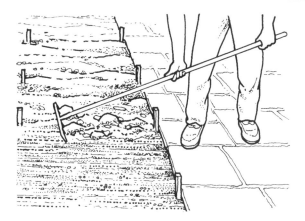

2 Rake the soil so that it reaches the level marked on the pegs. Fill any hollows with added topsoil and flatten bumps: although the lawn doesn't have to be perfectly level, these would create problems when mowing. Continue raking and levelling the entire site.

3 Once you have raked the whole site level, firm the surface by tramping over it evenly with your feet, or tamping with the back of rake. This will ensure that there are no soft spots that might later sink. Check the level again and fill any hollows as before.

4 When you are satisfied that the site is level and firm, rake it to a fine tilth and leave it for a few weeks so that any residual weeds can be dealt with. Before sowing grass seed or laying turf, scatter a general fertilizer over the site and lightly rake it in.

When you have prepared the site it's a good idea to let it stand idle for at least a month before you sow or turf; that way any resident weeds you overlooked will come up and show themselves and you can remove them smartly.

You'll probably have little choice when it comes to siting your lawn, but remember that grass grows poorly in heavy shade under trees, and is likely to be out of bounds for much of the year on really sticky, boggy soil.

When it comes to shape, that's something for you to decide, but remember that twiddly bits are hard on the eye and hard to mow. Try to avoid making square or rectangular lawns: go for sweeping, natural lines, which will show off your plants better and look a little more romantic and restful.

Fiddle around with the shape of the lawn by laying a hosepipe on it to mark out the area. Go inside the house and check your design from windows both upstairs and down until you hit upon the right shape.

Mark this out on the soil with a trail of sand. If you're being distinctly put off by the thought of going through all this rigmarole, there are a few shortcuts you can take in soil preparation. The weeds can be killed off with a herbicide such as Tumbleweed (glyphosate) – though you may need two or three applications – and the ground can then be rotavated. There are one or two disadvantages with this system. First, not all the weeds may have been killed and those that have survived will re-emerge later (probably chopped up into ten viable pieces). Secondly, the soil will be very fluffy and you'll have to make sure it's well firmed before sowing or turfing (shuffle around with your feet rather than using a roller, which may just flatten the surface). You'll still have to take as much care over levelling as if you were using a fork or spade.

SEED OR TURF?

It's tempting to turf a lawn rather than seed it because the effect is instant, but consider the disadvantages of turf as well. It is ten times more expensive than seed; it varies in quality from supplier to supplier, and you'll still have to wait for a few weeks before you can walk on it or the un-knit turves will skid around. What's more, there's a darned sight more labour involved in laying turf evenly than there is in scattering grass seed and raking it in.

> *"If the turf stays green and looks fine from a distance, then why worry if there's a bit of dock or dandelion in it?"*

The advantages of turf? Well, apart from being almost instant, you can lay it at any time of year when the soil is moist, rather than dusty, frozen or muddy. Seed is best sown in September or April and May.

Finding good turf is not easy. Look through the Yellow Pages under Turf Supplies and ring around for a few quotes. Beware of firms who offer just one type of turf – it's probably mown meadow turf, and even if it's described as 'weed treated' you're likely to find that it's as varied in make-up as a patchwork quilt. Settle for a good, hard-wearing turf from a specialist supplier; don't be talked into having flashy 'sea-washed' stuff which is far too luxurious for a resilient lawn. Arrange for delivery on a day when you know

you will be at home and ready to lay the stuff (weather permitting). Turf stacked for more than three days soon turns yellow and starts to die off. If you have to stack it yourself, remember to stack it grass to grass and soil to soil. Rolled turves can be left as they are, but do lay them quickly.

If you decide on seed, then you'll have to choose the kind of mixture you need. Don't get ideas above your station and sow a 'bowling green' type of mixture that looks good on the green-striped, pictorial packet. If you want a hard-wearing lawn that can tolerate children and picnics choose a mixture containing a dwarf variety of ryegrass. These mixtures make a dense, good-looking sward that wears well, and because the ryegrass is a dwarf strain it won't produce any of those long stems that refuse to be cut by the mower. The 'bowling green' mixtures are only suitable for lawns that won't be asked to take much wear. They don't contain ryegrass and need a much more comprehensive lawn care programme than those seed mixtures that do. They are likely to become overrun by alien grasses if not mown regularly, and fall prey to fungus diseases more easily. On the other hand, if you want to spend every waking hour producing a velvet lawn that is the envy of your neighbours, the fine mixture is the one to go for.

Slightly shady areas can be sown with grass seed mixtures that are made up from shade tolerant grasses – look for them in the garden centre.

Whether you choose seed or turf you'll still have to calculate how much you need. Turf is sold in square metres or square yards, as a rule, and seed by weight. The recommended sowing rate is 40 g (about 1½ oz) per square metre or yard; that will allow the birds a few beakfuls without spoiling your lawn.

LAYING TURF

Once the turf is neatly stacked near the site of your lawn-to-be and the earth is waiting to receive it, scatter a light dusting of general fertilizer over the soil (a handful to the square metre or yard will do) and lightly rake it in. Don't rake for hours or you'll find more stones than you know what to do with. The soil should be nicely moist – not dusty or so wet that it clings to your wellies.

You'll need a spade and a plank before you go any further: the spade for lifting and patting the turves into place (as well as adding and subtracting soil beneath them) and the plank to walk on.

Laying turf

Start at one end of the site and lay a row of turves overlapping the intended boundary. Lay them immediately in front of your plank so that you achieve a straight line right at the start. Butt them as close together as you can and pat them firm with the back of your spade (not so hard that they turn to mud). If any of them sit too far up or down, add or subtract a little soil beneath them. If you find, as you're laying the turves, that they don't sit quite flush with one another, take a bucket of soil with you and fill any gaps.

When the first row is laid, move your plank on top of them and lay the next row, staggering the joints like those of bricks in a wall. Continue like this, overlapping the boundary of the lawn all the way round – you can trim it up later.

When the entire area is covered, remove the plank and keep every member of the family off the lawn for at least ten days; that way the turf will have a chance to settle without being buffeted around.

1 Stand on a plank placed on the turves you have already laid. Work forwards and lay in a brick pattern.

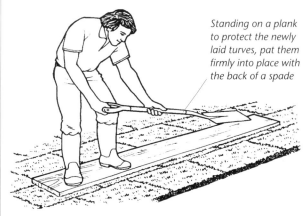

Standing on a plank to protect the newly laid turves, pat them firmly into place with the back of a spade

If any of the turves sit too high or too low, adjust the level of the soil beneath them

2 Pat down the turves so that they are firmly in contact with the levelled earth. Don't bash

3 Adjust the level of uneven turves by adding or subtracting soil underneath them as necessary.

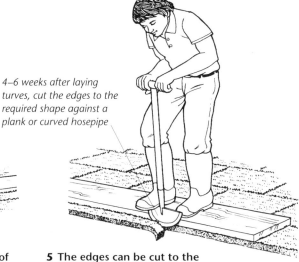

4–6 weeks after laying turves, cut the edges to the required shape against a plank or curved hosepipe

4 As the job progresses, brush fine soil (or a mixture of peat and sand) into any cracks between the turves.

5 The edges can be cut to the required shape with a spade or half-moon iron.

If you're turfing in spring or summer, have a hosepipe and sprinkler handy and turn it on over the completed lawn at the slightest suspicion of dryness. Left to bake, the turf will turn brown, refuse to knit together and shrink, causing large gaps to appear.

With any luck the lawn will be ready to walk on after four to six weeks, depending on the time of year (sooner in spring and summer; later in winter). It's at this stage that you can trim the edges against a plank or a curved hosepipe. You can start to mow, too, but take it slowly and don't cut the grass too short – just remove the top 1 cm (½ in) of grass once it has grown 5 cm (2 in) high. Soon you can mow more regularly, but it's still a good idea to avoid giving the grass too much wear, and to make sure it never dries out. The kinder you are at this stage, the more quickly will your lawn establish itself.

SOWING SEED

Soil preparation is exactly the same for sowing seeds as for laying turf: scatter a handful of general fertilizer over each square metre or square yard of soil and lightly rake it in. Shuffle over the soil with your feet to firm it, then rake again. The soil should be moist, not dusty or muddy. Lawns sown in September stand the best chance of establishing quickly: there is less likely to be a sudden burst of weed growth than there is with the April and May sowings, and the earth will be nicely warmed up after the summer sunshine and gently moistened by early autumn rains. The grass will also be expected to put up with less wear and tear through autumn and winter than it would through summer, so it's likely to grow thicker more quickly.

The recommended sowing rate of 40 g (about 1½ oz) per square metre or yard will allow the birds to have a nibble, so there's no need to be neurotic and rig up Heath Robinsonian devices using little metal bottle tops and steak-and-kidney pie dishes. Sparrows will only take dust baths on the soil if it's dusty which, as far as your grass seed is concerned, is a bad thing. Keep it moist with the aid of a sprinkler. The odd bit of disturbance won't really make any difference.

Don't go to the trouble of weighing out every 40 g (1½ oz) of the seed. Weigh one lot, put it into an old plastic yoghurt or cream carton and mark the side with a felt-tip pen. Use the measure for all subsequent work. I've never been conscientious enough to mark out the plot into square metres, but then I kid myself that I know what a metre looks like. If you don't, check

up and chalk it out on a path or patio. When it's imprinted on your mind, start sowing; for goodness sake don't mark out the entire area into little squares with canes and string.

Scatter each measure of seed evenly over its allotted area and, when the whole patch is sown, go over it with a rake, lightly raking the seed in. Don't roll it. If you've shuffled over the ground with your feet to firm it, that's all that's needed.

Turn a sprinkler on whenever the soil looks dry. It will seem ages before any grass shows, but after a few weeks, when you're bent double looking across the surface of the soil, you'll detect a faint green haze. That's the youngsters pushing their way up through the soil. Don't worry if the effect is patchy, even when the grass is a few centimetres or inches high. The seeds germinate erratically and may still come through a few weeks after the first ones showed.

The sweeping curve of the lawn, echoed by the brick path around its perimeter, draws the eye around the garden to the secluded dining area beyond, creating a pleasing sense of space and unhurried leisure.

When much of the grass is about 5 cm (2 in) high, go over the lawn either with a light roller (if you have one) or with a cylinder lawn mower that can be held so that only the back roller comes into contact with the soil. This rolling will make sure that the roots of the young plants are firmly anchored to the soil before they are pulled at by the mower.

The following day the lawn can receive its first mowing: take off just the top 1 cm (½ in) of grass, which will encourage the plants to produce sideshoots lower down, so thickening up the lawn. Cut again when the lawn has put on another 1 cm (½ in) of growth, and don't worry if there's a lot of weed growth present – most of it will be killed off by regular

Caring for your lawn

Most of us are rotten to our lawns; we cut them and bash them around without ever giving them regular meals or a wash and brush-up. Expert gardeners have complicated lawn-care programmes, but the following are the basic tasks necessary to produce a decent patch of greensward.

SCARIFYING

Scarifying involves the removal of dead grass known as thatch. It also pulls out moss. Use a wire-toothed 'springbok' rake for the job, or one of those excellent new electrically powered lawn rakers. Don't worry that the lawn looks a bit bare and tatty afterwards; it will soon pull round and grow away with renewed vigour. Timing: September.

SPIKING

Spiking the lawn with a fork or a hollow-tined aerator relieves surface compaction and improves drainage and soil condition. Ram the fork in to a depth of at least 10 cm (4 in) and wiggle it around a little. Stab it in at intervals of 15 cm (6 in). Timing: September, after scarifying.

After you've scratched or scarified your lawn, aerate it by spiking with a fork or a special hollow-tined aerator to relieve compaction and to improve surface drainage.

FEEDING

This is something that shouldn't be neglected. Apply a lawn fertilizer (or plain sulphate of ammonia at the rate of one clenched handful to the square metre or square yard) and water it in with a sprinkler if it doesn't rain within 24 hours. Timing: May and, if you're really keen, July as well.

WATERING

During dry periods in spring and summer, leave a sprinkler playing over the lawn for at least two hours. Oscillating sprinklers are better than the rotating type because they cover a sensible rectangular area rather than a circle, and they can be adjusted to throw in just one direction if you're having a picnic nearby. Timing: Spring and summer.

In autumn, lawns benefit from a good scratch with a wire-toothed rake to remove dead grass or 'thatch'.

mowing, and any weeds that remain can be treated later with a lawn weedkiller. If you are committed to organic gardening, avoiding the use of weedkillers in particular, then you will have to settle for a weedy lawn. Some weeds, such as dandelions and plantains, can be removed by hand with an old dinner knife; others are difficult to eradicate by mechanical means.

Any bare patches that remain after eight weeks can be resown with seed. Rake them over, scatter the seed on and rake again.

Lawns sown in September will need few mowings before the onset of winter, but those sown in spring can be progressively mown more regularly until they are being cut once or twice a week. Keep off the area until the grass looks well established and quite thick. After about eight weeks you should be able to tread your verdant sward and park a deckchair on it, but wait a little longer before giving the go-ahead for vigorous games of football. It will be some time before the roots of the young grass plants have explored deeply into the soil.

LEAF SWEEPING

Removing fallen leaves is vital if your lawn is not to become patchy and brown. Sweep all leaves from the surface as soon as possible and compost them. Timing: Autumn.

ROLLING

Rolling can help to even out bumps on a new lawn if your mower does not possess a hefty rear roller, but it's not essential. Timing: Spring.

TOPDRESSING

Topdressing is really only for the keen gardener. Scatter a mixture of sieved leaf mould and sand over the lawn and brush it in. One bucketful will do about 6 square metres (about 7 square yards). Timing: Autumn.

Follow up scarifying and spiking by topdressing with a mixture of leaf mould, sand and soil, raked well in.

THE IDLER'S LAWN

Any piece of ground that's fairly level and which has reasonable soil is a potential lawn. If you mow whatever grows on it – weeds, meadow- and weed-grasses – it will eventually turn into a lawn. The ironic thing is that after six or seven years you'll probably detect no difference between this type of lawn and one that was originally sown with a rye-grass mixture, unless the latter has been assiduously fed and treated against weeds. Where large areas of coarse turf are needed, under fruit trees and in paddocks, the mowing technique is well worth putting into practice.

MOWING

Everybody mows, but some mow better than others. The secret is to avoid cutting the grass too close. Far too many lawns are shaved, with the result that they wear badly and are susceptible to drought. Mowing is essential to encourage fine grasses and a thick carpet of growth, but it is far better for your grass (and for you) to mow regularly, taking off just a little, rather than to mow once a fortnight too close to the soil.

As a rule, mowing is necessary between March and October – more regularly at the height of the season than at each end. In June and July weekly or twice weekly mowing will be needed. I never mow closer than about 2 cm (¾ in), and when the weather is really dry I prefer to leave on about 2.5 cm (1 in) of grass. Really rough areas can be left with about 4 cm (1½ in) of grass after cutting.

If you've masses of lawn and are bone idle, you can

manage by mowing wide paths through it regularly, and cutting the long stuff occasionally. Not only will it save time, but it looks pleasant, too. If you don't treat your lawn with weedkiller you'll be surprised how many wild flowers it contains.

Take the clippings off the lawn when you mow, collecting them in a grassbox fitted to the mower, and compost them (taking care to mix them with other compost or they'll turn into a hot and smelly black gunge). If you can't be bothered to remove them, make sure you cut the grass regularly so that the clippings are small enough to be dried up by the sun and blown away by the wind. Left in large clods they'll kill out patches of grass and look very unsightly. Lawns from which the clippings are never removed will benefit from being scarified twice: once in June and once in September.

EDGING

Cutting the frayed edges from your lawn is a time-consuming and back-aching business. Use a pair of long-handled edging shears if you have lots of vertical lawn edges, but if possible try to get rid of them to save labour. A single row of bricks laid flush with the soil at the edge of the lawn will mean that you can run the mower over them and so keep the grass in trim without resorting to shears. When the grass does start to creep over the brickwork you can give it a yearly cut back with a spade or a half-moon iron sold especially for cutting new lawn edges.

WEEDS AND MOSS

I wish people didn't worry so much about weeds in lawns. If the turf stays green and looks fine enough from a distance then why worry that there's a bit of clover, dock or dandelion in it? If I banished all the daisies from my grass I'd be highly unpopular with both my daughters, so I'll continue to suffer the sideways glances of friends who think I ought to know better. If you feel you can't tolerate anything other than grass, then use a combined lawn weedkiller and fertilizer dressing in May, and again in August. There are certain weeds that are resistant to all manner of herbicides, and those that you can't shift by means of special lawn weedkillers will have to be put up with unless you want to get down on all fours and grub them out with a knife.

Individual weeds are easy to bump off with touch-

Caring for lawn edges

Replace damaged section with the damaged piece facing inwards

Firm the replaced turf into place. Fill the gap with sandy loam and sow grass seed

If only part of the lawn edge has been damaged, cut out a section containing that part. Replace the turf with the damaged part facing the lawn. Fill the gap with sandy loam, sow grass seed and water well.

Stand on a plank to protect the lawn as you work round the edges

An annual trim with a half-moon iron will keep lawn edges smart and trim. Cut against the solid edge of a plank or against a curved hosepipe for a neat finish.

weeders – aerosols or waxy sticks impregnated with herbicide that can be painted or sprayed on to isolated aliens. Before you use any weedkiller on a lawn do check that it won't kill the grass. It's surprising how many people think that Tumbleweed (glyphosate) can

Lawn renovation

If you take on an old lawn that's knee high in grass after months of neglect, don't start digging up the ground. Instead follow this course of action. You don't have to do the lot in one day. Spread it over a period of seven weeks by doing one job each week.

1 Clear away any bricks and debris.
2 Scythe or mow down the long grass with a rotary mower to a height of 5 cm (2 in).
3 Scarify to remove dead grass and thatch.
4 Mow to a height of 2.5 cm (1 in).
5 Apply a lawn fertilizer and weedkiller combined.
6 Mow regularly.
7 Treat as a normal lawn.

be used as a lawn weedkiller. It can, but don't expect any grass to survive.

Moss is another *bête noir*. You can pour on as much moss killer as you want, but unless you remedy the conditions that the moss finds favourable it will return and colonize the ground again after the initial killing off. Moss loves badly drained, poorly fed, acid soil, preferably with a bit of shade. Eliminate any of these problems and the moss will find it harder to survive. Scarifying helps to pull out the long, tufted mosses that give your lawn the springiness of a mattress, and I'd prefer to stick to this as a method of keeping it under relative control. Once again, if it's green and looks all right why worry what the neighbours think?

PESTS AND DISEASES

It's the fine lawn that is most troubled by disease; the coarser, more rugged grasses are seldom attacked by fungi apart from fairy rings. This fungus produces circles of dark green grass, often accompanied by toadstools. Only by digging out the infected turf and sterilizing the soil will you have any chance of eradicating it. Settle instead for mowing off the toadstools and telling the children about the fairies. The grass will come to no real harm.

Toadstools that arise from old tree stumps below the lawn are also a nuisance, but it's easier to mow them off than treat the area with a fungicide, which may only retain its effectiveness for a few weeks. Removal of stumps at lawn-making time is the only permanent answer.

Brown areas may be caused by fungus diseases, but are more likely to occur as a result of fertilizer scorch (if you've applied it clumsily and too heavily) or bitch urine. In both cases a good soaking with a lawn sprinkler (or even a watering can in the case of the bitch) will help to alleviate the problem. The grass will green up later in the season.

Black or dark green areas of slime are caused by algae. If your lawn is well drained and well fed you should be able to stop them appearing. If you want to bump existing infestations on the head, try watering each square metre (square yard) with 7 g (¼ oz) sulphate of iron in 2.5 litres (½ gallon) of water.

Moles are a pain in the neck and in the lawn. You'll read of umpteen old wives' cures for them, but if they infest the land around your garden there's absolutely nothing you can do to stop them coming into your plot. Traps laid in their runs will catch the individuals, and there are nasty little fuses to poison them out, but if I were you I'd enlist the help of the local mole catcher or rodent officer and enjoy using the soil from the molehills in your potting compost – it's wonderful stuff!

Worms should be tolerated. I know you'll read about how essential it is to kill them in lawns, but a healthy worm population means a healthy soil. The lawn occupies such a large proportion of most small gardens that if you bump off the worms there you'll lose them from most of your garden. Few lawns are really plagued by worm casts and only on really fine turf are they a severe handicap. Just sweep them off before mowing.

You'll gather from all this that I'm not the possessor of a manicured lawn. While this is true, I can still boast a patch of good-looking, fresh green turf that co-exists with wild flowers, animals and insects, and doesn't keep me occupied every waking hour.

Lawn-care calendar

■ *March*	Start to mow.	
■ *April*	Roll a new lawn if necessary.	
■ *May*	Apply fertilizer (and weedkiller if you must).	
■ *June/July*	Water when necessary.	
■ *August*	Apply fertilizer (and weedkiller if you must).	
■ *September*	Scarify and spike; topdress if you're keen.	
■ *October/November*	Stop mowing; sweep up leaves.	

patio gardening

Think of your patio as an

outdoor room where you can

relax when the weather is

fine. Furnish it with tubs,

baskets and small beds filled

with your favourite plants

I T'S NO USE HAVING A GARDEN IF YOU CAN'T make time to sit in it, so cobble together a patio and you'll be able to sit outdoors at any time of year, regardless of conditions under foot. Now the word 'patio' might conjure up an image of some Italian terrazzo, but it's lately come to mean any kind of stable surface on which a deckchair can be plonked.

PLANNING YOUR PATIO

The sunniest part of the garden is the most obvious place to put your pleasure patch, but it's also a good idea to position it near the house; that way the chef won't have to stagger too far with a heavy tray.

Reclining in the constant glare of summer sun palls after a while, so either allow room for a parasol, a good 2 m (6 ft) in diameter, or arrange for the sun to disappear behind a tree at a certain time of day. If you're no sun worshipper then there's nothing wrong with making a patio in the shade, surrounded by a leafy canopy; but remember that if it's really overhung you're likely to be dripped on in damp weather. (I speak as a gardener who eats out in any decent fine spell, winter or summer.)

With patio gardening, the back-yard owner comes into his or her own, for it matters not a jot that there's no soil for miles; it can all be imported and put into assorted containers. But more of that later.

LAYING PATIO MATERIALS

Having decided to construct a patio and worked out where to site it, the next question is what materials you are going to use and how you are going to lay them. Whatever hard surface you decide on, buy your materials from a builders' merchant; in most cases this is a far cheaper source of supply than a garden centre. A change of texture on the patio is easy to provide if small beds are left for plants, but you can also incorporate patches of cobbles, which have a similar effect. Don't overdo it though.

GRAVEL is by far the cheapest stuff of which patios are made. All you need to do is level and firm the soil before spreading over it a 2.5 cm (1 in) layer of washed pea shingle. Make the layer much thicker than this and you'll find that it's difficult to walk on and soon finds its way into the house. You'll always be sweeping the odd bit of gravel out anyway, but that's the price you pay for doing things on the cheap! (My patio is made of gravel.)

CONCRETE is the next most economical surface to gravel, but laying it involves much more slave labour. You'll have to lay it over a 10 cm (4 in) layer of rubble or 'hard core' to give it stability, and large areas can look rather dull unless they're broken up by lines of brick or patches of cobbles.

FLAGSTONES are pricey if you go for York stone or other natural materials, cheaper if they are reconstituted. Whatever you do, don't lay a patio of multicoloured pastel-shaded slabs: your sitting area should be a restful haven, not a technicolour dream. The plants will provide the colour.

Preparing the foundations for a patio

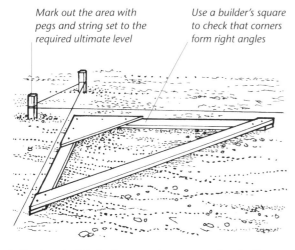

Mark out the area with pegs and string set to the required ultimate level

Use a builder's square to check that corners form right angles

1 Having decided where to site your patio, the first task is to prepare a firm foundation. Mark out the area with pegs and string, with the string at the final level of the patio. Use a builder's square to make sure that corners are set accurately at right angles.

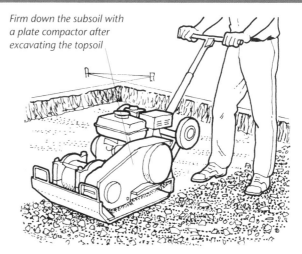

Firm down the subsoil with a plate compactor after excavating the topsoil

2 Dig out loose topsoil, removing any weeds or tree roots, until firm subsoil is reached. Allow for a 10 cm (4 in) layer of hardcore, covered with a 5 cm (2 in) layer of sand. Make sure that the subsoil is well packed down before adding the hardcore.

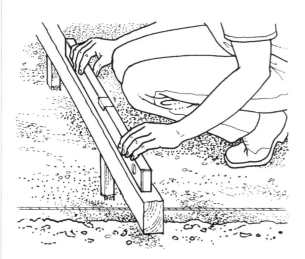

3 Drive in pegs over the area, 2 m (6 ft) apart, using a spirit level and plank to ensure that the tops are level with the string. Adjust the pegs to allow a slight slope for surface water to drain off, lowering them by approximately 2.5 cm (1 in) for each 2 m (6 ft) run.

Spread a hardcore layer over the excavated area to the required level

4 Spread a 10 cm (4 in) layer of hardcore over the entire site. On unstable soils, such as peat or heavy clay, a 15 cm (6 in) layer of hardcore is advisable. Firm it down until it is level, using the pegs as a guide. Cover the hardcore with sand to create a level surface.

Constructing patios

LAYING A CONCRETE PATIO

Concrete is an economical surface for a patio but it does require a lot of hard labour and a degree of DIY experience. After the site has been excavated to a depth of 20 cm (8 in) and levelled, construct a formwork of planks to hold the concrete in place until it sets. Spread hardcore 10 cm (4 in) deep and firm it down with a roller. Tip in the concrete until it is just proud of the formwork and work it well into the edges.

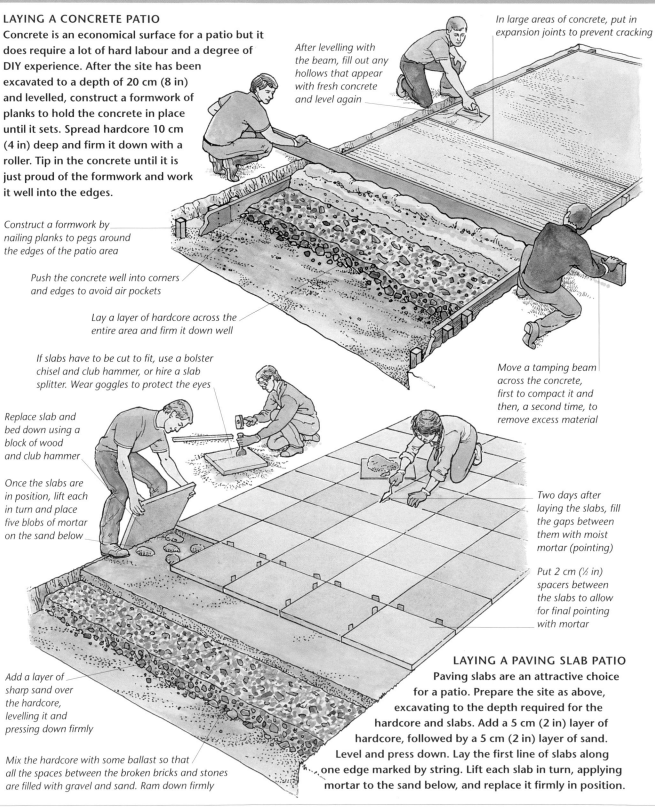

After levelling with the beam, fill out any hollows that appear with fresh concrete and level again

In large areas of concrete, put in expansion joints to prevent cracking

Construct a formwork by nailing planks to pegs around the edges of the patio area

Push the concrete well into corners and edges to avoid air pockets

Lay a layer of hardcore across the entire area and firm it down well

Move a tamping beam across the concrete, first to compact it and then, a second time, to remove excess material

If slabs have to be cut to fit, use a bolster chisel and club hammer, or hire a slab splitter. Wear goggles to protect the eyes

Replace slab and bed down using a block of wood and club hammer

Once the slabs are in position, lift each in turn and place five blobs of mortar on the sand below

Two days after laying the slabs, fill the gaps between them with moist mortar (pointing)

Put 2 cm (½ in) spacers between the slabs to allow for final pointing with mortar

Add a layer of sharp sand over the hardcore, levelling it and pressing down firmly

Mix the hardcore with some ballast so that all the spaces between the broken bricks and stones are filled with gravel and sand. Ram down firmly

LAYING A PAVING SLAB PATIO

Paving slabs are an attractive choice for a patio. Prepare the site as above, excavating to the depth required for the hardcore and slabs. Add a 5 cm (2 in) layer of hardcore, followed by a 5 cm (2 in) layer of sand. Level and press down. Lay the first line of slabs along one edge marked by string. Lift each slab in turn, applying mortar to the sand below, and replace it firmly in position.

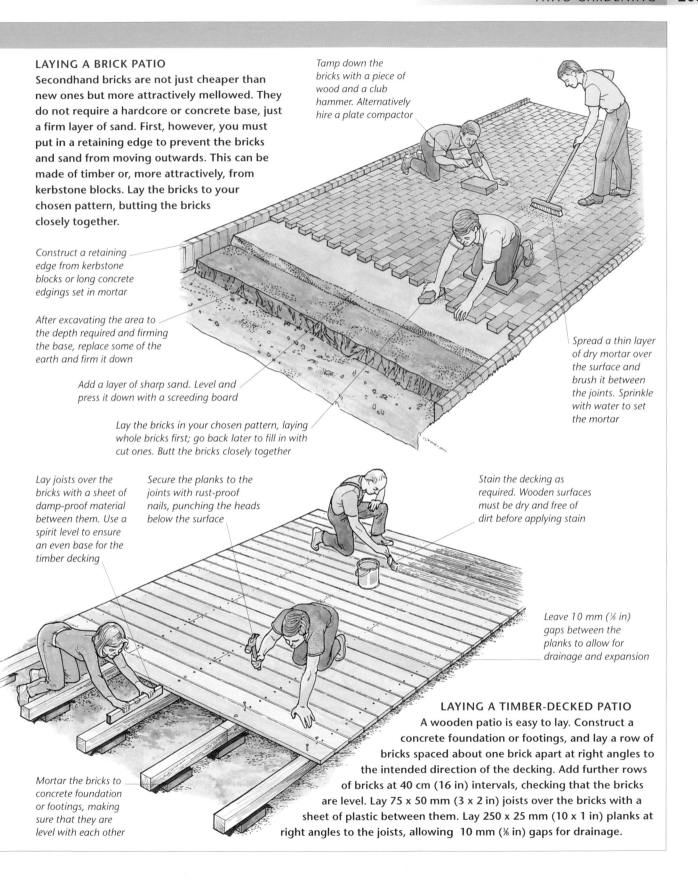

LAYING A BRICK PATIO

Secondhand bricks are not just cheaper than new ones but more attractively mellowed. They do not require a hardcore or concrete base, just a firm layer of sand. First, however, you must put in a retaining edge to prevent the bricks and sand from moving outwards. This can be made of timber or, more attractively, from kerbstone blocks. Lay the bricks to your chosen pattern, butting the bricks closely together.

Construct a retaining edge from kerbstone blocks or long concrete edgings set in mortar

After excavating the area to the depth required and firming the base, replace some of the earth and firm it down

Add a layer of sharp sand. Level and press it down with a screeding board

Lay the bricks in your chosen pattern, laying whole bricks first; go back later to fill in with cut ones. Butt the bricks closely together

Tamp down the bricks with a piece of wood and a club hammer. Alternatively hire a plate compactor

Spread a thin layer of dry mortar over the surface and brush it between the joints. Sprinkle with water to set the mortar

Lay joists over the bricks with a sheet of damp-proof material between them. Use a spirit level to ensure an even base for the timber decking

Secure the planks to the joists with rust-proof nails, punching the heads below the surface

Stain the decking as required. Wooden surfaces must be dry and free of dirt before applying stain

Leave 10 mm (⅜ in) gaps between the planks to allow for drainage and expansion

Mortar the bricks to concrete foundation or footings, making sure that they are level with each other

LAYING A TIMBER-DECKED PATIO

A wooden patio is easy to lay. Construct a concrete foundation or footings, and lay a row of bricks spaced about one brick apart at right angles to the intended direction of the decking. Add further rows of bricks at 40 cm (16 in) intervals, checking that the bricks are level. Lay 75 x 50 mm (3 x 2 in) joists over the bricks with a sheet of plastic between them. Lay 250 x 25 mm (10 x 1 in) planks at right angles to the joists, allowing 10 mm (⅜ in) gaps for drainage.

BRICKS are pricey if new, but quite cheap (and very good to look at) if you can find some mellowed secondhand stock. Lay both flagstones and bricks on an 8 cm (3 in) bed of sand spread over firmed and levelled soil. Use a straightedge and spirit level to make sure that your final surface is level (give it a slight 'fall' away from the house unless you want all the rain that lands on it to end up in your living room). Grout the bricks or slabs with a dry mortar mix (3 parts soft sand to 1 part cement) and allow the moisture that rises from below to set it.

A cautionary tale

Don't turn a hosepipe on your newly laid patio or you'll splash cement everywhere and discolour your bricks or flagstones. A mate of mine spent every weekend one year laying a brick patio and it nearly broke his heart when he washed in the grouting, only to find he had to spend days washing it out of his bricks again. If this disaster does befall you, try scattering damp coarse sand on the area and brushing it over the surface with a stiff broom (and no water). It should shift the cement deposit.

> "*Don't lay a patio of multicoloured slabs: the area should be a restful haven, not a technicolour dream.*"

FURNISHING YOUR PATIO

Achieving privacy

Screens might be necessary in small gardens if you want your patio to be private (and not many of us relish being watched while we idle our time away, whatever our state of dress). Trellis is an attractive proposition because it's cheap, but it also looks good if painted white and held firmly between posts and battens. Victorian arbours are seldom seen today, but they look delightful in shady or sunny parts of the garden where flowering climbers can be trained over them. Solid larch-lap fencing is certainly peep-proof but rather oppressive when it encloses a small area, and concrete screening blocks always look, to me, as though they've been left off a boat to Greece. If you like them, use them and ignore my rude comments.

If wooden screening doesn't appeal, use plants. There are plenty of climbers that can be trained up simple post and wire fences, or tall shrubs and hedges that can be planted densely enough to make an effective screen.

Choosing outdoor furniture

I haven't the nerve to tell you what you should be sitting on! However, a few tips gleaned from practical experience might save you a few bob. For a start, make your patio as big as possible because furniture takes up more room that you'd think. Those beautifully upholstered recliners are the best things on Earth to doze on, but they occupy a lot of space and you'll have to get them out and put them away every time you use them, which may make for storage problems. Invest in a couple by all means, but also have a pair of all-weather chairs and a table that can be left out even in winter if necessary. That way you can nip out there in a quick burst of sunshine for your morning cup of coffee without having to spend half an hour getting the posh stuff out of mothballs.

A parasol is not just decorative, it's also functional; read a book in scorching sunshine and you'll soon have a job to focus your eyes on anything else. If you do buy a parasol, go for one that's a plain colour rather than a floral print. Here I'm taking a liberty by inflicting my tastes on you, but it seems to me that the flowers in the garden should not have to compete with those on a William Morris parasol. Suit yourself!

Patio lighting

An illuminated patio is a luxury, but it becomes a bit of heaven on Earth on summer evenings when you can sit out late and admire the leaves and flowers as they bask in a carefully placed spotlight. Your electrician will advise you on installation and the kind of lamps needed, but bear in mind that plants always look best when lit from the side or from below, rather than flat on. Even in winter you can enjoy patio lighting from indoors if the illuminated plants are within view of your windows. If you're the outdoor type, patio lighting is a luxury worth saving for.

WHERE TO GROW PATIO PLANTS

On many plots the garden will surround the patio, bringing plants right up to the edge. In back yards or on rooftops, where a patio is all you've got, your plants will have to be grown in containers. You can plant in anything: wooden tubs, Greek urns, wall-mounted pots, large flower pots (small ones dry out too quickly), troughs, chimney pots (provided you remember they are bottomless and don't try to move them), growing bags and old porcelain sinks that have been treated to look like stone (see p.170).

Whatever your container, remember to place a layer of broken bricks, flowerpots or pebbles in the base to make for good drainage (all containers should have drainage holes) and, if the vessel is very large, stand it on a couple of bricks to keep it clear of the ground. With wooden tubs this helps to prevent rotting as well as allowing surplus water to escape unimpeded.

I would advise against the use of pots less than 23 cm (9 in) in diameter, simply because they dry out too quickly, and I would always use John Innes No. 2 potting compost in preference to the soilless types because, unlike them, if it dries out it won't shrink from the sides of the container and be difficult to re-wet. However, on rooftop and balcony gardens, peat-based composts have the advantage of being lightweight. (Always check with the appropriate authority before making a roof garden – it may save you a lot of heartache and expense later).

Leave a slight gap between the compost and the rim of all containers to allow for watering.

Windowboxes

Windows with outside sills lend themselves to being fitted with windowboxes that overflow with flowers all the year round. Spring and summer displays can be different (as with spring and summer bedding schemes) or some of the occupants can be permanent and a few bedders planted between them to vary the show from season to season.

Windowboxes are easy to make from old pieces of timber, screwed or nailed together with galvanized nails or brass screws. Treat them with preservative such as Cuprinol – not toxic creosote which kills plants – and equip them with short legs and drainage holes. Make sure that they sit firmly on the sill. If you lack outdoor sills the boxes can be held on steel brackets screwed to the wall. Make sure they're secure or you'll crown some unsuspecting passerby, who won't be able to see your floral tribute for stars.

Plants for windowboxes

PERMANENT RESIDENTS
- *Festuca glauca* (blue fescue grass)
- *Juniperus communis* '**Compressa**' (columnar dwarf conifer)
- *Hedera helix* varieties (common ivy)
- **Heathers** (*Erica* and *Calluna* – especially coloured-leafed varieties)
- *Euonymus* '**Emerald 'n' Gold**' (variegated evergreen leaves)
- *Hebe pinguifolia* '**Pagei**' (until it outgrows available space)
- *Buxus sempervirens* '**Suffruticosa**' (dwarf box)
- *Chamaecyparis obtusa* '**Nana**' (rounded dwarf conifer)
- *Thymus* spp. (thyme – especially coloured-leafed forms)

TEMPORARY RESIDENTS
Temporary residents are available in endless variety. Any spring or summer bedder that does not grow too tall will happily thrive, and dwarf bulbs will add to the spectacle in spring. Crocuses, dwarf irises and many of the compact narcissus varieties look superb, as do 'Universal' pansies, which can flower right through the winter. Dig them out before you plant the summer occupants.

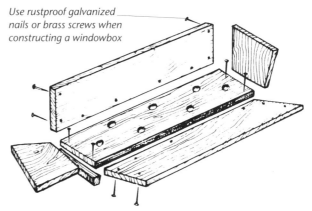

Use rustproof galvanized nails or brass screws when constructing a windowbox

Construct a simple windowbox from old pieces of floorboard; make sure that it is deep enough to hold 11.5 cm (6 in) of compost plus drainage material.

A drainage layer is as vital in a windowbox as it is in any other container, and the compost layer should be at least 15 cm (6 in) deep. Make your box large enough to allow for both.

Hanging baskets

These pendant floral features seem to have made a come-back in the last few years. Made of galvanized or plastic-covered wire, they can be slung from stout hooks or angle brackets outside doors and on plain house walls to brighten your life in summer. In winter they tend to get buffeted by the wind and the plants suffer.

To plant up the basket stand it on a large flowerpot or bucket. Line it with sphagnum moss (available from your florist) or old carpet underlay, or even three or four layers of newspaper cut to shape. Poke holes in the liner at intervals and insert suitable trailing plants from the outside, roots first, covering their roots with compost as soon as they appear inside the basket. When these are in place, plant up the top and then water the plants in. Bushy and trailing plants are naturally more suited to being grown in hanging baskets than stiff and starchy plants.

Keep the basket under cover for a few weeks after

Timber decking is an attractive choice for a patio surface, effortlessly extending the house into the garden and blending well with surrounding shrubs and trees. The timber theme in this garden includes raised beds constructed from reclaimed railway sleepers.

sides – the plants will have to cascade over the rim.

The secret of success with hanging baskets is watering. You'll have to soak them twice a day in midsummer, once a day even in dull weather: don't forget!

Plants for hanging baskets

It's the summer-flowering plants that make up hanging baskets. Experiment with different combinations each year, but rely on bushy and trailing plants, not those that grow tall and stiff. These are all first class:

- *Ageratum*
- *Alyssum*
- *Begonia pendula*
- *Begonia semperflorens*
- *Campanula isophylla* (Star of Bethlehem)
- *Centaurea gymnocarpa*
- *Helichrysum petiolatum*
- *Lobelia* (trailing)
- *Lysimachia nummularia* 'Aurea' (Creeping Jenny)
- *Mesembryanthemum* (Livingstone daisy)
- *Nasturtium*
- *Pelargonium, ivy-leaf* (ivy-leaf geranium)
- *Pelargonium, zonal* (geranium)
- *Petunia*
- *Senecio cineraria* (dusty miller)
- *Verbena*

PATIO PLANT CARE

Watering is certainly the most important job the patio gardener will undertake. All containers of compost dry out amazingly quickly on a sun-baked patch of hard standing, and plants that dry out soon die. Save your money and your temper, if not your time, by checking all containers morning and evening in summer – daily or, at the very least, every other day at other times of year.

Feed all container-grown plants once a fortnight in summer. Flowering plants love tomato fertilizer, which can be used at the same dilution as recommended for tomatoes.

planting to let its occupants establish themselves. Baskets are usually made up during late April and hung outdoors in late May or early June.

If a basket is to be hung directly over a door, you'd do well to invest in the kind with a built-in plastic drip-tray, but you won't be able to plant anything in the

Plants that are grown in pots for a number of years should either be potted on annually in spring, or topdressed, which involves scraping away the top layer of compost and replacing it with fresh. Both operations are described in Chapter 20 House Plants.

The removal of dead and diseased plants and the controlling of pests and diseases is as vital on the patio as it is anywhere else in the garden, but at least if you're lounging on a sunbed you'll notice quite quickly if there are pests on an overhanging branch – especially if they drop into your gin and tonic. Which brings me to weeding. If you're as fidgety as I am, you'll find that your patio beds and pots are the best-weeded parts of your garden. I'm forever leaping out of the chair to pull up a bit of groundsel or hairy bittercress!

CHOOSING PLANTS FOR PATIOS

I won't give you a long list of suitable patio plants, just a selection of those that I think are especially useful, because the truth of the matter is that you can grow almost anything in a pot for a limited period of time. There are certain plants that will not like being baked in the reflected heat that comes off your patio – rhododendrons for instance – but on a shady patio they'll do well. Other trees will refuse to stay in a tub for more than five or ten years, but that's not a bad life for any pot plant.

The greatest boon of patio gardening is that you can try anything, and you can move your plants around to give different effects from week to week (if you feel strong enough).

Don't forget that in summer your house plants will benefit greatly from a holiday in the garden, and on the patio they will receive shelter as well as welcome sunshine. Summer showers will refresh them rather than do them any harm.

Using evergreens and foliage plants

To make your potted show interesting all the year round, some of the plants should be evergreen and a lot of them should be foliage plants. Roses and other flowering shrubs will give a grand show in their season, but the evergreens will be the backbone of the display just as they are in the garden.

So long as you can give a shrub, border plant, rose or any other plant the conditions it would appreciate elsewhere in the garden, it will thrive in a container on your patio.

Potting on patio plants

1 **This container-grown conifer has outgrown its pot. Choose a new, larger container, and put a layer of crocks in the base to assist drainage.**

Foliage plants for patios

When planning your patio display, don't forget foliage plants and shrubs: they are just as important here as elsewhere in the garden. The following plants are especially striking if grown in gravel- or cobble-covered beds. After planting, firm down the soil then cover with a stone mulch of cobbles, pebbles, gravel or washed pea shingle. It will set off the plants, keep down weeds, and help to retain moisture.

BORDER PLANTS FOR PATIOS
(See Chapter 9 Border Plants for full details.)

- *Ajuga*
- *Alchemilla*
- *Artemisia*
- *Asplenium*
- *Ballota*
- *Bergenia*
- *Blechnum*
- *Carex*
- *Cynara*
- *Dryopteris*
- *Epimedium*
- *Euphorbia*
- *Festuca*
- *Glyceria*

2 Knock the conifer out of its old pot and tease away some of the compost from the roots. Put a layer of compost in the bottom of the new pot.

3 Set the conifer in the pot, ensuring that the top of the rootball will rest 2.5 cm (1 in) or so below the rim. Feed in compost around the rootball and firm it in.

- *Heuchera*
- *Hosta*
- *Iris*
- *Liriope*
- *Matteuccia*
- *Milium*
- *Persicaria*
  (syn. *Polygonum*)
- *Phormium*
- *Polygonatum*
- *Rheum*
- *Sedum*

Heuchera micrantha var. *diversifolia* 'Palace Purple' is a handsome foliage plant to grow in a patio container.

SHRUBS FOR PATIOS
Those marked ◆ are evergreen.
(See Chapter 5 Shrubs for full details.)

- *Aralia*
- *Arundinaria* ◆
- *Aucuba* ◆
- *Camellia* ◆
- *Chamaecyparis* ◆ (some)
- *Choisya* ◆
- *Cistus* ◆
- *Convolvulus* ◆
- *Cotinus*
- *Cotoneaster* ◆ (some)
- *Fatsia* ◆
- *Heathers* ◆
- *Hebe* ◆
- *Hedera* ◆

- *Ilex* ◆
- *Juniperus* ◆
- *Laurus* ◆
- *Lavandula* ◆
- *Lavatera*
- *Mahonia* ◆
- *Myrtus* ◆
- *Paeonia*
- *Pittosporum* ◆
- *Rhus*
- *Ruta* ◆
- *Sambucus*
- *Sarcococca* ◆
- *Yucca* ◆

part IV

THE FOOD CROPS

Experience the thrill of growing your own produce and discover the flavour of freshly picked fruit and vegetables

A well-tended vegetable garden is a pleasure to behold with its neat rows of ferny carrot tops and succulent heads of lettuce and cauliflower emerging from the fertile soil.

fruit growing

Even in a small garden or tiny backyard, the pleasures of fruit growing can be enjoyed, thanks to the dwarfing rootstocks and miniature varieties now available

THERE ARE FEW BRANCHES OF GARDENING as confusing as fruit growing. True enough, the cultivation of raspberries and gooseberries presents few problems, but once you get on to apples and pears, cherries and peaches, the pruning alone is enough to frighten anyone off. Here then, I've tried to simplify matters a little by not telling you too much. It's amazing how many gardeners grow tons of fruits without ever laying their hands on a pair of secateurs or loppers. The pruning techniques I've described are certainly necessary to make the best of your trees, but I defer to those gardeners with lofty apple trees, coated with lichen, that groan under the weight of a heavy harvest with amazing regularity.

I've dealt with most problems and operations under the individual fruit headings, but there are one or two general comments worth making.

TIPS ON FRUIT GROWING

SITE AND SOIL Remember that most fruits are expected to go on cropping year after year without being moved. Give them the best site and soil you can to help them achieve their aims.

POLLINATION Tree fruits generally need to be pollinated by another variety of the same fruit so that they can produce a good crop. Try to persuade your friends and neighbours to plant a tree that complements yours if you've no room for two.

PROPAGATION Don't propagate your own tree fruits – they are grafted on to vigour-controlling rootstocks and are best increased by the nurseryman. Two- or three-year-old trees will cost a little more than one-year-old 'maidens' but they will come into cropping more quickly and save you the complicated job of training them in the early stages.

JUNE DROP When it comes to technical terms, fruit growing has its quota. The 'June drop' is the name given to the shedding of immature tree fruits when they are quite small. It's the tree's natural way of thinning out its crop, so don't be alarmed. Just make sure that any thinning you do comes after this, otherwise you might find that the fruits you've left behind drop off too!

SETTING FRUIT Gardeners are frequently frustrated by trees that come into flower but refuse to set fruit. The reason is usually lack of pollination, but it may also be due to frosting. Grow your trees in a sheltered spot that is not on low-lying ground.

NON-FLOWERING If your trees refuse to flower, suspect one of the following: bird damage, frost damage, an excess of nitrogen or a lack of food in general. Faulty or very hard pruning can produce growth buds at the expense of fruit buds.

PRUNING When it's time for that terrifying job, pruning, use a sharp pair of secateurs to prevent diseases from gaining a foothold through torn tissue. Always prune to just above a bud – generally an outward facing one.

LEADERS, LATERALS AND SUB-LATERALS The branches themselves have technical names: leaders are the topmost, strongest-growing shoots; laterals are sideshoots. Sub-laterals are sideshoots that are growing from sideshoots.

Heavily laden espaliered apple and pear trees provide a luscious background to this border whose colourful display includes *Nicotiana*, *Limonium* (statice), *Cosmos*, and the exotic-looking *Cleome* (spider flower).

PLANTING A fruit tree or bush is planted in exactly the same way as an ornamental tree or bush, so throughout this chapter I've referred you to Chapter 4 Trees for planting details.

RESTRICTED FORMS Cordons and espaliers are usually planted against stout post and wire fences. Make sure that they are indeed stout. The posts, 10 cm (4 in) square in cross-section, should protrude 2 m (6 ft) from the ground. Treat them with a preservative other than creosote and bury to a depth of 60 cm (2 ft). They should occur every 2–2.5 m (6–8 ft) along the fence and the wire should be of a stout gauge. Spacings for the wires are recommended under individual fruits.

FRUIT CAGE If you intend to grow plenty of fruit, it really is worth investing in a fruit cage – home-made or shop-bought. It is not much to look at and it will cost quite a few pounds to make or acquire, but it will make sure that you eat the fruits before the birds do.

UNDERSTANDING ROOTSTOCKS

Fruit trees are not grown from pips; they are propagated in the nursery by a technique known as grafting. This involves the joining together of a scion (piece of stem) from a branch of the required variety and a rootstock. The rootstock is a plant that is especially grown to act as the root system for a chosen variety of fruit. If allowed to grow and crop itself it would have rather poor fruits because it's been selected, not for its own cropping ability, but for the effect it has on the vigour and cropping ability of the scion that is attached (grafted) to it. The two are spliced together in the nursery, a natural callus forms to glue them to one another, and the scion then forms the branch framework and the rootstock the roots.

> *"It's amazing how many gardeners grow tons of fruits without ever laying their hands on a pair of secateurs."*

There are hundreds of rootstocks; well, perhaps not hundreds but certainly enough to thoroughly confuse you. It is recommended that you ask for a tree on a particular rootstock number, so that you can be sure of getting a tree whose ultimate size is predictable. Apple rootstocks are prefixed by the letters M or MM (which stand for Malling and Malling Merton respectively).

ROOTSTOCK M.26 is the best one for general planting in small gardens. It is reasonably dwarfing and yet not so feeble that it needs to be staked all its life. Trees on M.26 grow 2.5–4 m (8–12 ft) high.

ROOTSTOCK M.9 is the dwarfest but it does need continuous staking and is a bit miffy on very poor or very heavy soils. Trees on M.9 grow to 2 or 3 m (6 or 10 ft).

ROOTSTOCK MM.106 is not quite as dwarfing as the previous two but it still keeps trees to a reasonable size. Trees on MM.106 grow 4–6 m (12–18 ft) high.

All three rootstocks will bring the trees into bearing quite early in their lives. Choose M.26 if you can; M.9 if you want a real midget and have good soil; MM.106 if you can't find M.26.

TREE FORMS

There's an added complication: you'll have to decide what shape of tree you want. You can buy 'maidens' (one-year-old trees that consist of a single stem) and train them if you want, but it's easier, and not that much more expensive, to buy two- or three-year-old trained trees in one of several forms: standard, half-standard, bush, dwarf pyramid, cordon, or espalier.

If terror is struck into your heart by the thought of having to train or prune any fruit tree, then you can simply plant a bush, half-standard or standard tree and leave it to its own devices. You'll risk owning a tree that is not very shapely and that crops neither as heavily, nor as early in its life as a trained tree, but if you are happy to live with such a tree, that's your affair and nobody else's.

Mind you, when you decide to prune it later you're in for a battle royal. Compromise by pruning it a little during its formative years to produce a good shape, then you can ignore it with less drastic results.

PLANTING FRUIT TREES

Planting distances

If you're growing more than one tree I suppose you can boast that you're planting an orchard (to an estate agent three trees constitute a small orchard). Plant bushes on M.9 and M.26 3 m (10 ft) apart; plant cordons 1 m (3 ft) apart with 2 m (6 ft) between rows; plant espaliers 3 m (10 ft) apart; plant dwarf pyramids 1 m (3 ft) apart in rows 2 m (6 ft) apart. You'll need to allow 6 m (20 ft) between standards and rather less between half-standards.

Fruit tree forms

STANDARDS

These trees have a branch framework at the top of a 2–2.25 m (6–7 ft) trunk. They are planted on vigorous rootstocks with numbers like M.2 and MM.111 and should really only be chosen if you want an ancient apple tree under which you can position a rustic seat for that cottage garden effect.

HALF-STANDARDS

In this form, the trunk is 1.25–1.5 m (4–4½ ft) tall and the tree will also be vigorous. Both standards and half-standards take longer to come into cropping than the dwarfer kinds.

2 m (6 ft) of clear stem   *1.25 m (4 ft) stem*

BUSHES

Bush trees (although it sounds a contradiction) have a bare stem of around 60 cm (2 ft), often rather less if they are on the dwarfing M.9 rootstock. They are a good choice for general garden planting because all cultivation techniques, from spraying to picking, are made easier. The bush is usually grown so that its branches make a goblet shape – open in the centre to allow good air circulation and freedom from disease.

60 cm (2 ft) stem

DWARF PYRAMIDS

Here the tree is grown into more of a conical shape and the central leading shoot is retained. The trunk is only 30 cm (12 in) high and the tree is even more accessible than the bush.

Leading shoot is retained

Branches trained at an angle of 90° to trunk

Trees trained at an angle of 45°

CORDONS

These are restricted trees grown on M.9 or M.26 rootstocks and planted against a fence or post and wire framework. They are trained on a single stem that runs at an angle of 45°. Pruning is carried out in summer – the laterals are nipped back and the central leader allowed to extend slowly.

ESPALIERS

These, too, are restricted trees; they are grown with one central stem rising vertically, and tiered pairs of branches trained at right angles to it. The yields of restricted trees are, not surprisingly, much lower than those of free-standing bushes.

When to plant

Plant bare-root trees from November to March and container-grown trees at any time of year. Planting instructions are exactly as for ornamental trees (see p.40). Cordons and espaliers are planted against a strong, 2 m (6 ft) high post and wire fence with horizontal wires at 60 cm (2 ft) intervals.

During the spring, after planting, scatter a good sprinkling of blood, bone and fishmeal around each tree and then lay a thick organic mulch. Make sure that the soil is not given a chance to dry out during establishment. Don't let grass grow up to the tree for at least three years. An annual spring feed with rose fertilizer is always appreciated.

A-Z OF *fruit crops*

APPLE

I've always fancied having an orchard full of old varieties of apple with quaint names like 'Norfolk Beefing', 'Devonshire Quarrenden' and 'Roundway Magnum Bonum' – the very sound of the names smacks of a bumper harvest. I've never yet got round to it; instead we have half a dozen hefty old trees scattered round the garden, but even these provide us with more apples than we know what to do with.

If you're keen on apples then you'll want to grow a few varieties that not only taste good but that also supply you with fruit over as long a season as possible, and that is the basis on which I have made my selection (see right). Romanticism aside, these are the varieties with some of the tastiest fruits, even if they don't have the most euphonious names. The early varieties should be eaten as soon as possible after picking; the late varieties are the best keepers.

I'm afraid I've not included 'Cox's Orange Pippin' – it requires too much spraying to keep it in good condition. 'Ribston Pippin' is easier and just as crisp and tasty. Neither have I included 'Golden Delicious'. We get far too many of these apples from France and, while they may be uniform in shape

and quality and crisp of flesh, they really do not possess a flavour that can rival a decent English pippin. Now there's prejudice for you!

WHERE TO PLANT Apples enjoy the classic situation: a site that's open and sunny, but sheltered at a distance from strong winds. Avoid frost pockets where the blossom will be killed off. Good drainage is vital and adequate soil preparation essential; dig the ground as deeply as you can and work in plenty of compost or manure, plus a good dusting of blood, bone and fishmeal a day or two before planting. Different varieties suit different situations, and while those that I've recommended will thrive in most gardens it's a good idea to rely on the advice of your local nurseryman, who knows what thrives in your neck of the woods.

POLLINATION Apple pollination is complicated in theory but usually simple in practice – there are so many apple trees around that the bees can usually do a good job at cross-

pollinating the flowers and ensuring a crop. Some apples won't set fruit with their own pollen so, to make sure of a good crop without having to rely on your neighbours, it's a good idea to plant two or three trees, even if they are restricted forms such as cordons and espaliers. Just make sure that they flower at the same time (see below).

PRUNING This varies depending on the form of tree, but basically aims to produce a healthy framework of branches and plenty of fruiting spurs. Proceed thus:

Bush After planting a two- or three-year-old bush, shorten all the leading shoots by half their length, cutting back to an outward-facing bud (see right). The following winter do exactly the same, but when the tree is in its fourth year only the laterals need be pruned, back to 10 cm (4 in). Leave plenty of unpruned laterals on 'Bramley's Seedling', which is a tip-bearing variety. Aim to produce a well-spaced framework of branches, and

Recommended apple varieties

VARIETY	IN SEASON	FLOWERING TIME*
EATERS		
'George Cave'	Late August/early September	1
'Discovery'	Late August/early September	1
'Ellison's Orange'	September/October	2
'James Grieve'	September/October	2
'Egremont Russet'	October/December	1
'Sunset'	October/December	2
'Ribston Pippin'	November/February	1
'Rosemary Russet'	December/March	2
'Tydeman's Late Orange'	December/March	2
COOKERS		
'Arthur Turner'	August/October	2
'Grenadier'	August/October	2
'Bramley's Seedling'	November/March	2
'Annie Elizabeth'	December/June	2
'Howgate Wonder'	November/February	2
'Lane's Prince Albert'	January/March	2

* Varieties marked **1** will flower before those marked **2**. For effective pollination, varieties within the same group should be planted together.

Pruning a newly planted bush apple tree

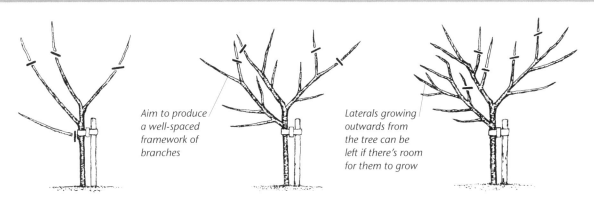

Aim to produce a well-spaced framework of branches

Laterals growing outwards from the tree can be left if there's room for them to grow

1 After planting a two-year-old bush (between November and March) shorten all the leading shoots by half their length, cutting to just above an outward-facing bud.

2 The following winter, repeat the process, cutting back the newly grown leading shoots by half. As before, cut back to just above an outward-facing bud.

3 One year later the pruning can be restricted to lateral shoots: cut them back to about 10 cm (4 in). It's a good idea to shorten some laterals every year.

Pruning a dwarf pyramid tree

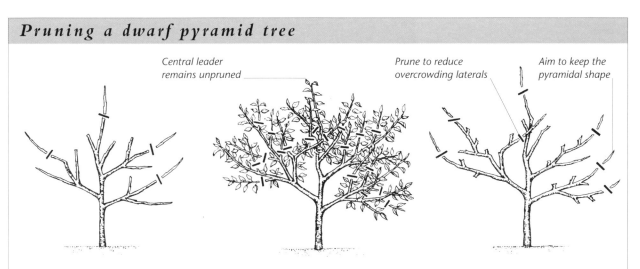

Central leader remains unpruned

Prune to reduce overcrowding laterals

Aim to keep the pyramidal shape

1 Buy a partially trained tree and after planting (between November and March) cut back all the main leading shoots to 23 cm (9 in) of new growth.

2 In July or August cut back all but the central leader to six leaves. Reduce all unwanted laterals to three leaves, and cut back sublaterals to the leaf above the lowest cluster.

3 The following winter cut back the central leader to 23 cm (9 in); once the tree has reached a height of 2 m (7 ft) the central leader can be cut back into old wood.

don't be afraid to cut out damaged, very old and badly placed stems completely if they are making a nuisance of themselves. But remember, the harder you prune, the more growth you'll get and the fewer apples you'll harvest.
Standards Prune as for bush trees.

Half-standards Prune as for bush trees.
Dwarf pyramid Buy a partially trained dwarf pyramid tree and then you can slip into the routine of simple twice-yearly pruning (see above).

In winter prune back all the main, leading shoots to leave just 23 cm (9 in) of new growth.

In July or August cut back all leaders except the central one, to six leaves. Any laterals not required as part of the branch framework can be reduced to three leaves, and sub-laterals (sideshoots that grow on sideshoots) can be cut to the leaf growing above the lowest cluster.

Pruning a cordon apple tree

Buy a partially trained cordon and concentrate on summer pruning – shortening any lateral shoots to three leaves to build up a spur system. Prune the leader once it has reached the topmost wire. The cordon can then be lowered slightly to give it more room to grow.

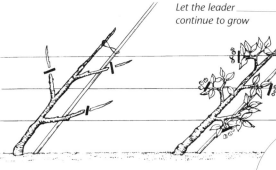

Let the leader continue to grow

Cut back any lateral shoots to leave three leaves above the basal cluster

In summer cut back to 2.5 cm (1 in) any shoots that attempt to take over from the leading shoot

When the leading shoot reaches the top wire cut it out each spring

1 Maiden trees can be trained to form cordons. Plant at an angle of 45°, with the graft union uppermost, and prune the lateral shoots back to four buds between November and March.

2 Remove any flowers that form one year later. Allow the leader to continue growing undisturbed, tying it in to the cane support as it extends.

3

Cut back sublaterals to one leaf above the basal cluster

3 In subsequent years, in late July and early August, cut back any lateral shoots emerging from the main stem to leave three leaves above the basal cluster (see inset). Further growth may occur in late summer and autumn. Cut back such shoots to two leaves.

The central leader can be cut back into old wood once the tree has reached a height of 2 m (7 ft). In subsequent years try to maintain the pyramidal shape of the tree; reduce overcrowded spurs and any vigorous shoots that sprout from within the framework.

Cordon See above.

Espalier Buy a trained tree and in summer prune the branches as for cordons so that a system of spurs is built up on each 'arm'.

THINNING After the natural June drop, remove one or two fruitlets from each cluster if they look overcrowded. Always pull the central fruit out first. This is the 'king fruit', which has a deformed lump next to the stalk. Leave two fruits to each cluster.

HARVESTING Pick the fruits as soon as they will part easily from the tree without tearing. The earliest will be ready from late July through August, and the later varieties in September and October. Pick any remaining apples in October and store them.

STORING The late varieties are the ones to store. It's a real fag wrapping them up in squares of greaseproof paper, so nip along to a friendly greengrocer and see if he can let you have some wooden 'Dutch trays' equipped with cardboard dividers (see right).

Store only sound fruits, and check them once a week to remove any that show signs of rotting. A cool but frostproof shed or garage is the best fruit store you'll find, unless you happen to have a cellar, where conditions will be ideal.

If you've found in the past that apples and pears shrivel while they're in store, put 1.6–1.8 kg (3–4 lb) in a polythene bag with the corners cut off and lay the bags in the trays so that they can be stacked. The polythene will keep the atmosphere around the fruits pleasantly moist. Sliced or puréed, the apples can also be frozen.

PESTS AND DISEASES Aphids, sawfly, codling moth, winter moth, apple

In late July and August, prune cordon apple trees by shortening sideshoots to three or four buds above the basal cluster.

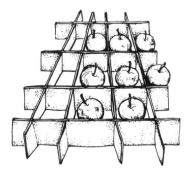

Store apples in wooden tomato trays fitted with cardboard dividers to separate the fruits and prevent any rot spreading. Keep them in a cool, dark, frostfree place.

sucker, capsid bugs, red spider mites, bitter pit, mildew, canker, scab, brown rot.

So many problems does the apple have to contend with that many gardeners adopt a spray programme. Coping with children and dogs, I've never felt that I could arrange for a comprehensive system of spraying. Idlers can spray with a tar oil wash such as Murphy Mortegg or ICI Clean Up in winter to remove hibernating eggs and bugs, and other infestations can be dealt with as they occur. It's not the perfectionist's way, but you'll still manage to harvest a good crop.

BLACKBERRY/LOGANBERRY

For growing against fences, and as productive screens against post and wire supports, these two fruits will produce a succulent harvest with very little bother. I'd choose 'Bedford Giant' or 'Oregon Thornless' when selecting blackberries; 'LY 59' or the thornless

'L 654' are by far the best of the loganberries. If you've never tried loganberries you're in for a treat. Mix them up with raspberries and smother them with cream! They crop in mid- to late summer.

WHERE TO PLANT Blackberries will tolerate a little shade; loganberries will too but they definitely prefer full sun. The soil should be well dug, well drained and enriched with manure or compost. Fork in a dusting of blood, bone and fishmeal just before planting.

SUPPORT Either equip a fence or wall with horizontal wires held in place by metal vine eyes at 45 cm (18 in) intervals, or make a 2 m (6 ft) post and wire fence with strands a similar distance apart. Each plant needs about 4 m (12 ft) of lateral fence space.

PLANTING Plant dormant canes between November and March – the earlier the better. Planting instructions are exactly the same as for ornamental trees and shrubs (see p.40). After planting, cut back the canes to 23 cm (9 in) above soil level, making your cuts just above a dormant bud.

CULTIVATION Dust the soil with blood, bone and fishmeal in February and lay a thick organic mulch in March. Tie the new canes to the support system as they grow, spacing them out in a fan

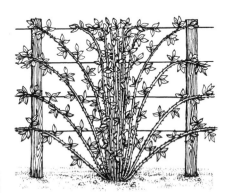

Space out the fruiting canes of blackberries and loganberries, training the new shoots up the centre as they grow. These can be spread out and tied in the following winter to replace the fruited stems, which are cut out at ground level.

formation and leaving a gap in the centre of the support system directly above the plant. Water well in dry weather. These canes will fruit in their second year while more new ones are growing. Train these up into the bare central area.

PRUNING When the canes have fruited, cut them out at ground level and then space out and tie in the new canes to replace them. Repeat the process in subsequent years.

HARVESTING Pick the fruits as soon as they are ripe. Hang old net curtains or muslin or close-weave plastic netting over them if birds are a problem. Pull the berries so that the 'plugs' are left behind.

STORING Jam; freeze surplus fruits.

PESTS AND DISEASES Aphids, raspberry beetle, cane spot, cane blight, spur blight, botrytis and viruses.

PROPAGATION During July, healthy shoot tips can be bent down and buried in the soil; hold them in place with a peg made from stout wire. Eventually a shoot will emerge. The new plant can be detached the following spring (with its own roots) and planted out where it is to grow.

BLACKCURRANT

Just the thing for vitamin C fanatics. The trouble is that blackcurrants are a bit greedy when it comes to space, but 'Ben Sarek' is compact and a heavy cropper and so the best choice for small gardens. It's a flavoursome mid-season cropper yielding its bounty during late July. Try 'Mendip Cross' and 'Tor Cross' for slightly earlier crops and 'Ben Lomond' for an August harvest.

WHERE TO PLANT Full sun or very gentle shade keep blackcurrants happy but, like all fruits, they can be hammered by frost if they are planted in hollows. Lime acid soil in autumn and dig it over, adding manure or compost during winter. Fork in a dusting of blood, bone and fishmeal just before planting.

PLANTING Two-year-old certified bushes are the best kind to buy; that way you have a guarantee that they are not infected with yield-reducing virus diseases. Plant all the varieties I've mentioned 1.5 m (5 ft) apart on the square (I told you they were a bit greedy). Planting instructions are exactly the same as for ornamental trees and shrubs (see p.40). It's a good idea to set the bushes about 5 cm (2 in) deeper than they were planted in the nursery so that the stem bases are encouraged to form roots and so give the plant more support and nourishment. Now cut all the shoots

> ## "Full sun or very gentle shade keep blackcurrants happy but, like all fruits, they can be hammered by frost if they are planted in hollows."

back to within 5 cm (2 in) of soil level. Use the prunings as cuttings: trim them above a bud at the top and below a bud at the base so that they are 25 cm (10 in) long. Insert them on the vegetable plot so that all but the top 5 cm (2 in) is buried. They'll grow next year and can be transplanted the following autumn.

CULTIVATION Mulch the soil around the plants with organic matter in spring. Don't let them go short of water during their first spring and summer. No fruits will be carried during the first year. Get into the habit of repeating the mulch each spring after scattering a little blood, bone and fishmeal over the soil.

PRUNING There's no need to prune after the first season's growth, but subsequently prune the bush each

winter, removing any spindly stems and a few old ones. Cut them all out at ground level. Never remove more than about one third of the plant's shoots, but aim to leave a well-spaced framework of branches.

HARVESTING Grow the bushes in a fruit cage or lay muslin or old net curtains over them when the fruits are coming to maturity: birds will enjoy them as much as you do. Cut off the sprigs of fruit when they are ripe – black and tender to the touch. If you can use the fruits immediately (rather than in a few days' time) pull them straight from the stalks. You should get around 4.5 kg (10 lb) fruit from one well-grown bush.

STORING Currants freeze and jam well.

PESTS AND DISEASES Birds, aphids, big bud mite, leaf spot, reversion virus, rust and American gooseberry mildew.

PROPAGATION Already described in planting information (left).

CHERRY

Until recently the only cherry recommended for small gardens was 'Morello' – an acid cherry that makes the most delicious pies and jam. Sweet cherries tend to make towering trees that need to be planted at least 10 m (30 ft) apart, and they are choosy as to how they perform. However, a new variety called 'Stella' has recently been introduced to gardens. Its main advantage is that, unlike other sweet cherries, it can set a good crop of fruits with its own pollen. 'Morello' is self-fertile, too.

WHERE TO PLANT Although they're tolerant of positions in the open garden, cherries are usually grown as fan-trained trees against walls. 'Morello' is often recommended for a north wall where it enjoys the cool conditions. Avoid frost pockets at all costs, and dig over and manure the

Glowing pale yellow, tinged with red, the firm-fleshed 'Bigarreau Napoleon' provides a sweet dessert cherry for cropping in late July.

ground in the autumn before planting.

SUPPORT Make sure that there are horizontal wires fastened at 30 cm (12 in) intervals up the brickwork. The stems can then be tied in and spaced out as they grow. The tree will need about 6 m (20 ft) of lateral space.

PLANTING To make life easier (if just a little more expensive), choose a tree that is already fan trained. It should be grafted onto a rootstock known as 'Colt', which is only semi-vigorous. Plant container-grown trees at any time of year, bare-root trees in November if possible. Planting is exactly as for trees and shrubs (see p.40). Set the tree about 30 cm (12 in) from the wall and tilt its branches towards the surface, tying the stems loosely to the wire. Cut back the stems by about one third of their length after planting, to encourage the production of sideshoots, which will form the basic

structure of the tree. Mulch the soil around the tree with organic matter in spring after dusting the soil with blood, bone and fishmeal. A dusting of rose or tomato fertilizer can be given each April. Never let the soil dry out.

PRUNING Prune cherries in spring or summer rather than winter. This lessens the likelihood of attack by silver leaf disease. Acid cherries flower on one-year-old wood and it is this that pruning aims to encourage. Thin out the shoots during spring and summer, cutting out any that grow directly away from the wall and any that are weak or overcrowding. The remaining shoots should be spaced about 15 cm (6 in) apart on the wall. After fruiting, cut out the cherry-bearing sideshoots, allowing them to be replaced by younger shoots that have arisen from their bases. If young growth is lacking as the tree matures, cut a few older branches back to young laterals so that new shoots are encouraged. At all times keep the framework well spaced and not overcrowded, and keep it young. Sweet cherries such as 'Stella' produce their fruit buds at the base of sideshoots that are one year old and which emerge from older wood. It follows that an older framework of branches is required on a sweet cherry than on an acid cherry, which is constantly being required to produce new wood for cropping. Pinch out the shoot tips of the new sideshoots on sweet cherries during the summer so that they are left with just five leaves. Further shorten these shoots in autumn to three buds. These buds will carry blossom and fruits the following summer.

HARVESTING 'Morello' matures in August and September, 'Stella' in July. Pick the fruits when they come to ripeness. The birds may have a go so use a large sheet of plastic netting that can be draped right over the plant. The longer the cherries are left before they are harvested, the less acid they will be, but the more likelihood there is of them being pecked. There's no need to thin the fruits.

STORING Pies can be frozen, as can the fruits themselves if they are stoned first.

PESTS AND DISEASES Aphids, birds, slugworm, winter moth, bacterial canker, brown rot, dieback, and silver leaf disease.

CURRANT, RED AND WHITE

I wish more folk were willing to plant red and white currants; they make a bright show in the flower border and possess the richest of flavours. Both can be used in jelly-making and wine-making and they fill a plump fruit pie with promise. 'Red Lake' is the best red currant for most gardens, yielding in late July. 'Laxton's No. 1' is earlier and 'Rondom' later. No white currant is better than 'White Versailles', but you'll also find 'White Dutch' and 'White Grape' good value.

WHERE TO PLANT Plant in the same kind of spot as blackcurrants, though these two are rather less tolerant of shade.

PLANTING Plant one- or two-year-old plants between November and March. Buy from a reputable supplier: there is no certification scheme for red and white currants so they cannot be guaranteed free from virus diseases. Plant the bushes 1.5 m (5 ft) apart on the square and at the same level as they were growing in the nursery (look for the soil mark on the stem). Each bush should have a short trunk or 'leg' and at least three branches. Cut these back to half their length after planting, preferably to just above an outward-facing bud.

CULTIVATION Dust the soil around the plants with blood, bone and fishmeal in February and then lay a mulch of organic matter. Repeat this operation

annually. Do not let the soil dry out during the first spring and summer, and each May scatter a handful of sulphate of potash around each bush to encourage fruit formation. Birds can eat the buds in winter and the fruits in summer if the bushes are not netted or caged.

PRUNING The system is quite different from that adopted for blackcurrants. Aim to build up a goblet-shaped bush of six or eight branches: the older branches keep on fruiting for several years. Remove one or two of the most ancient branches each year in winter. Shorten all sideshoots to six leaves in summer.

HARVESTING Pick the fruits individually when they are ripe, or cut off the sprigs if the fruits are to be kept for a few days before being used. Like blackcurrants, each bush should produce about 4.5 kg (10 lb) of fruit.

STORING Use in jellies or freeze.

PESTS AND DISEASES Aphids, birds, red currant blister aphid, capsid bug, currant sawfly, leaf spot and coral spot.

PROPAGATION As for gooseberries.

Damson and Gage See Plum

GOOSEBERRY

Gooseberries are not easy to prune, thanks to their thorns, but they're easy to eat in pies, jams, stewed and in that superb dessert gooseberry fool. There are culinary and dessert kinds and even

dual-purpose varieties. I reckon that those in the list below as some of the best.

WHERE TO PLANT Although they are tolerant of dappled shade, gooseberries grow best in full sun on ground that does not act as a frost pocket. Dig and manure the land in autumn before planting bare-root bushes between November and March. Scatter a dusting of blood, bone and fishmeal over the soil immediately before planting.

PLANTING Plant to the same level as the old soil mark on the stem after removing any suckers (shoots arising from the roots or from the portion of stem that will be below ground). Like red currants, gooseberries are grown on a short 'leg'. For full planting details see the instructions on planting trees and shrubs (see p.40). Space plants 1.5 m (5 ft) from their neighbours, or plant them in flower beds and borders as shrubs. Cut back all the stems by half their length after planting, preferably to an outward-facing bud. Varieties that have a tendency to trail their stems can be cut back to an upward-facing bud. Cut out any overcrowding sideshoots: aim to produce a bush with six or eight main stems.

CULTIVATION Dust the soil around the bushes with blood, bone and fishmeal in spring and then lay an organic mulch. Remove any suckers that form. Water well in dry spells. In succeeding years a little sulphate of potash can be

scattered around each bush in February before the general fertilizer and mulch are applied. Keep down weeds during the summer.

PRUNING Prune twice: in winter, cut back the main shoots by half and sideshoots back to three buds; completely remove one or two old stems. In summer, shorten sideshoots to about five leaves in early July.

HARVESTING The first pickings can be made in May when the fruits are thinned to leave them 5 cm (2 in) apart along the stems. Early pickings can be used in a pie. When the berries are fully fattened they will gradually soften and can then be harvested in one go.

STORING All manner of preserves can be made; both the fruits themselves and pies made with them can be frozen.

PESTS AND DISEASES Aphids, birds, gooseberry sawfly, American gooseberry mildew.

PROPAGATION Take hardwood cuttings in September or October. Shoot tips 30 cm (12 in) long can be cut above a bud at the top and below a bud at the base and relieved of all but the top four buds, which will form the branch framework of the new plant.

Insert the cuttings on the vegetable plot. The lowest bud on each cutting should be a few centimetres (inches) above ground level. Lift the rooted cuttings the following autumn and transplant them to where they can be allowed to grow permanently.

Recommended gooseberry varieties

VARIETY	COLOUR	ORDER OF RIPENING	CULINARY/DESSERT
'Careless'	white	2	C
'Golden Drop'	yellow	1	D
'Keepsake'	green	1	C/D
'Lancashire Lad'	red	2	C/D
'Langley Gage'	yellow	2	D
'Leveller'	yellow	2	C/D
'May Duke'	red	1	C/D
'Whitesmith'	green	3	C/D

GRAPE

We are now blessed with a good number of grapes that can be grown outdoors, but most gardeners find greater satisfaction in growing one vine in a greenhouse or conservatory, so with that excuse I'm going to stay under glass.

For a start you'll need a greenhouse or conservatory at least 4 m (12 ft) long, otherwise your rampant vine will boot everything else out of the way.

Don't be tempted to try that aristocrat of grapes 'Muscat of Alexandria' unless you're prepared to take a gamble. It's a temperamental customer and not likely to perform as well as either 'Royal Muscadine' (if you want a green grape) or 'Black Hamburgh' (if you prefer black).

PREPARING THE SOIL AND THE HOUSE

An Irishman once told me that the best thing to put under a grapevine was 'three dead dogs', but failing the availability of a canine trio I should stick to a good load of manure. Traditionally vines were always planted outside the greenhouse and the stem taken in through a hole in the wall. Today it's considered better to plant inside the house where the soil is warmer and you will have far more control over watering and feeding.

Growing happily in the border soil of this spacious conservatory, these vines are laden with tantalizingly healthy bunches of fat grapes.

Dig plenty of muck or compost into the border soil and a good sprinkling of general fertilizer. Fix training wires to the rafters of the house at 35 cm (15 in) intervals. The vine will be planted in the centre of one of the greenhouse borders and the stem or 'rod' led upwards to the eaves and then on to the ridge, which means that the growth will rest right against the glass. For this reason it's important to use 20–23 cm (8–9 in) long metal vine eyes to support the wire and allow maximum air circulation between the plant and the glass.

PLANTING Plant bare-root vines between November and December, container-grown vines at any time of year. Soak the soil thoroughly a few days before planting if it looks at all dry. Dig a hole large enough to take the roots of a bare-root vine, trim off any damaged roots with a sharp pair of secateurs, put the plant in the hole, spread out the roots and re-firm the soil with your feet. Set the plant 15 cm (6 in) from the greenhouse wall and make sure that the old soil mark on the stem is just level with the new surface. Container-grown vines should be tapped out of their pots but otherwise disturbed as little as possible (though any roots that are obviously trying to corkscrew themselves back into the rootball should be teased out). Lower the rootball into the hole and firm back the soil. Water the plant well to settle the soil around the roots and apply a thick mulch of manure or compost.

TRAINING AND PRUNING There are lots of frighteningly complicated methods of training a vine but this is the simplest I know (see below). Shorten the main rod (you'll have to get used to that word if you want to pass yourself off as an expert) to 60 cm (2 ft) and any lateral shoots to one bud after planting in December. When the buds start to grow, nip off all but the topmost shoot and allow this to grow to a length of 3 m (10 ft), then pinch out its tip. The shoot is most easily supported by tying it to a cane which is, in turn, tied to the wires so that it runs up the side of the house; another cane can be tied to the roof section. Sideshoots will emerge from the new main stem. Thin them out to leave one shoot every 35 cm (15 in), to correspond with the training wires. The shoots should be trained alternately to right and left. Carefully fasten these shoots to the wires as they grow. Pinch out their tips when they are 1 m (3 ft) long, leaving five leaves on each. Pinch back any laterals that form on these major sideshoots to just one leaf.

In the first autumn after planting, cut back the main laterals to two buds and shorten the main rod by two thirds of its length. In the years that follow, allow one lateral to grow from each stub or 'spur' and pinch out its tip two or three leaves after its flower cluster. Train the main rod as before, allowing it to retain an extra 60 cm (2 ft) each year until it is eventually pruned to just below the ridge.

Don't allow all the laterals to carry fruit in the second year – only the lower pair. Another tier can be allowed to fruit each year.

CULTIVATION Leave the house unheated and gently ventilated right through the winter until March. The rod is cleaned while it is dormant; lower it from the support wires and scrub it down with a stiff brush to remove flaking bark. Paint it with a winter wash to kill overwintering eggs of aphids, hibernating mealy bugs, red spider mites and scale insects. Heat can be applied as early as February but most folk are content to grow their grapes in an unheated greenhouse and settle for an August and September

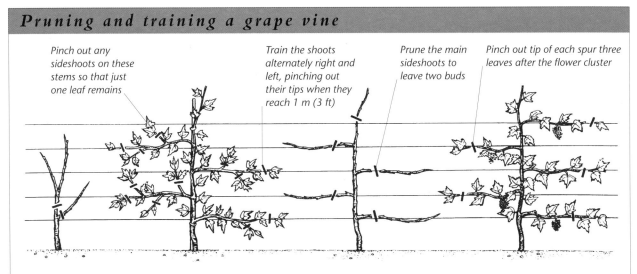

Pruning and training a grape vine

Pinch out any sideshoots on these stems so that just one leaf remains

Train the shoots alternately right and left, pinching out their tips when they reach 1 m (3 ft)

Prune the main sideshoots to leave two buds

Pinch out tip of each spur three leaves after the flower cluster

1 After planting a dormant vine, shorten the main rod to 60 cm (2 ft) and sideshoots to one bud.

2 Allow only the topmost bud to grow, fastening it to a cane as it extends. Sideshoots that emerge from this new stem should be thinned out so just one remains for each wire.

3 In the first winter after planting shorten the main sideshoots to leave just two buds. Cut back the leading shoot by two thirds.

4 Allow one shoot to grow from each stub or 'spur' in subsequent years, pinching out its tip three leaves after the flower cluster. Continue to pinch out sublaterals.

harvest. Close the ventilators in April and water the border soil well. Soon the buds will swell and training can begin. Leave the rod hanging down from the support system when you start it off, and tie it up again when the lower laterals have started to sprout.

Try to maintain a temperature of 16°C (60°F), gradually letting this rise to around 21°C (70°F) by late May (an automatic ventilating arm will be very useful here). Damp down daily in fine weather and spray the shoots with tepid rainwater once a day until the flowers open.

Shade when necessary from mid-May onwards. When the flowers open, dust over them with a fine paintbrush or a rabbit's tail to assist pollination. Try to maintain an average day temperature of 21°C (70°F) and a minimum night temperature of 13°C (55°F). Keep an eye on the border soil and really soak it before it has a chance to become dry. Apply a liquid feed (tomato fertilizer is best) every ten days once growth has started.

THINNING It's essential to thin out the fruit clusters if you want a healthy bunch of fat grapes. Thin the berries when they are pea-sized. Work from the bottom of the bunch to the top so that 1 cm (½ in) is left between all the remaining fruits. Use fine-pointed scissors and keep your fingers off the grapes or the white 'bloom' will be marked.

HARVESTING When the grapes start to ripen ease off watering and stop feeding or the fruits may over-expand and split. Snip off any that do. The grapes will be ready to cut in bunches about four weeks after they have changed colour. Once harvesting is completed, ventilate well and continue to ease off watering so that the vine gradually becomes dormant once more.

STORING Grapes can't be stored, but if you grow a suitable cultivar you might like to try your hand at winemaking with your own home-grown grapes.

PESTS AND DISEASES Aphids, mealy

bug, red spider mite, scale insects, scald, shanking.

PROPAGATION Tricky and not necessary if you only need one vine.

Loganberry See Blackberry

PEACH / NECTARINE

Exotic-sounding though it may be, the nectarine is nothing more than a peach without the fur coat. Grow it in exactly the same way. Don't waste your time growing a peach from a stone – it may never come to much. Instead buy a plant of a proven variety that can be relied on to produce plenty of succulent fruits. 'Peregrine' is my first choice. It ripens in August and is a good doer both under glass and in the open. 'Early Rivers' and 'Lord Napier' are among the best of the nectarines, ripening in July and August. If you insist on having peaches in July you'd better pick 'Duke of York'.

WHERE TO PLANT To keep them warm and in good order, peaches and nectarines are best trained as fan-shaped trees against a south- or west-facing wall or the rear wall of a lean-to greenhouse. Dig the soil deeply, working in plenty of manure or compost and improving drainage if necessary. Acid soil should be limed a few weeks after digging and a few weeks before planting.

SUPPORT Horizontal wires should be fastened to the wall, or to a sunny fence if that's all you've got, to allow tying in. Arrange the wires at 30 cm (12 in) intervals and hold them in place with metal vine eyes screwed into wall plugs.

PLANTING Plant a container-grown peach for preference. It can be planted at any time of year provided the soil against the wall is not allowed to dry out. It's easiest to plant a partially trained tree with the basis of the fan formation already established, but if you're mean, or just interested in doing the job yourself, you can buy a

'maiden' (a one-year-old tree) and start from scratch. Plant the tree (after watering it well) so that its rootball rests just below the surface of the soil. (See p.40 for full planting details.) Set the plant 15–30 cm (6–12 in) away from the wall. Scatter a little blood, bone and fishmeal around it during February and then apply an organic mulch.

TRAINING AND PRUNING When your maiden tree is planted, wait until the shoots start to grow in spring then cut it back to 60 cm (2 ft) just above a sprouting shoot. When two healthy shoots are observed growing in opposite directions from the base of the tree, but above the graft union, cut back the central stem to just above them and remove all other shoots. These two shoots will be taken up the wire framework in opposite directions at an angle of 45°. Fasten a cane to the wire to act as a marker and support for each shoot. Pinch out any sideshoots that form on these main laterals.

In winter, shorten the two laterals to about 1 m (3 ft) and allow four shoots to grow from each of them during the second summer. Make sure that these shoots are well spaced out on the framework, and at the end of the year cut them back to 1 m (3 ft), having pinched off their laterals during the summer.

During the third year shoots are allowed to grow from the established laterals at 23 cm (9 in) intervals, but only from the top sides of the shoots. Those growing out at other angles are removed. Pinch out the tips of these shoots when they are 45 cm (18 in) long. Allow the topmost bud that remains on each to grow on and extend the framework.

Peaches are carried on wood that is one year old and the aim should be to produce as much young wood on the mature framework as possible. Mature plants should have their fruiting sideshoots cut out as soon as the fruit is picked, and new ones tied in to replace them. Thin out overcrowding shoots in spring by simply pulling them off while they are soft and green.

UNDER GLASS There's no need to heat a peach under glass; it will have a head start simply by virtue of the fact that there's glass above it. Leave the ventilators open a little right through the winter, closing them in February and ventilating only when the temperature rises to 18°C (65°F). Ideally the plants want to be kept around 10°C (50°F) at night and 16°C (60°F) during the day, but in an unheated house you'll have to rely on the weather doing this for you (and in February it's not always kind). A good sprinkling of general fertilizer, followed by a thorough watering and mulching, will help to spur the plant into action, as will a daily spray with tepid water. Damp down the floor too. Soak the soil thoroughly whenever it shows signs of starting to dry out, and later in spring apply shading when there is a danger of sun scorch. Blinds are the best answer – they can be rolled up on dull days.

POLLINATION Peaches flower early, both in the open and under glass, and there are few bees around to do the job of pollinating for you. Use a soft paintbrush or a rabbit's tail to dust the pollen from flower to flower. If frost threatens, hang muslin or old net curtains over the flowering branches. When the fruitlets are the size of marbles, thin them out to leave one every 10 cm (4 in). Stop spraying the greenhouse plants with water now. When the fruits are as large as conkers, thin them to leave one every 23 cm (9 in).

HARVESTING Pick the fruits as soon as they are ripe – the flesh will suddenly soften at the shoulder of the fruit (the end nearest the stalk). Once the fruits have been picked the plant can be sprayed daily with water once more.

STORING The fruits can be stored for a few days by placing them in a container lined with soft material and keeping in a cool place.

PESTS AND DISEASES Aphids, scale insects, red spider mites, mildew,

peach leaf curl. The latter rarely attacks peaches under glass but almost always attacks peaches in the open. For this reason it's a good idea to give preventive sprays each year before the buds open.

PEAR

Perhaps the best all-round eating pear is 'Williams' Bon Chrétien', almost always known simply as Williams'. 'Doyenne du Comice' is certainly the juiciest and most succulent but it can be tricky in cold gardens. The long, slim 'Conference' is a good choice if you like your pears on the firm side, and if you want a good cooker try 'Catillac'.

WHERE TO PLANT Warmth, sun and shelter are the keys to success with pears. Give them a well-cultivated, well-manured soil in a bright spot and they should do well. The flowers open earlier than those of the apple, so keep the trees away from frost pockets at all costs or you'll lose your blossom. As well as being grown as free-standing trees, pears can also be trained as cordons, espaliers and fans (see p.217).

ROOTSTOCKS Like the apple, the pear is grafted on to a rootstock that controls its vigour. 'Quince A' is the name of the stock most frequently used. It is relatively dwarfing and brings the tree into bearing quite quickly when it's only a few years old.

POLLINATION It's as well to think about pollination before you plant. If your pear tree, or trees, don't receive the right kind of pollen they'll fail to set a crop. In practice there are often trees

in other gardens, and the bees are able to fly between them all doing a good job. If there are no other pears in the area you'd be well advised to plant two so that cross-pollination is ensured, but you'll have to plant pears that flower at the same time. 'Conference' will pollinate 'Williams', and vice versa; 'Doyenne du Comice' will pollinate 'Catillac' and that other favourite 'Beurre Hardy', and vice versa.

PLANTING If you are lucky enough to have room for a small orchard, plant bush trees 4 m (12 ft) apart on the square. Cordons should be planted 2 m (6 ft) apart on the support system; espaliers and fans 4.5 m (15 ft) apart.

Plant pears exactly as for ornamental trees (see p.40). Scatter a good dusting of blood, bone and fishmeal over the soil during the spring after planting and then lay a thick mulch of organic matter on the soil. Don't let grass grow within 1 m (3 ft) of the tree for at least three years or the roots of the grass will rob the soil of nutrients the pear could use.

TRAINING AND PRUNING Pruning of established trees is similar to the pruning of apples (see p.219 for fuller details). All the varieties I've mentioned carry their fruits on short sideshoots known as 'spurs'. To encourage the production of these the main shoots or 'leaders' are cut back by half their length during winter and the lateral shoots are shortened to three or four buds. Pears have a tendency to become overcrowded with fruiting spurs and the buds on these spurs can be reduced to three in number if you have the patience and determination.

Recommended pear varieties

VARIETY	PICK	DAYS TO RIPEN
'Williams' Bon Chrétien'	September	7–14
'Doyenne du Comice'	October	7–28
'Conference'	October	7–28
'Beurre Hardy'	Late September	14–28
'Catillac'	October	Keeps until April

It's not the end of the world if you don't prune your tree every year but it does help to keep it in shape. A yearly feed with rose fertilizer gives the tree a boost, especially in the first five years of its life. Scatter half a dozen handfuls on the soil around the trunk and lightly hoe it in during March. Thin the young fruits in mid-July to leave just two out of each cluster.

HARVESTING A tricky operation. Many pears need to be picked before they are ripe and allowed to come to maturity in store. The general rule for picking is that the fruit should be removed as soon as it parts easily from the tree. 'Catillac' remains hard right through storage, softening when cooked.

STORING As for apples, but do not wrap the fruits. Keep an especially close eye on pears for they suddenly ripen and are likely to be past it if you only check them once a week. As soon as a fruit starts to soften, bring it in from the store and eat it within a day or two. The polythene bag method of storage is especially useful for pears – it stops them from shrivelling. The early varieties will not keep for long; the later varieties last better.

PESTS AND DISEASES Aphids, red spider mite, pear midge, pear leaf blister mite, birds, codling moth, slugworm, pear sucker, pear sawfly, winter moth, canker, mildew, scab, brown rot, blossom wilt and fireblight.

PLUM / DAMSON / GAGE

Luscious fruits that are really easy to grow. There's little to master in the way of pruning and, if you choose the right variety, you'll not need to worry about planting more than one, for the tree can set a good crop of fruits with its own pollen. If you're baffled by all the different varieties, the following are among the best: 'Victoria' is an unbeatable plum. Sometimes it's so anxious to please that the branches are snapped off by the weight of its fruits. If your penchant is for gages, try 'Early

Transparent', a yellow fruit of incomparable sweetness. Both mature from mid- to late August. 'Czar' is a good culinary plum ripening earlier in the month, and 'Merryweather Damson' makes the most delectable dark red jam when it comes to maturity in September and October. Let your nurseryman tempt you with other goodies from his collection of varieties, but make sure you know whether they are dessert or culinary plums – the flavour of the culinary types is only appreciated after cooking.

WHERE TO PLANT The plum is happy on deep soil; it will grow on chalky ground but seldom on really shallow stuff. Lime acid ground in the autumn before digging and manuring. The soil

needs to be well cultivated to give the roots every chance to sink and establish themselves. Compared with other fruit trees, plums are comparatively shallow rooting and an annual spring mulch of manure is especially welcome. Avoid frost pockets, and make sure the trees have plenty of sun.

ROOTSTOCKS Plums, damsons and gages are usually grafted on to one of two rootstocks: St Julien A or Myrobalan B. The latter is used for vigorous standard trees, the former for

A typically heavy crop of 'Victoria' plum: the excellently flavoured, bright red fruit with golden-yellow flesh ripens in late August.

most others. In smaller gardens St Julien A is obviously a better choice, unless you have a craving for a tree seat in which case you'll plump for a standard. The new rootstock Pixy is more dwarfing than St Julien A but the trees are still quite large compared with bush apple trees.

PLANTING Having decided on a bush, pyramid, standard, half-standard or fan-shaped tree (see p.217 for details) you can think about planting. Like all trees, plums can be planted from containers at any time of year or as bare-root plants from November to March. Choose two- or three-year-old trees and plant as for ornamental trees and shrubs (see p.40). If you intend to plant them in an orchard, space bush trees 4 m (12 ft) apart, or 3 m (10 ft) apart if they are on Pixy rootstock; standards and half-standards 5.5 m (18 ft) apart. Fans should be trained against tall house walls of a southerly or westerly aspect for preference. They'll need a wire framework as recommended for peaches and acid cherries. Scatter a general fertilizer on the soil around the tree in spring and then lay a thick organic mulch. Avoid growing grass right up to plum trees: they resent the competition. Pay attention to watering during establishment.

PRUNING Prune your plums in spring or summer to lessen the risk of attack by silver leaf disease, which can enter wounds in winter. Newly planted trees should be pruned in March, just as the buds are starting to break. Cut all the shoots back by half their length. Remove completely any weak or overcrowding shoots. You can do this for a couple of years and then leave the tree to its own devices if you're really lazy. Prune when necessary in spring or summer to keep the tree shapely: cut back overlong leading shoots by one third of their length and snip the tips off laterals. Start off a fan-trained plum tree as described for peaches (see p.227). Some lateral shoots are retained as part of the framework each year; those that

are not required are pinched back to five leaves in summer to encourage the production of fruiting spurs. Cut out a portion of older wood each summer and replace it with strong, younger shoots. As with all fan-trained trees, cut out any shoots that grow directly away from the wall or towards it.

POLLINATION Most plums (and all those I've mentioned) will set a good crop of fruits with their own pollen, though the presence of another plum tree flowering at the same time will usually make for an even heavier crop. If frost threatens at blossom time, drape wall-trained trees with old net curtains or some other fabric to offer the blooms protection.

THINNING The tree will thin its own fruits to some extent in the June drop, but you can help out after this if you like by snipping off unwanted fruits to leave the remainder 5–8 cm (2–3 in) apart. If you don't thin 'Victoria', the boughs will often snap and can allow disease to enter. A tree that bears too heavily one year will often crop lightly the next. Prop up heavily laden branches with catapult-shaped poles.

HARVESTING Pick dessert plums when they are fully ripe – bite into one and see. Damsons and culinary plums can be picked with their stalks just before they are ripe. Try to harvest the fruits before birds and wasps eat their fill.

STORING Store in a cool place while you see to jam- and pie-making. They'll freeze well if you remove the stones first.

PESTS AND DISEASES Aphids, red spider mites, winter moth, pear leaf blister mite, plum sawfly, plum tortrix moth, mussel scale, wasps, silver leaf, bacterial canker, blossom wilt, brown rot.

RASPBERRY

It's a toss-up as to which is the more popular fruit in British gardens, the raspberry or the strawberry. The raspberry wins in mine. 'Malling Jewel' is easily the best flavoured of the summer fruiters, closely followed by

the slightly earlier 'Malling Promise'. Make sure you try the autumn fruiters 'Autumn Bliss' (the best) and 'Zeva', which extend the season well into October. Some folk claim that these autumn crops are not as fine flavoured as the summer harvest, but I wouldn't dream of complaining at that time of year.

WHERE TO PLANT Best in full sun, though the summer fruiters can take dappled shade. Choose a sheltered site on well-drained soil that has been well dug and well manured. Scatter a good dusting of blood, bone and fishmeal over the soil a few days before planting. The plants can be used as a screen and then a 45 cm (18 in) wide trench can be prepared for them rather than an entire patch of soil.

SUPPORT A 2 m (6 ft) high post and wire fence with stout horizontal wires at 45 cm (18 in) intervals is all that is necessary, or the plants can be trained against a fence fitted with wires at a similar spacing.

PLANTING Buy only certified raspberry canes that are free of virus diseases, which can cripple cropping. Plant from November to February. Soak the canes overnight in a bucket of water and then plant them at 45 cm (18 in) intervals along the foot of the support system, covering the roots with just 8 cm (3 in) of soil. Firm the earth well around the roots and then cut back the canes to 23 cm (9 in).

CULTIVATION Scatter a dusting of blood, bone and fishmeal over the soil along the row in March and then lay an organic mulch. Tie in the canes as they grow, spacing them 10 cm (4 in) apart. Cut off the old stump at ground level when the new stems grow. When the canes grow taller than the topmost wire, bend them downwards and tie them in. Cut them off level with the top wire during the winter. Keep the plants well watered at all times during the first spring and summer. Hand-weed among the plants and remove those that emerge too far away from the row.

PRUNING Summer fruiters will carry a crop in the second summer on the canes formed during their first year. The autumn fruiters will produce fruits in the first September after planting, so pruning from now on is different. All the canes of the autumn fruiters are cut out at ground level in February. As soon as the summer fruiters have been picked, the canes that carried the fruits are cut out at ground level and the new ones, which will carry next year's crop, are thinned out if necessary and tied into the framework again at 10 cm (4 in) intervals.

HARVESTING Make sure it is you who get the harvest, not the birds who will be fierce competition. Net or cage the crop if you can. Pick the berries, pulling them from their plugs, as soon as they are ripe. Check the canes every few days for ripening fruits. You should be able to harvest 900 g (2 lb) from every 30 cm (12 in) run of row with summer-fruiting varieties; around 225 g (½ lb) with the autumn fruiters.

STORING The fruits freeze well.

PESTS AND DISEASES Aphids, raspberry beetle, cane spot, cane blight, spur blight, botrytis and viruses.

PROPAGATION Dig up and transplant suckers in autumn. Only propagate from healthy, virus-free plants. Replace raspberry rows every eight years or so.

STRAWBERRY

The strawberry is more labour intensive than most fruits, but that doesn't seem to put gardeners off growing it. Don't stick by the ancient varieties, which are losing their vigour: go for some of the newcomers, but taste them before you commit yourself. I can heartily recommend the summer fruiters 'Tenira' and 'Pantagruella'. Varieties described as 'perpetual fruiting' crop late into the season; 'Aromel' and 'Rabunda' are both reliable even if they lack the full flavour of the first two.

WHERE TO PLANT An open, sunny spot in well-drained soil is what strawberries insist on. Don't whatever you do plant them in a frost pocket or you'll be lucky if you ever see a berry. Dig over the soil during spring and summer and add as much manure as you can spare. Scatter a general fertilizer over the soil a few days before planting and rake it into the surface.

PLANTING Buy certified strawberry plants that are guaranteed free from virus diseases. Water them well and plant while the soil is moist, during July and August and certainly no later than September. These plants can then be allowed to crop the following year. Perpetual fruiters that are not planted until spring can still be allowed to fruit in late summer and autumn, but the earlier fruiting varieties should be relieved of their flowers if they are spring planted. Conserve their strength for a bumper crop in one year's time. Plant the strawberries 45 cm (18 in) apart in rows 75 cm (2½ ft) apart. The crown of each plant should rest at soil level – not below it, nor too far above it. Water the plants in thoroughly with a sprinkler.

CULTIVATION Pay close attention to watering during the remainder of the summer and the following spring. I mulch my strawberry bed with pulverized bark immediately after planting. Pick off faded leaves and scatter tomato fertilizer among the plants in February at the rate of a handful to two plants; let the rain wash it in. Protect the plants from slugs and the fruits from birds: lay plastic netting over the rows or grow the plants in a fruit cage. Early in June push straw under the fruit clusters and around the plants to keep the crop clean. Bitumen strawberry mats and black plastic mulching are useful alternatives where straw is undesirable or in short supply. Remove any runners that form, unless you want to propagate from them. If you want to hasten fruit development and ripening, cover a row of strawberries with cloches in early February. Ventilate well when the flowers open, and remove the cloches when the crop has been picked.

As an alternative to straw or mats, support fruit-laden stems with loops made from lengths of galvanized wire

Strawberries are synonymous with summer, but it is possible to carry on harvesting this luscious soft fruit until late autumn. Keep fruit off the soil with clean straw or special mats.

HARVESTING Pick the fruits, with their stalks, as soon as they are ripe. When all the fruits have been picked, chop off all the foliage and burn it along with the straw to kill pests and diseases. The perpetual fruiters will be happier if you cut off just the older leaves and remove the straw.

STORING Strawberries make good jam and the new variety 'Totem' freezes well, even if it's not A1 when it comes to flavour.

PESTS AND DISEASES Aphids, birds, slugs, red spider mites, botrytis, viruses.

PROPAGATION To keep the plants in good condition, move the strawberry bed every three years. Allow runners to form during July and August in the third year, if the plants are still healthy and virus free, and peg these into 8 cm (3 in) pots of John Innes No. 1 potting compost sunk into the soil alongside the plants. Keep the compost moist and the plantlets will quickly send out roots. Sever them from their parents and plant them out individually six weeks later. If your plants have puckered or mottled leaves, burn them and buy in virus-free stock.

vegetable growing

Nothing can compare with the taste of home-grown vegetables, chosen for flavour, harvested in their prime and enhanced with a sprinkling of fresh, chopped herbs

I WISH I HAD A PENNY FOR EVERY TIME I'VE BEEN asked if it's really worth growing your own vegetables. If you're going to add up labour and the cost of seeds and fertilizers I doubt if it is. But how much do you allow for flavour, convenience, the thrill of the harvest and the fact that you can choose just what variety of vegetable you grow?

Gardeners who refuse to grow vegetables because it's easier to buy them from the shops must be desperately short of imagination as well as energy. Of course some crops fail, but isn't the magic moment of picking a good crop worth all that hassle? It is to me. So no more grumbling; on with the wellies and out with the spade!

Nobody should be without a handful of herbs to add flavour and aroma to their cooking, so I've included entries for the most popular culinary herbs at the end of the A–Z section.

PLANNING YOUR VEGETABLE PLOT

Choosing the best site

You might not have much choice but, if you can, try to pick a spot that's well lit, sheltered at a distance from wind and within easy reach of the house. Avoid frost pockets – dips in the land that will collect cold air and make for a slow start and rapid finish to the growing season. Vegetables are dependent upon generous supplies of water in summer, so make sure the hosepipe will reach them. If they are allowed to dry out, all development will stop and your yields will be down. It's no bad idea to start with a small plot and make it bigger as you need the space – that way you won't suddenly be faced with a massive patch of virgin soil to keep in trim.

Easy access

Paths around the plot will make access easier, and it's not a bad idea to make them out of loose-laid flagstones that can be lifted and relaid as necessary. I've divided my plot up with slabs laid on raked earth and it's easy to lift them for digging each winter. At just over one pound apiece they weren't too pricey, but I bought them a few at a time as the plot grew.

WHERE TO PLANT

I always feel a killjoy when I tell folk to plan their plots before they sow anything: most want to be out on the soil bunging in seeds for all they're worth. But if you stop to take out a pencil and paper for a few minutes you can decide which crop should go where and what can follow it. Can it be grown between two other crops that will not need the space at that time? If it is positioned next to crops that need the same kind of soil preparation, it will save you humping manure to all corners of the plot. Work out when the plant needs to be sown and when it is likely to be harvested and you'll know how it can be fitted into your cropping plan. This all sounds very grand, but a plan of campaign makes vegetable growing even more interesting.

Rotation

The rotation of crops is an ancient practice based on sound common sense. Farmers change their crops from field to field each year so that specific crop diseases do not get a chance to build up in any one area, and so that particular nutrients, which one crop might demand in quantity, do not become exhausted.

On the vegetable plot it is difficult to work out a really concrete rotation scheme (though I do try to divide my plot into three – liming one third, manuring another third and fertilizing the remainder) – but it is sensible to put vegetables in a different place each year. Don't keep your runner beans at the same end or your onions on one bed – even though some experts swear by this method. If disease does strike, it will be years before you can grow onions again.

What you can do in practice is to group together on the plot those crops that enjoy roughly the same soil conditions: those that like a freshly manured site, such as onions, leeks, peas and beans, and those that need lime if the ground is acid (most brassicas). Vegetables that just enjoy a little fertilizer (including most root crops) can be kept to one section of the plot and that section moved yearly.

IMPROVING THE SOIL

MANURING Those patches that need manuring every year can be enriched during digging in autumn, winter, or even spring, on light soils, with well-rotted manure or garden compost. If you can't get either (though you should always make your own compost – sorry to nag) use coarse peat laced with some general fertilizer. A bucketful to every running metre (yard) of trench will be fine (see p.15 for digging instructions).
LIMING Brassicas (members of the cabbage family) in particular grow best on a soil that is not too acid. Soil

test kits will tell you the status quo (see p.14) and a dressing of lime can be applied during winter, at least one month after manure, when necessary.
FERTILIZERS All crops need fertilizer so I've not mentioned its application to individual crops in the A–Z section. That's because it should be scattered over the plot about one week before sowing any crop. Two handfuls of blood, bone and fishmeal or Growmore can be scattered over each square metre (square yard) and raked in. This is known as a base dressing.

Topdressings are given to boost growing crops. With leafy crops, fertilizers high in growth-promoting nitrogen are beneficial (sulphate of ammonia and nitrochalk, for instance). Others will prefer a more balanced fertilizer containing equal amounts of nitrogen, phosphates and potassium, such as blood, bone and fishmeal and Growmore. I've indicated which crops like which.

> "If there's no room for a vegetable patch, fit your vegetables among the flowers."

Liquid feeds have the advantage of going straight into action and can give all crops a rapid boost.
MULCHING In flower beds and borders mulching is a common practice, but few folk mulch on the vegetable plot. That's a shame, for many crops grow better if surrounded with an organic mat. Beans and peas are especially grateful for a mulch of compost or even grass mowings in summer. Apply the mulch while the soil is moist and it will keep the moisture in as well as keeping down weeds.

WEED CONTROL

I'll speak only briefly of weed control but remember that it is vital (see Chapter 1 How to Start). If your crops have to compete with a forest of groundsel, chickweed, dandelions and couch grass they'll give up the ghost or, at the very best, become spindly and not worth harvesting.

A Dutch hoe pushed between the rows on a dry day is the best means of control for most annual weeds, and that's all that should be left after your preliminary cultivations, except, perhaps, the odd persistent dandelion or nettle. Hand-weeding between the plants is a bit of a chore but there's no finer method of getting to know your crops.

SOWING AND GROWING TECHNIQUES

There are various ways of sowing seeds on the vegetable plot, and there are some vegetables that need to be sown in a greenhouse or on a windowsill before being introduced to the great outdoors. I've dealt with the techniques for both methods in Chapter 2 Propagation, but here I want to mention a few wheezes that will enable you to get the best out of your plot.

Where and when to sow

SUCCESSIONAL SOWING This is the technique of sowing small quantities of one crop at intervals so that your harvest is spread. Don't sow three rows of lettuce or radish, for instance, all in one go. Sow half a row every

Even if your garden is too small to accommodate a full-scale vegetable plot, you can grow a few specimens in your flower beds and borders: many are handsome enough to show off flowers, such as these *Eschscholzia* 'Special Mixed' (Californian poppy), to advantage.

fortnight. That way you'll have a steady succession of crops instead of an embarrassing glut.

INTERCROPPING Here fast-growing crops such as radishes are sown between rows of slow-growing crops that will eventually need the space. The radishes will be mature by the time they are being jostled and you've managed to squeeze an extra harvest out of the soil.

CATCH CROPPING Fast-growing vegetables are used again here: not just radishes but spring onions, turnips and non-hearting lettuce too. Sow them on land that will not be planted up with another crop until later in the year. Your first crop will have matured and been picked by then. Only with careful planning will you be able to manage catch cropping.

Thinning and transplanting

THINNING Here's a job that's more vital than you think. Even the obliging radish will not grow unless it's thinned quickly. Do the job as soon as you can to give the crops that remain room to grow. You don't have to pull up the unwanted seedlings; you can simply nip them off at ground level (unless you'd rather fork them up and carefully transplant them).

PLANTING AND TRANSPLANTING When you're moving plants bear in mind a few golden rules: always water them well before transplanting and 'puddle' them in afterwards. Plant firmly and plant youngsters, not gnarled grandads. Use a trowel for most plants, a thick spade-handle dibber for brassicas if you like. Plant to the same depth as the plant was growing in the nursery bed – no shallower and no deeper.

Growing in bed systems

There's much fuss made of the modern technique of growing vegetables in beds rather than rows. It's a sensible scheme whereby several rows are spaced very close together (as close as the plants are spaced within the row) and a path left every 1 m (3 ft) or so between such blocks to allow weeding and other cultivations.

DEEP BED SYSTEM Here the soil within the beds is never walked on. It's double dug during the first year and enriched with compost and manure. In subsequent winters it is forked over and any additional enrichment worked in. A friend of mine swears by the method and I aim to try it myself. The first spell of double digging is hell on my flinty soil but I'm optimistic that the results will pay dividends.

Growing in the flower garden

Where there's simply no room for a conventional vegetable patch you'll have to fit your vegetables among the flowers. It's not as funny as it sounds. The foliage of beetroot, Swiss chard, frilly 'Salad Bowl' lettuce, and even leeks, is good to look at and can show off flowers a treat. There are even ornamental cabbages with pink or white hearts that can be eaten. So if you're desperate to fit vegetables in, squeeze up the antirrhinums and dahlias and stick in a few runner beans and carrots, curly kale and globe artichokes.

Growing in cloches

These are the mini-greenhouses of glass or plastic that are used to give vegetable crops an early start or a late finish. Think of them as umbrellas rather than hot-houses. They will shelter early sowings from wind and rain, but should not be thought of as making sowing possible in really foul conditions. Seeds buried in cold, muddy earth under cloches will die almost as quickly as those buried in muddy earth in the open, so you'll still be governed to some degree by the weather.

Nevertheless, the greedy vegetable grower should not be without cloches. They come in many different shapes and sizes, but all should be fitted with end pieces to prevent them from acting as wind tunnels. For best results cloches should be put in place two or three weeks before the crop is sown to keep the soil in good condition.

Water can be applied over the top of the cloches when necessary (it will seep through the soil to the crop roots), and don't forget to ventilate both cloches and plastic tunnels in warm weather.

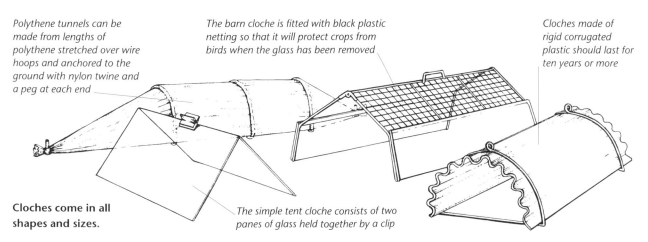

Polythene tunnels can be made from lengths of polythene stretched over wire hoops and anchored to the ground with nylon twine and a peg at each end

The barn cloche is fitted with black plastic netting so that it will protect crops from birds when the glass has been removed

Cloches made of rigid corrugated plastic should last for ten years or more

Cloches come in all shapes and sizes.

The simple tent cloche consists of two panes of glass held together by a clip

A-Z

OF

vegetables and herbs

VEGETABLE CROPS

ARTICHOKE, GLOBE

Don't sow seeds that can yield variable plants. Instead plant rooted offshoots of a variety like 'Vert de Laon'. For patient gourmets only.

WHERE TO PLANT Full sun and a very rich soil. A sheltered spot produces the biggest and best plants.

PLANT in spring, spacing the youngsters I m (3 ft) apart both ways.

CULTIVATION Topdress with compost or manure every May. Water well in dry spells. Remove all flowers during the first year. Cut the plants down to ground level in autumn and cover with straw or bracken. Scatter fertilizer around the plants in April and feed fortnightly in summer with liquid feed. Remove side buds to let only one flower develop on each head. Divide plants every four years.

HARVEST by cutting heads when firm and plump and when the scales are starting to expand. Don't wait until you can see the fuzzy flowerhead. In season from July to September.

STORE by cutting with 30 cm (12 in) long stalks and standing these in buckets of damp peat or sand. Globe artichokes will store for only a few days.

PROBLEMS Blackfly and slugs.

ARTICHOKE, JERUSALEM

'Fuseau' is a good, long, white variety that makes preparation a little easier. 'Boston Red' has ruddy skin. Both are dead easy to grow.

WHERE TO PLANT Sunny spot on well-drained and preferably well-manured soil. A good screen or windbreak for more tender plants.

PLANT tubers either in November or February and March (plant those bought from a greengrocer if you like). Set the tubers 15 cm (6 in) deep and 30 cm (12 in) apart allowing 1.25 m (4 ft) between rows or clumps. Label sites clearly.

CULTIVATION Water well in dry spells and earth up with soil if tubers start to push through the surface.

HARVEST by chopping down dead stems in autumn and lifting the tubers as they are needed. Dig up and replant any that remain in March.

STORE in the ground until required.

PROBLEMS Slugs.

ASPARAGUS

The show-off's vegetable. Previously popular varieties include 'Regal', 'Minerve' and 'Connover's Colossal', but now the all-male 'Lucullus' is proving a better cropper. Only for the very patient.

WHERE TO PLANT In full sun and a sheltered spot on well-cultivated, well-manured soil. Make sure the spot is entirely weedfree. Lime acid soil in the autumn before planting – but not at the same time as applying manure.

PLANT one-year-old crowns in April. Plant on slight ridges made in the bottom of 10 cm (4 in) deep and 30 cm (12 in) wide trenches, spacing the crowns 30 cm (12 in) apart. Return and firm the soil. Allow 60 cm–1 m (2–3 ft) between rows.

CULTIVATION Never let the bed dry out. Feed with liquid fertilizer monthly from June to September during the first year. Don't harvest any shoots for the first three years, but cut off all foliage

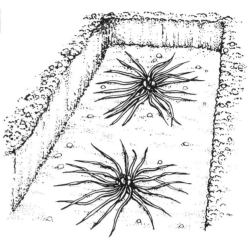

Plant one-year-old asparagus crowns on slight ridges made in the bottom of trenches 10 cm (4 in) deep and 30 cm (12 in) wide. Space them 30 cm (12 in) apart.

in autumn when it yellows. Apply a general fertilizer each spring, keep the bed weedfree and support the fern with canes and twine. In the third year, pull soil around the shoots as they start to grow; this will keep the bases white.

HARVEST by cutting all stems from the third year onwards. Harvest only from late April to late June, cutting the stems 8 cm (3 in) below ground level. Allow fern to grow after the final cutting date.

STORE by freezing if you have a surplus.

PROBLEMS Slugs, earwigs, asparagus beetle, violet root rot.

BEAN, BROAD

'The Sutton' and 'Bonny Lad' are good choices for spring and summer crops; 'Aquadulce' is for autumn sowing.

WHERE TO PLANT Full sun and a rich, well-cultivated soil. Lime acid soils in autumn.

SOW the seeds 5 cm (2 in) deep, 15 cm (6 in) apart in double rows 23 cm (9 in) apart. 'Bonny Lad' is a bush variety and can be sown in single rows. Sow 'Aquadulce' in November; cover with cloches if possible. Sow in spring from February to June. Can be sown under glass in peat pots in January; plant out in March under cloches.

CULTIVATION Weed and water as necessary. Pinch out shoot tips to prevent blackfly infestation once five flower clusters have opened. Support with a cane and string enclosure if tall varieties are grown. Remove cloches when weather improves or when the beans hit the glass.

HARVEST regularly as soon as the beans can be seen to be swollen within the pods, or pick young pods and cook as for French beans.

STORE by freezing or drying beans.

PROBLEMS Blackfly, pea and bean weevil and chocolate spot.

BEAN, FRENCH

The golden oldies 'The Prince' and 'Masterpiece' are still the most popular and reliable.

WHERE TO PLANT A sunny, sheltered spot in well-manured soil. Lime very acid ground in autumn.

SOW under cloches from mid-March to April; in the open from May to July. Sow the seeds at 8 cm (3 in) intervals along the bottom of a 5 cm (2 in) deep V-shaped drill. Don't sow in cold weather or soggy soil. Thin to leave one plant every 15 cm (6 in).

CULTIVATION Remove cloche coverings in May. Avoid drought at all costs, especially when the plants are flowering. If the plants flop, support them with brushwood.

HARVEST regularly from July to October.

STORE by freezing.

PROBLEMS Red spider mites and blackfly.

BEAN, RUNNER

'Butler' is a good stringless variety; the oldies 'Enorma' and 'Scarlet Emperor' will produce very long beans. 'Pickwick' is dwarf and grown without supports, like a French bean.

WHERE TO PLANT A sunny, sheltered spot in very rich soil. During winter, dig a trench along the line the plants will occupy and half fill it with compost before returning the earth. Moisture and food are vital.

SOW at the foot of 2.25 m (7½ ft) high wigwams or ridge-tent-like supports in May and June, planting two seeds at each station. Thin to leave one plant if both seeds grow. The canes should be 30–38 cm (12–15 in) apart. Alternatively sow seeds individually in peat pots under glass in April and plant out, one to each cane, in late May.

CULTIVATION A single twist-tie will make sure the shoots start to climb quickly. Weed regularly between plants and rows and really soak the soil in dry spells. Drought is detested. Mulch with manure or grass clippings or compost in June.

HARVEST regularly as soon as the beans are of a usable size (don't let them get too long and stringy). July to October is the runner bean season.

STORE by freezing.

PROBLEMS Blackfly and birds (which nip off flowers).

BEETROOT

'Boltardy' is best for early sowings until early April. The old favourite 'Detroit Little Ball' performs well if summer sown.

WHERE TO PLANT Full sun and a patch of ground that is well worked but not stony or heavily manured.

SOW seeds 8 cm (3 in) apart in drills 2.5 cm (1 in) deep and 30 cm (12 in) apart. Sow from March to July but cover all sowings made before late March with cloches until mid-April. Thin to leave one seedling at each 8 cm (3 in) station with the early sowings; one seedling every 1.5 cm (6 in) with later sowings (each capsule contains several beetroot seeds).

CULTIVATION Weed regularly and try to keep the soil evenly moist. Heavy watering during drought may split the roots.

HARVEST by pulling up the roots when they are large enough to be usable but before they reach the size of tennis balls. Twist off leaves to prevent bleeding. Harvest beetroot between June and October.

Make sure that climbers like runner beans (and sweet peas) are tied to supports early in their life.

STORE by pickling or by placing roots in boxes of dry peat or sand in a cool, dark, frostproof place.

PROBLEMS Blackfly and birds (which may shred young plants).

BEET, LEAF

Commonly known as Swiss chard, this is a space-saving dual-purpose vegetable. The broad leaf-stalks can be boiled for a few minutes and served with melted butter, and the leaves themselves make tasty spinach. There are white-stemmed (Swiss chard) and red-stemmed (Ruby chard) varieties, but the white is the better culinary proposition.

WHERE TO PLANT Full sun and a rich soil.

SOW the seeds 8 cm (3 in) apart in drills 2.5 cm (1 in) deep and 45 cm (18 in) apart in May and June. Thin to leave one plant every 30 cm (12 in).

CULTIVATION Keep weeded and

watered. Cut out any seedheads if some of the plants bolt.

HARVEST by pulling off large, outer leaves as they are needed. Harvest from August onwards.

STORE under cloches or straw *in situ*. May last right through winter.

PROBLEMS Slugs and snails.

BROCCOLI / CALABRESE

Broccoli is the late winter and spring vegetable; calabrese the late summer and early autumn type, which is not reliably frost hardy. Try 'Early Purple' and 'Late White' broccoli; 'Express Corona' and 'Corvet' calabrese are the green ones.

WHERE TO PLANT Full sun and a rich, well-cultivated yet firm soil. Apply lime in autumn if the ground is acid.

SOW the seeds thinly in a seedbed 1 cm (½ in) deep in small rows 23 cm (9 in) apart. Thin to leave one seedling every 8 cm (3 in). Sow broccoli in April and May; calabrese from April to June.

PLANT OUT the youngsters when they are 8 cm (3 in) high. Space them 60 cm (2 ft) apart in rows 60 cm (2 ft) apart. Firm well and water in.

CULTIVATION Earth up the stems if the plants lean. Weed and water as necessary. Scatter general fertilizer among the plants in July.

HARVEST calabrese from August to November (cut the central head first, then let side heads develop); broccoli from February to May.

STORE by freezing.

PROBLEMS Exactly as for cabbages.

BRUSSELS SPROUT

Tangy winter vegetables. 'Peer Gynt' will be ready to pick from September onwards; 'Wellington' from December. 'Rampart' and 'Widgeon' are two excellent varieties for prolonging cropping well into the New Year, often as late as April.

WHERE TO PLANT Full sun and a rich, well-cultivated and well-firmed soil. Lime in winter if the soil is acid.

SOW in a seedbed under cloches during February; during March and April in an outdoor seedbed. Sow the seeds thinly in 1 cm (½ in) deep drills spaced 23 cm (9 in) apart. Thin to leave one seedling every 8 cm (3 in).

PLANT OUT when the youngsters are 8 cm (3 in) high. Space the plants 60 cm (2 ft) apart on the square. Firm well and water in.

CULTIVATION Water and weed as necessary. Earth up the stems for stability as the plants grow. Stake with canes in exposed areas. Hoe in general fertilizer around the plants in summer. Remove yellow leaves in autumn.

HARVEST by pulling off the sprouts when large enough to eat. Start at the bottom and gradually work upwards.

STORE by leaving the sprouts on the plants through winter. End-of-season surpluses can be frozen.

PROBLEMS As for cabbage. Loose sprouts will be produced as a result of soft ground or overfeeding.

CABBAGE

A staple vegetable that can be harvested at any time of year if the sowings are planned. The chart (right) shows recommended varieties for a year-round supply of fat, firm hearts.

WHERE TO PLANT Full sun on a well-cultivated, well-firmed soil that was manured for a previous crop. Lime in winter if the soil is acid.

SOW in 1 cm (½ in) deep drills on a prepared seedbed, spacing the drills 23 cm (9 in) apart. Thin to leave one seedling every 8 cm (3 in).

PLANT OUT the seedlings when they are 8 cm (3 in) high. Firm well and puddle in. Space the plants 45 cm (18 in) apart, on the square. Spring cabbages ('April' and 'Harbinger') can be spaced 15 cm (6 in) apart, in rows 30 cm (12 in) apart and thinned to leave one plant every 30 cm (12 in) as soon as their leaves touch. Use the thinnings as spring greens.

Planting out cabbages

1 Use an old spade handle as a dibber to make a hole in the prepared soil.

2 (right) Drop in the plant and push back the earth as firmly as you can.

Recommended cabbages varieties

VARIETY	SOW	PLANT	HARVEST
'Hispi'; 'Golden Acre'	February/March (frame)	April/May	June/July
'Wiam'; 'Winnigstadt'	March/May	May/July	August/October
'Celtic'; 'Christmas Drumhead'	April/May	June/July	November/January
'January King' (savoy)	April/May	June/July	October/March
'April'; 'Harbinger'	July/August	September/October	April/May

CULTIVATION Water and weed as necessary. Guard against drought and pigeons, which will do the same. Scatter a dusting of nitrochalk among the plants in summer. Remove faded leaves. Feed spring cabbages with a dusting of general fertilizer in early April.

HARVEST the cabbages when they are large enough and firm enough to eat. For spring greens, cut a 'cross' shape in the stumps of harvested cabbages early in the year. Shoots will arise and can be harvested when of a decent size.

3 Puddle in the plant, using a watering can without a sprinkler head fitted.

STORE all varieties by leaving *in situ*.

PROBLEMS Aphids, caterpillars, cabbage root fly, flea beetles, pigeons, cabbage whitefly, clubroot, turnip gall weevil.

Calabrese See Broccoli

CARROT

A variety like 'Amsterdam Sweetheart' sown in a frame in March will give the earliest crops; 'Favourite' is certainly a favourite of most gardeners for April to June maincrop sowings. 'Autumn King', sown from May to early July, yields tasty late roots; the earlier you sow, the larger will be the carrots. 'Early French Frame' produces spherical roots that are easy to grow even on stony soil.

WHERE TO PLANT Very well-worked soil that is not stony or well manured (both conditions can cause root forking). Full sun is essential. Add peat to open up heavy soil. If your soil is heavy or stony make a raised carrot bed in a 23 cm (9 in) high enclosure of old floorboards or timber. Fill the enclosure with sieved soil, sand and peat.

SOW thinly in 1 cm (½ in) deep drills spaced 5 cm (2 in) apart. Avoid thinning the seedlings – it encourages carrot fly attack. Early crops sown in a frame or under cloches should be kept covered until mid-April.

CULTIVATION Weed between rows and aim to keep the soil evenly moist.

HARVEST as soon as of a usable size.

STORE *in situ* by covering with straw, or lift in October, trim off the tops and store the roots in boxes of dry peat or sand in a cool, dark, frostproof place.

PROBLEMS Carrot fly, slugs, carrot willow aphid.

CAULIFLOWER

Like cabbages, there are varieties to mature at different times of year (see p.240).

WHERE TO PLANT Full sun and shelter from wind. Avoid frost pockets. The ground should be well cultivated but firm and enriched with well-rotted compost or manure.

SOW in a seedbed as for cabbages.

PLANT OUT when 8 cm (3 in) high, spacing the summer-maturing types 45 cm (18 in) apart in rows 60 cm (2 ft) apart, and the autumn- and winter-maturing types 60 cm (2 ft) apart in rows 75 cm (2½ ft) apart. Seeds sown in heat during February can be pricked out and hardened off before being planted out in April. Firm well and puddle in.

CULTIVATION Weed and water copiously. A dusting of sulphate of ammonia will speed up the growth of slow plants in summer. Break two central leaves over developing curds (the white centre) to protect them from muck and weather.

HARVEST as soon as of a usable size.

STORE whole heads in boxes of straw; divided curds can be frozen.

Recommended cauliflower varieties

VARIETY	SOW	PLANT	HARVEST
'Andes'; 'Snowball'; 'All Year Round'	February (in heat)	March	June/July
'F1 Tuichan'; 'Snowball'; 'All Year Round'	March/April	April/May	July/August
'Wallaby'; 'Barrier Reef'; 'Autumn Glory'	Late April/May	June/July	August/December
'Asmer Pinnacle'; 'Walcheren Winter'	Late April/May	June/July	August/June

PROBLEMS As for cabbages. Failure to produce curds is usually caused by a check to growth – lack of water or food.

CELERIAC

Try 'Balder', 'Tellus' or 'Iram'.
WHERE TO PLANT In full sun on rich, moisture-retentive, but not soggy, soil. The roots won't fatten in poor earth.
SOW in pots in a heated frame or greenhouse during March. Prick out the seedlings into trays as soon as they can be easily handled; harden them off before planting out. Or sow outdoors under cloches in April, sowing the seeds thinly in 1 cm (½ in) deep drills.
PLANT OUT in late May or early June 30 cm (12 in) apart in rows 45 cm (18 in) apart. Don't plant too deeply. Thin the outdoor-sown seedlings to a similar spacing.
CULTIVATION Do not let the soil dry out. Feed with liquid fertilizer once a week. Remove a few leaves from the base of each plant as the roots start to swell; pull off sideshoots too.
HARVEST from September onwards as soon as the celeriac is fat enough to use. The turnip-like roots are celery flavoured and superb in soup or stew.
STORE all roots in boxes of dry peat or sand after trimming off leaves in October. Keep in a cool, dark, frostfree place.
PROBLEMS As for celery but less likely.

CELERY

Traditional 'trenched' celery is a labour-intensive crop. 'Giant White' is perhaps the most popular variety. Idlers can try self-blanching celery such as 'Golden Self-blanching' or 'Ivory Tower'. The self-blanchers won't stand frost.
WHERE TO PLANT On really rich, well-manured and moisture-retentive soil in full sun. Avoid frost pockets. Dig manure into the ground where self-blanching celery is to be grown; dig out a trench 38 cm (15 in) wide and 30 cm (12 in) deep. Spread plenty of compost or manure in the base and return the soil to within 10 cm (4 in) of the top, leaving the surplus at either side of the trench.
SOW in a heated greenhouse or frame in late March or early April. Prick out into trays and harden off.

Wrap maturing celery plants in 25 cm (10 in) cardboard collars when they are 30 cm (12 in) high The protective layer keeps them clean and excludes light to blanch the leaf stalks.

PLANT OUT in late May/early June. Plant the self-blanching types in blocks so the plants are 23 cm (9 in) apart. Don't plant in rows (in blocks the plants will exclude light from one another and so stay crisp).
Traditional celery plants are set out in a single row at 15 cm (6 in) intervals along the trench. Water them in and never let the soil dry out.
CULTIVATION Remove any sideshoots from traditional celery and wrap the plants in 25 cm (10 in) high cylinders of cardboard when they are 30 cm (12 in) high to keep the stems clean and in the dark. Pull a little soil around the 'collars' and earth up gradually over the next few weeks until none of the card is visible. Self-blanching celery needs no such treatment, but a good wedge of straw can be spread around the outside plants early in July to exclude light even more. Both crops could do with a light dusting of general fertilizer (or a good liquid feed or two) in summer.
HARVEST as soon as the leaf stalks are fat and crisp enough to eat. Start at the outside of the block with self-blanching celery, and at the end of the row with traditional types. The self-blanching celery should be harvestable from late July until October; the traditional from October to February.
STORE traditional celery *in situ* by piling straw over the green tops for frost protection. Celery will freeze, but can only be served cooked afterwards.
PROBLEMS Celery fly, leaf spot and soft rot.

Courgette See Marrow

KALE

The tastiest of the greens, I reckon. Also known as borecole. 'Pentland Brig' is the most popular, but 'Fribor' is a compact newcomer just 30 cm (12 in) high. 'Darkibor' is also very curly and is certainly well worth growing.

WHERE TO PLANT Full sun and a moderately rich but well drained soil. Lime in autumn if the ground is acid.

SOW in April and May in a seedbed. Sow seeds thinly in 1 cm (½ in) deep drills spaced 23 cm (9 in) apart. Thin to leave one seedling every 8 cm (3 in).

PLANT OUT from June to August when 10 cm (4 in) high, spacing the plants 38 cm (15 in) apart, in rows 45 cm (18 in) apart. Firm well and puddle in.

CULTIVATION Scatter a dusting of fertilizer around the plants during their second spring. Water and weed as necessary. Pull off faded foliage.

HARVEST leaves from late autumn right through to the following May.

STORE in situ. The plants are frost-hardy and can be harvested as required.

PROBLEMS As for cabbages.

KOHL RABI

Odd but interesting. Try the new varieties 'Rowel' and 'Lanro' for sowing between April and July.

WHERE TO PLANT Sunny spot and a soil that's good but not freshly manured. Lime in autumn if the ground is acid.

SOW thinly in drills 1 cm (½ in) deep and 30 cm (12 in) apart. Thin to leave one plant every 15 cm (6 in).

CULTIVATION Weed and water as necessary. An occasional liquid feed will be appreciated.

HARVEST from June to December when the roots are slightly smaller than tennis balls. Larger roots are hard and unpalatable. The leaves will cook like spinach.

STORE Storage is not advisable – the roots quickly become wizened.

PROBLEMS As for cabbages.

LEEK

'Musselburgh' and 'Lyon Prizetaker' are the old favourites; 'King Richard' is a long-stemmed newcomer.

WHERE TO PLANT Full sun and a very rich, moisture-retentive soil.

SOW thinly in March or April on a prepared seedbed in 1 cm (½ in) deep drills spaced 23 cm (9 in) apart.

PLANT OUT in June and July when the seedlings are 15 cm (6 in) or so high. Water them well before lifting. Select the largest seedlings and shorten their leaves by one third and their roots back to 2.5 cm (1 in). Drop the plants into 15 cm (6 in) deep holes made with a

Plant leeks by dropping them into 15 cm (6 in) deep holes made at 10 cm (4 in) intervals with a dibber. Puddle them in.

piece of broom handle at 10 cm (4 in) intervals along the row . Make the rows 30 cm (12 in) apart. Puddle the plants in and leave them to it. The soil will gradually fall back on its own to blanch the stem.

CULTIVATION Never let the plants go short of water. Weed when necessary and apply occasional liquid feeds.

HARVEST from November to May.

STORE in situ; or if the ground they occupy is needed lift and 'heel them in' on a corner of the plot: dig out a hole, lay the leeks in at an angle and cover their roots and lower stem with soil.

PROBLEM Leek rust.

LETTUCE

Another hearty crop that can be harvested almost all the year round. There are four basic types of lettuce: cos (with crispy upright leaves); butterhead (with soft leaves and spherical hearts); crisphead (similar but with crunchier leaves); and non-hearting (usually with frilly leaves that are cut-and-come-again).

WHERE TO PLANT Sun and a good but not heavily manured soil. Lime in autumn if ground is acid. Cos lettuces tolerate a little shade.

SOW thinly in 1 cm (½ in) deep drills spaced 30 cm (12 in) apart. Double rows under cloches can be 20 cm (8 in) apart. Sow sections of a row at fortnightly intervals for a succession. Thin gradually so that eventually the developing plants are about 23 cm (9 in) apart. 'Salad Bowl' can be closer and I've even got away without thinning it at all.

Recommended lettuce cropping plan

VARIETY	SOW	HARVEST
'Tom Thumb' (butterhead); 'Little Gem' (cos)	Early March (under cloches)	Early June
'Webb's Wonderful' (crisphead); 'Salad Bowl' (non-hearting)	March/June	June/August
'Avondefiance' (butterhead); 'Avoncrisp' (crisphead)	June/July (cloche in September)	September/December
'Valdor' (crisphead); 'Winter Density' (cos)	Late August/Early Sepember	May/June
'Unrivalled' (butterhead); 'May Queen' (butterhead)	October (under cloches)	Late March/May

CULTIVATION Keep the soil evenly moist to prevent 'bolting' (running to seed). Weed and control slugs regularly. Winter lettuces will enjoy a sprinkling of fertilizer in March.
HARVEST as soon as the plants are a reasonable size.
STORE Lettuces will not store.
PROBLEMS Aphids, birds, slugs, rabbits, mildew and botrytis (the diseases are more of a winter problem).

MARROW AND COURGETTE

Courgettes are simply marrow pups, and if you grow a variety like 'Zucchini' you can make sure of having both – just leave the courgettes to mature into monsters. If you want only marrows, grow 'Green Bush', which is less space consuming than the trailing varieties.
WHERE TO PLANT Prepare each planting site specially, working in masses of manure on the 45 cm (18 in) square patch that the plant will occupy. Some folk even plant on a mound of manure but I think that there's more danger of damaging drought if the spot is raised up. Marrows need full sun and shelter.
SOW seeds individually in peat pots on a windowsill or in a greenhouse. Late April is the best time. Harden off before planting out.
PLANT in late June after watering the peat pot well. It should be just below the surface of the soil when planted. Water well. Allow 60 cm (2 ft) between plants.
CULTIVATION Never let the plants go short of water. Mulch with compost or manure in June and then feed fortnightly with liquid tomato fertilizer. Manual pollination can boost fruit setting. Remove a male flower; tear off its petals and push it into the centre of a female flower,

which will possess an immature marrow behind its petals. Put pieces of slate or wood under developing marrows to keep them clean and slug-free. Lots of male flowers and few females are often produced early in the season or in cold weather.
HARVEST from July to September as soon as the fruits are large enough.
STORE marrows simply by standing them on shelves in a cool but frostproof shed or garage.
PROBLEMS Slugs, mildew, botrytis, mosaic.

ONION

I reckon it won't be long before we have onions from the garden all the year round. This is the state of play at the moment.
WHERE TO PLANT In full sun on soil that's as rich as can be. Some growers use the same rich soil on the bed every year, but there's more likelihood of disease striking with this technique. Lime acid soil in autumn.
SOW thinly in drills 1 cm (½ in) deep at the recommended time. Drills should be 30 cm (12 in) apart; 23 cm (9 in) apart for spring onions. Thin bulb onions to 10–15 cm (4–6 in) apart. Alternatively grow six rows of onions spaced 15 cm (6 in) apart and then leave wider paths from which to work. You'll save space but weeding may be more tricky. Autumn-sown onions should be thinned twice: once in autumn to 2.5 cm (1 in) and again in spring to 10 cm (4 in).
PLANT onion sets (small bulbs) with a

trowel so that they almost disappear from view. Space them 10 cm (4 in) apart and leave the same distance between rows as with onions raised from seeds. They are a convenient means of growing onions but the bulbs are never quite as large as those grown from seeds.
CULTIVATION Water and weed as necessary. Don't hoe too near the plants or you'll disturb the roots. Should a few bulbs run to seed, pull them up and use them at once – they won't store. When the leaves flop naturally in midsummer, bend them all over in between the rows to allow the sun to ripen the bulbs. Fork up the bulbs in August and leave them on the soil to ripen (cover them with cloches if you can). Onions growing through the winter will appreciate any cloche protection you can give them.
HARVEST at the recommended times. Only well-ripened bulbs will store. Autumn-sown and Japanese onions must be used as soon as possible.
STORE by plaiting into ropes, or by hanging up in old pairs of tights – there's a novel use for them! Keep the bulbs in the light or they'll sprout.
PROBLEMS Onion fly, eelworm, mildew, neck rot and white rot.

PARSNIP

'Avonresister' has small roots resistant to canker, and 'Gladiator' is longer but also resistant. Conservative gardeners almost always stick to 'Hollow Crown Improved' and 'True and Tender'.
WHERE TO PLANT On well-worked but

Recommended onion varieties

VARIETY	SOW SEEDS	PLANT SETS	HARVEST
'Ailsa Craig'; 'Bedfordshire Champion'	March/April	—	August onwards
'Sturon'; 'Stuttgarter Giant'	—	March/April	August onwards
'Express Yellow O–X'; 'Imai Early Yellow'	August	—	Late June
'Buffalo'	August	—	July
'White Lisbon' (spring onion)	March/August	—	May/March
'Unwin's First Early'	—	September/November	July onwards

not well-manured ground that is stone-free. Tolerant of just a little shade. Lime very acid soil in autumn.

SOW three seeds at 10 cm (4 in) intervals in 2.5 cm (1 in) deep drills spaced 30 cm (12 in) apart. Thin to leave one seedling at each station. The seeds are slow to come up. Sow from late February (in good years) to May.

CULTIVATION Weed and water as necessary.

HARVEST as needed from September to March.

STORE *in situ*. Parsnips are as hard as nails. Mark the position of the rows for the tops to die down. In frosty weather (when lifting is difficult) it is helpful to have some roots stored in boxes of sand or peat as for carrots. Lift any roots that remain when the land is needed for another crop and heel them in as for leeks.

PROBLEMS Carrot fly, celery fly and parsnip canker.

PEA

If you've eaten only frozen peas since you can't remember when, it's time you tried some fresh ones. Here's how to arrange for a succession (or even just one crop to remind you of the good old days). The mangetout peas are especially recommended: harvest the pods while they're young, boil them whole for barely five minutes and serve them with melted butter: knock-out!

WHERE TO PLANT Full sun on well-cultivated, well-manured soil not likely to dry out. Lime acid soil in autumn.

SOW the seeds 5 cm (2 in) apart in the bottom of 5 cm (2 in) deep and 23 cm (9 in) wide flat-bottomed drills. Never sow in cold, wet soil.

CULTIVATION Stake all peas with twiggy branches or cane and string enclosures when they are 10 cm (4 in) high.

Recommended pea varieties

VARIETY	SOW	HARVEST
'Hurst Beagle'; 'Little Marvel'	Late February/March (under cloches)	Late May/June
'Hurst Green Shaft'; 'Onward' 'Kelvedon Wonder'	Late March/June Late June/July	Early July/September October/November (cloche in September)
'Sugar Snap' (mangetout) 'Meteor'	March/June October/November (under cloches)	Early July/September May

Water well in dry weather – copiously during flowering – and protect the plant with netting if bird damage is likely. Lawn-mowing mulches are appreciated in early summer.

HARVEST as soon as the pods are filled. Don't delay.

STORE by freezing.

PROBLEMS Mice, slugs, pea and bean weevil, pea moth, birds, thrips, aphids, mildew and damping off.

POTATO

Even if space is short, a row of early potatoes is worth growing. Nothing matches that moment when the first tender spud of the year passes your lips! There are hundreds of varieties but these, I think, are some of the best: *First Early*: 'Maris Bard', 'Epicure'. *Second Early*: 'Vanessa', 'Catriona'. *Maincrop*: 'Desiree', 'Golden Wonder'.

WHERE TO PLANT Full sun and a rich, well-cultivated soil. Spuds are often grown to break down virgin clay soils. Their roots do shatter the soil a bit but it's your earthing up that is mainly responsible.

PLANT first early varieties in mid- to late March, second early and maincrop varieties in April. Sprout or 'chit' the tubers before you plant them. Stand them in egg boxes on a windowsill for six weeks prior to planting. The ends with the most buds should point upwards. When the shoots are 2.5 cm (1 in) or so long the tubers can be planted. Sprouted tubers tend to yield more heavily and rapidly than those

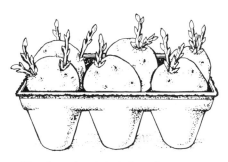

Stand seed potato tubers in egg boxes in good light for six weeks before planting, to encourage the shoots to grow. They will crop better as a result.

planted with dormant 'eyes'. Plant with a trowel so that the tubers are 5 cm (2 in) below the surface with their buds pointing upwards. Plant first earlies 30 cm (12 in) apart in rows 45 cm (18 in) apart; second earlies and maincrop varieties 45 cm (18 in) apart in rows 60 cm (2 ft) apart.

CULTIVATION As soon as the shoots appear, pull some soil around them with a rake or draw hoe. Continue to earth up gently in cold weather until the ridges are 23 cm (9 in) high. If it's mild, one good earthing up can be given when the shoots have risen 15 cm (6 in) above their first earthing up. Irrigate in a prolonged dry spell.

HARVEST first earlies in June or July; second earlies and maincrop from August onwards. Maturity often coincides with flowering.

STORE If your land has a heavy slug population, lift as soon as the tubers are ready and store in thick paper sacks in a cool, dark place. Otherwise lift as

Lift potatoes carefully with a fork and store in a thick paper sack in a cool dark place.

required, and lift the remainder for storing in October.

PROBLEMS Slugs, wireworm, eelworm, blight, scab, virus.

RADISH

The best vegetable for impatient gardeners. Ready in six weeks during summer. Try 'Cherry Belle' or 'Crystal Ball' if you like 'em round; 'French Breakfast' if you like 'em long.

WHERE TO PLANT Full sun or very slight shade in a well-worked but not freshly manured soil.

SOW sections of a row at fortnightly intervals from March to August (or from February under cloches). Sow thinly in drills 1 cm (½ in) deep between other crops to save space. Thin the seedlings to leave one every 2.5 cm (1 in).

CULTIVATION Water well in dry spells and weed as necessary. Slow-growing starved radishes will be hard as bullets.

HARVEST as soon as of a usable size from April to September.

STORE Storage is not recommended.

PROBLEMS Flea beetle.

RHUBARB

Yes, it is a vegetable and not a fruit. The newly developed varieties 'Cawood Castle' and 'Cawood Delight' are the ones to plant nowadays.

WHERE TO PLANT In full sun and a really rich soil that's been well manured. Plant in early spring, though on light soils autumn planting is often successful. Set the clumps or 'crowns' 5 cm (2 in) below the surface of the soil and 1 m (3 ft) apart. Firm the soil well.

CULTIVATION Don't cut anything during the first year except any flower spikes, which should always be removed as soon as they are seen. Mulch with manure every spring. Dig up and divide the plants every few years. For really early sticks, cover one plant with a bucket stuffed with straw in January. Tender pickings should be yours in March. Feed the plant well during the summer and don't force it again for a few years.

HARVEST from April to July, then let the plants build up their strength.

STORE by freezing.

PROBLEMS Honey fungus and crown rot.

SPINACH

You'll love or loathe spinach. If you love it you can enjoy it all the year round with a bit of thoughtful sowing.

WHERE TO PLANT Full sun and a rich soil. Perpetual spinach doesn't mind a bit of shade. Lime very acid ground in autumn.

SOW seeds at 8 cm (3 in) intervals in 2.5 cm (1 in) deep drills at the recommended time. Allow 30 cm (12 in) between rows. Thin to 23 cm (9 in) for winter spinach; 30 cm (12 in) for summer.

CULTIVATION Weed and water as necessary. Drought causes bolting: remove any flowerheads.

HARVEST as soon as leaves are large enough to use.

STORE by cooking and freezing.

PROBLEMS Birds, slugs, downy mildew.

SWEDE

There's nothing like a few mangels for warming you up in winter! I think 'Marian' is the best variety; it's tasty and resistant to clubroot and mildew.

WHERE TO PLANT Full sun and good but not freshly manured soil. Lime acid soils in autumn.

SOW in May and June thinly in 1 cm (½ in) deep drills spaced 38 cm (15 in) apart. Thin to 23 cm (9 in) in stages.

CULTIVATION Weed and water as necessary; if the ground becomes dry swelling will stop.

HARVEST from October onwards as soon as large enough to use. The roots should last until early spring.

STORE *in situ*; the roots are quite hardy. If frosty weather looks like making harvesting difficult, lift and store a few roots as for carrots.

PROBLEMS Clubroot, brown heart and flea beetle.

SWEET CORN

Dicey, but more reliable in the sunny south. Try 'Sundance' as the best all-rounder; 'Candle' is a 'supersweet' variety, best in the south.

WHERE TO PLANT In full sun on a rich soil in a sheltered spot.

SOW individually in peat pots under glass during April. Harden off before planting out.

Recommended spinach varieties

VARIETY	SOW	HARVEST
'Norvak'; 'Longstanding Round'	March/May	May/November
'Broad-leaved Prickly'	August/Sepember (can cloche in October)	November/March
Perpetual spinach	March/April	June/January
Perpetual spinach	July/August	November/May

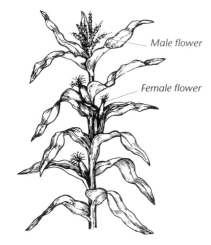

Male flower

Female flower

The female sweet corn flowers, which grow from the leaf axils, will produce the cobs. Tap the pollen from the male flower at the top to ensure fat, fully developed cobs.

PLANT OUT in late May or early June after watering the pots thoroughly. Space the plants 45 cm (18 in) apart on the square. Water the plants well.

CULTIVATION Water copiously in dry spells and keep down weeds. The male spires of bloom open at the top of the plants and should be regularly knocked to discharge their pollen on to the ladies below. Give a dilute liquid feed once a month in summer.

HARVEST when the cobs are fat and ripe. The tassels above them will turn brown and the cob will become angled away from the stem. Pull away the sheaths to see if the grains are fat and yellow. The old test of sticking a fingernail into a grain to see if it exudes milky rather than clear sap can obviously disfigure the cob.

STORE by freezing.

PROBLEMS Fruit fly and slugs.

TOMATO

There are many bush varieties for outdoor growing. 'Tornado' crops well in poor summers; 'Gardeners' Delight' is tops for flavour.

WHERE TO PLANT A sheltered spot in full sun on well-cultivated and rich but not freshly manured soil.

SOW seeds in a pot during March and germinate in a temperature of 18°C (65°F). Prick out seedlings into 8 cm (3 in) pots of John Innes No 1 potting compost or a peat-based equivalent.

PLANT OUT in late May or early June after hardening the plants off. Space the plants 45 cm (18 in) apart.

CULTIVATION Water regularly in summer; feed fortnightly with dilute liquid tomato fertilizer once the fruits have set. Don't remove the sideshoots from bush varieties. Spread dry straw underneath them in June to keep the fruits clean.

HARVEST as soon as ripe. Stand cloches over laid down plants in September to prolong the harvest.

STORE unripened fruits in October; ripen in a cool place (in a drawer or on a shelf, not necessarily in bright sun). Green fruits can be used in chutney.

PROBLEMS Whitefly, red spider mite, blossom end rot, blotchy ripening, greenback, eelworm, leaf mould, stem rot, root rot, potato blight, verticillium wilt, virus. (You won't get them all!)

TURNIP

An underrated vegetable. I recommend 'Snowball' and 'Golden Ball'.

WHERE TO PLANT Full sun and good but not freshly manured soil. Lime acid soil in winter.

SOW thinly in 1 cm (½ in) deep drills from March to September: under cloches in February. Use 'Snowball' for February to May sowings, 'Golden Ball' for later sowings. Space rows 23 cm (9 in) apart for early crops; 30 cm (12 in) apart for later crops. Thin early crops to 10 cm (4 in), later ones to 23 cm (9 in).

CULTIVATION Water when necessary and weed to relieve competition.

HARVEST early sown crops as young as possible and before they are tennis ball sized. Late sowings can be left in the ground and pulled as needed.

STORE as for carrots.

PROBLEMS Clubroot, mildew, soft rot and flea beetle.

HERBS

Shop-bought dried herbs bear no comparison to the freshly picked, home-grown variety.

Grow herbs on the vegetable plot if you like, but most are handsome-enough for the flower border or as edges to paths, where they will release their fragrance when you brush against them. Almost all herbs relish a warm sunny spot, which helps to bring out their full flavour.

Basil

The sweet aniseed flavour of basil is at its best in our kitchen on baked tomatoes and buttered carrots. Plant it in late June and pick and dry it for winter use (it will be killed by frost). Raise new plants from seed indoors in March or outdoors in May. Pinch out the shoot tips regularly and pick off any flowers.

Chives

A little clump of reed-shaped, onion-flavoured leaves. Happy in gentle shade if that's all you have to offer. Plant in spring or autumn: mature plants can be divided at that time and tired old plants cut down to ground level in early summer. Don't remove the flowers – they're lilac-pink and quite pretty. The plant is perennial.

Fennel

A hefty herb with 1.5 m (5 ft) stems of delicate feathery leaves. It tastes of aniseed and is usually used in fish dishes. Plant in spring and divide mature clumps at the same time. The plant dies down in winter and does not store very well.

Marjoram

Pot marjoram is the desirable perennial kind with a thyme-like flavour. Plant in spring and clip with shears when very

Drying and freezing herbs

DRYING

Herbs tend to have their maximum flavour just before they flower, so cut and dry them at that time for winter use. Put the shoots in brown paper bags and store them in a warm, dark place. Crush them when they are dry and put them in airtight containers from which the light can be excluded. That way they'll keep as much of their flavour as possible.

FREEZING

Herbs that lose their flavour when dried can often be successfully frozen. Sprigs of mint and parsley can be frozen in ice cubes for fruit cups; sprigs of herbs can be placed in polythene bags and put in the freezer compartment of a fridge. Although they won't keep their shape when defrosted they will often keep their flavour.

untidy. Divide clumps in spring to propagate. Freeze or dry for winter use.

Mint

Every gardener's bane if it gets loose. Plant it in a bottomless bucket sunk into the ground, but with the rim protruding – that will halt its spread. Plant in spring or autumn and propagate by division at those times. Dies down in winter. Dry or freeze for winter use. Make your own mint sauce with the stuff in summer and store a few bottles for winter. Can be frozen in ice cubes for use in fruit cups.

Parsley

Sow annually outdoors in April but be patient – seeds are slow to germinate. Cut off any flowers that form and protect with cloches in winter if you want to go on harvesting. The plant will perk up at the start of its second year but will gradually wear out. Can freeze for winter use.

Rosemary

A 1.5 m (5 ft) evergreen shrub that's very useful because it can be harvested at any time of year. The leaves have a warm, savoury flavour. Plant in spring and propagate by cuttings in a propagator at the same time. Severe winters will cause die-back. Essential in stuffings and with roast lamb.

Sage

Another evergreen bush but this time it's not so hefty at around 30 cm (12 in). Plant in spring and prune in summer to encourage fresh growth. There's not much leaf in winter but sometimes enough to harvest. The variegated varieties are prettiest and just as tasty. Cuttings can be rooted in a propagator in summer.

Tarragon

The French variety has the best flavour. Plant it in spring in a warm, sheltered spot. Protect with cloches or straw in winter. Propagate by division in spring. Freeze for winter use. Severe winters may see it off.

Thyme

Evergreen carpeter with savoury aromatic leaves. Grow against paths and in patios. Plant in autumn or spring. Cut back in spring to promote new growth and use the clippings as cuttings. Can be gathered fresh all the year round.

Although herbs are primarily known for their aromatic or medicinal uses, many are attractive enough to be grown for their decorative qualities, as in this planting of *Allium***, fennel, purple sage and French lavender (***Lavandula stoechas***).**

part V

THE UNDER COVER GARDEN

Gardening can be enjoyed all year round if you have a greenhouse and a collection of house plants to look after

A conservatory or lean-to greenhouse bridges the gap between house and garden, providing a pleasant retreat whatever the weather among a lush profusion of plants.

greenhouse gardening

The joy of a greenhouse is that

it enables you to continue

gardening through the

dark winter days, as well as

extending your range of

flowers, fruit and vegetables

HAVING A GREENHOUSE IS LIKE HAVING A dog: you might not want to be without one, but it does tie you down. You'll need to visit it every day, morning and evening, during the growing season, and you'll not be the most popular person in the household when you dive out to water your tomatoes just as dinner is being served.

But set against all this is the pleasure you'll get from growing a wider range of plants (and the frustration of a few failures), and the fact that you'll regularly be able to make a sizeable contribution to the meal you're about to eat. You'll be able to raise potfuls of flowers nearly all the year round, if your greenhouse is kept frostfree, and a few crops can be forced out of season to yield their bounty when shop prices are sky high.

So if you think you can risk the wrath of your spouse, or that you can placate it with out-of-season offerings for the table, take up the challenge and go in for gardening under cover.

CHOOSING YOUR GREENHOUSE

You'll find that there are dozens of greenhouses to choose from, all of which are capable of growing plants well. Two factors in particular will whittle down a few of the choices: price and design. You'll have to pick a greenhouse you can afford, and you're quite right to pick one that has an appealing shape. Whatever the practical qualities of a greenhouse, if you can't stand the sight of it there's not much point in owning it. Practical points are nevertheless important, so make sure that your chosen design can fulfil the following requirements:

1 Good light transmission.
2 Stability.
3 Good ventilation (one side and one ridge ventilator for every 2 m (6 ft) of the greenhouse's length).
4 Easily accessible, including a wide enough door to allow in a wheelbarrow if you feel this is necessary.

The most important consideration of all should be the use to which the house will be put. Pot plants are best in a house that has half-timbered sides, for then the 'understage' area can be hidden from view. Plants grown in the border soil will need a glass-to-ground greenhouse so that they receive plenty of light.

If you're intent on growing food crops, a glass-to-ground model is for you; if you aim to grow both tomatoes and pot plants then how about a house that's half glass-to-ground and half half-timbered? Manufacturers are making the decision even easier by

The anatomy of a greenhouse

Once you have decided to get a greenhouse, you will be overwhelmed by the choices available and the decisions you have to make. You will have to decide what you want from your greenhouse, whether to go for a timber or alloy frame, glass or plastic glazing, and whether the house should be half-timbered or all glass. Here is an example of a greenhouse designed to cope with pot plants on staging and crops growing both in the soil and on ring culture.

SPAN-ROOF GREENHOUSE
This is a traditional, timber-framed span-roof greenhouse. See p.252 for a full description.

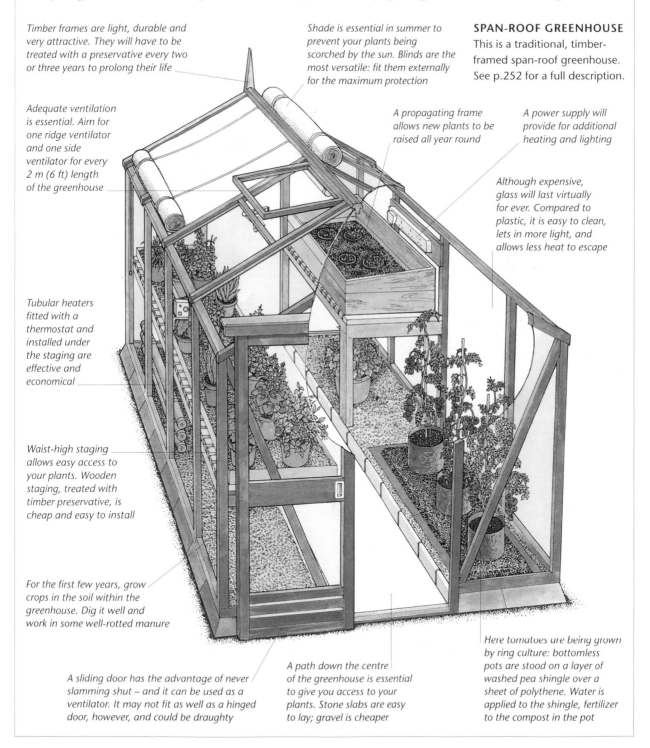

Timber frames are light, durable and very attractive. They will have to be treated with a preservative every two or three years to prolong their life

Shade is essential in summer to prevent your plants being scorched by the sun. Blinds are the most versatile: fit them externally for the maximum protection

A propagating frame allows new plants to be raised all year round

A power supply will provide for additional heating and lighting

Adequate ventilation is essential. Aim for one ridge ventilator and one side ventilator for every 2 m (6 ft) length of the greenhouse

Although expensive, glass will last virtually for ever. Compared to plastic, it is easy to clean, lets in more light, and allows less heat to escape

Tubular heaters fitted with a thermostat and installed under the staging are effective and economical

Waist-high staging allows easy access to your plants. Wooden staging, treated with timber preservative, is cheap and easy to install

For the first few years, grow crops in the soil within the greenhouse. Dig it well and work in some well-rotted manure

A sliding door has the advantage of never slamming shut – and it can be used as a ventilator. It may not fit as well as a hinged door, however, and could be draughty

A path down the centre of the greenhouse is essential to give you access to your plants. Stone slabs are easy to lay; gravel is cheaper

Here tomatoes are being grown by ring culture: bottomless pots are stood on a layer of washed pea shingle over a sheet of polythene. Water is applied to the shingle, fertilizer to the compost in the pot

Choosing a greenhouse design

Whichever design you decide on, buy the largest greenhouse you can possibly afford or accommodate – you'll soon find that it's bursting at the seams.

SPAN ROOF (See illustration on previous page)
This is the traditional greenhouse with vertical sides and two roof sections that slope down at an angle of roughly 45°. Glass-to-ground and half-timbered models are available, as are models with curved eaves. Remember that curved sections are plastic, not glass, and they will become opaque and need replacement in time. Span-roof greenhouses with a dividing partition are especially useful, for then only a portion of the house needs be heated in winter to protect frost-tender plants.

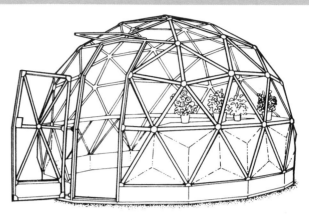

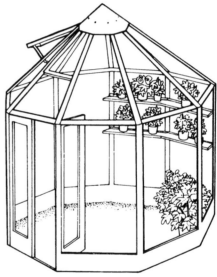

DOME
Dome-shaped greenhouses are for lovers of space-age designs. They are costly but allow exceptionally good light transmission. Check that there are plenty of vents.

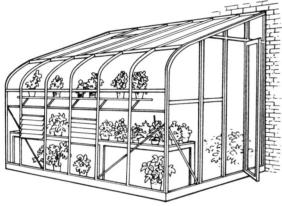

LEAN-TO
Designed to fit against the wall of a house, the lean-to has the advantages of being easily accessible, well insulated on one side and good to look at from inside the home if it is erected over a window. The installation of electricity and water, as well as an additional radiator from the central heating system, can be easily achieved. This design is now becoming very popular: glass-to-ground and half-timbered models are available, as well as mini versions that can be stood on patios and in back yards. A lean-to may affect your rates but it can enable you to get to the greenhouse in the foulest weather without getting your feet wet.

OCTAGONAL
Rather more ornamental than useful, except to the disabled gardener who will find that many plants can be easily tended from a wheelchair. Make sure that ventilation is adequate – on some models this is not the case.

supplying timber panels for their glass-to-ground greenhouses so that they can be rapidly transformed.

Framework considerations
Timber houses are the romantic gardener's favourite (and that includes me). They are usually made of western red cedar, which is amazingly light, extremely durable and very handsome. They have to be painted

with a preservative every two or three years to prolong their life, but they look good in the garden and blend beautifully with plants.

Cedar is not cheap, and wooden houses are now more expensive to buy than those made of alloy. Greenhouses made of Baltic pine are less pricey, but I can't recommend them because they have nothing like the durability of their cedar relations.

DUTCH HOUSE

This design has been around for many years. The panes are very large – roughly 1.5 m by 60 cm (5 ft by 2 ft) – and the sides slope outwards from the eaves. Light transmission is good, but breakages are expensive.

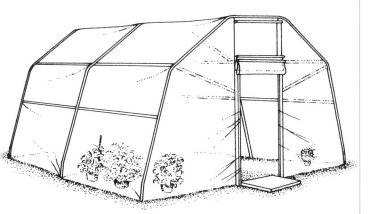

PLASTIC TUNNEL

Plastic tunnel houses are cheap but nothing like as durable as their glass counterparts. Access and ventilation are achieved via the doors at either end, and a tubular steel framework supports the replaceable polythene envelope. Anchor the edges firmly for stability by burying them 30 cm (12 in) deep in the soil.

Aluminium alloy greenhouses score because of their reasonable price, the fact that they need no maintenance other than the oiling of hinges, and because they are easy to glaze (the glass is held in position with clips or rubber strips). If you don't like the look of aluminium you can choose a model that has been coated with acrylic paint, which also stops the formation of that white powdery deposit.

Both timber and alloy houses will outlast you if they are treated well, so you pay your money and take your choice.

Glass or plastic?

If you want a permanent greenhouse, the answer has to be glass. It lasts virtually for ever, a fact that should counteract the initial expense. It allows in more light than plastic and allows heat to escape much more slowly. When it comes to cleaning, it takes little time to restore grimy glass to its former crystal-clear state, even if it has been painted with shading compounds to cut down summer glare.

Plastic has two great advantages – cheapness and safety where children are concerned – but the fact that it has to be replaced after a few years will often step up the cost. Certain plastics are now guaranteed a life of 15 years, but that's only a fraction of the time you can expect glass to last.

In time, all plastic becomes opaque and lets in less light; it loses heat rapidly, allows rapid temperature fluctuations and produces much condensation. In plastic tunnels ventilation is difficult and even though plastic houses may be easy to erect they can be equally quickly dismantled by a gale if not securely anchored to the ground.

After all that, you could be forgiven for thinking that plastic houses are useless! They're not, and they do have a lot to recommend them where temporary and easily movable forms of protection are needed.

PUTTING UP A GREENHOUSE

Laying the foundations

PURPOSE-MADE FOUNDATIONS Laying foundations is a real fag. Most gardeners are anxious to get cracking with putting up their greenhouse, and all that trench digging and concrete humping is a sizeable fly in the ointment.

By far the best solution is to buy a greenhouse for which tailor-made concrete kerb foundations can be bought. All you need to do then is lay the kerbs on firmed and levelled ground (checking that they themselves are level and square) and erect the greenhouse on top of them. Bolts will secure the base of the house to the prefabricated foundation, giving it stability in wind.

INTEGRAL BASE-PLATE Some greenhouses come equipped with an integral base-plate, which means that they can be erected straight onto firmed and levelled earth. Metal 'ground anchors' can be driven in at strategic points to offer wind resistance.

Digging and laying foundations

If no alternatives are available you'll just have to get out the pick and shovel. Dig a 23 cm (9 in) deep trench along the line of the foundation, ram 10 cm (4 in) of hardcore into the base and then top it with a layer of concrete shuttered between boards. A mix of 6 parts aggregate, 1 part sand and 1 part cement, mixed to a sticky consistency with water, should be tamped down between the boards, which have been checked for level and squareness. Coach bolts can be sunk into the concrete (threads uppermost) so that later the base of the house can be drilled to fit over them and the nuts screwed down to anchor the structure. It's all a real chore – you'd be better off with purpose-made foundations!

Erecting and glazing

Almost all greenhouses come with detailed instructions on erection, though the instructions very considerably in their degree of lucidity. Usually the structure is glazed after erection, though some manufacturers supply ready-glazed sections. This is a mixed blessing; it saves you the job of glazing but it makes erection a more nail-biting job, for there's always the risk of breakage.

Certain manufacturers offer an erection service: if you let them construct the house on site it can be bought free of VAT, which may offer a considerable saving of money and effort.

Greenhouses that can be glazed with clips or rubber strips make glazing a doddle, but some houses still come with a large bag of putty and a smaller bag of glazing sprigs.

It's always a good idea to have somebody around to help you glaze the greenhouse, especially if putty is involved. You'll become more proficient as you progress, but at first the putty gets everywhere except in the channels for which it is intended. Try to glaze the house in one day – if it's part-glazed and a wind gets up, you could be in for a hefty bill for glass replacement.

If you do have to use putty, start by glazing the roof,

Siting your greenhouse

I don't happen to subscribe to the idea that your greenhouse must run either north/south or east/west: it makes a difference where large commercial glasshouses are concerned, but not in your average back garden. The ideal spot for a greenhouse probably doesn't exist in a small garden, but bear the following points in mind when you're trying to shoe-horn it into the scheme.

1 Choose a spot that is well lit and not overshadowed by trees or buildings.

2 The site should be sheltered at a distance from strong winds, which will send heating bills soaring.

3 Avoid frost pockets – those dips in the land where cold air collects.

4 Avoid badly drained ground, otherwise greenhouse crops that are grown in the soil will always have a late start.

5 Try to find a level site: it makes foundation laying easier.

6 Site the greenhouse where water and electricity can easily be laid on.

7 Check with your local authority to see if planning permission is required before you erect the greenhouse.

---

strip by strip. Work putty into the rebates along the glazing bars (don't be too generous with it), and then insert the glass, starting at the bottom and leaving each pane overlapping the one below it by about 2.5 cm (1 in). Fasten the glass in position with glazing sprigs (making sure you put one under each side of the lower edge to prevent the glass from slipping) and then clean off the excess putty. Rub the glass immediately with a dry cloth to remove finger marks. You'll have a devil of a job to shift them once they're dry. Once the house is glazed you and your plants can move in without delay.

Make way for a path

Whether you grow plants in pots or on the floor, a path down the centre of the greenhouse is a must. Stone slabs are easy to lay and comfortable to walk on; gravel is cheaper and, where plants are to be grown in pots on the staging, it can be laid over the entire floor area to a depth of 2.5 cm (1 in). It looks good, keeps down weeds and holds moisture in summer when humidity is important. Buy the stuff from a builders' merchant, where it is described as washed pea shingle.

WHERE TO GROW THE PLANTS

Growing in border soil

If you plan to raise tomatoes, cucumbers, peppers and aubergines you can grow the crops in the soil within the greenhouse for a few years. Dig it well first and work in some well-rotted compost or manure. Don't grow the same crop in the same place year after year: practise a small rotation scheme and you should be able to grow good plants in the earth for three or four years. After this length of time the soil often becomes sick or exhausted and it's a good idea to move over to growing in pots, growing bags or, where tomatoes are concerned, to ring culture.

Some experts would have you ignore border soil from the outset, but I'd rather enjoy its cheapness and convenience for a couple of years before moving over to containers. You can always dig up and replace tired border soil with fresh, but it's an expensive and labour-intensive job.

Ring culture

If it's tomatoes you're growing, and the border soil becomes tired of them, turn to ring culture.

Lay a 15 cm (6 in) deep bed of washed pea shingle over a strip of polythene and retain it with boards at the edges. Alternatively, excavate a 15 cm (6 in) deep trench and lay the polythene and shingle in it. The gravel bed can stretch right down one side, or both sides, of the greenhouse.

Remove the bottoms from some 23 cm (9 in) plastic plant pots (a hacksaw will do the job), or buy special 'whalehide' rings, which are bottomless. (Conservationists please note: whalehide pots are made from bituminous paper.)

Sit the rings on the shingle, spacing them 45 cm (18 in) apart. Fill them with John Innes No. 3 potting compost and plant the young tomatoes in them. Water them well in and apply all subsequent waterings to the shingle. Only liquid fertilizer should be applied to the compost in the pot.

The plant will develop two root systems, one for absorbing water and one for absorbing food. At the end of the season the plants can be removed and the gravel thoroughly washed so that it is fit to use the following year.

Staging for pot plants

Pot plants need to be grown on shelves or on benches, which the greenhouse gardener calls staging. The most luxurious staging is made from timber or alloy and supports plastic trays that can be filled with gravel. During spring and summer, the moisture evaporating from the gravel keeps the air around the plants pleasantly humid and conducive to growth. In winter it can harbour too much moisture and lead to fungus attack, but it's a time-consuming job to remove all the gravel every autumn and replace it each spring. For this reason I always spread gravel on the floor of the greenhouse and have plain slatted wooden staging, which can be easily and relatively cheaply built from 5 x 2.5 cm (2 x 1 in) deal and painted with a red cedar timber preservative to match a cedar greenhouse. The gravel on the floor provides sufficient buoyancy in summer without being overpoweringly moisture retentive in winter.

A collection of alpines happily overwinters in an all-glass greenhouse. The pots sit on slatted timber staging, and gravel on the floor helps to maintain optimum humidity.

For ease of working, make the staging waist high and no more than 1 m (3 ft) deep, so that all plants can be reached from the front. If the house is very wide or intended to display flowering pot plants, the staging can be lower and tiered to present a bank of floral colour to the spectator. All staging should be strong. Pots full of compost may not feel very heavy on their own but collectively they weigh a ton.

Don't let the area underneath the staging lie idle. Shade-loving ferns and foliage plants will enjoy growing there.

Shelves fixed above the staging, down the sides and at the end of the greenhouse, provide more valuable space for growing pot plants. Fix them to metal angle brackets but make sure that they don't cast too much shade on the staging below. Shelves about 15 cm (6 in) wide should not cause much of a problem.

PROVIDING THE RIGHT CONDITIONS

Which type of heating?

To overwinter frost-tender plants and to make an early start with seed-raising in spring, your greenhouse will need heating. Certainly an unheated structure is valuable during the warmer months of the year and for growing winter lettuce, but a little heat will spread its usefulness over twelve months.

I'm not going to take up pages by going over all the forms of heating; instead I'll tell you quite simply that nothing beats electricity for efficiency or economy. Gone are the days when coal and paraffin offered cheap heat; thermostatically controlled electric heaters beat them hands down nowadays.

You'll have to enlist the help of an electrician to equip your greenhouse with the juice and to fit special waterproof plugs for safety. I use tubular heaters, which are slung underneath the staging and wired up to a rod-type thermostat set at 7°C (45°F) in winter (to keep my geraniums frostfree) and a little higher in spring. The thermostat is the key to economy. It switches the electricity off when the required temperature is reached – a feature lacking in paraffin and solid-fuel heating systems where burning continues regardless of temperature.

The other big advantage of electricity is that it produces dry heat. This is especially important in winter when excess humidity encourages fungus diseases. Paraffin heaters give out gallons of water every day and can also cause leaf scorch. Use them as emergency measures during winter power cuts, and

try to apply a little ventilation at all times so that poisonous fumes can escape. Use only those paraffin heaters expressly designed for greenhouses.

Tubular heaters are just one form of electrical air warmer; fan heaters designed for greenhouse use and air-warming cables can also be used, though the latter are really at their best in small structures where they can be clipped to the wall beneath the staging. Both types should be fitted with a thermostat for economy. Don't let a fan heater blow directly onto plants or it may brown their foliage.

Heaters running from natural gas might seem to be desirable, but they need to be connected up to the gas supply, which may be even more difficult than laying on electricity. They also produce water vapour and poisonous fumes and so cannot really compete with clean electricity.

Manufacturers will advise you on the size of heater needed for your structure. Make sure that the equipment you buy is capable of giving the heat you need. A maximum and minimum thermometer should hang in every greenhouse to check that your heater is functioning properly.

Providing lighting

If you're investing in electrical heating you might as well fit lighting too. A single fluorescent strip fastened to the ridge will provide plenty of working light on dark evenings – and mornings, too, in winter. If you just want enough light to check that no one's run off with your plants, then an ordinary lamp socket will do.

Lean-to greenhouses that are positioned over house windows can be lit for pleasure rather than practicality. A spotlight fitted to the back wall and angled to shine on the plants will provide colourful evening scenery.

Insulating the greenhouse

In winter, every step you take to prevent heat loss will save money. For a start check that doors and ventilators fit snugly. Stick-on household draught excluder can be used to plug any gaps. Mend all broken panes of glass before the bad weather arrives.

Keep all the glass clean so that every ray of sunlight can be utilized, and if your greenhouse is heated to a temperature of 10°C (50°F) or more, rig up some form of plastic insulation inside. Polythene sheeting or, better still, bubble polythene with built-in air pockets, should be fixed to the roof and sides of the house so that it creates an insulating layer of air. It's the 2.5 cm (1 in) gap between the polythene and the glass that does the insulating, rather than the polythene itself. Put up the insulating material in November and take it down in April. Don't cover the vents with the stuff – you'll still need them on warm days.

Double-glazed greenhouses are now on the market; they're efficient and amazingly strong, but they're rather expensive too.

Ensuring adequate ventilation

In a stagnant atmosphere fungus diseases are rife, so try to provide plants with a little fresh air at all times except in really cold or severe weather. In summer the ventilators are vital in letting in air to prevent the plants from baking, so when you buy a greenhouse make sure that it has plenty of ventilators. As a rule of thumb look for one ridge ventilator and one side ventilator for every 2 m (6 ft) of the greenhouse's length. If there are fewer than this, ask if more can be fitted. If they can't, shop elsewhere.

Ventilators on both sides of the house will allow you to vent on the leeward and prevent howling draughts. Louvre vents are efficient but not always draughtproof; ordinary hinged vents fitted with casement stays can usually be made to fit snugly.

The one piece of equipment you should not be without is an automatic ventilating arm. These devices are fastened to a ventilator and set to open and close it at a given temperature. If you have to be out at work during the day the arm will efficiently prevent your plants from being baked alive. The automatic ventilator is not expensive and needs no power supply; it is activated by the expansion and contraction of a substance confined in a special rod-shaped chamber.

Maintaining humidity

In spring and summer, high humidity in the greenhouse is essential to keep the plants in good health; in winter it will encourage diseases. The easiest way of maintaining a buoyant atmosphere is to damp down the floor of the greenhouse both morning and evening – the staging too if it is covered with gravel. The moisture will evaporate into the atmosphere and keep the plants perky. Don't damp down after late summer. From autumn until late spring the atmosphere wants to be on the dry side.

Providing summer shading

In summer, additional measures have to be taken to lower temperatures and prevent plants from being scorched by the sun. Shading is the solution. The cheapest form comes in a bottle: dilute it in water and paint it on so that a white film coats the glass. There are various products: one has the advantage of being easily removed with a dry duster and yet it stays firmly in place regardless of summer downpours. Another becomes translucent when wet, so allowing in more light on dingy summer days. Shading compounds such as these cannot be used effectively on all plastics; on some they will refuse to shift however hard you wash and scrub them in autumn.

Blinds are more expensive but more versatile, for they can be raised and lowered according to the weather. External blinds are preferable to those fixed inside the house for they will intercept the sun's rays before they have a chance to heat up the greenhouse atmosphere.

If you can't afford blinds, invest in some green plastic close-weave netting, which can be pinned or otherwise fixed to the outside of the greenhouse. Put it up in May and take it down in September.

> *"Don't let the area underneth the staging lie idle. Shade-loving ferns and foliage plants will enjoy growing there."*

ALL ABOUT WATERING

When I first worked in a nursery we had to water all the plants with a can. There were thousands of them. Eventually hosepipes were fitted, but the boss watched us like a hawk and came down like a ton of bricks if the hosepipe was running too fast. Whether you use a can (a long-spouted one is best) or a hosepipe, that's the secret – don't let it run too fast or the compost will be efficiently flushed out of the pot and splashed round to make a breeding ground for disease.

Tapwater or rainwater?

Tapwater does most plants no harm at all. Only if it's very hard and the plants are very sensitive will you encounter problems. In this case you can collect rainwater in a large tank, but make sure that leaves and other debris can be prevented from falling into it or it will turn into a bacterial broth. Rainwater that runs off the greenhouse roof can be channelled via the guttering into a tank sunk below the staging inside the house. Fasten a piece of nylon stocking over the inlet to keep out rubbish, and empty it regularly to prevent blockages. Some gardeners consider that water that is collected and stored in this way is full of disease. I've never found this to be the case. You can't grow plants in a sterile atmosphere and if they can't cope with a few germs in the rainwater then they are of a pretty sour constitution.

Automatic watering systems

Automatic watering saves a lot of time. It also takes some of the skill out of growing plants, but if you're busy it's worth the candle. Capillary benches are perhaps the best form of automatic watering. They are level and consist of waterproof trays on which is laid special nylon matting. This is kept constantly moist, from a reservoir or drip-feed system, and plants that are stood on it can take up just the water they need. Plastic pots with plenty of drainage holes are essential. Clay pots, unless they are fitted with a wick of the nylon material, cannot absorb the water because of the gap between the compost and the bottom of the pot. Various proprietary systems are available.

The spaghetti-tube watering system consists of a large Alkathene pipe from which small-bore spaghetti tubes emerge at intervals. Each tube is pegged into a plant pot and when the tap is turned on, water is delivered. The trouble with this system is that it is unselective: every plant is watered when the tap is turned on and there is consequently a risk of overwatering.

When to water

If you're watering by hand the time to water any pot plant is when the surface of the compost in the pot feels dry. You can also tell by lifting the pot up and testing its weight: the drier it is the lighter it will be. Most plants suffer no more from being allowed to dry out occasionally than we do from being thirsty, but regular drought causes leaf browning and flower drop; overwatering, on the other hand, will cause the plants to go into a wilt from which they will seldom recover.

Watering border soil

A final tip on watering plants in the greenhouse border soil. Sink a flowerpot into the earth alongside each plant at planting time. Subsequent waterings can be applied into the pot and will get straight to the roots without running off the surface.

John Innes composts

The John Innes composts were developed in the 1930s at a research institute carrying that man's name. They are now manufactured to the original formulae by many firms (look for the seal of the John Innes Manufacturers' Association on the bag to be sure that the compost is genuine). If you want to make them up at home, here are the recipes for the five different types of composts.

Note: a box measuring 25 x 25 x 55 cm (10 x 10 x 22 in) contains 36 litres (1 bushel) when filled to the brim.

JOHN INNES SEED COMPOST
A mixture in which all seeds can be sown.
- *2 parts by volume partially sterilized loam*
- *1 part by volume granulated peat*
- *1 part by volume coarse sand*
Plus:
- *40 g (1½ oz) superphospate of lime per 36 litres (1 bushel)*
- *20 g (¾ oz) ground limestone or chalk per 36 litres (1 bushel)*

JOHN INNES NO. 1 POTTING COMPOST (JIP 1)
Prick out bedding plants into this mixture and use it when potting up rooted cuttings.
- *7 parts by volume partially sterilized loam*
- *3 parts by volume granulated peat*
- *2 parts by volume coarse sand*
Plus:
- *110 g (4 oz) John Innes base fertilizer per 36 litres (1 bushel)*
- *20 g (¾ oz) ground limestone or chalk per 36 litres (1 bushel)*

COMPOSTS FOR POT PLANTS

Pot plants won't grow in garden soil: it is neither well drained enough nor nutritious enough to support them in such a confined space. For this reason gardeners have developed a range of composts for different purposes. Originally there was a different mix for each plant, but nowadays we have just a handful of recipes that can keep most plants happy. You can buy them ready-made, but if you want to make them up at home, the recipes are given above.

The ingredients

LOAM Kettering loam was originally prescribed in the formulae for composts, but by now Kettering must be in a gigantic valley. Good garden soil or, better still, soil derived from stacked turves, will do, but it should really be partially sterilized to kill harmful bacteria and weed seeds.

JOHN INNES NO. 2 POTTING COMPOST (JIP 2)
Suitable for most pot plants.
- *Loam, peat and sand as for John Innes No. 1 potting compost*

Plus:
- *225 g (8 oz) John Innes base fertilizer per 36 litres (1 bushel)*
- *40 g (1½ oz) ground limestone or chalk per 36 litres (1 bushel)*

JOHN INNES NO. 3 POTTING COMPOST (JIP 3)
Suitable for vigorous plants including tomatoes, chrysanthemums, cucumbers and melons.
- *Loam, peat and sand as for John Innes No. 1 potting compost*

Plus:
- *340 (12 oz) John Innes base fertilizer per 36 litres (1 bushel)*
- *60 g (2¼ oz) ground limestone or chalk per 36 litres (1 bushel)*

JOHN INNES ERICACEOUS COMPOST
Suitable for lime-hating plants such as rhododendrons, azaleas and heathers.
- *Loam, peat and sand as for John Innes No. 1 potting compost*

Plus:
- *110 g (4 oz) John Innes base fertilizer per 36 litres (1 bushel)*

Proprietary electric soil sterilizers are easy to use but pricey. The soil in them should be sterilized for 10 minutes at a temperature of 82°C (180°F). If you can't afford the equipment, find a large, old saucepan and boil 1 cm (½ in) water in the base before filling it to the brim with sieved soil and letting it simmer for 15 minutes. Tip out the soil afterwards and let it cool.

PEAT Granulated peat should be used and before it is mixed in, it must be moist. Pass it through a 1 cm (½ in) sieve. Peat is hard to replace in potting compost.

SAND Don't use bright yellow builder's sand. Coarse river sand is what is needed to make for good drainage.

FERTILIZER John Innes base fertilizer is available ready mixed from most garden shops or nurseries. It contains:
2 parts by weight hoof and horn;
2 parts by weight superphosphate of lime;
1 part by weight sulphate of potash.

Mixing and storing composts
Measure out the ingredients and tip them into a heap. Turn the heap three or four times with a shovel until the compost is well mixed. Store the compost in black plastic sacks or dustbins, but try to use it within two months. After this time it starts to turn sour. Mind you, I've used old John Innes compost on many occasions with no ill effects, but there's always a chance that some plants might not like it.

Other types of compost
PEAT- AND COIR-BASED COMPOSTS There are dozens of proprietary soilless composts, which at one time were based almost exclusively on peat with the addition of fertilizers. Now, due to a need to conserve our peat resources, other renewable organic resources are being experimented with. Many soilless composts today are based on coir – the fibres from coconut husks. Much has been written about the advantages and disadvantages of such composts. Only continuous experience will show us how they can best be managed, and which plants will and will not grow well in them. What all soilless composts have in common is an inability to hold on to nutrients for as long as loam-based composts, which means they need feeding regularly six weeks after potting. Heavy plants may overbalance in them, and they are best kept gently moist at all times: never let them dry out. Firm them only gently at potting time.

COMPOST FOR CUTTINGS One of the simplest and most effective composts for cuttings is 1 part granulated peat or coir to 1 part coarse river sand. Use it in pots or a propagator where it will provide a well-drained medium capable of inducing root formation.

CARING FOR GREENHOUSE PLANTS

Potting
Plants in the greenhouse grow rapidly and frequently need to be given larger containers of fresh compost. There are several different techniques.

POTTING UP Here a rooted cutting or seedling is put in its first pot. A 9–10 cm (3½ in) container is usually large enough. Some compost is placed in the bottom of the pot – over a layer of crocks or other drainage material if a loam-based compost is being used in a clay pot. The plant is then dug out of its seed tray or propagator with as much compost adhering to its roots as possible.

The plant is seated on the compost in the new pot,

Potting up a new arrival

1 Unpack plants obtained by mail order as soon as they arrive, and place in good light. Choose a pot large enough to hold the roots with a little room to spare.

2 Place some compost in the bottom of the pot, using a soilless potting compost or John Innes No 1 potting compost, and insert the plant.

3 Continue feeding in the compost around the plant, and then gently firm it with the fingertips to make sure there are no air pockets around the roots.

4 When potting is complete the crown of the plant should be level with the surface of the compost, which should be slightly below the rim of the pot.

and more compost fed round it and lightly firmed with the fingers. When potting up is completed the plant should sit at the same level at which it grew in its previous container, and there should be a gap of about 2 cm (¾ in) between the surface of the compost and the pot rim.

Water the plant in either by standing it in a shallow trough of water and allowing it to take up what it needs, or by gently soaking it with a can fitted with a fine rose.

POTTING ON Plants that have outgrown their existing container are moved on to a larger one. The technique is described fully on p.272. Plants growing in the greenhouse may require more than one new container each year if they are growing strongly prior to making flowers. Perennials that are kept for several years will usually be happy with one new pot a year, or maybe even one every second year. As a rule, pot on only during spring and summer when plants are growing actively.

Once a plant has completely filled its container with roots it should be potted on to a pot that is about 5 cm (2 in) larger in diameter.

REPOTTING A term that is often loosely used for any type of potting but which really indicates that a plant in a large pot is being knocked out, some of the compost removed from its rootball and replaced with fresh when the plant is returned to the same container.
TOPDRESSING Equally useful where plants are growing in large pots. Scrape away the top 5–8 cm (2–3 in) of compost and replace it with fresh.

When to feed greenhouse plants
Greenhouse plants have what you might call a high metabolic rate, thanks to good light and relatively high temperatures. For this reason they enjoy regular feeding during the growing season. Use dilute liquid fertilizers and apply them once every ten days during the growing season. Newly potted plants need not be fed for eight weeks if they are growing in loam-based compost such as John Innes, or for six weeks if they are in a peat-based compost.

Providing support and training
Just like house plants, greenhouse plants need pinching out from time to time to keep them bushy. Simply nip out the shoot tips between your forefinger and thumbnail to encourage the production of more sideshoots. Very dwarf plants won't need pinching, nor will plants being grown on a single stem.

Fuchsias and other plants being trained as standards on a tall, single stem should have their sideshoots removed so that the main stem is encouraged to grow to the required height. Then it can be pinched out and the bushy head developed at the top.

Support single-stemmed plants with canes to which the stem can be loosely tied with soft twine. Multi-stemmed plants can be held up with a few twiggy sticks, or by an enclosure made from split green canes and twine. All supports should be put in place before they are needed so that the plant can grow up and mask them.

Don't be frightened to cut old and straggly plants back quite hard in spring. They will often sprout vigorously and take on a new lease of life.

THE IMPORTANCE OF HYGIENE
Tidiness pays dividends in the greenhouse by keeping the risk of pest and disease attack to a minimum. Never leave dead or diseased plants among healthy ones, and always pick off faded leaves and flowers immediately you spot them.

Remove any weeds that sprout from the greenhouse floor, and act immediately when you spot a pest or disease outbreak by fumigating the house.

Once a year, in spring for preference, give the inside and outside of the house a good scrub down with horticulural disinfectant. It will remove dirt and grime as well as killing overwintering pests and their eggs. Keep the plants out of the way during the clean up – stand them under the staging and cover them with a sheet of polythene. Permanganate of potash, or one of the new algicides, will shift green algal deposits from paths if a stiff brush and elbow grease are used as well.

If gravel is present on the staging, put it in a sieve and swill it clean with a hosepipe bit by bit.

A-Z
OF
greenhouse plants

THERE'S NO REASON WHY YOUR greenhouse needs to be heated to tropical temperatures to keep you in flowers during winter. A minimum temperature of 7°C (45°F) at night, and just a fraction more during the day, will keep plenty of temperate plants blooming.

GREENHOUSE FLOWERS

The list includes flowering pot plants that can be grown from seeds to give year-round colour in a cool greenhouse, as well as more extensive advice on those four confirmed favourites: carnation, chrysanthemum, fuchsia and pelargonium.

Supplement this selection with plants included in Chapter 20 House Plants, and with pot-grown bulbs described in Chapter 11 Garden Bulbs. The measurements indicate the expected ultimate height.

Begonia semperflorens
15 cm (6 in)

Round, glossy leaves of green or brown; red, pink, salmon or white flowers from July to November.
SOW in February at 20°C (68°F).
PRICK OUT into trays in March–April.
POT UP into 10 cm (4 in) containers in May.

Browallia speciosa 'Blue Troll'
20 cm (8 in)

Starry flowers of sky-blue from October to March, on very compact, green-leafed plants.
SOW in July at 18°C (64°F).
POT UP into 10 cm (4 in) containers in August–September.

Calceolaria hybrids
23 cm (9 in)

Soft green leaves and pouch-like flowers, often with contrasting spotting, in April to July.
SOW in April–May at 15°C (59°F).
PRICK OUT into trays in June.
POT UP into 8 cm (3 in) containers in July–August and into 13 cm (5 in) containers in September.

Carnation

Perpetual-flowering carnations are those that you buy from the florist for wedding buttonholes. There are dozens of varieties with blooms of red, orange, yellow, pink, white and magenta; most of them are called something-or-other Sim: 'White Sim', 'Arthur Sim', 'Tangerine Sim' and so on.
POT UP young rooted cuttings into 8 cm (3 in) pots of JIP 1 in January, February or March. Specialist nurserymen will supply them at this time.
CULTIVATION Grow on in a temperature of 4–7°C (40–45°F): the plants insist on cool temperatures. Pot on into 13 cm (5 in) pots of JIP 2 when the plants have outgrown their previous containers, and stand them outdoors during the summer. Pot on into 20 cm (8 in) pots when necessary. Pinch out the central shoot when ten pairs of leaves have been formed, and pinch out sideshoots after eight pairs of leaves. 'Stop' the plants (pinch them out) at different times to stagger flowering. If you want winter flowers, don't stop the plants after June. Bring the pots into the greenhouse during September. The plants will grow to at least 1 m (3 ft) and will need some support. Canes and string are used by most gardeners, but special carnation supports are also available. Feed fortnightly with tomato fertilizer when the plants have been in their final pots for six or eight weeks. When the flower buds form, remove all but the large central one. Cut the blooms with a good length of stem just before they are fully open.
PROPAGATION Replace the plants with newly rooted cuttings every two years. Propagate them yourself by taking cuttings of sideshoots during December, January and February and rooting them in a propagator heated to 16°C (60°F).

Celosia argentea 'Fairy Fountains'
30 cm (12 in)

Plumes of orange, red or yellow flowers like waxy feathers in July to October.
SOW in March at 20°C (68°F).
PRICK OUT into trays in April.
POT UP into 10 cm (4 in) containers in May–June.

Chrysanthemum

The early-flowering chrysanthemums that bloom in September can be grown outdoors, but October- and late-flowering varieties are grown in pots so that they can be given greenhouse cover. Buy from a specialist grower who will offer a wide choice of varieties.
POT UP rooted cuttings in March or April – one plant to an 8 cm (3 in) pot of JIP 1. Grow on at a temperature of 10°C (50°F): the plants must be kept cool.
CULTIVATION Pot on the plants as they grow, first into 13 cm (5 in) pots and then into 20 cm (8 in) pots of JIP 3. Give each plant a 1.25 m (4 ft) cane when it is in its final pot. Pinch out the main shoot when it is 20 cm (8 in) tall and pinch out subsequent sideshoots when they, too, are 20 cm (8 in) long. Specialist nurseries will recommend

precise stopping dates for each of their varieties if you want to time your blooms for a flower show. The fewer stems you leave to develop, the larger will be the individual blooms. Lightly tie the stems to the cane with soft twine as they grow. Stand the plants outdoors on a path, patio, gravel or ash bed from late May onwards when there is no danger of frost. They should be sheltered from winds, which will blow them over, or else tied to a horizontal wire strained between two posts. Feed weekly eight weeks after planting the chrysanths in their final pots. If you want large, single blooms, remove all but the central bud on each stem. If you want sprays of flower, remove the central bud and let the rest develop. In late September bring the plants into the greenhouse, keeping them cool but frostfree and in good light. Nip off any extra sideshoots and dead leaves. Either cut the open blooms with long stems, or bring the entire pot into the house if you want colour in the home. Chrysanthemum leaf miner may be a problem.

PROPAGATION is easy from cuttings. Cut the plants down to within 5 cm (2 in) of the compost after flowering and box up these 'stools' in trays of JIP 1, having shaken most of the old compost from the roots. Keep the stools in a cool, well-lit greenhouse and they will eventually produce tough little shoots that can be taken as cuttings during January and February. Make them 5–8 cm (2–3 in) long and root them in a propagator in a temperature of 16°C (60°F).

Cobaea scandens

Climber

Bells of pale blue and white in August to October, on a vigorous, vine-like plant.
SOW in March at 18°C (64°F).
POT UP into 8 cm (3 in) containers in April and into 15 cm (6 in) containers in June.

Every inch of space in this well-stocked greenhouse is utilized to nurture a fine collection of plants, including pelargoniums, alpines, succulents and bulbs.

Cuphea ignea

15 cm (6 in)

Tiny, tubular red flowers tipped with purple and white in July to November.
SOW in March at 18°C (64°F).
POT UP into 8 cm (3 in) containers in April and into 13 cm (5 in) containers in May–June.

Exacum affine

15 cm (6 in)

Tiny lilac-blue flowers in September to March, on a neat, glossy-leaved plant.
SOW in April at 18°C (64°F).
POT UP into 8 cm (3 in) containers in May and into 13 cm (5 in) containers in June–July.

Fuchsia

Hardy fuchsias are shrubs that can be grown permanently in the garden, even though frost might cut them to the ground each winter. Tender fuchsias need frost protection and so are grown as greenhouse plants or bedded out in summer and brought under cover in autumn. There are hundreds of varieties. Some are suited to being grown as standards on a single stem; others make good hanging basket plants due to their pendulous habit; but the majority make shapely bushes.

POT UP rooted cuttings in spring or early summer in 8 cm (3 in) pots of JIP 1 or a peat-based equivalent.

CULTIVATION Pinch the shoot tips and subsequent sideshoots to encourage bushiness. Flowering will usually commence about six or eight weeks after pinching. To produce a standard fuchsia, first check that the variety is suitable, then remove all sideshoots and fasten the main stem to a cane as it grows. When the required height is reached, pinch out the shoot tip and keep pinching the terminal sideshoots to encourage the development of a bushy head.

Pot on the plants in JIP 3 or a peat-based equivalent as necessary. They are usually happy in 15 cm (6 in) pots. Plant pendant types in a hanging basket. The plants will flower continuously during summer and autumn. Stand them or hang them outdoors between June and September if you wish, but bring them back inside before frosts threaten. Feed fortnightly when in flower or bud. Keep the plants on the dry side in winter. Cut the shoots back to within a few centimetres or inches of compost level in spring to encourage shoots, which can be used in propagation or pinched to produce a shapely plant once more. Repot in fresh compost at the same time. The plants will need a winter minimum temperature of 7°C (45°F); 10°C (50°F) if they are to be kept growing rather than ticking over.

PROPAGATION is by shoot tip cuttings which can be removed and rooted in a propagator at any time during spring and summer. Maintain a temperature of 16–18°C (60–65°F) to induce rooting.

Gomphrena globosa 'Buddy'
23 cm (9 in)

Globular, crispy flowerheads of rich crimson-magenta from July to November, on compact plants.

SOW in March at 18°C (64°F).

PRICK OUT into trays in April.

POT UP into 10 cm (4 in) container in May–June.

Hypoestes phyllostachya
23 cm (9 in)

Dark green leaves spotted with bright pink.

SOW in March at 18°C (64°F).

POT UP into 8 cm (3 in) containers in April and then into 13 cm (5 in) containers in June.

Mimulus **Calypso Series**
15 cm (6 in)

Trumpet-shaped blooms of red, orange and yellow covered in contrasting spots in May to July.

SOW at 18°C (64°F) in March.

POT UP into 10 cm (4 in) containers in April.

Pelargonium
Geranium

Geraniums are real favourites with any gardener who appreciates brilliance and value for money. The zonal types are the commonest, with their attractively marked leaves and bright blooms; the miniature varieties are especially good because large numbers of them can be fitted into a small greenhouse to provide almost year-round colour. Scented-leaved pelargoniums should be tried too; their foliage may be scented of anything from peppermint to pineapples and is often finely cut.

POT UP rooted cuttings of named varieties obtained from specialist nurseries in February or March. Put them in 12 cm (4½ in) pots of JIP 2.

CULTIVATION Pelargoniums, more than most plants, prefer to dry out just a little between waterings, so don't keep them soggy. Pinch out the shoot tip of each plant when it is 10 cm (4 in) high. The miniatures will grow well without pinching. Pinch again later on to keep plants bushy. Feed fortnightly from May to September, and keep the plants in brilliant light. Pick off faded flowers and leaves as soon as they are seen. Stand the plants outdoors in summer if you wish, or plant them in bedding schemes. Bring them back under cover in September before the frosts. Keep the plants very much on the dry side in winter; singles may continue to flower, especially if they are disbudded during summer to save their energy, but doubles are less likely to do so. Maintain a minimum winter temperature of 7°C (45°F), though the plants can stand anything down to freezing point and still survive. Plants to be kept for a second year can be potted on into 13 or 15 cm (5 or 6 in) pots in their second spring, but most are best replaced annually from cuttings.

PROPAGATION Take shoot tip cuttings at any time between April and September. Make each cutting 8–10 cm (3–4 in) long and root cuttings around the edge of a 10 cm (4 in) pot of peat and sand. Maintain a temperature of 16–18°C (60–65°F) for rooting. Pot up as soon as roots are well developed. Hybrid pelargoniums can be raised from seeds sown in a temperature of 18–21°C (65–70°F) between January and March. The plants will flower from July onwards.

Pericallis hybrids
30 cm (12 in)

Daisy flowers of white, pink, blue, magenta or purple, often two-tone, from November to February.

SOW in April at 16°C (61°F).

PRICK OUT into trays in May.

POT UP into 8 cm (3 in) containers in

June–July and into 13 cm (5 in) containers in August.

Primula malacoides

30 cm (12 in)

Toothed leaves held in a rosette from which rise tiered heads of pink, blue or white flowers from February to April.
SOW at 18°C (64°F) in July.
POT UP into 8 cm (3 in) containers in August and into 13 cm (5 in) containers in September–October.

Schizanthus pinnatus 'Hit Parade'

30 cm (12 in)

'Poor man's orchid' with beautifully painted flowers from July to September, atop ferny green leaves.
SOW in April at 16°C (61°F).
POT UP into 8 cm (3 in) containers in April–May and into 13 cm (5 in) containers in May–June.

Solenostemon

30 cm (12 in)

Colourful leaves splashed with red, yellow, orange, green and purple.
SOW in April at 16°C (61°F).
POT UP into 8 cm (3 in) containers in May and into 13 cm (5 in) containers in June–July.

Streptocarpus hybrids

20 cm (8 in)

Long, downy leaves and elegant trumpet flowers of blue, white, pink or magenta from September to December.
SOW at 18°C (64°F).
POT UP into 8 cm (3 in) containers in February–March and into 10 cm (4 in) containers in May–June.

Thunbergia 'Orange Wonder'

Climber

Vine-like stems clothed in green leaves and decorated with orange, black-eyed

blooms from July to October.
SOW in March at 18°C (64°F).
POT UP into 8 cm (3 in) containers in April and into 13 cm (5 in) containers in May–June.

Torenia fournieri

30 cm (12 in)

Much-branched plants with pale blue and dark blue trumpets from July to October.
SOW in March at 16°C (61°F).
POT UP into 8 cm (3 in) containers in April–May and into 13 cm (5 in) containers in June.

Trachymene coerulea

45 cm (18 in)

Pale blue scabious flowers on tall stems in July to September.
SOW in March at 18°C (64°F).
POT UP into 8 cm (3 in) containers in April and into 13 cm (5 in) containers in May–June.

Vinca 'Dwarf Mixed'

30 cm (12 in)

Tender periwinkles with flowers of pink or white, often with a contrasting eye, from July to November.
SOW in March at 16°C (61°F).
PRICK OUT into trays in April.
POT UP into 10 cm (4 in) containers in May–June.

GREENHOUSE FOOD CROPS

You can grow all sorts of fruit and vegetables in a greenhouse, but here I include just the big five: tomatoes, cucumbers, aubergines, sweet peppers and melons. Grapes and peaches are included in Chapter 17 Fruit.

Aubergine

'Long Purple', 'Moneymaker' and 'Slice Rite' are three reliable and dark-purple-skinned varieties.
SOW thinly in a pot of seed compost in

January or February and germinate in a temperature of 16–18°C (60–65°F).
PRICK OUT individually into 8 cm (3 in) pots of peat-based compost or JIP 1.
CULTIVATION Pot on into 13 cm (5 in) pots of JIP 3 or a peat-based compost when the plants are 15 cm (6 in) high. Water well when necessary. Pinch out the shoot tip one week after potting on. Transfer to 20 cm (8 in) pots when the plants have outgrown their 13 cm (5 in) containers. Spray open flowers with tepid water, and give a fortnightly liquid feed of tomato fertilizer from this stage on. Allow six to eight fruits to remain on each plant. Pinch out any sideshoots. Stake if necessary.
HARVEST the fruits when they are a good size and while they are still shiny (they'll become tough when they turn dull). Watch out for the thorns!
STORE by freezing.
PROBLEMS Aphids, red spider mites and whitefly.

Cucumber

The 'all-female' varieties, which produce very few male flowers, are well worth growing. They save you the annoyance of bitter, misshapen cucumbers if you happen to miss just one masculine bloom (they should always be pinched off to prevent fertilization). 'Femspot', 'Femdan' and 'Pepinex' are all good.
SOW two seeds to an 8 cm (3 in) peat pot full of peat-based compost in March or April. Push the seeds 2.5 cm (1 in) deep and germinate them in a

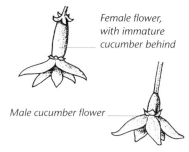

Female flower, with immature cucumber behind

Male cucumber flower

Pinch off any male cucumber flowers that occur: only female flowers have immature cucumbers behind them.

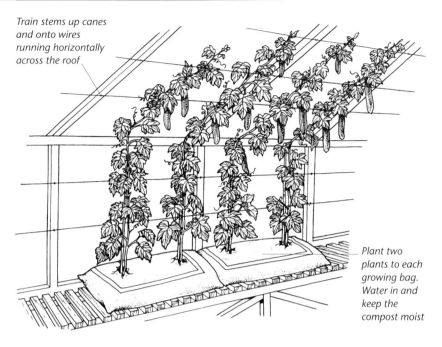

Train stems up canes and onto wires running horizontally across the roof

Plant two plants to each growing bag. Water in and keep the compost moist

temperature of 18°C (65°F). Should both seeds germinate, remove the weaker and grow the remaining one on in a temperature of 18°C (65°F). **CULTIVATION** Plant in growing bags or large pots of JIP 3 or a peat-based equivalent as soon as the young plants are 23 cm (9 in) high. Equip the sides and roof of the greenhouse with horizontal wires at 30 cm (12 in) intervals immediately above the site where the cucumbers are growing. Two plants will fit in a growing bag. Water well before planting, and plant so that the rim of the peat pot is just below the surface of the compost. Water in and keep the compost constantly moist, but never soggy, from now on. Place a cane alongside each plant and train the main stem upwards; pinch out sideshoots after three leaves have formed, and subsequent sideshoots after two leaves. Pinch out the tip of the main shoot when it reaches the ridge of the greenhouse. Spray daily with tepid water and keep the atmosphere moist by damping down. Pinch off any male flowers that do occur (female flowers have immature cucumbers behind them; males do not). Keep the plants shaded from bright sun. As soon as

The simplest way of training a cucumber plant is to pinch out sideshoots after three leaves have formed and subsequent sideshoots after two leaves. That way the plant takes up little space but crops well.

roots appear above the compost apply a topdressing. Feed fortnightly with dilute tomato fertilizer as soon as the fruits start to swell.
HARVEST the fruits as soon as they are of a decent size. The plant may continue to crop for many weeks if fruits are not allowed to mature fully.
PROBLEMS Whitefly, red spider mite, aphids, mildew, stem rot and mosaic virus.

Melon

The canteloupe melons 'Charantais' and 'Sweetheart' are old favourites; I rather like the earlier maturing 'Early Sweet', which is mouthwateringly succulent.
SOW exactly as for cucumbers.
CULTIVATION In the early stages the same instructions apply as for cucumbers, with regard to pinching and training, but do not remove the male flowers. As soon as four or five female flowers are open at the same

time (the females have miniature melons behind them), remove a male flower and push it into the centre of the females to assist pollination and subsequent fertilization. Do the job around midday when the humidity is high. If all four, or even five, fruits start to form, all well and good. If they don't, remove all the remaining females that were fertilized and wait for another batch of four to come along. Melons need to develop simultaneously because far less water must be given to them as they reach maturity. If some fruits were just starting to swell when others were almost ripe, it would be difficult to give the swelling fruits the water they required without causing the mature fruits to split. Feed weekly with liquid tomato fertilizer once the fruits have set. Pinch off subsequent female flowers. Topdress the compost when roots appear above the surface. When the fruits are tennis ball sized, support them in string bags slung from the framework of the greenhouse. Shade them from bright sunshine.
HARVEST the fruits as soon as the end furthest from the stalk gives a little when pressed. Just before this happens the fruits will start to exude that long-awaited melon aroma. This is the signal to cut down on the watering and let the compost become drier. Overwatering now will cause fruit split.
PROBLEMS aphids, whitefly, red spider mite and stem rot.

Sweet Pepper
(also known as **Capsicum**)

'Canape' and 'Worldbeater' are old favourites; the new 'Bellboy' is good too.
SOW seeds in a pot in March and germinate in a temperature of 16°C (60°F). Prick out individually into 8 cm (3 in) pots of JIP 1 or a peat-based equivalent. Grow on in a temperature of 16–18°C (60–65°F).
CULTIVATION Pot on into 15 cm (6 in) pots of JIP 3 or a peat-based equivalent when the plants are 15 cm (6 in) high.

Pinch out the shoot tips at the same time. Keep the compost gently moist at all times and shade the plants from bright sun. Spray the flowers with tepid water daily once they have opened, and feed weekly with dilute tomato fertilizer once the fruits have set.

HARVEST the fruits as soon as they are of a usable size and while they are still shiny and green. If left to turn red they will slow down the plant's growth rate and fewer fruits will come to maturity.

PROBLEMS Aphids and red spider mite.

Tomato

Everybody has their own favourite tomato variety; mostly 'Moneymaker'. Try 'Alicante' or 'Ailsa Craig' for a change, or the hefty-fruited 'Big Boy' if you like beefsteak tomatoes. 'Golden Boy' is a bright yellow tomato with an exquisite flavour.

SOW seeds in a pot during March and germinate in a temperature of 18°C (65°F). Prick out the seedlings individually into 8 cm (3 in) pots of JIP 1 or a peat-based equivalent.

CULTIVATION Grow on the plants in a temperature of around 18°C (65°F). When they are 23 cm (9 in) high, plant them out into the border soil (spacing them 45 cm (18 in) apart); into 23 cm (9 in) diameter pots of JIP 3 or a peat-based equivalent; into growing bags; or into rings (see p.255 for advice on ring culture). Water the plants well after planting and provide each one with a support – a stout cane or a string running up to the roof of the house. Remove any sideshoots as soon as they are seen. Tie the stem to the cane as it grows, or twist it carefully around the string. Try to keep the compost gently moist at all times. Sink a flowerpot into the soil alongside each border-grown plant and pour water into that instead of onto the surface of the soil: you'll prevent your tomatoes from becoming mud-spattered and the water will get straight to the roots. Spray open flowers with tepid water to encourage fruit setting. Feed weekly with diluted tomato fertilizer once the first fruits start to swell. Shade and ventilate as necessary. Pinch out the main shoot tip when six flower clusters or trusses have been formed. Cut away one or two leaves around each developing truss. Do not remove all the lower leaves as some growers do. It is not necessary and it weakens the plant.

HARVEST the fruits just as soon as they are ripe. Don't leave them on the plant too long or cropping will slow down.

STORE all remaining fruits in October. Strip the plants of their bounty and uproot them. The unripe fruits will slowly ripen if stored in a cool place. Put them in a drawer with a ripe banana if you want to speed up the process. Green tomatoes that refuse to blush can be used for chutney.

PROBLEMS Mindboggling, but you won't get them all: Whitefly, red spider mite, blossom end rot (especially on plants in growing bags), blotchy ripening, greenback, eelworm, leaf mould, stem rot, root rot, potato blight, verticillium wilt, virus.

FOOD CROPS TO FORCE

It sounds a bit cruel, but it's not really. You're just providing plants with favourable conditions that allow them rather than force them to start growing early, yielding their crops while prices are high in the shops.

French bean

Use our old friends 'The Prince' and 'Masterpiece'.

SOW four seeds 2.5 cm (1 in) deep in a 15 cm (6 in) pot of JIP 1 during December, January or February. Keep the compost moist and maintain a temperature of 16°C (60°F). Stake with a cane and string enclosure or short twiggy pea sticks as the plants grow. Feed fortnightly with tomato fertilizer once the flowers have opened.

HARVEST between 10 and 12 weeks after sowing. Pick the young pods regularly.

Potato

'Epicure' is about the best choice for forcing; 'Sharpe's Express' is also good.

POT in January. Half fill a 20 cm (8 in) pot with equal parts JIP 3 and peat-based compost. Plant three tubers 5 cm (2 in) deep. Keep the compost moist and maintain a temperature of 10°C (50°F). Topdress with more compost as the shoots grow.

HARVEST during April. Deliciously early!

Rhubarb

'Timperley Early' and 'Champagne' are both good.

PLANT the crowns close together in a 20 cm (8 in) deep box of moist peat at any time during November or December. The crowns should have been dug up a week before planting and left on the surface of the soil exposed to frost. Keep the boxes in the dark (blacked out with sacking or black polythene) in a temperature of 13–17°C (55–60°F). Check regularly and keep the compost moist.

HARVEST during January and February, cutting the pink sticks when they are about 30 cm (12 in) long. Discard the crown after cropping, unless you want to grow them on and rest them for a year before picking again.

Strawberry

'Tamella' and 'Cambridge Favourite' are both good forcers.

PLANT three rooted runners to a 20 cm (8 in) pot of JIP 3 in August. Stand the plants outdoors during the autumn and early winter, watching them carefully for dryness or, more likely, waterlogging. Bring the pots in during January. Try to maintain a temperature of 10°C (60°F) during February. Feed fortnightly with liquid fertilizer once the plants come into flower. Limit the number of fruits on each plant to 12.

HARVEST during April and May. Discard the plants after fruiting, or grow on in the garden if you are soft-hearted.

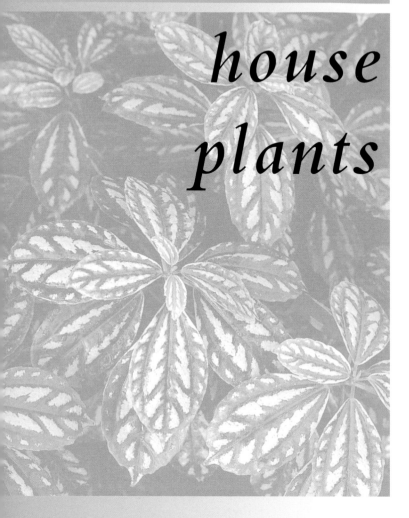

house plants

House plants have a place

in every home and office,

adding beauty, interest,

and a vital link with nature

to the environments in

which we live and work

WHAT MAKES A GOOD HOUSE-PLANT grower? Skill? Luck? Green fingers? Usually it's a smattering of all three and a hefty helping of common sense. No plants are more at your mercy than house plants: you control the amount of heat, water and light they receive and so you're directly responsible for their state of health.

Too many house plants are killed with kindness and a few are murdered by neglect but, if you choose the right plant for your particular situation and learn what it likes and loathes, then it will grow happily. A plant that is put in the kind of light it enjoys and at a temperature that suits it can only be killed by faulty watering. Master all three techniques and you'll win.

DIFFERENT TYPES OF HOUSE PLANT

There are basically three kinds of house plant: the foliage types, which last almost for ever and which are grown especially for their leaves; the flowering pot plants, which are perennial and which keep growing after blooming; and the short-term flowering pot plants that die once their blooms have faded. Most folk like a good number of foliage pot plants that offer year-round interest, plus a few flowering ones to brighten life at intervals.

Don't think of pot plants as single pieces of furniture – often they look good and feel more at home when grouped together, provided that they all have the same heat and light requirements.

BUYING HOUSE PLANTS

Spring and summer are the best times to buy house plants; then they can be transferred to your home with little check, and should carry on growing happily in a suitable environment. Christmas-flowering pot plants will obviously have to be bought in winter. Make sure that they are wrapped up well for their journey home, and don't leave them in an icy car while you complete your shopping.

If you can, buy from the nursery where the plant was grown, or from a garden centre where it has been kept in the conditions it likes. Buy from chain stores and supermarkets only when the plants are known to

Grouping several house plants together not only creates an attractive visual display, but benefits the plants by creating a higher level of humidity around them.

be fresh in. Buy from greengrocers' pavement displays at your peril: most of the plants will have been chilled and blasted by icy winds. They may be cheaper, but they'll suffer as a result of their ill treatment.

What to look for

Look for a healthy, shapely plant that has plenty of stems – unless it is purposely grown on a single stem. Avoid plants that are wilting, leafless at the base (unless this is part of their charm), brown at the leaf tips or showing signs of pest and disease attack. Flowering pot plants are best bought with a few blooms fully open and a few in bud. Plants in tight bud may not develop properly in the home; those in full flower will not last very long.

If there is a gap between the compost and the sides of the pot, leave the plant alone. It has been allowed to dry out too much and it may suffer when you get it home.

LOOKING AFTER YOUR HOUSE PLANT

Starting them off

When you get the plant home, unwrap it and stand it in the room where it is to be grown. A spot that is not in full sun is best at first, even for those plants that like bright sunlight. Keep a sun-loving plant in its temporary position for two or three days before moving it into a window. Most plants prefer a spot in good, indirect light and these can be put in their final positions straightaway, as can those plants that tolerate shade. Check the plant immediately for water. If the rootball is drier than a wrung-out flannel, then water it thoroughly.

> *"A plant will recover from wilting if it's too dry. If it wilts because it is too wet, you can wave it goodbye."*

Death traps

No house plant likes to grow directly above a radiator or other heat source, in a cold draught, or sandwiched between the curtains and the window on a winter's night. Plants placed where they are constantly brushed against will soon turn brown at the edges. Spiny plants placed where they are brushed against will soon bring forth bad language and blood.

Temperatures

There's no need to alter your central heating thermostat to suit your plants; buy instead those plants that can cope with your way of life. Most plants like to be warmer during the day than they are at night, and most houses fit conveniently into this pattern.

Plants recommended for unheated rooms will grow well in temperatures around 10–15°C (50–60°F), and can sometimes tolerate a chilly 5°C (40°F) – but they will stop growing. Those recommended for centrally heated rooms will be happy in 18–24°C (65–75°F).

Light

That mystical thing called 'good, indirect light' is the kind of brightness encountered a few feet from a window. Here the plants receive plenty of light, but not the direct rays of the sun. This is the situation that most of them enjoy.

Those plants that like full sun can be stood right against a window, but take care that they are not scorched by brilliant sunshine at the height of summer. Plants recommended for shade will not grow in a pitch-dark corner. If you can't read small print at arm's length in such a spot, it's too dark even for shade lovers.

Humidity

It's amazing what a bit of atmospheric moisture can do. House-plant owners who are used to their leaves turning brown at the edges can take heart: the problem is often solved if the pot is stood on a tray or saucer of gravel that is kept constantly moist. The water evaporates around the plant and creates an environment that is much more conducive to growth than hot, dry air. Ferns, especially, will appreciate such treatment.

If you're making a plant group, try standing the pots on a large tray or bowl of moist peat, part plunging them in the stuff. Not only will the humidity be improved, but the compost in the pots will dry out more slowly.

Large, glossy leaved plants can be sprayed with rainwater from a hand mister. Don't do this to hairy leaved plants: they'll probably rot.

Watering

Don't overdo it. Ninety-nine per cent of all household plants are killed by overwatering. Rhododendrons (Christmas azaleas), cyperus and ferns should be kept very moist at all times. All other plants need a good soak when they start to feel dry on the surface. Not before. If the compost feels like a wrung-out flannel, it is still moist.

Nearly all pot plants are happy being watered from above. Fill the pot to the brim with water and let it soak into the compost. When water runs out of the base of the pot, the plant has had enough (unless it has been allowed to dry out so much that the compost has shrunk from the sides of the pot and is letting the water run straight through).

A plant will recover from wilting if it is dry. If it wilts because it is too wet, you can wave it goodbye.

Plants like *Saintpaulia* (African violet) and *Cyclamen* may have such a tight dome of leaves that you can neither get your finger in to feel the compost, nor penetrate the rosette with a watering can or jug. Water these from below by standing them in a shallow container for half an hour and letting them take up what they want. Check for watering by weighing the pot in your hand. You'll soon become as efficient at predicting dryness as those ladies at church bazaars who can guess the weight of a cake to the nearest gram or ounce.

Check the plants daily in summer, weekly in winter. They'll need much less water during the darker months of the year. If you still fail (and I don't really believe you can be so unlucky), invest in a plant that is growing in a hydroculture unit (see p.272). Its roots will delve through a plastic basket of gravelly granules

Growing plants in a bottle garden

Small plants fond of high humidity can be grown really well in bottle gardens made in sweet jars, cider flagons, carboys and even goldfish bowls.

Spread 2.5 cm (1 in) of gravel in the base followed by 2.5 cm (1 in) of charcoal, which will prevent the compost from becoming sour. An 8 cm (3 in) layer of peat- or loam-based potting compost will keep the plants happy.

Nurseries and garden centres usually have a good selection of plants for bottle gardens, ready established in tiny pots. I'd recommend *Chamaedorea, Dionaea, Ficus pumila, Hedera helix* varieties, *Maranta, Peperomia, Pilea* and *Saxifraga*. Don't introduce anything too rampant, or slower growers will soon be swamped in a miniature jungle.

Tap the plants from their pots after watering them and plant them in the compost. If the neck of the bottle is narrow, scoop out a hole in the compost with a spoon fastened to a cane. Drop the plant into the hole and re-firm the soil with a cotton reel pushed on the other end of the cane. Plant at a spacing that allows for a little growth.

Water the plants in by running water down the inside of the bottle. Place the bottle in good indirect light; that way they won't steam up too much. Leave the top off altogether if you like, or put it in place after a few days.

Stoppered bottles will need hardly any watering at all; unstoppered bottles should be checked once a month, but it's doubtful whether they'll need watering every time.

   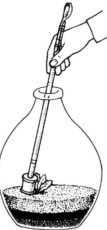 

1 Use a cardboard funnel to feed in a layer of gravel, then a layer of charcoal, and finally compost.

2 Dig holes in the compost with a teapoon fastened firmly to the end of a bamboo cane.

3 Water each plant before knocking it from its pot and dropping into the prepared hole.

4 Firm back the soil, with the aid of a cotton reel pushed onto the other end of the cane.

5 Settle the plants in by running water down the inside of the bottle – not too much!

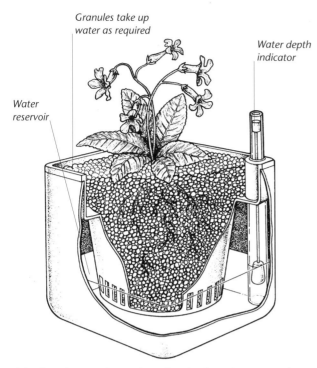

Granules take up water as required

Water depth indicator

Water reservoir

A hydroculture unit consists of a plastic water reservoir fitted with a water depth indicator. The plant grows in a perforated plastic pot filled with gravelly granules, and takes up the water as it needs it.

that sits over a water reservoir. All you have to do is keep the reservoir topped up with water. There's even a little indicator to help you out. Don't mistake a compost-filled self-watering pot for a hydroculture unit. Self-watering pots simply draw water through the compost from a reservoir below. They are difficult to manage and I've yet to see one that's full of happy plants.

Feeding

Give all pot plants a few square meals while they are growing actively. This is usually in spring and summer, but winter-flowering plants can be fed at that time too. Most vigorous plants will appreciate a fortnightly summer feed of diluted liquid pot-plant fertilizer; slow growers can be fed monthly. Flowering pot plants thrive on diluted liquid tomato fertilizer, and it's just the thing to coax shy *Saintpaulias* (African violets) into bloom.

Potting on

It's surprising how long a pot plant can carry on growing in the same container, but as we're in the business of growing plants well (rather than just keeping them alive) it's a good idea to give them a

new pot of compost every year. Spring is the best time to move them – just before growth begins with the warmer weather and improved light.

Pot on into a container that is 5 cm (2 in) larger in diameter than the existing one. Use a loam-based compost such as John Innes No. 2 or one of the proprietary soilless composts. Never use garden soil when repotting plants. It's just not good enough for them. Plastic pots have many holes in the base; clay pots have only one, so it's a good idea to lay a few pebbles in the bottom of a clay pot to prevent the hole becoming blocked by a plug of compost.

Water the plant well an hour before potting on. Place some moist compost in the bottom of the new pot (on top of the drainage layer if it is needed) and then tap the plant from its old pot so that the rootball comes out in one piece. Sit it on top of the compost in the new pot and check that the surface of the rootball rests 2.5 cm (1 in) or so below the rim. When potting is completed it should be fractionally below the surface of the new compost, yet there should still be a gap between the surface and the rim to allow for watering.

Fill in compost around the rootball, firming it lightly with your fingers. One rap with the palms of your hands on the sides of the pot will level the compost surface. Now all you need to do is water the plant well. At this stage the job is best done by standing the pot in a bowl of water; the compost can be easily displaced if it is soaked from above.

There are exceptions to all rules. A few house plants do not need repotting every year because they grow very slowly and prefer to be a little 'rootbound'. Large palms such as *Howeas*, *Aspidistras* and *Sansevieria* (mother-in-law's tongue) are three such examples, but as a general rule a plant needs a new pot when its roots are wrapped around the inside of the old one. Knock out the plant to see.

Hefty pot plants that are already in 30 cm (12 in) containers should not be repotted. Instead they can be topdressed. Scrape away the top 5 cm (2 in) of compost in spring and replace it with fresh.

GENERAL CARE

Keep them clean

When you're dusting the furniture, don't forget the plants. They collect just as much grime, and a leaf that is dirty can't manufacture food very well.

Clean hairy leaved plants with a dry paintbrush. Glossy leaves can be wiped clean with kitchen roll

In summer move house plants outdoors to a sheltered spot. Clean glossy leaves with kitchen roll dipped in a mixture of milk and rainwater.

dipped in tepid rainwater (or with a mixture of rainwater and milk if you insist on giving them a shine). Leafshine products may damage sensitive plants, but tissue 'leaf-shine wipes' seem to do a good job without causing any leaf burn.

Pinching out and staking

Pinch out the shoot tips of bushy plants to keep them that way, and stake any plants that need support. Single canes and string will keep up single stems; moss-covered sticks will keep vine-like plants with aerial roots happy, and small trellis or wire supports will hold up other climbers and scramblers.

Remove any wayward or unwanted shoots at any time of year if you're desperate to be rid of them. From the plant's point of view spring is the best time.

Summer break

During summer all house plants except ferns will appreciate a summer break outdoors on a sheltered patio. Bring them indoors early in September.

Holiday care

If you're due to go away on holiday, try to enlist the help of a neighbour and leave precise instructions on watering. If this isn't possible, plunge them in seed trays of moist peat in a shady room. They'll stay in reasonable condition for a fortnight like this.

Propagation

I've indicated in the A–Z section how each plant can best be increased. You'll find fuller details in Chapter 2 Propagation.

PESTS AND DISEASES

Relatively few pests and diseases attack house plants, but those that do make an amazing impact both on your temper and on the plant's health. I've dealt with them in Part V Pests, diseases and disorders, but for the record these are the beasts and blights most likely to attack.

Pests

Aphids (greenfly), caterpillars, earwigs, leafminers, mealy bug, red spider mite, scale insects, vine weevil, whitefly.

Diseases

Botrytis (grey mould), damping off, mildew, rust, sooty mould, viruses.

Disorders

These are caused by you. They occur as a result of unfavourable growing conditions, so take the necessary remedial action to put matters right. The most common disorders are:

BUD DROP Caused by dry air, draughts, dry compost, poor light or movement of the plant during bud formation.

FAILURE TO FLOWER Caused by underfeeding, lack of light, unsuitable temperatures or too large a pot of compost (the plant is busy growing roots).

LEAF FALL Caused by dry air, draughts, dryness at the roots or fluctuating temperatures.

LEAF SPOT Caused by sun scorch, splashed water, too much or too little water.

LEAF YELLOWING Caused particularly by overwatering and also by draughts, lack of light or nutrients. Remember that old leaves at the bottom of the plant naturally turn yellow before they fall.

SPINDLY SHOOTS Caused by lack of light.

STEM ROT Caused by soggy compost.

VARIEGATION FADING Caused by lack of light.

WILTING Caused by overwatering, underwatering, excessively high temperatures, vine weevil attack.

A-Z

OF

house

plants

ALMOST ALWAYS IT IS THE sight of a house plant in the shop or nursery that persuades you to buy it, rather than a glowing description in a catalogue. But what you do with it when you get it home is what matters, so in this section I have concentrated on providing information aout the growing conditions that each plant prefers. Check out the guidelines for your particular treasure and find the right spot for it in your home.

Adiantum capillus-veneris
Maidenhair Fern

30 x 45 cm (12 x 18 in)

FEATURES Foliage.
SEASON OF INTEREST All year round.
LIKES Good indirect light, cool temperature, and high humidity.
POT ON annually, in loam-based compost.
PROPAGATE by division.
SPECIAL INFORMATION Fronds brown if air or compost dry; cut back dead fronds.

Aechmea fasciata
Urn Plant

45 x 45 cm (18 x 18 in)

FEATURES Foliage/flowers. 'Vase' dies after flowering; offsets appear to replace parent plant.

SEASON OF INTEREST All year round.
LIKES Good indirect light, warm temperature, and high humidity.
POT ON every two years in soilless compost.
PROPAGATE by offsets.

Aphelandra squarrosa
Zebra Plant

30 x 30 cm (12 x 12 in)

FEATURES Foliage/flowers.
SEASON OF INTEREST All year round.
LIKES good indirect light, warm temperature, and high humidity.
POT ON annually in loam-based compost.
PROPAGATE by cuttings.
SPECIAL INFORMATION Cut off flowers as they fade, and cut back in spring.

Asparagus densiflorus
Asparagus Fern

30 x 45 cm (12 x 18 in)

FEATURES Foliage. Good in hanging baskets and pots.
SEASON OF INTEREST All year round.
LIKES good indirect light or semi-shade, cool or warm temperature, and high humidity.
POT ON annually in either loam-based or soilless compost.
PROPAGATE by division.

Asparagus setaceus
(syn. *A. plumosus*)
Asparagus Fern

30 x 30 cm (12 x 12 in)

FEATURES Foliage.

Hardy house plants

The following plants will tolerate almost any condition and are notoriously hard to kill:
- **Aspidistra**
- **Billbergia**
- **Chlorophytum**
- **Cissus**
- **Cyperus**
- **Fatshedera**
- **Fatsia**
- **Impatiens**
- **Philodendron**
- **Sansevieria**
- **Tradescantia**

SEASON OF INTEREST All year round.
LIKES good indirect light or semi-shade, cool or warm temperature, and high humidity.
POT ON annually in loam-based or soilless compost.
PROPAGATE by division.
SPECIAL INFORMATION Dry air or compost will cause leaf drop.

Aspidistra elatior
Cast Iron Plant

45 x 45 cm (18 x 18 in)

FEATURES Foliage.
SEASON OF INTEREST All year round.
LIKES good indirect light or semi-shade, and cool temperature.
POT ON in loam-based compost only when absolutely pot bound, perhaps every three years.
PROPAGATE by division.
SPECIAL INFORMATION Do not overwater.

Asplenium nidus
Bird's Nest Fern

60 x 60 cm (2 x 2 ft)

FEATURES Foliage.
SEASON OF INTEREST All year round.
LIKES semi-shade, warm temperature, and high humidity.
POT ON annually in soilless compost.
SPECIAL INFORMATION Dry air, bright sun and draughts cause leaf scorch.

Begonia maculata
Spotted Begonia

1.25 x 1 m (4 x 3 ft)

FEATURES Foliage/flowers.
SEASON OF INTEREST All year round.
LIKES good indirect light, warm temperature, and high humidity.
POT ON annually in loam-based compost.
PROPAGATE by cuttings.
SPECIAL INFORMATION Cut back hard in spring when spindly.

Begonia rex
Rex Begonia

45 cm x 1 m (18 in x 3 ft)

FEATURES Foliage. May be short-lived, and may not grow very large.
SEASON OF INTEREST All year round.
LIKES good indirect light, warm temperature, and high humidity.
POT ON annually in loam-based compost.
PROPAGATE by leaf cuttings.

Begonia semperflorens
Bedding Begonia

15 x 15 cm (6 x 6 in)

FEATURES Flowers.
SEASON OF INTEREST All year round.
LIKES good indirect light or direct sun, and cool to warm temperature. On a sunny windowsill will bloom through winter.
POT ON annually in loam-based compost.
PROPAGATE by cuttings.

Begonia x tuberhybrida
Tuberous Begonia

60 x 60 cm (2 x 2 ft)

FEATURES Flowers.
SEASON OF INTEREST Summer.
LIKES good indirect light, warm temperature, and high humidity.
POT ON annually in loam-based compost.
PROPAGATE by division.
SPECIAL INFORMATION Start dry tubers in February. Flowers fall if compost becomes dry.

Billbergia nutans
Queen's Tears

60 x 60 cm (2 x 2 ft)

FEATURES Flowers.
SEASON OF INTEREST Late winter.
LIKES good indirect light, cool to warm temperature, and high humidity.
POT ON every two years in soilless compost.
PROPAGATE by division.

SPECIAL INFORMATION Dry atmosphere causes brown leaf tips.

Calceolaria hybrids
Slipper Flower

30 x 30 cm (12 x 12 in)

FEATURES Flowers.
SEASON OF INTEREST Spring/summer.
LIKES good indirect light, cool temperature, and high humidity.
PROPAGATE by seed in soilless compost.
SPECIAL INFORMATION Sow early summer for spring flowering. Discard after blooming.

Capsicum annuum
Ornamental Pepper

30 x 15 cm (12 x 6 in)

FEATURES Fruits.
SEASON OF INTEREST Winter.
LIKES direct sun, cool temperature, and high humidity.
PROPAGATE by seed: sow in spring in soilless compost.
SPECIAL INFORMATION Discard after winter fruiting.

Chamaedorea elegans
Parlour Palm

60 x 45 cm (2 ft x 18 in)

FEATURES Foliage.
SEASON OF INTEREST All year round.
LIKES good indirect light, cool to warm temperature, and high humidity.
POT ON every two years in loam-based compost.
PROPAGATE by seed.
SPECIAL INFORMATION Good in bottle gardens.

Chlorophytum comosum
Spider Plant

45 x 60 cm (18 in x 2 ft)

FEATURES Foliage.
SEASON OF INTEREST All year round.
LIKES good indirect light, and cool to warm temperature.
POT ON annually in loam-based compost.

PROPAGATE by plantlets.
SPECIAL INFORMATION Starved or dry plants develop brown leaf tips.

Cissus antarctica
Kangaroo Vine

1 m x 60 cm (3 x 2 ft)

FEATURES Foliage.
SEASON OF INTEREST All year round.
LIKES good indirect light or semi-shade, and cool temperature.
POT ON annually in loam-based or soilless compost.
PROPAGATE by cuttings.
SPECIAL INFORMATION Train over a trellis or wire framework or plant in a hanging basket.

Cissus rhombifolia
Grape Ivy

Climber

FEATURES Foliage.
SEASON OF INTEREST All year round.
LIKES semi-shade or good indirect light, and cool to warm temperature.
POT ON every one or two years in loam-based or soilless compost.
PROPAGATE from cuttings.
SPECIAL INFORMATION Provide a large support system. Bomb-proof.

x citrofortunella microcarpa
Calamondin Orange

1 x 1 m (3 x 3 ft)

FEATURES Fruits.
SEASON OF INTEREST All year round; flowers in summer; fruits follow.
LIKES direct sun and cool temperature.
POT ON annually in loam-based compost.
PROPAGATE by seed or cuttings.

Codiaeum variegatum
Croton; Joseph's Coat

1 m x 45 cm (3 ft x 18 in)

FEATURES Foliage.
SEASON OF INTEREST All year round.
LIKES good indirect light, warm temperature, and high humidity.

Plants for shade and sun

FOR SHADY CORNERS
- Adiantum
- Asparagus
- Aspidistra
- Asplenium
- Cissus
- Fatshedera
- Fatsia
- Maranta
- Peperomia
- Philodendron
- Pilea
- Platycerium
- Sansevieria

FOR SUNNY WINDOWSILLS
- Capsicum
- Cyclamen
- Dionaea
- Erica
- Fuchsia
- Hedera
- Impatiens
- Pelargonium
- Primula
- Rhododendron
- Saintpaulia
- Sansevieria
- Saxifraga
- Schlumbergera
- Senecio
- Solanum
- Solenostemon
- Tradescantia

POT ON every two years in loam-based compost.

PROPAGATE by cuttings.

SPECIAL INFORMATION Leaves fall if humidity in short supply.

Cordyline indivisa
Mountain Cabbage Tree

1 m x 60 cm (3 x 2 ft)

FEATURES Foliage.

SEASON OF INTEREST All year round. Good outside in summer.

LIKES direct sun and cool temperature.

POT ON annually in loam-based compost.

PROPAGATE from seed.

Cordyline terminalis varieties
Dragon Tree; Ti Tree

1 m x 45 cm (3 ft x 18 in)

FEATURES Foliage.

SEASON OF INTEREST All year round.

LIKES good indirect light and warm temperature.

POT ON annually in loam-based compost.

PROPAGATE from seed or by air-layering.

SPECIAL INFORMATION Dry air and draughts cause leaf browning.

Cycas revoluta
Sago Palm

1 x 1 m (3 x 3 ft)

FEATURES Foliage.

SEASON OF INTEREST All year round.

LIKES good indirect light, cool to warm temperature, and high humidity.

POT ON every two to three years in loam-based compost.

PROPAGATE from seed.

PESTS AND DISEASES Mealy bug and scale are common pests.

Cyclamen hybrids
Cyclamen

30 x 30 cm (12 x 12 in)

FEATURES Flowers.

SEASON OF INTEREST Winter.

LIKES direct sun and very cool temperature.

POT ON Dry off after flowering and repot in late summer in a loam-based compost.

PROPAGATE from seed or tuber.

SPECIAL INFORMATION Must be kept cool.

Cyperus albostriatus
Cyperus

45 x 45 cm (18 x 18 in)

FEATURES Foliage.

SEASON OF INTEREST All year round.

LIKES good indirect light or semi-shade, and cool to warm temperature.

SPECIAL INFORMATION Stand in a saucer of water that is always kept topped up.

POT ON annually in a loam-based compost.

PROPAGATE by division.

Cyperus alternifolius
(syn. **C. involucratus**)
Umbrella Grass

1.25 m x 60 cm (4 x 2 ft)

FEATURES Foliage.

SEASON OF INTEREST All year round.

LIKES good indirect light or semi-shade, and cool to warm temperature.

POT ON annually in a loam-based compost.

PROPAGATE by division.

SPECIAL INFORMATION Stand in a saucer of water that is always kept topped up.

Dendranthema x morifolium
Pot Chrysanthemum

23 x 30 cm (9 x 12 in)

FEATURES Flowers. Plant in garden after blooming, where they will then grow taller.

SEASON OF INTEREST Any time of year.

LIKES direct sun and cool temperature.

PROPAGATE from cuttings in soilless compost.

Dieffenbachia seguine 'Amoena'
Dumb Cane

1 m plus x 45 cm (4 ft x 18 in)

FEATURES Foliage.

SEASON OF INTEREST All year round.

LIKES good indirect light or semi-shade, warm temperature, and high humidity.

POT ON every one or two years in soilless compost.

PROPAGATE from cuttings.

SPECIAL INFORMATION Chop back when leggy. Pull off yellow leaves. The sap is poisonous so handle carefully.

Dieffenbachia seguine varieties
Dumb Cane

1 m plus x 45 cm (4 ft x 18 in)

FEATURES Foliage.

SEASON OF INTEREST All year round.

LIKES good indirect light or direct sun, warm temperature, and high humidity.

POT ON every one or two years in soilless compost.

PROPAGATE from cuttings.
SPECIAL INFORMATION This variety needs more light than green-leaved types.

Dionaea muscipula
Venus Fly Trap

10 cm x 10 cm (4 x 4 in)

FEATURES Foliage.
SEASON OF INTEREST All year round.
LIKES direct sun, cool to warm temperature, and high humidity.
POT ON every two to three years in moss and soilless compost.
PROPAGATE by division.
SPECIAL INFORMATION Grow in live sphagnum moss under a transparent dome.

Dracaena species and varieties
Dragon Tree

1 m x 45 cm (3 x 18 in)

FEATURES Foliage.
SEASON OF INTEREST All year round.
LIKES good indirect light and warm temperature.
POT ON annually in loam-based compost.

PROPAGATE from seed or by air-layering.
SPECIAL INFORMATION Dry air and draughts cause leaf browning. Cut off flower spikes.

Erica 'Hyemalis'
Cape Heath

30 cm x 23 cm (12 x 9 in)

FEATURES Flowers.
SEASON OF INTEREST Winter.
LIKES direct sun, cool temperature, and high humidity.
POT ON Cut back and repot annually after flowering in peat-based compost.
PROPAGATE from cuttings.
SPECIAL INFORMATION Stand outside in summer.

Euphorbia pulcherrima
Poinsettia

1 x 1 m (3 x 3 ft)

FEATURES Bracts.
SEASON OF INTEREST Winter/spring.
LIKES good indirect light or direct sun, and warm temperature.
POT ON Cut back annually after flowering and repot in loam-based or soilless compost.

PROPAGATE from cuttings.
SPECIAL INFORMATION Long nights induce bract formation.

x Fatshedera lizei
Ivy Tree

2 x 1 m (6 x 3 ft)

FEATURES Foliage.
SEASON OF INTEREST All year round.
LIKES good indirect light or semi-shade, and cool temperature.
POT ON annually in loam-based or soilless compost.
PROPAGATE from cuttings.
SPECIAL INFORMATION Needs a moss-covered stick or frame to climb up.

Fatsia japonica
False Castor Oil Palm

1 x 1 m (3 x 3 ft)

FEATURES Foliage.
SEASON OF INTEREST All year round.
LIKES good indirect light or semi-shade, and cool temperature.
POT ON annually in loam-based or soilless compost.
PROPAGATE from seed or cuttings.

Ficus benjamina
Weeping Fig

2 x 1 m (6 x 3 ft)

FEATURES Foliage.
SEASON OF INTEREST All year round.
LIKES good indirect light, warm temperature, and high humidity.
POT ON every two years in loam-based compost.
PROPAGATE from cuttings.
SPECIAL INFORMATION A few leaves yellow and fall when first bought.

Ficus elastica varieties
Rubber Plant

3 m plus x 1 m plus (10 x 3 ft)

FEATURES Foliage.

Fatsia japonica is a popular and easy-to-grow house plant, which can also be grown outdoors.

SEASON OF INTEREST All year round.
LIKES good indirect light, cool to warm temperature, and high humidity.
POT ON every two to three years in loam-based compost.
PROPAGATE from leaf cuttings.
SPECIAL INFORMATION Easy to overwater. Tolerant of dryness.

Ficus pumila
Creeping Fig
5 x 50 cm (2 x 20 in)

FEATURES Foliage.
SEASON OF INTEREST All year round.
LIKES semi-shade, warm temperature, and high humidity.
POT ON annually in soilless compost.
PROPAGATE by cuttings.
SPECIAL INFORMATION A good choice for planting in bottle gardens and suspended pots.

Fuchsia hybrids
Fuchsia
60 x 60 cm plus (2 x 2 ft)

FEATURES Flowers.
SEASON OF INTEREST Summer.
LIKES direct sun and cool temperature.
POT ON Cut back and repot in spring in loam-based compost.
PROPAGATE by cuttings.
SPECIAL INFORMATION Don't move in flower or buds drop. With young plants, pinch out stem tips to promote bushy growth.

Hedera helix varieties
Ivy
Climber/trailer

FEATURES Foliage.
SEASON OF INTEREST All year round.
LIKES good indirect light or direct sun, cool temperature, and high humidity.
POT ON annually in loam-based or soilless compost.
PROPAGATE from cuttings.
PESTS AND DISEASES Dry air brings red spider.
SPECIAL INFORMATION Shade causes loss of variegation.

Hippeastrum hybrids
Amaryllis
60 x 30 cm (2 ft x 12 in)

FEATURES Flowers.
SEASON OF INTEREST Winter/spring.
LIKES good indirect light or direct sun, and warm temperature.
POT ON in autumn in loam-based or soilless compost and water gingerly at first.
PROPAGATE from seed.
SPECIAL INFORMATION Dry off after flowering.

Howea belmoreana
Kentia Palm
2 x 1 m (6 x 3 ft)

FEATURES Foliage.
SEASON OF INTEREST All year round.
LIKES good indirect light or semi-shade, warm temperature, and high humidity.
POT ON every two or three years in loam-based or soilless compost.
PROPAGATE from seed.
SPECIAL INFORMATION Leaves brown in dry air or draughts.

Howea forsteriana
Kentia Palm
2 x 1 m (6 x 3 ft)

FEATURES Foliage.
SEASON OF INTEREST All year round.
LIKES good indirect light or semi-shade, warm temperature, and high humidity.
POT ON every two or three years in loam-based or soilless compost.
PROPAGATE from seed.
SPECIAL INFORMATION Leaves not as curly as previous species. Equally sensitive.

Hoya carnosa
Wax Plant
Climber

FEATURES Foliage/flowers
SEASON OF INTEREST Spring/autumn.
LIKES direct sun, warm temperature, and high humidity. Be careful not to over-water.
POT ON every two or three years in loam-based compost.
PROPAGATE from cuttings or by layering.
SPECIAL INFORMATION Needs a support system around which to twine itself. Leave on old flower stalks – they bloom again.

Impatiens hybrids
Busy Lizzie; Balsam
60 x 60 cm (2 x 2 ft)

FEATURES Flowers.
SEASON OF INTEREST All year round.
LIKES direct sun, and cool to warm temperature.
POT ON Cut back and repot in spring in loam-based or soilless compost.
PROPAGATE from cuttings taken in late spring or early summer.
SPECIAL INFORMATION Plenty of food needed. When they become straggly, cut back hard.

Justicia brandegeeana
Shrimp Plant
60 x 60 cm (2 x 2 ft)

FEATURES Flowers.
SEASON OF INTEREST All year round.
LIKES direct sun, cool to warm temperature, and high humidity.
POT ON Cut back and repot in loam-based or soilless compost every spring.
PROPAGATE by cuttings.

Maranta species
Prayer Plant
15 x 30 cm (6 x 12 in)

FEATURES Foliage.
SEASON OF INTEREST All year round.
LIKES semi-shade, warm temperature, and high humidity. Hates soggy compost.
POT ON every two years in soilless compost.
PROPAGATE by division or cuttings.
SPECIAL INFORMATION Good in bottle gardens.

Find the right spot for your house plant

All too often the house plant comes as a present, which means that you're stuck with it whether it likes your conditions or not. You'll have to do your best to find it a suitable spot. If you're buying a plant, make sure you know exactly what it likes, dislikes and tolerates, and what it is supposed to do. The following plants are suitable for the conditions indicated.

PLANTS FOR CENTRALLY HEATED ROOMS
- *Aechmea*
- *Aphelandra*
- *Begonia*
- *Codiaeum*
- *Dieffenbachia*
- *Dracaena*
- *Euphorbia*
- *Ficus*
- *Howea*
- *Monstera*
- *Peperomia*
- *Philodendron*
- *Pilea*
- *Rhoicissus*
- *Saintpaulia*
- *Sansevieria*
- *Schefflera*
- *Sinningia*
- *Stephanotis*
- *Yucca*

PLANTS FOR UNHEATED ROOMS
- *Calceolaria*
- *Cordyline*
- *Cyclamen*
- *Dendranthema*
- *Erica*
- *Fatshedera*
- *Fatsia*
- *Hedera*
- *Primula*
- *Rhododendron*
- *Saxifraga*
- *Senecio*

PLANTS FOR WARM HUMID BATHROOMS
- *Adiantum*
- *Aechmea*
- *Aphelandra*
- *Asparagus*
- *Asplenium*
- *Begonia*
- *Cyperus*
- *Dieffenbachia*
- *Dionaea*
- *Maranta*
- *Nephrolepis*
- *Peperomia*
- *Pilea*
- *Platycerium*
- *Saintpaulia*
- *Tradescantia*

Monstera deliciosa
Swiss Cheese Plant

2 m plus x 2 m plus (6 x 6 ft)

FEATURES Foliage. Only leaves of older, well-fed plants are perforated.
SEASON OF INTEREST All year round.
LIKES good indirect light or semi-shade, warm temperature, and high humidity.
POT ON every two years in loam-based or soilless compost.
PROPAGATE from cuttings or by air-layering.
SPECIAL INFORMATION Tuck any aerial roots into the compost, where they can take up nutrients.

Nephrolepis exaltata
Ladder Fern

60 x 60 cm (2 x 2 ft)

FEATURES Foliage.
SEASON OF INTEREST All year round.
LIKES good indirect light or semi-shade, warm temperature, and high humidity.
POT ON every one or two years in soilless compost.
PROPAGATE by division.
SPECIAL INFORMATION Dry air and draughts cause leaf browning.

Nephrolepis exaltata 'Bostoniensis'
Boston Fern

60 cm x 1 m (2 x 3 ft)

FEATURES Foliage.
SEASON OF INTEREST All year round.
LIKES good indirect light or semi-shade, warm temperature, and high humidity.
POT ON every one or two years in soilless compost.
PROPAGATE by division.
SPECIAL INFORMATION As above. This variety is good in hanging baskets provided it can be kept moist. It will turn brown if allowed to dry out.

Pelargonium hybrids
Geranium

60 x 30 cm (2 ft x 12 in)

FEATURES Flowers.
SEASON OF INTEREST Spring/autumn.
LIKES some sun and cool temperature.
POT ON annually in loam-based or soilless compost.
PROPAGATE from cuttings and seed.
SPECIAL INFORMATION Bright light is vital. Leaves yellow in shade. Singles bloom in winter.

Peperomia species
Peperomia

15 x 15 cm (6 x 6 in)

FEATURES Foliage/flowers.
SEASON OF INTEREST All year round.
LIKES good indirect light or semi-shade, warm temperature, and high humidity. Hates soggy compost: allow to dry out before watering.
POT ON every one or two years in loam-based compost.
PROPAGATE from leaf cuttings.
SPECIAL INFORMATION Good in bottle gardens.

Perricallis x *hybrida*
Cineraria

30 x 30 cm (12 x 12 in)

FEATURES Flowers.
SEASON OF INTEREST Winter/spring.
LIKES direct sun and very cool temperature.
PROPAGATE from seed in loam-based compost.
PESTS AND DISEASES Loved by greenfly.
SPECIAL INFORMATION Easily overwatered. Discard after flowering.

Philodendron scandens
Sweetheart Plant

Climber

FEATURES Foliage.
SEASON OF INTEREST All year round.
LIKES good indirect light or semi-shade, and cool to warm temperature.

POT ON every one or two years in a soilless compost.

PROPAGATE from cuttings.

SPECIAL INFORMATION Needs a large support system such as a moss-covered pole. Thrives on neglect.

Pilea cadierei 'Minima'

Aluminium Plant

15 x 23 cm (6 x 9 in)

FEATURES Foliage. Good in bottle gardens.

SEASON OF INTEREST All year round.

LIKES good indirect light or semi-shade, warm temperature, and high humidity.

POT ON annually in loam-based compost.

PROPAGATE Renew regularly from cuttings.

Platycerium bifurcatum

Stag's Horn Fern

45 x 45 cm (18 x 18 in)

FEATURES Foliage.

SEASON OF INTEREST All year round.

LIKES semi-shade, warm temperature, and high humidity.

POT ON every one or two years in soilless compost.

SPECIAL INFORMATION Can grow in a wad of moss wired to a piece of cork bark.

Primula obconica

German Primrose

30 x 30 cm (12 x 12 in)

FEATURES Flowers.

SEASON OF INTEREST All year round.

LIKES direct sun and cool temperature.

POT ON annually in a loam-based or soilless compost.

PROPAGATE from seed or by division.

SPECIAL INFORMATION Can cause a rash on sensitive skin.

Rhododendron simsii

Azalea

30 x 45 cm (12 x 18 in)

FEATURES Flowers.

SEASON OF INTEREST Winter.

LIKES some direct sun, very cool temperature, and high humidity.

POT ON annually in soilless compost.

PROPAGATE from cuttings.

SPECIAL INFORMATION Never let the rootball dry out. Water with rainwater.

Saintpaulia ionantha varieties

African Violet

10 x 30 cm (4 x 12 in)

FEATURES Flowers.

SEASON OF INTEREST Spring/autumn.

LIKES direct sun, warm temperature, and high humidity.

POT ON every one or two years in soilless compost. Don't overpot.

PROPAGATE from leaf cuttings.

SPECIAL INFORMATION Dilute tomato fertilizer encourages flowering.

Sansevieria trifasciata 'Laurentii'

Mother-in-law's Tongue

1 m x 30 cm (3 ft x 12 in)

FEATURES Foliage.

SEASON OF INTEREST All year round.

LIKES direct sun, indirect light, or semi-shade, and cool to warm temperature.

POT ON every three or four years in loam-based compost.

PROPAGATE by division.

SPECIAL INFORMATION Almost indestructible, but do not overwater.

Saxifraga stolonifera varieties

Mother-of-thousands

Trailing

FEATURES Foliage.

SEASON OF INTEREST All year round.

LIKES good indirect light or direct sun, cool temperature, and high humidity.

POT ON in loam-based compost.

PROPAGATE from plantlets.

SPECIAL INFORMATION Good in hanging baskets.

Schefflera arboricola

Heptapleurum; Umbrella Tree

2 m plus x 45 cm plus (6 ft x 18 in)

FEATURES Foliage.

SEASON OF INTEREST All year round.

LIKES good indirect light, warm temperature, and high humidity.

POT ON every two years in loam-based or soilless compost.

PROPAGATE from seed.

SPECIAL INFORMATION Variegated kind needs good light.

Schefflera elegantissima

Finger Aralia

2 m x 60 cm (6 x 2 ft)

FEATURES Foliage.

SEASON OF INTEREST All year round.

LIKES semi-shade, warm temperature, and high humidity.

Plants for hanging pots and baskets

Trailing plants look particularly good when planted in suspended containers so that their stems can cascade into the air. Plant in soilless compost rather than the heavier soil-based types, and make sure that the pot or basket is securely fastened to the wall or ceiling. Built-in drip trays will prevent damage to furniture.

Plants in suspended pots and baskets tend to dry out more quickly than most pot plants, so check them regularly. They'll also go a bundle on extra humidity: spray them daily with tepid rainwater – but watch the furniture!

If you're short of inspiration when it comes to choosing plants try:

- *Asparagus*
- *Beloperone*
- *Chlorophytum*
- *Fuchsia*
- *Hedera*
- *Nephrolepis*
- *Philodendron scandens*
- *Saxifraga*
- *Schlumbergera*
- *Tradescantia*

Pilea cadierei **is an attractive foliage plant, with its distinctive silvery patterned quilted leaves.**

POT ON every two years in soilless compost.

PROPAGATE from seed.

SPECIAL INFORMATION Draughts, dry air, wet or dry compost cause leaf fall.

Schlumbergera x *buckleyi*
Christmas Cactus
Trailing

FEATURES Flowers. Superb in hanging baskets.

SEASON OF INTEREST Winter.

LIKES good indirect light, cool temperature, and high humidity.

POT ON every one or two years in loam-based compost.

PROPAGATE from cuttings.

SPECIAL INFORMATION Stand outside in summer.

Sinningia speciosa
Gloxinia
23 x 30 cm (9 x 12 in)

FEATURES Flowers.

SEASON OF INTEREST Summer.

LIKES direct sun, warm temperature, and high humidity.

POT ON Repot tubers in spring in soilless compost.

PROPAGATE from seed or tuber.

SPECIAL INFORMATION Dry off after flowering.

Solanum capsicastrum
Winter Cherry
30 x 30 cm (12 x 12 in)

FEATURES Fruits.

SEASON OF INTEREST Winter.

LIKES direct sun, cool temperature, and high humidity.

POT ON Cut back and repot annually after fruiting in loam-based compost.

PROPAGATE from seed or cuttings.

SPECIAL INFORMATION A teaspoon of Epsom salts in half a litre (one pint) of water prevents leaf yellowing.

Solenostemon
Flame Nettle
60 x 60 cm (2 x 2 ft)

FEATURES Foliage.

SEASON OF INTEREST All year round.

LIKES direct sun and warm temperature.

POT ON Chop back and repot in spring.

PROPAGATE by cuttings.

SPECIAL INFORMATION Tatty if light is poor in winter.

Stephanotis floribunda
Clustered Wax Flower
1 x 1 m (3 x 3 ft)

FEATURES Flowers.

SEASON OF INTEREST Spring/autumn.

LIKES good indirect light and warm temperature.

POT ON every two years in loam-based or soilless compost.

PROPAGATE from cuttings.

PESTS AND DISEASES Watch out for mealy bug.

SPECIAL INFORMATION Train over a support system.

Tradescantia species
Wandering Jew
Trailing

FEATURES Foliage.

SEASON OF INTEREST All year round.

LIKES direct sun and cool temperature.

POT ON annually in soilless compost.

PROPAGATE is very easy. Replace regularly from stem cuttings.

SPECIAL INFORMATION Feed well.

Tradescantia zebrina
Inch Plant
Trailing

FEATURES Foliage.

SEASON OF INTEREST All year round.

LIKES direct sun, and cool or warm temperature. Allow surface to dry out between waterings.

POT ON annually in soilless compost.

PROPAGATE Replace from cuttings.

Yucca aloifolia
Spanish Bayonet; Ti Tree
2 m x 60 cm (6 ft x 24 in)

FEATURES Foliage.

SEASON OF INTEREST All year round.

LIKES direct sun, and cool to warm temperature.

POT ON every two years in loam-based compost.

PROPAGATE from cuttings.

SPECIAL INFORMATION Stand outdoors in summer. Peel off faded leaves.

part VI

PESTS, DISEASES AND DISORDERS

Give your plants the conditions they require and problems are less likely to arise; but when they do tackle them without delay

Healthy, well-tended plants, like the inhabitants of this cottage garden in Devon, are less likely to be attacked by pests and diseases than malnourished weaklings.

THE LAST THING I WANT TO DO IS TURN you into a hypochondriac, but sooner or later your plants will be attacked by a beast or blight, and it's as well to know just how you can nurse them back to health.

Organic control

Like many people, in my own garden I now use no chemical spray because I value the balance of nature that exists there – the masses of birds, insects and animals (from deer to voles) – and I'd rather not upset them. I also find that plants supplied with plenty of soil enrichment in the form of garden compost, well-rotted manure and organic fertilizer do seem to resist epidemics. Surprisingly, my garden has not become a haven for pests and diseases because all the plants are mixed up and an epidemic cannot find sufficient concentration of any one thing to sustain it. I am a gardener who enjoys seeing the mullein moth eating my verbascums and Solomon's seal sawfly munching my polygonatums. But perhaps I'm an oddity and you may not feel the same way about pests and diseases.

Using chemical sprays

There are two schools of chemical thought on pests and diseases: one is that you spray immediately at the first sign of attack; the other is that you spray as a routine preventive measure before the pest or disease has a chance to raise its ugly thorax.

> *"Healthy, well-grown plants are more resistant to attacks than feeble weaklings."*

For those of you who do wish to use sprays, then the identification and control listings that follow will at least guide you in the right direction. Where really severe problems occur, and there are plenty of them, you should know exactly what remedies are available and when to take steps. That doesn't mean that you should be forever rushing out with a sprayer – let's face it, you'll seldom have more than a handful of pest and disease problems at any one time.

Bear in mind at all times that healthy, well-grown plants are more resistant to attacks than feeble weaklings, and some varieties have been bred for their resistance to particular diseases: these are always worth buying.

Try to use specific chemicals where possible; there's now a specific aphicide that kills greenfly yet leaves bees, ladybirds and beneficial lacewings unharmed. I've included it in the listings.

Using chemicals safely

Using chemicals is a bit terrifying, but rest assured that much research work has been carried out into these products, and you're more likely to do damage to wildlife if you start spraying with home-made concoctions of nettle leaves, rhubarb leaves and age-old quassia chips than with many of the new and more specific preparations. Now and again we have legitimate safety scares with chemicals, but by and large most of them are reliable and safe if used wisely.

When you've found the right remedy for a problem, make sure that you apply it safely, whether it's a dust, a spray, an aerosol, a fumigant or granules that are scattered on the soil.

- Store all chemicals in carefully labelled containers out of the reach of pets and children.
- Dispose of any surplus mixture down the lavatory.
- Wear rubber gloves when mixing up the solution or scattering granules, and wash your hands and the sprayer thoroughly afterwards. It seems a bit of a bind but it's only sensible; something that kills an insect is likely to give you stomachache.
- Spray on a still evening, rather than during the day when bees are active. Don't spray open flowers if you can avoid it. Keep children and pets indoors.
- Use hand sprayers that you can keep especially for insecticides and fungicides.
- Always allow the recommended interval between spraying and harvesting. However safe a product may be, always wash fruits and vegetables before eating them.
- Follow the instructions on the container to the letter. Never add more solution than is recommended.

Buy disease-free plants

Buy plants from a reputable supplier and, with fruit bushes, try to buy stock that is certified disease-free. Viruses are crippling, crop-reducing diseases that are transmitted by aphids, and you'd do well to make sure that the bushes you buy are not infected with them. There's no cure once the plants are under attack.

Practise crop rotation

Crop rotation is a cultivation technique that farmers have practised down the ages – and with good reason. Even in the garden it's risky to grow one type of plant in the same spot year after year so, with the exception of trees and shrubs, aim to rotate your plantings.

Correct cultivation techniques

Some plant problems are caused neither by pests nor diseases: they are caused by you, or by the faulty growing conditions you have provided for the plant. These are known as disorders and can usually be put right if your cultivation techniques are adjusted.

Identifying plant problems

When troubles do strike, correct identification is vital so that you can tackle the problem without delay. There are two methods of dealing with pests, diseases and disorders – chemical and cultural – and both are important. Use this illustration to help you identify the problem, then turn to the relevant A–Z entry for advice on treatment.

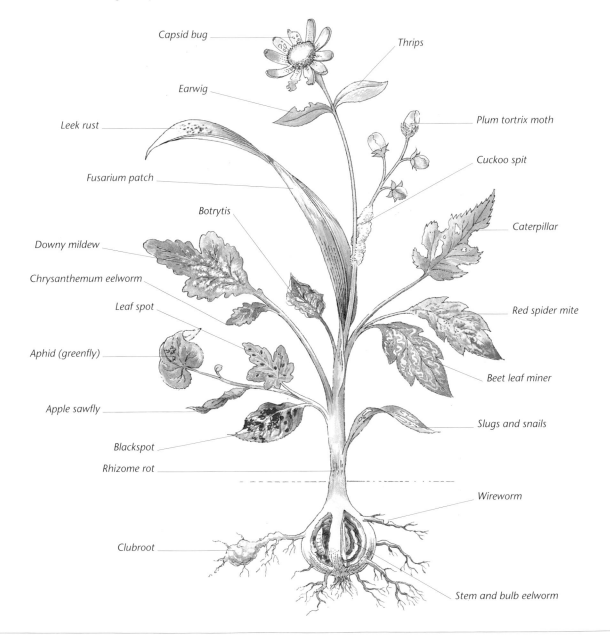

Capsid bug
Thrips
Earwig
Leek rust
Plum tortrix moth
Fusarium patch
Cuckoo spit
Botrytis
Downy mildew
Caterpillar
Chrysanthemum eelworm
Leaf spot
Aphid (greenfly)
Red spider mite
Apple sawfly
Beet leaf miner
Blackspot
Slugs and snails
Rhizome rot
Wireworm
Clubroot
Stem and bulb eelworm

A-Z

OF

*pests,
diseases
and
disorders*

FOR EASE OF REFERENCE, I HAVE compiled separate listings for the different plant groups – vegetables, fruit, ornamental plants, under cover plants (greenhouse and house plants), and lawns – and for each group a separate A–Z listing of pests, diseases, and disorders is given.

VEGETABLES

PESTS

Aphid (greenfly, blackfly)
CROPS ATTACKED **Wide range**

DAMAGE/SYMPTOMS Small insects suck sap, weaken plant, transmit viruses, secrete honeydew.
CONTROL Spray with specific aphicide such as Rapid Greenfly Killer.

Birds (sparrow, pigeon)
CROPS ATTACKED **Wide range**

DAMAGE/SYMPTOMS Leaves, pods and flowers torn.

CONTROL Netting is the only reliable long-term control.

Cabbage root fly
CROPS ATTACKED **Brassicas**

DAMAGE/SYMPTOMS Leaves wilt and turn blue; roots eaten by white maggots.
CONTROL Place black felt 'collars' around plants to prevent egg laying.

Cabbage whitefly
CROPS ATTACKED **Brassicas**

DAMAGE/SYMPTOMS Small, white, V-shaped flies suck sap and soil leaves.
CONTROL Spray with Miracle Picket or Bio Flydown.

Carrot fly
CROPS ATTACKED **Carrot, parsnip**

DAMAGE/SYMPTOMS Leaves turn reddish and wilt; roots tunnelled by grubs.
CONTROL Avoid by not thinning. Protect with horticultural fleece.

Caterpillar
CROPS ATTACKED **Wide range, especially brassicas**

DAMAGE/SYMPTOMS Leaves eaten; caterpillars or green droppings visible.
CONTROL Pick off small infestations. Spray with Miracle Picket or Bio Flydown.

Celery fly
CROPS ATTACKED **Celery**

DAMAGE/SYMPTOMS Leaves tunnelled and blistered by maggots.
CONTROL Spray with Malathion.

Eelworm
CROPS ATTACKED **Onion**

DAMAGE/SYMPTOMS Leaves distorted and bloated; bulbs soft and deformed.
CONTROL Destroy crops. Prevent by rotation. Keep onions, beans, parsnips and carrots off site for three years.

Eelworm (Root-knot)
CROPS ATTACKED **Tomato**

DAMAGE/SYMPTOMS Lower leaves yellow and wilting; galls on roots.
CONTROL Destroy plants. Replace border soil or grow in containers.

Flea beetle
CROPS ATTACKED **Radish and other seedlings**

DAMAGE/SYMPTOMS Tiny spots and holes in leaves.
CONTROL Dust with Derris at first sign of attack.

Frit fly
CROPS ATTACKED **Sweet corn**

DAMAGE/SYMPTOMS Young plants twisted and distorted; leaves ragged.
CONTROL Prevent by sowing seeds in greenhouse (not outdoors). Dust with Murphy Gamma-BHC Dust.

Gall weevil
CROPS ATTACKED **Brassicas, swede and turnip**

DAMAGE/SYMPTOMS Roots swollen and pierced by maggots; plants stunted.
CONTROL Dust soil around young plants with Miracle Sybol Dust.

Leek moth
CROPS ATTACKED **Onion, leek**

DAMAGE/SYMPTOMS Leaves tunnelled.
CONTROL Spray with Bio Fenitrothion.

Mealy cabbage aphid
CROPS ATTACKED **Brassicas**

DAMAGE/SYMPTOMS Leaves turn yellow; grey-coloured insects on undersides.
CONTROL Spray with Bio Fenitrothion.

Onion fly
CROPS ATTACKED **Onion**

DAMAGE/SYMPTOMS Leaves wilt and

turn yellowish; grubs eating roots.
CONTROL Prevent by crop rotation. Drench with spray-strength Miracle Sybol.

Pea and bean weevil

CROPS ATTACKED **Pea, broad bean**

DAMAGE/SYMPTOMS Leaf edges scalloped by chewing action of small, brown weevils.
CONTROL Tolerate if mild. Spray severe attacks with Bio Fenitrothion.

Pea moth

CROPS ATTACKED **Pea**

DAMAGE/SYMPTOMS Peas within pod found to be maggoty.
CONTROL Prevent by spraying with Bio Fenitrothion a week after flowers open.

Pea thrips

CROPS ATTACKED **Pea**

DAMAGE/SYMPTOMS Pods blotched and spotted silvery grey.
CONTROL Spray with Bio Fenitrothion.

Potato cyst eelworm

CROPS ATTACKED **Potato**

DAMAGE/SYMPTOMS Plants stunted; lower leaves brown and shrivelled; tiny nodules but few potatoes on roots.
CONTROL Grow resistant varieties. Do not replant infected soil with spuds for eight years.

Red spider mites

CROPS ATTACKED **French and runner bean**

DAMAGE/SYMPTOMS Leaves greyish or yellow; fine webs and tiny mites seen.
CONTROL Spray with Derris, Murphy Liquid Malathion or Murphy Systemic Action Insecticide.

Root aphid

CROPS ATTACKED **Lettuce**

DAMAGE/SYMPTOMS Stunted, wilting,

yellow leaves; insects on roots.
CONTROL Grow resistant varieties. Drench with spray-strength Malathion.

Slugs and snails

CROPS ATTACKED **Wide range**

DAMAGE/SYMPTOMS Leaves and stems eaten; silvery trails visible.
CONTROL Sink yogurt carton into soil and fill up with beer to trap. Surround susceptible plants with sharp grit.

Tomato moth

CROPS ATTACKED **Tomato**

DAMAGE/SYMPTOMS Leaves and fruits eaten by fat caterpillars.
CONTROL Prevent by weeding. Hand pick or spray with Bio Fenitrothion.

Wireworm

CROPS ATTACKED **Potato**

DAMAGE/SYMPTOMS Narrow tunnels appear in tubers.
CONTROL Harvest tubers quickly. Rake in Murphy's Gamma-BHC Dust.

DISEASES

Anthracnose

CROPS ATTACKED **French and runner bean**

DAMAGE/SYMPTOMS Leaves, stems and pods blotched brown.
CONTROL Burn all infected plants. Buy seeds from a reputable source.

Beet leaf miner

CROPS ATTACKED **Beetroot**

DAMAGE/SYMPTOMS Yellow or brown tunnels and blisters on leaves.
CONTROL Spray with Miracle Sybol or Doff Systemic insecticide.

Blackleg

CROPS ATTACKED **Potato**

DAMAGE/SYMPTOMS Stem bases black; leaves yellow and wilting.

CONTROL Dig up and destroy. Store only healthy tubers.

Black rot

CROPS ATTACKED **Turnip, swede**

DAMAGE/SYMPTOMS Leaf edges yellow; black veins; sliced root black around perimeter.
CONTROL Destroy infected plants. Improve drainage and rotate crops.

Buckeye rot

CROPS ATTACKED **Tomato**

DAMAGE/SYMPTOMS Grey or reddish areas on fruit, overlaid with brown concentric rings.
CONTROL Pick off and destroy. Water compost with Cheshunt compound.

Canker

CROPS ATTACKED **Parsnip**

DAMAGE/SYMPTOMS Upper areas of root turn soft and brown.
CONTROL Sow resistant varieties. Avoid over-manuring. Lime acid soils. Rotate crops.

Chocolate spot

CROPS ATTACKED **Broad bean**

DAMAGE/SYMPTOMS Leaves blotched with brown; leaves may die.
CONTROL Avoid applying too much nitrogen.

Clubroot

CROPS ATTACKED **Brassicas**

DAMAGE/SYMPTOMS Plants stunted and weak. Roots swollen and foul-smelling.
CONTROL Lime acid soil. Improve drainage. Dip roots of young plants in Bio Liquid Clubroot Control.

Crown rot

CROPS ATTACKED **Rhubarb**

DAMAGE/SYMPTOMS Buds and centre of plant brown and rotten.

CONTROL Dig up and burn. Improve drainage. Don't replant rhubarb on infected soil.

Downy mildew

CROPS ATTACKED **Brassicas, lettuce, spinach, onion, pea, beetroot**

DAMAGE/SYMPTOMS Leaves yellow above, whitish or purplish felted below.
CONTROL Spray with Bio Dithane 945 as soon as first symptoms are seen; repeat every fortnight as necessary; grow resistant varieties.

Dry rot

CROPS ATTACKED **Potato**

DAMAGE/SYMPTOMS Stored tubers wrinkle at one end; white or pink fungus visible.
CONTROL Prevent by lifting and storing carefully. Destroy infected tubers.

Foot rot

CROPS ATTACKED **French bean, pea, runner bean**

DAMAGE/SYMPTOMS Leaves yellow; stem bases black and rotten.
CONTROL Prevent by rotating crops. Water seedlings with Cheshunt compound.

Gangrene

CROPS ATTACKED **Potato**

DAMAGE/SYMPTOMS Stored tubers develop sunken brown areas and flesh rots.
CONTROL Prevent by storing healthy tubers in ideal conditions.

Ghost spot

CROPS ATTACKED **Tomato**

DAMAGE/SYMPTOMS Fruits develop white, circular spots centred with brown.
CONTROL Caused by grey mould, which thrives in damp conditions and poor air circulation. Prevent by ventilating well and watering carefully.

Grey mould

CROPS ATTACKED **Wide range**

DAMAGE/SYMPTOMS Brown, rotting areas are covered with grey fur.
CONTROL Prevent as for Ghost Spot. Spray with Bio Supercarb. Pull off affected leaves.

Halo blight

CROPS ATTACKED **French and runner bean**

DAMAGE/SYMPTOMS Brown, yellow-edged blotches on leaves; soggy blotches on pods.
CONTROL Prevent by buying seeds from a reputable supplier. Destroy infected plants.

Heart rot

CROPS ATTACKED **Celery**

DAMAGE/SYMPTOMS Centre of plant brown and rotten.
CONTROL Avoid damaging plants or applying too much nitrogen. Practise crop rotation.

Honey fungus

CROPS ATTACKED **Rhubarb**

DAMAGE/SYMPTOMS Plant dies; white fungus found on roots; black 'bootlaces' may be in soil.
CONTROL Dig up and burn. Replant new crowns on uninfected soil.

Leaf mould

CROPS ATTACKED **Tomato**

DAMAGE/SYMPTOMS Leaves yellowish above; purplish mould visible below.
CONTROL Prevent by growing resistant varieties. Ventilate well. Spray with Bio Supercarb.

Leaf spot

CROPS ATTACKED **Rhubarb, spinach, celery**

DAMAGE/SYMPTOMS Leaves spotted with brown – centres of spots fall out.

Spots on celery develop black 'pinheads'.
CONTROL Pull off infected leaves. Spray celery with Bio Dithane 945.

Leek rust

CROPS ATTACKED **Leek and occasionally onion**

DAMAGE/SYMPTOMS Leaves spotted with orange.
CONTROL Destroy infected foliage. Practise crop rotation.

Neck rot

CROPS ATTACKED **Onion**

DAMAGE/SYMPTOMS Stored bulbs become mouldy on upper surface.
CONTROL Prevent by storing ripe, well-dried onions.

Potato blight

CROPS ATTACKED **Potato, tomato**

DAMAGE/SYMPTOMS Leaves curled inwards and blotched brown. White mould on undersides. Tomato leaves brown at tips.
CONTROL To prevent blight in a wet summer, spray with Bio Dithane 945 from July onwards. Otherwise spray as soon as first symptoms appear. Grow resistant varieties of potato.

Powdery mildew

CROPS ATTACKED **Wide range**

DAMAGE/SYMPTOMS White powdery deposit, on leaves, shoots and pods.
CONTROL Sow resistant varieties. Space adequately. Spray with Miracle Nimrod-T.

Powdery scab

CROPS ATTACKED **Potato**

DAMAGE/SYMPTOMS Circular, dark brown scabs with raised edges found on tubers.
CONTROL Destroy infected tubers. Prevent by ensuring good drainage and practising crop rotation. Plant resistant cultivars.

Rust

CROPS ATTACKED **Broad bean**

DAMAGE/SYMPTOMS Raised orange spots on undersides of leaves.
CONTROL Spray only severe outbreaks with Bio Dithane 945.

Scab

CROPS ATTACKED **Potato**

DAMAGE/SYMPTOMS Tubers marred by rough brown scabs.
CONTROL Prevent by avoiding over-liming. Grow resistant varieties. Infected tubers still edible.

Shanking

CROPS ATTACKED **Onion**

DAMAGE/SYMPTOMS Central leaves turn yellow and wilt. Bulbs foul-smelling when sliced.
CONTROL Destroy infected plants. Prevent by practising crop rotation.

Smut

CROPS ATTACKED **Onion, sweetcorn**

DAMAGE/SYMPTOMS On onion, leaves and bulbs spotted with black; on sweetcorn, white outgrowths on cobs and stems.
CONTROL Destroy infected plants. Keep onions off infected ground for eight years.

Soft rot

CROPS ATTACKED **Carrot, swede, turnip**

DAMAGE/SYMPTOMS Stored or growing roots brown and rotten in centre.
CONTROL Destroy infected roots. Prevent by ensuring good drainage and avoiding over-manuring.

Spinach blight

CROPS ATTACKED **Spinach**

DAMAGE/SYMPTOMS Leaves roll inwards and turn yellowish.
CONTROL Destroy infected plants. Control aphids, which transmit viruses.

Spraing

CROPS ATTACKED **Potato**

DAMAGE/SYMPTOMS Tubers marked with red semi-circles when cut open.
CONTROL A virus disease. Prevent by rotating crops and planting certified potatoes. Infected roots still edible.

Stem rot (Didymella)

CROPS ATTACKED **Tomato**

DAMAGE/SYMPTOMS Black areas on stem bases; fruits may also become brown.
CONTROL Dig up and burn. Spray healthy plants with Bio Supercarb.

Verticillium wilt

CROPS ATTACKED **Tomato**

DAMAGE/SYMPTOMS Lower leaves yellow; plant wilts in sun.
CONTROL Topdress plants and water with Bio Supercarb. Grow resistant varieties.

Violet root rot

CROPS ATTACKED **Carrot**

DAMAGE/SYMPTOMS Roots felted with purple mould.
CONTROL Destroy infected roots. Practise rotation. Keep carrots off infected ground for four years.

Virus

CROPS ATTACKED **Wide range**

DAMAGE/SYMPTOMS Leaves puckered, distorted and mottled with yellow.
CONTROL Destroy infected plants. Keep down aphids, which transmit the diseases.

Wart disease

CROPS ATTACKED **Potato**

DAMAGE/SYMPTOMS Black, warty outgrowths on tubers of old varieties.
CONTROL Ministry of Agriculture must be informed. Grow new varieties that are immune. Destroy infected tubers.

DISORDERS

Blossom end rot

CROPS ATTACKED **Tomato**

DAMAGE/SYMPTOMS Black, sunken areas on undersides of fruits.
CONTROL Caused by erratic watering. Aim to keep compost evenly moist.

Blotchy ripening

CROPS ATTACKED **Tomato**

DAMAGE/SYMPTOMS Fruits ripen unevenly.
CONTROL Ventilate and shade well. Ensure adequate supplies of food and water.

Bolting

CROPS ATTACKED **Wide range**

DAMAGE/SYMPTOMS Plants form flowers and 'run to seed' prematurely.
CONTROL Prevent dryness at the roots. Do not transplant large plants.

Brown heart

CROPS ATTACKED **Turnip, swede**

DAMAGE/SYMPTOMS When sliced open, roots reveal brown centre.
CONTROL Caused by boron deficiency. Apply balanced fertilizer before sowing.

Fanging

CROPS ATTACKED **Carrot, parsnip, beetroot**

DAMAGE/SYMPTOMS Roots forked and distorted.
CONTROL Caused by stony or over-manured soil.

Greenback

CROPS ATTACKED **Tomato**

DAMAGE/SYMPTOMS Upper part of fruit remains green.
CONTROL Shade from bright sun. Feed well. Do not defoliate. Plant resistant varieties.

Green tubers

CROPS ATTACKED **Potato**

DAMAGE/SYMPTOMS Tubers green both outside and inside.
CONTROL Caused by sunlight. Earth up tubers adequately.

Hearts (lack of)

CROPS ATTACKED **Cabbage**

DAMAGE/SYMPTOMS Plants remain leafy and open – no solid heart formed.
CONTROL Plant in firm, well-manured soil that does not dry out.

Hollow heart

CROPS ATTACKED **Potato**

DAMAGE/SYMPTOMS Tubers undamaged outside but hollow inside.
CONTROL Caused by heavy rain or irrigation after drought.

Root split

CROPS ATTACKED **Carrot**

DAMAGE/SYMPTOMS Roots split lengthways.
CONTROL Caused by heavy rain or irrigation after drought. Keep evenly moist.

Scald

CROPS ATTACKED **Tomato**

DAMAGE/SYMPTOMS Sunken, straw-coloured patches on fruits or leaves.
CONTROL Shade from bright sunshine.

Split fruit

CROPS ATTACKED **Tomato**

DAMAGE/SYMPTOMS Fruits split open when ripe.
CONTROL Caused by heavy watering after dryness. Keep evenly moist.

Tip burn

CROPS ATTACKED **Lettuce**

DAMAGE/SYMPTOMS Leaf edges marked with brown.

CONTROL Caused by dryness at the roots.

Weedkiller damage

CROPS ATTACKED **Tomato**

DAMAGE/SYMPTOMS Leaves narrow and distorted; stems twisted; fruits oval and hollow.
CONTROL Keep all weedkillers away from tomatoes and use a separate watering can.

Whiptail

CROPS ATTACKED **Brassicas**

DAMAGE/SYMPTOMS Leaves reduced to just the midrib. No pest damage visible.
CONTROL Water with 28 g (1 oz) sodium molybdate in 9 litres (2 gallons) water to each 8.3 square metres (10 square yards) of soil.

FRUIT

PESTS

Aphid

CROPS ATTACKED **Wide range**

DAMAGE/SYMPTOMS Sap sucked; plant weakened; viruses transmitted; honeydew secreted.
CONTROL Spray trees in winter with Murphy Mortegg to kill eggs. Spray in summer with Rapid Greenfly Killer.

Apple sawfly

CROPS ATTACKED **Apple**

DAMAGE/SYMPTOMS Fruitlets fall; tunnels visible. Remaining fruits possess ribbon-like scars.
CONTROL Spray with Bio Fenitrothion when most petals have fallen.

Apple sucker

CROPS ATTACKED **Apple**

DAMAGE/SYMPTOMS Flowers turn brown; green, aphid-like insects observed among them.

CONTROL Spray trees in winter as for aphids. Spray with a systemic insecticide before flowers open.

Big bud mite

CROPS ATTACKED **Blackcurrant**

DAMAGE/SYMPTOMS Dormant buds fat and spherical.
CONTROL Prune out and burn infected shoots. Spray with Bio Supercarb as flowers open.

Birds (sparrow, bullfinch, pigeon)

CROPS ATTACKED **Wide range**

DAMAGE/SYMPTOMS Fruits pecked or wholly eaten.
CONTROL Invest in a fruit cage or try 'Stay Off' spray.

Blossom weevil

CROPS ATTACKED **Strawberry**

DAMAGE/SYMPTOMS Unopened flowers wither and turn brown; stalks eaten through.
CONTROL Pick off and burn any infected flowers.

Brown scale

CROPS ATTACKED **Peach, grape and gooseberry**

DAMAGE/SYMPTOMS Stems covered with small, brown, limpet-like scales.
CONTROL Spray in winter as for aphids. Spray in summer with Malathion.

Capsid bug

CROPS ATTACKED **Wide range**

DAMAGE/SYMPTOMS Tiny brown holes in leaves; raised brown areas on fruits.
CONTROL Spray with Bio Fenitrothion.

Caterpillar

CROPS ATTACKED **Wide range**

DAMAGE/SYMPTOMS Leaves eaten; caterpillars or droppings visible.
CONTROL Spray with Miracle Picket.

Cherry fruit moth

CROPS ATTACKED **Cherry**

DAMAGE/SYMPTOMS Small green caterpillars eat buds, flowers and green fruits.
CONTROL Spray trees in winter with Murphy Mortegg.

Codling moth

CROPS ATTACKED **Apple, pear**

DAMAGE/SYMPTOMS Holes tunnelled in ripe fruits; fruits are maggoty when harvested.
CONTROL Spray with Bio Fenitrothion: once in June and once in July.

Currant blister aphid

CROPS ATTACKED **Red/white currant**

DAMAGE/SYMPTOMS Upper leaves twisted and blistered; often tinged red.
CONTROL Spray in winter as for aphids. Spray in summer with systemic insecticide.

Currant sawfly

CROPS ATTACKED **Currant**

DAMAGE/SYMPTOMS Leaves eaten, and only veins left.
CONTROL Spray with Derris (if fruits near maturity) or Bio Fenitrothion.

Gooseberry sawfly

CROPS ATTACKED **Gooseberry**

DAMAGE/SYMPTOMS Leaves eaten by larvae of sawfly species, and only veins left.
CONTROL Spray with Derris (if fruits near maturity) or Bio Fenitrothion.

Leaf and bud mite

CROPS ATTACKED **Raspberry**

DAMAGE/SYMPTOMS Leaves blotched yellow on upper surface; no reduction in vigour or cropping.
CONTROL None. Do not confuse with mosaic virus, which is accompanied by distortion and poor cropping.

Leaf midge

CROPS ATTACKED **Currant**

DAMAGE/SYMPTOMS Shoot tips distorted and withered.
CONTROL Spray with systemic insecticide just before flowers open.

Mealy bug

CROPS ATTACKED **Grape and occasionally other crops**

DAMAGE/SYMPTOMS Small, white, mealy insects visible on stems; suck sap; secrete honeydew.
CONTROL Spray with Malathion. Brush down rods in winter and spray with Murphy Mortegg.

Mussel scale

CROPS ATTACKED **Plum**

DAMAGE/SYMPTOMS Tiny, mussel-shaped scales plastered on stems.
CONTROL Spray with Malathion. Spray in winter with Murphy Mortegg.

Pear leaf blister mite

CROPS ATTACKED **Pear and sometimes plum**

DAMAGE/SYMPTOMS Spots (pale green, then pink, then black) appear on leaves.
CONTROL Pick off and burn infected leaves if possible. Keep tree well fed and watered.

Pear midge

CROPS ATTACKED **Pear**

DAMAGE/SYMPTOMS Fruits fall when small. Lots of small yellow maggots inside.
CONTROL Destroy infected fruitlets. Spray with Bio Fenitrothion just before flowers open.

Pear sawfly

CROPS ATTACKED **Pear**

DAMAGE/SYMPTOMS Fruitlets fall and are tunnelled by a single maggot.

Ribbon-like scars on remaining fruits.
CONTROL Spray with Bio Fenitrothion when most petals have fallen.

Pear sucker

CROPS ATTACKED **Pear**

DAMAGE/SYMPTOMS Flowers turn brown; green, aphid-like insects among them.
CONTROL Spray trees in winter as for aphids. Spray with systemic insecticide before flowers open.

Plum sawfly

CROPS ATTACKED **Plum**

DAMAGE/SYMPTOMS Fruitlets fall before they are fully developed, and are tunnelled.
CONTROL Spray with Bio Fenitrothion one week after petals have fallen.

Plum tortrix moth

CROPS ATTACKED **Plum**

DAMAGE/SYMPTOMS Leaves bound with silken web; caterpillars inside.
CONTROL Spray in winter as for aphids. Spray in summer with Bio Fenitrothion.

Rabbits/deer

CROPS ATTACKED **Wide range**

DAMAGE/SYMPTOMS Leaves or bark gnawed away.
CONTROL Difficult. Plastic tree guards help. Try 'Stay Off' spray.

Raspberry beetle

CROPS ATTACKED **Raspberry**

DAMAGE/SYMPTOMS Fruits eaten by small maggots.
CONTROL Spray with Derris when fruits turn pink.

Red spider mite

CROPS ATTACKED **Apple, plum, peach**

DAMAGE/SYMPTOMS Leaves bleached and mottled; webs spun; tiny yellow green or brown mites visible.

CONTROL Spray in winter as for aphids. Spray in summer with systemic insecticide.

Slugworm

CROPS ATTACKED **Pear, cherry**

DAMAGE/SYMPTOMS Small, slimy, black, slug-like creatures eating leaf surfaces.

CONTROL Spray only very severe infestations with Derris; otherwise ignore.

Tortrix moth

CROPS ATTACKED **Apple**

DAMAGE/SYMPTOMS Surface of fruit eaten; leaf stuck over damage; caterpillar may be seen.

CONTROL Spray in winter as for aphids. Spray at fruitlet stage with Bio Fenitrothion.

Wasp

CROPS ATTACKED **Wide range, especially plum**

DAMAGE/SYMPTOMS Fruits eaten as they approach ripeness.

CONTROL Tolerate. Drape wall-trained trees with old net curtains to keep wasps out.

Winter moth

CROPS ATTACKED **Apple, pear, plum, cherry**

DAMAGE/SYMPTOMS Young leaves and open flowers eaten by small, green caterpillars.

CONTROL Fasten grease bands around trees from September to March. Spray in spring with Bio Fenitrothion.

Woolly aphid

CROPS ATTACKED **Wide range**

DAMAGE/SYMPTOMS Stems covered in greyish white, wool-covered insects.

CONTROL Spray with systemic insecticide. Insect causes canker on apple and pear.

DISEASES

American gooseberry mildew

CROPS ATTACKED **Gooseberry, blackcurrant**

DAMAGE/SYMPTOMS Leaves, shoots and fruits become covered in white powder, which turns to light brown felt.

CONTROL Prevent by pruning well. Don't apply too much nitrogen. Spray with Bio Supercarb.

Bacterial canker

CROPS ATTACKED **Cherry, plum**

DAMAGE/SYMPTOMS Gum oozes from flattened cankers on stem; leaves full of holes; tree weak.

CONTROL Cut out and burn infected wood and treat wounds with special paint. Spray with Copper Fungicide.

Blossom wilt

CROPS ATTACKED **Apple, pear, cherry, plum**

DAMAGE/SYMPTOMS Flowers wilt and turn brown; leaves may die.

CONTROL Cut out infected wood. Spray before flowers open with Bio Supercarb.

Botrytis (Grey Mould)

CROPS ATTACKED **Raspberry, strawberry**

DAMAGE/SYMPTOMS Fruits covered with fluffy grey mould.

CONTROL Pick off infected fruits. Spray open flowers with Bio Supercarb.

Brown rot

CROPS ATTACKED **Apple, pear, plum, cherry**

DAMAGE/SYMPTOMS Fruits develop soft brown areas on the skin, and concentric rings of buff pustules throughout the flesh.

CONTROL Dispose of infected fruits (do not compost). Store only undamaged fruits.

Cane blight

CROPS ATTACKED **Raspberry**

DAMAGE/SYMPTOMS Leaves wither; dark areas on canes at ground level; canes become brittle.

CONTROL Cut out and burn infected canes. Sterilize secateurs. Spray with Murphy Copper Fungicide.

Cane spot

CROPS ATTACKED **Raspberry**

DAMAGE/SYMPTOMS Small purple spots on canes; eventually turn grey; fruits and leaves spotted later.

CONTROL Cut out and burn infected canes.

Canker

CROPS ATTACKED **Apple, pear**

DAMAGE/SYMPTOMS Shoots wounded and, in winter, filled with reddish fruiting bodies.

CONTROL Prune out infected wood. Control woolly aphid.

Coral spot

CROPS ATTACKED **Wide range, especially currant**

DAMAGE/SYMPTOMS Orange pustules appear on dead or dying stems.

CONTROL Cut out infected wood.

Crown gall

CROPS ATTACKED **Blackberry, loganberry**

DAMAGE/SYMPTOMS Swollen galls visible on stems at soil level or higher.

CONTROL Cut out and burn. Replant on uninfected soil.

Fireblight

CROPS ATTACKED **Apple, pear, cherry and others**

DAMAGE/SYMPTOMS Shoots wither and turn brown; leaves do not fall; wounds visible at stem bases.

CONTROL Cut out damaged wood well back into healthy wood.

Honey fungus (Armillaria)

CROPS ATTACKED **Wide range**

DAMAGE/SYMPTOMS Trees die back; honey-coloured toadstools may appear; white fungal threads in soil; black 'bootlaces' in soil on occasions.
CONTROL Dig up and burn badly infected plants. Manure others to maintain vigour.

Leaf spot

CROPS ATTACKED **Currant**

DAMAGE/SYMPTOMS Small brown spots on leaves coagulate; leaves eventually fall.
CONTROL Burn fallen leaves.

Peach leaf curl

CROPS ATTACKED **Peach, apricot, nectarine**

DAMAGE/SYMPTOMS Leaves become puckered and bright pink in colour.
CONTROL Spray with a Liquid Copper Fungicide before buds open in January and as they burst. Destroy infected leaves.

Powdery mildew

CROPS ATTACKED **Wide range**

DAMAGE/SYMPTOMS Leaves and shoots covered in white powder.
CONTROL Spray with systemic fungicide.

Reversion disease

CROPS ATTACKED **Blackcurrant**

DAMAGE/SYMPTOMS Leaves distorted; flowers pinkish purple.
CONTROL Burn. Control big bud mite, which spreads this virus disease.

Rust

CROPS ATTACKED **Plum, currant**

DAMAGE/SYMPTOMS Leaves spotted yellow on undersides; may fall early.
CONTROL Keep tree well fed and watered. Spray with Bio Dithane 945.

Shot hole

CROPS ATTACKED **Cherry, plum**

DAMAGE/SYMPTOMS Leaves full of small holes and spotted brown. No gummosis visible.
CONTROL Feed tree well and apply water. If gum oozing from bark, see Bacterial canker.

Silver leaf

CROPS ATTACKED **Plum and sometimes cherry, peach, nectarine**

DAMAGE/SYMPTOMS Leaves silvery in appearance on one or more branches; wood stained brown within.
CONTROL Cut out infected branches back to healthy tissue. Burn them. (See False silver leaf: Fruit Disorders)

Spur blight

CROPS ATTACKED **Raspberry, loganberry**

DAMAGE/SYMPTOMS Purplish areas develop around buds; buds fail to grow and soon wilt.
CONTROL Burn infected canes. Spray others with Bio Supercarb.

Stem rot (Collar rot)

CROPS ATTACKED **Melon**

DAMAGE/SYMPTOMS Stem base turns brown and rots.
CONTROL Prevent by not planting too deeply and by using sterilized compost.

Strawberry mildew

CROPS ATTACKED **Strawberry**

DAMAGE/SYMPTOMS Leaves purple blotched above, white beneath.
CONTROL Dust fortnightly with sulphur, from flower bud formation onwards.

Virus

CROPS ATTACKED **Raspberry, strawberry and others**

DAMAGE/SYMPTOMS Leaves distorted, twisted and often mottled yellow; yields down and vigour reduced.
CONTROL Dig up and burn affected plants. Control aphids, which spread the disease.

DISORDERS

Bitter pit

CROPS ATTACKED **Apple**

DAMAGE/SYMPTOMS Fruits spotted dark brown; flesh affected too. Tastes bitter.
CONTROL Keep trees well watered. Spray with calcium nitrate (28 g (1 oz) in 9 litres (2 gallons) water in mid-June and twice more at fortnightly intervals.

False silver leaf

CROPS ATTACKED **Cherry, plum**

DAMAGE/SYMPTOMS Leaves on entire tree turn silvery; no die-back.
CONTROL Water well and spray with foliar feed.

Frost damage

CROPS ATTACKED **Strawberry**

DAMAGE/SYMPTOMS Centres of flowers turn black.
CONTROL Cover flowering plants with straw, newspaper or cloches if frost threatens.

Fruit drop

CROPS ATTACKED **Apple, pear, plum**

DAMAGE/SYMPTOMS Fruitlets fall early; no sign of insect damage.
CONTROL There is a natural June drop in which the tree thins out its fruits. If they all drop, suspect lack of food, water or suitable pollinator.

Fruit not forming

CROPS ATTACKED **Wide range**

DAMAGE/SYMPTOMS Flowers appear but no fruit follows.
CONTROL Check that a suitable pollinator is present. Frost damage may produce the same symptoms.

Gummosis

CROPS ATTACKED **Cherry, plum**

DAMAGE/SYMPTOMS Clear gum oozing from trunk or main branch; no other symptoms.
CONTROL Cut off hardened gum. Feed tree with general fertilizer.

Nutrient deficiency

CROPS ATTACKED **Wide range**

DAMAGE/SYMPTOMS Areas between veins on leaves become yellow. No distortion.
CONTROL Enrich surrounding soil with general fertilizer.

Scald

CROPS ATTACKED **Grape**

DAMAGE/SYMPTOMS Berries scorched on side nearest glass.
CONTROL Shade and ventilate as necessary. Cut out affected fruits.

Shanking

CROPS ATTACKED **Grape**

DAMAGE/SYMPTOMS Fruit stalks wither; berries fail to develop and turn brown.
CONTROL Remove affected grapes. Keep soil evenly moist. Thin grape bunches.

ORNAMENTAL PLANTS

PESTS

Aphid

PLANTS ATTACKED **Wide range**

DAMAGE/SYMPTOMS Suck sap, weaken plant, secrete honeydew, transmit viruses.
CONTROL Spray with a specific aphicide such as Rapid Greenfly Killer.

Birds

PLANTS ATTACKED **Wide range**

DAMAGE/SYMPTOMS Leaves, shoots, flowers and fruits pecked.

CONTROL Netting is the only solution. Spray with 'Stay Off'.

Broom gall mite

PLANTS ATTACKED **Broom**

DAMAGE/SYMPTOMS Green or grey-brown, lumpy outgrowths appear on stems.
CONTROL Cut off and burn galls. Destroy badly infected plants.

Bulb scale mite

PLANTS ATTACKED **Narcissus**

DAMAGE/SYMPTOMS Bulbs in store are soft, lightweight and brown; slice open and specks are visible in tissue.
CONTROL Destroy infected bulbs.

Capsid bug

PLANTS ATTACKED **Wide range, especially rose**

DAMAGE/SYMPTOMS Leaves punctured with brown holes and distorted.
CONTROL Spray with systemic insecticide as the leaves unfold.

Carnation fly

PLANTS ATTACKED **Carnation**

DAMAGE/SYMPTOMS Maggots tunnel into stems, leaves, roots.
CONTROL Spray with Derris dust.

Caterpillar

PLANTS ATTACKED **Wide range**

DAMAGE/SYMPTOMS Leaves eaten; caterpillars or droppings visible.
CONTROL Pick off small infestations. Spray larger outbreaks with Miracle Sybol.

Chrysanthemum eelworm

PLANTS ATTACKED **Chrysanthemum**

DAMAGE/SYMPTOMS Leaves turn dark brown between the veins; eventually entirely brown.
CONTROL Burn infected plants and buy new stock. Plant in sterilized compost.

Cuckoo spit (Froghopper)

PLANTS ATTACKED **Wide range**

DAMAGE/SYMPTOMS Green insect shelters in blob of spittle on stem.
CONTROL Rub off or spray with Bio Fenitrothion.

Earwig

PLANTS ATTACKED **Dahlia and others**

DAMAGE/SYMPTOMS Flowers and leaves eaten.
CONTROL Trap in flowerpots stuffed with straw and inverted on garden canes. Tip into boiling water. Apply Bio Flydown or Miracle Picket at dusk.

Leaf cutter bee

PLANTS ATTACKED **Rose**

DAMAGE/SYMPTOMS Large pieces cut from leaf to leave scalloped effect.
CONTROL None. You'll just have to lump it! Leaf cutting bees are of some benefit as pollinating insects.

Leaf miner

PLANTS ATTACKED **Chrysanthemum, cineraria, holly**

DAMAGE/SYMPTOMS Leaves tunnelled by small grubs.
CONTROL Spray with Miracle Sybol where practicable, or pick off infected leaves.

Leaf rolling sawfly

PLANTS ATTACKED **Rose**

DAMAGE/SYMPTOMS Leaves curled under; caterpillars may be inside.
CONTROL Pick off isolated leaves. Spray with Bio Fenitrothion in May and again in June before attack.

Lily beetle

PLANTS ATTACKED **Lily and relations**

DAMAGE/SYMPTOMS Leaves eaten; scarlet beetles observed.
CONTROL Spray with Miracle Sybol. Only found in Surrey, Berkshire, Hampshire.

Narcissus fly

PLANTS ATTACKED *Narcissus*

DAMAGE/SYMPTOMS No flowers produced, only weak, grassy leaves. Cut bulbs reveal maggot.
CONTROL Destroy infested bulbs. Buy from reputable supplier. Dust naturalized bulbs with Murphy Gamma-BHC Dust after flowering.

Rhododendron bug

PLANTS ATTACKED **Rhododendron**

DAMAGE/SYMPTOMS Leaves mottled yellow above, brown beneath.
CONTROL Spray undersides of leaves with Miracle Sybol.

Slugs and snails

PLANTS ATTACKED **Wide range**

DAMAGE/SYMPTOMS Leaves and flowers eaten; silvery trails observed.
CONTROL As for slugs on vegetable crops.

Stem and bulb eelworm

PLANTS ATTACKED **Narcissus**

DAMAGE/SYMPTOMS Leaves distorted and yellow mottled; lack of flowers; brown rings within bulbs.
CONTROL Destroy infected bulbs. Buy from reputable supplier.

Stem eelworm

PLANTS ATTACKED **Phlox**

DAMAGE/SYMPTOMS Leaves narrow and distorted; stems split; growth stunted.
CONTROL Dig up and burn infected plants.

Thrips

PLANTS ATTACKED **Rose, gladiolus**

DAMAGE/SYMPTOMS Silvery grey discoloration on flowers and leaves and tiny black spots on upper leaf surface.
CONTROL Water plants regularly. Spray with Bio Fenitrothion.

Vine weevil

PLANTS ATTACKED **Rhododendron**

DAMAGE/SYMPTOMS Lower leaves eaten and shredded.
CONTROL Dust lower leaves and soil with Murphy Gamma-BHC Dust.

DISEASES

Azalea gall

PLANTS ATTACKED **Azalea**

DAMAGE/SYMPTOMS Green, red and then white swellings appear on leaves.
CONTROL Burn galls. Spray with Murphy Copper Fungicide.

Blackleg

PLANTS ATTACKED **Pelargonium (geranium)**

DAMAGE/SYMPTOMS Base of stem becomes black and soft; grey fur develops.
CONTROL Prevent by using sterile compost and by ventilating well. Pull off dead leaves.

Black slime

PLANTS ATTACKED **Hyacinth**

DAMAGE/SYMPTOMS Leaves turn yellow and collapse. Black resting bodies found between scales of bulb.
CONTROL Destroy infected bulbs. Do not replant in infected area. Use sterile composts.

Blackspot

PLANTS ATTACKED **Rose**

DAMAGE/SYMPTOMS Large black spots appear on leaves; leaves eventually fall.
CONTROL Pick off and burn infected leaves. Spray with Miracle Nimrod-T from April onwards.

Botrytis

PLANTS ATTACKED **Wide range**

DAMAGE/SYMPTOMS Parts of plant rotting and covered with grey fur.

CONTROL Pick off infected parts. Spray with Bio Supercarb.

Bud blast

PLANTS ATTACKED **Rhododendron**

DAMAGE/SYMPTOMS Buds turn brown and do not open; black 'pinheads' appear on them.
CONTROL Cut off and burn infected buds. Spray in late summer with Bio Fenitrothion to control leaf hoppers which spread the disease.

Canker

PLANTS ATTACKED **Rose**

DAMAGE/SYMPTOMS Rough, brown, sunken areas appear on stem.
CONTROL Cut out and burn infected stems. Spray with copper fungicide.

Carnation leaf spot

PLANTS ATTACKED **Carnation**

DAMAGE/SYMPTOMS Purplish brown spots appear on leaves.
CONTROL Burn badly infected leaves. Spray with Bio Dithane 945.

Clematis wilt

PLANTS ATTACKED **Clematis**

DAMAGE/SYMPTOMS One or more stems wilt, then collapse completely.
CONTROL Prune out infected shoots at ground level. Drench plant and soil with Bio Supercarb. Be patient.

Clubroot

PLANTS ATTACKED **Wallflower**

DAMAGE/SYMPTOMS Plants wilt and looked stunted; swollen, knobbly roots.
CONTROL Dip roots in Bio Liquid Clubroot Control. Lime acid soil.

Dutch elm disease

PLANTS ATTACKED **Elm**

DAMAGE/SYMPTOMS Trees look burned; eventually whole tree will die.

CONTROL None. Fell, then strip off the bark and burn it. Timber unaffected.

Grey bulb rot

PLANTS ATTACKED **Hyacinth**

DAMAGE/SYMPTOMS Top of bulb becomes dry and grey; black fungal resting bodies found.
CONTROL Burn infected plants. Do not plant bulbs in soil known to be infected.

Honey fungus (Armillaria)

PLANTS ATTACKED **Wide range, especially trees and shrubs**

DAMAGE/SYMPTOMS Trees or shrubs die back; honey-coloured toadstools may appear; white fungal threads and black 'bootlaces' in soil.
CONTROL Dig up and burn badly infected plants. Manure to improve vigour.

Ink disease

PLANTS ATTACKED **Bulbous irises**

DAMAGE/SYMPTOMS Black patches develop on bulb, and on leaves and flowers in wet weather.
CONTROL Burn infected bulbs. Prevent by spraying emerging leaves with Bio Dithane 945.

Leaf blight

PLANTS ATTACKED **Lily**

DAMAGE/SYMPTOMS Leaves covered with brown blotches.
CONTROL Remove and destroy infected growth. Spray with copper fungicide in wet weather.

Leaf spot

PLANTS ATTACKED **Dahlia, rhizomatous iris**

DAMAGE/SYMPTOMS Brown spots appear on leaves and eventually coalesce.
CONTROL Pull off and destroy infected leaves.

Powdery mildew

PLANTS ATTACKED **Rose, chrysanthemum and others**

DAMAGE/SYMPTOMS Leaves and shoots covered in white powder.
CONTROL Spray roses with Miracle Nimrod-T, other plants with bio Benlate.

Rhizome rot

PLANTS ATTACKED **Rhizomatous irises**

DAMAGE/SYMPTOMS Leaves turn brown from tips backwards; rhizomes rot and become slimy.
CONTROL Dig up and burn. Control slugs. Spray with copper fungicide. Improve drainage.

Rust

PLANTS ATTACKED **Rose, pelargonium, antirrhinum, hollyhock**

DAMAGE/SYMPTOMS Rusty brown marks appear on underside of leaves.
CONTROL Pick off badly infected leaves. Spray with Bio Dithane 945.

Scab

PLANTS ATTACKED **Gladiolus**

DAMAGE/SYMPTOMS Red-brown spots on leaves; growth may topple; black areas on corm.
CONTROL Destroy infected plants. Keep gladioli off infected ground.

Smoulder

PLANTS ATTACKED **Narcissus**

DAMAGE/SYMPTOMS Stored bulbs rot; growing leaves spotted and rotten; black resting bodies on bulb.
CONTROL Destroy infected stored bulbs. Spray growing ones with systemic fungicide.

Tulip fire

PLANTS ATTACKED **Tulip**

DAMAGE/SYMPTOMS Leaf tips scorched; straw-coloured streaks on leaves and flowers.

CONTROL Burn infected bulbs. Do not plant tulips in infected soil. Prevent by spraying with Bio Dithane 945.

Virus

PLANTS ATTACKED **Wide range**

DAMAGE/SYMPTOMS Leaves mottled with yellow and distorted.
CONTROL Destroy infected plants. Control aphids, which spread virus diseases.

Wilt

PLANTS ATTACKED **Michaelmas daisy**

DAMAGE/SYMPTOMS Leaves at stem bases wilt and shrivel; effect spreads up stem.
CONTROL Destroy infected plants. Do not replant on infected soil.

DISORDERS

Blind shoots

PLANTS ATTACKED **Narcissus**

DAMAGE/SYMPTOMS Leaves produced but flowers fail to appear.
CONTROL Make sure bulbs do not dry out in spring. Feed after flowering.

Bud drop

PLANTS ATTACKED **Camellia and others**

DAMAGE/SYMPTOMS Flower buds fall before they have a chance to open.
CONTROL Caused by dryness at roots – keep evenly moist and mulch.

Chlorosis

PLANTS ATTACKED **Wide range**

DAMAGE/SYMPTOMS Leaves yellow between veins. No distortion.
CONTROL Caused by food shortage. Feed well. Water plants on chalky soil with Iron Sequestrene.

A beautiful, well-planned garden, brimful of healthy plants that give year-round colour and interest, is the goal and reward of gardening.

Oedema

PLANTS ATTACKED *Pelargonium*

DAMAGE/SYMPTOMS Blisters form on undersides of leaves; eventually burst.
CONTROL Caused by overwatering and high humidity.

Peony wilt

PLANTS ATTACKED **Peony**

DAMAGE/SYMPTOMS Tree peony: unopened buds turn grey and rot. Herbaceous peony: leaf bases turn brown and collapse.
CONTROL Cut out infected growth.

UNDER COVER PLANTS

Hygiene is an important factor in reducing the risk of plant problems in the greenhouse (see p.261), whereas most house plant disorders can be avoided by providing your plants with the right growing conditions.

PESTS

See also under Ornamental Plants

Aphid

PLANTS ATTACKED **Wide range**

DAMAGE/SYMPTOMS Sap sucked; plant weakened; honeydew secreted; viruses transmitted.
CONTROL Spray with a specific aphicide such as Rapid Greenfly Killer.

Caterpillars

PLANTS ATTACKED **Wide range**

DAMAGE/SYMPTOMS Leaves eaten; caterpillars or green droppings visible.
CONTROL Fumigate greenhouse with Fumite Whitefly Smoke; hand pick from house plants.

Earwig

PLANTS ATTACKED **Wide range**

DAMAGE/SYMPTOMS Young leaves and flowers eaten.

CONTROL Fumigate greenhouse with pest smoke. Scrub down greenhouse in winter.

Mealy bug

PLANTS ATTACKED **Wide range**

DAMAGE/SYMPTOMS Oval bugs covered in white wax suck sap and secrete honeydew.
CONTROL Spray with Bio Flydown.

Red spider mite

PLANTS ATTACKED **Wide range**

DAMAGE/SYMPTOMS Leaves bleached; webs spun; tiny mites visible on foliage.
CONTROL Discourage by maintaining a humid atmosphere. Spray with Bio Fenitrothion or Malathion. Fumigate with Murphy Pest and Disease Smoke.

Root aphid

PLANTS ATTACKED **Small range**

DAMAGE/SYMPTOMS Plant wilts and looks stunted; aphids found among roots.
CONTROL Destroy isolated infections. Water compost with diluted Malathion.

Scale insect

PLANTS ATTACKED **Wide range**

DAMAGE/SYMPTOMS Brown, limpet-like scales on stems and leaves; honeydew secreted.
CONTROL Spray with Bio Flydown.

Slugs and snails

PLANTS ATTACKED **Wide range**

DAMAGE/SYMPTOMS Leaves and flowers eaten; silvery trails visible.
CONTROL Pick off pot plants. Use beer traps in greenhouse borders.

Symphilid

PLANTS ATTACKED **Small range**

DAMAGE/SYMPTOMS Plants wilt and

look stunted and blue-grey; tiny, white grubs with 12 pairs of legs can be found among roots.
CONTROL Treat affected plants with diluted Murphy Gamma BHC Dust.

Thrips

PLANTS ATTACKED **Wide range**

DAMAGE/SYMPTOMS Leaves and flowers speckled with white.
CONTROL Spray with Bio Sprayday or fumigate with Fumite Whitefly Smoke.

Vine weevil

PLANTS ATTACKED **Small range including cyclamen**

DAMAGE/SYMPTOMS Plants wilt and look sick. Fat, 1 cm (½ in) long creamy white grubs may be found among eaten roots.
CONTROL Destroy infected plants. Use sterile compost or Levington's compost containing Intercept.

Whitefly

PLANTS ATTACKED **Wide range**

DAMAGE/SYMPTOMS White V-shaped flies on undersides of leaves; honeydew secreted.
CONTROL Spray with Bio Flydown or Sprayday. Fumigate as for thrips.

DISEASES

Algae

PLANTS ATTACKED **Paths, pots and compost surface**

DAMAGE/SYMPTOMS Green, slimy growth on paths, pots and compost surface.
CONTROL Scrub off paths. Add sharp grit to improve surface drainage of compost.

Blackleg

PLANTS ATTACKED **Pelargonium (geranium)**

See under Ornamental Plants.

Damping off

PLANTS ATTACKED **Wide range of seedlings**

DAMAGE/SYMPTOMS Seedlings keel over at stem bases and die off.
CONTROL Prevent by sowing thinly, ventilating well and watering with Cheshunt Compound.

Sooty mould

PLANTS ATTACKED **Wide range**

DAMAGE/SYMPTOMS Black felt appears on leaves and stems.
CONTROL Grows on honeydew secreted by aphids etc. Control the pest; sponge off the mould.

LAWNS

It is fine lawns that are most troubled by disease: the coarser more rugged grasses are seldom attacked by fungi, Brown areas are most likely caused by fertilizer scorch or bitch urine.

PESTS

Ants

DAMAGE/SYMPTOMS A nuisance where picnics are popular. Fine soil brought to surface to provide a spot for weeds and moss.
CONTROL Dust nests with Ant Killer.

Birds

DAMAGE/SYMPTOMS Only a nuisance when lawns are being sown because they eat the seeds. They also eat lawn pests.
CONTROL Sow enough seeds for the lawn and the birds.

Dogs

DAMAGE/SYMPTOMS Bitches in season have strong urine that burns the grass.
CONTROL Spike area with a fork and water immediately to reduce caustic effect.

Leatherjackets

DAMAGE/SYMPTOMS Patches of grass turn yellow. If watered and covered with polythene overnight, grey grubs will be found on the surface in the morning.
CONTROL Water turf in autumn with Miracle Sybol Dust.

Moles

DAMAGE/SYMPTOMS Molehills appear.
CONTROL Set traps in runs to catch offending mole – release it where it can do no harm. If adjacent to farmland there's no way of controlling moles.

Worms

DAMAGE/SYMPTOMS Wormcasts appear on surface.
CONTROL Brush them off. Worms should be tolerated on all except bowling green lawns.

DISEASES

Algae

DAMAGE/SYMPTOMS Dark green slimy areas appear, usually in damp, shady spots.
CONTROL Spike and aerate lawn. Treat with Bio Mosskiller or Murphy Tumblemoss.

Damping off

DAMAGE/SYMPTOMS Newly germinated grass seedlings wilt, turn brown and die – especially in humid weather.
CONTROL Water with Cheshunt Compound at the earliest sign of disease.

Dollar spot

DAMAGE/SYMPTOMS Straw-coloured patches 2.5–5 cm (1–2 in) across appear on lawn in late summer; they enlarge and join together.
CONTROL Feed lawn well. Water each square metre (square yard) of the infected lawn with 7 g (¼ oz) sulphate of iron diluted in 2.25 litres (4 pints) water.

Fairy rings

DAMAGE/SYMPTOMS Dark green rings appear on lawn, often accompanied by toadstools.
CONTROL Water with 500 g (1 lb) sulphate of iron in 7 litres (1½ gallons) water – enough for 3 square metres (square yards).

Fusarium patch

DAMAGE/SYMPTOMS Grass patches turn yellow then brown before dying off. White or pink fungus strands visible.
CONTROL Prevent by keeping lawn well fed. Water each square metre (square yard) of infected lawn with 7 g (¼ oz) sulphate of iron diluted in 2.25 litres (4 pints) water.

Moss

DAMAGE/SYMPTOMS Moss colonizes areas of soil between grass – especially under trees and in shade.
CONTROL Improve drainage, do not mow so close, feed lawn well, relieve shady conditions, relieve acidity. Moss killers will kill existing moss but will not remove cause.

Red thread

DAMAGE/SYMPTOMS Small patches of pale pink to red fungal growth appear on the lawn in summer and autumn, the patches later become bleached. 'Stag's horn' fruiting bodies are produced. The lawn is very rarely killed completely.
CONTROL Spike lawn regularly and feed well to prevent attack. Scatter 14 g (½ oz) sulphate of ammonia over each square metre (square yard) of affected lawn. Water in.

index

Page numbers in *italic* refer to illustrations

Abelia x *grandiflora*, 56
Abutilon vitifolium, 92
Acaena, 174
Acanthus, 118
Acer griseum, 46, 47; *A. japonicum* 'Vitifolium', 46; *A. negundo* 'Variegatum', 46; *A. palmatum*, 56; *A. pseudoplatanus* 'Brilliantissimum', 46; *A. shirasawanum* 'Aureum', 56
Achillea, 118, *151*
Acid soils, 14, 167
Aconite, winter, *158-9*
Aconitum, 118
Acorus calamus, 186
Acrolinium, 142
Actinidia kolomikta, 92
Adam's needle, 79
Adiantum capillus-veneris, 274
Adonis aestivalis, 142
Aechmea fasciata, 274
Aethionema, 174
African violet, 24, 25, 280
Agapanthus, 118
Ageratum, 147; *A. houstonianum* 'Navaria', *147*
Agrostemma 'Milas', 142
Ajuga, 118
Alcea, 118
Alchemilla, *111*, 118
Alder, golden, 46
Algae, 298, 299
Alkaline soils, 14, 167
Allium, 156; *A. cristophii*, *156-57*
Almond, 73
Alnus glutinosa 'Aurea', 46
Aloysia, 97
Alpines, 166-77
Alstroemeria, *118-20*
Althaea, *123*
Alum root, 128
Aluminium plant, 280
Alyssum, 142, 174
Amaranthus caudatos, 145; *A.* 'Illumination', *147*
Amaryllis, 278
Amaryllis belladonna, 156-7
Amberboa moschata, 146
Amelanchier canadensis, 56
American gooseberry mildew, 292
Anagallis 'Coerulea', *147*
Anaphalis, 120
Anchusa, 120; *A. capensis* 'Blue Angel', 142
Androsace, 174
Anemone, 120, 157
Angelica tree, Japanese, 56-7
Angel's fishing rod, 124
Annuals, 138-51
Antirrhinum, 147, *151*
Ants, 299
Aphelandra squarrosa, 274
Aphids, *285*, 286, 290, 294, 298
Aponogeton distachyos, 186
Apple, 218-21; cherry, 48; Japanese crab, 48
Apple sawfly, *285*, 290

Apple sucker, 290
Aquatic plants, 182-3, 186-7
Aquilegia, 120, *123*
Arabis, 174
Aralia, finger, 277
Aralia elata, 56-7
Arbours, 89
Arbutus unedo, 46
Arches, climbers, 89-90
Arctotis, 147
Argemone, 142
Armeria, 174
Arrowhead, 187
Artemisia, 120
Artichoke: Globe, 236; Jerusalem, 236
Arum, 120
Arum, bog, 186
Aruncus, 120
Arundinaria, 57
Asparagus, *236*
Asparagus densiflorus, 274; *A. setaceus*, 274
Asperula azurea setosa, 142
Aspidistra elatior, 274
Asplenium, 120; *A. nidus*, 274
Aster, 120-1, *134*, 147
Astilbe, 121
Astrantia, 121
Atriplex hortensis var. *rubra*, 142
Aubergine, 265
Aubrieta, 174
Aucuba japonica, 84; *A. japonica* 'Variegata', 57
Aunt Eliza, 123
Avens, 127; mountain, 175
Azalea, 73-4, 280
Azalea gall, 295
Azolla caroliniana, 187

Baby blue eyes, 145
Baby's breath, 127
Bacterial canker, 292
Balloon flower, 132
Ballota, 121
Balsam, 279
Bamboo, 57
Barberry, 57, 84
Bark, shrubs, 69
Barrenwort, 126
Basil, 245
Bay, sweet, 68-9
Bean: broad, 236-7; French, 237, 267; runner, *237*
Bear's breech, 118
Bed systems, vegetables, 235
Bedding plants, 138-51
Bee balm, 131
Beech, 82, 85
Bees, 189
Beet, leaf, 237-8
Beet leaf miner, *285*, 287
Beetroot, 237
Begonia, 22; *B. maculata*, 274; *B. rex*, 25-6, 275; *B. semperflorens*, 147, 262, 275; *B.* x *tuberhybrida*, 275
Bellflower, 121-2, 174
Bellis perennis, 150
Bells of Ireland, 145

Berberis darwinii, 57, 84; *B.* x *ottawensis* f. *purpurea*, 57; *B.* x *stenophylla*, 57, 84; *B. thunbergii*, 57-8
Bergamot, 131
Bergenia, 121
Berries: hedges, 86; shrubs, 69
Betony, 136
Betula ermanii, 46; *B. papyrifera*, 46; *B. pendula* 'Laciniata', 46; *B. utilis* var. *jacquemontii*, 46-7
Biennials, 139, 141, 150-1
Big bud mite, 290
Billbergia nutans, 275
Birch: Erman's, 46; Kashmir, 46-7; paper-bark, 46; Swedish, 46
Birds, 189-90, 286, 290, 294, 299
Bishop's hat, 126
Bitter pit, 293
Black-eyed Susan, 134
Black rot, 287
Black slime, 295
Blackberry, 221
Blackcurrant, 221-3
Blackleg, 287, 295, 298
Blackspot, *285*, 295
Blackthorn, 82
Bladderwort, 186
Blanket flower, 126-7, 149
Blechnum, 121
Bleeding heart, 124
Blind shoots, 296
Blood, bone and fishmeal, 14
Blossom end rot, 289
Blossom weevil, 290
Blossom wilt, 292
Bog bean, 187
Bog plants, 182, 187
Bolting, 289
Bonemeal, 14-15
Border plants, 112-37
Botrytis, *285*, 292, 295
Bottle gardens, *271*
Bouncing Bet, 134
Bowles' golden grass, 131
Box, 59, 83, 84; dwarf, 84
Brachyscome, 148
Brandy bottle, 186
Brick, patios, 205, 206
Broccoli, 238
Broom, 62, 64-5; Moroccan, 94-5
Broom gall mite, 294
Browallia speciosa 'Blue Troll', 262
Brown rot, 292
Brown scale, 290
Brunnera, 121
Brussels sprout, 238
Buckeye rot, 287
Bud blast, 295
Bud drop, 296
Buddleja alternifolia, 58; *B. davidii*, 58-9
Bugbane, 122
Bugle, 118
Bulb scale mite, 294
Bulbs, 27, *152-63*
Bull bay, 97
Butomus umbellatus, 186
Butterflies, 188-9
Butterfly bush, 58-9
Buxus sempervirens, 59, 84, *86-87*; *B. sempervirens* 'Suffruticosa', 84

Cabbage, *238-9*; ornamental, 142
Cabbage root fly, 286
Cabbage whitefly, 286
Cacalia, 142
Cactus, Christmas, 281

Calabrese, 238
Calamintha, 121
Calamondin orange, 275
Calandrinia umbellata, 148
Calceolaria, 22, 262, 275; *C.* 'Sunshine', 148
Calendula, 142
Calla palustris, 186
Calluna, 65
Caltha palustris, 186
Camassia, 157
Camellia, 25, 26; *C. japonica*, 92; *C. japonica* 'Tricolor', *93*; *C.* x *williamsii*, 59
Campanula, 121-2, 174; *C. medium*, 150; *C. speculum* 'Violetta', *143*
Canary creeper, 142
Candytuft, 143; perennial, 176
Cane blight, 292
Cane spot, 292
Canker, 287, 292, 295
Canterbury bell, 150
Capsicum annuum, 275
Capsid bug, *285*, 290, 294
Cardinal flower, 129-30
Cardoon, 123
Carex, 122
Carnation, 124, 148, 262
Carnation fly, 294
Carnation leaf spot, 295
Carpenteria californica, 92
Carpinus betulus, 84
Carrot, 239
Carrot fly, 286
Caryopteris x *clandonensis*, 59
Cast iron plant, 274
Castor oil plant, 150
Catananche, 122
Catch cropping, 234-5
Catchfly, 177
Caterpillars, *285*, 286, 290, 294, 298
Catmint, 131
Cauliflower, 239-40
Ceanothus, 92-3
Celeriac, 240
Celery, *240*
Celery fly, 286
Celosia argentea 'Fairy Fountains', 262
Centaurea, 122; *C. cyanus*, 143; *C. gymnocarpa*, 148; *C. moschata*, 146
Centranthus, 122
Cerastium, 174
Ceratostigma, 122
Cercis siliquastrum, 47
Chaenomeles, 93
Chalky soils, 14
Chamaecyparis, 59; *C. lawsoniana*, 47, 84
Chamaedorea elegans, 275
Cheiranthus allionii, 151; *C. cheiri*, 151
Chemical pest and disease control, 284
Cherry, 73, 222-3; 'Bigarreau Napoleon', *222*; Japanese, 49; purple-leaf sand, 86; Sato, 49; Tibetan, *39*, 49; winter, 49-50, 281
Cherry fruit moth, 291
Chilean fire bush, 63
Chilean glory, 95
Chilean potato tree, 98
Chinese lantern flower, 132
Chionodoxa forbesii, 157
Chives, 245
Chlorophytum comosum, 275
Chlorosis, 296

Chocolate spot, 287
Choisya ternata, 59
Christmas box, 76
Christmas rose, 127-8
Chrysanthemum, 122, 262-3;
  C. carinatum, 143;
  C. x *morifolium*, 275
Chrysanthemum eelworm, *285*, 294
Cimicifuga, 122
Cineraria, 279
Cinquefoil, 73, 133
Cissus, 280; *C. antarctica*, 275;
  C. rhombifolia, 275
Cistus, 60; *C.* 'Silver Pink', *60-61*
x *citrofortunella microcarpa*, 275
Clarkia elegans, 143
Clary, 146
Clay soils, 12, 13
Clematis, 25, 26, 94-5: *C. montana*
  'Elizabeth', *89*; *C. Montana* var.
  rubens, *33*
Clematis wilt, 295
Cleome spinosa, 148, *215*
Climbers, 88-99; roses, 101, 110-11
Cloches, *235*
Clubroot, *285*, 287, 295
Cobaea scandens, 263
Codiaeum variegatum, 275
Codling moth, 291
Coir-based composts, 259
Colchicum, 157-8
Colour: bedding plants, 138;
  single-colour schemes, 113
Columbine, 120
Compost, *13*
Composts, pot plants, 258-9
Coneflower, 134, 146; purple, 125
Conifers: dwarf, 175; hedges, 82, 83
Containers: bulbs, 154-5; climbers
  in, 90; composts, 258-9; on
  patios, 206-11; staging, 255-6
Convallaria, 122
Convolvulus 'Blue Flash', 143;
  C. cneorum, 60
Coral bells, 128
Coral berry, 77
Coral spot, 292
Cordons, 216, *217*, 220
Cordyline indivisa, 276;
  C. terminalis, 276
Coreopsis, 122, 143
Corms, 27, 152, *153*
Corn cockle, 142
Cornflower, 122, 143
Cornus alba, 60; *C. kousa*, 60
Cortaderia, 122-3
Corydalis, 123
Corylus avellana 'Contorta', 60;
  C. maxima 'Purpurea', 60, 84
Cosmos, 148, *215*
Cotinus coggygria, 62
Cotoneaster, fishbone, 94
Cotoneaster, 62; *C. horizontalis*, 94;
  C. simonsii, 84
Cotton lavender, 76
Courgette, 242
Crambe, 123
Crataegus monogyna, 84;
  C. laevigata 'Paul's Scarlet', 47
Creeping Jenny, 130
Crepis rubra, 143
Cress: purple rock, 174; rock, 174;
  stone, 174
Crocosmia. 123; *C. paniculata*, 123
Crocus, 158
Crocus, autumn, 157-8
Crop rotation, 185, 233

Croton, 276
Crowfoot, water, 186
Crown gall, 292
Crown imperial, 159
Crown rot, 287-8
Cuckoo pint, 120
Cuckoo spit, *285*, 294
Cucumber, *265-6*
Cup flower, 176
Cuphea ignea, 263
Cupid's dart, 122
x *Cupressocyparis leylandii*, 81, 84
Currant: flowering, 75, 82
Currant blister aphid, 291
Currant sawfly, 291
Cuttings, 23-6; composts for, 259
Cunninghamia lanceolata, 47
Cycas revoluta, 276
Cyclamen, 158, 276
Cydonia, 93
Cynara, 123
Cyperus albostriatus, 276;
  C. alternifolius, 276
Cypress, 59; Lawson, 47, 84;
  Leyland, 81, 84
Cytisus, 62; *C. battandieri*, 94-5

Daboecia, 65
Daffodil, 161-2; winter, 162
Dahlia, 148, 158
Daisy: African, 147; double, 150;
  Livingstone, 149; Shasta, 122;
  Swan River, 148
Daisy bush, 70; New Zealand, 85
Damping off, 299
Damson, 229-30
Daphne, 62
Davidia involucrata, 47
Deadheading: border plants, 116-17; roses, 104
Deadnettle, 129
Delphinium, *123-4*, 144, 148
Dendranthema, 276
Deutzia x *magnifica*, 62
Dianthus, 124, 175; *D. barbatus*, 151; *D. heddewigii*, 148
Diascia, 175
Dibbers, *32*
Dicentra, 124
Dictamnus, 124
Dieffenbachia seguine, 276;
  D. seguine 'Amoena', 276;
Dierama, 124
Diervilla, 79
Digging, *15-17*, 114
Digitalis, 124, 150, *151*
Dimorphotheca, 143
Dionaea muscipula, 277
Dipsacus fullonum, 150
Diseases *see* Pests
Dittany, 124, 176
Division, 23
Dogwood, 60
Dollar spot, 299
Doronicum, 125
Dove tree, 47
Downy mildew, *285*, 288
Dracaena, 277
Dracocephalum moldavica, 143
Dragon tree, 276, 277
Drainage, 12; rock gardens, 166
Drills, sowing seeds, *21*
Dry rot, 288
Dryas, 175
Dryopteris, 125
Dumb cane, 276-7
Dusty miller, 148
Dutch elm disease, 295-6

Earwigs, 294, 298
Eccremocarpus scaber, 95

Echinacea, 125
Echinops, 125; *E. ritro*, *125*
Echium, 143
Edelweiss, 176
Eelworm, 286
Elaeagnus pungens 'Maculata', 62-3
Elder, 76; box, 46
Elephant's ears, 121
Elodea canadensis, 186
Embothrium coccineum, 63
Emilia, 143
Epilobium, 126
Epimedium, 126
Equipment, *28-35*
Eranthis hyemalis, *158-9*
Eremurus, 126
Erica, 65; *E.* 'Hyemalis', 277
Erigeron, 126, 175
Erinus, 175
Erodium, 175
Eryngium, 126
Erysimum x *allionii*, 151; *E. cheiri*, 151
Erythronium, 159
Escallonia 'Donard Star', 63;
  E. rubra var. *macrantha*, 84-5
Eschscholzia, 143; *E.* 'Special
  Mixed' *234*
Espaliers, 216, *217*
Eucalyptus pauciflora ssp.
  niphophila, 47
Eucryphia x *nymansensis*
  'Nymansay', 63
Euonymus europaeus, 64; *E. fortunei*
  'Emerald 'n' Gold', 64;
  E. japonicus, 85
Euphorbia, 126, 175;
  E. pulcherrima, 277
Evening primrose, 131
Evergreens: in containers, 210;
  shrubs, 65
Exacum affine, 263

F1 hybrid seeds, 21
Fagus sylvatica, 85
Fairy rings, 201, 299
Fairy wand flower, 124
Fallopia baldschuanica, 98
False silver leaf, 293
x *Fatshedera lizei*, 277
Fatsia japonica, 64, *277*
Feather grass, 136
Fennel, 245
Fern: asparagus, 274; bird's nest,
  274; Boston, 279; hart's tongue,
  120; ladder, 279; maidenhair,
  274; male, 125; ostrich plume,
  130; stag's horn, 280
Fertilizers, 13, 14-15; border
  plants, 116; bulbs, 155;
  climbers, 91; composts, 259;
  containers, 209; greenhouse
  plants, 261; house plants, 272;
  lawns, 198; roses, 104; shrubs,
  55; vegetable gardens, 233
Fescue grass, 126
Festuca, 126
Ficus, 25, 26; *F. benjamina*, 277;
  F. elastica, 277; *F. pumila*, 278
Fig: creeping, 278; weeping, 278
Figwort, 124
Filbert, purple-leafed, 60
Fir, Chinese, 47
Fireblight, 292
Firethorn, 86, 98
Fish, 183-4
Flag, 128; sweet, 186; yellow, 187
Flame nettle, 276
Flax, 129; New Zealand, 132
Flea beetle, 286

Fleabane, 126, 175
Floss flower, 147
Flower of a day, 137
Focal points, shrubs, 52-3, 63
Foliage, plants for, 74, 210-11
Foliar feeds, 15
Foot rot, 288
Forget-me-not, 151; water, 187
Forsythia x *intermedia* 'Lynwood',
  64; *F.* x *intermedia* 'Spectabilis',
  85
Fountains, 185
Four o'clock plant, 149
Foxglove, 124, 150, *151*
Fremontia, 95
Fremontodendron californicum, 95
Frit fly, 286
Fritillaria, 159
Frogbit, 187
Frost damage, 293
Fruit, 214-31; greenhouses, 265-7;
  hedges, 86; pests and diseases,
  290-4; trees, 51
Fuchsia, Californian, 177
Fuchsia, 263-4, 278;
  F. magellanica, 64, 85
Fumitory, 123
Fungi, in lawns, 201
Funkia, 128
Fusarium patches, *285*, 299

Gage, 229-30
Gaillardia, 126-7, 148
Galanthus, 159
Galega, 127
Gall weevil, 286
Galtonia candicans, 159
Gangrene, 288
Garrya elliptica, 95
Gaultheria mucronata, 64-5, 72
Gazania, 149
Genista, 65
Gentiana, 127, 175
Geranium (*Pelargonium*), 23, 264-5, 279
Germination, seeds, 21
Geranium (Cranesbill), *111*, 127, 175
Geum, 127
Ghost spot, 288
Gilia 'Summer Song', 143
Ginkgo biloba, 47
Gladiolus, 159-60
Gleditsia triacanthos 'Sunburst',
  48, *138*
Globe flower, 137
Glory of the snow, 157
Gloxinia, 22, 281
Glyceria, 127; *G. maxima* var.
  variegata, 186
Goat's beard, 120
Goat's rue, 127
Godetia, 143
Gold dust, 174
Golden bells, 64, 85
Golden club, 187
Golden rod, 135-6
Gomphrena globosa 'Buddy', 264
Gooseberry, 224; fuchsia-flowered,
  98
Gooseberry sawfly, 291
Gorse, 82, 86
Gourd, 149
Grafting, fruit trees, 216
Grape hyacinth, 161
Grapes, 225-7
Grass: lawns, 192-201;
  naturalizing bulbs in, 153, 154
Gravel: gravel beds, 113-14;
  patios, 202
Greenfly, *285*

Greenhouses, *250-67*; pests and diseases, 298-9
Grey bulb rot, 296
Grey mould, 288
Gromwell, 176
Ground cover: border plants, 113, 136; roses, 111; shrubs, 58
Growmore, 14
Gum, snow, 47
Gummosis, 294
Gunnera, 127
Gypsophila, 127; *G. elegans*, 143

Half-hardy annuals, 139, 140-1, 147-50
Halo blight, 288
Hamamelis mollis, 65
Hanging baskets, 207-9, 280
Hardwood cuttings, *24*, 25
Hardy annuals, 139-41, 142-6
Hardy perennials, 112
Hattie's pincushion, 121
Hawksbeard, 143
Hawthorn, 82; quick, 84; water, 186
Hazel, 82; corkscrew, 60; purple-leafed, 84
Heart rot, 288
Heath: Cape, 277; prickly, 72
Heather, 27, 66
Heating: greenhouses, 256; house plants, 270
Hebe, 66-7
Hedera, 67, 96, 278
Hedges, 80-7; roses, 107
Helenium, 127
Helianthemum, 176
Helianthus, 146
Helichrysum, 149
Heliotrope, 149
Helipterum manglesii, 146
Helleborus, 127-8
Hemerocallis, 128
Heptapleurum, 280
Herbicides, 18-19
Herbs, 245-6
Heron's bill, 175
Heuchera, 128
Hibiscus syriacus, 67
Hippeastrum, 278
Hoheria lyallii, 96
Holly, 68, 82, 85; variegated, 48
Hollyhock, 118, *123*
Honesty, 151
Honey fungus, 288, 293, 296
Honey locust, 48
Honeysuckle, 97; bush, 79; Himalayan, 69
Hop, golden-leafed, 96
Hornbeam, 82, 84; hop, 48-9
Hosta, 128
Hottonia palustris, 186
House plants, 268-81
Houseleek, 177
Houttuynia cordata 'Flore Pleno', 187
Howea belmoreana, 278; *H. forsteriana*, 278
Hoya carnosa, 278
Humidity: greenhouses, 257; house plants, 270
Humulus lupulus 'Aureus', 96
Humus, 12
Hyacinthus, 160
Hydrangea macrophylla, 67; *H. paniculata*, 68; *H. petiolaris*, 96
Hydrocharis morsus-ranae, 187
Hydroculture, *271-2*
Hygiene, greenhouses, 261
Hypericum, 68, 176

Hypertufa, 170
Hypoestes phyllostachya, 264

Iberis, 143, 176
Ice plant, 135
Ilex x *altaclerensis* 'Golden King', 48; *I. aquifolium*, 68, 85
Impatiens, 24, 149, 278
Incarvillea, 128
Inch plant, 281
Ink disease, 296
Insulation, greenhouses, 256-7
Intercropping, 234
Ionopsidium, 143
Ipomoea, 149
Iris, 23, 128, 160-1; *I. laevigata*, 187; *I. pseudacorus*, 187; *I. reticulata*, *160*
Ironwood, Persian, 49
Island beds, 112
Ivy, 66-7, 96, 278; Boston, 97; grape, 280
Ivy tree, 277

Jacob's ladder, 132-3
Japonica, 93
Jasmine: rock, 174; winter, 96
Jasminum nudiflorum, 96
John Innes composts, 258-9
Joseph's coat, 276
Judas tree, 47
Juncus effusus 'Spiralis', 187
Juniper, 68
Juniperus, 68
Justicia brandegeeana 278

Kale, 240-1
Kangaroo vine, 275
Kansas gayfeather, 129
Kerria japonica 'Pleniflora', 69
Kingcup, 186
Kirengeshoma, 129
Knapweed, 122
Kniphofia, 129
Knotweed, 133, 176
Kochia, 143
Kohl rabi, 241

Labelling, rock plants, 173
Laburnum x *wateri* 'Vossii', 48
Lad's love, 120
Lady's mantle, 118
Lamb's ears, 136
Lamium, 129
Land clearance, 12
Larch: European, 48; golden, 50
Larix decidua, 48
Larkspur, 123-4, 143
Lathyrus, 129; *L. latifolius*, 96; *L. odoratus*, 146
Laurel, 82, 83; cherry, 73, 86; spotted, 57, 84; victor's, 68-9
Laurel magnolia, 97
Laurus nobilis, 69
Laurustinus, 82, 86
Lavandula, 69, 85; *L. stoechas*, 246
Lavatera, 144; *L.* 'Rosea', 69
Lavender, 69, 85; cotton, 76; French, 246; sea, 150
Lawn mowers, 35
Lawns, 192-201; pests and diseases, 199
Layering, *26-7*
Layia elegans, 144
Leaf and bud mite, 291
Leaf blight, 296
Leaf cutter bee, 294
Leaf cuttings, *24-6*
Leaf midge, 291
Leaf miner, 294
Leaf mould, 13-14, 288

Leaf rolling sawfly, 294
Leaf spot, *285*, 288, 293, 296
Leatherjackets, 299
Leek, *241*
Leek moth, 286
Leek rust, *285*, 288
Legousia speculum-veneris, 144
Leontopodium, 176
Leopard's bane, 125
Leptosiphon, 144
Lettuce, 241-2
Leucojum, 161
Lewisia, 176
Leycesteria formosa, 70
Leyland cypress, 81, 84
Liatris, 129
Lighting: greenhouses, 256; house plants, 270; patios, 206
Ligustrum ovalifolium, 85
Lilac, 77; Californian, 92-3
Lilium, 161
Lily, 27, 161; arum, 137; belladonna, 156-7; blue African, 118; day, 128; diamond, 162; foxtail, 126; Kaffir, 162; Peruvian, 118-20; spire, 159; sword, 159-60; trout, 159; wood, 177
Lily beetle, 294
Lily of the field, 162
Lily-of-the-valley, 122
Lily-of-the-valley bush, 73
Lime trees, 44
Liming, vegetable gardens, 233
Limnanthes, 144; *L. douglasii*, 144
Limonium, 215
Linaria, 129; *L.* 'Fairy Bouquet', 144
Liners, pools, 179-81
Ling, 65
Linum, 129; *L. grandiflorum* 'Rubrum', 144
Lippia citriodora, 97
Liriope, 129
Lithodora, 176
Lithospermum, 176
Loam, 258-9
Lobelia, 22, 129-30, 149
Loganberry, 221
Lonas inodora, 144
Lonicera, 97; *L. nitida*, 82, 85
Loosestrife, 130
Lords and ladies, 120
Love-in-a-mist, 145
Love-lies-bleeding, 144
Lunaria, 151
Lungwort, 133
Lupinus, *130*
Lychnis, 130
Lysimachia, 130

Macleaya, 130
Madwort, 174
Magnolia, 70; *M. grandiflora*, 97
Mahonia, 70
Maidenhair tree, 47
Mallow, 130, 144; tree, 69
Malope, 145
Malus floribunda, 47, 48; *M.* 'John Downie', 48
Malva, 130
Maltese cross, 130
Manuring, vegetable gardens, 233
Maple: downy Japanese, 46; Japanese, 56; paperbark, 46
Maranta, 278
Marigold: African, 149, 150; Afro-French, 149; French, 149, 150; marsh, 186; pot, 143
Marjoram, 245-6
Marrow, 242

Masterwort, 121
Matricaria 'Golden Ball', 149
Matteuccia, 130
Matthiola longipetula, 145
Meadow rue, 136
Mealy bug, 291, 298
Mealy cabbage aphid, 286
Meconopsis, 130-1
Megasea, 121
Melon, 266
Mentha aquatica, 187
Mentzelia, 145
Menyanthes trifoliata, 187
Mesembryanthemum, 149
Mespilus, snowy, 56
Metasequoia glyptostroboides, 48, 85
Mexican orange blossom, 59
Michaelmas daisy, 120-1
Mignonette, 145
Mile-a-minute, 98
Milfoil, water, 186
Milium, 131
Mimulus, 131, 149; *M.* Calypso Series, 264
Mint, 246; water, 187
Mirabilis, 149
Mock orange, 72; Californian, 92
Moles, 201, 299
Moluccella, 145
Monarda, 131
Monkey flower, 131, 149
Monkshood, 118
Monstera deliciosa, 279
Montbretia, 123
Morina, 131
Morning glory, 149
Morus nigra, 48
Moss, 299; fairy floating, 187; in lawns, 201
Mother-in-law's tongue, 280
Mother-of-thousands, 280
Mountain ash, 51
Mountain cabbage tree, 276
Mowing lawns, 199-200
Mulberry, black, 48
Mulches, 12, 15; border plants, 117; hedges, 81; roses, 104; shrubs, 55; trees, 43; vegetable gardens, 233
Mullein, 137, 151, 177
Muscari, 161
Mussel scale, 291
Myosotis, 151; *M. scorpiodes*, 187
Myriophyllum, 186
Myrtle, 70
Myrtus communis, 70, *71*

Naked ladies, 157-8
Narcissus, 161-2
Narcissus fly, 295
Nasturtium, *145*
Neck rot, 288
Nectarine, 227-8
Nemesia, 149
Nemophila, 145
Nepeta, 131, *145*; *N. sibirica* 'Souvenir d'André Chaudron', *37*
Nephrolepis exaltata, 279; *N. exaltata* 'Bostoniensis', 279
Nerine bowdenii, 162
Nicandra, 145
Nicotiana, 149, *215*
Nierembergia, 176
Nigella, 145
Nolana 'Lavender Gown', 149
Nuphar lutea, 186
Nymphaea, 186
Nyssa sylvatica, 48

Obedient plant, 132
Oedema, 298
Oenothera, 131
Olearia, 70; *O.* x *haastii*, 85
Oleaster, 62-3
Onion, 242; ornamental, 156
Onion fly, 286-7
Orach, 142
Organic pest control, 284
Origanum, 176
Ornithogalum umbellatum, 162
Orontium aquaticum, 187
Osmanthus, 82
Osmanthus delavayi, 71-2
Ostrya carpinifolia, 48-9
Oswego tea, 131
Othonna, 176
Oxalis, 176

Paeonia, 72, 131
Pagoda tree, 51
Painted tongue, 150
Palm: Chusan, 51; false castor oil,
    64, 277-8; Kentia, 278-9;
    parlour, 275; sago, 276
Pampas grass, 122-3
Pansy, 137, 151
Papaver, 131-2, 176; *P. nudicaule*,
    151
Parrotia persica, 49
Parsley, 246
Parsnip, 242-3
Parthenocissus, 97
Pasque flower, 177
Passiflora caerulea, 97-8
Passion flower, 97-8
Patio gardening, 202-11
Pea, 243; everlasting, 96; sweet,
    146
Pea and bean weevil, 287
Pea moth, 287
Pea thrips, 287
Peach, 73, 227-8
Peach leaf curl, 293
Pear, 228-9; willow-leafed, 50
Pear leaf blister mite, 291
Pear midge, 291
Pear sawfly, 291
Pear sucker, 291
Pearly everlasting, 120
Peat, 259
Peat beds, 168-70
Peaty soils, 12, 13
Pelargonium, 23, 264, 279
Penstemon, 132, 149, 151;
    P. glaber, 156
Peony, 131; tree, 71-2
Peony wilt, 298
Peperomia, 279
Pepper: ornamental, 275; sweet,
    266-7
Perennials, 112; tender, 139,
    141
Pergolas, 89-90
Pericallis, 264; *P.* x *hybrida*, 279
Perilla, 146
Periwinkle, 79
Persicaria, 132, 176
Pests, 283-99; fruit, 290-4; house
    plants, 273, 298-9; lawns, 201,
    299; ornamental plants, 294-8;
    roses, 105; vegetables, 286-90
Petunia, 22, 149
pH, soil, 14
Phacelia campanularia, 146
Pheasant's eye, 142
Philadelphus, 72
Philodendron scandens, 279
Phlomis fruticosa, 72
Phlox, 118, 132, 176;
    P. drummondii, 149

Phormium, 132
Photinia x *fraseri* 'Red Robin', 72
Phygelius capensis, 98
Physalis, 132
Physostegia, 132
Picea breweriana, 49; *P. omorika*,
    49; *P. pungens* 'Koster', 49
Pickerel weed, 187
Pieris formosa var. *forrestii*, 72-3
Pilea cadierei, 281; *P. cadierei*
    'Minima', 280
Pinching out, house plants, 273
Pincushion flower, 150
Pink, 124, 175; sea, 174
Pittosporum tenuifolium, 73, 85
Planning, 10-12, 115-16
Plantain lily, 128
Planting: border plants, 116;
    bulbs, 153, 155; cabbages, 238-
    9; climbers, 90-1; fruit trees and
    bushes, 216-17; hedges, 81-2;
    leeks, 241; rock plants, 171-3;
    roses, 103; shrubs, 53-4; trees,
    40-3; water plants, 182-3
Platycerium bifurcatum, 280
Platycodon, 132
Pleached trees, 44
Plum, 73, 229-30; 'Victoria', 229
Plum sawfly, 291
Plum tortrix moth, 285, 291
Plumbago, hardy, 122
Plume poppy, 130
Poached egg flower, 144
Pocket handkerchief tree, 47
Poinsettia, 277
Polemonium, 132-3
Polyanthus, 133
Polygonatum, 133
Polygonum baldschuanicum, 98
Pondweed: Canadian, 186; curled,
    186
Pontederia cordata, 187
Pools, 178-87, 190, 191
Poplar, variegated balm of gilead,
    49
Poppy, 131-2; alpine, 176;
    Californian, 143, 234;
    Himalayan blue, 130-1; Iceland,
    151; 'Pink Chiffon', 146; prickly,
    142; Shirley, 146; tree, 75;
    Welsh, 130-1
Populus x *candicans* 'Aurora', 49
Portulaca, 149
Potamogeton crispus, 186
Potato, 243-4, 267
Potato blight, 288
Potato cyst eelworm, 287
Potentilla, 133; *P. fruticosa*, 73,
    85
Potting on, 210, 261, 272
Potting up, 259-61
Powdery mildew, 288, 293, 296
Powdery scab, 288
Pratia, 177
Prayer plant, 279
Pricking out seedlings, 23
Prickly heath, 72
Primrose, German, 280
Primula, 133; *P. malacoides*, 265;
    P. obconica, 280
Privet, 81, 82, 83, 85
Propagation, 20-7; annuals,
    biennials and bedding plants,
    139-41; cuttings, 23-6; division,
    23; fruit trees, 216; hedges, 83;
    layering, 26-7; roses, 105;
    seeds, 20-3; shrubs, 55
Propagators, 22
Pruning: apple trees, 219, 220;
    clematis, 94-5; climbers, 91;
    fruit trees and bushes, 215;

grape vines, 226; hedges, 82-3;
    rock plants, 173; roses, 103-4;
    shrubs, 54-5; tools, 32-4; trees,
    43-5
Prunus, 73; *P.* x *cistena*, 86;
    P. laurocerasus, 86; *P. serrula*, 39,
    49; *P. serrulata*, 49;
    P. x *subhirtella* 'Autumnalis',
    49-50
Pseudolarix amabilis, 50
Pulmonaria, 133
Pulsatilla, 177
Pumps, water features, 185
Purslane, rock, 148
Pyracantha, 98; *P. rogersiana*, 86
Pyrethrum 'Golden Moss', 150;
    P. 'Silver Lace', 150
Pyrus salicifolia 'Pendula', 50

Quamash, 157
Queen's tears, 275
Quince, Japanese, 93

Radish, 244
Ramanas rose, 86
Ranunculus aquatilis, 186
Raspberry, 230-1
Raspberry beetle, 291
Red hot poker, 129
Red spider mites, 285, 287,
    291-2, 298
Red thread, 299
Redcurrant, 223-4
Redwood, dawn, 48, 85
Reseda odorata, 145
Reversion disease, 293
Rheum, 133-4
Rhizome rot, 285, 296
Rhizomes, 152, 153
Rhodanthe, 146
Rhodanthe chlorocephala ssp. *rosa*,
    142
Rhododendron, 73-4; *R. ponticum*,
    86; *R. simsii*, 280
Rhododendron bug, 295
Rhoicissus rhomboidea, 280
Rhubarb, 133-4, 244, 267; prickly,
    127
Rhus typhina, 74
Ribes sanguineum, 74;
    R. speciosum, 98
Ricinus, 150
Ring culture, 255
Robinia pseudoacacia 'Frisia', 50
Rock gardens, 166-77; bulbs, 154
Rock rose, 176
Rockfoil, 177
Rodger's bronze leaf, 134
Rodgersia, 134
Romneya coulteri, 74
Root aphid, 287, 298
Root cuttings, 26
Rootstocks, fruit trees, 216
Rosa eglanteria, 86; *R. gallica*
    'Versicolor', 104; *R. rugosa*, 86
Rosemary, 75, 86, 246
Roses, 100-11
Rosmarinus officinalis, 74, 86-87
Rotation of crops, 185, 233
Rowan, 51
Rubber plant, 25, 26, 278
Rudbeckia, 134, 146
Rue, 75
Rush: corkscrew, 187; flowering,
    186; zebra, 187
Russian vine , 98
Rust, 289, 293, 296
Ruta graveolens 'Jackman's Blue',
    75

Saffron, meadow, 157-8

Sage, 134, 246; Jerusalem, 72
Sagittaria sagittifolia 'Flore Pleno',
    187
St John's wort, 68, 176
Saintpaulia, 24, 25; *S. ionantha*,
    280
Salix, 75; *S. babylonica* var.
    pekinensis 'Tortuosa', 51; *S.* x
    sepulcralis var. *chrysocoma*, 51
Salpiglossis, 150
Salvia, 134; *S.* 'Blaze of Fire', 150;
    S. viridis, 146
Sambucus, 75-6
Sand, composts, 259
Sandy soils, 12
Sansevieria trifasciata 'Laurentii',
    280
Santolina, 76
Sanvitalia procumbens, 150
Saponaria, 134, 177; *S. vaccaria*,
    146
Sarcococca confusa, 76
Savin, 68
Saxifraga, 177; *S. stolonifera*, 280
Scab, 289, 296
Scabiosa, 134
Scabious, 134, 150
Scald, 294
Scale insect, 298
Scarifying lawns, 198
Scent: roses, 108; shrubs, 77
Schefflera arboricola, 280;
    S. elegantissima, 280
Schizanthus pinnatus 'Hit Parade',
    265
Schizostylis coccinea, 162
Schlumbergera x *buckleyi*, 281
Scilla, 162; *S. sibirica*, 160
Scirpus tabernaemontani
    'Zebrinus', 187
Scotch flame flower, 98-9, 137
Scree beds, 168
Sea holly, 126
Sedge, 122
Sedum, 135, 177; 'Autumn Joy',
    134
Seedlings, pricking out, 23
Seeds: annuals, biennials and
    bedding plants, 139-41; lawns,
    194, 196-9; sowing, 20-3;
    vegetables, 234-5
Sempervivum, 23, 177
Senecio cineraria, 150; *S. cruentus*,
    281
Shade: greenhouses, 257; plants
    for, 154, 276; rock plants, 173;
    roses for, 108
Shanking, 289, 294
Shoo-fly plant, 145
Shot hole, 293
Shrimp plant, 275
Shrubs, 52-79; growing climbers
    through, 90; for patios, 211;
    shrub roses, 101-2, 106-8
Sidalcea, 135
Silene, 177
Silk tassel bush, 95
Silver leaf, 293
Sink gardens, 170-1
Sinningia speciosa, 281
Sisyrinchium, 177
Skimmia, 76
Slipper flower, 275
Slugs, 285, 287, 295, 298
Slugworm, 292
Smilacina, 135
Smoke tree, 62
Smoulder, 296
Smut, 289
Snails, 285, 287, 295, 298
Snapdragon, 147

Sneezeweed, 127
Snow in summer, 174
Snowberry, 77, 82
Snowdrop, 159
Snowflake, 161
Soapwort, 134, 177
Soft rot, 289
Softwood cuttings, 24
Soil: borders, 114; climbers, 90;
    digging, 15-17; drainage, 12;
    improving, 13-15; land
    clearance, 12; pH, 14; rock
    gardens, 166-7; roses, 102;
    types, 12; vegetable gardens,
    233
Solanum capsicastrum, 281;
    S. crispum, 98
Soldiers and sailors, 133
Solenostemon, 265, 281
Solidago, 135-6
Solomon's seal, 133
Sooty mould, 299
Sophora japonica, 51
Sorbus aucuparia 'Beissneri', 51;
    S. 'Joseph Rock', 51
Sorrel, wood, 176
Sowbread, 158
Sowing *see* Seeds
Spanish bayonet, 281
Spider flower, 148, *215*
Spider plant, 275
Spiderwort, 137
Spikenard, false, 135
Spiking lawns, *198*
Spinach, 244
Spinach blight, 289
Spindle tree, 64
Spiraea, 76, 121; blue, 59
Spraing, 289
Spruce: Brewer's weeping, 49;
    Koster's blue, 49; Serbian, 49
Spur blight, 293
Spurge, 126, 175
Squill, 162
Stachys, 136; *S. byzantina*, *156*
Staging, greenhouses, 255-6
Star of Bethlehem, 162
Star of the Veldt, 143
Stardust, 144
Statice, 150, *215*
Stem and bulb eelworm, *285*, 295
Stem cuttings, 23-5
Stem eelworm, 295
Stem rot, 289, 293
Stephanotis floribunda, 281
Sternbergia, 162
Stewartia pseudocamellia, 51
Stipa, 136
Stock: Brompton, 151; night-
    scented, 145; ten-week, 150
Stonecrop, 135, 177
Stony soils, 12, 13
Stratiotes aloides, 187
Strawberry, 231, 267
Strawberry mildew, 293
Strawberry tree, 46
Strawflower, 149
Streptocarpus, 265
Successional sowing, 234
Suckers, 44; roses, *104-5*
Sulphate of ammonia, 14
Sumach, stag's horn, 74
Sun rose, 60
Sunflower, 146
Supports: annuals, *140*; border
    plants, *117*; climbers, 89-90, *91*;
    greenhouse plants, 261; house
    plants, *273*
Swede, 244
Sweet briar, 86
Sweet corn, *244-5*

Sweet pea, 146
Sweet pepper, 266
Sweet Sultan, 146
Sweet William, 151
Sweetheart plant, 279
Swiss cheese plant, 279
Sycamore, 46
Symphilid, 298
Symphoricarpos, 77
Syringa, 72, 77

Tagetes, 150
Tamarisk, 78, 82, 86
Tamarix gallica, 86; *T. ramosissima*,
    77
Tarragon, 246
Tassel flower, 142
Taxus baccata, 51, 86; *T. baccata*
    'Fastigiata Aurea', 51
Teasel, fuller's, 150
Tender annuals, 139
Tender perennials, 139, 141
Thalictrum, 136
Thinning vegetable seedlings,
    235
Thistle, globe, 125
Thorn, Paul's scarlet, 47
Thorny hedges, 84
Thrift, 174
Thrips, *285*, 295, 298
Thuja plicata, 86; *T. plicata*
    'Zebrina', 51
Thunbergia 'Orange Wonder', 265
Thyme, 246
Thymus, 177
Tibetan cherry, *39*, 49
Ti tree, 276, 281
Tickseed, 122
Tidy tips, 144
Tithonia, 150
Toadflax, 129, 144
Tobacco plant, 149
Tomato, 245, 267
Tomato fertilizer, 15
Tomato moth, 287
Tools, *28-35*
Topdressing: greenhouse plants,
    261; lawns, *199*
Topiary, 53
Torenia fournieri, 265
Tortrix moth, 291, 292
Trachycarpus fortunei, 51
Trachymene coerulea, 265
Tradescantia, 137, 281; *T. zebrina*,
    281
Training: blackberries, 221;
    climbers, 91; cordons, 220;
    grape vines, 226; greenhouse
    plants, 261
Transplanting: shrubs, *54*;
    vegetable seedlings, 235
Trees, 38-51; growing climbers
    through, *90*; staking, *42, 43*
Trillium, 177
Trollius, 137
Tropaeolum, 137; *T. majus*, *145*;
    T. peregrinum, 143; *T. speciosum*,
    98-9
Tub pools, *185*
Tubers, 152, *153*
Tufa, 167
Tulip fire, 296
Tulipa, 162-3
Tunnels, 253
Tupelo, 48
Turf, laying lawns, *194-6*
Turnip, 245

Ulex europaeus, 86
Umbrella grass, 276
Umbrella tree, 280

Urn plant, 274
Ursinia, 150
Utricularia vulgaris, 186

Valerian, 122
Variegated foliage, shrubs, 74
Vegetables, 232-45; greenhouses,
    265-7; pests and diseases,
    286-90
Venus fly trap, 277
Venus looking glass, 143
Verbascum, 137, 151, 177
Verbena, 150
Verbena, lemon, 97
Veronica, 137
Veronica, shrubby, 65-6
Verticillium wilt, 289
Vervain, 150
Viburnum, 78-9; *V. x bodnantense*,
    79; *V. carlesii*, 79; *V. farreri*, 79;
    V. opulus, 79; *V. plicatum
    tomentosum*, 79; *V. tinus*, 79,
    86
Vinca, 79; *V.* 'Dwarf Mixed', 265;
    V. minor 'Azurea Flore Pleno', *78*
Vine weevil, 295, 298
Vines, 99
Viola, 137, 151
Violet, 137; dog's tooth, 159;
    water, 186
Violet cress, 143
Violet root rot, 289
Viper's bugloss, 143
Virginia creeper, 97
Virgin's bower, 94
Virus diseases, 289, 293, 296
Viscaria 'Blue Angel', 146
Vitis, 99

Wall plants, 88-99
Wallflower, 151; Siberian, *151*
Walls, dry, 168
Wandering Jew, 281
Wart disease, 289
Wasps, 292
Water gardens, 178-87
Water lily, *183*, 186; yellow,
    186

Water soldier, 187
Watering, 15; border plants, 116;
    containers, 209; equipment,
    34-5; greenhouses, 257-8;
    house plants, 270-2; lawns, *198*;
    roses, 104
Wax flower, clustered, 281
Wax plant, 279
Weedkillers, 18-19, 290
Weeds, 12, *17-19*; in lawns,
    200-1; vegetable gardens, 233
Weigela, 79
Whiptail, 290
White currant, 223-4
Whitefly, 298
Wild flowers, 191
Wildlife, 183-4, 188-91
Willow, 75; dragon's claw, 51;
    golden weeping, 51
Willowherb, rose bay, 126
Wilt, 296
Wind protection, shrubs, *55*
Windflower, 120, 157
Windowboxes, 207
Winter aconite, *159*
Winter moth, 292
Wireworm, *285*, 287
Wisteria, Chinese, 99
Wisteria sinensis, 99
Witch hazel, 65
Wolfsbane, 118
Woodbine, 97
Woodruff, annual, 142
Woolly aphid, 292
Worms, 201, 299

Xeranthemum, 146

Yarrow, 118
Yellow foliage, shrubs, 74
Yew, 51, 82, 83, 86
Yucca aloifolia, 281; *Y. filamentosa*,
    79

Zantedeschia, 137
Zauschneria, 177
Zebra plant, 274
Zinnia, 150

ACKNOWLEDGEMENTS

Illustrations by Alan Burton, Pamela Dowson and Nils Solberg

The publishers gratefully acknowledge the following for
granting permission to reproduce colour photographs:

Edward Barber 2; 7.
Bob Challinor 41; 42; 65; 91; 101; 130; 138–9; 159; 160;
169; 170; 184; 238–9; 255.
Jerry Harpur 8–9; 93; 114–15; 164–5; 172; 179; 196–7;
208–9; 248–9; 269; 277.
Marcus Harpur 234–5.
Clive Nichols/Jonathan Baillie 33; Clive Nichols/Butterstream,
Eire 119; Clive Nichols 123; Clive Nichols/Waterperry
Gardens, Oxfordshire 134–5; Clive Nichols/Preen Manor,
Shropshire 151; Clive Nichols/Coton Manor, Northamptonshire
156–7; Clive Nichols/Mainau, Lake Constance 163; Clive
Nichols/Design: N. Hancock/Mathew Bell 246–7.
Andrew Lawson 36–7; 39; 50; 61; 66–7; 71; 78–9; 87; 89; 99;
110–11; 124–5; 144; 145; 147; 148; 191; 210–11 (bottom);
212–13; 215; 222–3; 224–5; 229; 263; 281; 282–3; 297.
Michael Stead 43; 44; 55; 83; 167; 171; 187; 198–9; 210;
211 (top); 220; 237; 260; 273.
Alan Titchmarsh 102.